P9-CCY-710

English Skills

with Readings

JOHN LANGAN
Atlantic Community College

SHARON WINSTANLEY
Seneca College

**McGraw-Hill
Ryerson**

Toronto Montréal Burr Ridge, IL Dubuque, IA Madison, WI New York San Francisco
St. Louis Bangkok Bogotá Caracas Kuala Lumpur Lisbon London Madrid
Mexico City Milan New Delhi Santiago Seoul Singapore Sydney Taipei

The McGraw·Hill Companies

McGraw-Hill Ryerson

ENGLISH SKILLS WITH READINGS
Third Canadian Edition

ISBN: 0-07-089164-8

1 2 3 4 5 6 7 8 9 10   TCP   0 9 8 7 6 5

Printed and bound in Canada

Care has been taken to trace ownership of copyright material contained in this text; however, the publisher will welcome any information that enables them to rectify any reference or credit for subsequent editions.

Vice President, Editorial and Media Technology: Patrick Ferrier
Sponsoring Editor: Leanna MacLean
Senior Marketing Manager: Sharon Loeb
Managing Editor, Development: Jennifer DiDomenico
Senior Production Coordinator: Madeleine Harrington
Supervising Editor: Anne Nellis
Cover Design: Liz Harasymczuk /Sharon Lucas
Interior Designer: Liz Harasymczuk
Composition: Bill Renaud/Accutype
Printer: Transcontinental Printing Group

Library and Archives Canada Cataloguing in Publication

Langan, John, 1942–
    English skills with readings / John Langan, Sharon Winstanley.

3rd Canadian ed.
Includes index.
ISBN 0-07-089164-8

1. English language — Rhetoric.   I. Winstanley, Sharon.   II. Title.

PE1408.L28 2004   808'.0427   C2004-905584-4

xplaining a Process • *Examining Cause and Effect* • *Comparing or Contrasting* • *Definin*
erm • *Dividing and Classifying* • *Describing a Scene or Person* • *Narrating an Event* • *Argu*
Position • *Explaining a Process* • *Examining Cause and Effect* • *Comparing or Contrastin*
efining a Term • *Dividing and Classifying* • *Describing a Scene or Person* • *Narrating an Ev*
Arguing a Position • *Explaining a Process* • *Examining Cause and Effect* • *Comparing*

Contents

laining a Process · Examining Cause and Effect · Comparing or Contrasting · Defining a
m · Dividing and Classifying · Describing a Scene or Person · Narrating an Event · Arguing
sition · Explaining a Process · Examining Cause and Effect · Comparing or Contrasting
ining a Term · Dividing and Classifying · Describing a Scene or Person · Narrating an Even
rguing a Position · Explaining a Process · Examining Cause and Effect · Comparing o

Readings Listed by Rhetorical Mode

Note: Some selections are listed more than once because they illustrate more than one rhetorical* mode of development.

Narration

Description

Examples

* The word "rhetorical" refers to a particular structuring method or format chosen by a writer for its effectiveness in communicating the selection's message to an audience. Many of these selections, and most writers, make use of more than one rhetorical mode or format in any one piece of writing; for example, an essay may be *narrative* in basic style, but may also *contrast* two different ideas.

Process

Cause and Effect

Comparison or Contrast

Definition

Division and Classification

Argumentation

*The word "rhetorical" refers to a particular structuring method or format chosen by a writer for its effectiveness in communicating the selection's message to an audience. Many of these selections, and most writers, make use of more than one rhetorical mode or format in any one piece of writing; for example, an essay may be *narrative* but may also *contrast* two different ideas.

laining a Process • Examining Cause and Effect • Comparing or Contrasting • Defining
m • Dividing and Classifying • Describing a Scene or Person • Narrating an Event • Arguin
osition • Explaining a Process • Examining Cause and Effect • Comparing or Contrasting
ining a Term • Dividing and Classifying • Describing a Scene or Person • Narrating an Even
rguing a Position • Explaining a Process • Examining Cause and Effect • Comparing o

Preface

English Skills with Readings, Third Canadian Edition, helps students understand, learn, and apply the basic principles of effective writing and reading comprehension. This book focuses on challenges faced by first-semester and first-year Canadian college students. This edition has been extensively revised to present each set of skills and each subject area in goal-oriented, staged units of information to encourage confidence and a sense of mastery in the student learner as he or she proceeds.

Like previous editions, the Third Canadian Edition of *English Skills with Readings* relies on a direct, prescriptive, and supportive approach that encourages the student writer. *English Skills with Readings* bases its approach on four essential principles that are keys to effective writing for any medium: **unity, support, coherence, and sentence skills.** The four principles or bases are highlighted on the inside front cover and reinforced throughout the book.

- Section One, "Basic Principles of Effective Writing," focuses on the first three bases while introducing the fourth base.
- Section Two applies the four bases to paragraph development.
- Section Three applies the four bases to multiple-paragraph essays.
- Section Four serves as a concise handbook of sentence skills.
- Section Five contains fifteen reading selections that prompt students to see how professional writers use these principles, and again demonstrates their application in writing assignments for both paragraphs and essays.

THE *ENGLISH SKILLS WITH READINGS* APPROACH

The time-tested philosophy behind the Langan/Winstanley texts is based on a number of assumptions about reading and writing and aims to decomplicate writing as much as possible and to encourage hesitant or unwilling writers. This edition contains new coverage as well as new exercises and activities that reinforce and build on the text's basic philosophy.

- First, the four bases described above constitute a readily understandable and workable approach to good writing, mainly because they are so clearly and easily demonstrated in concrete terms. In this new edition, these bases are reinforced more intensively in the stages of the writing process, in pedagogy for rhetorical modes, and in writing assignments.
- This new edition also reflects the belief that, in addition to the four bases, other significant factors are involved in writing effectively. These factors have added importance for remedial-level college writers, students writing in a second language, and students previously perplexed or defeated by writing tasks. First is the student's recognition and acceptance that writing is a process made doable by working in stages. This edition devotes even more attention to each stage of the writing process, with particular focus on prewriting and revising as essential activities. Next, writing is consistently presented as a learnable skill. The text's presentation of good writing as an attainable goal that requires genuine

effort offers realistic encouragement to the student willing to engage in the process of learning to communicate effectively. Finally, the writer's attitude both toward the act of writing and toward himself or herself as a writer is given careful consideration. This edition emphasizes attitudinal issues related to self-expression and difficulties experienced by student writers at various stages of the writing process.

- This edition of *English Skills with Readings* acknowledges that writing from personal experience is a good way for "under-prepared" or unwilling students to begin writing. However, it also emphasizes that after students master the skill of presenting a point and providing support from personal experience, they are ready to write from a more objective stance that is more relevant to career-based writing tasks. Students are asked to write in the third-person voice where appropriate and to extrapolate from their own reasoning or externally derived sources of information. In Sections Two and Three, students are asked to write on both experience-based and more objective topics, with emphasis on and preference given to the third-person voice and viewpoint. Additionally, some writing assignments require the use of basic online research skills.

- Another premise basic to *English Skills with Readings*, Third Canadian Edition, is that mastery of the paragraph should precede extension of basic compositional principles and skills into the longer essay. Thus, Section One illustrates the basic principles of composition using paragraph models, and the assignments in Section Two aim to develop the student's ability to support ideas within a variety of paragraph forms. The essential skills of writing an effective paragraph are then extended and applied to the traditional college essays in Section Three. Finally, in Section Five, each reading selection is followed by two paragraph assignments and one or more essay assignments.

- The book continues in its assumption that beginning writers at a college level are more likely to learn composing skills through contact with lively, engaging, and realistic models than through encountering material remote from common everyday experiences and interests. When one writer, for example, explains the annoyances of her college's Internet server, or another relates his sadness at the withering away of his Lake Erie shore hometown, or yet another warmly recalls how her grandmother's cooking led her into training to be a chef, students are more apt to remember and follow the writing principles involved. After reading student samples from predominantly Canadian contexts and the varied and stimulating professional selections in Section Five, students have a firmer grasp of the power that good writing can exert. They are then more likely to aim for similar honesty, realism, and detail in their own work.

- Especially central to this text is the assumption that reading and writing are inextricably connected skills. Practising one helps the other. Section Five enables students to practise critical thinking and to work on becoming better readers as well as better writers. The introduction to Section Five offers a series of tips on effective reading, and ten questions after each selection provide practice in key reading comprehension skills. Discussion questions following each selection deepen students' understanding of content and sensitize them to the ways various authors achieve structural, stylistic, and tonal effects. The writing assignments for each selection offer guidelines to help students work through these assignments.

- Finally, since no two people will use an English text in exactly the same way, this book works on the assumption that its material should be organized in a highly accessible way. Because each of the five sections of the book deals with a distinct area of the text's subject, instructors can turn easily to the skills and knowledge they wish to present.

WHAT'S NEW IN THE THIRD CANADIAN EDITION?

The Third Canadian Edition of *English Skills with Readings* contains additions and revisions to existing content, fresh examples, new activities for both individual students and groups, eight new readings, and extended support in the form of an Online Learning Centre, which can be accessed at www.mcgrawhill.ca/college/langan. All the changes speak to the needs of the first-semester Canadian college student, who faces new and varied demands on his or her writing and reading comprehension abilities. Responding to comments from instructors across Canada, we have included a stronger focus on prewriting and revising, including a new Chapter 5; structural changes that ensure that each chapter clearly builds upon concepts introduced in previous chapters; new writing assignments to accustom students to a greater range of career-related possibilities for writing in various modes; and a wider range of examples and activities that stress the third-person voice.

Here is an overview of major changes in the Third Canadian Edition.

SECTION ONE: BASIC PRINCIPLES OF EFFECTIVE WRITING

- Section One has been restructured into six chapters to place greater emphasis on the prewriting and revising stages of composing.
- Section One introduces new material on structuring paragraphs, and on paragraph length as it relates to different print media.
- Chapter 1 now focuses squarely on reducing the college entry-level or ESL writer's anxiety about communicating clearly in writing. Writing, from this opening chapter on, is presented as a skill learnable in stages, and as a process to be managed and worked on step by step. The aim is to encourage students to understand their attitudes, preconceptions, and misconceptions about themselves as writ-

ers and to see the practical and motivational benefits of learning to write effectively.

- The introduction of the concept of the "rhetorical triangle" or "writer's triangle" of subject, purpose, and audience is an important addition to this book. This essential set of considerations is continually reinforced throughout Sections One, Two, and Three, as well as in the writing assignments in Section Five. Considering shifts of audience and purpose can help beginning student writers to move away from mainly personal concerns and to grasp notions of tonal and vocabulary variation. The "triangle" itself is fully explained in Chapter 7, where students begin to work with methods of paragraph development. The relationship of purpose, audience, and subject knowledge is strongly related to students' future career writing and communication tasks. Student writers in the pedagogical narratives deal with adjusting tone, detail, wording, and purpose in several cases, including "Lessons from the Gym" in Chapter 2 and "Torture by Telephone" in Chapter 4, which is repurposed into an essay in Section Three.
- Chapter 2 treats prewriting and structural aspects of the paragraph in greater depth than previous editions, with explanations and rationales for each technique. The text repeatedly advises students to spend significant time on prewriting in order to clarify as well as discover their ideas. Prewriting is emphasized as an iterative activity, and examples demonstrate students doing at least two stages of prewriting, often trying different types for different purposes as they generate and order content.
- Chapter 2 also presents stronger emphasis on outlining, with outline diagrams appearing in most student writing exemplar narratives. Outlining is treated as essential, and given greater focus and a more detailed explanation. Techniques for preparing an effective outline have been added.
- Chapter 3 offers new activities to help students recognize, then create solid support in paragraphs, as many instructors find that

weak, general, or repetitive support is a frequent point of weakness in student writing. New and distinctly Canadian exemplars appear, showing the third-person viewpoint as a reasonable, if not preferable, alternative to the first-person viewpoint. This sets a good example for students and asks for a stretch away from purely personal writing.

- New group activities appear in this edition, such as those on page 68 in Chapter 3.

- The new Chapter 5, "The Fourth Step in Writing," covers revision in a standalone chapter. It contains fresh material on sentence-level revision and editing to increase students' attention to and proficiency at revision. This focus on the fourth base of effective writing, solid sentence skills, now appears at an appropriate point for both instructors and students—before the students begin writing in the various modes. There are new exemplars, new material on computer grammar checkers and their pitfalls, and new exercises and review tests to reinforce the importance of revising.

- Common problems in sentence structure, consistency, and word use have been incorporated in Chapter 5 to help students write better paragraphs sooner, thereby increasing their confidence in themselves as writers. Concerns including parallel structure, consistency of verb tenses and pronoun point of view, specificity and conciseness of word choice, and basic sentence types are now treated as part of the fabric of paragraph and essay writing and revision, rather than as items relegated to a grammar handbook.

SECTION TWO: PARAGRAPH DEVELOPMENT

- Each chapter in Section Two has been extensively revised to help students manage and master writing situations. The first two assignments in the chapter for each rhetorical mode have been rewritten to guide students step by step through a writing task from prewriting through revising, to decomplicate the initial stages of writing, and to encourage hesitant or unwilling writers by showing "students at work." These scenarios show students dealing with the particular challenges of each mode.

- Section Two opens with revised explanations of the various rhetorical modes, showing that these methods reflect certain human thinking patterns rather than existing as arbitrary impositions on students.

- The "writer's triangle" is thoroughly explained in Chapter 7 as an essential set of concepts with which to begin any writing task. Subject knowledge, audience, and purpose are clearly explained, with strategies for understanding each concept and a new activity that can be done individually or in groups.

- In the chapters "Narrating an Event" and "Describing a Scene or Person," new material on subjective and objective forms shows the college and career uses of narrative and descriptive writing.

- To reinforce this edition's added emphasis on revision, a "Development through Revising" section appears in the chapter for each rhetorical mode.

- Self-checking questions have been added to several assignments in each of these chapters to reinforce each chapter's and the book's teaching points, and to allow professors to use these as marking criteria and guidelines for independent or group use.

SECTION THREE: ESSAY DEVELOPMENT

- Section Three offers new content to strengthen the student's understanding of the connections between paragraph and essay structures. Opening paragraphs, thesis statements, supporting paragraphs, transitional material, and concluding paragraphs are covered in greater depth and detail, with new activities added for each topic.

- Careful reinforcement of such material as structuring supporting paragraphs is provided in new boxed sections, as on page 285.

- A new exemplar essay appears in Section Three ("Tele-Torture") that reflects a previously mentioned student's revision, expansion, and repurposing of a single-paragraph assignment. Reinforcement, additional pedagogy, and new activities based on recognizing and applying the four principles of effective writing to parts of the essay are incorporated into the section.
- The section "Common Methods of Introduction" has been expanded to include the concept of presenting context or necessary background information, especially in situations where students must write about technological subjects. A new exemplar about DVD technology has been added to demonstrate this method of introduction.
- New material on focusing topics to write effective thesis statements has been added as a stepped process, including information on writing thesis statements for different modes.

SECTION FOUR: SENTENCE SKILLS (GRAMMAR, MECHANICS, PUNCTUATION, WORD USE, AND PRACTICE)

- Material on consistent verb tense, parallelism, and sentence variety (formerly Chapters 24, 30, and 42) is now introduced in Section One, Chapter 5.
- Overall, a number of changes and refinements appear in Section Four. Examples have been freshened and revised throughout, with considerable revision appearing in Chapter 22, "Run-ons and Comma Splices." Chapter 24, "Subject-Verb Agreement," contains a new introduction and new material explaining singular and plural subjects and verbs. Additionally, Chapter 26 now presents the concept of cases as applied to pronouns, and Chapter 27 offers new content on comparative and superlative forms of adverbs.

- Chapter 30, "Manuscript Form," has been revised, corrected, and updated to reflect more frequent computer use.
- Chapter 33, in an effort to halt the often inappropriate use of apostrophes, contains new material on matters such as non-apostrophized plurals of acronym abbreviations, such as CD.
- Chapter 34 includes a new, more current exemplar, and new content on semicolon and colon placement with quotation marks.
- Chapter 37's new material on "chatroom" and "text-messaging" usages and their inappropriateness in college writing will be a welcome addition for many instructors, as will the vocabulary improvement websites added to Chapter 38.
- Chapter 41, "ESL Pointers," has been revised, with added material on gerund and infinitive idioms and participial adjectives, and the introduction to
- Chapter 43's editing tests includes new editing hints.

SECTION FIVE: READINGS

- More than half of the fifteen readings in this Third Canadian Edition of *English Skills with Readings* are new. Six of these new selections are Canadian. An effort has been made to provide a wide range of styles, tones, and lengths in the selections. The readings now offer a range of reading levels to allow instructors to accommodate the diverse nature of remedial or entry-level English or communications classes. An instructor may work with students at one reading level or may choose to build in complexity over the course of a semester.
- The six new Canadian readings present uncomplicated, humorous pieces such as "Mrs. Squirrel and I Negotiated Terms" and "What's in Your Fridge," which may stimulate classroom discussion, as well as more challenging and mildly controversial selections like "Here's to a Long and Unhappy Life."

More serious current social or technology-related issues are addressed in "Welcome to the Matrix" and "The Oldest Profession: Shopping," and "Language Out, Style In" looks at language use in colleges and the media today, from a communication specialist's perspective.

- Two American selections new to this edition offer subject matter of interest to students: "Bullies in School" and "Anxiety: Challenge by Another Name."

- New writing assignments that require modest Internet research appear with the selections "What's in Your Fridge," "Language Out, Style In," "Here's to a Long and Unhappy Life," and "Bullies in School." Each of these assignments provides instructions for students to help them link to research information on the Online Learning Centre and conduct focused online searches.

INSTRUCTOR RESOURCES

i-LEARNING SALES SPECIALIST

Your **Integrated Learning Sales Specialist** is a McGraw-Hill Ryerson representative who has the experience, product knowledge, training, and support to help you assess and integrate any of the products, technology, and services listed below into your course for optimum teaching and learning performance. Whether it's using our Online Learning Centres, helping your students improve their grades, or putting your entire course online, your *i*-Learning Sales Specialist is there to help you do it. Contact your local *i*-Learning Sales Specialist today to learn how to maximize all of McGraw-Hill Ryerson's resources!

i-LEARNING SERVICES PROGRAM

McGraw-Hill Ryerson offers a unique *i*-Services package designed for Canadian faculty. Our mission is to equip providers of higher education with superior tools and resources required for excellence in teaching. For additional information visit www.mcgrawhill.ca/highereducation/eservices/.

INSTRUCTOR'S MANUAL

The Instructor's Manual contains a wealth of teaching resources, including hints and tips for approaching the course, a model syllabus, and supplementary activities and tests. The Instructor's Manual is available for download in the passcode-protected Instructor's Centre of the Online Learning Centre (www.mcgrawhill.ca/college/langan).

ONLINE LEARNING CENTRE

The Online Learning Centre for *English Skills with Readings*, Third Canadian Edition (www. mcgrawhill.ca/college/langan), features learning and study tools, as well as a passcode-protected Instructor's Centre with downloadable supplements, including the complete Instructor's Manual and Microsoft PowerPoint™ presentations for Sections One through Four.

PAGEOUT™

Visit www.mhhe.com/pageout to create a Web page for your course using our resources. PageOut™ is the McGraw-Hill Ryerson Web site development centre. This Web page-generation software is free to adopters and is designed to help faculty create an online course, complete with assignments, quizzes, links to relevant Web sites, and more—all in a matter of minutes.

In addition, content cartridges are available for the course management systems **WebCT and Blackboard**. These platforms provide instructors with user-friendly, flexible teaching tools. Please contact your local McGraw-Hill Ryerson *i*-Learning Sales Specialist for details.

STUDENT RESOURCES

ONLINE LEARNING CENTRE

The Online Learning Centre for *English Skills with Readings*, Third Canadian Edition (www.mcgraw hill.ca/college/langan), features learning and study tools such as learning outcomes, writing prompts, self-quizzes, weblinks, a searchable glossary, and bonus material on study and research skills.

ALLWRITE! CANADIAN VERSION 2.0

A self-paced, interactive tutorial, *AllWrite!* includes an online handbook that provides details on all the information students would find in a typical print handbook: grammar, the writing process, documentation, and special types of writing, as well as thousands of interactive exercises that allow students to develop and assess their skills. With optional testing and course management capabilities, *AllWrite!* is the number one Web-based grammar resource for Canadian students and instructors! To learn more, visit www.mcgrawhill.ca/college/allwrite.

ACKNOWLEDGEMENTS

Once again, I am grateful for the continuing support and assistance of the editors at McGraw-Hill Ryerson. Their dedication to excellence and attention to detail have been an inspiration, and their good humour, ideas, and "voices at the other end of the phone" have been invaluable. I would especially like to thank Jennifer DiDomenico, Managing Editor, Development, Leanna McLean, Sponsoring Editor, and Anne Nellis, Supervising Editor, whose work contributed so much to the completion of this project. My thanks also, as always, go to my students at Seneca @ York, who continue to teach, inspire, delight, and amuse me.

Finally, I would like to thank the reviewers who provided helpful ideas and feedback for the Third Canadian Edition:

Bev Allix, Humber College
Arlene Davis-Fuhr, Grant MacEwan College
Maxine Evans, Red Deer College
Gary Lipschutz, Centennial College
Jane Marinakis, North Island College
Peter C. Miller, Seneca College
Kay Oxford, George Brown College
Sharren Patterson, Mount Royal College
Pamela Robinson, St. Lawrence College
Suzanne Schiller, Humber College

SHARON WINSTANLEY

Basic Principles
of Effective Writing

PREVIEW

Section One begins by introducing you to the book and to paragraph form. As you work through the brief activities in "An Introduction to Writing," you will gain a quick understanding of the book's purpose, how it is organized, and how it will help you develop your writing skills. After presenting a series of important general factors that will help you create good paragraphs, Section One describes four basic steps that can make you an effective writer. The four steps are:

1   Make a point.
2   Support the point with specific evidence.
3   Organize and connect the specific evidence.
4   Write clear, error-free sentences.

Explanations, examples, and activities are provided to help you master the steps. (You will also be referred to Section Four of the book for more detailed treatment of the fourth step.) After seeing how these steps can help you write effective paragraphs and essays, you will learn how they lead to four standards, or "bases," of effective writing: unity, support, coherence, and sentence skills. You will then practise evaluating a number of paragraphs in terms of these four bases.

Explaining a Process · Examining Cause and Effect · Comparing or Contrasting · Defining a Term · Dividing and Classifying · Describing a Scene or Person · Narrating an Event · Arguing a Position · Explaining a Process · Examining Cause and Effect · Comparing or Contrasting Defining a Term · Dividing and Classifying · Describing a Scene or Person · Narrating an Event · Arguing a Position · Explaining a Process · Examining Cause and Effect · Comparing

CHAPTER 1

An Introduction to Writing

LEARNING OUTCOMES

After reading this chapter and completing its activities, you will

- see writing as a learnable skill and a process of discovery;
- realize the benefits of paragraph and essay writing;
- have a sense of the basics of effective writing;
- apply those basics in writing a simple paragraph; and
- understand the overall organization of this book.

English Skills with Readings, third Canadian edition, grows from the experiences of Canadian students who, each semester, begin their post-secondary education.

First-semester students in Canadian colleges face an array of challenges, many of which relate to the need to communicate effectively. Although you and your fellow students arrive in the classroom from diverse backgrounds and educational experiences, you share thc desire to build a future for yourselves. This future and your career in the twenty-first century will depend on your ability to communicate clearly in English. This book's general aim is to help you to do so.

First-semester students often share a feeling about the writing demands they face in college—a feeling of anxiety. Anxiety is nearly always what keeps these students from communicating their ideas clearly, whether it is rooted in past school experiences or in the difficulties associated with writing in a second or third language. The specific aim of *English Skills with Readings* is to release students from such "communication anxiety" by providing a realistic, experience-based, step-by-step approach to college writing tasks.

This book explains in a clear and direct way *how* to write clearly and effectively—basic principles and skills you can learn and practise and apply in every college subject. *English Skills with Readings* provides you with practice materials and exercises, so that you can master writing skills one step at a time and review each skill until you make it a habit. Each chapter begins with specific learning outcomes to show you what you can achieve as you work through that chapter's content and activities.

First, consider writing for what it is: communicating in a set of characters or symbols to express some meaning. Writing is just one significant part of your life-long process of communicating with others. Writing clearly is not a mystery or a gift; virtually no one is a "born writer." All writers must learn the same lessons if they are to reach an *audience* for whatever *purpose* they may have. The lessons and rules for effective writing arose gradually from the success or failure of those who tried to write in various ways. Patterns and rules grew from seeing "what worked." Writing is mainly a matter of practice, perseverance, and gradually increasing skill. Becoming an effective writer involves no mysteries and no impossible tasks.

APPROACHING WRITING

The main themes reinforced throughout this book are introduced in the box below.

- Writing is a skill; anxiety and confusion decrease as writers learn to follow clearly set out and workable methods and practices.

- Writing often depends on the attitude of the writer. Because writing is self-expression, it is closely tied to feelings of self-worth, and its quality may suffer if the writer feels incompetent. Working on writing in stages and being determined to write well are keys to a good attitude about writing.

- Writing is a process of discovering, arranging, and revising thoughts, and clear expression of ideas results from understanding and following this process.

- Writing the traditional paragraph or essay, whose main point is logically supported, is the best preparation for effective communication in most media.

Begin by considering each of these themes in turn, knowing that they can help you approach writing with more confidence and stronger motivation.

WRITING IS A SKILL

Students feel uncertain or anxious about writing and English classes for many reasons. Indeed, most people, if they are honest, feel discomfort about putting thoughts on paper. Writing exposes the writer: to himself or herself, and to others. Thoughts and feelings are on paper, language difficulties are manifested, and writers feel vulnerable. Perhaps nowhere is anyone more vulnerable than in the classroom, where judgments have mark values. Students feel *they*, not their writing skills, are being judged.

While feeling unsure or unvalued, students may jump to two wrong conclusions: first, that only they find writing difficult; and, second, that they lack the talent to write well. Such attitudes lead to avoidance behaviours; students avoid trying to improve and even avoid writing. In this self-fulfilling prophecy, trying results in failing, so there is no reason to try. To break out of this cycle of self-defeat, the student must resist the temptation of hopelessness and be open to a different attitude about writing.

Replace hopelessness with reality: begin with the idea that *writing is a skill*. All skills are acquired and mastered in stages. Like learning to cook, drive, or design websites, learning to write is a step-by-step process. Writing requires the willingness to learn, the patience to revise and correct, and the determination to work through each step.

Writing well consists of a series of tasks; it is not a gift, nor does it result from a flash of inspiration. Clear writing requires intense thinking and analytic skills—challenges for anyone. Finding words and phrases that translate ideas to paper is demanding. Deciding what is worth keeping, out of hours of writing, is difficult. Discovering that an apparently simple topic has become complex is frustrating. *Writing well is hard work*. But learning any skill requires work. The reward is the achievement of owning that skill—and communicating effectively is a significant skill to possess.

Now, think about some attitudes about writing that may keep you from seeing the writing process realistically.

WRITING IS AFFECTED BY ATTITUDE

Bad experiences and personal uncertainties colour almost everyone's attitudes about writing. Begin building a realistic view of writing by giving some honest consideration to the questions that follow.

How would you answer these questions?

- ■ *How do you feel when you face beginning a writing task?* Most people feel *vulnerable*. They feel their shortcomings will be exposed on paper, whether in their ideas or in the way they express them, or both. A good way to manage this feeling is to write *only for yourself* when you are working on the first stages of the writing process; visualize yourself as *your only audience* as you begin. The more often do this, the less exposed you will feel.
- ■ *Do you worry about your instructor's evaluation of your first assignments?* Every student does. You do not know your audience the first few times you submit an assignment in a new course. You may worry that your professor will see you as less than intelligent or "bad at writing" when he or she marks your first submissions. In reality, your college English or communications instructor is waiting to help you and is *the audience you need*, not your enemy. Your instructor is willing to see your work positively and share his or her knowledge with you. Ask for help and do not expect perfection of yourself.

WRITING IS A PROCESS OF DISCOVERY

Believing that writing is a natural gift leads students to another false assumption: that writing flows in a single straight line from the writer's mind to the page. Good writing is never a simple one-draft trip to a flawless final text.

Writing is a process of discovery—a series of steps. The process loops and zigzags in many directions as the writer finds new ideas and connections between thoughts and associated feelings and mental images. Most writers do not know what they want to say or what their focus will be until they follow the paths of their thoughts in writing. Look at the following illustrations of the writing process:

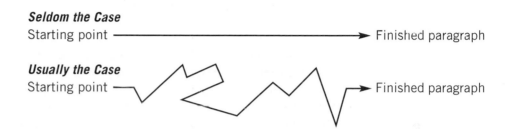

Writing is usually a process of continuing discovery; as you write, you find new avenues of thought, change direction, or even go backwards. An example would be Farida, the writer of this chapter's sample paragraph. She was asked to write about some aspect of college life. Only after freewriting on a wild assortment of college-related topics did she realize that most of her details concerned using the computer screen in front of her and her college's server. She discovered her subject in the course of writing.

You may work out an opening sentence and realize suddenly that this is your conclusion. Or you may find yourself caught up in explaining some detail, only to find it could be the main point of your paragraph. Chapter 2 will treat the writing process directly. What is important now, as you begin to write, is to know that writers usually do not know their precise destination when they start out. Be relaxed and patient with yourself; the directional shifts in the writing process are *not* mistakes. You are discovering what you want to say as well as the shape and direction of your paper.

WRITING PARAGRAPHS AND ESSAYS OFFERS MANY BENEFITS

Now you know some reassuring facts about writing in general. Before moving on to the paragraph as a specific form, consider the benefits of writing paragraphs and essays, benefits that may surprise and motivate you.

Mastering the structural requirements of paragraphs and essays gives you the foundation for all college writing assignments. For other courses, you will be assigned a variety of writing forms that will be variations on paragraph and essay forms: exam answers, short reports, analyses, business or technical documents, response papers, and even website text. You begin with paragraphs because these serve as the basic building blocks of essays, the most common form of writing in college.

Looking ahead, and to other media, paragraph writing readies you for the requirements of electronic communication. During your career, you may write online as often as on paper. Stating a point and backing it up concisely are the essentials of time-efficient e-mail correspondence and website content. Screen readers impatiently scan a document's opening for its point and spend only seconds to check for evidence of support and explanation, expecting to see the patterns and skills you learn from writing effective paragraphs.

Disciplines you acquire in paragraph and essay writing strengthen other essential communication skills: reading and listening. During college and your career, you will be evaluated on how well you absorb, use, and transmit information. Learning to manage ideas in paragraphs makes you a more perceptive reader. As you clarify your own ideas and learn to support them, your awareness of how other writers handle ideas and proof grows stronger. You become more critically aware of other writers' and speakers' ideas and the evidence they provide.

Most important, paragraph and essay writing makes you a stronger thinker. Writing a clearly reasoned paragraph or essay requires mental discipline and close attention to a set of logical rules. Each time you meet the challenge of writing a topic sentence or thesis statement supported by well-reasoned, convincing evidence, your ability to express, order, and defend ideas grows stronger.

AN INTRODUCTION TO THE BASIC PRINCIPLES OF EFFECTIVE WRITING

These are the four steps to follow each time you begin a paragraph or essay writing assignment:

1 Discover and start with a clearly stated point.
2 Provide logically ordered, detailed support for your point.
3 Organize and connect your supporting material.
4 Revise and edit so that your content is concise and well stated and your sentences error-free.

Section One of this book explains each of these steps in detail and provides many practice materials to help you master them. Now, however, we will begin by examining two basic elements of effective college writing: point and support.

Point and Support: An Important Difference between Writing and Talking

Every act of communication has a point. Humans are rarely aimless creatures; even when we wave to a friend in the hall, we have a reason to do so. Speech is even more purposeful: in everyday conversation, we make all kinds of points. We may say, "I love my job," "Sherifa's a really generous person," or "That exam was unfair." The points may concern personal matters or larger issues: "A lot of doctors are arrogant" or "Rises in tuition fees make students suffer."

Points raised in conversation often lack support, for two reasons. First, conversations are brief, unless we intend to argue or pursue a point more thoroughly. Second, the people with whom we speak do not always challenge us to support our statements. They may know why we feel as we do, or they may already agree with us, or they simply may not want to put us on the spot. Thus, they do not always ask "Why?" But the people who *read* what we write may not know us, agree with us, or feel in any way obliged to us.

Points made in print need support. First, we rarely write as briefly as we speak. Second, a reading audience may have many viewpoints. Readers' knowledge of you and of the context for your ideas is usually limited to the words you have written. You are not there to interrupt your text and explain what you mean, so you must give detailed support for your points. Third, and perhaps most significant, print allows readers to consider our views at their leisure and form their own responses. As well, reading even a paragraph asks something of readers: time and some concentration. Readers don't like wasting time and energy; they want to know what you are writing about and why you are writing.

Therefore, communicating effectively means making a point understood by the audience. To communicate effectively with readers, an effective writer provides solid evidence for any point he or she makes. An important difference between writing and talking is that *in writing, any idea advanced must be supported with specific reasons or details.*

Readers are generally reasonable people. They will not take our views on faith, but they *are* willing to consider what we say *as long as we support it.* Therefore, we must remember to support any statements that we make with specific evidence.

Point and Support in a Paragraph

You read print in blocks of sentences, or paragraphs. The look of a group of sentences placed together and surrounded by white space suggests a paragraph's purpose: it is a container for a series of thoughts tied to one idea. A paragraph is a basic unit of writing of 150 words or more. It usually consists of an opening point called a *topic sentence* followed by a *series of specifics*, in the form of sentences, that support the point. Much of the writing featured in this book will be paragraphs.

A Sample Paragraph: Following is a paragraph on why Farida, a student writer, finds her college's Internet server annoying.

Net Eats Student's Time!

Using my college's server can be a terrible waste of time. Yesterday evening was typical of how irritating "collegenet" can be. First of all, the server itself was down for two hours. This happened on the evening when I wanted to check the college library site for an article my marketing professor mentioned. I was determined to find the article, so I kept trying my connection, and I was too restless to concentrate on my accounting assignment. Once the server started up again at 10:30 p.m., I found the article, printed it, and then decided to check my e-mail. The second stage in my growing irritation began with the twenty-three pointless messages I found. A lot of mail that the college sends out means nothing to me, like postings about parking charges at other campuses and announcements from student groups I've never heard of, so scrolling through these e-mails just to delete and trash them is a time-waster. The final stage in my annoyance was still waiting for me. Unlike the college notices, these were mysterious posts that took forever to download. As I sat there at midnight, yawning and drumming my fingers on the desk, the mystery mails finally revealed themselves as chain letters with huge address lists on them. These were the names and e-mail addresses of dozens of students—everyone the sender knew. Students who send these chain letters, complete with the usual threats about "breaking the chain," obviously have more time on their hands than I do.

Notice what the details in this paragraph do. They provide you, the reader, with a basis for understanding why the writer feels as she does. Through specific evidence, the writer has explained and communicated her point successfully. The evidence that supports the point in a paragraph often consists of a series of reasons or subtopics introduced by signal words (*first of all, second*, and the like) and followed by examples and details that support the reasons or expand on the subtopics. That is true of the sample paragraph above: three reasons are provided, followed by examples and details that back up those reasons.

Activity 1

Complete the following outline of the sample paragraph. Summarize in a few words the details that develop each reason, rather than writing the details out in full.

Point: _____

_____

Reason 1: _____

    Details that develop reason 1: _____

_____

_____

Reason 2: _____

    Details that develop reason 2: _____

_____

_____

Reason 3: _____

    Details that develop reason 3: _____

_____

_____

Activity 2

Complete the statements below.

1. An important difference between writing and talking is that in writing we absolutely must _____ any statement we make.

2. A _____ is a collection of specifics that support a point.

Writing a Paragraph: An excellent way to get a feel for the paragraph is to write one. Your instructor may ask you to do that now. The only guidelines you need to follow are the ones described here and on the previous pages. There is an advantage to writing a paragraph right away, at a point where you have had almost no instruction. This first paragraph will give a quick sense of your needs as a writer and will provide a benchmark or baseline—a standard of comparison that you and your instructor can use to measure your writing progress during the semester.

WRITING YOUR FIRST PARAGRAPH

Activity

Write a paragraph on the best or worst job you have ever had. Provide three reasons why your job was the best or the worst, and give plenty of details to develop each of your three reasons. Note that the sample paragraph, "Net Eats Student's Time," has the same format your paragraph should have. The author:

1 states a point in her first sentence,
2 gives three reasons to support the point,
3 introduces each reason clearly with signal words (*first of all, second,* and *finally*), and then
4 provides details that develop each of the three reasons.

Write your paragraph on a separate sheet of paper.

AN INTRODUCTION TO THIS BOOK

How the Book Is Organized

English Skills with Readings is divided into five sections. Read the Table of Contents, then skim through Sections One and Two. Brief questions about Sections One through Four appear below, not to test you but simply to introduce you to the central ideas in the text and the organization of the book. Your instructor may ask you to write the answers in class or just to note the answers in your head.

1. According to Chapters 3, 4, and 5 of Section One, what are the first, second, third, and fourth steps in writing?
    - How many of these steps have you used as parts of previous writing experience?
    - How many stages do you feel there would be in writing an effective paragraph or essay, using these steps?
    - What would those stages be, according to your experience?

2. The final chapter of Section One, "Four Bases for Evaluating Writing," introduces you to four goals for all your writing. These goals are referred to as "the four bases" in this book. List them and discuss briefly what each term means to you at this time. (You will find these bases summarized on the inside front cover of this text.)

3. Section Two is concerned with the different ways of developing your ideas within a paragraph or essay's structure.
    - How many methods of development are listed in the Table of Contents?
    - How many of these patterns have you already encountered?

4. Section Three deals with essay writing.
    - Based on your previous experience, how is an essay similar to a paragraph, and in what ways is it different?

5. Section Four is the largest section of the text; why do you think this is the case?
    - Which specific aspects of sentence skills do you wish to work on this semester?

AS YOU BEGIN. . .

English Skills with Readings will help you learn, practise, and apply the writing skills you need to communicate clearly and effectively. But the starting point must be your determination to do the work needed to become an effective writer. If you decide—*and only you can decide*—that you want to learn to write effectively, this book will help you reach that goal.

REVIEWING THE LEARNING OUTCOMES FOR CHAPTER 1

To assure yourself that you have understood and met the learning outcomes for this chapter, answer the following questions.

1   What does the idea of "writing as a learnable skill" mean to you, based on your own experiences?
2   How will writing paragraphs and essays specifically benefit you during your college years and your career?
3   What are the four basic steps in effective writing?
4   How were you able to put some of this chapter's ideas to specific use in writing your first paragraph?
5   What are the five main sections of this book?

Visit the *English Skills with Readings* Online Learning Centre at **www.mcgrawhill.ca/college/langan** to access self-quizzes, bonus material on study and research skills, web resources, and other learning and study tools.

*xplaining a Process • Examining Cause and Effect • Comparing or Contrasting • Defining erm • Dividing and Classifying • Describing a Scene or Person • Narrating an Event • Argui Position • Explaining a Process • Examining Cause and Effect • Comparing or Contrasting efining a Term • Dividing and Classifying • Describing a Scene or Person • Narrating vent • Arguing a Position • Explaining a Process • Examining Cause and Effect • Compari

CHAPTER 2

The Writing Process

LEARNING OUTCOMES

After reading this chapter and completing its activities, you will

- know the four steps in writing an effective paragraph or essay;
- understand the main purposes for writing and the importance of writing for a specific purpose;
- know your audience and its expectations each time you write;
- understand how to choose a subject and how to discover information about your subject;
- know why prewriting is important and know four different ways to discover ideas;
- understand the importance of outlining and how to create an effective outline; and
- know what revising is, why it is essential, how to revise, and how revising differs from editing and proofreading.

Chapter 1 introduced you to the paragraph form and some basics about writing. The chapters that follow in Section One will explain the steps in writing a paragraph and standards for evaluating a paragraph. This chapter sets you on the road to effective writing by introducing you to *writing as a process with a purpose*. The focus will be on prewriting, outlining, and revising: strategies that help you create solid paragraphs every time you use them.

Four steps for creating effective paragraphs are set out below. Internalizing these steps and making them constant habits will guide you every time you approach a writing task.

Four Steps to Effective Writing

- Discover your point—often through prewriting.
- Develop logical, detailed support for your point—through more prewriting.
- Organize your point and supporting material into an outline.
- Write a first draft, then revise and edit in further drafts.

Each of these steps uses different parts of your mind and different ways of thinking. Learning how the writing process works at each step will help you to focus your mind for that step and lessen your confusion about writing effectively. The chapters that follow cover the steps in detail, allowing you to practise them and absorb the sequence thoroughly.

Before you "test drive" the writing process, you may face common first-semester challenges: discovering your purpose and audience and choosing a topic. Here is some advice to help you with these preliminary tasks.

WRITING FOR A SPECIFIC PURPOSE AND AUDIENCE

The three most common purposes of writing are *to inform*, *to persuade*, and *to entertain*. Most of the writing you will do in this book will involve some form of persuasion. You will advance a point in your topic sentence and then support it in a variety of ways. To some extent, you will also write papers to inform: to provide readers with information about a particular subject.

Your audience will be primarily your instructor and sometimes other students as well. Your instructor is really a symbol of the larger audience you should see yourself as writing for: an educated, adult audience that expects you to present your ideas in a clear, direct, and organized way. If you can learn to write to persuade or inform such a general audience, you will have accomplished a great deal. Section Two of this book includes assignments asking you to write with very specific purposes in mind, and for very specific audiences.

KNOWING OR DISCOVERING YOUR SUBJECT

KNOWING YOUR SUBJECT

Whenever possible, try to write on a subject that interests you. You will then find it easier to put more time and energy into your work. More important, try to write on a subject that you already know something about. If you do not have direct experience with the subject, you should at least have indirect experience: knowledge gained through thinking, prewriting (to be explained on page 16), reading, or talking about the subject.

If you are asked to write on a topic about which you have no experience or knowledge, do enough research to gain the information you need. Without direct or indirect experience, or the information you gain through research, you will be unable to provide the specific evidence needed to develop the point you are trying to make. Your writing will be starved for specifics.

To find the information you need, visit your college or local library or use an Internet search engine to find websites on your topic. At the library, look up your topic in the subject index of the computerized catalogue. Note the titles of books or of articles in journals or magazines that seem most related to your topic. (See the Online Learning Centre for information on basic research techniques.) Be prepared to spend some time scanning material relevant to your assignment. Remember to write down the author, the title of the publication or website, and the page number of any material you want to quote or paraphrase in your own words. If you use the Internet for your research, use your topic and synonyms for it as search keywords. Be ready to spend some time reading and perhaps printing information from sites most related to your topic. Bookmark these sites on your own computer or write down the titles of the sites and their URLs.

DISCOVERING YOUR TOPIC AND YOUR FOCUS

Sometimes you will not know your subject when you start writing. At other times you will be given a broad subject area and will need to find a definite topic within it. You will often discover your topic at one point or another during the writing process. When a student named Paul was given the general subject "learning from experience" (page 37), *experience* acted as a keyword for him and triggered some thoughts about working out. At first, his prewriting showed a focus on all the reasons why he had started going to the gym. When he tried asking himself questions, however, he found that his topic was really the benefits he had gained from maintaining his workout schedule. Paul *thought* he knew where his focus lay when he finished his freewriting. In fact, he *discovered* his true focused topic *during the process of writing*.

Another student, Alexa, started with a broad assigned subject: part-time jobs. She immediately thought that because she had quit high school and worked at several jobs, her topic might be how boring such jobs were. But as she accumulated details, she realized that she was really more challenged and sometimes even upset at work—*bored* did not, in fact, describe her true feelings. She sensed that the strongest source of her real feelings was the memory of her nightly routine as a telemarketer. "That was it," Alexa explained. "I had a picture in my head of every step I went through five nights a week. I knew I had something to turn into a paragraph." Then it was just a matter of detailing exactly how her work routine felt each evening. Her paragraph, "Torture by Telephone," is on page 77. Alexa changed her topic focus again when she turned her paragraph into the essay that appears on pages 278-79.

Sometimes you must write a bit in order to find out just what you want to write. Writing can help you think about and explore your topic and decide just what direction your essay will finally take. The techniques presented in "Prewriting"— the section starting on page 16—will suggest specific ways to discover and develop a subject.

ALLOWING YOUR IDEAS TO EMERGE

Do not feel that you must proceed in a linear fashion when you write. As noted in Chapter 1, the writing process is not a direct line from your central point to supporting detail 1 to supporting detail 2 to supporting detail 3 to your conclusion. Instead, as you draft the paragraph, proceed in whatever way seems most comfortable. You may want to start by writing the closing section or by developing your third supporting detail.

Do whatever is easiest. As you get material down on the page, it will make what you have left to do a bit easier. Sometimes as you work on one section, a new focal point for your paragraph will emerge. If your writing tells you that it wants to be something else, then revise or start over as needed to take advantage of that discovery. Do not be rigid or critical of yourself. The discovery stage of the writing process is not a time for linear, "by the rules" thinking. Your goal is to wind up with a paragraph that solidly makes and supports a point. Be ready and open to change direction and to make whatever adjustments are needed to reach your goal.

Activity 1

Answer the following questions.

1. What are three ways of gaining information to write a paragraph?
2. How does having enough information about a subject make the writing process easier?
3. You are freewriting to discover material for a paragraph on using technology at college and find that most of the points you have written down concern your enjoyment of computer graphics software. What has happened? What should you do?

Activity 2

Write for five minutes about the house, residence, or apartment where you live. Simply write down whatever details come to you. Don't worry about being neat; just pile up as many details as you can.

Afterwards, go through the material. Try to find a potential focus within all those details. Do the details suggest a simple point that you could make about the place where you live? If so, you've seen a small example of how writing about a topic can be an excellent way of discovering a point about that topic.

A NOTE ABOUT PARAGRAPH LENGTH

Every time you read a paragraph from a newspaper article, a website, or a novel, the paragraph's look sends you a message. Its appearance signals to you that it covers a single idea, but some paragraphs are so short that they look like "print bites." You know that proving your point in print requires more words than you might use in conversation, but you may wonder how long a paragraph should be.

Paragraph length depends on three main considerations:

- the purpose of the paragraph,
- the reading audience's needs, and
- the medium and format in which the paragraph appears.

Paragraphs range from one sentence to several pages in length. Short paragraphs in newspapers—a disposable medium—give easy-to-manage information quickly to a wide variety of readers. Because article paragraphs are printed in narrow columns, they are purposely broken into short pieces to attract busy readers. Websites entertain and inform in a competitive electronic environment. Screens are harder to read than pages; scroll bars, back buttons, colour, animation, and graphics tempt readers away from long periods of focus. Web-based paragraphs may appear brief, but in fact they often use "three-dimensional support"—hypertext links to material on other parts of the same page or other sites. Stories and novels imitate life in entertaining ways. Their paragraphs may be only a single line of dialogue or may run to twenty sentences of intense action or vivid description—their purpose is to carry leisure-time readers along in a fictional world.

Essays, reports, textbooks, non-fiction books, and career writing formats inform or persuade readers. These formats are generally printed so that readers can consider, judge, and sometimes act on their content. Paragraph length depends on making a point and supporting it with logical and sufficient explanation. This is the type of writing that you are doing now, and this is why short paragraphs are rarely found in college writing. Instead of asking how long your paragraph should be, ask yourself, "Does my paragraph make my point clear?"

AN OVERVIEW OF THE WRITING PROCESS

A blank page or screen can intimidate anyone. As you sit wondering how to develop a paragraph, you may develop a mental block instead. The blank, confused feeling is usually the result of "mental clutter," trying to think of too many things at once.

Beginning to write is difficult, but these two strategies will help you immediately:

1 Review the four steps to effective writing in the box below, and see how these steps mesh with and lead to the four clear-cut goals for an effective paragraph. Doing so will give you a structure and path to follow.

2 Focus on *one* writing task at a time. No one can come up with a point before knowing what his or her thoughts are; no one writes a final draft in one sitting. Begin at the beginning—this chapter will show you where and how to begin to write good paragraphs.

Four Steps to Effective Writing

1 **Discover** a point.
2 **Develop** solid support for the point.

3 **Organize and connect** supporting details by outlining and drafting.
4 **Write and revise** to develop your point most clearly through supporting details and to ensure that language or mechanical errors do not interfere with your message.

Four Goals for Effective Writing

1 **Unity:** The point guides and controls all details.
2 **Support:** There are sufficient supporting details and each is clearly explained.
3 **Coherence:** Supporting details are in an appropriate order; transitions connect ideas.
4 **Effective Sentence Skills:**
Sentences, spelling, and punctuation are free of errors; readers will see your point without interference.

Don't worry about trying to memorize the four steps or the four goals; this book will remind you of them. As you work through this text, these steps and goals will become parts of your "writing equipment."

When you start to write a paragraph, you begin a process that is not straightforward. For most writers, getting started is difficult. First of all, discovering what you think will take time and energy. Your mind is not blank; it is full of ideas and connections—writing, like drawing, speaking, or making music, is a way of finding out what your ideas are, then giving them a shape.

The writing process has four general stages, and each calls for a different approach. The "discovery" stage, or *prewriting*, requires different mental processes than the "shaping" stages—*outlining* and *drafting*—or the "polishing," or *revising*, stage of the writing process.

In the following pages, you will learn how to best use your abilities during the different stages of writing, and you will explore tested strategies to help you over blocks and problems—skills you can practise in writing situations for the rest of your life.

STAGE 1: PREWRITING

Prewriting describes the first stage of the writing process, the creative discovery period. During prewriting, you free your mind to discover the directions in which your ideas flow most freely. This is not a time to use "ordering" or "correcting" functions in your mind—those work against the relaxed, open mental state you need for exploratory prewriting.

By trial and error, writers have found techniques, sometimes referred to as "brainstorming," to help open up their minds and imaginations. The following pages describe four of these techniques to help you discover and develop a topic and get words down on paper:

1 Freewriting
2 Questioning
3 List making
4 Clustering

1 FREEWRITING

When you do not know what to write about a subject or when you are blocked in writing, freewriting sometimes helps. In *freewriting*, you write on your topic for ten minutes. Do not worry about spelling or punctuating correctly, about erasing mistakes, or about finding exact words. Just write without stopping. If you get stuck for words, write "I am looking for something to say," or repeat words until something comes. Do not be inhibited, since mistakes do not count and you do not have to hand in what you've written.

Freewriting will limber up your writing muscles and make you familiar with the act of writing. It is a way to break through mental blocks about writing and overcome the fear of making errors. Simply concentrate on discovering what you want to say about a subject. Your initial ideas and impressions will often become clearer once they are down on paper. Through continued practice in freewriting, you will develop the habit of thinking as you write. And you will learn a technique that is a helpful way to get started on almost any writing task.

Freewriting to Generate Ideas: A Student Model

Terry was assigned a paragraph on the general topic of a change that had affected him. He began with some freewriting about any changes he could think of. His spelling and grammar errors have been corrected for readability in the text below; but in freewriting, do not worry about such things. Concentrate on chasing your thoughts and feelings.

> There've been so many changes in the last while I can't think where to start here. Coming to Toronto was one of them. Funny, I used to dream about living in Toronto and now it doesn't seem that much better than home. It's just more expensive and bigger. College is another change, and I think it's a good one. At least I hope I end up with a job at the end so I don't have to worry about moving home and not getting work. There's not much left to my town any more, and I don't think some people in my class who grew up in a city could understand what it's like to watch the place you live die out. It felt so deserted, like a ghost town, when I went home for Thanksgiving. I didn't even want to walk down Queen Street because it was even emptier than what I remembered—you feel more attached to streets and places maybe than you would in a city.

Focused Freewriting

That evening after class, Terry read over his notes and realized he had a few potential topics. He asked himself if there was some point he could make that he could cover in a paragraph. What had he written the most about? What did he feel most strongly about? In Terry's case, his freewriting ended up mainly concerned with how his hometown was suffering. He decided that he would narrow his topic down to the changes in his town. Then he did some focused freewriting to pile up details on the topic he had discovered.

> Two years ago, the town where I grew up on the shore of Lake Erie started to dry up and disappear. The biggest employer, the car-parts factory, had just closed down for its third strike in five years, and the labour problems were getting worse and worse. More workers were being laid off as more and more parts were being made in Mexico or in Asia. Last night's paper said the U.S. parent company is going to close the factory for good. There isn't anywhere near here for all those hundreds of people to work. Will all those families still be able to live here? One of the two big chain stores just outside of town closed in the last year, and the other one became part of an American chain. Wal-Mart took over the big discount store, but they brought in their own management and people from some of their other stores, so a third of the original store's employees didn't end up working at the new store. The saddest

sight of all is Queen Street, the town's old main street. Everybody used to walk along Queen Street; it always looked like it would never change and it was the real heart of town. A year ago, a big new mall was built just outside of London, only a half-hour's drive away. People drive there to do all their shopping, and even to do their banking, or go to the movies. Half the stores on Queen Street are closed and empty today, and two of the bank branches have shut down. No one has any reason to "go downtown" any more. Right now, it feels like my hometown is on the way to becoming a ghost town.

Terry's next step was to use the freewriting as the basis for a list and an outline for a paragraph about the causes of the changes in his hometown. An effective paragraph that eventually resulted from freewriting, an outline, and a good deal of rewriting appears on pages 208-9.

Tips and Comments

- Freewriting is *for you*; you are the audience and no one is checking over your shoulder.
- The whole point of freewriting is to go with the flow of your ideas; don't stop as you discover what's in your mind—get ideas down just as they come to you.
- Correcting problems is a different mental process from exploring; shifting mental gears or trying to "get it right" can slow or stop the discovery stage of the writing process.

Activity

To get a sense of freewriting, use a sheet of paper to freewrite about your everyday worries. See how many ideas and details you can accumulate in ten minutes.

2   QUESTIONING

Questioning as a technique works in a different way than freewriting. If you are an order-oriented, methodical person who enjoys linear thinking, questioning may offer a comfortable framework to use. Freewriting bypasses the ordering parts of your mind; questioning requires you to confront yourself with a set of specific demands. Questioning's structured approach gives a sense of direction to prewriting. Ask yourself as many questions as you can think of about your subject; your answers will be a series of different takes or focuses on it. Such questions include "Why?" "When?" "Where?" "Who?" and "How?"

To begin, divide your page or screen into two columns: "Questions" and "Answers," as you see below. Leave enough space in the "Answers" column so that you can return to a particular response if more details come to you later. Next, ask yourself this preliminary question: "What's my subject?" Write your answer as a reference point for the rest of your question and answer series. If one question stops you, just go on to another.

Here is an example of how one student, Mark, used questioning to generate material for a paragraph. Mark felt that he could write about a painful moment he had experienced, but he was having trouble getting started after doing some freewriting. So he asked himself a series of questions about the experience. As a result, he accumulated a series of details that provided the basis for the paragraph he finally wrote.

Here are the questions Mark asked and the answers he wrote.

Questions	Answers
<u>Where</u> did the experience happen?	In my younger brother's residence room at the University of Alberta
<u>When</u> did it happen?	A week before his first-year spring break
<u>Who</u> was involved?	My brother Josh, his roommate, and I
<u>What</u> happened?	I found out my brother was failing every course but one, and wasn't even planning to tell our parents. His marks in December weren't good, and his bulletin board was covered with tests with big red Fs on them. He'd even changed the address for his spring transcripts by claiming his main residence was his roommate's mother's house.
<u>Why</u> was the experience so painful?	My brother always did better than I did in school, and my parents were paying for his tuition and residence fees. They really wanted him to succeed at university. I worked for five years before I started putting myself through college for the last two years. The trip from Winnipeg cost me a lot of money, and I was really looking forward to it.
<u>How</u> did my brother react?	He tried to lie to me at first, pretending that nothing was wrong when I asked how his marks were. Then he got tense and defensive, saying he wasn't sure what he was doing yet anyway and that he needed time off to travel.
<u>How</u> did I react?	I was in a rage. I couldn't believe how dishonest he was and how he could let down our parents this way. I wanted to get out of there and call home, then I thought better of it. I was jealous of all the advantages he was ready to waste. Then I decided to wait and see if he would admit what he was doing to the family.

After discovering all these details from his questioning, Mark's next step was to prepare an outline. He then worked his way through several drafts of the paper, focusing on revealing his own responses to his disappointment with his brother. The effective paragraph that eventually resulted from Mark's prewriting techniques appears in Chapter 8, "Narrating an Event," on page 155.

Tips and Comments

Questioning works well as a second stage for your prewriting, too. If you have done some general freewriting but are still not sure of a focus for your paper, then try questioning, using your freewriting as a reference.

- Questioning may reveal your focus quickly when one answer in particular is more detailed than others.
- Questioning can yield answers that may be rich sources of *connected* details—making some of your organizing and outlining a little easier.
- Questioning can show you directions for paragraphs; if you have many answers to "Why?" your mind may want to explore the causes of a subject.

Activity

To get a sense of questioning, use a sheet of paper to ask yourself a series of questions about a restaurant you particularly enjoy. See how many details you can accumulate about that place in ten minutes.

3 LIST MAKING

Making a list is another way to get your ideas flowing. Simply list as many different items as you can think of about your topic. Do not worry about repeating yourself, and do not allow yourself to be sidetracked into the ordering stage of sorting out major ideas from lesser ones or supporting details. Spelling and punctuation are not concerns here; you are the only audience. A list's lack of structure works for you—there are no sentences to be concerned about; write in point form. Your goal is to accumulate as much raw material related to your topic as possible.

Jennifer, a first-semester student in a digital media program, was assigned a paragraph on the general subject of "an important decision." First she made a list to focus her topic. She listed all the decisions she could think of that she had made within the past six months and noticed that she was adding points to one item in particular.

Here is Jennifer's first try at list making, when she was narrowing her topic for her paragraph.

Decisions (my topic)

1. renting an apartment
   —finding roommates—rent
2. cutting my hair ?
3. applying to Sheridan
   —not going to university

4. taking digital media
    —want to design video games, I love to play them
    —really interested in digital graphics and how games work
    —jobs in the gaming industry?
    —never thought I could work at something that's fun
5. buying my own computer

Making this list clearly showed Jennifer one good topic focus for a paragraph: her decision to enter a digital media program.

Next Jennifer prepared a second list, to generate ideas for her paragraph. She felt more confident now, because making the first list had revealed to her that she had lots of thoughts about why she had registered in her program. Following is the list she made to accumulate all her ideas and details on the topic she had discovered with her first list.

Decision—to take digital media

1. it will let me take courses in game design
2. love working with graphics (spend hours with Photoshop— thought I was wasting my time)
3. playing v.g. almost an obsession (want to know how to make them myself)
4. making up stories about characters for games
5. orientation for program—talked about jobs in the gaming industry
6. I could work at something I really love
7. kinds of games—first person

Notice that with this list, Jennifer is starting to expand on her items. She puts parentheses around some notes to herself of ideas and details that relate to, explain, and expand on the items she thinks of. Very often, as you make a list, you will discover ways to develop your writing. Jot down any ideas that connect to your list items.

Tips and Comments

List making works as a first or second stage of prewriting. As a first stage, listing is a quick, easy method that you are already familiar with from making everyday to-do lists.

- List making frees you of concerns about your sentences in prewriting; simply list your ideas as phrases.
- List making works if you like to make notes to yourself as you work; just include something like "good first idea" in parentheses after an item.

List making is an effective second stage of prewriting. You may find it useful to make a list by referring to your page of freewriting.

- List making after freewriting can stimulate your mind so you think of more points and details.
- Listing your ideas after freewriting, questioning, or clustering displays your thoughts in simple uncluttered form, so you can proceed to evaluate them.

■ Listing is an excellent sorting method; number your points and ideas in your preferred order before outlining, or sort out points and their related supporting details from your list.
■ Listing is useful for writers who like to connect ideas graphically with lines and circles—you can quickly sketch in relationships between ideas and note anything special.

Activity

To get a sense of making a list, use a sheet of paper to list specific hopes you will have for this semester. See how many ideas and details you can accumulate in ten minutes.

4 CLUSTERING

Clustering, also known as *mapping* or *diagramming*, is another prewriting activity that can help you generate ideas and details about a topic. In clustering, you use lines, boxes, arrows, and circles to show relationships among the ideas and details that come to you.

Clustering is helpful to people who like to think visually. Whether you use a diagram, and just how you proceed with it, is up to you.

To use clustering to generate ideas, or as a first stage in prewriting, state your subject in a few words in the centre of a blank sheet of paper. Then, as ideas and details come to you, write them inside circles or boxes. When you discover connections between ideas and between groups of ideas, draw lines to connect them to one another and to your central idea.

There is no right or wrong way to diagram or cluster; it is a way to think on paper about how various ideas relate to one another. Below are the beginnings of some first-stage clustering done by a student named Devon, as he began to prepare for a paragraph on his job as a police officer.

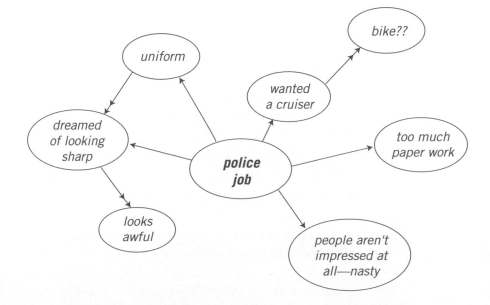

Below is the second stage of Devon's diagramming for that paragraph. He now knew he could write about the differences between his job as he imagined it and as it turned out to be. The cluster diagram, with its clear picture of relationships, was especially helpful for the comparison-contrast paragraph that Devon was doing. His final draft appears on page 227.

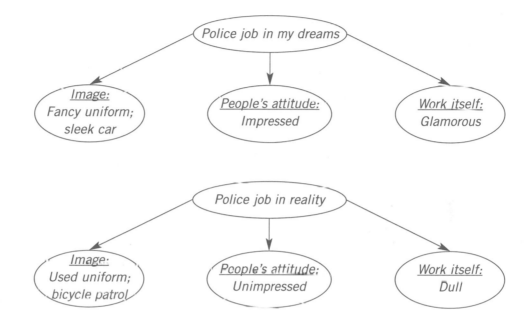

Tips and Comments

Clustering excels as a prewriting tool for the visually minded writer, for both the first and the second stages of prewriting. As a primary method of generating ideas, clustering frees you from the linearity of the page or screen.

- Clustering prevents "sentence block"; you note points and details in words and phrases.
- Clustering instantly shows you connections between ideas as you use lines and arrows to link one thing with another. If one idea seems to branch off from another, try using double arrows to show that connection, as in Devon's first-stage cluster diagram.

Clustering's only disadvantage is that your page may become too messy to follow. Avoid this by starting a second page where you distinguish visually between possible subtopics and details. Refer to both of Devon's diagrams for techniques to help you clarify levels of support, possible structures, and connections.

As a second stage of prewriting, clustering demonstrates relationships between ideas and details, as it has done for Devon. Clustering can also "preview" your paragraph's content and focuses.

- Cluster diagrams reveal clearly both a paragraph's focus and the possible levels of details within a paragraph.
- Clustering as a second stage, if you show levels of links between points and details, prepares you for outlining and drafting.

Activity

To get a sense of diagramming, use a sheet of paper to make a diagram of differences between two instructors or two jobs. See how many ideas and details you can accumulate in ten minutes.

USING ALL FOUR TECHNIQUES

Prewriting techniques are designed to open up your mind, to allow you to discover ideas and the connections between those ideas. No rules govern your use of prewriting techniques; go with what works for you. You may use several techniques almost simultaneously when writing. You may, for example, ask questions while making a list; you may diagram and perhaps sort through a list as you write it; you may ask yourself questions and then freewrite answers to them. And keep in mind that if you try one technique and are not satisfied, you can simply go on to another one. All the techniques are at your disposal. Choose those that work best for you.

Activity 1

Answer the following questions.

1. Which prewriting technique have you used previously?
2. Which prewriting technique do you think might work best for you? Why?
3. Why do people prewrite at all, rather than trying immediately to write a first draft?

Activity 2

Following are examples of how the four prewriting techniques could be used to develop the topic "inconsiderate drivers." Identify each technique by writing *Q* (for *questioning*), *F* (for *freewriting*), *C* (for the *cluster*), or *L* (for the *list*) in the answer space.

_____   High beams on

Weave in and out at high speeds

Treat street like a garbage can

Open car door onto street without looking

Stop on street looking for an address

Don't use turn signals

High speeds in low-speed zones

Don't take turns merging

Use horn when they don't need to

Don't give walkers the right of way

_____

What is one example of an inconsiderate driver?	A person who suddenly turns without using a signal to let the drivers behind know in advance.
When does this happen?	At city intersections or on smaller country roads.
Why is this dangerous?	You have to be alert to slow down yourself to avoid rear-ending the car in front.
What is another example of inconsiderateness on the road?	Drivers who come toward you at night with their high beams on.

_____

I was driving home last night after class and had three people try to blind me by coming at me with their high beams on. I had to zap them all with my high beams. Rude drivers make me crazy. The worst are the ones that use the road as a garbage can. People who throw bags and cups and hamburger wrappings and other stuff out the car windows should be tossed into a trash can themselves. If word got around that this was the punishment maybe they would wise up. Other people do dumb things as well. I hate the person who will just stop in the middle of the street and try to figure out directions or look for a house address. Why don't they pull over to the side of the street? That hardly seems like too much to ask. Instead, they stop all traffic while doing their own thing. Then there are the people who keep what they want to do a secret. They're not going to tell you they plan to make a right- or left-hand turn. Instead, you've got to figure it out yourself when they suddenly slow down in front of you.

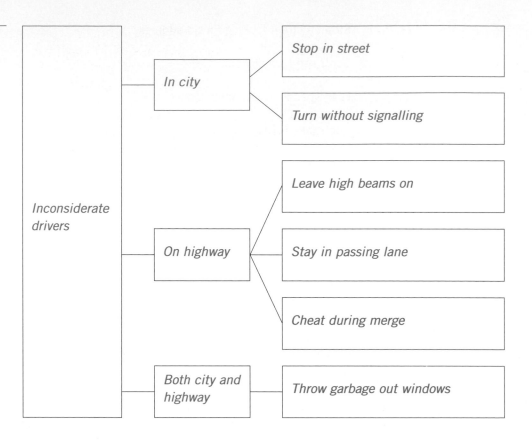

STAGE 2: OUTLINING

Outlining is the essential second stage in the writing process. You may first have to do a fair amount of prewriting to discover your topic and focus on the point you want to make; many writers spend over 60 per cent of their time on this first stage. Generally, you will create an outline from your prewriting, followed by a first draft: this is the sequence this book demonstrates. Outlining and sometimes re-outlining are needed to untangle and clarify your prewriting.

The quality of your outline can determine the success or failure of your paragraph. A paragraph is effective when its content is logically arranged and sufficiently detailed to make a point and support it thoroughly. Such a paragraph does not result from patching together random pieces of prewriting into a final draft. Paragraphs written without good outlines are as ramshackle as buildings constructed without blueprints.

- Creating a formal outline requires three thought processes: sorting, ordering, and evaluating. These are decision-making activities: you will consider your point and supporting details. The quality and the arrangement of your raw material are what add up to a solid paragraph.
- Sorting, ordering, and evaluating are organizational skills that develop your ability to think clearly and logically. Outlining lets you work on the bare

bones of your paragraph without the distracting clutter of phrases and sentences. You will see both your ideas and the connections between them.

- A good outline allows you to relax and write your first draft without worrying about what you will say next—you have your "blueprint" at hand.

Before you become intimidated by the prospect of outlining, know that with your prewriting done, you already have most of your content. There are some sorting techniques you can use to bridge the gap between rough notes, lists, or clusters and a finished outline.

CREATING AN OUTLINE FOR AN EFFECTIVE PARAGRAPH

The outlining process may not proceed in exactly the order set out below. You may find it easier to note your main subtopics before you are able to write a suitable topic sentence. Discovering the structure within your prewriting is one of the values of making an outline.

Students sometimes avoid making outlines, or they make quick and often odd-looking outlines *after* writing paragraphs. Outlining takes work, but it exposes repeated or similar ideas and weak connections between ideas. Outlining makes writing a good paper much easier. Rather than avoiding outlining, use it to map your thoughts and keep your intentions for your paragraph clear.

A good time to make an outline is after you have done some prewriting. Pause for a while so that you see your ideas with fresh eyes. Remember that outlines tend to change as you work on them, so try not to judge yourself harshly while you work.

There are many ways to start an outline, but the following method works if you allow yourself the time to go through it a step a time.

1 Copy the outline form on page 28. Write it by hand, leaving spaces to fill in, or key it in, saving it as a blank document that you can copy for repeated use.

2 Before you begin your outline, take a clean piece of paper or open a new document onscreen. Ask yourself two questions: "What is my point?" and "Why do I believe my point is true?" Write out your point in one sentence—now you have a topic sentence, a trial statement of your point. Be prepared to change the sentence if you find your point changing. Now list any words or phrases that bring to mind facts or situations that back up your point; these are your subtopics.

3 Next, look at your prewriting as well as at the page or screen document where you just noted your point and reasons for that point. See if some reasons are more important than others; if so, put your reasons—your subtopics—in order of importance, in order of time, or in another order that seems appropriate to you. Look back at your trial topic sentence to see if it is general enough to cover your subtopics; if not, revise it.

4 For each subtopic, list in point form the related details from your prewriting or any new details that occur to you. To ensure balance in your paragraph, it is desirable to have approximately the same number of details to support each subtopic.

5 You are ready to start your outline. Don't worry if you change or eliminate examples or think of a new way to explain a detail. If you are stalled at some point, fill in another section of the outline—you do not have to work from top to bottom in a straight line. The point of outlining is to see and shape your thoughts; you can always rearrange parts of your outline. A messy outline is usually a good outline.

The exercises following this section will help you to discern the difference between more general subtopics and the specific details that clarify, explain, or make vivid those subtopics.

PARAGRAPH OUTLINE FORM

To write an effective paragraph, first prepare an outline. Photocopy this outline form, or set it up as a blank document to save to your computer disk.

Point

  Topic Sentence: _____

  _____

Support

  Subtopic 1: _____

  _____

  Supporting Details (examples, explanations):

    a. _____

    b. _____

    c. _____

  Subtopic 2: _____

  _____

  Supporting Details (examples, explanations):

    a. _____

    b. _____

    c. _____

  Subtopic 3: _____

  _____

  Supporting Details (examples, explanations):

    a. _____

    b. _____

    c. _____

The following series of exercises will help develop the outlining skills that are so important to writing an effective paper.

Activity 1

One key to effective outlining is the ability to distinguish between general ideas and specific ideas. Read each group of specific ideas below. Then circle the letter of the general idea that tells what the specific ideas have in common. Note that the general idea should not be too broad or too narrow. Begin by trying the example item, and then read the explanation that follows.

Example   *Specific ideas:* egg salad; tuna salad; bacon, lettuce, and tomato; peanut butter and jelly
The general idea is:
a.   foods.
b.   sandwich fillings.
c.   salads used as sandwich fillings.

Explanation: It is true that the specific ideas are all food, but they have in common something even more specific—they are all sandwich fillings. Therefore, answer *a* is too broad; the correct answer is *b*. Answer *c* is too narrow because it doesn't cover all of the specific ideas: two of the sandwich fillings are not salads.

1. *Specific ideas:* Easter, Thanksgiving, Valentine's Day, New Year's Day
   The general idea is:
   a. days.
   b. holidays.
   c. religious holidays.

2. *Specific ideas:* hide and seek, tag, jacks, hopscotch
   The general idea is:
   a. games.
   b. toys.
   c. children's games.

3. *Specific ideas:* runny nose, coughing, sneezing, sore throat
   The general idea is:
   a. cold symptoms.
   b. symptoms.
   c. throat problems.

4. *Specific ideas:* yes, no, maybe, okay
   The general idea is:
   a. negative answers.
   b. positive answers.
   c. answers.

5. *Specific ideas:* OPEN, STOP, FIRE EXIT, YIELD
   The general idea is:
   a. words.
   b. words on signs.
   c. words on traffic signs.

Activity 2

In the following items, specific items are given but general ideas are unstated. Fill in each blank with a general heading that accurately encompasses the list provided.

Example   *General idea:*   <u>Breakfast choices</u>
                 Specific ideas: doughnuts
                                       bacon and eggs
                                       cereal
                                       pancakes

1. *General idea:* _____
    Specific ideas: birthday
                      anniversary
                      get well
                      graduation

2. *General idea:* _____
    Specific ideas: robbery
                      assault
                      murder
                      kidnapping

3. *General idea:* _____
    Specific ideas: salesperson
                      hairstylist
                      welder
                      insurance agent

4. *General idea:* _____
    Specific ideas: washing dishes
                      preparing meals
                      taking out garbage
                      dusting

5. *General idea:* _____
    Specific ideas: writing
                      listening
                      speaking
                      reading

Activity 3

Major and minor ideas, or subtopics and details, are mixed together in the two paragraphs outlined below. Place subtopics in the numbered spaces. Place each appropriate detail or minor idea under each subtopic in the spaces labelled *a* and *b*.

A. *Topic sentence:* People can be classified by how they treat their cars.
    Seldom wax or vacuum car
    Keep every mechanical item in top shape
    Protective owners
    Deliberately ignore needed maintenance
    Indifferent owners

Wash and polish car every week
Accelerate too quickly and brake too hard
Abusive owners
Inspect and service car only when required by provincial law

1. _____

   a. _____

   b. _____

2. _____

   a. _____

   b. _____

3. _____

   a. _____

   b. _____

B. *Topic sentence:* Living with an elderly parent has many benefits.
Advantages for elderly person
Live-in babysitter
Learn about the past
Advantages for adult children
Serve useful role in family
Help with household tasks
Advantages for grandchildren
Stay active and interested in young people
More attention from adults

1. _____

   a. _____

   b. _____

2. _____

   a. _____

   b. _____

3. _____

   a. _____

   b. _____

Activity 4

Again, major and minor ideas (subtopics and details) are mixed together. In addition, in each outline one of the three major ideas or subtopics is missing and must be added. Put the subtopics and details in logical order by filling in the outlines that follow (summarizing as needed) and adding a third major idea or subtopic.

A. *Topic sentence:* Extending the school day would have several advantages.
Help children academically

Parents know children are safe at the school
More time to spend on basics
Less pressure to cover subjects quickly
More time for extras like art, music, and sports
Help working parents
More convenient to pick up children at 4 or 5 p.m.
Teachers' salaries would be raised

1. _____

    a. _____

    b. _____

2. _____

    a. _____

    b. _____

3. _____

    a. _____

    b. _____

B. *Topic sentence:* By following hints about food, exercise, and smoking, you can increase your chances of dying young.

Don't ever walk if you can ride instead.
Choose foods such as bacon and lunch meats that are laced with nitrates and other preservatives.
Be very selective about what you eat.
If you begin to cough or feel short of breath, keep smoking.
If a friend invites you to play an outdoor sport, open a beer instead and head for your reclining chair.
Resist the urge to exercise.
Choose foods from one of four essential groups: fat, starch, sugar, and grease.
Smoke on a regular basis.

1. _____

    a. _____

    b. _____

2. _____

    a. _____

    b. _____

3. _____

    a. _____

    b. _____

Activity 5

Read the following student paragraph. Then outline it in the space provided. Write out the topic sentence and summarize in a few words the subtopics. Then note the supporting details that fit under each subtopic.

Cooking Is My Life

I love to cook for many reasons; in fact, cooking will truly be my life when I graduate from the culinary arts program at Niagara College. My love of cooking begins in my childhood, so my first reason must be early memories of wonderful smells and funny kitchen conversations with my grandmother. Today I still prefer the fragrance of her white cornbread baking to the scent of any perfume. Some day I hope to attract customers to a restaurant of my own with the aromas of the Portuguese soups and stews she made for the family. I also associate cooking with laughter, because my grandmother had the interesting habit of talking to food. If a piece of meat she was trimming would not do what she wanted it to, she would say, "Come on, Senhor Lamb Leg, you must obey me." The meat, the fish, and the vegetables always understood her and obeyed, even the potatoes she hated peeling and occasionally cursed. Talk and laughter were always part of family dinners, so they are the second reason I love to cook. Dinners lasted at least an hour. They held us together as a family because meals were often the only times I saw my older sisters and brothers and my father. Even though I liked sharing in the conversations, what I loved best about those dinners was the respect and love my grandmother received for everything she put on the table. Each dish was always tasted, smelled, and praised when it arrived on the table. Finally, perhaps the most important reason I love to cook is that from a very early age, I always received my share of praise for cooking. When my grandmother kneaded bread dough, she would hand me a piece, put me on a stool at the counter beside her, and let me pound the dough any way I pleased. Even if I made a mess, she would always bake my little "loaf" beside her big ones, and give everyone some of my bread at dinner so they could say how good it was. For all these reasons, I can say that I look forward to a lifetime of cooking ... and talking to the food as I cook.

Topic sentence: _____

_____

Subtopic 1. _____

    a. _____

    b. _____

Subtopic 2. _____

    a. _____

    b. _____

Subtopic 3. _____

      a. _____

      b. _____

STAGE 3: WRITING FIRST DRAFTS

Writing an effective paragraph is never done all at once. First, prewrite until you feel confident about your topic, subtopics, and supporting details. Then work with your prewriting until you are satisfied that you can create a complete and logical paragraph outline. Now you are ready for the third stage of the writing process: creating a first draft. (Chapters 3 and 4 will give you more details about this stage.)

All your work on the first two stages will now pay off. Instead of staring at that blank screen or empty sheet of paper, you have ideas and details ready to turn into sentences. If possible, allow some time between outlining and writing a draft. A day or even a few hours will let you approach your material with a fresh outlook and a new perspective on what you want to say. Here are some tips on creating a first draft.

- Never try to make a first draft a *final* draft. You will defeat the purpose of working on writing as a process. A first draft is only one part—*the third stage after prewriting and outlining*—in creating your effective paragraph. It represents your first try at putting your ideas and structure into sentence and paragraph form. Second, you will inhibit yourself by trying to make each sentence "perfect." Saying exactly what you mean in the way you want to say it takes time. In your first draft, concentrate on getting the points and details on your outline down as sentences. Trying to write a finished piece of work in one draft forces your mind to do too many things at once: creating, choosing the right words, spelling correctly, and all the other tasks you perform as you write. Do one thing at a time. *Concentrate on your content.*
- Write on every other line, or, after typing in your draft, highlight it and change it from single spacing to double spacing. Doing so enables you to make changes and to add and subtract ideas, words, and phrases in your revision drafts.
- Do not worry about spelling errors or sentence problems. Correcting these belongs to the final stage of the writing process: *revising, editing, and proofreading.* Focus on getting your ideas down in sentences. Any other concern will only distract you.
- Do not worry if you leave out an idea or detail in your outline or add some new point or detail. The writing process is never straightforward. Do not sacrifice a potentially good idea or vivid example for the sake of sticking rigidly to your outline. You can always revise your outline, and you will be revising your draft.

Your instructor may want you to include your first draft with the draft you submit, so be sure to save it. Alternatively, you may participate in peer evaluations of your first draft with your classmates. In such evaluations, focus is always on *content*: how clear is your point, and how well is it supported?

STAGE 4: REVISING, EDITING, AND PROOFREADING

REVISING CONTENT

Revising is the first part of the fourth stage of the writing process. Revising means literally "re-seeing" material; *it focuses on content* and how accurately or fully that content is expressed. Working with your first draft, you shape, add to, and perhaps subtract from your raw material as you take your paragraph through two or more drafts.

To revise the content of your paper, recall the four goals for effective writing from page 15, and ask the following questions.

1 Is my paper **unified**?
- Do I have a main idea that is clearly stated at the beginning of my paragraph?
- Do all my supporting points truly support and back up my main idea?

2 Is my paper **supported**?
- Are there separate subtopics for the main idea?
- Do I have *specific* evidence for each subtopic?
- Is there *enough* specific evidence for the subtopics?

3 Is my paper **coherent**?
- Do I have a clear method of organizing my paragraph?
- Do I use transitions and other connecting words?

The next two chapters will give you practice in achieving **unity**, **support**, and **coherence** in your writing.

Your goal in revising is to *make clear the single point* of your paragraph. Achieving this goal involves working on two activities: development of evidence and organization of evidence.

1 *Develop fully* the specific evidence needed to support your point.

- Be sure that your paragraph's main point is fully developed. Ask yourself, "What's missing?" Remember that your audience does not see your point through your eyes. For another person to "see" your point through your words, he or she needs you to be as specific and complete as possible. Either leave some time between drafts so that you read your work with fresh eyes, or have someone else read your paragraph.
- Look for *balance* in the distribution of your supporting details for each of your subtopics. If you have two examples as details to support one subtopic, but four examples detailing each of your other subtopics, then your paragraph will not seem *balanced,* and one subtopic may seem weak. You must add more support to one of your subtopics and delete your weakest items from your other subtopics.
- Check for *repetition,* ideas or details that do not add to your point but merely say the same thing in different words. Delete such repetitions and supply examples and details that are different, distinct, and aimed at making your point clear.

2 *Organize* and *connect* the specific evidence. Look at the way you explained or backed up your point.

- Are your subtopics set out in the order in which they happened? If you have used *time order,* be sure all your material follows this order.
- Is one of your points more important than the others? If you want to *emphasize* this point, place it last so that your other subtopics and details lead up to it.
- To ensure that your reader sees the *connections and relationships* between your subtopics, be sure to use *transition words and phrases.* If the *sequence* of your subtopics is important, use words like *first, next, second,* and so on. If there is a growing *order of importance* to your subtopics, use words like *more* and *most* when you introduce these increasingly important points. If one idea simply follows another *in time,* use phrases like *then, next,* or *after that,* and if one idea is *caused by* another, use words like *because* or *therefore.*

REVISING SENTENCES: EDITING AND PROOFREADING

Editing and proofreading are the final activities in this fourth stage of the writing process.

You *edit* the next-to-final draft; that is, you check it carefully for sentence skills—grammar, mechanics, punctuation, and usage. Run the spell checker on your final draft, or note and look up any words you are likely to have misspelled.

To revise individual sentences in your paragraph, ask the following questions.

1 Do I use *parallelism* to balance my words and ideas?

2 Do I have a *consistent point of view*?

3 Do I use *specific words*?

4 Do I use words effectively by avoiding *slang, clichés, pretentious language,* and *wordiness*?

5 Do I *vary my sentences* in length and structure?

Chapter 5 will give you practice in revising your sentences, and page references for all sentence-skills issues appear on the inside front cover.

Finally, you *proofread* the final copy of the paragraph for any mistakes in keying or handwriting.

Editing and proofreading are important steps that some people avoid, often because they have worked so hard (or so little) on the previous stages.

Ideally, you should have enough time to set your writing aside for a while, so that you can check it later from a fresh point of view. Remember that locating and correcting sentence-skills mistakes can turn an average essay into a better one and a good essay into an excellent one. A later section of this book will give you practice in editing and proofreading in a series of editing tests (Chapter 43).

PRACTICE IN SEEING THE ENTIRE WRITING PROCESS

This section will show you the stages, as covered in this chapter, in writing an effective paragraph. You will see what one student, Paul, did in preparing a paragraph about learning from experience.

There is no single sequence that all people follow in writing a composition. However, the different stages in composing that Paul went through in writing his paragraph should give you some idea of what to expect. Paul did not just sit down and proceed neatly from start to middle to finish. Writing seldom works like that.

STAGE 1: PREWRITING

Paul's assignment was to write a paragraph on learning unexpected things from experience. His first step was to do some freewriting on his topic.

> I've learned a lot from experience, for sure. Things I didn't expect were usually bad things, but sometimes I think I learn only by experiencing things. Starting to work out taught me a lot. Nothing bad there. Except being really stiff and not wanting to go sometimes. But I've changed a lot from when I started going to the gym. I've stopped avoiding stuff as much as I used to. I feel a lot better and I'm more confident about myself. I guess this is one of the best things I've ever done. Just feeling better kept me going back a lot of the time, even when I didn't feel like it. My self-esteem is a lot better than it was, even at school, in classes. I feel like I can face challenges better than I used to—I don't put things off as much. I've got more energy, too. And then when the gym offered me a job as a trainer, I knew I didn't just learn to do my routines well and build up my strength. All of a sudden, someone thought I was good enough at something to get paid for it. I like helping people to learn how to train. Some of them remind me of myself.

Note: To keep Paul's work as readable as possible, his spelling and sentence-skills mistakes have been corrected throughout this section. Ordinarily, a number of such mistakes might be present, and editing his work to remove them would be the final part of the writing process.

At this point, Paul has found a specific focus for his topic: some unexpected benefits he realized from working out. He then decided to move on to another prewriting technique—making up a list of details about what he learned from going to the gym consistently. Here is Paul's list.

How working out worked for me

went because I felt out of shape
Clothes didn't fit and I felt bad all the time
(What did I learn though?)
learned to go even when I didn't feel like it
learned to follow routines, even when I thought I could jump past something
Saw other people there in worse shape than me
it hurt a lot at first, but I started to get stronger and have more endurance

could run up the stairs at school without panting
feel like I can do all kinds of things now
stopped procrastinating so much
my jeans fit better—I bought a smaller size—like shopping for clothes
learned some discipline and patience
stuck with routines the way the trainer said to
got a job, get paid to go to the gym

STAGE 2: MORE PREWRITING AND CREATING AN OUTLINE

Freewriting and list making helped Paul to accumulate material for his paragraph. He *thought* he was ready to start lining up his details about things he hadn't expected to learn from working out. As he looked over his list, something occurred to him. Did he really want to discuss why he went to the gym in the first place? Did that really relate to learning unexpected things? He decided it did not, and he opted to omit those items. Paul also thought he could fill out some of the list items with more details to explain how important each of those benefits was to him.

Before trying to order the list items he thought were of value and risking frustration or forgetting which items he wished to add to, Paul decided to "step backwards." He tried another type of prewriting: asking himself questions. He thought of asking himself what were the *things he had learned* at the gym. Then he asked himself what were the *most unexpected benefits* he had gained. When he tried this, he found he had many details to add about what benefits he had gained and which of these were most important to him.

I learned a lot of unexpected things by going to the gym. What were they?
1. I could stick at something
   —hated doing the exercises at first
   —but I had paid for it
   —went when I didn't feel like it
   —used to give up on things easily
2. learned to follow instructions
   —did what the trainer told me to
   —hated it sometimes—felt like I was just repeating stuff for no reason
3. I felt better
   —stopped panting on stairs
   —lost weight
4. got good enough at working out to get a job
5. self-esteem—really didn't expect this

Paul felt, at this point, that he was not coming up with anything new, and he worried that he might lose track of some of the details he wanted to add to his list. As well, as he wrote the final two items on the list above, he realized he wanted to discuss the most important things he had learned from fitness training. He decided to move on to ranking what he had learned by asking himself what were the *most unexpected things* he had learned.

What was <u>most</u> unexpected?

1. Learning to stick with something
   —used to just give up on games when I didn't do well
   —gave up on schoolwork when it was too hard
   —would get impatient at following rules and instructions, and give up before I finished—learning drafting
2. Felt better because I kept going—self-esteem improved
   —compliments on looking better
   —buying smaller jeans
   —got more patient—stopped giving up on hard assignments
   —felt like I was actually changing in a lot of ways
3. Being offered a job at the gym
   —total surprise
   —never had a job I cared about
   —never had jobs where I was rewarded for being good at something
   —I'm responsible for showing people what I can do and what I learned—big thing to me

Looking at the two steps he had worked through, Paul now knew he had some organization for his points, and he could create a reasonable outline. He started to fill in the copy of the Paragraph Outline Form (page 28) he had saved on his disk. As he did so, he found new details to add.

Point

Topic Sentence: The experience of working out at the gym taught me some unexpected lessons.

Support

Subtopic 1: I learned to stick with something I started.

Supporting Details (examples, explanations):

a. bought a gym membership

b. after a few times, I was ready to stop

c. so out of shape that the exercises left me stiff and in pain at first

d. But my jeans fit better, so I pushed myself to go back—vanity?

e. first time I didn't quit something—I was surprised when I realized this

f. same thing as schoolwork?

Subtopic 2: I learned discipline and patience.

Supporting Details (examples, explanations):

a. impatient with repetitions and learning routines—thought I knew better

b. didn't listen to the trainer at first—breathing improved—could run on stairs

c.   made a chart, started to track myself

d.   started building up routines—trainer knew what she was talking about

e.   felt like I was "relaxing"—got more patient—same thing happened with a couple of assignments—I actually kept at them, didn't avoid doing them

Subtopic 3:   My self-esteem really improved and I'm more responsible.

Supporting Details (examples, explanations):

a.   six months later, I'm not just working out, I do endurance running

b.   gym offered me part-time job as training assistant

c.   stopped procrastinating with school and chores—feel good about myself

d.   best thing—responsible for showing people what I learned

Notice that Paul changed his subtopics. He decided that he wanted to focus on three things he had learned, so he worked these into his outline.

STAGE 3: WRITING A FULL DRAFT

Paul now moved on to a first full draft.

> Sticking with my workout program has taught me some unexpected lessons. I used to be ashamed of being a quitter. When I bought a gym membership, I wanted to stop after two weeks. But I had paid for it, so I felt worse about quitting. Besides, the exercises made me stiff and sore. I think I went back only because my clothes started to fit better. It turned out that this was probably the first time I didn't quit something I started. I learned a lot about discipline and patience from working with my trainer. She made me keep doing repetitions ~~of the same things~~. Then I started to relax and enjoy following my routines. Having discipline made me work better at college, too. I stopped avoiding things so much. I have a lot more self-esteem ~~because of this~~. Now I do endurance running and, best of all, the gym gave me a part-time job as a training assistant. I do more now and I stopped procrastinating so much with schoolwork. For the first time, I feel good about myself. I know I can count on myself, and now I am responsible for showing people what I have learned.

Notice that Paul, after writing his first draft, was still trying to make his details more specific. He struck out vague phrases.

STAGE 4A: REVISING

Paul put his work aside for a day and began to revise his paragraph the next morning. Revising is as important a part of the writing process as prewriting and writing the first draft. *Revising* means that you rewrite a draft, building on what has been done to make it stronger and better. One writer has said about revision, "It's like cleaning house—getting rid of all the junk and putting things in the right order." A typical revision means *writing at least one or two more drafts.*

Shown below is Paul's revised second draft. He copied and pasted his first draft into a new document as "Gym Draft 2." Notice that he double spaced this draft, so that he could make changes easily. He made his changes in green, so that he could see them clearly. Phrases and sentences that Paul removed are shown as struck out, although he would simply have deleted them in his second draft.

> [1]Starting and sticking with my workout program have taught me some unexpected lessons. [2]First, I have learned not to give up so easily. [3]~~I used to be ashamed of being a quitter.~~ [4]When I bought a gym membership, I wanted to stop after two weeks. [5]But I had paid for it, ~~so I felt worse about quitting~~ so I kept going, even though [6]~~Besides,~~ the exercises made me stiff and sore. [7]~~I think~~ I ~~only~~ went back at first because my clothes started to fit better, so maybe vanity inspired me. [8]~~It turned out that~~ This was probably the first time I didn't quit something I started. [9]The next thing I learned ~~a lot about~~ was discipline and patience ~~from working with my trainer.~~ [10]~~She~~ My trainer made me slow down, keep doing repetitions, and work on the way I performed my exercises, so ~~of the same things.~~ [11]~~Then~~ I started to relax and enjoy following my routines. [12]I worked at getting better, not just at getting things over with. [13]Learning to be ~~Having~~ disciplined made me work better at college, too. [14]I stopped avoiding things so much. [15]I have a lot more self-esteem because my marks are better and I feel better physically. ~~because of this.~~ [16]Now I do endurance running and, best of all, the gym gave me a part-time job as a training assistant. [17]~~I do more now and I stopped procrastinating so much with schoolwork.~~ [18]For the first time, ~~I feel good about myself.~~ [19]I know I can count on myself, and now I am responsible for showing people what I have learned.

Activity

Fill in the missing words or sentence numbers, and underline the correct goal in the parentheses.

1. To clarify the organization or coherence of his paragraph, Paul added at the beginning of the first supporting point the transitional word _____, and he set off the second supporting point with the phrase _____

   _____.

2. In the interest of (*unity, support, coherence*), he crossed out sentence number_____. Paul realized that this sentence was not a relevant detail to support the idea of learning not to give up.

3. To eliminate wordiness, he removed the words _____ in sentence 7 of his revision.

4. To add more (*unity, support, coherence*), Paul added the phrases _____ _____ and _____ to sentence 10.

5. For greater sentence variety, he combined sentences 10 and 11 with the word _____.

STAGE 4B: EDITING AND PROOFREADING

Paul now printed a next-to-final draft of his paragraph. He marked in pen any areas where he was unsure of his sentence skills and circled words to look up in his dictionary. When you reach the editing and proofreading stage, you, like Paul, will have finished revising the content and organization of your draft. Print a double-spaced copy of your paragraph, leaving room for grammar and spelling corrections.

Editing and proofreading, the final activities in the writing process, mean checking the work carefully for spelling, grammar, punctuation, and other errors. You are ready for this stage when you are satisfied with your content: your choice of subtopics and supporting details; the order in which they are presented; and the way they and your topic sentence are worded.

Using the hints in the box below, read through your paragraph carefully. Check for typing errors, spelling errors, omitted words, and any other errors you may have missed so far. Refer to Section Four of this book for help with grammar and sentence-skills questions. Use your dictionary to be certain of any choices you made with the spell checker and to check spellings of any words of which you are still uncertain. At this stage such close and attentive work is often hard to do—students have spent so much time on their writing, or so little, that they want to avoid any more work. But if it is done carefully, this important final stage will ensure that an essay looks as good as possible.

Hints for Editing and Proofreading

- One helpful technique is to read your writing out loud. You will probably hear awkward wordings and become aware of spots where the punctuation needs to be improved. Make the changes needed for your sentences to read smoothly and clearly.
- Another technique is to use a sheet of paper to cover your paragraph so that you can expose and check carefully just one line at a time.
- A third strategy is to read your paragraph backward, from the last sentence to the first. Doing so helps keep you from getting caught up in the flow of the paragraph and missing small mistakes—which is easy to do, since you are so familiar with what you meant to say.

After editing and proofreading, Paul wrote the final draft of his paragraph.

Lessons from the Gym

Starting and sticking with my workout program have taught me some unexpected lessons. First, I have learned not to give up so easily. When I bought a gym membership, I wanted to stop after two weeks. But I had paid for it, so I kept going, even though the exercises made me stiff and sore. At first, I probably went back because my clothes started to fit better. Maybe vanity inspired me, but this was the first time I didn't quit something I started. The next things I learned were discipline and patience. My trainer made me slow down, keep doing repetitions, and work on the way I performed my exercises, so

I started to relax and enjoy following my routines. I worked at getting better, not just at getting things over with. Learning to be more disciplined made me work more carefully on assignments at college, too. I faced challenges, instead of avoiding them. My self-esteem has increased because my marks are higher and I feel better physically. Best of all, the gym gave me a part-time job as a training assistant. For the first time, I know I can count on myself, and now I am responsible for showing people what I have learned.

Activity 1

Here are five of six stages one student worked through in the process of composing a paragraph titled "My Favourite Places":

1. Prewriting (list)
2. Prewriting (freewriting and questioning)
3. First draft
4. Second draft
5. Final draft

The five stages appear in scrambled order below. Write the number *1* in the blank space in front of the first stage of development, and number the remaining stages in sequence.

_____

There are some places that always make me feel happy. For example, video rental stores. ~~The posters out front and on the walls~~ The posters for new movies outside the front door ~~make me excited and eager to see what's new~~ draw me inside and make me eager to see movies I've heard about. I also feel happy whenever I walk into the animation lab at college. ~~On days when I have computer animation classes, I just feel happy. Even at eight o'clock in the morning, I feel quite cheerful.~~ Any day when I have an animation class or lab time is a happy day, because I love the whole process of creating pictures and stories. ~~Not many people feel as happy as I do in a room full of computers.~~ I feel happiest of all in the bedroom of my new apartment … a big room on the third floor, with a huge bay window … built-in shelves for my books and treasures … shiny wood floors … my stereo and VCR … an old dresser I spent months refinishing …

_____

Favourite Places
the park at the end of my block
movie houses and video stores
feel happy in the animation lab
with a small group of my best friends   at a show, or just hanging out together
music stores
flea markets in the country
with my dogs at my parents' house
the bus on the way home from college

My Favourite Places

I have three favourite places that make me feel happy for different reasons. Video stores, for example, always brighten me up. The brightly coloured posters in the windows excite me, making me curious and eager to see new movies I've heard about. Inside the stores, the shelves full of thousands of movies seem like an endless buffet of entertainment. I feel I will never really be bored or unhappy as long as there are so many movies to take me away from my worries. My spirits also lift every time I enter the computer animation lab at college. Whenever I walk through the door, I'm in an environment where I really enjoy myself, and where every skill I learn adds to my happiness. I love the whole process of making images on the screen, and then making those images act out stories. But I most enjoy creating bizarre new creatures out of bits and pieces of images that were never together before. The place where I am happiest of all is the bedroom of my new apartment; it's a world all its own. Every time I climb the stairs to the top floor, I peek in just to see my kingdom. Part of my pleasure comes from the sheer size; my room is big, airy, and always full of light from its bay window. I can sit on the built-in window seat and look out over the treetops at the street, or I can look into my room and enjoy the shiny wood floors, my old iron-frame bed, and the shelves full of my books, stereo equipment, and personal treasures. Maybe the fact that the room is a reflection of me is what makes me happy there. I feel like I have three "secret weapons" for when I'm down: the video store, the animation lab, and my room.

There are some places that always make me happy. For example, I always feel excited and happy in video stores. When I stand outside looking at the posters, I feel excited and eager to see the new movies, and then I see all the shelves full of movies. The computer animation lab at college is another favourite place of mine. I love to sit at the computer and create images and stories. And to design whole new creatures on screen. I love learning anything new in animation. The place where I'm happiest is my big new third-floor bedroom. There is a bay window with a window seat where I can sit, and shiny wood floors. I love to sit and look at the shelves full of my belongings and all the things that reflect me. Video stores, the animation lab, and my bedroom are three of my favourite places to be.

Some places just make me happy. For example, I always enjoy going into video stores and seeing the posters and all the movies. Sitting on the shelves waiting for me. Also I cheer up every time I walk into the animation lab for a class or free time. My bedroom and the park at the end of my street are the best, though. I feel like myself in those places.

Why am I so happy in the animation lab?	What makes my bedroom my favourite place?
Learn new things all the time	Big bay window and seat, shiny floors
Making new creatures	Shelves with all my favourite things
Telling stories with pictures on screen	Light, trees outside, looking outside
I'm good at what I do there	Things I've worked on—the dresser, the bed

Activity 2

The author of "My Favourite Places" in Activity 1 made a number of revising and editing changes between the second draft and the final draft. Compare the two drafts and identify five of the changes in the spaces provided below.

1. _____
2. _____
3. _____
4. _____
5. _____

REVIEWING THE LEARNING OUTCOMES FOR CHAPTER 2

To assure yourself that you have understood and met the learning outcomes for this chapter, answer the following questions.

1. What are the four steps involved in writing an effective paragraph or essay?
2. What are the three main purposes for writing? Which will you encounter most often in college? Why?
3. Describe your main reading audience. What is your audience looking for in a paragraph or essay that you write?
4. What should be your guide as you choose a subject to write about? Why? How will you acquire information about a subject of which you have no experience or knowledge?
5. What is the goal of all prewriting techniques? Why do several different techniques exist?
6. At what point in the writing process will you create an outline? What are the two main sections of a paragraph outline? What are the purposes of outlining?
7. What is revising? Why and how is revising different from editing? What is proofreading?

Explaining a Process · Examining Cause and Effect · Comparing or Contrasting · Definin
erm · Dividing and Classifying · Describing a Scene or Person · Narrating an Event · Argu
Position · Explaining a Process · Examining Cause and Effect · Comparing or contrastin
efining a Term · Dividing and Classifying · Describing a Scene or Person · Narrating
vent · Arguing a Position · Explaining a Process · Examining Cause and Effect · Compar

CHAPTER 3

The First and Second Steps in Writing

LEARNING OUTCOMES

After reading this chapter and completing its activities you will

- be prepared to begin a paragraph by making a single, clear point;
- know the relationship between a paragraph's topic sentence and the rest of the paragraph;
- understand the difference between a subtopic and supporting details;
- know the two main functions of specific supporting details; and
- know why writers must provide enough supporting details.

Chapter 2 emphasized the ways in which prewriting and revising can help you become an effective writer. This chapter will focus on the first two steps in writing an effective paragraph:

1 Begin with a point.
2 Support the point with specific evidence.

Chapters 4 and 5 will then look at the third and fourth steps in writing:

3 Organize and connect the specific evidence.
4 Write clear, error-free sentences.

STEP 1: MAKE A POINT

Your first step in writing is to think about your subject, decide what point you want to make about that subject, and write that point in a single sentence. The point is commonly known as a *topic sentence*. As a guide to yourself and to the reader, put that point in the first sentence of your paragraph. Everything else in the paragraph should then develop and support in specific ways the single point given in the first sentence.

Activity

Your goal is to develop your awareness of two things: a clear, single point and focused, specific support for that point.

Read the two paragraphs below, written by students on the topic "cheating in everyday life." Which paragraph clearly supports a single point? Which paragraph fails to start with a clear point and rambles on in many directions, introducing a number of ideas but developing none of them?

Paragraph A

Cheating

Cheating has always been a part of life, and it will be so in the future. An obvious situation is that students have many ways of cheating in school. This habit can continue after school is over and become part of their daily lives. There are steps that can be taken to prevent cheating, but many teachers do not seem to care. Maybe they are so burned out by their jobs that they do not want to bother. The honest student is often the one hurt by the cheating of others. Cheating at work also occurs. This cheating may be more dangerous, because employers watch out for it more. Businesses have had to close down because cheating by employees took away a good deal of their profits. A news story recently concerned a server who was fired for taking a steak home from the restaurant where he worked, but his taking the steak may have been justified. Cheating in the sense of being unfaithful to a loved one is a different story because emotions are involved. People will probably never stop cheating unless there is a heavy penalty to be paid.

Paragraph B

Everyday Cheating

Cheating is common in everyday life. For one thing, cheating at school is common. Many students will borrow a friend's homework and copy it in their own handwriting. Other students take or buy essays from Internet sites and claim them as their own. People also cheat on the job. They use the postage meter at work for personal mail, spend hours of company time sending personal e-mails, or take home office supplies such as tape, paper, or pens. Some people who are not closely supervised or who are out on the road may cheat an employer by taking dozens of breaks or using work time for personal chores. Finally, many people cheat when they deal with large businesses. For instance, few customers will report an incorrect bill in their favour. Visitors in a hotel may take home towels, and restaurant patrons may take home silverware. A customer in a store may change price tags because "this is how much the shirt cost last month." For many people, daily cheating is an acceptable way to behave.

Complete the following statement: Paragraph _____ is effective because it makes a clear, single point in the first sentence and goes on in the remaining sentences to support that single point.

Paragraph B starts with a *single idea,* that people cheat in everyday life, and then supports that idea with several different examples. But paragraph A does not begin by making a definite point. Instead, we get two broad, obvious statements: that cheating "has always been a part of life" and "will be so in the future." Because the author has not focused on a clear, single point, what happens in this paragraph is inevitable.

The line of thought in paragraph A swerves about in various directions. In the second sentence, we read that "students have many ways of cheating in school," and we think for a moment that this will be the author's point: he or she will give us supporting details about different ways students cheat in school. But the next sentence makes another point: that after school is over, students may continue to cheat as "part of their daily lives." We therefore expect the author to give us details backing up the idea that students who cheat continue to cheat after they leave or finish school. However, the next sentence makes two additional points: "There are steps that can be taken to prevent cheating, but many teachers do not seem to care." These are two more ideas that could be, but are not, the focus of the paragraph. By now we are not really surprised at what happens in the following sentences. Several more points are made: "The honest student is often the one hurt by the cheating of others," cheating at work "may be more dangerous," an employee who stole a steak "may have been justified," and cheating by being unfaithful is different "because emotions are involved." *No single idea is developed; the result is confusion.*

In summary, while paragraph B is unified, paragraph A shows a complete lack of unity.

STEP 2: SUPPORT THE POINT WITH SPECIFIC EVIDENCE

The first essential element in writing effectively is to *start with a clearly stated point.* The second basic step is to *support that point with specific evidence.* Following are the two examples of supported points that you have already read, on pages 7-8 and on page 47.

Example A

Point

Using the college's server can be a waste of time.

Subtopics

1. The server can go down for hours.
2. The college sends out a lot of e-mail I do not need.
3. Students clog up e-mail with chain letters.

Example B

Point

Cheating is common in everyday life.

Subtopics and Supporting Details

1. At school
   a. Copying homework
   b. Cheating on essays
2. At work
   a. Using postage meter and company server for personal purposes
   b. Stealing office supplies
   c. Taking breaks and doing errands on company time
3. With large businesses
   a. Not reporting error on bill
   b. Stealing towels and silverware
   c. Switching price tags

The subtopics and supporting details are needed so that we can see and understand for ourselves that each writer's point is sound. By providing us with particulars about her experiences with the college server, the first writer shows why she believes it can be a waste of time. We can see that she has made a sound point. Likewise, the author of "Everyday Cheating" has supplied specific supporting examples of how cheating is common in everyday life. That paragraph, too, has provided the evidence (in the form of subtopics and details to support each) that is needed for us to understand and agree with the writer's point.

Activity 1

Consider the following paragraph.

Give Summer Courses a Break

Taking summer courses at college is a good idea for students who can make some sacrifices. The first benefit is getting a course or two out of the way by taking them ahead of time. If people are willing or able to give up part of their summer break, they can use that time for courses that could be more difficult for them. It is a lot easier to concentrate on a complicated subject like C++ or get through an English course with a lot of assignments when there aren't four or five other courses to worry about at the same time. The next big plus of summer school is that classes are usually smaller, so students get more personal attention. With complex programming courses, students may have a lot of questions that a teacher with only fifteen students will have the time to answer. With subjects like English, many students enjoy smaller, more relaxed classes where they can discuss their ideas and problems and get to know their classmates. Finally, though going to school part-time in summer means students cannot work as much to pay for the next fall's tuition, it can also save those same students from spending as much as they might otherwise. Going to school two or three days a week can lead to spending evenings doing assignments rather than going out with friends. This doesn't sound like a benefit, but movies, malls, and concerts cost more than doing homework any time. So these students give up the odd thing, but they end up with their own kind of "summer breaks."

The author's point is that taking summer courses is for the most part a good idea. Summarize in the spaces below the three reasons she gives to support her point.

1. _____

2. _____

3. _____

Notice what the supporting details in this paragraph do. They provide the reader with a basis for understanding why the writer feels the way she does. Through specific evidence, the writer has explained and communicated her point successfully. The evidence that supports the point in a paragraph often consists of a series of reasons (subtopics) introduced by transitions or signal words (the author uses *first*, *next*, and *finally*) and followed by examples and details that support and explain the reasons. That is true of the sample paragraph above: three reasons are provided, followed by examples and details that back up those reasons.

Activity 2

Your goal for this activity is to develop a sense of the varied and specific details that let a reader "see" the writer's point.

Both of the paragraphs that follow resulted from this assignment: "Write a paper that details your reasons for being in college." Both writers make the point that they have various reasons for attending college.

- Which paragraph then goes on to provide plenty of specific evidence to back up its point?
- Which paragraph is vague and repetitive and lacks the concrete details needed to show us exactly why the author decided to attend college?

Hint: Imagine that you've been asked to make a short film based on each paragraph. Which one suggests specific pictures, locations, words, and scenes you could shoot?

Paragraph A

Reasons for Going to College

I decided to attend college for various reasons. One reason is self-respect. For a long time now, I have felt little self-respect. I spent a lot of time doing nothing, just hanging around or getting into trouble, and eventually I began to feel bad about it. Going to college is a way to start feeling better about myself. By accomplishing things, I will improve my self-image. Another reason for going to college is that things happened in my life that made me think about a change. For one thing, I lost the part-time job I had. When I lost the job, I realized I would have to do something in life, so I thought about school. I was in a rut and needed to get out of it but did not know how. But when something happens that is out of your control, then you have to make some kind of decision. The most important reason for college, though, is to fulfill my dream. I know I need an education, and I want to take the courses I need to reach the position that I think I can handle. Only by gaining confidence and experience can I get what I want. Going to college will help me fulfill this goal. These are the main reasons why I am attending college.

Paragraph B

Why I'm in School

There are several reasons I'm in school. First of all my father's attitude made me want to succeed in school. One night last year, after I had come in at 3 a.m., my father said, "Sean, you're losing all respect for yourself. When I look at my son, all I see is a young man who doesn't care about himself." I was angry, but I knew my father was right in a way. I had spent the last two years working at odd jobs delivering pizza and repairing bikes, then spending all night at raves with my friends. That night, though, I decided I would prove my father wrong. I would go to college and be a success. Another reason I'm in college is my girlfriend's encouragement. Marie has already been in school for a year, and she is doing well in her computer technology courses. Marie helped me fill out my application and register for courses. She even lent me a hundred dollars for textbooks. On her day off, she lets me use her car so I don't have to take the bus. The main reason I am in college is to fulfill a personal goal: I want to finish something, for the first time in my life. For example, I quit high school at the end of grade eleven. Then I enrolled in a provincial job-training program, but I dropped out after six months. I tried to get my grade twelve certificate, but I started missing classes and eventually gave up. Now I am registered as a mature student in a special program where I will make up my missing high-school credits at night as part of first-semester work. I am determined to accomplish this goal and to then go on and work for a diploma in broadcast technology.

Complete the following statement: Paragraph _____ provides clear, vividly detailed reasons why the writer decided to attend college.

Paragraph B is the one that solidly backs up its point. The writer gives us specific reasons why he is in school. On the basis of such evidence, we can clearly understand his opening point. The writer of paragraph A offers only vague, general reasons for being in school. We do not get specific examples of how the writer was "getting into trouble," what events occurred that forced the decision, or even what kind of job he or she wants to qualify for. We sense that the feeling expressed is sincere; but without particular examples we cannot really see why the writer decided to attend college.

THE IMPORTANCE OF SPECIFIC DETAILS

As you read in Chapter 2 (page 29), a paragraph's content moves from a somewhat general opening position to more specific statements.

The point that opens a paper is a general statement. The evidence that supports a point is generally made up of subtopics and their specific details, reasons, examples, and facts.

Specific details have two key functions:

- Details and specific ideas *excite the reader's interest.* They make writing a pleasure to read, for we all enjoy learning particulars about other people—what they do and think and feel.
- Details *support and explain a writer's point;* they give the evidence needed for us to see and understand a general idea.

For example, the writer of "Net Eats Student's Time!" in Chapter 1 provides details that make vividly clear why she feels using the college's server wastes her time. She specifies a precise occasion when she had to wait while the server was down (and how long she had to wait—two hours) and describes how restless and distracted she was while waiting for service to resume. She mentions checking her e-mail and finding many messages from the college to scroll through, then goes on to specify exactly why these posts were a waste of time (they were irrelevant to her and she had to read them to discover this and then delete them). She then tells us two specific details of her final reason for frustration with spending time on the Net: (1) she finds a number of messages so heavily weighted with addresses that they take a long time to load, and (2) the messages turn out to be student "chain letters."

The writer of "Why I'm in School" provides equally vivid details. He gives clear reasons for being in school (his father's attitude, his girlfriend's encouragement, and his wish to fulfill a personal goal) and backs up each reason with specific details. His details give us many sharp pictures. For instance, we hear the exact words his father spoke: "Sean, you're losing all respect for yourself." He tells us exactly how he was spending his time ("delivering pizza and repairing bikes, then spending all night at raves with my friends"). He describes how his girlfriend helped him (filling out the college application, lending money and her car). Finally, instead of stating generally that "you have to make some kind of decision," as the writer of "Reasons for Going to College" does, he specifies that he has a strong desire to finish college because he dropped out of schools and programs in the past: high school, a job-training program, and another try at high school.

In both "Net Eats Student's Time!" and "Why I'm in School," the vivid, exact details capture our interest and enable us to share in the writer's experience. We see people's actions and hear their words; the details provide pictures that make each of us feel "I am there." The particulars also allow us to understand each writer's point clearly. We are *shown* exactly why the first writer finds the college server a time-waster and exactly why the second writer is attending college.

Activity

In this activity, you will continue to sharpen your sense of what makes good specific support. Each of the five points below is followed by two attempts at support (*a* and *b*). Write S (for *specific*) in the space next to the one that succeeds in providing specific support for the point. Write *X* in the space next to the one that lacks supporting details.

1. My two-year-old son was in a stubborn mood today.
    a. When I asked him to do something, he gave me nothing but trouble. He seemed determined to make things difficult for me, for he had his mind made up.
    b. When I asked him to stop playing in the yard and come indoors, he looked me square in the eye and shouted "No!" and then spelled it out, "N … O!"

2. The prices in the amusement park were outrageously high.
    a. The food seemed to cost twice as much as it would in a supermarket and was sometimes of poor quality. The rides also cost a lot, and so I had to tell the children that they were limited to a certain number of them.
    b. The cost of the log flume, a ride that lasts roughly three minutes, was $5.75 a person. Then I had to pay $2 for a 250 mL soft drink and $3.75 for a hot dog.

3. My brother-in-law is accident-prone.
    a. Once he tried to open a tube of Krazy Glue with his teeth. When the cap came loose, glue squirted out and sealed his lips shut. They had to be pried open in a hospital emergency room.
    b. Even when he does seemingly simple jobs, he seems to get into trouble. This can lead to hilarious, but sometimes dangerous, results. Things never seem to go right for him, and he often needs the help of others to get out of one predicament or another.

4. The so-called "bargains" at the yard sale were junk.
    a. The tables at the yard sale were filled with useless stuff no one could possibly want. They were the kinds of things that should be thrown away, not sold.
    b. The "bargains" at the yard sale included two headless dolls, blankets filled with holes, scorched pot holders, and a plastic Christmas tree with several branches missing.

5. The key to success in college is organization.
    a. Knowing what you're doing, when you have to do it, and so on is a big help for a student. A system is crucial in achieving an ordered approach to study. Otherwise, things become very disorganized, and it is not long before your grades begin to drop.
    b. Organized students never forget paper or exam dates, which are marked on a calendar above their desks. And instead of having to cram for exams, they study their clear, neat classroom and textbook notes on a daily basis.

Comments: The specific support for point 1 is answer *b*. The writer does not just tell us that the little boy was stubborn but provides an example that shows us. In particular, the detail of the son's spelling out "N … O!" makes his stubbornness vividly real for the reader. For point 2, answer *b* gives specific prices ($5.75 for a ride, $2 for a soft drink, and $3.75 for a hot dog) to support the idea that the amusement park was expensive. For point 3, answer *a* vividly backs up the idea that the brother-in-law is accident-prone by detailing an accident with Krazy Glue. Point 4 is supported by answer *b*, which lists specific examples of useless items that were offered for sale—from headless dolls to a broken plastic Christmas tree. We cannot help agreeing with the writer's point that the items were not bargains but junk. Point 5 is backed up by answer *b*, which identifies two specific strategies of organized students: they mark important dates on calendars above their desks, and they take careful notes and study them daily.

In each of the five cases, the specific evidence enables us to see for ourselves that the writer's point is valid.

THE IMPORTANCE OF ADEQUATE DETAILS

One of the most common and most serious problems in students' writing is inadequate development. You must provide *enough* specific details to support fully the point you are making. You could not, for example, submit a paragraph about how your brother-in-law is accident-prone and provide only a single short example. You would have to add several other examples or provide an extended example of your brother-in-law's accident-proneness. Without such additional support, your paragraph would be underdeveloped.

At times, students try to disguise an undersupported point by using repetition and wordy generalities. You saw this, for example, in paragraph A ("Reasons for Going to College") on pages 50-51. Be prepared to do the plain hard work needed to ensure that each of your paragraphs has full and solid support.

Activity

Your goal in this activity is to develop a sense of when support is sufficient to make a point clear. The following paragraphs were written on the same topic, and each has a clear opening point.

- Which one is adequately developed?
- Which one has few particulars and uses mostly vague, general, wordy sentences to conceal the fact that it is starved for specific details?

Paragraph A

New Uses for Public Parks

Canadians are finding new ways to use city parks. Instead of visiting large parks for playgrounds or for walks among the trees, people may go to the park to exercise in groups. People of every age do Tai Chi stretches every morning, while others band together for organized walks each evening. Each park has its joggers, runners, and cyclists, while others bring their weights to do workouts in the park's fresh air and quiet. Canadian city parks also host concerts, art shows, and plays. Suburban and waterfront parks offer children's festivals every summer; musicians return to parks for annual folk and world music events, and Shakespeare comes to stages in Toronto parks every July. Perhaps the most interesting "new" use of parks is really an old one: public rental gardens. Large parks rent "allotment gardens" where apartment dwellers plant and cultivate gardens each year. These park-gardeners fence off their spaces, plant flowers, fruits, and vegetables, and faithfully tend their plots every day. Allotment gardens began in the Depression when families on tight budgets tried to supplement their diets, and recently a group of U of T students started growing fruit and vegetables for the university's food bank, to help feed hungry people in today's economy. Some gardeners are from cultures used to growing their own produce, and still others simply enjoy the contact with nature and the seasons. Parks are made for people, and today, people are finding new ways to use and enjoy the peace, space, and land that parks offer.

Paragraph B

Uses for Public Parks

People use parks for many hobbies and activities. Exercising in the open air is healthy, and many people choose to take advantage of this in a variety of ways. Different types of people can be seen every day getting different forms of exercise in various parks. In fact, every season is suitable for some form of exercise in the park. But working at fitness in the fresh air is not the only reason people go to parks. Parks offer entertainment of every kind these days, which benefits the cultural life of the cities where the parks are located and draws many visitors. Many of these people might not otherwise visit a public park. Today, parks are full of children and their parents, people working at fitness, people admiring the trees and flowers, and people walking their pets. It is certainly obvious that parks have many attractions for people in today's cities.

Complete the following statement: Paragraph _____ provides an adequate number of specific details to support its point.

Paragraph A offers a series of detailed examples of new ways in which people are using public parks. Paragraph B, on the other hand, is underdeveloped. Paragraph B mentions only "different types of people … getting different forms of exercise," while paragraph A refers specifically to people who "do Tai Chi stretches … joggers, runners, and cyclists," and weightlifters and groups of walkers. Paragraph B talks generally of "entertainment of every kind" in parks, while paragraph A specifies "concerts, art shows, and plays," as well as children's festivals, music events, and Shakespeare in outdoor park theatres. Moreover, there is no parallel in paragraph B for paragraph A's point and details about allotment gardens and the people who cultivate them. In summary, paragraph B lacks the full, specifically detailed support needed to develop its opening point convincingly.

■ Review Activity

To check your understanding of the chapter so far, see if you can answer the following questions.

1. Someone has observed: "To write well, the first thing that you must do is decide what nail you want to drive home." What is meant by *nail*?

2. How do you *drive home the nail* in a paper?

    _____

3. What are the two reasons for using specific details in your writing?

    a. _____

    b. _____

PRACTICE IN MAKING AND SUPPORTING A POINT

You now know the two most important steps in competent writing: (1) making a point and (2) supporting that point with specific and adequate evidence. The purpose of this section is to expand and strengthen your understanding of these two basic steps.

You will first work through a series of activities on *making* a point:

1 Identifying Common Errors in Topic Sentences
2 Understanding the Two Parts of a Topic Sentence
3 Selecting a Topic Sentence
4 Writing a Topic Sentence: I
5 Writing a Topic Sentence: II

You will then sharpen your understanding of specific details by working through a series of activities on *supporting* a point:

6 Recognizing Specific Details: I
7 Recognizing Specific Details: II
8 Providing Specific Supporting Evidence
9 Identifying Adequate Supporting Evidence
10 Adding Details to Complete a Paragraph
11 Writing a Simple Paragraph

1 IDENTIFYING COMMON ERRORS IN TOPIC SENTENCES

When writing the main point in a topic sentence, people sometimes make mistakes that undermine their chances of producing an effective paper. One mistake is to substitute an *announcement of the topic* for a true topic sentence. Other mistakes include *writing statements that are too broad or too narrow.* Here are examples of all three errors, along with contrasting examples of effective topic sentences.

Announcement

My Ford Escort is the concern of this paragraph.

The statement above is a simple announcement of a subject, rather than a topic sentence in which an idea is expressed about the subject.

Statement That Is Too Broad

Many people have problems with their cars.

The statement above is too broad to be supported adequately with specific details in a single paragraph.

Statement That Is Too Narrow or Does Not Take a Position

My car is a Ford Escort.

The statement above is too narrow to be expanded into a paragraph. Such a narrow statement is somctimes called a *dead-end statement* because there is no place to go with it. "My car is a Ford Escort" is a simple fact; it does not take a position on the car and therefore does not call for any support.

Effective Topic Sentence

I hate my Ford Escort.

The statement above expresses an opinion that could be supported in a paragraph. The writer could offer a series of specific supporting reasons, examples, and details to make it clear why he or she hates the car.
Here are additional examples.

Announcements

The subject of this paper will be my apartment.
I want to talk about increases in the divorce rate.

Statements That Are Too Broad

The places where people live have definite effects on their lives.
Many people have trouble getting along with others.

Statements That Are Too Narrow or Do Not Take a Position

I have no hot water in my apartment at night.
Almost one of every two marriages ends in divorce.

Effective Topic Sentences

My apartment is a terrible place to live.
The divorce rate is increasing for several reasons.

Activity 1

For each pair of sentences below, write *A* beside the sentence that only *announces* a topic. Write *OK* beside the sentence that *advances an idea* about the topic.

1. _____ a. This paper will deal with flunking math.

   _____ b. I flunked math last semester for several reasons.

2. _____ a. I am going to write about my job as a gas station attendant.

   _____ b. Working as a gas station attendant was the most demanding job I ever had.

3. _____ a. Telemarketing is the subject of this paragraph.

   _____ b. People should know what to do when they receive a tele-marketing phone call.

4. _____ a. In several ways, my college library is very easy to use.

   _____ b. This paragraph will deal with the college library.

5. _____ a. My paper will discuss the topic of procrastinating.

   _____ b. The following steps will help you stop procrastinating.

Activity 2

For each pair of sentences below, write *TN* beside the statement that does not take a position or is *too narrow* to be developed into a paragraph. (Such a narrow statement is also known as a *dead-end sentence*.) Write *OK* beside the statement in each pair that calls for support or development of some kind.

1. _____ a. I do push-ups and sit-ups each morning.

   _____ b. Exercising every morning has had positive effects on my health.

2. _____ a. Farid works nine hours a day and then goes to school three hours a night.

   _____ b. Farid is an ambitious man.

3. _____ a. I started college after being away from school for seven years.

   _____ b. Several of my fears about returning to school have proved to be groundless.

4. _____ a. Parts of the NFB film *Get a Job* are interesting to college students.

   _____ b. Our class watched the NFB film *Get a Job* yesterday.

5. _____ a. My brother was depressed yesterday for several reasons.

   _____ b. Yesterday my brother had to pay seventy dollars for an engine tune-up.

Activity 3

For each pair of sentences below, write *TB* beside the statement that is *too broad* to be supported adequately in a short paper. Write *OK* beside the statement that makes a limited point.

1. _____ a. Professional hockey is a dangerous sport.

   _____ b. Professional sports are violent.

2.   _____   a. Married life is the best way of living.

           _____   b. Teenage marriages often end in divorce for several reasons.

3.   _____   a. Aspirin has several beneficial side effects.

           _____   b. Drugs have different effects on different people.

4.   _____   a. I've always done fairly well in school.

           _____   b. I got an A in math last semester for several reasons.

5.   _____   a. Computers are changing our society.

           _____   b. Using computers to teach children is having excellent results.

2 UNDERSTANDING THE TWO PARTS OF A TOPIC SENTENCE

The point that opens and controls the content of a paragraph is expressed in a *topic sentence*. When you look closely at a topic sentence, you can see that it is made up of two parts:

1 The *topic*

2 The writer's *attitude* about the topic

The writer's attitude, position, or idea is usually expressed in one or more *keywords*. All the details in a paragraph should support the idea expressed in the keywords. In each of the topic sentences below, a single line appears under the topic and a double line under the idea or attitude about the topic (expressed in a keyword or keywords).

My girlfriend is very assertive.

Highway accidents are often caused by absent-mindedness.

The kitchen is the most widely used room in my house.

Voting should be required by law in Canada.

My pickup truck is the most reliable vehicle I have ever owned.

In the first sentence, the topic is *girlfriend*, and the keyword that expresses the writer's idea about his topic is that his girlfriend is *assertive*. In the second sentence, the topic is *highway accidents*, and the keyword that determines the focus of the paragraph is that such accidents are often caused by *absent-mindedness*. Notice each topic and keyword or keywords in the other three sentences as well.

Activity

For each point below, draw a single line under the topic and a double line under the idea about the topic.

1. Billboards should be abolished.

2. My boss is an ambitious woman.

3. Politicians are often self-serving.

4. The apartment needed repairs.

5. Television commercials are often misleading.

6. My parents have rigid racial attitudes.

7. The middle child is often a neglected member of the family.

8. The language in many movies today is offensive.

9. Doctors are often insensitive.

10. Homeowners today are more energy-conscious than ever before.

3 SELECTING A TOPIC SENTENCE

Remember that a paragraph is made up of a topic sentence and a group of related sentences that develop and support the topic sentence. It is also helpful to remember that the topic sentence is a somewhat *general* statement. The other sentences provide specific support for the general statement. Supporting sentences include *subtopics*, which are subsections or categories of the topic presented. Each subtopic requires *specific supporting details* or examples to make it clear.

Activity

Each group of sentences below could be written as a short paragraph. Circle the letter of the topic sentence in each case. To find the topic sentence, ask yourself, "Which is a general statement supported by the specific details in the other three statements?"

Begin by trying the example item below. First circle the letter of the sentence you think expresses the main idea. Then read the explanation.

Example   a.   Substitute water for coffee or pop at least once a day.
b.   Park farther away from the mall or the college, so you walk more.
c.   By changing a few habits, you can live a healthier life.
d.   Change one "empty calorie" snacking pattern a month.

Explanation: Sentence *a* describes one healthy habit. Sentences *b* and *d* also offer definite healthful behaviour choices. In sentence *c*, however, no one specific habit is mentioned. The words "changing a few habits" refer only generally to such habits. Therefore, sentence *c* is the topic sentence; it expresses the author's main idea. The other sentences support that idea by providing examples.

1.   a.   "I couldn't study because I forgot to bring my book home."
b.   "I couldn't take the final because my grandmother died."
c.   Students give instructors some common excuses.
d.   "I couldn't come to class because I had a migraine headache."

2.   a.   Its brakes are badly worn.
b.   My old car is ready for the junk pile.

    c. Its floor has rusted through, and water splashes on my feet when the highway is wet.

    d. My mechanic says its engine is too old to be repaired, and the car isn't worth the cost of a new engine.

3. a. Tobacco is one of the most addictive of all drugs.
    b. Selling cigarettes ought to be against the law.
    c. Non-smokers are put in danger by breathing the smoke from other people's cigarettes.
    d. Cigarette smoking kills many more people than all illegal drugs combined.

4. a. Contract workers are valuable commodities for employment agencies and for employers with specific needs.
    b. Contract workers are self-employed, for tax purposes, so they can write off many expenses such as gas used during the drive to work and back.
    c. Contract workers earn slightly less than permanent employees but may have the same net income because of fewer company deductions.
    d. Contract workers have distinct advantages in the workplace of the twenty-first century.

5. a. The last time I ate there, I discovered two new flavours I now love: lemon grass and coriander.
    b. Although it is only a small local restaurant, it has received great reviews.
    c. The new Thai restaurant near my house is a favourite of mine and of people from all over Vancouver.
    d. The seafood is really fresh, and all the dishes are cooked to order.

4 WRITING A TOPIC SENTENCE: I

Activity

The following activity will give you practice in writing an accurate topic sentence—one that is neither too broad nor too narrow for the supporting material in a paragraph. Sometimes you will construct your topic sentence after you have decided what details you want to discuss. An added value of this activity is that it shows you how to write a topic sentence that will exactly match the subtopics or supporting details you have developed.

1. *Topic sentence:* _____

    _____

    a. Some are caused by careless people tossing matches out of car windows.
    b. A few are started when lightning strikes a tree.
    c. Some result when campers fail to douse cooking fires.
    d. The majority of forest fires are deliberately set by arsonists.

2. *Topic sentence:* _____

_____

   a. The bistro owner greeted us with a smile and seated us at a window table as soon as we arrived.
   b. Our appetizers and main courses were delicious.
   c. Our server brought us extra bread and more water.
   d. The desserts were homemade and garnished with whipped cream.

3. *Topic sentence:* _____

_____

   a. My server goes dead at certain times of the day.
   b. When I am online, I experience slow loading times.
   c. The line to the server does not always connect quickly.
   d. Sometimes, the server connection will cut out in mid-session.

4. *Topic sentence:* _____

_____

   a. The crowd scenes were crudely spliced from another film.
   b. Mountains and other background scenery were just poorly done computer graphics.
   c. The "sync" was off, so that the audience heard voices even when the actors' lips were not moving.
   d. The so-called monster was just a spider that had been filmed through a magnifying lens.

5 WRITING A TOPIC SENTENCE: II

Often you will start with a general topic or a general idea of what you want to write about. You may, for example, want to write a paragraph about some aspect of school life. To come up with a point about school life, begin by narrowing your topic. One way to do this is to make a list of all the subtopics you can think of that fit under the general topic.

Activity

On the following pages are four general topics and a series of subtopics that fit under them. Make a point out of *one* of the subtopics in each group.

Hint: To create a topic sentence, ask yourself, "What point do I want to make about _____ (*my subtopic*)?"

Example   Recreation
   • Movies
   • Dancing

- TV shows
- Reading
- Sports parks

Your point: *Sports parks today have some truly exciting games.*

1. Your college
   - Instructor
   - Cafeteria
   - Specific class
   - Particular room or building
   - Particular policy (attendance, marking, etc.)
   - Classmate

Your point: _____

2. Job
   - Pay
   - Boss
   - Working conditions
   - Duties
   - Co-workers
   - Customers or clients

Your point: _____

3. Money
   - Budgets
   - Credit cards
   - Dealing with a bank
   - School expenses
   - Ways to get it
   - Ways to save it

Your point: _____

4. Cars
   - First car
   - Driver's licence test
   - Road conditions
   - Accident
   - Speed limit
   - Safety problems

Your point: _____

6 RECOGNIZING SPECIFIC DETAILS: I

Specific details are examples, reasons, particulars, and facts. Such details are needed to support and explain a topic sentence effectively. Each subtopic sentence needs specific details to clarify and explain it, as well. Specific details provide the evidence needed for readers to understand, as well as to feel and experience, a writer's point. Specific details allow readers to *see* your point clearly.

Here is a topic sentence followed by two sets of supporting sentences. Which set provides sharp, specific details?

Topic Sentence

Some poor people must struggle to make meals for themselves.

Set A

> They gather up whatever free food they can find in fast-food restaurants and take it home to use however they can. Unless they have access to food banks, they base their diet on anything they can buy that is cheap and filling.

Set B

> Some add hot water to the free packets of ketchup they get at fast-food places to make tomato soup. Others buy cheap canned dog food and fry it like hamburger.

Set B provides specific details: instead of a general statement about "free food they can find in fast-food restaurants and take … home to use however they can," we get a vivid detail we can see and picture clearly: "free packets of ketchup they get at fast-food places to make tomato soup." Instead of a general statement about how the poor will "base their diet on anything they can buy that is cheap and filling," we get exact and vivid details: "Others buy cans of cheap canned dog food and fry it like hamburger."

Specific details are often like the information we might find in a movie script, as we mentioned on page 50. They provide us with such clear pictures that we could make a film of them if we wanted to. You would know just how to film the information given in set B. You would show a poor person breaking open a packet of ketchup from some fast-food place and mixing it with water to make a kind of tomato soup. You would show someone opening a can of dog food and frying its contents like hamburger.

In contrast, the writer of set A fails to provide the specific information needed. If you were asked to make a film based on set A, you would have to figure out for yourself just what particulars you were going to show.

When you are working to provide specific supporting information in a paper, it might help to ask yourself, "Could someone easily film this information?" If the answer is yes, you probably have good details. Your specific details help you to *show*, not *tell*.

Activity

Your aim in this activity is to strengthen your "eye" for specific details. Each topic sentence below is followed by two sets of supporting details (*a* and *b*). Write S (for *specific*) in the space next to the set that provides specific support for the point. Write G (for *general*) next to the set that offers only vague, general support.

1. *Topic sentence:* My roommate is messy.

    _____ a. He doesn't seem to mind that he can't find any clean clothes or dishes. He never puts anything back in its proper place; he just drops it wherever he happens to be. His side of the room looks as if a hurricane has gone through.

    _____ b. His coffee cup is covered inside with a thick layer of green mould. I can't tell you what colour his easy chair is; it has disappeared under a pile of dirty laundry. When he turns over in bed, I can hear the crunch of cracker crumbs beneath his body.

2. *Topic sentence:* Antonetta is very assertive.

    _____ a. Her assertiveness is apparent in both her personal and her professional life. She is never shy about extending social invitations. And while some people are turned off by her assertiveness, others are impressed by it and enjoy doing business with her.

    _____ b. When she meets a man she likes, she is quick to say, "Let's go out for coffee sometime." In her job as a furniture salesperson, she will call potential customers to let them know when new stock is coming in.

3. *Topic sentence:* Our new kitten causes us lots of trouble.

    _____ a. He has shredded the curtains in my bedroom with his claws. He nearly drowned when he crawled into the washing machine. And my hands look like raw hamburger from his playful bites and scratches.

    _____ b. He seems to destroy everything he touches. He's always getting into places where he doesn't belong. Sometimes he plays too roughly, and that can be painful.

7 RECOGNIZING SPECIFIC DETAILS: II

Activity

At several points in the following paragraphs you are given a choice of two sets of supporting details. Write *S* (for *specific*) in the space next to the set that provides specific support for that point. Write *G* (for *general*) next to the set that offers only vague, general support.

Paragraph A

The Caribana festival in Toronto may look and sound like a big party, but there is more to it than just a good time. For one thing, Caribbean carnivals have more history than people realize.

    _____ a. Caribana began in the Caribbean islands with various carnivals. On these islands, slaves could not get together socially or celebrate their heritage or African history. When they were freed, they began to hold parades for which they created songs and dances that mixed old and new ideas. They made fancy costumes and masks, and people wearing these misbehaved sometimes. Carnivals or masquerades could be quite wild events where people could speak their minds in songs and act out their thoughts in exciting dances. Caribbean festivals are now organized competitions.

_____ b. Caribana's beats and costumes began with carnivals on Trinidad and Tobago. When slavery ended on "T&T" in the 1830s, islanders celebrated the start of Lent with African drumming and dancing. They made their own versions of European gowns and fancy jackets in silks and satins to make fun of their former masters. Some costumes turned into full masquerade disguises like bats, clowns, and Indian rajahs. People could criticize bosses and politicians from behind their masks, and the parades grew longer, louder, and more organized. In the twentieth century, calypso singers spoke their minds in songs, and steel drums gave more new sounds to the carnivals. Soon people of all races were dressing up and "playing mas."

In Toronto, Caribana has an interesting story behind it as well.

_____ c. Over thirty-five years ago, it began as a community project for Canada's centennial. The people who started Caribana intended to show off Caribbean culture and how it belonged in Canada. Their first small parade started near Bloor and St. George and continued down Yonge Street for only a few blocks. At this one-day affair, participants simply went home after the parade or ended up at family parties. Now that one-day festival is a two-week event with nearly 300,000 visitors from New York, Ohio, Michigan, Pennsylvania, and Illinois. Caribana is now North America's largest Caribbean festival.

_____ d. Caribana was a little get-together for islanders when it started out. Most cultural groups had events they wanted to contribute to Canada's centennial celebrations, and West Indians were no exception. From a short parade with some lively music and dancers, the festival has turned into a marathon cultural show with picnics and parties. This major event lasts a couple of weeks and brings many visitors and tourist dollars to Toronto.

Finally, the best thing about Caribana might be the way it brings all kinds of people together.

_____ e. Caribana today isn't only for West Indians. Everyone can come and enjoy the party. People like to try different foods, and after listening to the mas bands, they want to try various ways of dancing along with the paraders, too. Now Spanish culture is starting to become part of the festival, with its Latin rhythms and spicy foods. Everyone loves a party, it seems.

_____ f. The first Caribana welcomed other West Indian countries, including Jamaica, the Bahamas, Antigua, and Barbados. Everyone brought his or her island's music, food, and costumes—from Jamaican ska to Trinidadian roti. Today floats from Brazilian entrants pulse with samba beats, and festival visitors try out their Spanish to order a *café* or sandwich *Cubano.* As the festival grows, more faces and sounds from Toronto's cultures appear at Caribana's functions.

Paragraph B

Many adult children move back in with their parents for some period of time. Although living with Mom and Dad again has some advantages, there are certain problems that are likely to arise. One common problem is that children may expect their parents to do all the household chores.

_____ a. They never think that they should take on their share of work around the house. Not only do they not help with their parents' chores, they don't even take responsibility for the extra work that their presence creates. Like babies, they go through the house making a mess that they expect their parents to clean up. It's as if they think their parents are their servants.

_____ b. They expect meals to appear on the table as if by magic. After they've eaten, they go off to work or play, never thinking about who's going to do the dishes. They drop their dirty laundry beside the washing machine, assuming that Mom will attend to it and return clean, folded clothes to their bedroom door. And speaking of their bedroom: every day they await the arrival of Mom's Maid Service to make the bed, pick up the floor, and dust the furniture.

Another problem that frequently arises is that parents forget their children are no longer adolescents.

_____ c. Parents with kids living at home want to know everything about their adult children's lives. They don't think their kids, even though they are adults, should have any privacy. Whenever they see their children doing anything, they want to know all the details. It's as though their children are still teenagers who are expected to report all their activities. Naturally, adult children get irritated when they are treated as if they were teenagers.

_____ d. They may insist upon knowing far more about their children's comings and goings than the children want to share. For example, if such parents see their adult son heading out the door, they demand to know: Where is he going? Who will he be with? What will he be doing? What time will he be back? In addition, they may not let their adult child have any privacy. If their daughter and a date are sitting in the living room, for instance, they may join them there and start asking the young man questions about his family and his job, as if they were interviewing him for the position of son-in-law.

Finally, there may be financial problems when an adult child returns to live at home.

_____ e. Having an extra adult in the household creates extra expenses. But many adult children don't offer to help deal with those extra costs. Adult children often eat at home, causing the grocery bill to climb. They may stay in a formerly unused room, which now needs to be heated and lit. They produce extra laundry to be washed. They use the telephone, adding to the long-distance bill. For all these reasons, adult children should expect to pay a reasonable amount to their parents for room and board.

_____ f. It's expensive to have another adult living in the household. Adult children would be paying a lot of bills on their own if they weren't staying with their parents. It's only fair that they share the expenses at their parents' house. They should consider all the ways that their living at home is increasing their parents' expenses. Then they should insist upon covering their share of the costs.

8 PROVIDING SPECIFIC SUPPORTING EVIDENCE

This activity can be done by students individually or in groups.

Individual Activity

Provide three details that logically support the points made in each of the following topic sentences. Your details can be drawn from your own experience, or they can be invented. In each case, the details should show in a specific way what the point expresses in only a general way. State your details briefly in phrases rather than in complete sentences.

Group Activity

In each group of five students, have each person select one of the following topic sentences. Each student will provide three details to specifically support and illustrate his or her point. Students may then exchange papers within the group and evaluate the quality of one another's supporting evidence, or groups may compare responses.

Example   The student had several ways of passing time during the dull lecture.

a. *Shielded his eyes with his hand and dozed for a while*

b. *Read the sports magazine he had brought to class*

c. *Made an elaborate drawing on a page of his notebook*

1. I could tell I was coming down with the flu.

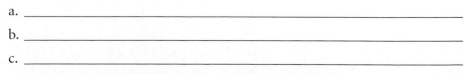

a. _____

b. _____

c. _____

2. Canadians should vacation in their own country.

   a. _____

   b. _____

   c. _____

3. I had car problems recently.

   a. _____

   b. _____

   c. _____

4. When your money gets tight, there are several ways to economize.

   a. _____

   b. _____

   c. _____

5. Some people are excellent drivers.

   a. _____

   b. _____

   c. _____

9 IDENTIFYING ADEQUATE SUPPORTING EVIDENCE

Activity

Two of the following paragraphs provide clear subtopics and sufficient details to support their topic sentences convincingly. Write *AD,* for *adequate development,* beside those paragraphs. There are also three paragraphs that, for the most part, use vague, general, or wordy sentences as a substitute for clear subtopics and concrete details. Write *U,* for *underdeveloped,* beside those paragraphs.

_____   1.

My Husband's Stubbornness

My husband's worst problem is his stubbornness. He simply will not let any kind of weakness show. If he isn't feeling well, he refuses to admit it. He will keep on doing whatever he is doing and will wait until the symptoms get almost unbearable before he will even hint that anything is the matter with him. Then things are so far along that he has to spend more time recovering than he would if he had a different attitude. He also hates to be wrong. If he is wrong, he will be the last to admit it. This happened once when we went shopping, and he spent an endless amount of time going from one place to the next. He insisted that one of them had a fantastic sale on things he wanted. We never found a sale, but the fact that this situation happened will not change his attitude. Finally, he never listens to anyone else's suggestions on a car trip. He always knows he's on the right road, and the results have led to a lot of time wasted getting back in the right direction. Every time one of these incidents happens, it only means that it is going to happen again in the future.

_____   2.

Street Hockey: Tradition or Torture?

Street hockey has always been popular with boys and girls in Red Deer, Alberta, so we feel we have a tradition to keep up, but it is becoming an increasingly dangerous pastime. Games are constantly interrupted by cars and trucks. This fall, one of the new girl players, who was captain of her school's field hockey team, believed she had to prove herself to us. Unaware of the amount of traffic on seemingly quiet streets, she plowed forward, head down, eyes focused on the ball, and nearly wound up as the hood ornament on a minivan. Late-night drinking drivers make street hockey even more hazardous. Bottles thrown out the windows shatter on the pavement, and large chunks of glass get picked up by hockey sticks as we chase the ball. Two players ended up in Emergency: one with a dangerous cut over his eye, the other with six stitches in his forearm; both injuries were caused by flying glass. The most dangerous incident, though, had nothing to do with traffic; it was a combination of ordinary carelessness and modern lawn care. A wild shot sent the ball onto someone's newly treated front yard. Our forward sprinted to retrieve the ball, tripped over the "dangerous chemical" sign, and fell face forward into damp grass, freshly soaked in weed killer. He turned out to be violently allergic to the ingredients and went into something like an asthma attack. We had to call 911 for paramedics with inhalers and oxygen. So a traditional teenage prairie sport has lost some of its appeal these days and, in fact, has become more of a hazard than a tradition for its players.

_____   3.

Attitudes about Food

Attitudes that we form as children about food are not easily changed. In some families, food is love. Not all families are like this, but some children grow up with this attitude. Some families think of food as something precious and not to be wasted. The attitudes children pick up about food are hard to change in adulthood. Some families celebrate with food. If a child learns an attitude, it is hard to break this later. Someone once said: "As the twig is bent, so grows the tree." Children are very impressionable, and they can't really think for themselves when they are small. Children learn from the parent figures in their lives and later from their peers. Some families have healthy attitudes about food. It is important for adults to teach their children these healthy attitudes. Otherwise, the children may have weight problems when they are adults.

_____   4.

Qualities in a Friend

There are several qualities I look for in a friend. A friend should give support and security. A friend should also be fun to be around. Friends can have faults, like anyone else, and sometimes it is hard to overlook them. But a friend can't be dropped because he or she has faults. A friend should stick by a friend, even in bad times. There is a saying that "a friend in need is a friend indeed." I believe this means that there are good friends and fair-weather friends. The second type is not a true friend. He or she is the kind of person who runs when there's trouble. Friends don't always last a lifetime. Someone believed to be a best friend may lose contact if a person moves to a different area or goes around with a different group of people. A friend should be generous and understanding. A friend does not have to be exactly like you. Sometimes friends are opposites, but they still like each other and get along. Since I am a very quiet person, I can't say that I have many friends. But these are the qualities I believe a friend should have.

_____   5.   **Schoolyard Card Sharks**

There is something odd about the evenings-only men's club in the nearby school playground. As dusk gathers over Halifax, under the arc lights provided for the children's protection, a group of gentlemen like to get together. The members of this society have a uniform: ballcaps worn back to front, XXL-size shirts, and unlaced athletic shoes. Sheltering behind the wooden climbing castle, they arrange their chosen furniture, worn folding chairs stolen from the neighbourhood's front porches. Next, raised ritual handgrips are exchanged, and the fraternal greetings are heard: "How the h--- are ya?" "So where were ya last night?" As a rough circle is formed by the players' chairs, packs of Export A emerge from pockets and sleeves, and the sacramental beverages of Molson Ex and Gatorade are readied for the tense action to follow. Finally, the stakes are agreed upon, and the equipment is carefully placed on a pilfered card table: two dog-eared decks of playing cards. Is their game five-card stud or blackjack, deuces wild? No, it's euchre—the same game their grandparents play in their retirement homes. Youth and age meet in odd ways, in odd locations.

10 ADDING DETAILS TO COMPLETE A PARAGRAPH

Activity

Each of the following paragraphs needs specific details to back up its supporting points. In the spaces provided, add a sentence or two of realistic details for each supporting point. The more specific you are, the more convincing your details are likely to be.

1.   **An Inspiring Instructor**

After only a class or two, it was clear that the new computer graphics instructor was very good at her job. First of all, she made personal contact with every student in the class. _____

_____

_____

_____

_____

In addition, she gave out extremely clear course requirements. _____

_____

_____

_____

Finally, she encouraged all the students to ask questions. _____

_____

_____

_____

_____

2.   **Helping a Parent in College**

There are several ways a family can help a parent who is attending college. First, family members can take over some of the household chores that the parent usually does. _____

_____

_____

_____

Also, family members can make sure that the student has some quiet study time. _____

_____

_____

_____

Last, families can take an interest in the student's problems and accomplishments. _____

_____

_____

_____

1 1 WRITING A SIMPLE PARAGRAPH

You know now that an effective paragraph does two essential things: (1) it makes a point, and (2) it provides specific details to support that point. You have considered a number of paragraphs that are effective because they follow these two basic steps or are ineffective because they fail to follow them.

You are ready, then, to write a simple paragraph of your own. Choose one of the three assignments below, and follow carefully the guidelines provided.

■ Assignment 1

Turn back to the activity on pages 68-69 and, if you did that activity individually, select the point for which you have the best supporting details. Otherwise, choose a point for which you could develop strong support. Develop that point into a paragraph by following these steps.

a If necessary, rewrite the point so that the first sentence is more specific or suits your purpose more exactly. For example, you might want to rewrite the second point so that it includes a specific place: "Taking a vacation in and around Vancouver has many attractive possibilities."

b Use one or two methods of prewriting to generate details about your topic. When you are satisfied with what you have accumulated, see if the details can be grouped under more general or subtopic headings. You are looking for three subtopics for your topic. For example, a student writing about vacationing near Vancouver might find that he or she has details that fit under three headings: city attractions like Stanley Park, Whistler and ski resorts, and Victoria and the coastal islands. You may find it useful to reread Paul's experience with the writing process on pages 37-43.

c Using your disk copy or a photocopy of the Paragraph Outline Form on page 28, provide several details to develop fully each of your three subtopics. Make sure that all the information in your outline truly supports your point.

d Write your first draft based on your outline. Conclude your paragraph with a sentence that refers to your opening point. This last sentence "rounds off" the paragraph and lets the reader know that your discussion is complete. For example, the second paragraph about cheating on page 47 begins with "Cheating is common in everyday life." It closes with a statement that refers to and echoes the opening point: "For many people, daily cheating is an acceptable way to behave."

e Revise your first draft. Does each sentence truly support your topic? Is the order in which you stated your ideas reasonable? Check to make sure that you use transition words like *first of all, second* or *next,* and *finally, most,* or *last* to introduce your three supporting details.

f Supply a title based on the point. For instance, point 4 on page 69 might have the title "Ways to Economize."

g Read your paragraph aloud, if possible, or to yourself. If any sentences do not sound right, correct them; refer to Section Four of this book where needed. If you have been drafting on the computer, run the spell checker and double-check your spelling choices with the dictionary. If you are handwriting your draft, use a dictionary to check any words of which you are not certain.

Use the following list to check your paragraph for each of the above items.

YES	NO	
_____	_____	Do you begin with a point?
_____	_____	Do you provide relevant, specific details that support the point?
_____	_____	Do you use the words *first of all, second,* and *finally* to introduce your three supporting details?
_____	_____	Do you have a closing sentence that refers back to your opening point?
_____	_____	Do you have a title based on the point?
_____	_____	Are your sentences clear and free from obvious errors?

■ **Assignment 2**

In this chapter you have read two paragraphs (pages 50-51) on reasons for being in college. For this assignment, write a paragraph describing your own reasons for being in college. You might want to look first at the following list of common reasons students give for going to school. Use the ones that apply to you (making them as specific as possible) or supply your own. Select three of your most important reasons for being in school as subtopics, and generate specific supporting details for each reason.

Before starting, reread paragraph B on page 51. *You must provide comparable specific details of your own.* Make your paragraph truly personal; do not fall back on vague generalities like those in paragraph A on pages 50-51. Use the checklist for Assignment 1 as a guideline as you work on the paragraph.

APPLY IN MY CASE	*Reasons Students Go to College*
_____	• To acquire employment-related skills
_____	• To prepare for a specific career
_____	• To please their families
_____	• To educate and enrich themselves
_____	• To be with friends
_____	• To take advantage of an opportunity they didn't have before
_____	• To see if college has anything to offer them
_____	• To do more with their lives than they've done so far

_____   • To take advantage of provincial or federal assistance programs or other special funding

_____   • To earn the status that they feel comes with a college diploma

_____   • To get a new start in life

▪ Assignment 3

Write a paragraph about stress in your life. Choose three of the following stressful areas and provide specific examples and details to develop each area.

Stress at school
Stress at work
Stress at home
Stress with a friend or friends

Use the checklist for Assignment 1 as a guideline while working on the paragraph.

REVIEWING THE LEARNING OUTCOMES FOR CHAPTER 3

To assure yourself that you have understood and met the learning outcomes for this chapter, answer the following questions.

1 What is the first sentence in an effective paragraph called? What does that first sentence do?

2 How do the rest of the sentences in an effective paragraph relate to this sentence?

3 How does a subtopic differ from a supporting detail?

4 What are three reasons why specific supporting details are necessary for an effective paragraph?

5 Why must there be adequate supporting details for each subtopic?

Visit the _English Skills with Readings_ Online Learning Centre at **www.mcgrawhill.ca/college/langan** to access self-quizzes, bonus material on study and research skills, web resources, and other learning and study tools.

Explaining a Process · Examining Cause and Effect · Comparing or Contrasting · Defining
Term · Dividing and Classifying · Describing a Scene or Person · Narrating an Event · Argu
Position · Explaining a Process · Examining Cause and Effect · Comparing or Contrasti
Defining a Term · Dividing and Classifying · Describing a Scene or Person · Narrating
Event · Arguing a Position · Explaining a Process · Examining Cause and Effect · Compar

CHAPTER 4

The Third Step in Writing

LEARNING OUTCOMES

After reading this chapter and completing its activities, you will

- know how to achieve coherence by organizing your paragraph's support with an appropriate ordering method;
- be ready to create coherence by using transitions to organize and connect supporting material;
- know six types of transitional signal words and phrases;
- know three methods of indicating transition or connection between ideas; and
- know why reading audiences require transitional words and phrases.

You now know from Chapter 3 that the first two steps in writing an effective paragraph are making a point and supporting that point with specific evidence. This chapter will explore two aspects of the third step:

1 Structure supporting material according to an appropriate method of organization.

2 Create a coherent paper by using transitions and other connecting words.

You will learn and practise the main ways to organize and connect the supporting information in a paragraph or essay.

Chapter 5 will then focus on the fourth step in writing: revising and editing for clear, error-free sentences.

STEP 3: ORGANIZE AND CONNECT THE SPECIFIC EVIDENCE

At the same time that you are generating the specific details needed to support a point, you should be thinking about ways to organize and connect those details.

All the details in your paper must **cohere**, or **stick together**; when they do, your reader is able to move smoothly and clearly from one bit of supporting information to the next. This chapter will discuss the following ways to organize and connect supporting details: (1) common methods of organization, (2) transitions, and (3) other connecting words.

COMMON METHODS OF ORGANIZATION: TIME ORDER AND EMPHATIC ORDER

Time order and emphatic order are common methods used to organize the supporting material in a paper. You will learn more specialized methods of development in Section Two of the book.

Time order simply means that details are listed as they occur in time: *first* this is done; *next* this; *then* this; *after* that, this; and so on. Here is a paragraph that organizes its details through time order.

Torture by Telephone

When I left high school in grade eleven, I turned into an expert in the field of depressing short-term jobs. Every one of these jobs involved a routine, but none could compare to my nightly ritual as a telemarketer. First, my shift started every evening at five, just when everyone else was leaving work, The elevators kept letting out all these relaxed people, and there I was, waiting to go up to the twelfth floor and start work. After that, I walked down empty hallways and entered my torture chamber, where the fluorescent lights glared and computers hummed twenty-four hours a day. I started each shift by trying to adjust my chair, but it never worked, so I hunched over and turned on my computer terminal. I reached for my headset and silently prayed that it was clean. Then, when I turned on the set, I waited for the crackling sound that would rustle through every call all night long. I was never disappointed. The next step before actually starting to call people involved some suspense— would the right program open up on my terminal? I had to follow a script that appeared on the screen, and even if I had the right program, sometimes it ran so slowly that I ran out of things to say to the poor person on the other end of the line. The final treats every night were the supervisor's visits, when she always told me to do the impossible: "Smile and dial."

Fill in the missing words: "Torture by Telephone" uses the following words to help show time order: _____, _____, _____, _____, and _____.

Emphatic order is sometimes described as "save-the-best-till-last" order. It means that the most interesting or important detail is placed in the last part of a paper. (In cases where all the details seem equal in importance, the writer should impose a personal order that seems logical or appropriate to the details in question.) The last position in a paper is the most emphatic position because the reader is most likely to remember the last thing read. *Finally, last of all,* and *most important* are typical words showing emphasis. The following paragraph organizes its details through emphatic order.

Riding the Cranky Turtle

Who doesn't enjoy taking the car to school? Public transportation is not necessarily "the better way" for everyone. Many people do not enjoy using buses and subways, for a variety of reasons. First of all, at morning and evening rush hours, when most students are going to or leaving college, packs of people throng the bus stops and subway platforms. Riders lose their manners while fighting for a way through the narrow vehicle doorways. Rush-hour crowds can also mean standing during the ride, while carrying heavy bookbags or equipment. This discomfort should be multiplied by the number of people who push, shove, act rudely, or, worse, smell nasty. Additionally, there is the "turtle factor." Buses are often behind schedule and drivers seem to schedule coffee stops just when students are worrying about getting to nine-o'clock classes. Subway trains have their mysterious dark pauses, usually inside tunnels, leaving riders unable even to read their watches. But most awful of all are the prices charged for all this inconvenience. Those who suffer most are students who live far from school and need to use several different bus systems that cost double or triple fares. Generally, fares are over two dollars for a one-way ride, and service barely exists. Drivers can be unpleasant or short-tempered from overwork, so asking even a simple question about a stop could result in a snarled answer or no answer at all. The four or five dollars spent on two tickets could pay for a day's parking and maybe even enough gas for the trip. If college students look tired or sour, perhaps it's the result of riding on a very cranky and expensive turtle.

Fill in the missing words: The paragraph lists a total of _____ different reasons why students dislike public transportation. The writer of the paragraph feels that the most important reason is _____ . He or she signals this reason by using the emphasis words _____.

Some paragraphs use a *combination of time order and emphatic order.* For example, "Net Eats Student's Time!" on pages 7-8 includes time order: it moves from the time the writer tried to access the server to the end of the evening. In addition, the writer uses emphatic order, ending with her greatest source of irritation, signalled by the words "the final stage in my annoyance."

TRANSITIONS

Transitions are *signal words and phrases* that help readers *follow the direction of the writer's thought.* They show the relationship between ideas, connecting one thought with the next. They can be compared to road signs that guide travellers.

To see the value of transitions, look at the following pairs of examples. Put a check beside the example in each pair that is easier and clearer to read and understand.

1. _____ a. Our building manager recently repainted our apartment. He replaced our faulty air conditioner.

   _____ b. Our building manager recently repainted our apartment. Also, he replaced our faulty air conditioner.

2. _____ a. I carefully inserted a disk into the computer. I turned on the power button.

   _____ b. I carefully inserted a disk into the computer. Then I turned on the power button.

3. _____ a. Moviegoers usually dislike film monsters. Filmgoers loved Chucky and could not wait for him to return and take a bride.

   _____ b. Moviegoers usually dislike film monsters. However, filmgoers loved Chucky and could not wait for him to return and take a bride.

You should have checked the second example in each pair. The transitional words in those sentences—*also, then,* and *however*—make the relationship between the sentences clear. Like all effective transitions, they help connect the writer's thoughts.

In the following box are common transitional words and phrases, grouped according to the kind of signal they give readers. Note that certain words provide more than one kind of signal. In the paragraphs you write, you will often use addition signals: words like *first of all, also, another,* and *finally* will help you move from one supporting reason or detail to the next.

Transitions

Addition signals: first of all, for one thing, second, the third reason, also, next, another, and, in addition, moreover, furthermore, finally, last of all

Time signals: first, then, next, after, as, before, while, meanwhile, now, during, finally

Space signals: next to, across, on the opposite side, to the left, to the right, in front, in back, above, below, behind, nearby

Change-of-direction signals: but, however, yet, in contrast, otherwise, still, on the contrary, on the other hand

Illustration signals: for example, for instance, specifically, as an illustration, once, such as

Conclusion signals: therefore, consequently, thus, then, as a result, in summary, to conclude, last of all, finally

---

Activity

1. Underline the three *addition* signals in the following paragraph.

   I am opposed to provincial lotteries for a number of reasons. First of all, by supporting lotteries, provinces are supporting gambling. I don't see anything morally wrong with gambling, but it is a known cause of suffering for many people who do it to excess. Provinces should be concerned with improving people's lives, not causing more misery. Another objection I have to the provincial lotteries is the kind of advertising they do on television. The commercials promote the lotteries as an easy way to get rich. In fact, the odds against getting rich are astronomical. Last, the lotteries take advantage of the people who can least afford them. Studies have shown that people with lower incomes are more likely to buy lottery tickets than people with higher incomes. This is the harshest reality of the lotteries: provinces are encouraging people of limited means not to save their money but to throw it away on a provincial pipe dream.

2. Underline the four *time* signals in the following paragraph.

A few things make it easy for a Canadian to know that he or she is home when crossing the border. First is always seeing the word "Douanes" underneath the word "Customs." Of course, unless someone is entering Quebec, it is unlikely that the traveller will actually hear any French, but there is something comforting and familiar about two languages on all the signs. Then, back on the highway, another signal tips off the Canadian that he or she is home: no more trying to figure out how far 276 miles might be. Road signs are in kilometres again. Next, if a glance at the gas gauge shows the needle pointing to *E*, the driver returns to the joy of buying gas in little litres, not in large U.S. gallons. And finally, desperate for a few minutes' rest and a snack, the returning Canadian stops at a doughnut shop named for a hockey player and is again able to order the one thing never seen south of the border: a butter tart.

3. Underline the three *space* signals in the following paragraph.

Standing in the burned-out shell of my living room was a shocking experience. Above my head were charred beams, all that remained of our ceiling. In front of me, where our television and stereo had once stood, were twisted pieces of metal and chunks of blackened glass. Strangely, some items seemed little damaged by the fire. For example, I could see the TV tuner knob and a dusty CD under the rubble. I walked through the gritty ashes until I came to what was left of our couch. Behind the couch had been a wall of family photographs. Now, the wall and the pictures were gone. I found only a waterlogged scrap of my wedding picture.

4. Underline the four *change-of-direction* signals in the following paragraph.

In some ways, train travel is superior to air travel. People always marvel at the speed with which airplanes can zip from one end of the country to another. Trains, on the other hand, definitely take longer. But sometimes longer can be better. Travelling across Canada by train allows people to experience the trip more completely. They get to see the cities and towns, the Rockies, and the prairies that too often pass by unnoticed when they fly. Another advantage of train travel is comfort. Travelling by plane means wedging into a narrow seat with knees bent and bumping the back of the seat in front and being handed a "snack" consisting of a bag of ten roasted peanuts. In contrast, the seats on most trains are spacious and comfortable, permitting even the longest-legged traveller to stretch out and watch the scenery just outside the window. And when train travellers grow hungry, they can get up and stroll to the dining car, where they can order anything from a simple snack to a complete meal. There's no question that train travel is definitely slow and old-fashioned compared with air travel. However, in many ways it is much more civilized.

5. Underline the three *illustration* signals in the following selection.

At the start of the twenty-first century, the most desirable status symbols are the smallest ones, and they are all powered by microchips. The home computer everyone secretly craves, for instance, is <u>not</u> the powerful-looking model with external drives, modems, and speaker boxes hanging off its side. No, the status computer is probably one of those cute little flip-up screen models or a titanium laptop that weighs less then some magazines. Or it might be a nearly invisible model, with a tiny console that fits in a drawer and an elegant flat screen mounted on a collapsible arm. But there is an even trendier example of tiny technology, something for the person who really wants to look organized: the Palm Pilot. With the arrival of the millennium, the big leather-bound daybook went out of style. Instead, the busy person lists all of his or her appointments, phone numbers, and vital information on a little piece of equipment that looks like a grown-up GameBoy. And when this busy individual wants to make a call, he or she uses the tiniest piece of status technology of all: specifically, one of the itty-bitty new cellphones. These wee marvels are smaller than a deck of cards, fit into a pocket or purse, and let their owners "reach out and touch someone," play a video game, or even access their e-mail. Status symbols are shrinking all the time; who knows if one day they will be built right into their owners?

6. Underline the *conclusion* signal in the following paragraph.

A hundred years ago, miners used to bring caged canaries down into the mines with them to act as warning signals. If the bird died, the miner knew that the oxygen was running out. The smaller animal would be affected much more quickly than the miners. In the same way, animals are acting as warning signals to us today. Baby birds die before they can hatch because pesticides in the environment cause the adults to lay eggs with paper-thin shells. Fish die because the Great Lakes are contaminated with acid rain or poisonous mercury. The dangers in our environment will eventually affect all life on earth, including humans. Therefore, we must pay attention to these early warning signals. If we don't, we will be as foolish as a miner who ignored a dead canary—and we will die.

OTHER CONNECTING WORDS AND TRANSITIONAL METHODS

In addition to transitions, there are three other kinds of connecting words that help tie together the specific evidence in a paper: repeated words, pronouns, and synonyms. Each will be discussed in turn.

Repeated Words

Many of us have been taught not to repeat ourselves in our writing. On the other hand, repeating keywords can help tie a flow of thought together. In the paragraph that follows, the word *retirement* is repeated to remind readers of the key idea on which the discussion is centred. Underline the word the five times it appears.

> Oddly enough, retirement can pose more problems for the spouse than for the retired person. For a person who has been accustomed to a demanding job, retirement can mean frustration and a feeling of uselessness. This feeling will put pressure on the spouse to provide challenges at home equal to those of the workplace. Often, these tasks will disrupt the spouse's well-established routine. Another problem arising from retirement is filling up all those empty hours. The spouse may find himself or herself in the role of social director or tour guide, expected to come up with a new form of amusement every day. Without sufficient challenges or leisure activities, a person can become irritable and take out the resulting boredom and frustration of retirement on the marriage partner. It is no wonder that many of these partners wish their spouses would come out of retirement and do something—anything—just to get out of the house.

Pronouns

Pronouns (*he, she, it, you, they, this, that,* and others) are another way to connect ideas as you develop a paper. Using pronouns to take the place of other words or ideas can help you avoid needless repetition. Be careful, though, to use pronouns with care in order to *avoid unclear or inconsistent pronoun reference,* as described on pages 98-99 and 357-58 of this book. Underline the seven pronouns in the passage below, noting at the same time the words to which the pronouns refer.

> A professor of nutrition at a major university recently advised his students that they could do better on examinations by eating lots of sweets. He told them that the sugar in cakes and candy would stimulate their brains to work more efficiently, and that if the sugar was eaten for only a month or two, it would not do them any harm.

Synonyms

Using synonyms (words that are alike in meaning) can also help move the reader clearly from one thought to the next. In addition, the use of synonyms increases variety and reader interest by avoiding needless repetition of the same words. Underline the three phrases used as synonyms for *ATMs* in the following passage.

ATMs make it too tempting for the average Canadian to overspend. Because bank machines run "twenty-four/seven," we can take out another forty dollars any time of day or night instead of waiting for the bank to open and perhaps reconsidering how much we really need that extra money. Automated cash windows are temptingly placed nearly everywhere just for our spending convenience. "Instant tellers" sit in convenience stores, at gas stations, and all over malls, waiting to catch us when we are weakest. ATMs look so bright, friendly, and appealing that somehow we feel less guilty about withdrawing money from them than we might after filling out a withdrawal slip, waiting in line, and facing a teller. Perhaps it is just easier to face a screen that reads "Insufficient funds" than it is to hear a live bank teller say, "I'm sorry, but your account is overdrawn."

Activity

To sharpen your sense of how *coherence*, or a sense of connection, is maintained throughout a paper, read the selection below and then answer the questions about it that follow.

The Worst Experience of My Week

[1]The registration process at McKenzie College was a nightmare. [2]The night before registration for my course officially began, I went to bed anxious about the whole thing, and nothing that happened the next day eased any of my tension. [3]First, even though I had paid my registration fee early last spring, the staff in the registration office had no record of my payment. [4]For some bizarre reason, they wouldn't accept the receipt I had. [5]Consequently, I had to stand in a special numbered line for two hours, waiting for someone to give me a paper that stated that I had, in fact, paid my registration fee. [6]The need for this new receipt seemed ridiculous to me, since, all along, I had proof that I had paid. [7]Next, I was told that I had to see my program coordinator in the International Business Faculty and that this faculty was in Section C, Phase 2, of the Champlain Building. [8]I had no idea what or where the Champlain Building was. [9]Finally, I found the ugly cinder-block structure. Then I began looking for Section C and Phase 2. [10]When I found these, everyone there was a member of the Communications Department. [11]No one seemed to know where International Business had gone. [12]Finally, one instructor said she thought International Business was in Section A. [13]"And where is Section A?" I asked. [14]"I don't know," the teacher answered. "I'm new here." [15]She saw the bewildered look on my face and said sympathetically, "You're not the only one who's confused." [16]I nodded and walked numbly away. [17]I felt as if I were fated to spend the rest of the semester trying to complete the registration process, and I wondered if I would ever become an official college student.

▨ Questions

1. How many times is the key idea *registration* repeated? _____;

2. Write here the pronoun that is used for *staff in the registration office*

(sentence 4): _____; for *Section C, Phase 2* (sentence 10): _____; for *instructor* (sentence 15): _____.

3. Write here the words that are used as a synonym for *receipt* (sentence 5):

    _____;

    the words that are used as a synonym for *Champlain Building* (sentence 9):

    _____;

    the word that is used as a synonym for *instructor* (sentence 14):

    _____.

■ **Review Activity**

To check your progress with the learning outcomes for this chapter, complete the following statements.

1. The four steps in writing a paper are:

    a. _____

    b. _____

    c. _____

    d. _____

2. *Time order* means _____

    _____

3. *Emphatic order* means _____

    _____

4. What are *transitions?* What is their function?   _____

    _____

5. In addition to transitions, three other kinds of connecting words that help

    link sentences and ideas are repeated words, _____, and

    _____.

PRACTICE IN ORGANIZING AND CONNECTING SPECIFIC EVIDENCE

You now know the third step in effective writing: *organizing the specific evidence used to support the main point of a paper.* You also know that the fourth step—writing clear, error-free sentences—will be treated in detail in Section Four of this book. As you work through the activities in this section, you will expand and strengthen your understanding of the third step in writing. You will achieve mastery of this chapter's learning outcomes connected to gaining and increasing your competence in organizing and linking ideas.

To do so, work through the following series of activities:

1 Organizing through Time Order
2 Organizing through Emphatic Order
3 Organizing through a Combination of Time Order and Emphatic Order
4 Identifying Transitions
5 Providing Transitions
6 Identifying Transitions and Other Connecting Words

1 ORGANIZING THROUGH TIME ORDER

Activity

Use time order to organize the scrambled list of sentences below.

First choose the point that all the other sentences support, and write the number *1* next to it. Then choose one of three methods for completing the exercise:

1 Read all the items through, and write a number for each supporting sentence as it occurs in time sequence in the spaces provided.
2 Type each supporting item and use the cut and paste functions on your computer to move the sentences around until they are in the correct time sequence. Number the sentences, and then print your document.
3 Write the sentences on a sheet of paper, leaving spaces between them, and then cut out each item. Move around the strips of paper containing the sentences until they are in time sequence; then number the sentences. Transfer the numbers for the correctly ordered sentences to the spaces below.

_____ The table is right near the garbage pail.

_____ So you reluctantly select a glue-like tuna-fish sandwich, a crushed-in apple pie, and watery, lukewarm coffee.

_____ You sit at the edge of the table, away from the garbage pail, and gulp down your meal.

_____ Trying to eat in the cafeteria is an unpleasant experience.

_____ Suddenly you spot a free table in the corner.

_____ With a last swallow of the lukewarm coffee, you get up and leave the cafeteria as rapidly as possible.

_____ Flies are flitting in and out of the pail.

_____ By the time it is your turn, the few things that are almost good are gone.

_____ There does not seem to be a free table anywhere.

_____ Unfortunately, there is a line in the cafeteria.

_____ The submarine sandwiches, doughnuts, and iced tea have all disappeared.

_____   You hold your tray and look for a place to sit down.

_____   You have a class in a few minutes, and so you run in to grab something to eat quickly.

2 ORGANIZING THROUGH EMPHATIC ORDER

Activity

Use emphatic order (order of importance) to arrange the following scrambled list of sentences. Write the number *1* beside the point that all the other sentences support. Then, using one of the three methods suggested in the preceding activity, number each supporting sentence, starting with what seems to be the least important detail and ending with the most important detail.

_____   The people in my area of Swift Current are all around my age and seem to be genuinely friendly and interested in me.

_____   The place where I live has several important advantages.

_____   The schools in this neighbourhood have a good reputation, so I feel that my daughter is getting a good education.

_____   The best thing of all about this area, though, is the school system.

_____   Therefore, I don't have to put up with public transportation or worry about how much it's going to cost to park each day.

_____   The school also has an extended daycare program, so I know my daughter is in good hands until I come home from work.

_____   First of all, I like the people who live in the other apartments near mine.

_____   Another positive aspect of this area is that it's close to where I work.

_____   That's more than I can say for the last place I lived, where people never seemed to say hello.

_____   The office where I'm a receptionist is only a six-block walk from my house.

_____   In addition, I save a lot of wear and tear on my car.

3 ORGANIZING THROUGH A COMBINATION OF TIME ORDER AND EMPHATIC ORDER

Activity

Use a *combination* of time order and emphatic order to arrange the scrambled list of sentences below. Write the number *1* beside the point that all the other sentences support. Then, using one of the three methods suggested in the two preceding activities, number each supporting sentence. Paying close attention to transitional words and phrases will help you organize and connect the supporting sentences.

_____ I did not see the snake but visited my friend in the Gravenhurst hospital, where he suffered for days because of the snakebite venom.

_____ We were taking our time, dawdling along side roads, when we decided to eat lunch in the woods by the roadside.

_____ As I walked back to the car, I saw a long dark shape on the path in front of me.

_____ After my two experiences, I suspect that my fear of snakes will be with me for life.

_____ The first experience occurred when my best friend received a bite from a massasauga rattler.

_____ I looked down at my feet, but it was shady and dark in the woods and my legs were shaking.

_____ I had two experiences when I was eighteen that are the cause of my herpeto-phobia, or terrible and uncontrollable fear of snakes.

_____ We stopped the car at the side of the road and took out our lunches, and then I decided to walk into the woods a little farther.

_____ When I got back in the car, I felt sick to my stomach, light-headed, and faint.

_____ I saw the huge bandage on his calf and the discoloured, puffy swelling when the bandage was removed.

_____ Then it curved its horrible slinky body off sideways out of my way and slithered into the dark bushes nearby.

_____ I sat in the car for an hour afterward, shaking and sweating, trying to reassure myself that snakes could not open car doors.

_____ But my more direct experience with snakes happened one day when another friend and I were driving south to Barrie to buy concert tickets.

_____ Nearly touching the toe of my running shoe was a long, fat, grey snake, with a huge diamond-shaped head, looking straight at me.

_____ Most of all, I saw the ugly red scabs on his leg where the snake's fangs had ripped the flesh of his calf.

_____ I imagined the evil, muscular-looking snake lunging at me, opening its mouth wide, and attaching itself to my ankle.

_____ At the same time I cried out "Arghh!" and ran toward the car, and I never looked back.

_____ For a long, horrible second, the snake raised its head and eyed me coldly, as if it were thinking about how I would taste.

4 IDENTIFYING TRANSITIONS

The following three activities will increase your awareness of various transitional methods and your competence in using them. In meeting this learning outcome, you will achieve two necessities for effective writing: (1) you will connect your supporting ideas and details in ways that reflect your intention as a writer, and (2) you will make your point and the sequence of your supporting material easier to follow for your readers.

Activity

Locate the major transitions used in the following two selections. Then write the transitions in the spaces provided. Mostly, you will find addition words such as *another* and *also*. You will also find several change-of-direction words such as *but* and *however*.

1.   **Watching Hockey on TV**

Watching a hockey game on television may seem like the easiest thing in the world. However, like the game of hockey itself, watching a game correctly is far more complicated than it appears. First is the matter of the company. The ideal number of people depends on the size of your living-room floor. Also, at least one of your guests should be rooting for the opposite team. There's nothing like a little rivalry, the potential for a fight, to increase the enjoyment of hockey. Next, consider the refreshments. Make sure you have plenty of everyone's favourite drinks, along with the essential chips, dips, and pretzels. You may even want something more substantial on hand, like wings or pizza. If you do, make everyone wait until the moment the puck is dropped before eating. Waiting will make everything taste much better. Finally, there are the last items to have on hand or, in this case, on upper body: team jerseys. The purpose of these garments is not to keep people warm but to reinforce loyalties during the game—and to use as weapons after. If your team happens to be getting trounced, you may just decide to wrap up your friends in the Oilers jerseys in your blue-and-white Leafs sweaters.

a. _____

b. _____

c. _____

d. _____

e. _____

2.   **Avoidance Tactics**

Getting down to studying for an exam or writing a paper is hard, and so it is tempting for students to use one of the following five avoidance tactics in order to put the work aside. For one thing, students may say to themselves, "I can't do it." They adopt a defeatist attitude at the start and give up without a struggle. They could get help with their work by using such college services as tutoring programs and access and learning resources. However, they refuse even to try. A second avoidance technique is to say, "I'm too busy." Students may take on an extra job, become heavily involved in social activities, or allow family problems to become so time-consuming that they cannot concentrate on their studies. Yet if college really matters to a student, he or she will make sure that there is enough time to do the required work. Another avoidance technique is expressed by the phrase "I'm too tired." Typically, sleepiness occurs when it is time to study or go to class and then vanishes when the school pressure is off. This sleepiness is a sign of work avoidance. A fourth excuse is to say, "I'll do it later." Putting things off until the last minute is practically a guarantee of poor grades on tests and papers. When everything else seems more urgent than studying—watching TV, calling a friend, or even cleaning the oven—a student may simply be escaping academic work. Last, some students avoid work by saying to themselves, "I'm here and that's what counts." Such students live under the dangerous delusion that, since they possess a student card, a parking sticker, and textbooks, the coursework will somehow take care of itself. But once a student has a student card, he or she has only just begun. Doing the necessary studying, writing, and reading will bring real results: good grades, genuine learning, and a sense of accomplishment.

a. _____

b. _____

c. _____

d. _____

e. _____

f. _____

g. _____

h. _____

5 PROVIDING TRANSITIONS

Activity

In the spaces provided, add logical transitions to tie together the sentences and ideas in the following paragraphs. Use the words in the boxes that precede the paragraphs.

1.

| however | a second | last of all |
| for one thing | also | on the other hand |

Why School May Frighten a Young Child

Schools may be frightening to young children for a number of reasons.

_____, the regimented environment may be a new and disturbing experience. At home children may have been able to do what they wanted when they wanted to do it. In school,

_____, they are given a set time for talking, working, playing, eating, and even going to the toilet. _____ source of anxiety may be the public method of discipline that some teachers use. Whereas at home children are scolded in private, in school they may be held up to embarrassment and ridicule in front of their peers. "Fatima," the teacher may say, "why are you the only one in the class who didn't do your homework?" Or "David, why are you the only one who can't work quietly at your seat?" Children may _____ be frightened by the loss of personal attention. Their little discomforts or mishaps, such as tripping on the stairs, may bring instant sympathy from a parent; in school, there is often no one to notice, or the teacher is frequently too busy to care and just says, "Go do your work. You'll be all right." _____, a child may be scared by the competitive environment of the school. At home, one hopes, such competition for attention is minimal. In school,

_____, children may vie for the teacher's approving glance or tone of voice, or for stars on a paper, or for favoured seats in the front row. For these and other reasons, it is not surprising that children may have difficulty adjusting to school.

2.

as a result	once	finally
second	when	first of all
	but	

Joining a Multicultural Club

Canadians are proud of the "diversity" of our population, but I learned first-hand about diversity when I joined a multicultural club.

_____, the club has helped me become friends with a diverse group of people. At any time in my apartment, I can have someone from Pakistan chatting about music to someone from Portugal, or someone from Russia talking about politics to someone from Uganda.

_____ I watched an Israeli student give falafels to three students from China. They had never eaten such things, but they liked them.

A _____ benefit of the club is that it's helped me realize how similar people are. _____ the whole club first assembled, we wound up having a conversation about dating and sex that included the perspectives of fifteen countries and six continents!

It was clear we all shared the feeling that sex was fascinating. The talk lasted for hours, with many different persons describing the wildest or funniest experience they had had with the opposite sex. Only a few students, particularly those from Canada and Japan, seemed bashful.

_____, the club has reminded me about the dangers of stereotyping. Before I joined the club, most of my experience with Chinese Canadians was limited to some shy fellow high-school students.

_____, I believed that most Chinese people worked

in the computer or food service industries. _____ in the club, I met Chinese people who were soccer players, English majors, and graphic designers. I've also seen Jewish and Muslim students, people who I thought would never get along, drop their preconceived notions and become friends. Even more than my classes, the club has been an eye-opener for me.

6 IDENTIFYING TRANSITIONS AND OTHER CONNECTING WORDS

Activity

This activity will give you practice in identifying *transitions, repeated words, synonyms,* and *pronouns* that are used to help tie ideas together.

Section A: Transitions In the space provided, write the transitional words.

1. I decided to pick up a drop-add form from the registrar's office. However, I changed my mind when I saw the long line of students waiting there.

   _____

2. In England, drivers use the left-hand side of the road. Consequently, steering wheels are on the right side.

   _____

3. Crawling babies will often investigate new objects by putting them in their mouths. Therefore, parents should be alert for any pins, tacks, or other dangerous items on floors and carpets.

   _____

4. One technique that advertisers use is to have a celebrity endorse a product. The consumer then associates the star qualities of the celebrity with the product.

   _____

Section B: Repeated Words In the space provided, write the repeated words.

5. We absorb radiation from many sources in our environment. Our colour television sets and microwave ovens, among other things, give off low-level radiation.

   _____

6. Many researchers believe that people have set points of weight that their bodies try to maintain. This may explain why many dieters return to their original weight.

   _____

7. At the end of the Sum 41 concert, thousands of fans held up disposable lighters in the darkened area. The sea of lighters signalled that the fans wanted an encore.

   _____

8. Establishing credit is important for a woman. A good credit history is often necessary when she is applying for a consumer loan or a mortgage.

   _____

Section C: Synonyms   In the space provided, write the synonym for the underlined word.

9. I checked my <u>car's</u> tires, oil, water, and belts before the trip. But the ungrateful machine blew a gasket about fifty kilometres from home.

   _____

10. Women's <u>clothes</u>, in general, use less material than men's clothes. Yet women's garments usually cost more than men's.

    _____

11. Temperance movements in various provinces sought to ban <u>alcohol</u>. Drinking liquor, movement leaders said, led to violence, poverty, prostitution, and insanity.

    _____

12. For me, <u>apathy</u> quickly sets in when the weather becomes hot and sticky. This listlessness disappears when the humidity decreases.

    _____

Section D: Pronouns   In the space provided, write the word referred to by the underlined pronoun.

13. At the turn of the century, bananas were still an oddity in North America. Some people even attempted to eat <u>them</u> with the skins on.

    _____

14. Canning vegetables is easy and economical. <u>It</u> can also be very dangerous.

    _____

15. There are a number of signs that appear when students are under stress. For example, <u>they</u> start to have trouble studying, eating, and even sleeping.

REVIEWING THE LEARNING OUTCOMES FOR CHAPTER 4

To assure yourself that you have understood and met the learning outcomes for this chapter, answer the following questions.

1 What is the first way to achieve coherence in a paragraph? What are the two main methods of ordering support?

2 What are transitions?

3 What are six types of transitional signals? Name two examples of each type.

4 What are three other methods of indicating transition or connection between ideas?

5 What are the main purposes for providing transitional words and phrases?

Visit the *English Skills with Readings* Online Learning Centre at **www.mcgrawhill.ca/college/langan** to access self-quizzes, bonus material on study and research skills, web resources, and other learning and study tools.

CHAPTER 5

The Fourth Step in Writing

LEARNING OUTCOMES

After completing the activities, you will

- know five strategies to help you revise your sentences so that they are clear and effective;
- know two aspects of sentence structure where a consistent point of view is essential;
- use specific words to capture readers' interest and make your meanings clear;
- use concise words to convey your meaning economically;
- revise your sentences to create variety and interest in your paragraphs by using four different methods; and
- know how to edit and proofread your sentences for correct use of sentence skills.

So far this book has emphasized the first three bases for writing an effective paragraph: unity, support, and coherence. This chapter will focus on the fourth base for writing effectively: sentence skills. You will learn a "close focus" skill: how to revise a paragraph so that your sentences flow smoothly and clearly to present the meaning you intend. Next, you will concentrate on how to edit a paragraph's sentences for errors in grammar, punctuation, and spelling.

STEP 4: REVISE TO WRITE CLEAR, ERROR-FREE SENTENCES

The work of revising your sentences means two things: first, reading your sentences with fresh eyes to discover what you wish to change; and, second, rewriting your sentences so that they say clearly just what you mean. Always leave some time between writing a draft and revising to give you distance from what you have written, so that you can view your work as objectively as possible. When revising, try to see your paragraph as your readers will—ask yourself where meanings are not clear, where sentences do not flow easily from one to the next, and where a group of sentences sound repetitive.

This chapter will sharpen your awareness of possible sentence problems and show you these strategies for writing sentences that express your meaning in a way that readers will follow easily:

- Use Parallel Structures
- Use Consistent Verb Tenses and Pronouns
- Use Specific Words
- Use Concise Wording
- Vary Your Sentence Types

USE PARALLEL STRUCTURES

Words in a pair or a series should have a parallel structure. By balancing the items in a pair or a series so that they have the same kind of structure, you will make a sentence clearer and easier to read. Notice how the parallel sentences that follow read more smoothly than the non-parallel ones.

Non-Parallel (Not Balanced)	*Parallel (Balanced)*
I made resolutions to lose weight, to study more, and *watching* less TV.	I made resolutions to lose weight, to study more, and to watch less TV. (A balanced series of *to* verbs: *to lose, to study, to watch*)
A consumer group rates my car as noisy, expensive, and *not having much safety.*	A consumer group rates my car as noisy, expensive, and unsafe. (A balanced series of descriptive words: *noisy, expensive, unsafe*)
Pei-Ti likes wearing soft sweaters, eating exotic foods, and *to bathe* in scented bath oil.	Pei-Ti likes wearing soft sweaters, eating exotic foods, and bathing in scented bath oil. (A balanced series of *-ing* words: *wearing, eating, bathing*)
Single life offers more freedom of choice; *more security is offered by marriage.*	Single life offers more freedom of choice; marriage offers more security. (Balanced verbs and word order: *single life offers … ; marriage offers …*)

You need not worry about balanced sentences when writing first drafts. But when you revise, you should try to put matching words and ideas into matching structures.

Errors in parallel structure show up most often in lists of items within sentences, as the activity below demonstrates. When you write college essays, your thesis statement frequently contains just this kind of list; when you set out your three supporting ideas in a thesis, try to make your ideas match grammatically. Mastering parallelism will improve and smooth your writing style.

Activity

The unbalanced part of each of the following sentences is *italicized*. Rewrite the unbalanced part so that it matches the rest of the sentence. The first one is done for you as an example.

1. Mike Myers's films are clever, well-acted, and *have a lot of humour.*

   _____humorous_____

2. Filling out an income tax form is worse than wrestling a bear or *to walk* on hot coals. _____

3. The study-skills course taught me how to take more effective notes, read a textbook chapter, and *preparing* for exams. _____

4. Nadine plans to become a model, a lawyer, or *to go into nursing.*

   _____

5. Elaine likes *to water* her garden, walking her fox terrier, and arguing with her husband. _____

6. Filled with talent and *ambitious,* Eduardo plugged away at his sales job.

   _____

7. When I saw my roommate with my girlfriend, I felt worried, angry, and *embarrassment* as well. _____

8. Cindy's cat likes sleeping in the dryer, lying in the bathtub, and *to chase* squirrels. _____

9. The bacon was fatty, *grease was on the potatoes,* and the eggs were cold.

   _____

10. People in the lobby munched popcorn, sipped pop, and *were shuffling* their feet impatiently.

USE CONSISTENT VERB TENSES AND PRONOUNS

See if you can find and underline the two mistakes in verb tense in the following passage.

Kyle's eyes burned and itched all day long. When he looked at them in a mirror, he also discovers there were red blotches on his neck. He spoke to his mother about the symptoms, and she said that maybe he was allergic to something. Then he remembers he had been cuddling the kitten that Sarah had just bought the day before. "Good grief. I must be allergic to cats," he said to himself.

If you underlined *discovers* and *remembers*, you are correct. *Discovers* and *remembers* are present-tense verbs, and the paragraph is written in the past tense. The tense shifts are errors and disruptive for readers.

CONSISTENCY OF VERB TENSES

Do not shift verb tenses unnecessarily. If you begin writing a paper in the present tense, don't shift suddenly to the past. If you begin in the past, don't shift without reason to the present. Notice the inconsistent verb tenses in the following example.

The shoplifter *walked* quickly toward the front of the store. When a clerk *shouts* at him, he *started* to run.

The verbs must be consistently in the present tense:

The shoplifter *walks* quickly toward the front of the store. When a clerk *shouts* at him, he *starts* to run.

Or the verbs must be consistently in the past tense:

The shoplifter *walked* quickly toward the front of the store. When a clerk *shouted* at him, he *started* to run.

Activity

In each item, one verb must be changed so that it agrees in tense with the other verbs. Cross out the incorrect verb and write the correct form in the space provided.

Example   _____*carried*_____ Kareem wanted to be someplace else when the dentist ~~carries~~ in a long needle.

1. I played my CDs and watched television before I decide to do some homework. _____

2. The hitchhiker stopped me as I walks from the highway rest area and said, "Are you on your way to Red Deer?" _____

3. Some students attend all their classes in school. They listen carefully during lectures but they don't take notes. As a result, they often failed tests.

   _____

4. His parents stayed together for his sake; only after he graduates from college were they divorced. _____

5. In the movie, artillery shells exploded on the hide of the reptile monster. It just grinned, tosses off the shells, and kept eating people. _____

6. Several months a year, monarch butterflies come to live on Point Pelee along the Lake Erie shore. Thousands and thousands of them hang from the trees and fluttered through the air in large groups. _____

7. After waking up each morning, Neil stays in bed for a while. First he stretches and yawned loudly, and then he plans his day. _____

8. The salespeople at Biggs's Department Store are very helpful. When people asked for a product the store doesn't carry or is out of, the salesperson recommends another store. _____

9. Part-time workers at the company are the first to be laid off. They are also paid less, and they received no union representation. _____

10. Smashed cars, ambulances, and police cars blocked traffic on one side of the highway. On the other side, traffic slows down as drivers looked to see what happened. _____

CONSISTENCY OF PRONOUNS

Pronouns should not shift their point of view unnecessarily. When writing a paper, be consistent in your use of first-, second-, or third-person pronouns.

Type of Pronoun	*Singular*	*Plural*
First-person pronouns	I (my, mine, me)	we (our, ours, us)
Second-person pronouns	you (your, yours)	you (your, yours)
Third-person pronouns	he (his, him)	they (theirs, theirs, them)
	she (her, hers)	
	it (its)	

Note: Any person, place, or thing, as well as any indefinite pronoun like *one, anyone, someone,* and so on (page 356), takes a pronoun in the third person.

For instance, if you start writing in the third-person singular, using *she,* don't jump suddenly to the second person, *you,* or to the plural, *they.* Or if you are writing in the first person, using *I,* don't shift unexpectedly to *one.* Look at the examples.

Inconsistent	*Consistent*
I enjoy movies like *The Ring* that frighten *you.* (The most common mistake people make is to let *you* slip into their writing after they start with another pronoun.)	I enjoy movies like *The Ring* that frighten *me.*

As soon as a person walks into Helen's apartment, *you* can tell that Helen owns a cat.
(Again, *you* is a shift in point of view from "a person.")

As soon as a person walks into Helen's apartment, *he or she* can tell that Helen owns a cat.
(See also the note on *his or her* references on page 357.)

Activity

Cross out incorrect pronouns in the following sentences, and write the correct form of the pronoun above each crossed-out word.

Example   My dreams are always the kind that haunt ~~you~~ *me* the next day.

1. Whenever we take our children on a trip, you have to remember to bring snacks, tissues, and toys.

2. In our society, we often need a diploma before you are hired for a job.

3. A worker can take a break only after a relief person comes to take your place.

4. If a student organizes time carefully, you can accomplish a great deal of work.

5. Although I know you should watch your cholesterol intake, I can never resist an ear of corn dripping with melted butter.

6. A good conversationalist has the ability to make the person she is talking to feel as if they are the only other person in the room.

7. We almost never go to Wild Sushi any more, because you wait so long to be seated and the servers make mistakes with the orders.

8. I'm careful about talking to people on the subway because one can get into some really weird situations.

9. We can't afford to move right now, because you need not only the first month's rent but also an extra month's security deposit.

10. In my job as a department manager, I'm supposed to be nice to the customer even if they are being totally unreasonable.

USE SPECIFIC WORDS

To be an effective writer, you must use specific, rather than general, words. Specific words create pictures in the reader's mind. They help capture the reader's interest and make your meaning clear.

General	*Specific*
The boy came down the street.	Voytek ran down Woodlawn Avenue.
A bird appeared on the grass.	A blue jay swooped down onto the frost-covered lawn.

| She stopped the car. | Wanda slammed on the brakes of her Escort. |

The specific sentences create clear pictures in your reader's mind. The details *show* readers exactly what has happened.

Here are four ways to make your words and sentences specific.

1   Use exact names.

> *She* loves her *motorbike*.
> *Kellie* loves her *Honda*.

2   Use lively verbs.

> The garbage truck *went* down Front Street.
> The garbage truck *rumbled* down Front Street.

3   Use descriptive words (modifiers) before nouns.

> A girl peeked out the window.
> A *chubby, six-year-old* girl peeked out the *dirty kitchen* window.

4   Use words that relate to the five senses: sight, hearing, taste, smell, and touch.

> That woman is a karate expert.
> That *tiny, silver-haired* woman is a karate expert. (*Sight*)

> When the dryer stopped, a signal sounded.
> When the *whooshing* dryer stopped, a *loud buzzer* sounded. (*Hearing*)

> Natasha offered me an orange slice.
> Natasha offered me a *sweet, juicy* orange slice. (*Taste*)

> The real estate agent opened the door of the closet.
> The real estate agent opened the door of the *cedar-scented* closet. (*Smell*)

> I pulled the blanket around me to fight off the wind.
> I pulled the *scratchy* blanket around me to fight off the *chilling* wind. (*Touch*)

Activity 1

This activity will give you practice in replacing vague, indefinite words with sharp, specific words. Add three or more specific words to replace the general word or words underlined in each sentence. Make changes in the wording of a sentence as necessary.

Example   My bathroom cabinet contains <u>many drugs</u>.

> *My bathroom cabinet contains Aspirin, antibiotics, herbal sedative,*
> *and cough medicine.*

1.   At the shopping centre, we visited <u>several stores</u>.

_____

_____

2. Sunday is my day to take care of <u>chores</u>.

    _____

    _____

3. Hoi Yee enjoys <u>various activities</u> in her spare time.

    _____

    _____

4. I spent most of my afternoon doing <u>homework</u>.

    _____

    _____

5. We returned home from vacation to discover that <u>several pests</u> had invaded the house.

    _____

    _____

Activity 2

Again, practise changing vague, general, and indefinite words into lively, image-filled writing that captures your reader's interest and makes your meaning clear.

Using the methods described in the preceding activity, add specific details to the ten sentences that follow, on a separate sheet of paper. Note the examples below.

Examples   The person got out of the car.

The elderly man painfully lifted himself out of the white station wagon.

The fans enjoyed the victory.

Many of the fifty thousand fans stood, waved Leafs sweaters, and

cheered wildly when Tretiak scored the winning goal.

1. The lunch was not very good.
2. The animal ran away.
3. An accident occurred.
4. The instructor came into the room.
5. The machine did not work.
6. The crowd grew restless.
7. I relaxed.
8. The room was inviting.
9. The child threw the object.
10. The driver was angry.

USE CONCISE WORDING

Wordiness—using more words than necessary to express a meaning—is often a sign of lazy or careless writing. Your readers may resent the extra time and energy they must spend when you have not done the work needed to make your writing direct and concise.

Here are examples of wordy sentences.

Anna is of the opinion that the death penalty should be allowed.

I would like to say that my subject in this paper will be the kind of generous person that my father was.

Omitting needless words improves the sentences.

Anna supports the death penalty.

My father was a generous person.

The following box lists some wordy expressions that could be reduced to single words.

Wordy Form	Short Form	Wordy Form	Short Form
a large number of	many	in every instance	always
a period of a week	a week	in my own opinion	I think
arrive at an agreement	agree	in the event that	if
at an earlier point in time	before	in the near future	soon
at the present time	now	in this day and age	today
owing to the fact that	because	large in size	large
during the time that	while	plan ahead for the future	plan
for the reason that	because	postponed until later	postponed

VARY YOUR SENTENCE TYPES

Varied types of sentences add interest to your writing. If every sentence follows the same pattern, writing becomes monotonous to read. This section explains four ways to create variety in your writing style. Coordination and subordination are important techniques for achieving different kinds of emphasis in writing.

Here are four methods you can use when revising to make your sentences more varied and more sophisticated:

1 Add a Second Complete Thought (coordination)
2 Add a Dependent Thought (subordination)
3 Begin with a Special Opening Word or Phrase
4 Place Adjectives or Verbs in a Series

Each method will be discussed in turn.

ADD A SECOND COMPLETE THOUGHT

When you add a second complete thought to a simple sentence, the result is a compound (or double) sentence. The two complete statements in a compound sentence are usually connected by a comma plus a joining, or coordinating, word *(and, but, for, or, nor, so, yet)*.

Use a compound sentence when you want to give equal weight to two closely related ideas. The technique of showing that ideas have equal importance is called *coordination*.

Following are some compound sentences. Each contains two ideas that the writer regards as equal in importance.

> Barry has stopped smoking cigarettes, but he is now addicted to chewing gum.
>
> I repeatedly failed the math quizzes, so I decided to drop the course.
>
> Stan turned all the lights off, and then he locked the office door.

Activity

Combine the following pairs of simple sentences into compound sentences. Use a comma and a logical joining word *(and, but, for, so)* to connect each pair.

Note: If you are not sure what *and, but, for,* and *so* mean, see pages 333–34.

Example   • The car crept along slowly
            • Visability was poor in the heavy fog.

            The car crept along slowly, for visibility was poor in the heavy fog.

1. • The line at the deli counter was long.
    • Jake took a numbered ticket anyway.

    _____

2. • Vandals smashed the car's headlights.
    • They slashed the tires as well.

    _____

3. • I married at age seventeen.
    • I never got a chance to live on my own.

    _____

4. • Mould grew on my leather boots.
    • The closet was warm and humid.

    _____

5. • My father has a high cholesterol count.
    • He continues to eat red meat almost every day.

    _____

ADD A DEPENDENT THOUGHT

When you add a dependent thought to a simple sentence, the result is a complex sentence.* A dependent thought begins with a word or phrase like those in the box below.

Dependent Words		
after	if, even if	when, whenever
although, though	in order that	where, wherever
as	since	whether
because	that, so that	which, whichever
before	unless	while
even though	until	who, whoever
how	what, whatever	whose

A complex sentence is used when you want to emphasize one idea over another within a sentence. Look at the following complex sentence:

Although I lowered the thermostat, my heating bill remained high.

The idea that the writer wants to emphasize here—*my heating bill remained high*—is expressed as a complete thought. The less important idea—*Although I lowered my thermostat*—is subordinated to this complete thought. The technique of giving one idea less emphasis than another is called *subordination*.

Following are other examples of complex sentences. In each case, the part starting with the dependent word is the less emphasized part of the sentence.

Even though I was tired, I stayed up to watch the horror movie.
Before I take a bath, I check for spiders in the tub.
When Ivy feels nervous, she pulls on her earlobe.

Activity

Use logical subordinating words to combine the following pairs of simple sentences into sentences that contain a dependent thought. Place a comma after a dependent statement when it starts the sentence.

Example • Our team lost.
 • We were not invited to the tournament.

 Because our team lost, we were not invited to the tournament.

1. • I receive my diploma in June.
 • I will begin applying for jobs.

*The two parts of a complex sentence are sometimes called an *independent clause* and a *dependent clause*. A *clause* is simply a word group that contains a subject and a verb. An independent clause expresses a complete thought and can stand alone. A dependent clause does not express a complete thought in itself and "depends on" the independent clause to complete its meaning. Dependent clauses always begin with a dependent, or subordinating, word.

2. • Kyra doesn't enjoy cooking.
   • She often eats at fast-food restaurants.

_____

_____

3. • I sent several letters of complaint.
   • The hydro company never corrected my bill.

_____

_____

4. • Marc's car went into a skid.
   • He took his foot off the gas pedal.

_____

_____

5. • The final exam covered sixteen chapters.
   • The students complained.

_____

_____

BEGIN WITH A SPECIAL OPENING WORD OR PHRASE

Among the special openers that can be used to start sentences are (1) *-ed* words, (2) *-ing* words, (3) *-ly* words, (4) *to* word groups, and (5) prepositional phrases. Here are examples of all five kinds of openers.

-ed **word**	Tired from a long day of work, Sharon fell asleep on the sofa.
-ing **word**	Using a thick towel, Chan dried his hair quickly.
-ly **word**	Reluctantly, I agreed to rewrite the paper.
to **word group**	To get to the church on time, you must leave now.
prepositional phrase	With Mark's help, Samantha planted the evergreen shrubs.

Activity

Combine the simple sentences into one sentence by using the opener shown in the margin and omitting repeated words. Use a comma to set off the opener from the rest of the sentence.

Example   *-ing* word   • The toaster refused to pop up.
   • It buzzed like an angry hornet.

   Buzzing like an angry hornet, the toaster refused

   to pop up.

-ed word

1. • Dimitri was annoyed by the poor TV reception.
   • He decided to get a satellite dish.

   _____

   _____

-ing word

2. • The star player glided down the court.
   • He dribbled the basketball like a pro.

   _____

   _____

-ly word

3. • Food will run short on our crowded planet.
   • It is inevitable.

   _____

   _____

to word group

4. • Andrew rented a limousine for the night.
   • He wanted to make a good impression.

   _____

   _____

prepositional
phrase

5. • Ayesha answered the telephone.
   • She did this at 4 a.m.

   _____

   _____

-ed word

6. • Nathan dreaded the coming holidays.
   • He was depressed by his recent divorce.

   _____

   _____

-ing word

7. • The people pressed against the doors of the theatre.
   • They pushed and shoved each other.

   _____

   _____

-ly word

8. • I waited in the packed emergency room.
   • I was impatient.

   _____

   _____

to word group

9. • The little boy likes to annoy his parents.
   • He pretends he can't hear them.

   _____

   _____

prepositional
phrase

10. • People must wear white-soled shoes.
    • They must do this in the gym.

    _____

    _____

PLACE ADJECTIVES OR VERBS IN A SERIES

Various parts of a sentence may be placed in a series. Among these parts are adjectives (descriptive words) and verbs. Here are examples of both in a series.

Adjectives   The *black, smeary* newsprint rubbed off on my *new butcher-block* table.

Verbs   The quarterback *fumbled* the ball, *recovered* it, and *sighed* with relief.

Activity

Combine the simple sentences in each group into one sentence by using adjectives or verbs in a series and by omitting repeated words. If you are not sure whether to use a comma between the adjectives or verbs in a series, see page 412.

Example   • Before Christmas, I made fruitcakes.
             • I decorated the house.
             • I wrapped dozens of toys.

             Before Christmas, I made fruitcakes, decorated the house, and

             wrapped dozens of toys.

1. • My lumpy mattress was giving me a cramp in my neck.
   • It was causing pains in my back.
   • It was making me lose sleep.

   _____

   _____

2. • Lights appeared in the fog.
   • The lights were flashing.
   • The lights were red.
   • The fog was grey.
   • The fog was soupy.

_____

_____

3. • Before going to bed, I locked all the doors.
   • I activated the burglar alarm.
   • I slipped my wallet under my mattress.

_____

_____

4. • Joanna picked sweater hairs off her coat.
   • The hairs were fuzzy.
   • The hairs were white.
   • The coat was brown.
   • The coat was suede.

_____

_____

5. • The contact lens fell onto the floor.
   • The contact lens was thin.
   • The contact lens was slippery.
   • The floor was dirty.
   • The floor was tiled.

_____

_____

EDITING SENTENCES

Once you have revised sentences in a paragraph so that it has some variety and so that your sentences flow smoothly and clearly reflect your meaning, you need to *edit* the sentences for mistakes in grammar, punctuation, mechanics, usage, and spelling.

This looks like a long list of requirements, but even if your paragraph is otherwise well written, it will make an unfavourable impression on your reading audience if it contains such mistakes. Mechanical errors are sometimes called "noise," a term that vividly describes the effect of errors on readers' ability to understand or be persuaded by your point.

To edit a paragraph, do not rely greatly on the grammar checker in your word-processing program. These "editing applications," which may insert wiggly green lines under words or phrases on your screen, rely on pre-programmed "acceptable" word strings or patterns. Grammar checkers do not take into account the meanings of words and phrases; they simply recognize patterns. As a result, they may offer incorrect or bizarre substitutions for something they analyze as incorrect.

Instead, print your paragraph and check it against the agreed-upon rules and conventions of written English called *sentence skills* in this book. Here are the most common conventions.

1 Use parallel grammatical structure for items in a series in sentences.
2 Keep verb tenses consistent within a paragraph.
3 Keep pronouns consistent in sentences and paragraphs.
4 Use specific and concise words that express your meaning most effectively.
5 Vary your sentence structures to reflect your intended meaning and create a paragraph whose flow is appealing to readers.
6 Eliminate careless errors through careful editing and proofreading.
7 Write complete sentences rather than fragments.
8 Do not write run-ons or comma splices.
9 Use verb forms correctly.
10 Make sure subjects and verbs agree.
11 Use pronoun forms and types correctly.
12 Use adjectives and adverbs correctly.
13 Eliminate faulty modifiers.
14 Use capital letters where needed.
15 Use the following punctuation marks correctly: apostrophe, quotation marks, comma, semicolon, colon, hyphen, dash, and parentheses.
16 Use correct manuscript form.

These sentence skills are explained in detail, and activities are provided, in Section Four, where they can be referred to easily as needed. A diagnostic test on pages 301-5 will help you identify skills you may need to review. Your instructor will also identify such skills in marking your papers and may use the correction symbols shown on the inside back cover. Note that the correction symbols and the checklist of sentence skills on the inside front cover include page references, so that you can turn quickly to those skills that give you problems.

HINTS FOR EDITING

Here are hints that can help you edit the next-to-final draft of a paper for sentence-skills mistakes.

1 Have at hand two essential tools: a good dictionary (see page 427) and a grammar or sentence-skills handbook (you can use the one in this book in Section Four).
2 Use a sheet of paper to cover your paragraph as you read so that you expose only one sentence at a time. Look for errors in grammar, spelling, and typing. It may help to read each sentence out loud. If a sentence does not read clearly and smoothly, chances are that something is wrong.
3 Pay special attention to the kinds of errors you tend to make. For example, if you tend to write run-ons or fragments, be especially on the lookout for those errors.

4   Try to work on a word-processed draft, where you'll be able to see your writing more objectively than you can on a handwritten page; use a pen with coloured ink so that your corrections will stand out. If you make too many corrections, retype the page or enter corrections into your document file and reprint the page.

PRACTICE IN REVISING SENTENCES

You now know the basics of the fourth step in effective writing: revising and editing sentences. You also know that practice in *editing* sentences is best undertaken after you have worked through the sentence skills in Section Four.

Here you will practise *revising* sentences: using a variety of methods to ensure that your sentences flow smoothly and are clear and interesting. Your sentences and therefore your paragraphs will more clearly reflect your ideas and feelings, and readers will see your points more readily.

Work through these review tests to consolidate your understanding of sentence revision:

1   Using Parallel Structures
2   Using Consistent Verb Tenses and Pronouns
3   Using Specific Words
4   Using Concise Wording
5   Varying Your Sentence Types

USING PARALLEL STRUCTURES

Review Test 1

Cross out the unbalanced part of each sentence. Then revise the unbalanced part so that it matches the other item or items in the sentence. The first one is done for you as an example.

1. Our professor warned us that he would give surprise tests, the assignment of term papers, and allow no makeup exams.

    assign term papers

2. Pesky mosquitoes, humidity that is high, and sweltering heat make summer an unpleasant time for me.

3. I want a job that pays high wages, provides a complete benefits package, and offering opportunities for promotion.

4. My teenage daughter enjoys shopping for new clothes, to try different cosmetics, and reading teen magazines.

_____

5. My car needed the brakes replaced, the front wheels aligned, and recharging of the battery.

_____

6. I had to correct my paper for fragments, misplaced modifiers, and there were apostrophe mistakes.

_____

7. They did not want an ordinary TV set, but a flat-screen set could not be afforded.

_____

8. The neighbourhood group asked the town council to repair the potholes and that a traffic light be installed.

_____

9. Having a headache, my stomach being upset, and a bad case of sunburn did not put me in a good mood for the evening.

_____

10. Senior Link is an organization that not only aids older citizens but also providing information for their families.

_____

■ Review Test 2

Cross out the unbalanced part of each sentence. In the space provided, revise the unbalanced part so that it matches the other item or items in the sentence.

1. While you're downtown, please pick up the dry cleaning, return the library books, and the car needs washing, too.

_____

2. Making dinner is a lot more fun than to clean up after it.

_____

3. Canada Post brought advertisements that were unwanted, bills I couldn't pay, and catalogues I didn't like.

_____

4. Our house has a dented garage door, shutters that are peeling, and a crumbling chimney.

_____

5. Fantastic special effects are part of the *Star Wars* movies, but dialogue that is believable is not.

_____

6. I fell into bed at the end of the hard day, grateful for the sheets that were clean, soft pillow, and cozy blanket.

_____

7. We do not want to stay home during reading week, but a trip is not something we can afford.

_____

8. Stumbling out of bed, a cup of coffee that he drinks, and listening to the weather report make up Todd's early-morning routine.

_____

9. Ron's wide smile, clear blue eyes, and expressing himself earnestly all make him seem honest, even though he is not.

_____

10. Mastering programs like Director is time-consuming, could be hard to understand, and is challenging.

_____

USING CONSISTENT VERB TENSES AND PRONOUNS

■ Review Test 1

Change verb tenses as needed in the following passage so that they are consistently in the past tense. Cross out each incorrect verb and write the correct form above it, as shown in the example below. You will need to make nine corrections.

Late one rainy night, Mei Ling woke to the sound of steady dripping. When
she got out of bed to investigate, a drop of cold water ~~splashes~~ *splashed* onto her arm.
She looks up just in time to see another drop form on the ceiling, hang
suspended for a moment, and fall to the carpet. Stumbling to the kitchen,
Mei Ling reaches deep into one of the cabinets and lifts out a large roasting
pan. As she did so, pot lids and baking tins clattered out and crash onto the
counter. Mei Ling ignored them, stumbled back to the bedroom, and places
the pan on the floor under the drip. But a minute after sliding her icy feet
under the covers, Mei Ling realized she is in trouble. The sound of each drop

hitting the metal pan echoed like a cannon in the quiet room. Mei Ling feels like crying, but she finally thought of a solution. She got out of bed and returns a minute later with a thick bath towel. She lined the pan with the towel and crawls back into bed.

■ Review Test 2

Cross out the incorrect pronouns in the following sentences and revise by writing the correct form of the pronoun above each crossed-out word.

Example   I dislike working as a server, for ~~you~~ can never count on a fair tip.

1. My kitchen is so narrow that one can't open the refrigerator without turning sideways first.

   _____

2. Wanting relief from her headaches, Carla asked her doctor if acupuncture could really do you any good.

   _____

3. I love Jell-O because one can eat about five bowls of it and still not feel full.

   _____

4. As we entered the house, you could hear someone giggling in the hallway.

   _____

5. I hate going to the supermarket because you always have trouble finding a parking space there.

   _____

6. In this company, a worker can take a break only after a relief person comes to take your place.

   _____

7. Sometimes the Bradleys take the express highway, but it costs you five dollars in tolls.

   _____

8. As we sat in class waiting for the test results, you could feel the tension.

   _____

9. My brother doesn't get enough regular exercise, even though he knows exercise is good for you.

   _____

10. My favourite subject is abnormal psychology because the case studies make one seem so normal by comparison.

_____

USING SPECIFIC WORDS

■ **Review Test 1**

Revise the following sentences, replacing the vague, indefinite words in italics with sharp, specific ones.

1. When I woke up this morning, I had *several signs of a cold*.

   _____

   _____

2. Lin brought *lots of reading materials* to keep her occupied in the dentist's waiting room.

   _____

   _____

3. To succeed in college, a student must possess *certain qualities*.

   _____

   _____

4. The table at the wedding reception was full of a *variety of appetizers*.

   _____

   _____

5. As I grew older and less stupid, I realized that money cannot buy *certain things*.

   _____

   _____

■ **Review Test 2**

With the help of the methods described on page 100, add specific details to the sentences that follow.

1. The crowd grew restless.

   _____

   _____

2. I relaxed.

_____

_____

3. The room was cluttered.

_____

_____

4. The child threw the object.

_____   _____

_____

5. The driver was angry.

_____

_____

USE CONCISE WORDING

■ Review Test 1

Rewrite the following sentences, omitting needless words.

1. There was this one girl in my class who rarely if ever did her assignments.

_____

_____

2. Judging by the looks of things, it seems to me that it will probably snow very soon.

_____

_____   _____

3. Seeing as how the refrigerator is totally empty of food, I will go to the super-market in the very near future.

_____

_____

4. In this day and age it is almost a certainty that someone you know will be an innocent victim of criminal activity.

_____

_____

5. In my personal opinion it is correct to say that the spring season is the most beautiful period of time in the year.

_____

_____

■ **Review Test 2**

Rewrite the following sentences, omitting needless words.

1. Workers who are on a part-time basis are attractive to a business because they do not have to be paid as much as full-time workers for a business.

    _____

    _____

2. During the time that I was sick and out of school, I missed a total of three math tests.

    _____

    _____

3. The game, which was scheduled for later today, has been cancelled by the officials because of the rainy weather.

    _____

    _____

4. At this point in time, I am quite undecided and unsure about just which classes I will take during this coming semester.

    _____

    _____

5. An inconsiderate person located in the apartment next to mine keeps her radio on too loud a good deal of the time, with the result being that it is disturbing to everyone in the neighbouring apartments.

    _____

    _____

VARYING YOUR SENTENCE TYPES

■ **Review Test 1**

Using coordination, subordination, or both, combine each of the following groups of simple sentences into one longer sentence. Omit repeated words. Various combinations are possible, so for each group, try to find the combination that flows most smoothly and clearly.

1. • My grandmother is eighty-six.
   • She drives to Florida alone every year.
   • She believes in being self-reliant.

2. • His name was called.
   • Luis walked into the examining room.
   • He was nervous.
   • He was determined to ask the doctor for a straight answer.

3. • They left twenty minutes early for class.
   • They were late anyway.
   • The car overheated.

4. • Jake failed the midterm exam.
   • He studied harder for the final.
   • He passed it.

5. • A volcano erupts.
   • It sends tonnes of ash into the air.
   • This creates flaming orange sunsets.

6. • Fernando got home from the shopping mall.
   • He discovered that his rented tuxedo did not fit.
   • The jacket sleeves covered his hands.
   • The pants cuffs hung over his shoes.

7. • The boys waited for the bus.
   • The wind shook the flimsy shelter.
   • They shivered with cold.
   • They were wearing thin jackets.

8. • The engine almost caught.
   • Then it died.
   • I realized no help would come.
   • I was on a lonely road.
   • It was very late.

9. • Miriam wanted white wall-to-wall carpeting.
   • She knew it was a bad buy.
   • It would look beautiful.
   • It would be very hard to clean.

10. • Gordon was leaving the store.
    • The shoplifting alarm went off.
    • He had not stolen anything.
    • The clerk had forgotten to remove the magnetic tag.
    • The tag was on a shirt Gordon had bought.

■ **Review Test 2**

Part A   Combine the simple sentences into one sentence by using the opener shown in the margin and omitting repeated words. Use a comma to set off the opener from the rest of the sentence.

-ed word

1. • We were exhausted from four hours of hiking.
   • We decided to stop for the day.

   _____

   _____

-ing word

2. • Enoch was staring out the window.
   • He did not hear the instructor call on him.

   _____

   _____

-ly word

3. • Nobody saw the thieves steal our bikes.
   • This was unfortunate.

   _____

   _____

to word
group

4. • Matt rented a limousine for the night.
   • He wanted to make a good impression.

   _____

   _____

prepositional
phrase

5. • Giovanna goes online to visit her friends.
   • She does this during her lunch breaks.

   _____

   _____

Part B   Combine the simple sentences into one sentence by using adjectives or verbs in a series and by omitting repeated words.

6. • The photographer waved a teddy bear at the baby.
   • She made a funny face.
   • She quacked like a duck.

   _____

   _____

7. • The bucket held a bunch of daisies.
   • The bucket was shiny.
   • The bucket was aluminum.
   • The daisies were fresh.
   • The daisies were white.

   _____

   _____

8. • Amanda poured herself a cup of coffee.
   • She pulled her hair back into a ponytail.
   • She opened her textbook.
   • She sat down at her desk.
   • She fell asleep.

   _____

   _____

9. • The box in the dresser drawer was stuffed with letters.
   • The box was cardboard.
   • The dresser drawer was locked.
   • The letters were faded.
   • The letters were about love.

   _____

   _____

10. • The boy asked the girl to dance.
    • The boy was short.
    • The boy was self-confident.
    • The girl was tall.
    • The girl was shy.

    _____

    _____

REVIEWING THE LEARNING OUTCOMES FOR CHAPTER 5

To assure yourself that you have understood and met the learning outcomes for this chapter, answer the following questions.

1   What are the five strategies that will help you revise your sentences for clarity and effectiveness?

2   What are two aspects of sentence skills in which maintaining consistency is important, and why?

3 How exactly does using specific words help your readers?

4 Why are concise word choices more appealing to readers than wordy phrases?

5 What are four different methods for revising sentences to create variety and interest?

6 What is the difference between revising your sentences and editing and proof-reading your sentences?

Visit the *English Skills with Readings* Online Learning Centre at **www.mcgrawhill.ca/college/langan** to access self-quizzes, bonus material on study and research skills, web resources, and other learning and study tools.

xplaining a Process • Examining Cause and Effect • Comparing or Contrasting • Defining
rm • Dividing and Classifying • Describing a Scene or Person • Narrating an Event • Argui
Position • Explaining a Process • Examining Cause and Effect • Comparing or Contrasting
efining a Term • Dividing and Classifying • Describing a Scene or Person • Narrating
ent • Arguing a Position • Explaining a Process • Examining Cause and Effect • compari

CHAPTER 6

Four Bases for Evaluating Writing

LEARNING OUTCOMES

After completing the activities in this chapter, you will

- know two guidelines for revising a paragraph for *unity*;
- revise for effective *support* by asking three questions;
- know how to revise for *coherence* with the use of an appropriate ordering method and transitional devices;
- be ready to identify and correct errors to meet the goal of *effective sentence skills*; and
- understand why and how to evaluate a paragraph for each base of effective writing.

As you complete these activities based on the four bases of effective writing, you will prepare for the writing, revising, and editing stages of writing tasks in the following chapters of this text. Your confidence in your ability to write effectively will increase.

In the preceding three chapters, you learned four essential steps in writing an effective paragraph. The box on page 122 shows how these steps lead to four bases, or standards, you can use in evaluating your work.

BASE 1: UNITY

UNDERSTANDING UNITY

The two paragraphs on pages 122-23 were written by students on the topic "why students drop out of college." Read them and decide which one makes its point more clearly and effectively, and why.

Four Steps ⟶	*Four Bases* ⟶	*Four Goals Defined*
1 If you make a point and stick to that point,	your writing will have *unity.*	**Unity:** a single main idea pursued and supported by the points and details of your writing
2 If you back up the point with specific evidence,	your writing will have *support.*	**Support:** for each supporting point, specific and definite details
3 If you organize and connect the specific evidence,	your writing will have *coherence.*	**Coherence:** supporting points and details organized and connected clearly
4 If you write clear, error-free sentences,	your writing will reflect effective *sentence skills.*	**Effective Sentence Skills:** sentence structure, grammar, spelling, and punctuation free of errors

Paragraph A

Why Students Drop Out

Students drop out of college for many reasons. First of all, some students are bored in school. These students may enter college expecting non-stop fun or a series of undemanding courses. When they find out that college is often routine, they quickly lose interest. They do not want to take dull required courses or spend their nights studying, and so they drop out. Students also drop out of college because the work is harder than they thought it would be. These students may have gotten decent marks in high school simply by showing up for class. In college, however, they may have to prepare for two-hour exams, write lengthy reports, or make detailed presentations to a class. The hard work comes as a shock, and students give up. Perhaps the most common reason students drop out is that they are having personal or emotional problems. Younger students, especially, may be attending college at an age when they are also feeling confused, lonely, or depressed. These students may have problems with roommates, family, boyfriends, or girlfriends. They become too unhappy to deal with both hard academic work and emotional troubles. For many types of students, dropping out seems to be the only solution they can imagine.

Paragraph B

Student Dropouts

There are three main reasons students drop out of college. Some students, for one thing, are not really sure they want to be in school and lack the desire to do the work. When exams come up, or when a course requires a difficult project or demanding essay, these students will not do the required studying or research. Eventually, they may drop out because their grades are so poor they are about to fail anyway. Such students sometimes come back to school later with a completely different attitude about school. Other students drop out for financial reasons. The pressures of paying tuition, buying textbooks, and possibly having to support themselves can be overwhelming. These students can often be helped by the school or the province because financial aid is available, and some schools offer work-study programs. Finally, students drop out because they have personal problems. They cannot concentrate on their courses because they are unhappy at home, they are lonely, or they are having trouble with boyfriends or girlfriends. Instructors should suggest that such troubled students see counsellors or join support groups. If instructors would take a more personal interest in their students, more students would make it through troubled times.

Fill in the blanks: Paragraph _____ makes its point more clearly and effectively

because _____

_____

_____

Comment: Paragraph A is more effective because it is *unified.* All the details in paragraph A are *on target;* they support and develop the single point expressed in the first sentence: that there are many reasons students drop out of college. On the other hand, paragraph B contains some details irrelevant to the opening point: that there are three main reasons students drop out. These details should be omitted in the interest of paragraph unity. Go back to paragraph B and cross out the sentences that are off target—the sentences that do not support the opening idea.

You should have crossed out the following sentences: "Such students sometimes … attitude about school"; "These students can often … work-study programs"; and "Instructors should suggest … through troubled times."

The difference between these two paragraphs leads us to the first base of effective writing: *unity.* To achieve unity is to have all the details in your paper *related to the single point* expressed in the topic sentence, the first sentence. Each time you think of something to put in, ask yourself whether it relates to your main point. If it does not, leave it out. For example, if you were writing about a certain job as the worst job you ever had and then spent a couple of sentences talking about the interesting people that you met there, you would be missing the first and most essential base of good writing.

CHECKING FOR UNITY

To check a paper for unity, ask yourself these questions:

1 Is there a clear opening statement of the point of the paper?
2 Is all the material on target in support of the opening point?

BASE 2: SUPPORT

UNDERSTANDING SUPPORT

The following student paragraphs were written on the topic "a quality of some person or animal you know." Both are unified, but one communicates more clearly and effectively. Which one, and why?

Paragraph A

Laziness Defined

Cats may be the laziest creatures on earth, but they are also the smartest. Every day is divided up according to their pleasures and needs. They always find time to eat, without ever having to cook or prepare a meal. Enough complaining will make sure that their dishes are filled on time. Cats know they need exercise, too, so they take care of that by climbing the furniture and suddenly running up and down the stairs, usually at night. If they need someone to play with, they know enough not to strain themselves. Their radar can usually locate an owner who is busy at the computer or snoozing in front of the television, all ready for an eager furry playmate to nudge him or her into cooperating. Cats know their greatest need is for many hours of deep soothing sleep. Any time is the right time to sleep, and any place where humans are busy or where a fuzzy patch of cat fur will be appreciated is the right spot. Meeting all three needs keeps a cat healthy and occupied and shows humans just how smart a lazy creature can be.

Paragraph B

My Generous Grandfather

My grandfather is the most generous person I know. He has given up a life of his own in order to give his grandchildren everything they want. Not only has he given up many years of his life to raise his children properly, but he is now sacrificing many more years to his grandchildren. His generosity is also evident in his relationship with his neighbours, his friends, and the members of his church. He has been responsible for many good deeds and has always been there to help all the people around him in times of trouble. Everyone knows that he will gladly lend a helping hand. He is so generous that I almost have to feel sorry for him. If one day he suddenly became selfish, it would be earth-shaking. That's my grandfather.

Fill in the blanks: Paragraph _____ makes its point more clearly and effectively because _____

_____

_____

Comment: Paragraph A is more effective, for it offers *specific examples that show* us the laziness of cats in action. We see for ourselves why the writer describes cats as extremely lazy but clever. Paragraph B, on the other hand, gives us no specific evidence. The writer of paragraph B *tells us repeatedly* that the grandfather is generous *but never shows us* examples of that generosity. Just how, for instance, did the grandfather sacrifice his life for his children and grandchildren? Did he hold two jobs so that his son could go to college or so that his daughter could have her own car? Does he give up time with his wife and friends to travel every day to his daughter's house to babysit? Does he wear threadbare suits and coats and eat inexpensive meals (with no desserts) so that he can give money to his children and toys to his grandchildren? We want to see and judge for ourselves whether the writer is making a valid point about the grandfather, but without specific details we cannot do so. In fact, we have almost no picture of him at all. The best writing *shows*; it does not *tell*.

Consideration of these two paragraphs leads us to the second base of effective writing: *support*. After realizing the importance of specific supporting details, one student writer revised an essay she had done on a restaurant job as the worst job she ever had. In the revised essay, instead of talking about "unsanitary conditions in the kitchen," she referred to such specifics as "green mould on the bacon" and "ants in the potato salad." All your writing should include many vivid details.

CHECKING FOR SUPPORT

To check a paragraph for support, ask yourself these questions:

1 Are there *specific subtopics* to support the opening point?

2 Is there *enough specific evidence*?

3 Are *specific details* included?

BASE 3: COHERENCE

UNDERSTANDING COHERENCE

The following two paragraphs were written on the topic "the best or worst job you ever had." Both are unified and both are supported. However, one communicates more clearly and effectively. Which one, and why?

Paragraph A

Pantry Helper

My worst job was as a pantry helper in one of Vancouver's well-known restaurants. I had an assistant from three to six in the afternoon who did little but stand around and eat the whole time she was there. She kept an ear open for the sound of the back door opening, which was a sure sign the boss was coming in. The boss would testily say to me, "You've got a lot of things to do here, Lina. Try to get a move on." I would come in at two o'clock to relieve the woman on the morning shift. If her day was busy, that meant I would have to prepare salads, prepare soup stocks, and so on. Orders for appetizers and cold plates would come in and have to be prepared. The worst thing about the job was that the heat in the kitchen, combined with my nerves, would give me an upset stomach by seven o'clock almost every night. I might be going to the storeroom to get some supplies, and one of the servers would tell me she wanted an order of fried calamari. I would put the fryer basket on and head for the supply room, and a waitress would holler out that her customer was in a hurry. Flies would come in through the torn screen in the kitchen window and sting me. I was getting paid only $6.50 an hour. At five o'clock, when the dinner rush began, I would be dead tired. Roaches scurried in all directions whenever I moved a box or picked up a head of lettuce to cut.

Paragraph B

My Worst Job

The worst job I ever had was as a server at the Westside Inn. First of all, many of the people I waited on were rude. When a baked potato was hard inside or a salad was limp or their steak wasn't just the way they wanted it, they blamed me, rather than the kitchen. Or they would ask me to pick up their cutlery from the floor, or bring them different wineglasses, or even take their children to the bathroom. Also, I had to contend not only with the customers but with the kitchen staff as well. The cooks and bussers were often undependable and surly. If I didn't treat them just right, I would wind up having to apologize to customers because their meals came late or their water glasses weren't filled. Another reason I didn't like the job was that I was always moving. Because of the constant line at the door, as soon as one group left, another would take its place. I usually had only a twenty-minute lunch break and a ten-minute break in almost nine hours of work. I think I could have put up with the job if I had been able to pause and rest more often. The last and most important reason I hated the job was my boss. She played favourites, giving some of the servers the best-tipping repeat customers and preferences on holidays. She would hover around during my break to make sure I didn't take a second more than the allotted time. And even when I helped out by working through a break, she never had an appreciative word but would just tell me not to be late for work the next day.

Fill in the blanks: Paragraph _____ makes its point more clearly and effectively because _____

_____

_____

Comment: Paragraph B is more effective *because the material is organized clearly* and logically. Using emphatic order, the writer gives us a list of four reasons why the job was so bad: rude customers, unreliable kitchen staff, constant motion, and—most of all—an unfair boss. Further, the writer includes transitional words that act as signposts, making movement from one idea to the next easy to follow. The major transitions are *first of all, also, another reason,* and *the last and most important reason.*

Although paragraph A is unified and supported, the writer does not have any clear and consistent way of organizing the material. Partly, emphatic order is used, but this is not made clear by transitions or by saving the most important reason for last. Partly, a time order is used, but it moves inconsistently from two to seven to five o'clock.

These two paragraphs lead us to the third base of effective writing: *coherence.* The supporting ideas and sentences in a composition must be organized so that they cohere or "stick together." As has already been mentioned, key techniques for tying material together are:

- a clear method of organization (such as time order or emphatic order),
- transitions, and
- other transitional phrases and connecting words.

CHECKING FOR COHERENCE

To check a paper for coherence, ask yourself these questions:

1 Does the paper have a clear method of organization?
2 Are transitions and other connecting words used to tie the material together?

BASE 4: SENTENCE SKILLS

UNDERSTANDING SENTENCE SKILLS

Two versions of a paragraph are given below. Both are *unified, supported,* and *organized,* but one version communicates more clearly and effectively. Which one, and why?

Paragraph A

Falling Asleep Anywhere

[1]There are times when people are so tired that they fall asleep almost anywhere. [2]For example, there is a lot of sleeping on the bus or subway on the way home from work in the evenings. [3]A man will be reading the newspaper, and seconds later it appears as if he is trying to eat it. [4]Or he will fall asleep on the shoulder of the stranger sitting next to him. [5]Another place where unplanned naps go on is the classroom. [6]In some classes, a student will start snoring so loudly that the professor has to ask another student to shake the sleeper awake. [7]A more embarrassing situation occurs when a student leans on one elbow and starts drifting off to sleep. [8]The weight of the head pushes the elbow off the desk, and this momentum carries the rest of the body along. [9]The student wakes up on the floor with no memory of getting there. [10]The

worst time to fall asleep is when driving a car. [11]Police reports are full of accidents that occur when people lose consciousness and go off the road. [12]If the drivers are lucky, they are not seriously hurt. [13]One woman's car, for instance, went into the river. [14]She woke up in a metre of water and thought it was raining. [15]When people are really tired, nothing will stop them from falling asleep—no matter where they are.

Paragraph B

"Falling Asleep Anywhere"

[1]There are times when people are so tired that they fall asleep almost anywhere. [2]For example, on the bus or subway on the way home from work. [3]A man will be reading the newspaper, seconds later it appears as if he is trying to eat it. [4]Or he will fall asleep on the shoulder of the stranger sitting next to him. [5]Another place where unplanned naps go on are in the classroom. [6]In some classes, a student will start snoring so loudly that the professor has to ask another student to shake the sleeper awake. [7]A more embarrassing situation occurs when a student leans on one elbow and starting to drift off to sleep. [8]The weight of the head push the elbow off the desk, and this momentum carries the rest of the body along. [9]The student wakes up on the floor with no memory of getting there. [10]The worst time to fall asleep is when driving a car. [11]Police reports are full of accidents that occur when people conk out and go off the road. [12]If the drivers are lucky they are not seriously hurt. [13]One womans car, for instance, went into the river. [14]She woke up in a metre of water. [15]And thought it was raining. [16]When people are really tired, nothing will stop them from falling asleep—no matter where they are.

Fill in the blanks: Paragraph _____ makes its point more clearly and effectively because _____

_____

_____

Activity

Paragraph A is more effective because it incorporates *sentence skills,* the fourth base of competent writing. See if you can identify the ten sentence-skills mistakes in paragraph B. Do this, first of all, by going back and underlining the ten spots in paragraph B that differ in wording or punctuation from paragraph A. Then try to identify the ten sentence-skills mistakes by circling what you think is the correct answer in each of the ten statements below.

Note: Comparing paragraph B with the correct version may help you guess correct answers even if you are not familiar with the names of certain skills.

Sentences have been designated "word groups," because some of the paragraph's "sentences" do not fulfill the grammatical requirements for a sentence. Answers are on page 130.

1. The title should not be set off with
   a. capital letters
   b. quotation marks

2. In word group 2, there is a
   a. missing comma
   b. missing apostrophe
   c. fragment
   d. dangling modifier

3. In word group 3, there is a
   a. run-on
   b. fragment
   c. mistake in subject-verb
      agreement
   d. mistake involving an
      irregular verb

4. In word group 5, there is a
   a. fragment
   b. spelling error
   c. run-on
   d. mistake in subject-verb
      agreement

5. In word group 7, there is a
   a. misplaced modifier
   b. dangling modifier
   c. mistake in parallelism
   d. run-on

6. In word group 8, there is a
   a. non-standard English verb

   b. run-on
   c. comma mistake
   d. missing capital letter

7. In word group 11, there is a
   a. mistake involving an irregular
      verb
   b. fragment
   c. slang phrase
   d. mistake in subject-verb agree-
      ment

8. In word group 12, there is a
   a. missing apostrophe
   b. missing comma
   c. mistake involving an irregular
      verb
   d. fragment

9. In word group 13, there is a
   a. mistake in parallelism
   b. mistake involving an irregular
      verb
   c. missing apostrophe
   d. missing capital letter

10. In word group 15, there is a
    a. missing quotation mark
    b. mistake involving an irregular
       verb
    c. fragment
    d. mistake in pronoun point of
       view

Section Four of this book explains these and other sentence skills. You should review all the skills carefully. Doing so will ensure that you know the most important rules of grammar, punctuation, and usage—rules needed to write clear, error-free sentences.

PRACTICE IN USING THE FOUR BASES

You are now familiar with four bases or goals of effective writing: unity, support, coherence, and sentence skills. In this closing section, you will expand and strengthen your understanding of the four bases as you work through the following activities:

1 Evaluating Outlines for Unity
2 Evaluating Paragraphs for Unity

  3 Evaluating Paragraphs for Support
  4 Evaluating Paragraphs for Coherence
  5 Revising Paragraphs for Coherence
  6 Evaluating Paragraphs for All Four Bases: Unity, Support, Coherence, and Sentence Skills

---

You should have chosen the following answers for the questions on page 129:

1. b	3. a	5. c	7. c	9. c
2. c	4. d	6. a	8. b	10. c

---

1 EVALUATING OUTLINES FOR UNITY

The best time to check a paragraph for unity is when it is in outline form. An outline, as explained on pages 26-29, is one of the best techniques for getting started with a paragraph.

Look at the rough beginning of an outline that one student prepared and then corrected for unity:

I had a depressing weekend.

1. Hay fever bothered me

2. Had to pay seventy-seven-dollar car bill

3. ~~Felt bad~~

4. Boyfriend and I had a fight

5. ~~Did poorly on my math test today as a result~~

6. My mother yelled at me unfairly

Four reasons support the opening statement that the writer was depressed over the weekend. The writer crossed out "Felt bad" because it was not a reason for her depression. Saying that she felt bad is only another way of saying that she was depressed. She also crossed out the item about the day's math test because the point she is supporting is that she was depressed over the weekend.

Activity

In each outline, cross out items that do not support the opening point. These items must be omitted in order to achieve paragraph unity.

1. The cost of raising a child keeps increasing.
    a. Education taxes get higher every year.
    b. A pair of children's running shoes now costs over a hundred dollars.
    c. Overpopulation is a worldwide problem.
    d. Providing nutritious food is more costly because of inflated prices.
    e. Children should work at age sixteen.

2. My father's compulsive gambling hurt our family life.
    a. We were always short of money for bills.
    b. Luckily, my father didn't drink.
    c. My father ignored his children to spend time at the racetrack.
    d. Gamblers Anonymous can help compulsive gamblers.
    e. My mother and father argued constantly.

3. There are several ways to get better mileage in your car.
    a. Check air pressure in tires regularly.
    b. Drive at no more than ninety kilometres per hour.
    c. Orange and yellow cars are the most visible.
    d. Avoid jackrabbit starts at stop signs and traffic lights.
    e. Always have duplicate ignition and trunk keys.

2 EVALUATING PARAGRAPHS FOR UNITY

Activity

Each of the following three paragraphs contains *sentences that are off target*—sentences that do not support the opening point—and so the paragraphs are *not unified*. In the interest of paragraph unity, such sentences must be omitted.

Cross out the irrelevant sentences and write the numbers of those sentences in the spaces provided. The number of spaces will tell you the number of irrelevant sentences in each paragraph.

Paragraph A

A Kindergarten Failure

¹In kindergarten I experienced the fear of failure that haunts many schoolchildren. ²My moment of panic occurred on my last day in kindergarten at Laurier Public School in Dauphin, Manitoba. ³My family lived in Manitoba for three years before we moved to Toronto, where my father was a human resources manager for the Co-operators Insurance Company. ⁴Our teacher began reading a list of names of all those students who were to line up at the door in order to visit the grade one classroom. ⁵Our teacher was a pleasant-faced woman who had resumed her career after raising her own children. ⁶She called every name but mine, and I was left sitting alone in the class while everyone left, the teacher included. ⁷I sat there in absolute horror. ⁸I imagined that I was the first kid in human history who had flunked things like crayons, sandbox, and swings. ⁹Without getting the teacher's permission, I got up and walked to the bathroom and threw up into a sink. ¹⁰Only when I ran home in tears to my mother did I get an explanation of what had happened. ¹¹Since I was to go to a separate school in the fall, I had not been taken with the other children to meet the grade one teacher at the public school. ¹²My moment of terror and shame had been only a misunderstanding.

The numbers of the irrelevant sentences: _____ _____

Paragraph B

How to Prevent Cheating

[1]Instructors should take steps to prevent students from cheating on exams. [2]To begin with, instructors should stop reusing old tests. [3]A test that has been used even once is soon known via the student grapevine. [4]Students will check with their friends to find out, for example, what was on Dr. Thompson's marketing final last term. [5]They may even manage to find a copy of the test itself, "accidentally" not turned in by a former student of Dr. Thompson's. [6]Instructors should also take some common sense precautions at test time. [7]They should make students separate themselves, by at least one seat, during an exam, and they should watch the class closely. [8]The best place for the instructor to sit is in the rear of the room, so that a student is never sure if the instructor is looking at him or her. [9]Last of all, instructors must make it clear to students that there will be stiff penalties for cheating. [10]One of the problems with our educational systems is a lack of discipline. [11]Instructors never used to give in to students' demands or put up with bad behaviour, as they do today. [12]Anyone caught cheating should immediately receive a zero for the exam. [13]A person even suspected of cheating should be forced to take an alternative exam in the instructor's office. [14]Because cheating is unfair to honest students, it should not be tolerated.

The numbers of the irrelevant sentences: _____   _____

Paragraph C

Other Uses for Cars

[1]Many people who own a car manage to turn the vehicle into a garbage can, a clothes closet, or a storage room. [2]People who use their cars as garbage cans are easily recognized. [3]Empty snack bags, hamburger wrappers, pizza cartons, pop cans, and doughnut boxes litter the floor. [4]On the seats are old CDs, blackened fruit skins, crumpled receipts, crushed candy boxes, and used tissues. [5]At least the garbage stays in the car, instead of adding to the litter on our highways. [6]Other people use a car as a clothes closet. [7]The car contains several pairs of shoes, pants, or shorts, along with a suit or dress that's been hanging on the car's clothes hanger for over a year. [8]Sweaty, smelly gym clothes will also find a place in the car, a fact passengers quickly discover. [9]The world would be better off if people showed more consideration of others. [10]Finally, some people use a car as a spare garage or basement. [11]In the back seats or trunks of these cars are bags of fertilizer, beach chairs, old textbooks, chainsaws, or window screens that have been there for months. [12]The trunk may also contain an extra spare tire, a dented hub cap, a four-litre container of window washer fluid, and old stereo equipment. [13]If apartments offered more storage space, probably fewer people would resort to using their cars for such storage purposes. [14]All in all, people get a lot more use out of their cars than simply the kilometres they travel on the road.

The numbers of the irrelevant sentences: _____   _____   _____

3 EVALUATING PARAGRAPHS FOR SUPPORT

Activity

The three paragraphs that follow lack sufficient supporting details. In each paragraph, identify the spot or spots where more specific details are needed.

Paragraph A

Chicken: Our Best Friend

[1]Chicken is the best-selling meat today for a number of good reasons. [2]First of all, its reasonable cost puts it within everyone's reach. [3]Chicken is popular, too, because it can be prepared in so many different ways. [4]It can, for example, be cooked by itself, in spaghetti sauce, or with noodles and gravy. [5]It can be baked, boiled, broiled, or fried. [6]Chicken is also convenient. [7]Last and most important, chicken has a high nutritional value. [8]Two hundred and fifty grams of chicken contains twenty eight grams of protein, which is almost half the recommended daily dietary allowance.

Fill in the blanks: The first spot where supporting details are needed is after sentence number _____. The second spot is after sentence number

_____.

Paragraph B

Tips on Bringing Up Children

[1]In some ways, children should be treated as mature people. [2]For one thing, adults should not use baby talk with children. [3]Using real words with children helps them develop language skills more quickly. [4]Baby talk makes children feel patronized, frustrated, and confused, for they want to understand and communicate with adults by learning their speech. [5]So animals should be called cows and dogs, not "moo-moos" and "bow-wows." [6]Second, parents should be consistent when disciplining children. [7]For example, if a parent tells a child, "You cannot have dessert unless you put away your toys," it is important that the parent follow through on the warning. [8]By being consistent, parents will teach children responsibility and give them a stable centre around which to grow. [9]Finally, and most important, children should be allowed and encouraged to make simple decisions. [10]Parents will thus be helping their children prepare for the complex decisions that they will have to deal with in later life.

Fill in the blank: The spot where supporting details are needed is after sentence number _____.

Paragraph C

Culture Conflict

[1]I am in a constant tug-of-war with my parents over conflicts between their Vietnamese culture and Canadian society. [2]To begin with, my parents do not like me to have so many friends from Canada. [3]They think that I should spend all my time with other Vietnamese people and speak English only when necessary. [4]I get into an argument whenever I want to go to a fast-food restaurant or a movie at night with my friends from school. [5]The conflict with my parents is even worse when it comes to plans for a career. [6]My parents want me to get a degree in science and then go on to medical school. [7]On the other hand, I think I want to become a teacher. [8]So far I have been taking science courses, but soon I will have to apply for Carleton's education program. [9]The other night my father made his attitude about what I should do very clear. [10]The most difficult aspect of our cultural differences is the way our family is structured. [11]My father is the centre of our family, and he expects that I will always listen to him. [12]Although I am twenty-one years old, I still have a nightly curfew at an hour which I consider insulting. [13]Also, I am expected to help my mother perform certain household chores that I've really come to hate. [14]My father expects me to live at home until I am married to a Vietnamese man. [15]When that happens, he assumes I will obey my husband just as I obey him. [16]I do not want to be a bad daughter, but I want to live like my Canadian female friends.

Fill in the blanks: The first spot where a supporting detail or details are needed is after sentence number _____. The second spot is after sentence number _____. The third spot is after sentence number _____.

4 EVALUATING PARAGRAPHS FOR COHERENCE

Activity

Answer the questions about coherence that follow each of the two paragraphs below.

Paragraph A

Living Just Enough for the City

[1]There are so many good reasons to live in the city that it is hard to know why suburbs even exist. [2]Most important, there is no reason ever to sit inside, become a TV-bound vegetable, trapped in a maze of courts, crescents, and curving streets going nowhere. [3]Any day or evening, the city and its attractions are only a walk or subway ride away. [4]There is no need to rely on a car and add to the general pollution by driving to a movie, a concert, a museum, or an interesting stretch of stores or clubs. [5]Anything new listed in the paper or discussed in class is easily accessible to the city dweller and never involves a

carefully planned or lengthy expedition "downtown." [6]Walking the streets is one secret pleasure of city folks; they can walk everywhere. [7]And city streets are fascinating and full of life. [8]These streets may not be as well manicured or as spacious as suburban residential areas, but they are "people-sized" and meant for walking and looking. [9]Each store window has its stories to tell, and every old house is unique. [10]There are no vast empty parking lots or stretches of closed business strip malls; every block is cluttered with people, dogs, storefronts, and sidewalk displays. [11]Every metre of city streets grabs the attention; the walker's eye is never starved for something interesting. [12]Walking only a block or so to shop every day at small stores where the owners say hello makes shopping a pleasure, not a chore. [13]The fruits and vegetables are fresh and not sealed under plastic so cleverly that the bruises don't show. [14]And the friendly human contact makes the city person's shopping a social activity as much as a consumer activity. [15]Somehow, living in the city makes it easier to be alert, alive, and human.

a. The paragraph should use emphatic order. Write *1* before the reason that seems slightly less important than the other two, *2* before the second-most-important reason, and *3* before the most important reason.

   _____ Closeness to attractions

   _____ Ability to shop near home

   _____ The pleasures of walking

b. Before which of the three reasons could the transitional words *first of all* be added? _____

c. Before which of the three reasons could the transition *in addition* be added? _____

d. What words show emphasis in sentence 2? _____

e. How many times are the keywords *city, city folks*, and *city dwellers* repeated in the paragraph? _____

Paragraph B

Apartment Hunting

[1]Apartment hunting is a several-step process. [2]Visit and carefully inspect the most promising apartments. [3]Check each place for signs of unwanted guests such as roaches or mice. [4]Make sure that light switches and appliances work and that there are enough electrical outlets. [5]Turn faucets and flush the toilet to be sure that the plumbing works smoothly. [6]Talk to the building manager for a bit to get a sense of him or her as a person. [7]If a problem develops after you move in, you want to know that a capable person will be there to handle the matter. [8]Find out what stores and services that match your interests are available in the neighbourhood. [9]Your local newspaper and real

estate offices can provide you with a list of apartments for rent. [10]Family and friends may be able to give you leads. [11]And your college may have a housing office that keeps a list of apartments for rent. [12]Decide just what you need. [13]If you can afford no more than six hundred dollars a month, you need to find a place that will cost no more than that. [14]If you want a location that's close to work or school, you must take that factor into account. [15]If you plan to cook, you want a place with a workable kitchen. [16]By taking these steps, you should be ready to select the apartment that is best for you.

a. The paragraph should use time order. Write *1* before the step that should come first, *2* before the intermediate step, and *3* before the final step.

_____ Visit and carefully inspect the most promising apartments.

_____ Decide just what you need.

_____ Find out what's available that matches your interests.

b. Before which of the three steps could the transitional words *the first step is to* be added? _____

c. Before which step could the transitional words *after you have decided what you are looking for, the next step is to* be added? _____

d. Before which step could the transitional words *the final step* be added?

_____

e. To whom does the pronoun *him or her* in sentence 6 refer? _____

f. What is a synonym for *building manager* in sentence 7? _____

g. What is a synonym for *apartment* in sentence 13? _____

5 REVISING PARAGRAPHS FOR COHERENCE

The two paragraphs in this section begin with a clear point, but in each case the supporting material that follows the point is not coherent. Read each paragraph and the comments that follow it on how to organize and connect the supporting material. Then do the activity for the paragraph.

Paragraph A

A Difficult Period

Since I arrived on the West Coast in midsummer, I have had the most difficult period of my life. I had to look for an apartment. I found only one place that I could afford, but the owner said I could not move in until it was painted. When I first arrived in Vancouver, my thoughts were to stay with my father and stepmother. I had to set out looking for a job so that I could afford my own place, for I soon realized that my stepmother was not at all happy about having me live with them. A three-week search led to a job shampooing rugs for a house-cleaning company. I painted the apartment myself, and at least that problem was solved. I was in a hurry to get settled because I was starting school at Simon Fraser in September. A transportation problem developed because my stepmother insisted that I return my father's bike, which I was using at first to get to school. I had to rely on a bus that often arrived late, with the result that I missed some classes and was late for others. I had already had a problem with registration in early September. My counsellor had made a mistake with my classes, and I had to register all over again. This meant that I was one week late for class. Now I'm riding to school with a classmate and no longer have to depend on the bus. My life is starting to order itself, but I must admit that at first I thought it was hopeless to stay here.

Comments: The writer of this paragraph has provided a good deal of specific evidence to support the opening point. The evidence, however, needs to be organized. Before starting the paragraph, the writer should have decided to arrange the details by using time order. He or she could then have listed in an outline the exact sequence of events that made for such a difficult period.

Activity 1

Here is a list of the various events described by the writer of paragraph A. Number the events in the correct time sequence by writing *1* in front of the first event that occurred, *2* in front of the second event, and so on.

Since I arrived on the West Coast in midsummer, I have had the most difficult period of my life.

_____ I had to search for an apartment I could afford.

_____ I had to find a job so that I could afford my own place.

_____ My stepmother objected to my living with her and my father.

_____ I had to paint the apartment before I could move in.

_____ I had to find an alternative to unreliable bus transportation.

_____ I had to reregister for my courses because of a counsellor's mistake.

Your instructor may now have you rewrite the paragraph on a separate sheet of paper. If so, be sure to use time signals such as *first, next, then, during, when, after,* and *now* to help guide your reader from one event to the next.

Paragraph B

Sometimes Dreams Pay Off

When I was in elementary school, there was one boy my friends and I called "David the Dreamer," and we thought there were lots of good reasons for that nickname. Most of the time in class, David looked half asleep. In fact, he had long floppy bangs and rather droopy eyelids that seemed to cover his light blue eyes, and we usually knew he was drifting away at his desk because teachers would startle him from his snoozy posture each time they called his name during classes. Every year, we heard some teacher ask, "David, are you awake, or does none of this interest you?" Instead of looking sheepish or guilty, David always smiled, dreamily. He never showed any concern, he just went back to whatever he was thinking about as he slumped with his head on his elbows. We knew from talking to him in the schoolyard that he loved comic books. He had a huge collection and knew every character and all the artists who drew the characters. Those comics characters seemed more real to him than we were, so we decided that *they* were what he was dreaming about in class. At recess, he loved to make up stories of his own about the characters and to give them whole new adventures. When he was spinning his "X-Men" stories, he did not look sleepy at all, and his blue eyes were wide open and fixed on his listeners. Even in gym class, he leaned sleepily against a tree or the gym wall, unfazed by the loud insults of the gym teacher, who called him "Mr. Relaxation" and never chose him for a single team. David had his own world that he was happy enough to share, but he just never worried much about anyone else's world. A year ago, I was reading the arts section of the newspaper, and I realized how busy David had been during all that dreaming. There was a picture of David, floppy bangs, sleepy blue eyes and all, winning an award at the Toronto International Film Festival for best independent film. Apparently, he made the winning team, after all.

Comments: The writer of this paragraph provides a number of specifics that support the opening point. However, the supporting material has not been organized clearly. Before writing this paragraph, the author should have (1) decided to arrange the supporting evidence by using emphatic order and (2) listed in an outline the reasons why David's dreaminess was so intriguing and all-consuming, and the supporting details for each reason. The writer could also have determined which reason to use in the emphatic final position of the paper.

Activity 2

Create a clear outline for paragraph B by filling in the scheme below. The outline is partially completed.

When I was in elementary school, there was one boy my friends and I called "David the Dreamer," and we thought...

SUBTOPIC   1. *David's appearance* _____

SUPPORTING DETAILS   a. _____

                         b. _____

SUBTOPIC   2. _____

SUPPORTING DETAILS   a. _____

                         b. *Dozing at desk* _____

                         c. _____

                         d. _____

SUBTOPIC   3. *His fascination with comic books* _____

SUPPORTING DETAILS   a. _____

                         b. _____

                         c. _____

Your instructor may have you rewrite the paragraph on a separate sheet of paper. If so, be sure to introduce each of the subtopics or reasons with transitions such as *first, second, another reason*, and *finally*. You may also want to use repeated words, pronouns, and synonyms to help tie your sentences together.

6 EVALUATING PARAGRAPHS FOR ALL FOUR BASES: UNITY, SUPPORT, COHERENCE, AND SENTENCE SKILLS

Activity

In this activity, you will evaluate paragraphs in terms of all four bases: *unity, support, coherence*, and *sentence skills*. Evaluative comments follow each paragraph below. Circle the letter of the statement that best applies in each case.

Paragraph A

Drunk Drivers

People caught driving while drunk, even first offenders, should be jailed. Drunk driving, first of all, is more dangerous than carrying a loaded gun. In addition, a jail term would show drivers that society will no longer tolerate such careless and dangerous behaviour. Finally, severe penalties might encourage solutions to the problem of drinking and driving. People who go out for a good time and intend to have several drinks should follow media advice and always designate one person, who would stay completely sober, as the driver.

a. The paragraph is not unified.
b. The paragraph is not adequately supported.
c. The paragraph is not well organized.
d. The paragraph does not show a command of sentence skills.
e. The paragraph is well written in terms of the four bases.

Paragraph B

A Frustrating Moment

A frustrating moment happened to me several days ago. When I was shopping. I had picked up a tube of toothpaste and a jar of skin cream. After the cashier rang up the purchases, which came to $4.15. I handed her $10. Then got back my change, which was only $0.85. I told the cashier that she had made a mistake. Giving me change for $5 instead of $10. But she insist that I had only gave her $5, I became very upset and insist that she return the rest of my change. She refused to do so instead she asked me to step aside so she could wait on the next customer. I stood very rigid, trying not to lose my temper. I simply said to her, I'm not going to leave here without my change for $10. Giving in at this point a bell was rung and the manager was summoned. After the situation was explain to him, he ask the cashier to ring off her register to check for the change. After doing so, the cashier was $5 over her sale receipts. Only then did the manager return my change and apologize for the cashier mistake.

a. The paragraph is not unified.
b. The paragraph is not adequately supported.
c. The paragraph is not well organized.
d. The paragraph does not show a command of sentence skills.
e. The paragraph is well written in terms of the four bases.

Paragraph C

A Change in My Writing

A technique in my present English class has corrected a writing problem that I've always had. In past English courses, I had major problems with commas in the wrong places, bad spelling, capitalizing the wrong words, sentence fragments, and run-on sentences. I never had any big problems with unity, support, or coherence, but the sentence skills were another matter. They were like little bugs that always appeared to infest my writing. My present instructor asked me to rewrite papers, concentrating just on sentence skills. I thought that the instructor was crazy because I didn't feel that rewriting would do any good. I soon became certain that my instructor was out of his mind, for he made me rewrite my first paper four times. It was very frustrating, for I became tired of doing the same paper over and over. I wanted to curse at my instructor when I'd show him each new draft and he'd find skills mistakes and say, "Rewrite." Finally, my papers began to improve and the sentence skills began to fall into place. I was able to see them and correct them before turning in a paper, whereas I couldn't before. Why or how this happened I don't know, but I think that rewriting helped a lot. It took me most of the semester, but I stuck it out and the work paid off.

a. The paragraph is not unified.
b. The paragraph is not adequately supported.
c. The paragraph is not well organized.
d. The paragraph does not show a command of sentence skills.
e. The paragraph is well written in terms of the four bases.

REVIEWING THE LEARNING OUTCOMES FOR CHAPTER 6

To assure yourself that you have understood and met the learning outcomes for this chapter, answer the following questions.

1 What are two characteristics that must be present in order for a paragraph to be *unified*?

2 What three elements must the body of paragraph have for it to be well *supported*?

3 What activities are involved in creating a paper that is *coherent*? How do these two writing and revising activities lead to this standard?

4 Where in this book will you find help with revising for effective *sentence skills*? At which stage of the writing process is identifying and correcting sentence-skills and grammatical errors appropriate, and why?

5 Why are evaluating activities needed at different stages of the writing process?

Visit the *English Skills with Readings* Online Learning Centre at **www.mcgrawhill.ca/college/langan** to access self-quizzes, bonus material on study and research skills, web resources, and other learning and study tools.

Paragraph Development

PREVIEW

Section Two introduces you to paragraph development and gives you practice in the following common types of paragraph development:

- Narrating an Event
- Describing a Scene or Person
- Providing Examples
- Explaining a Process
- Examining Cause and Effect
- Comparing or Contrasting
- Defining a Term
- Dividing and Classifying
- Arguing a Position

After a brief explanation of each type of paragraph development, student paragraphs illustrating each type are presented, followed by questions about those paragraphs. The questions relate to the bases for effective writing described in Section One. You are then asked to write your own paragraph. In each case, writing assignments progress from personal-experience topics to more formal and objective topics; some topics require simple research, and the last assignment in each section asks you to write with a specific purpose and audience in mind. At times, points or topic sentences for development are suggested, so that you can concentrate on (1) making sure your evidence is on target in support of your opening idea, (2) providing plenty of specific supporting details to back up your point, and (3) organizing your supporting material clearly.

plaining a Process • Examining Cause and Effect • Comparing or Contrasting • Defining
rm • Dividing and Classifying • Describing a Scene or Person • Narrating an Event • Arguin
Position • Explaining a Process • Examining Cause and Effect • Comparing or Contrasting
fining a Term • Dividing and Classifying • Describing a Scene or Person • Narrating a
ent • Arguing a Position • Explaining a Process • Examining Cause and Effect • comparin

C H A P T E R 7

Introduction to Paragraph Development

LEARNING OUTCOMES

After reading this chapter and completing its activities you will

- understand the main methods of paragraph development and their functions;
- know how to work through the chapters in Section Two of this book;
- begin to understand the relationship of subject, purpose, and audience to each piece of writing; and
- be prepared to use two tools to assist you in revision: peer review and a personal review.

NINE PATTERNS OF PARAGRAPH DEVELOPMENT

Traditionally, writing has been divided into the following patterns of development:

- Narration
- Description
- Exposition

Examples	Comparison or contrast
Process	Definition
Cause and effect	Division and classification

- Argumentation or persuasion

Individual chapters within Section Two are devoted to each of the methods for developing and patterning ideas listed above.

- **Narration** and **description** are basic modes of expression and are present, to some degree, in all methods of development.

  Narration is the shaping or storytelling voice of writing. Much writing relies on narrative to support other methods of development, but when narration is dominant, the reader mainly follows the "narrative line" of actions or the writer's voice through a series of events.

Description is the sharp drafting pencil or paintbrush of writing. Description lends specificity, vividness, and clarity to most writing. Describing in words is the attempt to translate the mind's images of people, places, and things into word-pictures. When description predominates in a piece of writing, these word-pictures make the writer's point.

- **Exposition** includes a group of methods of development which *explain* or expose evidence for a point. In any method of *exposition,* the writer provides information about a particular subject. Exposition's main goal is always to clarify, with fine focus on limited areas of its subject. Exposition explains something by breaking it down into smaller units that open up into specific details. Exposition may be achieved by (1) giving examples, (2) detailing the process of doing or making something, (3) analyzing causes or effects, (4) comparing or contrasting, (5) defining a term or concept, or (6) dividing something into parts or grouping it into categories. Each of the six patterns of exposition is presented in a separate chapter.

- **Argumentation** is an attempt to prove a point or defend an opinion. *Argumentation* is writing with a single goal; it generally makes use of a variety of methods of exposition and specific techniques to reach its goal most effectively. Since writing tasks in this text are aimed at making a clear point, most paragraph and essay writing will contain some elements of argumentation or persuasion.

LEARNING PATTERNS OF DEVELOPMENT

Patterns of development are not a set of independent categories or styles. These "ways of arranging ideas" exist in most forms of non-fiction and fictional writing and, to varying degrees, in other communications forms such as graphic design as well. All the methods you will learn about in this book have developed from universal habits of the human mind as it tries to understand and express its thoughts and feelings about itself and the world around it. Writing patterns have emerged because some subjects simply lend themselves better to different ways of treating them. People instinctively compare two different ideas or objects; no one has to teach them to do so. Therefore, the practical exercises and ways of structuring your ideas that you will find in the following chapters will prepare you for challenges in expressing yourself in many college and career situations.

Each of the nine patterns of development has its own internal logic and provides its own special strategies for imposing order on ideas. As you practise each pattern, keep the following two points in mind.

- In each paragraph you write, one pattern will predominate, but very often one or more additional patterns may also be involved. For instance, "Net Eats Student's Time!"(pages 7-8) presents a series of causes leading to an effect: that the writer feels using the college's server wastes her time. But the writer also presents examples to explain each of the causes (the server's two-hour downtime left her too anxious to concentrate, college e-mail was irrelevant and time-consuming to read, students' chain letters clogged the mail and slowed down service). There is also an element of narration, as the writer presents examples that occur from the beginning to the end of an evening meant for homework.

■   More important, a paragraph you write in almost any pattern will probably involve some form of argumentation. You will advance a point and then go on to support it. To convince the reader that your point or thesis is valid, you may use a series of examples, or narration, or description, or some other pattern of organization. Among the paragraphs you will read in Section Two, one writer supports the point that a certain pet shop is depressing by providing a number of descriptive details. Another writer advances the opinion that good horror movies can be easily distinguished from bad horror movies and then supplies comparative information about both to support her claim. Much of your writing will have the purpose of persuading your reader that the idea you have advanced is valid.

HOW TO USE SECTION TWO

In each chapter of Section Two (after this one), a single method of paragraph development is explained—why it exists, how to write using this method, and what its potential uses are. Student papers then illustrate the method, followed by questions about the paragraphs. As you absorb the approach used in each type of development, the questions remind you of the four bases of effective writing introduced in Section One. The questions reinforce your awareness of the importance of *unity*, *support*, *coherence*, and *sentence skills*.

You are then asked to write your own paragraph. In most cases, the first assignment is fairly structured and provides a good deal of guidance for the writing process. Other assignments offer a wide choice of writing topics. The fourth assignment always requires some simple research, and the fifth assignment asks you to write for a specific purpose and a specific audience.

IMPORTANT CONSIDERATIONS AS YOU BEGIN TO WRITE

Whether or not you have found writing difficult in the past, and even if you are writing in your second (or third) language, you are now making a fresh start in college. If you approach each writing task in any subject by considering the three important ideas that follow, you may find writing less confusing.

If you know something about your subject, you will be able to concentrate on how to express what you know. If you know what your purpose is—whether it is to report objectively on some matter or to give your personal views on a situation—then you can judge how to shape your information and details. Finally, once you have determined who your audience is, you will find it easier to choose the right words and tone to carry your message effectively. As with any activity, when you narrow the field and focus on one thing at a time, you will find writing less intimidating.

Look at the "writer's triangle" below. Each time you receive a writing assignment, draw yourself a triangle like this one. Before you even begin to brainstorm or do another form of prewriting, ask yourself the questions you see here. Your answers will make your prewriting easier in two ways: you will begin to focus on your subject area and feel less confusion, and you will see right away whether you should do a bit of research before prewriting.

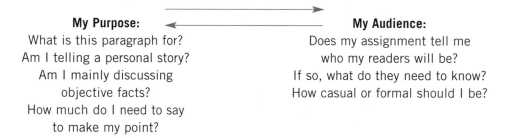

My Subject:
What do I know about it?
Do I need more information?
Where will I find more information?

My Purpose:
What is this paragraph for?
Am I telling a personal story?
Am I mainly discussing
objective facts?
How much do I need to say
to make my point?

My Audience:
Does my assignment tell me
who my readers will be?
If so, what do they need to know?
How casual or formal should I be?

Most of the writing you will do at college prepares you for career writing tasks. Most career writing is aimed at definite groups of readers and has definite purposes. You will always need to know enough about your subject to satisfy those readers' needs. Each point of this triangle relates to the others, as the arrows demonstrate. So begin now to consider "what" (subject knowledge), "why" (purpose), and "for whom" (audience) each time you write. Every time you do so, you will refine your writing skills and become a more effective writer.

The chapters that follow will remind you of these three considerations with activities and writing assignments that lead you to think of your subject knowledge, purpose, and audience each time you write.

KNOWING YOUR SUBJECT

Knowing your subject is not the impossible task it may seem. Here are three simple strategies for approaching a list of subjects or coming up with one of your own.

1 Follow Your Interests

Whenever possible, try to write about a subject that interests you. Your interest will give you energy and enthusiasm that come through in your writing. You will also find it easier to put more time into your work.

2 Discover What You Already Know

Try to write on a subject that you already know something about. You may know some things because you have direct personal experience with them. Sometimes your knowledge may come from prior indirect experience; you may have read, thought, or talked about subjects. Either direct or indirect knowledge may be enough, but that depends on the aim of your paper and how deeply you wish to pursue your subject.

3 Do Some Basic Research

The word *research* tends to make people anxious, but learning more about a subject could be as straightforward and easy as talking to someone who knows about it. Never hesitate to discuss a subject in which you're interested with a few people; it may help you to generate ideas of your own or stimulate you to do some book or Internet research.

   If you are asked to write about a topic that requires more than casual research or a topic about which you have no experience or knowledge, you will want to set aside some time to spend online or at the library. "Research Skills," available on the Online Learning Centre, will show you how to look up relevant information and use it effectively.

Direct or indirect experience and research provide you with the specific evidence you need to develop the point you wish to make. Knowing your subject is an essential part of writing effectively.

KNOWING YOUR PURPOSE

Generally, the main purpose for writing is to inform, to persuade, or to entertain. These are broad headings that sometimes confuse students who are simply trying to write a paragraph or essay. Try seeing each one in a different way by thinking about the explanations below. Remember as well that you may have and probably will have a main purpose and a secondary purpose. Each time you start writing, think of your audience as you consider your purpose or purposes.

1 Writing to Inform

Writing to inform actually means writing to explain what you mean in some detail to readers. "Writing to clarify" might be another way of expressing this idea; in business or technical communication, the phrase might mean "writing to transmit information" or "writing to report on something." Even a paragraph relating a personal story informs readers about the writer and his or her life and thoughts. What "writing to inform" does *not* mean is simply restating research; writing must always make a point and show your own ideas or response to others' ideas. Much of your college writing will have this general purpose. In fact, whenever you make a point and explain its validity with specific proof, you are writing to inform.

2 Writing to Persuade

As stated in Section One, most paragraphs that present a point and proof for that point seek to persuade readers to varying degrees. The best type of persuasion is the clear and convincing presentation of factual details. Paragraphs that mainly use description or other methods of development to make their point may be quite persuasive, in fact. If you intend to put across a strong point of view, then your main purpose is usually persuasion. In Chapter 16, you will learn some techniques specific to stating an argument.

3 Writing to Entertain

Although entertaining your readers (or your professor) will rarely be your main purpose, you may be naturally humorous or entertaining. College writing will rarely ask you to entertain, so use your judgment and knowledge of your subject and your audience—mainly your instructor—to guide you when entertaining readers is your secondary purpose.

KNOWING YOUR AUDIENCE

You already know something about writing for different audiences. When you e-mail a friend, you use a way of speaking that is familiar to both parties, and you know roughly what you want to say. If you have written to your college or applied for a job, you wrote a bit more formally and were concerned about what to put in those letters. In other words, you are probably aware of the need to change your tone, content, and wording to suit your reader.

When you submit writing assignments in college, your audiences are mainly your instructors and sometimes other students. These people represent a generalized peer group, a typical educated adult audience. They expect you to present your ideas in a clear, direct, organized way. If you learn to write to persuade or inform such a general audience, you should feel confident that you have accomplished a great deal.

As you work through the chapters that follow, you will write some papers for more specific audiences. By doing so, you will develop a skill that you will refine throughout your life: the ability to choose words and adopt a tone of "writing voice" that is just right for a given purpose and a given group of people.

1 What Do Readers Need to Know?

Begin by putting yourself "in the shoes" of your reader. How much does this person know about your subject? How much background information does he or she need to be able to follow your point through its proof to its conclusion? Your reader cannot see into your thoughts and experiences and does not know why you hold the views you do.

2 What Kind of Language Will Readers Expect?

General readers want one thing: to understand easily what you have to say. Therefore, your language in college writing should always aim for clarity, for a neutral middle ground of language. Slang or overly casual, conversational word use carries the risk of losing readers who may not know you. Too formal or too grand words with many syllables may lose readers; people may not see your points clearly or easily if the points are hidden behind a forest of words. Aim for accuracy when you choose your words.

3 What Tone or Degree of Formality Is Best?

A sense of tone develops with time and with frequent writing practice. Your own experience can guide you in the beginning. Begin by visualizing your reader for an assignment: how well does he or she know you? Then consider the circumstances of your writing task; you will generally write more formally, less casually to someone in an organization or business situation than you would to your peers.

The exercise below will help you to see the connection between subject, purpose, and audience more concretely.

Section Two includes assignments that ask you to write with a very specific purpose in mind and for a very specific audience. You will be asked, for example, to write as someone advising your MPP about possible effects of privatizing health care in Canada, as an aide at a daycare centre preparing instructions for children, as a member of a panel of college and university students speaking to high-school students, or as an employee writing a description of a new job opening at your workplace. Through these and other assignments, you will learn how to adjust your style and tone to a given writing situation.

Activity

This activity will stimulate your awareness of the relationship between subject, purpose, and audience. You may work on this activity alone or as part of a group; if you do this assignment as a group, compare all groups' results in class.

Imagine yourself as your English instructor; you are trying to come up with a set of new writing assignments. Develop five subjects; then consider what you would want readers to know, and why; and for whom you would logically write. One example of subject, purpose, and audience is supplied for you below.

Subject	*Purpose*	*Audience*
Example		
everyday fashion	how to shop for great cheap clothes	readers of college paper
1._____	_____	_____
2._____	_____	_____
3._____	_____	_____
4._____	_____	_____
5._____	_____	_____

USING PEER REVIEW

In addition to having your instructor as an audience for your writing, you will benefit by having another student in your class as an audience. On the day an assignment is due, or on a day when you are writing in class, your instructor may ask you to pair up with another student. That student will read your work, and you will read his or her work.

Ideally, try to read the other paragraph aloud while your partner listens. If that is not practical, read the assignment in a whisper while he or she looks on. As you read, both you and your partner should look and listen for spots where the paragraph does not flow smoothly and clearly. Check or circle the trouble spots where your reading hesitates.

Your partner should then read your paragraph, marking possible trouble spots while doing so. Then each of you should do three things: (1) identify yourself, (2) make an X-ray outline, and (3) make comments.

1 Identification

On a separate sheet of paper, write at the top the title and author of the assignment you have read. Underneath that, put your name as the reader of the paragraph.

2 X-Ray Outline

"X-ray" the paragraph for its inner logic by making up an outline. The outline need be no more than twenty words or so, but it should show clearly the logical foundation on which the paragraph is built. It should identify and summarize the overall point of the paragraph and the three areas of support for the main point.

Your outline could look like this.

Point: _____

Support:

1. _____

2. _____

3. _____

For example, here is an outline of the paragraph on a new puppy in the house on page 208:

Point: A new puppy can have drastic effects on a house.

Support:

1. Keeps family awake at night

2. Destroys possessions

3. Causes arguments

3 Comments

Under the outline, write the heading "Comments." Here is what you should comment on.

■   First, make note of something you really liked about the paragraph, such as good use of transitions or an especially realistic or vivid specific detail.

■   Look at the spots where your reading of the paragraph hesitated: Are words missing or misspelled? Is there a lack of parallel structure? (See pages 95-96.) Are there mistakes in punctuation? Is the meaning of a sentence confused? Try to figure out what the problems are and suggest ways of fixing them.

■   Are there spots in the paragraph where you see problems with *unity, support,* or *coherence?* If so, offer comments. For example, you might say, "More details are needed in the first subtopic" or "Some of the details in the last subtopic don't really back up your point."

After you have completed your evaluation of the paragraph, give it to your partner. Ideally you will make revisions in light of this feedback. Remember to weigh your peer marker's comments against your own views. Whether or not you have time to rewrite, be sure to hand in the peer evaluation form with your paragraph.

DOING A PERSONAL REVIEW

After you have completed your next-to-final draft of a paragraph, there are three ways you should check it yourself. You should *always* do the first two checks, which take only a couple of minutes. Ideally, you should take the time to do the detailed final check as well.

1   Read the paragraph *out loud.* If it does not sound right—that is, if it does not read smoothly and clearly—then make the changes needed to ensure that it does.

2   Make sure you can answer clearly and concisely two basic questions: "What is the point of my paragraph or essay? What are the three distinct bits of support for my point?"

3   Your last task with your next-to-final draft is always to review it carefully, using the checklist on page 153 and on the inside front cover. Pay special attention to *sentence skills* on this final pass, and revise or edit as needed until your paper is completely reviewed and corrected.

REVIEWING THE LEARNING OUTCOMES FOR PARAGRAPH DEVELOPMENT

To assure yourself that you have understood and met the learning outcomes for this chapter, answer the following questions.

1   What are the main functions of narration and description?

2 What is the main function of exposition, and what are the major forms of exposition?

3 Why is argumentation nearly always an element of most writing?

4 How does knowledge of your subject relate to writing for a specific purpose and audience?

5 What must you do to prepare for peer review of your work?

Visit the *English Skills with Readings* Online Learning Centre at **www.mcgrawhill.ca/college/langan** to access self-quizzes, bonus material on study and research skills, web resources, and other learning and study tools.

Checklist of the Four Bases in Effective Writing

Use the questions below as a guide in both writing and evaluating an assignment. Numbers in parentheses refer to the pages that explain each skill.

Base 1: Unity

☐ Clear opening statement of the point of your paragraph or essay? (46-48; 56-63)

☐ All material on target in support of opening point? (121-23)

Base 2: Support

☐ Specific evidence? (48-54; 68-69; 124-25)

☐ Plenty of it? (54-56; 69-72)

Base 3: Coherence

☐ Clear method of organization? (76-78; 125-27)

☐ Transitions and other connective devices? (78-84)

Base 4: Sentence Skills

☐ Faulty parallelism eliminated? (96)

☐ Inconsistent verb tenses corrected? (96-97)

☐ Faulty pronouns eliminated? (98-99; 355-58; 361-65)

☐ Sentences varied? (102-8)

☐ Careless errors removed through editing and proofreading? (108-10)

☐ Fragments eliminated? (314-24)

☐ Run-ons and comma splices eliminated? (329-38)

☐ Correct verb forms? (342-45)

☐ Subject and verb agreement? (349-52)

☐ Faulty modifiers eliminated? (371-72; 374-76)

☐ Correct manuscript form? (378-79)

☐ Capital letters used correctly? (383-89)

☐ Punctuation marks where needed?

    a Apostrophe (395-402)

    b Quotation marks (404-9)

    c Comma (411-17)

    d Colon; semicolon (420-22)

    e Dash; hyphen (423-24)

    f Parentheses (424-25)

☐ Possible spelling errors checked? (438-47)

☐ Effective word choice? (449-52)

Explaining a Process • Examining Cause and Effect • Comparing or Contrasting • Defini Term • Dividing and Classifying • Describing a Scene or Person • Narrating an Event • Arg a Position • Explaining a Process • Examining Cause and Effect • Comparing or Contrasti Defining a Term • Dividing and Classifying • Describing a Scene or Person • Narrating Event • Arguing a Position • Explaining a Process • Examining Cause and Effect • Compa

CHAPTER 8

Narrating an Event

LEARNING OUTCOMES

By working through the activities and writing tasks in this chapter you will create a narrative paragraph that

- displays the point of internal or external conflict within an experience: i.e., the focus of your narrative;
- shows careful selection of details related to your point;
- organizes and sequences your supporting material in time order to create an accurate and coherent narrative paragraph;
- is revised to include vivid and important details to "show" readers your point and recreate your events as accurately as possible; and
- concludes by returning to its point, rather than ending with its last event.

Narrative paragraphs and essays work toward the same purpose as the forms of exposition: such papers seek *to explain*. Narrative-based writing uses a storyline to explain and deepen the meaning of its point. Unlike a made-up story or fictional narrative where the meaning may reveal itself slowly as the story unrolls, a narrative announces its meaning in its topic sentence. Expository narrative, then, (1) makes a point *clear* by relating a detailed storyline about something that has happened and (2) presents its details *in the order in which they happened*.

Here is a typical narrative illustrating the point "I was embarrassed yesterday."

> I was hurrying across campus to get to a class. It had rained heavily all morning, so I was hopscotching my way around puddles in the pathway. I called to two friends ahead to wait for me, and right before I caught up to them, I came to a large puddle that covered the entire path. I had to make a quick choice of either stepping into the puddle or trying to jump over it. I jumped, wanting to seem cool, since my friends were watching, but didn't clear the puddle. Water splashed everywhere, drenching my shoes, socks, and pants cuffs, and spraying the pants of my friends as well. I felt the more embarrassed because I had tried to look so casual.

This narrative or linked sequence of details is a vivid and real explanation of the writer's embarrassment: we see and understand just why he felt as he did.

Narrative's uses in college and career writing are numerous. Child care and social services workers write narrative-based case studies and reports; course writing and career writing in business and technology require reports of situations and procedures written as accurate recountings of events. Law enforcement officers must record every situation with which they are involved.

In this section, you will be asked to write narratives that illustrate a specific point. The paragraphs below both present narrative experiences that support a particular point. Read them, and then answer the questions that follow.

PARAGRAPHS TO CONSIDER

A Loss of Faith

[1]My younger brother Josh was always the "star" of the family, so six months ago our parents rewarded his good marks by paying for university tuition and residence fees. [2]A week before reading week in February, I used my own break from college to fly out to see him at the University of Alberta. [3]When I knocked on the door of his room, he looked surprised, but not in a pleasant way. [4]He introduced me to his roommate, who looked uncomfortable and quickly left. [5]I asked Josh how classes were going, and because Josh's jumpiness was making me nervous, I started to look around the room; the first thing I noticed was the big bulletin board above the desk. [6]As I focused my eyes on the board, dozens of papers tacked up there caught my eye. [7]Most of the papers were tests and lab reports, each one marked with either a big red F or an O, but the largest paper up there was an official document from the university—an official notice of change of address for Josh McKenna. [8]"What's going on?" I said. [9]I stood there stunned and then felt my anger start to grow. [10]"Who lives at 488 West 3rd Street in Calgary?" I asked. [11]Josh just shrugged and said, "What's it to you? Are you supposed to report back on me?" [12]I don't really remember all that he told me, except that he tried to lie at first, to pretend his marks were all right, before he admitted the truth: he was failing nearly every course and had stopped going to classes—he had even arranged to send his next transcripts to his roommate's mother's house, the Calgary address. [13]I felt a sharp pain in the pit of my stomach, and I wanted to be anywhere but in that residence room. [14]I wanted to hit him or tear down the papers and run out to call our parents, but I did nothing. [15]Clumsily I pulled on my jacket. [16]My stomach felt sick, and I worried that my rage would take control of my body. [17]I opened the room door, and suddenly more than anything I wanted to slam the door on my brother and his lies. [18]Instead, I managed to close the door quietly. [19]I walked away understanding what is meant by a loss of faith.

A Childhood Disappointment

[1]The time I almost won a car when I was ten years old was probably the most disappointing moment of my childhood. [2]One hot summer afternoon I was wandering around a local Bay store, waiting for my mother to finish shopping.

[3]Near the toy department, I was attracted to a crowd of people gathered around a bright blue car that was on display in the main aisle. [4]A sign indicated that the car was the first prize in a sweepstakes celebrating the store's tenth anniversary. [5]The sign caught my attention because of the tiny lights embedded in the words "win" and "car." [6]White entry cards and shiny yellow pencils were scattered on a card table nearby, and the table was just low enough for me to write on, so I filled out a card. [7]Then, feeling very much like an adult, I slipped my card into the slot of a heavy blue wooden box that rested on another table nearby. [8]I then proceeded to the toy department, completely forgetting about the car. [9]However, about a month later, just as I was walking into the house from my first day back at school, the telephone rang. [10]When my mother answered it, a man asked to speak to a Jeff Wellesley. [11]My mother said, "There's a Jeff Castaldo here, but not a Jeff Wellesley." [12]He asked, "Is this 862-9715 at 29 Castaldo Street?" [13]My mother said, "That's the right number, but this is 29 Wellesley Street." [14]She then asked him, "What is this all about?" and he explained to her about the sweepstakes contest. [15]My mother then called me to ask if I had ever filled out an application for a sweepstakes drawing. [16]I said that I had, and she told me to get on the phone. [17]The man by this time had realized that I had filled in my first name and street name on the line where my full name was to be. [18]He told me I could not qualify for the prize because I had filled out the application incorrectly. [19]For the rest of the day, I cried whenever I thought of how close I had come to winning the car. [20]I am probably fated for the rest of my life to think of the "almost" prize whenever I fill out any kind of contest form.

■ **Questions**

About Unity

1. Which paragraph lacks a topic sentence?

   _____

   Write a topic sentence for the paragraph:

   _____

   _____

   _____

2. Which sentence in "A Childhood Disappointment" should be omitted in the interest of paragraph unity? (*Write the sentence number here.*) _____

About Support

3. What is for you the best (most real and vivid) detail or image in the paragraph "A Loss of Faith"?

   _____

   _____

What is the best detail or image in "A Childhood Disappointment"?

_____

_____

What is the most effective detail in "A Loss of Faith"?

_____

_____

4. Which paragraph or paragraphs provide details in the form of the actual words used by the participants?

_____

_____

About Coherence

5. Do the two paragraphs use time order or emphatic order to organize details?

_____

6. List the transition words used in one of the two paragraphs:

    a. _____

    b. _____

    c. _____

    d. _____

FORMS OF NARRATIVE WRITING

All narratives relate a time-ordered series of events, but not all narrative writing is personal or deeply emotional.

Personal Narratives

- This chapter includes personal narrative paragraphs which show *why* people feel the way they do or *how* they learned some lesson in life. Narratives often point to a moral or teach a lesson.
- Personal narratives are often effective because of their intimate connection between reader and writer. The use of "I," the first-person singular point of view, offers this immediacy when the writer's purpose is to to share his or her experience.

Other Forms of Narrative

- Many narratives, including some personal stories, may be less personal in focus or tone. Writing a narrative in the third-person point of view places the reader's focus on the events or experience itself, rather than on the writer. There is no "I" to distract the reader. Such narratives allow readers more "distance" between themselves and the subject matter; their tone is cooler, less intimate.

■ More objective third-person narratives may also relate the "story" of a marketing campaign, the stages in a technical process, or the events occurring as part of an accident. Such narratives must naturally be more impersonal, but their general purpose is the same as that of all narrative: the vivid and accurate recreation of some experience or events.

Writers must decide whether their purpose is to focus on the events they narrate or on their connection to these events. The writer's decision dictates both the point of view used and the ultimate tone of the narrative.

DEVELOPING A NARRATIVE PARAGRAPH

Development through Prewriting

Mark's instructor was helping her students think of topics for their narrative paragraphs. "A narrative is just a story that illustrates a point," she said. "That point is often about a strong emotion you felt. Looking at a list of emotions may help you think of a topic. Ask yourself what incident in your life has led you to feel any of these emotions."

The instructor then jotted these feelings on the board:

Anger
Embarrassment
Jealousy
Amusement
Confusion
Thankfulness
Loneliness
Sadness
Terror
Relief

As Mark looked over the list, he remembered several experiences in his life. "The word *anger* made me think about a time when I was a kid. My brother took my skateboard without telling me, and he left it in the park, where it got stolen. *Amusement* made me think of a school trip to Quebec City and watching Terry Levesque, who claimed he spoke French, try to bargain with a street vendor. He got in such a flap that he ended up paying more than what the vendor asked for. When I got to *sadness*, though, I thought about my brother again and hit on something that still bothers me now. I visited my brother only a few months ago, and I still feel angry and sad about that. *Sad* isn't really a strong enough word, though— I felt angry and deceived. So I decided to write about losing my faith in someone."

Mark's first step was to do some freewriting. Without worrying about spelling or grammar, he just sat down at the computer and let fly all the thoughts and emotions he'd been worrying over since his visit to his brother. Here is what he came up with.

> I was really looking forward to seeing Josh last spring. He went off to University of Alberta six months ago. I saved up enough for a discount plane fare from working at the garage part-time, and I was excited about going out west on my own. Travelling alone was a major thing for me. But from the moment I got to his residence room, I think I knew something was wrong. He looked so surprised when he saw me at the door and I didn't know why—he knew I was coming. His roommate left as soon as I got there and Josh was nervous and jumpy. And not just full-of-energy jumpy, either. All over his bulletin board were these failed assignments, like he was proud of them. There were cartons of beer bottles all over the floor, and garbage everywhere. I didn't know what to do. I didn't know what to say either, so I asked him about the address I saw on a university letter—it wasn't his address. Making me feel kind of sick. Even before he admitted anything I kept thinking about our parents. He was lying to them and hiding things. Josh was always the favourite, the guy who couldn't do anything wrong, and he was lying to everybody now. I wanted to hit him or yell at him or something. Instead I shut my mouth and realized I felt lied to, too. I couldn't believe anything he was saying, and I just wanted to go home.

Development through Revising

Mark knew that his first freewriting needed work, but he also knew he had something to work with. After he reread it the following day, he said, "Although my point is supposed to be that my visit to my brother taught me about losing faith in someone, I didn't really get that across. I needed to say more about how the experience felt to me, and why it felt that way.

"I've included stuff, information that doesn't really support my point. For instance, how I paid for my plane ticket isn't important here, and maybe the mess in his room isn't either. And I think I spend too much time talking about getting to the visit itself. I want to get more quickly to the point where I arrived at Josh's room.

"Maybe I should try putting in some conversation, too. That might show people how this whole thing felt to me, and how it seemed like there was this wall between my brother and me."

Mark used two strategies—the self-critique, above, and questioning—to generate material. He created an outline, then revised his paragraph until he produced the version that appears on page 155.

WRITING A NARRATIVE PARAGRAPH

How to Write a Narrative Paragraph

1   Think of an event or experience that seems meaningful to you. Such an experience will probably have caused you to change, learn something, or grow in some way.

2   Prewrite to pile up details of your experience. Do not be concerned if you do not immediately find an easy-to-state single point.

3   After your initial prewriting, look for a *conflict*, some moment when your actions or expectations met with something unexpected, causing you to change direction. This is probably your "moment of enlightenment," your focus for your paragraph. Try to state what you learned at this moment, or try to name your dominant emotion: this will become the topic, the point of your paragraph.

4   Write out your point as a topic sentence and create an outline for your narrative. *Organize* your details in time sequence as they occurred. *Select* details from your prewriting that (1) cover only a limited amount of time, and (2) truly support your point.

5   Draft and revise your paragraph with one aim: to *recreate* emotions, actions, and speech as vividly as possible. "Show" readers your experience, and achieve accuracy in your writing by doing so.

■ **Writing Assignment 1**

Write a paragraph about an experience in which a certain emotion was predominant. The emotion might be fear, pride, satisfaction, embarrassment, or any of the following:

Frustration	Sympathy	Shyness
Love	Bitterness	Disappointment
Sadness	Violence	Happiness
Terror	Surprise	Jealousy
Shock	Nostalgia	Anger
Relief	Loss	Hate
Envy	Silliness	Nervousness

The experience should be *limited in time*. Note that the two paragraphs presented in this chapter detail experiences that occurred within relatively short periods. One writer describes the anger he felt at his brother's dishonesty during a brief visit; another describes the disappointing loss of a prize.

A good way to recreate an event is to *include some dialogue*, as the writers of the two paragraphs in this chapter have done. Repeating what you have said or what you have heard someone else say helps make the situation come alive. First, though, be sure to check Chapter 34, on quotation marks.

Prewriting

a Begin by prewriting. Think of an experience or event in your life in which you felt a certain emotion strongly. Then spend ten minutes freewriting about the experience. Do not worry at this point about such matters as spelling or grammar or putting things in the right order; instead, just try to get down all the details you can think of that seem related to the experience.

b This preliminary writing will help you decide whether your topic is promising enough to develop further. If it is not, choose another emotion. If it is, do three things:

  - First, write your topic sentence, underlining the emotion you will focus on. For example, "My first day in kindergarten was one of the *scariest* days of my life."
  - Second, make up a list of all the details involved in the experience. Then arrange these details in time order.
  - Third, write an outline or detailed plan for your paragraph.

c Using the list and outline as guides, prepare a rough draft of your paper. Use time signals such as *first, then, next, after, while, during,* and *finally* to help connect details as you move from the beginning to the middle to the end of your narrative. Be sure to include not only what happened but also how you felt about what was going on.

Revising

Put your first draft away for a day or so. When you return to it, read it over, asking yourself these questions:

  - Does my topic sentence clearly state what emotion the experience made me feel?
  - If it is appropriate to my paragraph, have I included some dialogue to make the experience come alive?
  - Have I explained how I felt as the experience occurred?
  - Have I used time order to narrate the experience from beginning to end?
  - Have I used time signals to connect one detail to the next?
  - Have I checked my paper for sentence skills, including spelling, as listed on the inside front cover of this book?

Continue revising your work until you can answer yes to all these questions.

Writing Assignment 2

Narrate a real-life event you have witnessed. Listed below are some places where interesting personal interactions often happen. Think of an event that you saw occur at one of these places, or visit one of them and take notes on an incident to write about.

The dinner table at your home or someone else's

A lineup at the college cafeteria, supermarket, ticket counter, movie theatre, or government office

A doctor's or dentist's office
A traffic court or small claims court
A restaurant
A concert or sports event

Prewriting

a Decide what point you will make about the incident. What one word or phrase characterizes the scene you witnessed? Your narration of the incident will emphasize and use that characteristic to focus its details. This word or phrase is the "keynote" or dominant emotion that will tie your paragraph together.

b Write your topic sentence. The topic sentence should state where the incident happened as well as your point about it. Here are some possibilities; notice the keynote word or phrase in each:

> Yesterday at Harvey's, there was an encounter that *warmed my heart.*
> Two fans at last night's Oilers game got into a *hilarious* argument.
> A *bizarre* discussion went on at traffic court last night.
> The scene at my family's dinner table Monday was one of total *confusion.*

c Use the questioning technique to remind yourself of details that will make your narrative come alive. Ask yourself questions like these and write down your answers:

> Whom was I observing?
> How were they dressed?
> What were their facial expressions?
> What tones of voice did they use?
> What did I hear them say?

d Using the Paragraph Outline Form on page 28, create an outline that begins with your topic sentence, in which you have underlined or italicized your keynote word or phrase. Be sure that your subtopics and supporting details all explain and illustrate that main emotion or descriptive phrase.

e Drawing details from your notes and your outline, write the first draft of your paragraph. Remember to use time signals such as *then, after that, during, meanwhile,* and *finally* to connect your details and sentences together.

Revising

After you have put your paragraph away for a day, read it to a friend or fellow student who will give you honest feedback. Both of you should consider these questions:

■ Does the topic sentence make a general point about the incident and state the "keynote" word or phrase?

■ Do descriptions of the appearance, tone of voice, and expressions of the people involved paint a clear picture that illustrates the keynote word or phrase?

■ Is the sequence of events made clear by transitional words such as at *first, later,* and *then*?

Continue revising your work until you and your reader can answer yes to all these questions. Then check to make sure your paragraph is free of sentence-skills mistakes, including spelling errors. Use the list on the inside front cover of this book.

■ Writing Assignment 3

Write a paragraph that shows, through some experience you have had, the truth *or* falsity of a popular belief. You might write about any one of the following statements or some other popular saying.

Every person has a price.
Haste makes waste.
Don't count your chickens before they're hatched.
A bird in the hand is worth two in the bush.
It isn't what you know, it's who you know.
Borrowing can get you into trouble.
What you don't know won't hurt you.
Keeping a promise is easier said than done.
You never really know people until you see them in an emergency.
If you don't help yourself, nobody will.
An ounce of prevention is worth a pound of cure.
Hope for the best but expect the worst.
Never give advice to a friend.
You get what you pay for.
A stitch in time saves nine.
A fool and money are soon parted.
There is an exception to every rule.
Nice people finish last.

Begin your narrative paragraph with a topic sentence that expresses your attitude, your agreement or disagreement, with a popular saying. For example, "My sister learned recently that 'keeping a promise is easier said than done.'" Or "'Never give advice to a friend' is not always good advice, as I learned after helping a friend reunite with her boyfriend."

Refer to the suggestions for prewriting, outlining, and revising on pages 162-63. Remember that the purpose of your story is to *support* your topic sentence. Feel free to select carefully from your experience and even add to it so that the details truly support the point of your story.

■ Writing Assignment 4

Write an account of a memorable personal experience. Make sure that your story has a point, expressed in the first sentence of the paragraph. If necessary, tailor your narrative to fit your purpose. Use *time order* to organize your details (*first* this happened; *then* this; *after* that, this; *next*, this; and so on). Concentrate on providing as many specific details as possible so that the reader can really "see" and share your experience. Try to make it as vivid for the reader as it was for you when you first experienced it.

You might want to use one of the topics below, or a topic of your own choosing. Regardless, remember that every sentence of your story must illustrate or support a point stated in the first sentence of your paragraph.

The first time you felt like an adult
A major decision
A moment you knew you were happy
Your best or worst date
A foolish risk
An argument you will never forget
An incident that changed your life
A time when you did or did not do the right thing
Your best or worst holiday or birthday
A time you learned a lesson or taught one to someone else
A triumph in sports or some other event

You may want to refer to the suggestions on prewriting and revising in Writing Assignment 1.

■ Writing Assignment 5

Imagine that a younger brother or sister or a young friend has to make a difficult decision of some kind. Perhaps he or she must decide how to go about preparing for a job interview, whether to get help with a difficult class, or what to do about a co-worker who is taking money from the cash register. Write a third-person narrative based on your own experience (or that of someone you know) that will teach a younger person something about the decision he or she must make. In your paragraph, include a comment or two about the lesson your story teaches. You may narrate an experience about any problem young people face, including any of those already mentioned or those listed below. (See "My Ghost Town" on pages 208-9 for an example of a third-person narrative.)

Should he or she save a little from a weekly paycheque?
Should he or she live at home or move to an apartment with some friends?
How should he or she deal with a group of friends who are involved with drugs, stealing, or both?

■ Writing Assignment 6

Writing about a Reading Selection: Read Margot Devlin's article "Mrs. Squirrel and I Negotiated Terms" on pages 510-12. Many relationships with others begin if not in conflict, then in mutual misunderstanding. Change, as you have learned in this chapter, is the essence of a good narrative. Sometimes, during the process of getting to know something about someone else, we come to see the individual differently—we change our attitude and consequently our behaviour toward him or her. We change, the other person changes, and "terms" are "negotiated."

Write a narrative about some person (or creature) toward whom your attitude changed as you got to know him or her. What did you learn as a result of "negotiating terms" and coming to a new understanding with the other party?

REVIEWING THE LEARNING OUTCOMES FOR NARRATIVE WRITING

When you complete any of the writing assignments in this chapter, review your work to decide how well you have met the learning outcomes for narrative writing. Decide how well your paragraph meets each of these requirements.

1 Does your paragraph open with a clear statement of its point about the emotion, experience, or lesson that is its subject?
2 Does each detail of your storyline contribute specifically to clarifying your point or lesson?
3 Are your details arranged in time order, with transitional words and phrases to show the relationships between events?
4 Are your details specific and vividly described: do they recreate your experience?
5 Do you conclude with a return to your point, rather than with the last event in your story?

 Visit the *English Skills with Readings* Online Learning Centre at **www.mcgrawhill.ca/college/langan** to access self-quizzes, bonus material on study and research skills, web resources, and other learning and study tools.

Explaining a Process • Examining Cause and Effect • Comparing or Contrasting • Defini
Term • Dividing and Classifying • Describing a Scene or Person • Narrating an Event • Arg
a Position • Explaining a Process • Examining Cause and Effect • Comparing or Contrast
Defining a Term • Dividing and Classifying • Describing a Scene or Person • Narrating an E
Arguing a Position • Explaining a Process • Examining Cause and Effect • Comparin

CHAPTER 9

Describing a Scene or Person

LEARNING OUTCOMES

By working through the activities and writing tasks in this chapter, you will create a descriptive paper that

- opens with a dominant impression of its subject in its topic sentence;
- offers a rich, focused, careful selection of sense-oriented details to confirm and strengthen aspects of your dominant impression;
- guides your readers with a clear point of view and a consistent method of tracking observations about your subject; and
- concludes with a thought that fixes your dominant impression in the reader's mind.

Descriptive writing gives readers pictures in words. Describing is a basic communication activity that serves all forms of writing. Narration succeeds because of the power of its descriptive details; readers' thoughts and emotions are touched directly by description that provokes reactions or persuades. Locations, technical processes, or situations are explained and recreated in words by accurate description.

Descriptive "word-pictures" may have many purposes, but to be effective, they must be as vivid and real as possible. You perceive the subject you describe through your senses, so you must, in turn, record your subject in specific details to appeal to your readers' senses: sight, hearing, taste, smell, and touch. More than any other type of writing, a descriptive paragraph needs sharp, colourful details.

Here is a description in which only the sense of sight is used:

A rug covers the living-room floor.

In contrast, here is a description rich in sense impressions:

A thick, forest green, plush broadloom rug stretches wall to wall across the living-room floor. The deep and densely woven fibres of the carpet hush your steps as you walk through them in your bare feet, and as your feet relax into the cushiony pile, the soft wool pushes back at you with a spongy resilience.

How many senses do the writer's details speak to?

- Sight: *thick, forest green, plush broadloom rug; stretches wall to wall; walk through them in your bare feet; cushiony pile*
- Hearing: *hush*
- Touch: *bare feet, deep and densely woven fibres, pushes back, spongy resilience*

Sharp, vivid images provided by the sensory details create a clear picture of the rug: we are able to share in the writer's experience.

Descriptive writing skills and techniques are essential to any college assignment where an event, procedure, human behaviour pattern, or strategy must be carefully tracked and recreated. Advertising and sales rely on description; training manuals require careful description of objects, gestures, and processes; in fact, every form of career writing demands the accuracy, precision, and careful detail selection of effective descriptive writing.

In this section, you will be asked to describe a person, place, or thing for your readers by using words rich in sensory details. To help you prepare for the assignment, read the next two paragraphs and answer the questions that follow.

PARAGRAPHS TO CONSIDER

An Athlete's Room

[1]As I entered the bright, cheerful space, with its beige walls and practical, flat-pile carpet, I noticed a closet to my right with the door open. [2]On the shelf above the bunched-together clothes were a red baseball cap, a fielder's glove, and a battered brown gym bag. [3]Turning from the closet, I noticed a single bed with its wooden headboard against the far wall. [4]The bedspread was a brown, orange, and beige print of basketball, football, and baseball scenes. [5]A lamp shaped like a baseball and a copy of Sports Illustrated were on the top of a nightstand to the left of the bed. [6]A sports schedule and several yellowing newspaper clippings were tacked to the cork bulletin board on the wall above the nightstand. [7]A desk with a bookcase top stood against the left wall. [8]I walked toward it to examine it more closely. [9]As I ran my fingers over the items on the dusty shelves, I noticed some tarnished medals and faded ribbons for track accomplishments. [10]These lay next to a heavy gold trophy inscribed "MVP: Windsor Varsity Basketball." [11]I accidentally tipped an autograph-covered, slightly deflated basketball off one shelf, and the ball bounced with dull thuds across the width of the room. [12]Next to the desk was a window with brightly printed curtains that matched the bedspread. [13]Between the window and the left corner stood a dresser with one drawer half open, revealing a tangle of odd sweat socks and a few stretched-out T-shirts emblazoned with team insignias. [14]As I turned to leave the room, I carefully picked my way around scattered pairs of worn-out athletic shoes.

A Depressing Place

[1]The pet shop in the mall is a depressing place. [2]A display window attracts passersby who stare at the prisoners penned inside. [3]In the right-hand side of

the window, two puppies press their forepaws against the glass and attempt to lick the human hands that press from the outside. ⁴A cardboard barrier separates the dogs from several black-and-white kittens piled together in the opposite end of the window. ⁵Inside the shop, rows of wire cages line one wall from top to bottom. ⁶At first, it is hard to tell whether a bird, hamster, gerbil, cat, or dog is locked inside each cage. ⁷Only an occasional movement or clawing, shuffling sound tells visitors that living creatures are inside. ⁸Running down the centre of the store is a line of large wooden perches that look like coat racks. ⁹When customers pass by, the parrots and mynahs chained to these perches flutter their clipped wings in a useless attempt to escape. ¹⁰At the end of this centre aisle is a large plastic tub of dirty, stagnant-looking water containing a few motionless turtles. ¹¹The shelves against the left-hand wall are packed with all kinds of pet-related items. ¹²The smell inside the entire shop is an unpleasant mixture of strong chemical deodorizers, urine-soaked newspapers, and musty sawdust. ¹³Because so many animals are crammed together, the normally pleasant, slightly milky smell of the puppies and kittens is sour and strong. ¹⁴The droppings inside the uncleaned birdcages give off a dry, stinging odour. ¹⁵Visitors hurry out of the shop, anxious to feel fresh air and sunlight. ¹⁶The animals remain there.

▨ Questions

About Unity

1. Which paragraph lacks a topic sentence?

_____

2. Which sentence in the paragraph in "A Depressing Place" should be omitted in the interest of paragraph unity? (*Write the sentence number here.*)

_____

About Support

3. Label as *sight, touch, hearing,* or *smell* all the sensory details in the following sentences taken from the three paragraphs. The first one is done for you as an example.

          touch   *sight*   *sight*
a. I accidentally tipped an autograph-covered, slightly deflated basketball off

          sight   *hearing*   *sight*
one shelf, and the ball bounced with dull thuds across the width of the room.

b. Because so many animals are crammed together, the normally pleasant,

slightly milky smell of the puppies and kittens is sour and strong.

c. As I ran my fingers over the items on the dusty shelves, I noticed some

tarnished medals and faded ribbons for track accomplishments.

4. After which sentence in "A Depressing Place" are specific details needed?

    _____

About Coherence

5. Space signals (*above, next to, to the right,* and so on) are often used to help organize details in descriptive paragraphs. List four space signals that appear in "An Athlete's Room":

    _____

    _____

    _____

    _____

FORMS OF DESCRIPTIVE WRITING

All effective description records its subject by using a consistent and clear method of tracking or viewing that subject and by using the most accurate and vivid details appropriate for its purpose. While subjectively focused description relies on the writer's impressions of a subject, objective description seeks to present an impersonal and accurate word picture recorded by a camera-like "invisible writer."

Subjective Descriptions

- This chapter shows primarily personally based subjective descriptions. The writer's response to a subject is the essence of a subjective descriptive paragraph. The writer's dominant impression of some place, object, or person derives from and is coloured by his or her involvement with that subject. Descriptive paragraphs based on such personal response rely on details that consistently convey the writer's attitude toward the subject.
- The focus of a personal or subjective description may be subtly shifted by the writer's use of third-person point of view. An example of this difference in focus is the paragraph "A Depressing Place"; it focuses on the pet shop itself, not on the writer's feelings as she walks through it. Many details included could be considered objective details; anyone entering the pet shop would observe the sights, sounds, and smells. This choice of third-person focus often makes the paragraph more persuasive.

Objective Descriptions

- Some college and career writing requires more objectivity—less personal involvement in description. Objective descriptions are always written in the third-person point of view; the writer's aim is to record his or her subject with the impersonal accuracy of a camera.
- The focus of objective description is totally on its subject and on offering the reader an obvious and clear path to follow as he or she reads the description. The dominant impression in objective description is simply an overview of

the object or situation to be described; it does not include any indication of the writer's presence.

A writer approaching a writing task that requires effective description must first decide whether the purpose of that writing is to provide a personal response to the subject or to record that subject as accurately and impersonally as possible.

DEVELOPING A DESCRIPTIVE PARAGRAPH

Development through Prewriting

When Mariana was assigned a descriptive paragraph, she thought at first of describing her cubicle at work. She started by listing the details she noticed while looking around a place she knew inside out.

> adjustable black chair
> white Formica desk
> piles of paper
> computer and printer
> picture of Sebastian
> desk calendar

But Mariana quickly became bored with the very idea of putting together a paragraph. She said later, "As I wrote down what I saw in my cubicle, I was thinking, 'What a drag this assignment is.' I gave up and did some filing. Later that evening I told my friend Nestor that I was going to write a boring paragraph about my boring office. He started laughing at me. I asked what was so funny, and he said, 'You're so sure that an English assignment has to be boring that you deliberately picked a subject that bores you. Why don't you write about something you care about?' At first I was annoyed, but then I realized he was right. When I hear the words *writing* and *assignment* I automatically think 'boring pain in the neck' and just want to get it over with."

Mariana's attitude is anything but uncommon. Many students who are hesitant or inexperienced writers don't take the time to find a topic that interests them. They tend to leave facing their assignment until the last moment, then grab the first topic at hand and force themselves to write about it just for the sake of handing in the assignment. Like Mariana, they ensure that they (and probably their instructors, too) will be bored with the task.

In Mariana's case, she decided that this assignment would be different. Later that evening, when she talked to her mother on the phone, she mentioned a trip to the mall the two had made a few days earlier. Her mother was looking for a new collar and some toys for Sebastian, the family spaniel, so they went to a pet store. Mariana found the pet store a horrible place. "As I remembered the store, a lot of nasty details came back to me—sounds, smells, and sights. I didn't really want to recall them, but they made an impact on me," Mariana said. "I realized not only that it would be a lot easier to describe a place like that than my bland office cubicle, but that I might find it an interesting challenge to make a reader see it through my words. For me to realize writing could be enjoyable was a shock!"

Now that Mariana had her subject, she began to make a list of details about the pet shop.

Sawdust, animal droppings on floors of cages
Unhappy-looking puppies and kittens
Screech of birds
Chained parrots
Tanks with green dirty water
No place for animals to play
Bored-looking clerks
Animals scratching cages for attention
Strong urine smell

As she looked over her list of details, the word that came to mind was *depressing*. She decided this was the strongest feeling she'd had and that her topic sentence would be "The pet store in the mall is depressing." She then outlined her paragraph.

Topic Sentence: The pet store in the mall is <u>depressing</u>.

Subtopic 1: Puppies and kittens look miserable
Supporting Details:
a. scratching
b. trapped in small cages

Subtopic 2: Parrots and turtles
Supporting Details:
a. parrots are chained and wings are clipped
b. turtles in filthy tubs

Subtopic 3: Nasty smells
Supporting Details:
a. cleaning stuff, droppings, musty
b. should smell nice, like young animals

Mariana quickly tried to recapture her impressions in a first draft.

The pet store in the mall is depressing. There is sawdust and animal droppings all over the floor. Sad-looking puppies and kittens scratch on their cages for attention. In too many cages stacked up. Dead fish and motionless turtles float in tanks of greenish water. The loud screeching of birds is everywhere, and parrots with clipped wings try to fly off when customers get too near. Everywhere there is the smell of animal urine that has soaked through the sawdust and newspapers. The clerks, who should be cleaning the cages or patting the animals, stand around talking to each other and ignoring the animals.

Development through Revising

After class the next day, Mariana's instructor went over the students' first drafts. This is what he wrote on Mariana's paper:

This is a very good beginning. You have given strong details that appeal to readers' senses of smell, hearing, and sight.

In your next draft, organize your paragraph by using spatial order. Do this by describing your "way around the room" in some logical physical order—maybe from left to right, or from front to back. This way, you're taking readers through the store just the way they might go themselves.

I recommend that you be even more specific in your details—in what way did the puppies and kittens seem sad? Try to include some sharp descriptive words in each sentence so your picture in words is really vivid.

In response to her professor's suggestion about a spatial order or path through the store, Mariana rewrote the paragraph, beginning with the display window that attracts visitors, then going on to the store's right-hand wall, the centre aisle, and the left-hand wall. She ended the paragraph by taking the reader back outside the shop. Thinking about the store this way helped Mariana to remember and add a number of new specific details as well. She then wrote the second draft of "A Depressing Place" that appears on pages 167-68.

WRITING A DESCRIPTIVE PARAGRAPH

> ### How to Write a Descriptive Paragraph
>
> 1   Use all of your senses as you remember or observe your subject. In your prewriting, accumulate as many kinds of details as you can come up with. Try questioning yourself: "What do I feel when I touch this?" "What do I see when I look at it from this angle?"
>
> 2   When you have recorded as many details as possible, decide on the best way to track your progress as you describe your subject. If you describe a place, how will you take your reader along with you? If you describe a person or an object, where will you begin, and what path will you follow as you show your subject to your reader?
>
> 3   Decide on your main impression of or feeling about your subject, and write this down as a trial topic sentence.
>
> 4   Begin your formal outline with this topic sentence, and order your details in the outline according to the way your reader will view your subject along with you.
>
> 5   As you begin to draft your paragraph, revise and select only those details that contribute to your dominant impression. Try to use the most precise and accurate descriptive words possible for your details.
>
> 6   Conclude with a sentence that reminds the reader of your opening dominant impression.

■ **Writing Assignment 1**

Write a paragraph describing a special kind of room. Use as your topic sentence "I could tell by looking at the room that a _____ lived there."

There are many kinds of people who could be the focus for such a paragraph. You can select any one of the following, or think of some other type of person.

Photographer	Music lover	Carpenter
Cook	Video game addict	Baby
Student	Camper	Cat or dog lover
Musician	Grandparent	World traveller
Slob	Hockey player	Alcoholic
Outdoors person	Actor	Skateboarder

Prewriting

a   After choosing a topic, spend a few minutes making sure it will work. Prepare a list of all the details you can think of that support the topic. Next, list the five senses, and group as many details as possible under each sense heading. For example, the writer of "An Athlete's Room" made this list.

Sports trophy
Autographed basketball
Sports Illustrated
Baseball lamp
Sports schedule
Medals and ribbons
Sports print on bedspread, curtains
Sweat socks, T-shirts
Baseball cap
Baseball glove
Gym bag
Sports clippings

b   Using the Paragraph Outline Form on page 28, create an outline. Be sure your subtopics and supporting details follow a path or spatial method of organization. If you don't have enough details, choose another type of person, and check your new choice with a list of details before committing yourself to the topic. If your outline seems to lack details, try another prewriting technique.

c   As you begin to work on the first draft of your paragraph, keep in mind all four bases of effective writing.

Base 1: Unity. Develop your dominant impression and work to support it. Everything in the paragraph should support your point. For example, if you are writing about a soccer player's room, all the details should serve to show that the person loves soccer. Other details—a computer, a fish tank—should be omitted. Then, after your paragraph is finished, imagine omitting the keyword in your topic sentence. Your details alone should make it clear to the reader what word should fit in that empty space.

Base 2: Support. Sharpen your focus. Description depends on the use of *specific* rather than *general* descriptive words. For example:

General	*Specific*
Mess on the floor	Broken CD cases, wadded-up socks, and a pile of permanently open books
Ugly turtle tub	Large plastic tub of dirty, stagnant-looking water containing a few motionless turtles
Unpleasant smell	Unpleasant mixture of strong chemical deodorizers, urine-soaked newpapers, and musty sawdust

Remember that you want your readers to *see* or experience the room vividly as they read. Your words should be as detailed as a clear photograph and should give your readers a clear idea of the room. Use as many senses as possible in describing the room. Chiefly you will use sight, but to some extent you may be able to use touch, hearing, and smell as well.

Base 3: Coherence. Track your subject carefully. Organize your descriptive paragraph by using spatial order. Spatial order means that you move as a visitor's eye might move, from right to left or from larger items to smaller ones. For instance, the writer of "An Athlete's Room" presents an orderly description in which the eye moves from right to left around the room. Here are transition words that will help you connect your sentences as you describe the room:

to the left	across from	on the opposite side
to the right	above	nearby
next to	below	

Such transitions will help prevent you—and your reader—from getting lost as the description proceeds.

d Review your first draft with your outline. You may want to make a quick "map outline" of your prewriting or draft. Here is one possible map outline of a paragraph about a soccer player's room. Note that the details are organized according to spatial order—the author leads readers from the edges of the room toward the centre.

> Topic Sentence: I could tell by looking at the room that a soccer player lived there.
>
> 1. Walls
> 2. Bookcase
> 3. Desk
> 4. Chair
> 5. Floor

e Revise any parts of your prewriting or draft that do not follow the spatial order or path that you have decided on.

Revising

Read your descriptive paragraph out loud to a friend. Ask the friend to close his or her eyes and try to picture the room as you read. Read it aloud a second time. Ask your friend to answer these questions:

- Does every detail in the paragraph support the dominant impression in the topic sentence? Here's one way to find out: Ask your friend to imagine omitting the keyword or keywords (in the example above, *soccer player*) in your topic sentence. Would readers know what word or phrase should fit in that empty space?
- Are the details specific and vivid rather than general?
- Has the writer included details that appeal to as many senses as possible?
- Does the paragraph follow a logical spatial order?
- Has the writer used transitions (such as *on top of, beside, next to, to the left of*) to help the reader follow that order?

Continue revising your work until you and your reader can answer yes to all these questions.

Base 4: Sentence Skills. In the later drafts of your paragraph, edit carefully for sentence-skills mistakes, including spelling errors. Refer to the checklist of these skills on the inside front cover of this book.

Writing Assignment 2

Write a paragraph about a particular place that you can observe carefully or that you already know well. It might be one of the following or some other place:

Student lounge area	Hair salon
Car showroom	Doctor's or dentist's office
Gymnasium	Classroom
Fast-food restaurant	Bank
Inside of a car	Dressing room
Ladies' or men's washroom	Attic
Movie theatre	Street market
Auto repair garage	Place where you work
Music store	Porch

Prewriting

a **Consider the dominant impression you want to create.** Remember that, like all paragraphs, a descriptive paper must have an opening point. This point, or topic sentence, should state a dominant impression about the place you are describing. State the place you want to describe and the dominant impression you want to make in a single short sentence. The sentence can be refined later. For now, you just want to find and express a workable topic, an overview to guide your readers. You might write, for example, a sentence like one of the following:

The student lounge was hectic.
The music store was noisy.
The car's interior was very clean.
The dressing room in the department store was stifling.
The dentist's office was soothing.
The movie theatre was freezing.
The gymnasium was tense.
The attic was gloomy.
The restaurant was elegant.
The office where I work was strangely quiet.

b **Accumulate supporting details.** Now make a list of all the details you can think of that support the general impression. For example, the writer of "A Depressing Place" made the following list.

A Depressing Place
Puppies behind glass
Unpleasant smell
Chained birds
Rows of cages
Dirty tub of turtles
Stuffy atmosphere
Kittens in window
Sounds of caged animals
Droppings and urine on newspapers

c **Make your details specific and appealing to the senses.** Use as many senses as possible in describing a scene. Chiefly you will use sight, but to some extent you may be able to use touch, hearing, smell, and perhaps even taste as well. Remember that it is through the richness of your sense impressions that the reader will gain a picture of the scene.

d **Choose a method of organization to track your subject.** Organize your paper by using a spatial method of organization. For instance, the writer of "A Depressing Place" organizes the paper in terms of physical order (from one side of the pet shop to the centre to the other side).

Revising

As you are working on the drafts of your paper, refer to the checklist on the inside front cover. Make sure you can answer yes to the questions about unity, support, coherence, and sentence skills.

■ **Writing Assignment 3**

Write a paragraph describing a person. Here are some examples of people you might want to write about.

TV or movie personality	Co-worker
Instructor	Clergyperson
Employer	Police officer
Child	Store owner or manager
Older person	Bartender
Close friend	Joker
Enemy	Neighbour

Prewriting

a Begin by thinking of one thing, one characteristic that makes your subject most like himself or herself. That one characteristic is your dominant impression, your guiding focus for your paragraph; it can be an aspect of that person's personality, appearance, or behaviour.

Once you have chosen the person you will write about and the impression you plan to portray, put that information into a topic sentence.

Here are some possible topic sentences that mention a particular person and the dominant impression of that person. Your instructor may let you develop one of these or may require you to write your own.

Brendan gives the impression of being permanently nervous.
The old man was as faded and brittle as a dying leaf.
The child was an angelic little figure.
Our high-school principal resembled a cartoon drawing.
The young woman seemed to belong to another era.
Our neighbour is a fussy person.
The rock singer seemed to be plugged in to some special kind of energy source.
The drug addict looked as lifeless as a corpse.
My friend Mike is a slow, deliberate person.
The owner of that grocery store seems burdened with troubles.

b Make a list of the person's qualities that support or illustrate your topic sentence. Write quickly; don't worry if you find yourself writing down something that doesn't quite fit. You can always edit the list later. For now, just write down all the details that occur to you that support the dominant impression you want to convey. Include details that involve as many senses as possible (sight, sound, hearing, touch, smell). For instance, here's a list one writer jotted down to support the topic sentence "The child was an angelic little figure."

soft black ringlets of hair
pink cheeks
wide shining eyes
shrieking laugh
joyful smile
starched white dress
white flowers in hair

c Edit your list, striking out details that don't support your topic sentence and adding others that do. The author of the paragraph on the angelic child crossed out one detail from the original list and added a new one.

> soft black ringlets of hair
> pink cheeks
> wide shining eyes
> ~~shrieking laugh~~
> joyful smile
> starched white dress
> white flowers in hair
> *sweet singing voice*

d Decide on a spatial order of organization. In the example above, the writer ultimately decided to describe the child from head to toe.

e Write an outline for your paragraph, based on the organization you have chosen.

f Then write the first draft of your paragraph.

Revising

Put your paragraph away for a day or so if at all possible. When you read it and your later drafts, ask yourself these questions:

- Does my topic sentence clearly state my dominant impression of my subject?
- If I left out the keywords in my topic sentence, the words that state my dominant impression, would a reader know what idea fits there?
- Does every detail support my topic sentence?
- Are the details I have used specific rather than vague and general?
- Have I used a logical spatial organization that helps my reader follow my description?
- Have I checked my paper for sentence skills, as listed on the inside front cover of this book?

Continue revising until you can answer yes to all these questions.

■ Writing Assignment 4

Write a paragraph describing an animal you have spent some time with—a pet, a friend's pet, an animal you've seen in a park or zoo or even on television. Write this paragraph about how the animal looks and behaves. Select details that support a dominant impression of your subject. Once you decide on the impression you wish to convey, compose a topic sentence, such as either of those below, to summarize the details you wish to use.

> Joker the gorilla's appearance gives no hint of his intelligence and gentleness.
> The plushy grey squirrel who has decided to live in my yard shows surprising agility and energy.

Remember to provide colourful, detailed descriptions to help your readers picture the features and behaviour you are writing about. Note the contrast in the two items below.

Lacks rich descriptive details: The squirrel was grey and enjoyed the back steps.

Includes rich descriptive details: On our back steps, the plushy-furred grey squirrel dug a hole in the dirt in a planter full of marigolds. He then carefully deposited an acorn in the hole and covered it with soil, his fluffy tail bobbing energetically the whole time.

■ Writing Assignment 5

Option A: Imagine that you are an interior designer. A new residence is going to be built on your college campus, and you have been asked to create a model residence room for two students. Write a paragraph describing your design of the room, specifying what it would include and how it would be arranged. In your prewriting for this assignment, you might list all the relevant student needs you can think of, such as a good study space, storage space, and appropriate lighting and colours. Then put all the parts together so that they work well as a whole. Use a spatial order in your paragraph to help readers "see" your room. If you are short on ideas, look up a few colleges and universities on a search engine and see if there is information on residence facilities on their websites.

Begin with the following topic sentence or something like it:

My design for a residence room offers both efficiency and comfort for two students.

Feel free to use a less than serious tone.

Option B: Alternatively, write a paragraph describing your ideal design of another type of room, including any of the following:

Classroom	Kitchen
Porch	Restaurant
Game room	Bakery

■ Writing Assignment 6

Writing About a Reading Selection: Read the selection "Bullies in School" by Kathleen Berger on pages 521–25. The article describes behaviours of those who bully others. In fact, everyone, male or female, can relate in some way either to being a bully or to being bullied at some time. Many people have been on both the giving and receiving ends of bullying.

Write a descriptive paragraph about a bully you have encountered. Focus on three aspects of this person: his or her appearance, actions, and effects on others. Help your reader vividly imagine the bully by providing concrete details that illustrate each aspect. Your topic sentence could be something like the following: "In grade eight, I attracted the attention of Margot Fenner and became a member of what she called 'the Losers Club.'"

REVIEWING THE LEARNING OUTCOMES FOR DESCRIPTIVE WRITING

When you complete any of the writing assignments in this chapter, review your work to decide how well it meets the following tests.

1 Does your paragraph begin with a well-focused statement of your dominant impression of your subject? Is this dominant impression supported by each idea and supporting detail in your paragraph?

2 Are all your details specific and vivid? Are your descriptive words as precise as they can be? Do your details appeal to several different senses?

3 Can your reader follow your descriptive path as you move through or around your subject? Have you provided transitional words and phrases to help the reader and to reinforce your tracking of your subject?

4 Does your concluding sentence return to and reinforce your dominant impression?

Visit the *English Skills with Readings* Online Learning Centre at **www.mcgrawhill.ca/college/langan** to access self-quizzes, bonus material on study and research skills, web resources, and other learning and study tools.

Explaining a Process • Examining Cause and Effect • Comparing or Contrasting • Defining
rm • Dividing and Classifying • Describing a Scene or Person • Narrating an Event • Argui
Position • Explaining a Process • Examining Cause and Effect • Comparing or Contrasting
efining a Term • Dividing and Classifying • Describing a Scene or Person • Narrating
ent • Arguing a Position • Explaining a Process • Examining Cause and Effect • Compari

CHAPTER 10

Providing Examples

LEARNING OUTCOMES

By completing the activities and writing tasks in this chapter, you will write a paragraph that explains its point with examples and effectively

- opens with a topic sentence or controlling idea that makes a specific and clear point about a subject;
- offers three subtopics that are primary examples to support your point;
- supplies supporting details (which may themselves be secondary examples) for each subtopic; and
- ends with a conclusion that returns to your main point and sums up what your examples have clarified or explained.

Examples in exposition provide readers with clarifications or explanations of the writer's ideas. If narration offers sharing of experience, and description offers sharing of impressions, exposition with examples offers a chance to share knowledge or understanding of a subject. Each time an idea is supported with apt, specific, and sharply written examples, the reader's ability to grasp that idea is increased; examples help readers to see fully what the writer means.

Our daily conversations are full of *examples*—that is, details, particulars, specific instances—to *explain or make clear* statements that we make.

Statement	*Example*
The IGA was crowded today.	There were at least four carts lined up at each of the checkout counters, and it took me forty-five minutes to get through a line.

Examples sometimes provide *reasons why* we make a particular point and may help to prove to readers the truth of that statement.

Statement	*Example*
The corduroy shirt I bought is badly made.	The first time I washed it, the colour began to fade, one button cracked and another fell off, and the sleeves shrank almost five centimetres.

181

Examples offer *specifics*, or hooks, for readers to grasp and remember.

The cat can be very annoying.	She howls for fifteen minutes at a time and uses her claws to climb the curtains, only to get stuck at the top and howl some more.

In each case, the examples help us *see for ourselves* the truth of the statement that has been made. In paragraphs, too, explanatory examples help the audience fully understand and perhaps be persuaded by a point. Lively, specific examples also add interest to a paragraph. Consider the sentences you have just read; they are *examples* used to support the point that examples are essential to effective writing. Instructors and textbooks teach by constantly using examples.

All forms of expository and persuasive writing required during college and careers make use of examples; explaining by example is a basic and essential skill that is practised throughout life.

In this chapter, you will be asked to provide a series of examples to support a topic sentence. First read the next two paragraphs; they both use examples to develop their points. Then answer the questions that follow.

PARAGRAPHS TO CONSIDER

The Cruelty of Children

[1]Children can be very cruel. [2]For one thing, they start very early to use words that wound. [3]Three-year-olds in nursery school, for example, call each other "dum-dum" or "weirdo," and slightly older children use nicknames like "fatty" or "four-eyes" to tease their schoolmates. [4]Children who are just a bit older learn facts about other kids from their parents and use those facts to make someone break down and cry. [5]Perhaps even more harmful, children attack one another physically. [6]For instance, whenever a group of elementary-school children come home from school, there is a lot of pushing, tripping, punching, and pinching. [7]An argument may end in shoving and hair-pulling. [8]But far worse than harsh words or physical violence is the emotional hurt that children can cause their classmates by their cruelty. [9]By junior high school days, for example, young teenagers start to shut out the people they do not like. [10]They ignore the kids whose looks, clothes, interests, or finances differ from their own. [11]Popular kids form groups, and the unpopular ones are left to face social isolation, loneliness, and depression. [12]Many adults think that childhood is an ideal time, but terribly cruel things can happen at this stage in life.

Office Politics

[1]Office politics may be Canada's real national sport, a destructive game played everywhere by several kinds of people. [2]A part-time worker often has a clearer view of these goings-on. [3]For instance, two supervisors may get into a conflict over how to do a certain job. [4]Instead of working out an agreement like adults, they carry on a power struggle that turns the poor employees working

under them into human hockey pucks being shot back and forth between two angry players. ⁵Another common example of office politics is the ambitious worker who takes credit for other people's ideas. ⁶He or she will chat in a friendly fashion with new or less experienced employees, getting their ideas about how to run things more smoothly. ⁷These people seem so pleasant at first. ⁸Next thing anyone knows, Mr. or Ms. Idea-Stealer is having a private meeting with the boss and getting promotion points for his or her creativity. ⁹Yet another star player in office politics is the spy. ¹⁰This employee acts very chummy with other workers, often dropping little comments about things he or she doesn't like in the workplace. ¹¹The spy encourages people to talk about their problems at work, how they don't like their boss, the pay, and the working conditions. ¹²Then the spy goes straight back and repeats all he or she has heard to the management, and the employees get blamed for their "poor attitude." ¹³A final example of office politics is people who gossip. ¹⁴Too often the players on the office politics team can turn a perfectly fine work situation into a stressful one.

■ **Questions**

About Unity

1. Which two sentences in "Office Politics" are irrelevant to the point about people's office behaviour? *(Write the sentence numbers here.)* _____
    _____

About Support

2. In "The Cruelty of Children," how many examples are given of children's cruelty?

    _____ one _____ two _____ three _____ four

3. After which sentence in "Office Politics" are specific details needed?

    _____

About Coherence

4. What are the three main transition words used in "The Cruelty of Children"?

    a. _____

    b. _____

    c. _____

5. What are two of the transition words in "Office Politics"?

    a. _____

    b. _____

6. Which paragraph clearly uses emphatic order to organize its details, saving for last what the writer regards as the most important example?

_____

_____

DEVELOPING AN EXAMPLES PARAGRAPH

Development through Prewriting

Backing up your statements with clear, specific illustrations is the key to a successful examples paragraph. When Vince, the writer of "Office Politics," was assigned an examples paragraph, he at first did not know what to write about.

Then his instructor made a suggestion. "Imagine yourself having lunch with friends," he said. "You're telling them *how* you feel about something and *why*. Maybe you're saying, 'I am so fed up with my graphics instructor!' or 'The White Stripes are really incredible.' You wouldn't just stop there—you'd go on to say what that instructor does that is so annoying, or in what ways that group is so good. In other words, you would make a general point and back it up with examples. That's what you need to do in this paper."

Later, Vince was on the phone with his brother. He was complaining about the office where he worked. "Suddenly I realized what I was doing," he said. "I was making a statement—I hate the game-playing at work—and giving examples of those political moves people make. I knew what I could write about."

Vince hung up and started scribbling down everything he could think of about politics at his job. He freewrote for ten or fifteen minutes, and this is what he came up with.

> Of all the places I've worked since I was in high school this one is the worst that way. Can't trust anybody there—everybody's playing some kind of game and hoping to score. Maybe they think I can't see them doing stuff because I'm only part-time there. Worst of all is Mr. Simchuk and the way he pretends to be friendly with people. Gets them to complain about Ms. Wyland and Mr. Martinez and then runs back to them and reports everything. He ought to realize that people are catching on to his game and figuring out what a jerk he is. Melissa steals people's ideas and then takes the credit for them. Anything to get brownie points. She's always out for herself first, you can tell. Then there's all the gossip that goes on. You think you're in a soap opera or something and it's kind of fun in a way but it's also very distracting people always talking about each other and worrying about what they say about you. And people always talk about our bosses a lot. Nobody knows why Ms. Wyland and Mr. Martinez hate each other so much but they each want the workers on their side. You do something one boss's way, but then the other boss appears and is angry you're not doing it another way. You don't know what to do sometimes to keep people happy.

Vince read over his freewriting and still felt a little confused about what he was trying to say. He then spent some time asking questions about his paragraph. (You may find a second stage of prewriting, one in which you try another technique, to be very effective.) "Exactly what do I want my point to be?" he asked. "And exactly how am I going to support that point?" Keeping those questions in mind, he tried a few different outlines and wound up with the following short-form outline.

Office politics are ruining the office:

1. Simchuk reports people's complaints
   —his weaselly 'chats'
2. Melissa steals ideas
   —'oh, how would <u>you</u> do this?'
3. People gossip
4. Ms. Wyland and Mr. Martinez make workers pick sides
   —nobody feels safe or knows what to do

Working from his sketch outline, Vince then tried the following first draft.

My office is being ruined by office politics. Maybe they think I don't see things because I only work half-time. It seems like everybody is trying to play some kind of game to get ahead and don't care what it does to anybody else. One example is Simchuk. Although he pretends to be friendly with people, he isn't sincere. What he is trying to do is get them to complain about their bosses. Once they do, he goes back to the bosses and tells them what's been said and gets the worker in trouble. I've seen the same kind of thing happen at one or two other places I've worked. Melissa is another example of someone who plays office politics games. She steals other people's ideas and takes the credit for them. I had a good idea once to save paper. I told her we ought to use mostly e-mail for office memos instead of printing them all out. She went to Ms. Wyland and pretended the idea was her own. I guess I was partly to blame for not acting on the idea myself. And Ms. Wyland and Mr. Martinez hate each other and try to get us to take sides in their conflict. Then there is all the gossip that goes on. People do a lot of backbiting and you have to be very careful about your behaviour or people will start talking about you. All in all, office politics is a real problem where I work.

Development through Revising

After completing his first draft, Vince put it aside until the next day. When he reread it, he said, "I think the paragraph would be stronger if I made it about office politics in general, as a kind of 'national thing,' instead of just politics in my office. The things I was writing about happen all over the place, not just where I work. Also, it sounds a bit like I'm just ranting here. The professor wants us to try some third-person writing so this is a good time for it, I think. Also, I need some transitions to help people follow when I move from one example to another."

With these thoughts in mind, Vince started revising his paper, and after several drafts he produced the paragraph that appears on pages 182-83.

WRITING AN EXAMPLES PARAGRAPH

How to Write a Paragraph That Explains with Examples

1   Begin by prewriting to accumulate details about your subject. Questioning, list making, and clustering are good methods for generating examples. Visualizing a place, person, or situation helps you discover your ideas.

2   Write a few trial topic sentences, then decide which one best states a clear point of view or controlling attitude about your subject. Examples paragraphs sometimes begin by specifying how many subtopic examples the paragraph will provide: for example, "Three situations that occurred last week show how stubborn my friend Javier can be."

3   Begin your paragraph outline with your best topic sentence, and select three primary examples as subtopics to explain, clarify, or prove your topic's point. Write these as subtopic sentences (subtopic + attitude). Next, note in point form under each subtopic any supporting details or secondary examples that further illustrate your subtopics. (See Writing Assignment 1 for an illustration of outlining.)

4   As you draft and revise, ask yourself if your major or primary examples and details or secondary examples truly support your point. Eliminate non-supporting material and add any clarifying details that may occur to you.

5   In your concluding sentence, sum up the way in which your examples have demonstrated your point.

■ **Writing Assignment 1**

The assignment here is to complete an unfinished paragraph outline that has as its topic sentence "My husband Sean is a selfish person." Provide the supporting details needed to fill out the subtopic examples of Sean's selfishness. The first subtopic example out of four has been supplied for you.

How to Proceed

For this assignment, you will provide secondary examples, examples that support the main subtopic examples provided on the outline form on the following page. Note that this paragraph outline will show two types of examples: primary or subtopic examples (refusal to move, Sean's constant choice of vacations, selfish spending habits, and ignoring child care) and secondary supporting examples for each subtopic.

Point

Topic Sentence: My husband Sean is a selfish person.

Support

Subtopic 1: For one thing, he refuses to move out of the city, even though it is a bad place to raise the children.

Supporting Details (examples, explanations):

a.   We inherited some money when my parents died, and it might be enough for a down payment on a small house in a nearby town. But Sean says he would miss his buddies in the neighbourhood.

b. _____

c. _____

Subtopic 2: Also, when we go on vacation, we always go where Sean wants to go.

Supporting Details (examples, explanations):

a _____

b. _____

c. _____

Subtopic 3: Another example of Sean's selfishness is that he always spends any budget money that is left over.

Supporting Details (examples, explanations):

a. _____

b. _____

c. _____

Subtopic 4: Finally, Sean leaves all the work of caring for the children to me.

Supporting Details (examples, explanations):

a. _____

b. _____

c. _____

Prewriting

a On a separate piece of paper, jot down a couple of answers for each of the following questions:

- What specific vacations did the family go on because Sean wanted to go? Give places, length of stay, time of year. What vacations has the family never gone on (for example, to visit the wife's relatives), even though the wife wanted to?
- What specific items has Sean bought for himself (rather than for the whole family's use) with leftover budget money?
- What chores and duties involved in the everyday caring for the children has Sean never done?

Your instructor may ask you to work with one or two other students in generating the details needed to develop the three examples in the paragraph. Someone from each group may then be asked to read the group's details aloud, with the class deciding which details are the most effective for each example.

Here and in general in your writing, try to generate *more* supporting material than you need. You are then in a position to choose the *most convincing details* for your paper.

b Read over the details you have generated and decide which sound most effective. Jot down additional details as they occur to you.

c Take your best details, reshape them as needed, and use them to complete the paragraph about Sean.

Revising

Read over your paragraph. Ask yourself these questions or discuss them in your group:

- Do the examples really support the idea that Sean is selfish?
- Are there enough examples to make each subtopic or primary example clear?
- Are there enough examples to make the overall point about Sean and have people agree with it?
- Are any of the examples too similar to one another?
- Have I or we checked the paragraph for spelling and other sentence skills, as listed on the inside front cover of this book?

Continue revising until you can answer yes to all these questions.

Writing Assignment 2

Write a paragraph providing examples that clarify and explain one quality of a person you know well. The person might be a member of your family, a friend, a roommate, a boss or supervisor, a neighbour, an instructor, or someone else. Following are some descriptive words that can be applied to people. They are only suggestions; you can write about any other specific quality.

Honest	Hard-working	Jealous
Bad-tempered	Supportive	Materialistic
Ambitious	Suspicious	Sarcastic
Bigoted	Open-minded	Self-centred
Considerate	Lazy	Spineless
Argumentative	Independent	Good-humoured
Soft-hearted	Stubborn	Cooperative
Energetic	Flirtatious	Disciplined
Patient	Irresponsible	Sentimental
Reliable	Stingy	Defensive
Generous	Trustworthy	Dishonest
Persistent	Aggressive	Insensitive
Shy	Courageous	Unpretentious
Sloppy	Compulsive	Tidy

Prewriting

a Select the individual you will write about and the quality of this person that you will focus on.

b Make a list of examples that will support and clearly explain the point of your topic sentence. For example, if you decide to write about your brother's irresponsibility, jot down several examples of times when he showed this quality. Part of your list might look like this.

> Lost rent money
> Forgot to return borrowed textbooks
> Didn't show up for big family dinner
> Left dog alone in the apartment for two days
> Left my bike out in the rain
> Missed conference with instructor

Another way to get started, or a second way of prewriting, is to ask yourself questions about your topic and write down the answers. Again, if you were writing about your brother's irresponsibility, you might ask yourself questions such as these.

> *How* has he been irresponsible?
> *What* are examples of times he's shown this quality?
> *What* happened on these occasions?
> *Who* was involved?
> *What were the results* of his actions?

The answers to these questions should serve as an excellent source of details for the paragraph.

c   Think about categories or subtopics. Read over your list or your answers to the questions and see how you might group the items into categories. The list above, for example, could be broken into three categories that might make good subtopics: apartment, home, and college.

> Lost rent money (apartment)
> Forgot to return borrowed textbooks (college)
> Didn't show up for big family dinner (home)
> Left dog alone in the apartment for two days (apartment)
> Left my bike out in the rain (home)
> Missed conference with instructor (college)

Another way of categorizing these details might be to consider who the irresponsibility affects most—the brother himself and other people.

d   **Make an outline showing subtopics and support.** Your outline should be made up of the strongest examples from the prewriting material you have generated. As you make this outline, group related details together according to the catagories you chose, creating subtopics or subheadings. For example, the items in the list about the irresponsible brother can be categorized into subtopics as follows.

> At apartment
> Lost rent money
> Left dog alone in apartment
>
> At home
> Missed family dinner
> Left bike in rain
>
> At school
> Didn't return textbooks
> Missed conference

e   **Write the topic sentence containing your subject and overall attitude toward it.** This first sentence should tell the name of the person you are writing about, your relationship to the person, and the specific quality you are focusing on. For example, you might write, "Linda is a flirtatious girl I know at school," or "Stubbornness is Uncle Carl's outstanding characteristic."

   Do not begin with more than one quality ("I have a cousin named Jamal who is soft-hearted and generous") or with a vague general quality ("My boss is a good person"). Focus on *one specific quality.*

f   **Develop enough specific and typical examples.** Remember that you don't want to *tell* readers about the person; rather, you want to *show* the person by detailing words, actions, or both. Provide *enough* specific details so that you solidly support your point.

g   **Write a concluding sentence that sums up your examples and reinforces your point.**

Revising

It is very hard to criticize your own work honestly, especially right after you've done it and it's still "warm" from your efforts. If it is at all possible, put your paragraph away for a day or so and return to it with fresh eyes. Better yet, wait a day and read it aloud to someone whose judgment you trust.

Read the paragraph with these questions in mind:

- Does my topic sentence clearly state whom I am writing about, what that person's relationship is to me, and what quality of that person I am going to focus on?
- Do the examples I provide truly show that my subject has the quality I'm writing about?
- Have I provided enough specific details in my paragraph to solidly illustrate and back up my point that my subject has a certain quality?
- Have I organized the details in my paragraph into several clearly defined categories or subtopics?
- Have I used transition words such as *also, in addition, for example*, and *for instance* to help the reader follow my train of thought?
- Have I summed up my view of my subject in my closing sentence?
- Have I checked my paragraph for sentence skills, as listed on the inside front cover of this book?

Continue revising your work until you and your reader can answer yes to all these questions.

■ Writing Assignment 3

Write a paragraph that uses examples to develop one of the following statements or a related statement of your own.

1. _____ is a distracting place to try to study.

2. The daily life of a student is filled with conflicts.

3. Abundant evidence exists that Canada has become a health-conscious nation.

4. Despite computerized techniques, animated films are still time-consuming to make!

5. One of my instructors, _____, has some good [*or* unusual] teaching techniques.

6. Wasted electricity is all around us.

7. Life in Canada [*or* your city or town] is faster-paced than ever before.

8. Violence on television [*or* video games] is widespread.

9. Women [*or* men] today are wearing some ridiculous fashions.

10. Some students here at _____ do not care about learning [*or* are overly concerned about marks].

Be sure to choose specific and related examples that truly support your point. They should be relevant facts, statistics, personal experiences, or incidents you have heard or read about. Organize your paragraph by grouping several examples that support your point. Save the most vivid, most convincing, or most important example for last.

■ Writing Assignment 4

Write a paragraph with this topic sentence: "The diet of the average Canadian is unhealthy." Using strategies described in "Research Skills" on the Online Learning Centre, find three strong pieces of support for this point. Be sure to give credit for paraphrased material and to cite any quoted phrases correctly.

■ Writing Assignment 5

Imagine that you are a television critic for a local newspaper. Your job is to recommend to viewers, every day, which programs are most worth watching. Today you have decided there is nothing particularly good on TV. Therefore, your plan is to write a one-paragraph column about TV commercials, supporting this point: "Television commercials are more entertaining than the programs they interrupt."

To prepare for this article, spend some time watching television, taking detailed notes about some of the advertisements. Decide on two or three ways in which ads are entertaining; these will be the main subtopics in your outline. Then choose at least one commercial to use as a specific example to illustrate each of those points. Listed below are some entertaining qualities that may be seen in commercials:

Humour
Music
Cartoons or animation
Beauty
Cleverness
Suspense

■ Writing Assignment 6

Writing about a Reading Selection: Read the selection "Anxiety: Challenge by Another Name" by James Lincoln Collier on pages 515-17. One of Collier's corollaries to his basic rule about anxiety is "You can't learn if you don't try." Write a paragraph using this statement as your main idea. Support it with examples from your own experience, someone else's experience, or both. For instance, you could write about a time when you learned something useful by daring to give a new experience a try. You may then provide other similar examples of your own or, alternatively, examples of times when you did not dare to try something different. In your conclusion, include a final thought about what you learned from the sum of the examples your paragraph presents.

REVIEWING THE LEARNING OUTCOMES FOR PROVIDING EXAMPLES

After completing any of the writing assignments in this chapter, review your work, using the following questions, to see how well it meets the learning outcomes for this chapter.

1 Do you open with a topic sentence that makes a specific and clear point about your subject?

2 Is your main point supported by three subtopics that are your primary examples?

3 For each subtopic or primary example, are there enough specific details or secondary examples to explain or clarify your subtopics and add to your main point?

4 Do you conclude with a statement that returns to your main point and sums up the meaning of your paper?

Visit the *English Skills with Readings* Online Learning Centre at **www.mcgrawhill.ca/college/langan** to access self-quizzes, bonus material on study and research skills, web resources, and other learning and study tools.

plaining a Process • Examining Cause and Effect • Comparing or Contrasting • Defining a
ividing and Classifying • Describing a Scene or Person • Narrating an Event • Arguing a Po.
xplaining a Process • Examining Cause and Effect • Comparing or Contrasting • Defining a
ividing and Classifying • Describing a Scene or Person • Narrating an Event • Arguing a Po.
Explaining a Process • Examining Cause and Effect • Comparin

CHAPTER 11

Explaining a Process

LEARNING OUTCOMES

The goal of any process writing is for its readers to be able to successfully complete the procedure it sets out. By completing this chapter's activities and carefully following the instructions for writing assignments, you will write a process paragraph that

- is appropriate to the knowledge level and ability of its readers;
- opens with a clear statement of the value and purpose of the process to be followed and of its approximate degree of difficulty;
- tells readers exactly what they will need (equipment, time, space, tools, and so on) to complete the process successfully;
- offers complete, carefully ordered steps and explanations for each stage of the process;
- mentions both possible problems and potential difficulties that may occur; and
- concludes with a reassurance of the value of the process for the reader.

Process writing explains how to do something or describes how something occurred. The most common and useful form of process writing is *instructive*; its purpose is to explain *how to* do something and *why* following its instructions will achieve the desired result. Process writing always sets out its goal or end product and offers a time-sequenced series of steps for reaching that goal.

Everyone performs activities that are processes, or series of steps carried out in a definite order. Many of these processes are familiar and automatic: tying shoelaces, using a vending machine, and starting a car. Similarly, everyone routinely follows written instructions every day: working through textbook exercises or even following the commands in any word-processing program. In other cases, when we are asked for directions to a particular place or when we try to read and follow the directions for some new piece of technology, we are painfully conscious of the whole series of steps involved in the process. Process writing requires us to become aware of the steps in a procedure and of the stages into which we group these steps for ease of following them.

Process writing skills and techniques are used constantly in college and career writing. Students in business, human services, and technology programs must frequently write both instructions and step-by-step descriptions of procedures and changes in situations.

In this chapter, you will be asked to write a process paragraph—one that explains clearly how to do or make something. To prepare for this assignment, you should first read the student process paragraphs and respond to the questions that follow.

Note: In process writing, where you are often giving instructions, the pronoun *you* can appropriately be used. One of the model paragraphs here uses *you*. Indeed, much of this book, which gives instruction on how to write effectively, uses *you*, a style known as direct address.

PARAGRAPHS TO CONSIDER

Sneaking into the House at Night

[1]Your first step is bringing your key along with you. [2]Obviously, you don't want to have to knock on the door at 1:30 in the morning and rouse your parents out of bed. [3]Second, make it a point to stay out past midnight. [4]If you come in before then, your father might still be up. [5]You would find it hard to face his disapproving look after a night out. [6]All you need in your life right now is for him to make you feel guilty. [7]Trying to make it as a college student is as much as most people are ready to handle. [8]Next, be careful to be very quiet upon entering the house. [9]This involves lifting the front door up slightly as you open it, so that it does not creak. [10]It also means treating the floor and steps like a minefield, stepping carefully over the spots that squeak. [11]Finally, stop briefly in the bathroom without turning on the light and then tiptoe to your room, put your clothes in a pile on a chair, and slip quietly into bed. [12]With this careful method of sneaking into the house at night, you can avoid some major hassles with your parents.

How Shareen Broke the D Barrier

[1]Shareen decided she wanted to excel when she returned to college at twenty-nine, but she just was not sure how. [2]Her first-semester transcripts were a long list of Bs, with a glaring D in English. [3]First, she acknowledged the biggest problem she had to tackle: the D, with the writing problems it represented. [4]The fact that she couldn't seem to write clearly was dragging down her marks on written assignments in business courses as well. [5]So after avoiding the campus tutorial centre for three months, she decided her second move would be to gather up her red-ink-scarred essays and register for weekly sessions with a tutor. [6]At the same time, Shareen realized she had to face another potential problem: time. [7]As a next step, she would either have to cut back on hours at her part-time job or keep her daughter in daycare for several more hours a day. [8]Shareen decided the best decision was to stop working

Wednesday evenings. [9]A stroke of luck followed her decision: her aunt Bharati offered to loan Shareen her computer and printer, so she could work at home instead of waiting to use the college computers. [10]Now she could work more conveniently, without paying for extra daycare; she was motivated to follow her tutor's advice and not try to write every essay in a single draft. [11]The computer allowed Shareen to take the final step toward improving her writing. [12]She started to spend twice as long revising a paper as she had spent writing her first draft. [13]Because Shareen no longer felt the need to try to write a "perfect" first draft, she actually started to enjoy writing, seeing it as a puzzle to solve. [14]The final step was pure lucky coincidence, because Shareen was a born problem-solver. [15]The result of her decision, her follow-up, and her revising efforts began to arrive when three English papers came back to her with Bs and encouraging comments on them, instead of Ds. [16]And the final, most satisfying moment arrived in the last week of classes, when Shareen received an A on both a business report and an English research paper. [17]She had broken both the B and the D barriers and was on the way to excelling at college.

Note: This paragraph *describes* a process or a transitional series of stages. The writer is analyzing a situation or result and tracing the steps by which his or her subject arrived at that result. *Descriptive process writing* does not show "how to"; it analyzes a result and describes each stage that led to it. Students in technological and science-based programs will find descriptive process writing skills extremely useful.

■ Questions

About Unity

1. Which paragraph lacks a topic sentence?

   _____

2. Which two sentences in "Sneaking into the House at Night" should be eliminated in the interest of paragraph unity? (*Write the sentence numbers here.*)

   _____ _____

About Support

3. After which sentence in "How Shareen Broke the D Barrier" are supporting

   details needed? _____

4. Summarize the four steps in the process of breaking the D barrier.

   a. _____

   b. _____

   c. _____

   d. _____

About Coherence

5. Do these paragraphs use time order or emphatic order?

    _____

6. List the four main transition words in "Sneaking into the House at Night."

    a. _____   c. _____

    b. _____   d. _____

DEVELOPING A PROCESS PARAGRAPH

Development through Prewriting

To be successful, a process paragraph or essay must explain clearly each step in an activity or sequence of events. The key to preparing to write such an assignment is thinking through the activity or sequence as though you are doing it or experiencing it for the first time. Shareen is the author of "How Shareen Broke the D Barrier." As her paragraph relates, she had done poorly in her English classes before she put her mind to doing better. She debated possible topics for her paragraph, then realized that her previous semester's improvement in writing skills involved a process worth describing.

She started by doing something she never used to do: she did some prewriting, making a list of the realizations and steps she went through on the path to writing better papers.

> Borrowed Auntie's computer
> Couldn't work at college on computers there
> No time because of looking after Kerima
> Went for weekly tutoring
> Spent a lot of time on tutorial work
> Too many work hours every week
> Learned to take writing "one step at a time"
> Not trying to fix everything at once
> Daycare was expensive
> Could work at home and not use daycare

Next, she numbered the steps she had gone through in the order in which she'd experienced them. She crossed out some items she realized weren't parts of the process of becoming a better writer and added some revisions and new items that seemed necessary.

> *6* Borrowed Auntie's computer
> *4* Couldn't work at college on computers there—used a lot of time waiting
> ~~No time because of looking after Kerima~~
> *2* Went for weekly tutoring
> ~~Spent a lot of time on tutorial work~~
> *3* Too many work hours every week—cut down on nights
> *7* Started to work on essays on computer at night—it was not hard
> ~~Learned to take writing "one step at a time"~~

8 Not trying to fix everything at once

9 Fixing and changing more important than just writing—getting it right takes time

~~Daycare was expensive~~

5 Could work at home and not use daycare

1 Admitted I needed some outside help

Then Shareen grouped her items into four stages: (1) admitting she had to face her problem and doing something about it; (2) realizing she needed more time to work on her writing and figuring out what to do; (3) giving up work one evening and being loaned a computer, which made it easier to work at home; (4) starting to follow her tutor's advice and take writing "one step at a time," leaving lots of time for revision.

Shareen was ready to write her first draft now.

> I was always a perfectionist. So returning to college as a mature student offered me a lot of challenges, the worst of which was English. At the end of my first semester, it was my only D. So, if you are facing problems with English and writing, you may want to find out how I faced this challenge. I didn't want to admit that I needed help (after all, I'm an adult), but my grade point average was getting pulled down by that D, and I wanted to stay in International Business. Finally, I went to the tutoring centre—they were really nice there. But I had another problem to cope with. I didn't have enough extra time to devote to writing drafts and going over them because I worked three nights a week. So I knew I'd either have to keep Kerima in daycare longer or give up one of those evenings of work. Plus the computer rooms at college are always full, and I felt pressured trying to work there and too tired to think after waiting for my chance. My next stage was a lucky break—my auntie Bharati lent me her computer and printer! So now, after I got Kerima to sleep, I could sit comfortably in my sweatpants and follow the steps my tutor showed me. At first I didn't want to keep going back to the same page of writing. But really it was like I stopped trying to be perfect, and somehow got better—weird. In fact, the most amazing part of this process is that I get at least Bs now, and sometimes As on both my business and English papers.

Development through Revision

After Shareen wrote her first draft, she showed it to a classmate for her comments. Here are the notes her classmate made.

> *In order to make this a good process paragraph, I think you need to do a couple of things here.*
>
> *First, although this paper is based on what you went through, I think it's a little too much about your own experience. I wonder if other people can relate to it. I don't mean you should take yourself out of it completely—this is kind of inspiring, so your personal stuff helps make it strong that way. But I think what I mean is this paragraph needs to be more about the process you went through, so someone could realistically try some of these things if they needed to. Do you see what I mean?*

Second, and we've heard this one often enough—you need a good topic sentence that explains what process you're going to describe.

Third, you've got some transitions in there, so I have a rough idea of what happened when, but you could use some more. And I think the stages themselves could be clearer. Maybe you could sort out some of those details into neater "packages."

But don't be offended, because I think this is a great inspiration to people—just tell them how you did it, and kind of step into the background a bit.

When Shareen read her classmate's comments, she agreed with most of them. Because she enjoyed a challenge, she decided to try for a "descriptive process" paragraph, rather than a "how-to" paragraph. She then wrote the version of "How Shareen Broke the D Barrier" that appears on pages 195-96.

WRITING A PROCESS PARAGRAPH

How to Write a Process Paragraph

1 Decide how much your readers are likely to know about the process you will describe. Ask yourself what information they would need to understand and follow your instructions successfully.

2 Prewrite until you have listed details, pieces of equipment, possible problems, and steps: any ideas about your process that occur to you.

3 Note considerations such as time involved, equipment, ingredients, or other items at the top of another page. Under these notes, begin to number and order the steps in your process in point form.

4 Group the steps in your process into approximately three general stages, using time order.

5 Transfer your stages and steps to an outline form. The stages in your process paragraph are your three subtopics. Leaving space for additional details or examples that may be needed, add the necessary number of steps involved in each stage.

6 Write a topic sentence that gives the purpose, value, and relative level of difficulty of your process; then draft your paragraph from your outline.

7 Revise your paragraph to ensure
   - that you have mentioned any possible warnings needed or problems that might occur, and have not omitted any details; and
   - that you have used transitional words and phrases to assist understanding of your process.

8 Conclude by refocusing on the value or importance of having performed the actions described.

■ **Writing Assignment 1**

Choose one of the topics below to write about in a process paragraph.

How to change a car or bike tire
How to bathe a dog or cat
How to get rid of house or garden pests such as mice, cockroaches, or wasps
How to fall asleep (if you need to and can't)
How to play a simple game like checkers, tic-tac-toe, or an easy card game
How to load a van
How to choose the right college for you
How to live on a limited budget
How to plant a garden
How to use a search engine on the Internet
How to fix a leaky faucet, a clogged drain, or the like
How to enjoy a Canadian winter
How to study for an important exam
How to paint a ceiling
How to wash dishes efficiently, clean a bathroom, do laundry, or the like

Prewriting

a Begin by freewriting for ten minutes on the topic you have chosen. Do not worry about spelling, grammar, or organization. Just write whatever comes into your head regarding the topic.

Write for more than ten minutes if added details about the topic occur to you. This freewriting will give you a base of raw material that you can draw on in the next phase of your work on the paragraph. After freewriting, you should have a sense of whether there is enough material available for you to write a process paragraph about the topic. If so, continue as explained below. If not, choose another topic and freewrite about *it* for ten minutes.

b Write a clear, direct topic sentence stating the process you are going to describe or give directions for. For instance, if you are going to describe a way to study for major exams, your topic sentence might be "My study-skills instructor has suggested a good way to study for major exams." In this topic sentence, you can count on an audience of other students who recognize the value of your topic. A very good type of topic sentence tells its readers the topic and the number of steps involved: "My technique for building a charcoal barbecue fire involves four main steps."

c List all the steps you can think of that may be part of the process. Don't worry, at this point, about how each step fits or whether certain steps overlap. Here, for example, is the list prepared by the author of "Sneaking into the House at Night."

Quiet on stairs
Come in after Dad's asleep
House is freezing at night
Bring key
Know which steps to avoid

Lift up front door
Late dances on Saturday night
Don't turn on bathroom light
Avoid squeaky spots on floor
Get into bed quietly

d   Number your items in time order and revise for completeness. Strike out items that do not fit in the list; add others that come to mind.

~~Quiet on stairs~~
2   Come in after Dad's asleep
~~House is freezing at night~~
1   Bring key
5   Know which steps to avoid
3   Lift up front door
~~Late dances on Saturday night~~
6   Don't turn on bathroom light
4   Avoid squeaky spots on floor
8   Get into bed quietly
7   *Undress quietly*

e   Use your list as a guide to write the outline and first rough draft of your paper. As you write, try to think of additional details that will support your opening sentence. Group the details of your process into three or more stages, or subtopics. Make sure each stage omits no needed details. Do not expect to finish your paper in one draft. You should, in fact, be ready to write a series of lists and drafts as you work toward the goals of unity, support, and coherence.

Revising

After you have written your first draft, set it aside for a while. Then read it out loud, either to yourself or to a friend or classmate who will be honest with you about how it sounds. Process writing requires you to be especially aware of your readers because your purpose is to either teach them how to do something or describe exactly how something is done.

■   Consider how much your reader knows about your topic. A reader cannot follow a process or do so with much interest if he or she does not have any idea about the general nature of your subject. For example, if you are writing about how to install a particular piece of software, you may need to explain some terms to readers who are unfamiliar with either computers or your particular software. Have you included any necessary background information about equipment, ingredients, or terms?

■   Be sure that the pronoun point of view in your paragraph is consistent. For instance, if you open with "How I got rid of mice" (first person), do not switch to "*You* must buy the right kind of traps" (second person). Have you written your paragraph consistently in the first person (*I, we*), or as an address to your reader in the second person (*you*), or in the third person as Shareen did in her descriptive process paragraph?

- The goal of all process writing is to be clear and easy to follow. Are the steps in your paragraph described in a clear, logical way? Is your sequence correct? Have you omitted any steps or stages that would keep readers from following your process? Have you informed your readers about any difficulties with your process?

- Transitions are essential in a process paragraph or essay. Have you used transitions to reassure readers of the order in which your steps or stages are presented, while making sure that your paragraph moves smoothly from one step to another?

- Look at your topic sentence again. There are three very effective ways to open an effective process paragraph. Your challenge is to engage your readers' interest or to get them to try your process. Your choice of topic sentence pattern will depend on three things: (1) your reading audience, (2) the level of difficulty involved in the process involved, and (3) your readers' knowledge, likely understanding, or interest in your topic.

    One effective type of topic sentence states the importance of your subject to your readers ("Knowing how to study effectively for a major exam can mean the difference between passing and failing a course"). Another method offers your opinion of the value of your process ("My technique for building a charcoal barbecue fire is almost foolproof"). A third opener presents the results of the process to give readers an idea of the goal ("A delicious plate of crispy samosas awaits anyone who follows my formula").

    Does your topic sentence reflect the interests and knowledge of your reading audience? Have you used an appropriate version of one of the types of topic sentence suggested above?

- Return to your closing sentences. Have you taken your process beyond its final step? Have you summed up your process, reassured readers of its value or results, or encouraged readers to see the wider value of your process?

- Have you corrected any sentence-skills errors that you noticed while reading your paper out loud? Have you checked the paper carefully for sentence skills, including spelling, as listed on the inside front cover of this book?

Continue revising until you and your reader can answer yes to all these questions.

Transitions for Process Paragraphs		
first	next, then	finally
as you begin	while this is happening	to finish
first of all	during this step	at last
to start out	the second (third, fourth) step	as a last step
the first step	after you have	to complete

■ Writing Assignment 2

Write a paragraph about one of the following processes. For this assignment, you will be working with more general topics than those in Writing Assignment 1. In fact, many of the topics are so broad that entire self-help books have been written about them. A big part of your task, then, will be to narrow the topic down enough so that it can be covered in one paragraph.

You will find, in many cases, that you must invent your own steps in a particular process. You will also have to make decisions about how many steps to include, the order in which to present them, and the number of stages or subtopics in your process.

How to break a bad habit such as smoking, overeating, or excess drinking
How to improve a course you have taken
How to make someone you know happy
How to go about meeting people
How to discipline a child
How to improve the place where you work
How to show appreciation to others
How to make someone forgive you
How to make yourself depressed
How to get over a broken relationship
How to enjoy a day off
How to procrastinate

Prewriting

a Choose a topic that appeals to you. Then ask yourself, "How can I make this general topic narrow enough to be covered in one paragraph?" One way is to choose a section of some process, the one that you believe is most important. Another way to proceed is to think of a particular time you have gone through this process. For example, if the general topic is "how to decorate economically," you might think about a time when you decorated your own apartment.

b Write a topic sentence about the process you are going to describe. Your topic sentence should clearly reflect the narrowed-down topic you have chosen. If you chose the topic mentioned in step *a*, for example, your topic sentence could be "I made my first apartment look nice without spending a fortune."

c Make a list of as many different items as you can think of that concern your topic. Don't worry about repeating yourself, about putting them in order, about whether details are major or minor, or about spelling. Simply make a list of everything about your topic that occurs to you. Here, for instance, is a list of items generated by a student writing about decorating her apartment on a tight budget.

Bought fabric ends and used them as wall hangings
Trimmed overgrown bushes in the yard
Used old jars and bottles as vases for flowers from the yard
Found an oriental rug at a warehouse sale
Painted unmatched kitchen chairs in bright yellow
Kept dishes washed and put away
Bought a slipcover for a ratty couch

Used pink light bulbs
Hung sheets over the windows

d Next, decide what order you will present your items in and number them. (As in the example of decorating an apartment, there may not be an order that the steps *must* be done in. If that is the case, you should decide on a sequence that makes sense or that you followed yourself.) If you think of any potential problems or setbacks that you or others might experience, list those as well and put them into your sequence. As you number your items, strike out any that do not fit in the list and add others you think of, like this.

6 Bought fabric ends and used them as wall hangings
~~Trimmed overgrown bushes in the yard~~
7 Used old jars and bottles as vases for flowers from the yard
4 Found an oriental rug at a warehouse sale
2 Painted unmatched kitchen chairs in bright yellow
~~Kept dishes washed and put away~~
1 Bought a slipcover for a ratty couch
8 Used pink light bulbs
5 Hung sheets over the windows
3 *Built bookcases out of bricks and boards*

e Write an outline for your paragraph. Begin by putting down your topic sentence. Then try to group your steps or stages into related items. Think about details that might fill out any stage or step or might explain it better.

f Referring to your outline and list, write the first draft of your paragraph. Add any additional steps or details as they occur to you.

Revising

If you can, put away your first draft for at least a day and then return to it. Read it out loud to yourself or to a friend who will give you honest feedback.

Here are the questions to ask yourself as you read over your first draft and the drafts to follow:

- Have I included a clear topic sentence that tells the limits of the process I will be describing? Should I give an idea of the value of my process in my topic sentence?
- Have I included all the essential information so that anyone reading my paper could follow the same process? Did I mention any potential problems that could occur and what to do about them?
- Have I grouped any steps that naturally belong together?
- Have I made the sequence of steps easy to follow by using transitions like *first, second, then, next, during,* and *finally*?
- Have I written a closing sentence or two to sum up the process and reassure readers of its value or relative easiness?
- Can I answer yes to other questions about unity, support, and coherence found on the inside cover of the book?

■ Have I corrected sentence-skills mistakes, including spelling errors?

Continue revising your work until you can answer yes to all these questions.

Writing Assignment 3

Everyone is an expert at something. Write a *descriptive* process paragraph that explains some skill that you can perform very well. The skill might be, for example, playing goalie, putting up a tent, making an ice cream soda, becoming a long-distance runner, or fine-tuning a car engine. Write from the point of view that "this is how _____ should be done." Be sure that your paragraph *describes* and *explains* how your process occurs. *Descriptive* process writing does *not* give instructions.

Writing Assignment 4

Write a process paragraph on how to succeed at a job interview. Using strategies described on the Online Learning Centre, do some research on the topic. Take a look at job search websites like Monster.ca, for instance. Such research will help you think about how to proceed with this assignment.

Condense the material you have found into three, four, or five basic steps. Choose the steps, tips, and pointers that seem most important to you or that recur most often in the material you examine. Remember that you are doing research only to obtain background information for your paragraph. Do not copy material or repeat someone else's words or phrases in your own work.

Writing Assignment 5

Option A: You have a part-time job helping out in a daycare centre. The director, who is pleased with your work and wants to give you more responsibility, has assigned you to be in charge of a group activity (for example, an exercise session, an alphabet lesson, or a valentine-making project). But before you actually begin the activity, the director wants to see a summary of how you would go about it. What advance preparation would be needed, what supplies or equipment would be needed, and what exactly would you be doing throughout the time of the project? Write a paragraph explaining the steps you would follow in conducting the activity.

Option B: Alternatively, write an explanation that you might give to a friend at college who is *not in your program*. Examples might include explaining how a particular piece of software is used, how to do some special activity in a lab, how to make a demo tape, or another specialized activity unique to your program. Explain each step of the task in a way that a friend would understand.

Writing Assignment 6

Writing about a Reading Selection: Read "Power Learning" on pages 529-35. Then write a process paragraph on how you could go about improving your study skills. Your topic sentence or thesis might be "To become a better student, I will take the following steps to strengthen my time control, my classroom note-taking, and my textbook study."

To get started, read through "Power Learning" again and jot down a list of all the suggestions that will be helpful for you. Then pull out the five or six that seem most important. Next, put the steps into a sequence: put hints on time control first, hints on note-taking second, and hints on textbook study third. Then prepare a rough draft of your paragraph in which you present each step and explain briefly why it is valuable for you. Use transitions and synonyms such as *one step, another way, a third study aid, next, a fifth means*, and *last* as you develop your ideas.

REVIEWING THE LEARNING OUTCOMES FOR PROCESS WRITING

After completing any of the writing assignments in this chapter, answer the following questions to decide how well your paragraph meets the learning outcomes for process writing.

1 Overall, have you supplied enough information or background material to make your process understandable to your readers? Have you explained any technical or specialized points you have included?

2 Do you open with a topic sentence that states the value of your process and perhaps its approximate level of difficulty?

3 Have you mentioned any necessary equipment or supplies? Have you indicated the amount of time needed for your process and its stages?

4 Are your steps grouped into logical stages?

5 Is each step completely and carefully described with enough details or examples to make it clear and easy to follow? Have you mentioned any possible problems that may occur while following your instructions?

6 Do you conclude with a reassurance of the value of the process to the reader?

Visit the *English Skills with Readings* Online Learning Centre at **www.mcgrawhill.ca/college/langan** to access self-quizzes, bonus material on study and research skills, web resources, and other learning and study tools.

plaining a Process · Examining Cause and Effect · Comparing or Contrasting · Defining
rm · Dividing and Classifying · Describing a Scene or Person · Narrating an Event · Arguin
Position · Explaining a Process · Examining Cause and Effect · Comparing or Contrasting
fining a Term · Dividing and Classifying · Describing a Scene or Person · Narrating a
ent · Arguing a Position · Explaining a Process · Examining Cause and Effect · Comparin

CHAPTER 12

Examining Cause and Effect

LEARNING OUTCOMES

By carefully working through this chapter's activities and successfully completing one or more of its writing assignments, you will write a cause and effect paragraph that

- opens with a topic sentence that states your point of view on your subject and indicates whether you will examine causes or effects;
- shows a selection of causes and/or effects focused on proving the point of the paragraph;
- uses true and logical causes and/or effects to support its point;
- presents its subtopic causes and/or effects in order of importance;
- supports its subtopic causes and/or effects with sufficient and specific details; and
- concludes with a reassurance that its point is effectively supported.

Cause and effect writing examines the *reasons why* things happen (cause) and the *results* of those things happening (effects). Writing a paragraph that discusses causes and/or effects demands clear thinking and observation; this type of thinking is called *analysis*. To analyze is to break a subject down into its component parts. An event or situation may appear to have many causes and many effects, but not all these may be true causes or effects; they may simply have happened before or after the event or situation. So to write about causes or effects, a writer must first break down the subject into component events to examine whether they are truly causes or effects. As a form of exposition, cause and effect writing seeks to explain causal or resultant relationships between events.

Every day we ask questions about why things happen; this is a normal response to our environment. We ask why someone seems unhappy or why our car stopped working, and we look for answers. We realize that many actions do not occur without causes, and we also realize that a given action can have a series of effects—good or bad. By examining the causes or effects of an action, we seek to understand and explain things that happen in our lives.

Much career and college writing and speaking focuses on cause and effect. Why does a product not sell? Why is a specific piece of software inefficient? Why does a particular biochemical process yield these results? The skills and techniques in analyzing and communicating cause and effect are in constant use in any number of communications formats.

In this section, you will be asked to examine the causes or the effects of something. First read the two paragraphs that follow and answer the questions about them. Both paragraphs support their opening points by explaining a series of causes or a series of effects.

PARAGRAPHS TO CONSIDER

New Puppy in the House

[1]Buying a new puppy can have drastic effects on a quiet household. [2]For one thing, the puppy keeps the entire family awake for at least two solid weeks. [3]Every night when the puppy is placed in its box, it begins to howl, yip, and whine. [4]Even after the lights go out and the house quiets down, the puppy continues to moan. [5]Since it is impossible to sleep while listening to a heartbroken, trembling "Woo-woooo," the family soon begins to suffer the effects of loss of sleep. [6]Soon people become hostile, short-tempered, depressed, and irritable. [7]A second effect is that the puppy tortures the family by destroying its material possessions. [8]Every day something different is damaged. [9]Family members find chewed belts and shoes, gnawed table legs, and leaking sofa cushions. [10]In addition, the puppy usually ruins the wall-to-wall carpeting and makes the house smell like a public washroom at a big-city bus station. [11]Worst of all, though, the puppy causes family disagreements. [12]Parents argue with children about who is supposed to feed and walk the dog. [13]Children argue among themselves about whose turn it is to play with the puppy. [14]Everyone argues about whose idea it was to get the puppy in the first place. [15]These continual arguments, along with the effects of sleeplessness and the loss of valued possessions, seriously disrupt a household. [16]Only when the puppy gets a bit older will the house become peaceful again.

My Ghost Town

[1]My hometown near Lake Erie is drying up and disappearing. [2]First, there are an increasing number of problems for employees of the company that used to be the biggest employer in town. [3]The huge car-parts factory supported hundreds of families, but there have been three strikes in five years, and the workers' complaints never seem to be addressed. [4]Also, more workers are being laid off because more and more parts are made in Mexico or Asia. [5]Then this week the U.S. parent company admitted the plant is unprofitable and said it will close the factory completely. [6]Another reason the town looks unhappy and deserted is that one of our largest stores closed down and relocated last year. [7]The other chain store was sold to Wal-Mart, an American company. [8]The Wal-Mart store brought in management and employees from other locations, so one third of the old discount store's workers were out of a job and either looked for a new job, moved away, or both. [9]There are very few new jobs

available, and there are no new companies opening near here. ¹⁰But the most visibly depressing cause of all for my town's empty streets is a half-hour's drive away: a big new mall built last year. ¹¹People drive there for entertainment as they do their shopping and banking. ¹²No one wants to use the little family-owned businesses on the main street any more. ¹³So more Queen Street stores sit empty every week and the two banks are closing their branches, which means fewer jobs for even fewer people. ¹⁴All these changes leave my town looking and feeling as lonely and sad as a frontier ghost town.

■ Questions

About Unity

1. Which sentences in "New Puppy in the House" repeat an idea already stated and so should be omitted? (*Write the sentence numbers here.*) _____

2. Which sentence in "My Ghost Town" does not directly support the paragraph's point? (*Write the sentence number.*)

_____

About Support

3. How many causes are given to support the opening idea in "My Ghost Town"?

_____ one   _____ two   _____ three   _____ four

4. How many effects of bringing a new puppy into the home are given in "New Puppy in the House"?

_____ one   _____ two   _____ three   _____ four

About Coherence

5. What are the five major transition words used in "My Ghost Town"?

a._____   c._____   e. _____

b._____   d. _____

6. Which words signal the most important effect in "New Puppy in the House"?

_____

DEVELOPING A CAUSE AND EFFECT PARAGRAPH

Development through Prewriting

Cause and effect writing requires an extra step in logical thinking that can be done effectively only during your prewriting stage. In order to write a good cause and effect paragraph, you must clearly define an effect (*what* happened) and the contributing causes (*why* it happened). Alternatively, you will define some cause and its resulting effects. In addition, you will need to provide details that support and explain the causes and effects you're writing about.

Terry is the student author of "My Ghost Town." His assignment was to write a paragraph about some change that he had experienced. Chapter 2 shows Terry's initial freewriting, during which he discovered his focus—how his hometown had changed. He decided to do some focused freewriting; he knew he had his *effect* (his hometown was losing people and businesses) but thought he could come up with more details. Finally, to clarify his thinking, he made a list based on his focused freewriting of *causes* (reasons for the town's problems). This is what he came up with.

Car-parts plant in trouble
Plant will close now
Big store closed and moved
No new jobs
The Westland Mall—everybody goes there
Stores and banks shut down

He found it hard to think of his causes clearly, so he labelled each one, then listed the details in point form under each. He knew he had to hand in his outline with his paragraph, so he thought he could work out a clearer outline by making the list below.

Cause #1 Car-parts plant is biggest employer & it's in trouble
    —three strikes
    —layoffs—cause? Lower production
    —plant will close down

Cause #2 Big stores closing and changing hands
    —one store closed completely—new one near Simcoe
    —big discount store turned into Wal-Mart—brought in outside people
    —No new jobs
    —People moved away, on unemployment

Cause #3 Westland Mall opened up
    —no one shops in town any more
    —the movie house closed
    —banks closing

Terry now had his effect and three causes with details, and he knew he had most of a good outline done, as well. Based on his work, he wrote a first draft.

My hometown is drying up and shutting down. That's one of the reasons why I'm here in London at college. The car-parts plant has always been where most people worked, including my father. Now they don't even try to settle with workers after three strikes. They're making the same parts cheaper in Mexico or Asia now, so they keep laying people off. And the last straw was last week when the American parent company decided to close it down completely. I don't know what my dad is going to do. The big chain stores where everybody shopped, even people from the other places around here, are either closed or have new owners, too. Sears closed and it only has a little catalogue office now, so that put a lot of people out of work. The big discount store turned into a Wal-Mart, and all its managers and a lot of staff are from other places, so nearly a third of its employees lost their jobs. Also the new Westland Mall is just killing the local stores and businesses. Even the Festival Theatre closed, and the banks will only have machines or branches in the mall. Nobody goes downtown any more, and my town looks as empty as a ghost town.

Development through Revising

In his next class, Terry traded papers with his classmate Roger. This is what Roger wrote about Terry's first draft.

> *The biggest criticism I have is that you haven't used a lot of transitions to tie your sentences together. You've got a lot of good stuff here, but it feels bumpy. There are a lot of facts, but it's not very smooth.*
>
> *Is one of these reasons more important than the others? Which of these things really is the biggest reason why your town's hurting? If you know, it would be good if you told people that.*
>
> *You could add some more details in some places, too. Why is the mall hurting your town so much? Why do people go there so much? And the other thing I notice is that sometimes you're telling a story about yourself, and sometimes this is about the town.*

As Terry read over his own paper, the first thing he realized was that he'd run out of steam toward the end. "I was so careful with my outline that I hurried with the draft, especially the last part. I didn't explain how big an effect the mall is having on our main street. I went back to some of the stuff about Queen Street in my freewriting for more details about how empty it is. Also, this is supposed to be a cause and effect paragraph, so I guess my story doesn't belong here. I think I put it in because I was worrying about my father."

Using Roger's comments and his own thoughts, Terry rewrote his first draft, fixing the point of view and producing the paragraph that appears on pages 208-9.

Activity

In this exercise you will create a cause and effect outline that will help you tell the difference between *reasons* that back up a point and the supporting *details* that go with each of the reasons or subtopics. The scrambled list below contains both reasons (subtopics) and supporting details. Complete the outline following the list by writing the reasons in the numbered blanks (*1, 2, 3*) and the appropriate supporting details in the lettered blanks (*a, b, c, d*). Arrange the reasons in what you feel is their order of importance. Summarize the reasons and details in a few words rather than writing them out completely.

Point: There are a number of reasons why college students find first semesters difficult.

There are so many kinds of expensive supplies to buy, like drafting materials and zip disks.

Reading, doing assignments, and attending labs take up many hours.

Assignments are often more difficult than previous school tasks.

Most students work several hours a week at part-time jobs.

Travelling to and from college is costly, whether the student pays for a car, gas, and parking or whether the student must buy monthly public transit passes.

College classes and coursework are demanding and unfamiliar to many students.

Classes usually take up at least twenty hours a week

Students find time management to be a problem.

It is hard for a student who lives away from home to pay for tuition, rent, and food.

Lectures are often an intimidating experience for students used to informal classes.

Attending college is frequently financially draining.

Managing assignments for four or more courses, attending required lab hours, and attempting extracurricular interests can be a major worry.

Textbooks for several courses may cost hundreds of dollars.

Almost all the course material is totally new to students and may be quite difficult to grasp.

Students often find there is no time left for families, friends, or children.

Outline

1. _____

    a. _____

    b. _____

    c. _____

    d. _____

2. _____

    a. _____

    b. _____

    c. _____

    d. _____

3. _____

    a. _____

    b. _____

    c. _____

    d. _____

A Note about Causes, Effects, and Logic

Two types of problems occur in cause and effect writing. The first is an error in logic caused by confusing time order with causality, and the second is caused by assuming there is only a single cause or effect in any situation.

- Sometimes facts or events appear to be causes or effects when they merely *precede* or *follow* something *in time*. For instance, if a dog crossed the road just before your car stalled, the dog was not the cause of the breakdown. The dog's crossing the road simply occurred before your car stalled, but the two events have no causal relationship.
- There are also often multiple or underlying causes and effects. If a writer states that catching frequent colds is caused by being in constant contact with people with colds, he or she could be ignoring other less apparent causes, such as low resistance due to fatigue or persistent conditions like asthma.

WRITING A CAUSE AND EFFECT PARAGRAPH

How to Write a Cause and Effect Paragraph

1   Look at your topic. Does it require a paragraph on causes only or effects only, or could it be treated either way? After deciding on either a causes or an effects paragraph, begin to prewrite.

2   Use listing or questioning to create either causes or effects for your topic. Examine your lists or notes to be sure that your points are true and logical causes or effects; are there other or deeper causes or effects that you may have missed in your prewriting?

3   Number and try to group points or details that are related or similar. Check to be sure that similar points are not merely repetitions of each other. If you have several points that are related, group them under a common subheading as a possible subtopic cause or effect. (See Writing Assignment 1 below for an example.)

4   Use your outline to list your major or subtopic causes or effects and the details that support each. Write a topic sentence that both states your point of view on your subject and indicates whether your paragraph is about causes or about effects.

5   As you work on drafts based on your outline, use an order that is most effective for your subtopics and supporting details: is one cause or effect more important than the others? Is the order in time in which your causes or effects occur important to your point?

6   Be sure to use transitional words and phrases appropriate to cause and effect writing to help readers to follow your thoughts.

7   Conclude by reinforcing your main point with a reference to the evidence you have presented.

- **Writing Assignment 1**

Choose one of the three topic sentences and brief outlines below. Each is made up of three subtopics (causes or effects). Your task is to turn the topic sentence and outline into a causes or an effects paragraph.

Option A

Topic sentence: There are several reasons why some high school graduates are unable to read or write adequately for college requirements.

1. Failure of parents (*cause*)
2. Failure of schools (*cause*)
3. Failure of students themselves (*cause*)

Option B

Topic sentence: Attending college has changed my personality in positive ways.

1. More confident (*effect*)
2. More knowledgeable (*effect*)
3. More assertive (*effect*)

Option C

Topic sentence: Living with roommates (*or* family) makes attending college difficult.

1. Late-night hours (*cause*)
2. More temptations to cut class (*cause*)
3. More distractions from studying (*cause*)

Prewriting

a   After you have chosen the option that appeals to you most, jot down all the details you can think of that might go under each of the subtopics. Use separate sheets of paper for each list. Don't worry yet about whether you can use all the items—your goal is to generate more material than you need. Here, for example, are some of the details generated by the writer of "New Puppy in the House" while working on the paragraph.

Whines and moans	Loss of sleep
Arguments about walking dog	Visits to vet
Arguments about feeding dog	Short tempers
Purchase collar, leash, food	Accidents on carpet
Chewed belts and shoes	Chewed cushions and tables
Arguments about playing with dog	

b   Edit, order, and select details. Look for possible subtopics. Decide which details you will use to develop the paragraph. Also, number the details in the order in which you will present them. Here is how the writer of "New Puppy in the House" made decisions about the details that were the *effects* of having a puppy.

2   Whines and moans
6   Arguments about walking dog
6   Arguments about feeding dog

~~Purchase collar, leash, food~~
4   Chewed belts and shoes
6   Arguments about playing with dog
1   Loss of sleep
~~Visits to vet~~
3   Short tempers
5   Accidents on carpet
4   Chewed cushions and tables

Notice that the writer has found possible subtopics and put the same number in front of certain details that go together. For example, there is a *"4"* in front of "Chewed belts and shoes" and also in front of "Chewed cushions and tables."

c Organize your subtopics and details. Group details that are related (as indicated by numbers), and arrange them in a rough trial outline form under subtopic headings. At this stage, causes and effects may still be scrambled.

1.   Lack of sleep
   a) puppy whines alone in its box—cause
   b) short tempers—effect

2.   Damage to house and belongings
   a) clothes, shoes, table legs, cushions—chewing
   b) carpet smells—dog isn't trained

3.   Causes arguments
   a) parents & children—who should walk the puppy?
   b) who gets to play with the puppy?
   c) whose idea was the puppy?

Topic sentence? Having a puppy in the house is disruptive...

d Revise your outline, taking care to cover only causes or effects and to supply sufficient details to support each cause or effect. Here is the final outline for the "New Puppy in the House" paragraph on page 208.

Topic Sentence: Having a new puppy disrupts the household.

1. Keeps family awake
   a. Whines at night
   b. Howls
   c. Loss of sleep

2. Destroys possessions
   a. Chews belts & shoes
   b. Chews furniture
   c. Has accidents on couch & carpet

3. Causes arguments
   a. Arguments about walking dog
   b. Arguments about feeding dog
   c. Arguments about who gets to play with dog

e Now you are ready to write your paragraph. With cause and effect paragraphs and essays, *outlining is essential* because of the need to sort out causes from effects, as well as the need (as with any paper) to supply sufficient supporting details. Be sure to develop each of the subtopics from your outline into a complete sentence, and then back it up with the best of the details you have generated.

Revising

Revise your paragraph with these questions in mind:

- Have I begun the paragraph with the topic sentence provided?
- Is each subtopic stated in a complete sentence?
- Have I provided effective details, and enough of them, to back up each subtopic?
- Have I used transitions such as *in addition*, *another thing*, and *also* to make relationships between the sentences clear?
- Have I proofread the paragraph for sentence-skills errors, including spelling mistakes?

Revise your paragraph until you are sure the answer to each question is yes.

Transitions for Cause and Effect Paragraphs	
Transitions for Causes	*Transitions for Effects*
is a result of; results from	so, so that, so then
the reason for	is a consequence of, consequently
since	therefore, thus, then
because (of)	for this reason
is caused by	as a result

▪ Writing Assignment 2

Most of us criticize others readily, but we find it more difficult to give compliments. For this assignment, write a one-paragraph letter praising someone. The letter may be to a person you know (parent, relative, friend); to a public figure (actor, politician, musician, sports star, and so on); or to a company or organization (for example, the people who manufactured a product you own, a newspaper, a TV network, or a government agency).

Prewriting

a The fact that you are writing this letter indicates that its recipient has had an *effect* on you: you like, admire, or appreciate the person or organization. Your job will be to put into words the *causes*, or reasons, for this good feeling. Begin by making a list of reasons for your admiration. Here, for example, are a few reasons why a person might praise a car manufacturer.

> My car is dependable.
> There was prompt action on a complaint.
> The car is well designed.
> The price was reasonable.
> The car dealer was honest and fair.
> The car has needed little maintenance.

Reasons for admiring a parent might include these.

> You are patient with me.
> You always listen to me.
> You have a great sense of humour.
> You encourage me in several ways.
> I know you have made sacrifices for me.

Develop your own list of reasons for admiring the person or organization you have chosen.

b Now that you have a list of reasons, you need details to back up each reason. Jot down as many examples or supporting details as you can for each reason. Turn your list of reasons and details into an outline, using the order you think best. Here is what the writer of the letter to the car manufacturer might do.

> My car is dependable.
> Started during last winter's coldest days when neighbours' cars wouldn't start
> Has never stranded me anywhere
>
> The price was reasonable.
> Compared to other cars in its class, it cost less
> Came with more options than other cars of the same price
>
> I received prompt action on a complaint.
> When I complained about a rattling door, manufacturer arranged for a part to be replaced at no charge
>
> The car is well designed.
> Controls are easy to reach
> Dashboard gauges are easy to read
>
> The car dealer was fair and honest.
> No pressure, no fake "special deal only today" price
>
> The car has needed little maintenance.
> Haven't needed anything but tune-ups and oil changes

c Next, select from your outline list the three or four reasons that you can best support with effective details. These will make up the body of your letter.

d For your topic sentence, make the positive statement you wish to support. For example, the writer of the letter to the car manufacturer might begin like this: "I am the very satisfied owner of a 2004 Toyota."

e Now combine your topic sentence, reasons, and supporting details, and write a draft of your letter.

Revising

If possible, put your letter aside for a day. Then read it aloud to a friend. As you and he or she listen to your words, you should both keep these questions in mind:

- Is my topic sentence a positive statement that is supported by all my details?
- Do I clearly state several different reasons why I like or admire the person or organization I'm writing to?
- Do I support each of those reasons with specific evidence?
- Have I linked my sentences together with transitional words and phrases?
- Is my letter free of sentence-skills errors, including spelling mistakes?

Continue revising until you and your friend can answer yes to all these questions.

■ **Writing Assignment 3**

Below are ten topic sentences for a causes or effects paragraph. In outline form on a separate sheet of paper, provide brief subtopics for five of the ten statements.

List the Causes

1. There are several reasons why so many accidents occur on

   _____ (*name a local road, highway, or intersection*).

2. _____ is [*or* is not] a good instructor [*or* employer], for several reasons.

3. _____ is a sport that cannot be appreciated on television.

4. _____ is the most difficult course I have ever taken.

5. For several reasons, many students live at home while going to school.

List the Effects

6. Watching too much American TV can have a bad effect on Canadians.

7. When I heard the news that _____, I was affected in various ways.

8. Conflicts between parents can have harmful effects on a child.

9. Breaking my bad habit of _____ has changed my life [*or* would change my life].

10. My fear of _____ has affected my everyday life.

Decide which of your outlines would be most promising to develop into a paragraph. Make sure that your causes or effects are logical ones that truly support the point in the topic sentence. Then follow the directions on prewriting and revising for Writing Assignment 1.

■ Writing Assignment 4

Option A: Canada's federal and provincial governments are changing health care policies today, sometimes making them more like U.S. policies. Imagine an extreme outcome of such a change. There would no longer be government-funded insurance to cover medical procedures, operations, hospitalization, or doctor's appointments. What would be some of the effects of such a change? Spend some time thinking about specific results, good or bad, that could occur.

Now, taking into account both any opinions you may have read about such changes and your own personal views and experiences, write a letter to your local MPP detailing your thoughts about the results of such a change.

Option B: Your roommate has been complaining that it is impossible to succeed in Mr. X's class because the class is too stressful. You volunteer to attend the class and see for yourself. Afterwards, you decide to write a letter to the instructor, calling attention to the stressful conditions in the class and suggesting concrete ways that he could deal with these conditions. Write this letter, dealing with the causes and effects of stress in the class.

■ Writing Assignment 5

Investigate the reasons behind a current news event. For example, you may want to discover the causes behind one of the following events.

A labour strike or other protest

A tax increase

Changes in education

A traffic accident, fire, or other disastrous event

A military action by a government

Research the reasons for the event by reading current newspapers (especially the national papers, which may cover a story in detail), reading a newsmagazine such as *Maclean's*, watching the television news, or checking various news websites.

Decide on the major cause or causes of the event and their specific effects. Then write a paragraph explaining in detail the causes and effects. Below is a sample topic sentence for this assignment.

Recent charges of racial profiling by Toronto police have set off a variety of angry reactions.

Note how this topic sentence uses general descriptive words (*angry reactions*) that can summarize specific supporting details. Support for the words *angry reactions*, for example, might include specific ways in which police, city officials, and the public have responded to these allegations.

■ Writing Assignment 6

Writing about a Reading Selection: Read the selection "Why Should We Hire You?" by Jim Maloney on pages 544-47. In his second paragraph, Maloney describes a feeling most of us know all too well: "a sinking feeling in my stomach, and a quickening of my pulse: the sensations that come with being caught." The situations in which we have been "caught" unprepared may be serious or trivial, and the consequences or effects of being caught may be significant or insignificant. Think about one situation for which you were unprepared—a situation where you felt "caught." Why did you feel this way?

Write a causes paragraph that begins by explaining this situation and your feelings about it. Your topic sentence might be something like "There is nothing that causes feelings of guilt and stupidity like arriving at the right time for the wrong exam." As you develop each cause for why you ended up in your particular situation, use cause transitions and order-of-importance transitions to emphasize the order of your reasons. Conclude with your most important point.

As an alternative, you could write about the consequences or effects of being unprepared for this situation. Once again, be sure to include effects and supporting details in order of importance.

REVIEWING THE LEARNING OUTCOMES FOR CAUSE AND EFFECT WRITING

After completing any of the writing assignments in this chapter, review your work to decide how well it meets the following tests.

1 Does your paragraph open with a topic sentence that states your point of view on your subject and indicates whether your paragraph deals with causes or effects?

2 Is each cause or effect in your paragraph truly a cause or effect? Does each clearly support the point you make?

3 Are your causes or effects presented in an effective order, with appropriate transitions to guide your reader and reinforce your point?

4 Are your subtopics adequately supported by adequate and specific details?

5 Do you conclude with a reinforcement of your point that sums up your paragraph?

 **Online LearningCentre**

Visit the *English Skills with Readings* Online Learning Centre at **www.mcgrawhill.ca/college/langan** to access self-quizzes, bonus material on study and research skills, web resources, and other learning and study tools.

Explaining a Process • Examining Cause and Effect • Comparing or Contrasting • Defin-
erm • Dividing and Classifying • Describing a Scene or Person • Narrating an Event • Arg
Position • Explaining a Process • Examining Cause and Effect • Comparing or Contrast
efining a Term • Dividing and Classifying • Describing a Scene or Person • Narrating an E
Arguing a Position • Explaining a Process • Examining Cause and Effect • Compari

CHAPTER 13

Comparing or Contrasting

LEARNING OUTCOMES

By working through this chapter's activities, practising the skills used in both types of comparison or contrast patterns of development, and completing one or more of its writing assignments, you will write a comparison or contrast paragraph that

- compares or contrasts limited aspects of two subjects that have a logical reason to be considered together;
- begins with a focused, clear topic sentence stating (1) both its subjects, (2) its intention either to compare or to contrast, and (3) your point in comparing or contrasting these subjects;
- uses either the one-side-at-a-time or the point-by-point method to state and develop its comparison or contrast;
- carefully compares or contrasts each subject within one of these structures according to several major points or bases for comparing or contrasting; and
- concludes with a summing-up of the results of comparing or contrasting your two subjects and a confirmation of your point of view or judgment on these results.

Papers that *compare* two things show *similarities;* papers that *contrast* two things show *differences.* Comparison papers may *inform* readers by showing them similarities between familiar concepts and unknown or seemingly dissimilar concepts. Contrast papers may *persuade* readers by allowing them to examine the differences between two points, then align their views with one side or the other. Both types of paper involve *analysis,* or thinking that breaks down concepts into their component ideas. Both types of papers begin with a judgment (or viewpoint) on the part of the writer and lead to a judgment on the part of the reader.

Comparing and contrasting are two thought processes we constantly perform in everyday life. We compare or contrast two brand-name products: for example,

Fila versus Reeboks shoes, two television shows, two instructors, two friends, or two possible courses of action in a situation. We compare or contrast to understand each of the two things more clearly and to make judgments about them. Comparison and contrast writing structures simply imitate and extend our thinking habits.

Comparing and contrasting occur constantly in college and career writing. Why is digital reproduction superior to photographic processing? How does one accounting software package compare with another? How does one advertising campaign's use of media coverage differ from another's? Responding to any such question requires competence in the techniques of comparing or contrasting to structure your thinking and achieve the response you desire from readers.

In this chapter, you will be asked to write a paragraph of comparison or contrast. First, however, you must learn the two common methods of developing a comparison or contrast paragraph. Read the two paragraphs that follow and try to explain the difference in the two methods of development.

PARAGRAPHS TO CONSIDER

Last Dance

[1]My graduation dance was nothing like what I had expected it to be. [2]From the start of grade twelve, I had pictured getting dressed in a blue gown that my aunt would make and that would cost five hundred dollars in any store. [3]No one else would have a gown as attractive as mine. [4]I imagined my boyfriend coming to the door with a lovely blue corsage, and I pictured myself happily inhaling its perfume all evening long. [5]I saw us setting off for the evening in his brother's Audi. [6]We would make a flourish as we swept in and out of a series of parties before the dance. [7]Our evening would be capped by a delicious steak dinner and by dancing close together into the early morning hours. [8]The formal was held on May 17, 2002, at the Riding Club on the Pembina Highway. [9]However, because of sickness in her family, my aunt had no time to finish my gown and I had to buy an ugly pink one at the last minute for eighty dollars. [10]My corsage of yellow carnations looked terrible on my pink gown, and I do not remember its having any scent. [11]My boyfriend's brother was out of town, and I stepped outside to the stripped-down Chevy that he used at races on weekends. [12]We went to one party where I drank a glass of wine that made me sleepy and upset my stomach. [13]After we arrived at the dance, I nibbled on a roll and some celery sticks. [14]Worst of all, we left early without dancing because my boyfriend and I had had a fight several days before, and at the time, we did not really want to be with each other.

Day versus Evening Students

[1]As a part-time college student who has taken both day and evening courses, I have observed notable differences between day and evening students. [2]First of all, the students in my daytime classes are all about the same age, with similar clothing styles and similar interests. [3]Most are in their late teens to early twenties, and whether male or female, they pretty much dress alike. [4]Their uniform consists of jeans, T-shirts, running shoes, baseball

caps, and maybe a gold earring or two. [5]They use the same popular slang, talk about the same movies and TV shows, and know the same musical artists. [6]But students in my evening courses are much more diverse. [7]Some are in their late teens, but most range from young married people in their twenties and thirties to people my grandparents' age. [8]Generally, their clothing is more formal than the day students'. [9]They are dressed for the workplace, not for a typical college classroom. [10]Many of the women wear suits, while the men often wear dress shirts or sweaters. [11]As well, they are more comfortable talking about their mortgages or work schedules or child care than about what was on TV last night. [12]Second, for day students, college is generally their only major responsibility. [13]They have plenty of time to study and get assignments done. [14]However, evening students lead much more complicated lives than most day students. [15]They may come to campus after putting in a nine-to-five day at work. [16]Most have children to raise or grandchildren to babysit. [17]When they miss a class or hand in an assignment late, it's usually because of a real problem, such as a sick child or an important deadline at work. [18]Finally, day and evening students definitely have different attitudes toward school. [19]Day students often seem more interested in the view out the window or the attractive classmate in the next row than in what the instructor is saying. [20]They doze, draw cartoons, whisper, and write notes instead of paying attention. [21]Evening students sit up straight, listen hard, and ask the instructor lots of questions. [22]They obviously are there to learn, and they don't want their time wasted. [23]In short, day students and night students are as different as ... day and night.

Complete this comment: The difference in the methods of contrast in the two paragraphs is _____

_____

_____

_____

_____

_____

Compare your answer with the following explanation of the two methods of development used in comparison or contrast paragraphs.

METHODS OF DEVELOPMENT

There are two common methods, or formats, of development in a comparison or contrast paper. Details can be presented *one side at a time* or *point by point*. Each format is illustrated below.

One Side at a Time

Look at the outline of "Last Dance":

Topic sentence: My senior prom was nothing like what I had expected it to be.

1. Expectations (*first half of paper*)
    a. Gown (expensive, blue)
    b. Corsage (lovely, fragrant, blue)
    c. Car (Audi)
    d. Partying (much)
    e. Dinner (steak)
    f. Dancing (all night)
2. Reality (*second half of paper*)
    a. Gown (cheap, pink)
    b. Corsage (wrong colour, no scent)
    c. Car (stripped-down Chevy)
    d. Partying (little)
    e. Dinner (roll and celery sticks)
    f. Dancing (didn't because of quarrel)

When you use the one-side-at-a-time method, follow the same order of points of contrast or comparison for each side, as in the outline above. For example, both the first half of the paper and the second half begin with the subtopic of what dress would be worn. Then both sides go on to the corsage, the car, and so on.

Point by Point

Now look at the outline of "Day versus Evening Students":

Topic sentence: There are notable differences between day and evening students.

1. Age and related tastes in clothing and interests
    a. Youthful nature of day students
    b. Older nature of evening students
2. Amount of responsibility
    a. Lighter responsibilities of day students
    b. Heavier responsibilities of evening students
3. Attitude toward school
    a. Casual attitude of day students
    b. Serious attitude of evening students

The outline shows how the two kinds of students are contrasted point by point under three subtopics, or bases of comparison. First, the writer compares the ages, clothing styles, and interests of the young daytime students and the older evening students. Next, the writer compares the limited amount of responsibility of the daytime students with the heavier responsibilities of the evening students. Finally, the writer compares the casual attitudes toward school of the daytime students with the serious attitudes of the evening students.

When you begin a comparison or contrast paper, you should decide right away whether you are going to use the one-side-at-a-time format or the point-by-point format. Your subject matter will often help you determine which format is preferable. Following are some of the advantages and disadvantages of each format.

One-side-at-a-time format (also called *block* format) is most effective when you wish to explore each idea in great depth. When you present one side of your subject in an uninterrupted way, you are able to examine any complexities at length or build a detailed or dramatic argument or description. *But* presenting one side at a time requires you, in the second part of your paper, to carefully remind readers of each point of comparison or contrast as you present the other side of your subject.

Point-by-point format works best with brief, specific points of comparison or contrast for two subjects or two aspects of the same subject. The reader sees both sides one after the other; he or she is constantly reminded of the comparing or contrasting activity and is less likely to forget points being examined. Point-by-point format is also best for a subject with numerous bases of comparison or contrast for this reason.

An outline is an essential step in helping you decide which format will be more workable for your topic.

Activity

Complete the partial outlines provided for the two paragraphs that follow.

How My Parents' Divorce Changed Me

In the three years since my parents' divorce, I have changed from a spoiled brat to a reasonably normal college student. Before the divorce, I expected my mother to wait on me. She did my laundry, cooked and cleaned up after meals, and even straightened up my room. My only response was to complain if the meat was too well done or if the sweater I wanted to wear was not clean. In addition, I expected money for anything I wanted. Whether it was an expensive ski trip or my own cellphone, I expected Mom to hand over the money. If she refused, I would get it from Dad. However, he left when I was fifteen, and things changed. When Mom got a full-time job to support us, I was the one with the free time to do housework. I did the laundry, started the dinner, and cleaned not only my own room but the whole house. Also, I no longer asked her for money since I knew there was none to spare. Instead, I got a part-time job on weekends to earn my own spending money. Today I have my own car that I am paying for, and I am putting myself through college. Things have been hard sometimes, but I am glad not to be that spoiled kid any more.

Topic sentence: In the three years since my parents' divorce, I have changed from a spoiled brat to a reasonably normal college student.

1. Before the divorce

    a. _____

    b. _____

2. After the divorce

    a. _____

    b. _____

Complete the following statement: This paragraph uses a _____ method of development.

Good and Bad Horror Movies

A good horror movie is easily distinguished from a bad one. A good horror movie, first of all, has both male and female victims. Both sexes suffer terrible fates at the hands of monsters and maniacs. Therefore, everyone in the audience has a chance to identify with the victim. Bad horror movies, on the other hand, tend to concentrate on women, especially half-dressed or seemingly sluttish ones. These movies are obviously prejudiced against half the human race. Second, a good horror movie inspires compassion for its characters. For example, the audience will feel sympathy for the victims of Freddy or Dracula, and also for Freddy or Dracula, who are themselves shown to be sad victims of fate. In contrast, a bad horror movie encourages feelings of aggression and violence in viewers. For instance, in the <u>Halloween</u> or <u>Scream</u> films, the murder scenes use the murderer's point of view. The effect is that the audience stalks the victims along with the killer and feels the same thrill he does. Finally, every good horror movie has a sense of humour. In <u>Dracula</u>, the Count says meaningfully at dinner, "I don't drink wine," as he stares at Jonathan Harker's juicy neck. Humour provides relief from the horror and makes the characters more human. A bad horror movie, though, is humourless and boring. One murder is piled on top of another, and the characters are just cardboard figures. Bad horror movies may provide cheap thrills, but the good ones touch our emotions and live forever.

Topic sentence: A good horror movie is easily distinguished from a bad one.

1. Kinds of victims

   a. _____

   b. _____

2. Effect on audience

   a. _____

   b. _____

3. Tone

   a. _____

   b. _____

Complete the following statement: This paragraph uses a _____ method of development.

ADDITIONAL PARAGRAPHS TO CONSIDER

Read these additional paragraphs of comparison or contrast, and then answer the questions that follow.

My Broken Dream

[1]When I became a police officer in Hamilton, the job was not as I had dreamed it would be. [2]I began to dream about being a police officer at about age ten. [3]I could picture myself wearing a handsome blue uniform and having an impressive-looking badge. [4]I could also picture myself driving a powerful patrol car through town and seeing everyone stare at me with envy. [5]But most of all, I dreamed of working on a SWAT team using all the equipment that "TV cops" use. [6]I just knew everyone would be proud of me. [7]I could almost hear the guys on the block saying, [8]"Boy, Devon made it big. Did you hear he's a cop?" [9]I dreamed of leading an exciting life, solving big crimes, and meeting lots of people. [10]I just knew that if I became a cop everyone in town would look up to me. [11]However, when I actually did become a police officer, I soon found out that the reality was different. [12]My first disappointment came when I was sworn in and handed a well-used, baggy uniform. [13]My disappointment continued when I was given a badge that looked like something pulled out of a cereal box. [14]I was assigned bicycle patrol duty and given a used bike. [15]I got to wear navy Bermuda shorts and knee socks while dodging traffic. [16]Disappointment seemed to continue. [17]I soon found out that I was not the envy of all my friends. [18]When I cycled through town, they acted as if they had not seen me. [19]I was told I was crazy doing this kind of job by people I thought would look up to me. [20]My job was not as exciting as I had dreamed it would be either. [21]Instead of solving robberies and murders every day, I found that I spent a great deal of time comforting a local resident because a neighbourhood dog had watered his favourite bush.

Two Views on Toys

[1]There is a vast difference between children and adults where presents are concerned. [2]First, there is the matter of taste. [3]Adults pride themselves on taste, while children ignore the matter of taste in favour of things that are fun. [4]Adults, especially grandparents, pick out educational and tasteful toys that go unused, while children love the trendy playthings advertised on television. [5]Then, of course, there is the matter of money. [6]The new games on the market today are a case in point. [7]Have you ever tried to lure a child away from some expensive game in order to get him or her to play with an old-fashioned game or toy? [8]Finally, there is a difference between an adult's and a child's idea of what is educational. [9]Adults, filled with memories of their own childhoods, tend to be fond of the written word. [10]Today's children, on the other hand, concentrate on anything electronic. [11]These things mean much more to them than to adults. [12]Next holiday season, examine the toys that adults choose for children. [13]Then look at the toys the children prefer. [14]You will see the difference.

■ **Questions**

About Unity

1. Which sentence in "My Broken Dream" does not directly add to the support for its topic? (*Write the sentence number.*)

2. Which paragraph has a topic sentence that is too broad?

_____

About Support

3. Which paragraph contains virtually no specific details?

_____

4. Which paragraph do you feel offers the most effective details?

_____

About Coherence

5. What method of development (one side at a time or point by point) is used in "My Broken Dream"?

_____

6. What transitional words are used in "Two Views on Toys"?

_____

DEVELOPING A COMPARISON OR CONTRAST PARAGRAPH

Development through Prewriting

Randi, the author of "Last Dance," had no trouble thinking of a topic for her comparison or contrast paragraph.

"My communications instructor said, 'You might compare or contrast two individuals, jobs you've had, or places you've lived,'" Randi said. "Then he added, 'Or you might compare or contrast your expectations of a situation with the reality.' My friends and I had just been talking about high-school dances, and no one could remember a good experience. My expectations for my grade twelve formal were so different from the reality! I thought it would be the high point of my last year, but instead it was a total disaster."

Because she likes to think visually, Randi started her preparations for her paragraph by clustering. She found this a helpful way to "see" the relationships between the points she was developing. Her diagram looked like this:

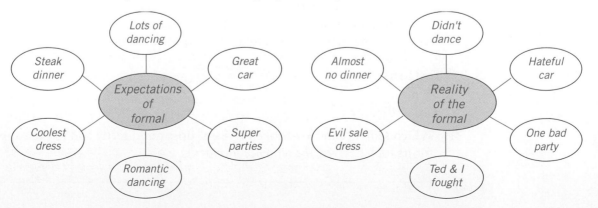

Taking a detail first from the "Expectations" part of the diagram, then from the "Reality" part of the diagram, then another from "Expectations," and so on, Randi began to write her paragraph using the point-by-point format.

> My graduation dance was nothing like what I expected. First of all, I expected to be wearing a beautiful dress that my aunt would make for me. But because she couldn't finish it in time, I had to buy a cheesy one on sale at the last minute. Second, I thought I'd have a wonderful romantic evening with my boyfriend. But we'd been fighting a few days earlier and by the time the formal came around we were barely speaking. I thought we'd have a great time stopping in at lots of parties before the dance, too, but we went to only one—a really dull one—and I left with an upset stomach.

Randi stopped there, because she wasn't satisfied with the way the paragraph was developing. "I wanted the reader to really picture the way I had imagined that last dance, and I didn't like interrupting that picture with the nasty reality of the evening. I wanted to show the dream, then the reality. So I decided to try the one-side-at-a-time approach instead." Here is Randi's first draft.

> My graduation dance was nothing like what I expected. I imagined myself wearing a beautiful, expensive-looking dress that my aunt would make. I thought my boyfriend and I would have a wonderful romantic evening together. We'd dance all through the night and we would cruise around in Ted's brother's hot new Audi. We would stop in at a lot of the best of the pre-dance parties, I thought, and we'd have an excellent steak dinner at the club. But instead my uncle Pete had a gallbladder attack that they thought might be a heart attack, and my aunt went to the hospital with him instead of finishing my dress. I had to run to the mall at the last minute and buy the most pathetic dress that nobody else had wanted off the sale rack. Ted and I had been fighting for days. Because he played minor-league hockey and they were in playoffs and he had a part-time job, too, we didn't have much time together and he still wanted to go out weekends with the boys. So by the night of the dance we were hardly speaking to each other. We went to only one really dull party before the dance and I left it feeling sick. And the room at the club where the dance was was so crowded that I hardly got anything to eat and it was only a buffet anyway. Because we were angry at each other, we didn't dance at all. And instead of his brother's luxury car, we ended up in Ted's friend Lou's stripped-down stock car.

Development through Revising

Randi's instructor reviewed the in-class first drafts of students who wanted his feedback. Here are his comments on Randi's work.

> *All this is very promising and full of details, but some of those details are out of order—you mention the pre-dance parties after the dance itself. Be sure to follow the evening's sequence of events.*
>
> *More descriptive details of some of the important issues here are needed! For instance, what was that "beautiful" dress supposed to look like, and why was the one you ended up with "pathetic"?*

You've got some unnecessary information in here: for example, the details of your uncle's illness. Everything in your paragraph should support your topic sentence.

Taking her instructor's suggestions (and remembering a few more details she wanted to include), Randi wrote the version of her paragraph that appears on page 222.

WRITING A COMPARISON OR CONTRAST PARAGRAPH

How to Write a Comparison or Contrast Paragraph

1   An effective comparison or contrast paragraph examines two subjects that have some relationship to each other and examines the same specific aspects of each subject. Do your two subjects share a common quality or category so you can find points or bases on which to compare or contrast them? Can you focus your two-part topic enough to create a *limited* comparison or contrast paper that addresses specific points about both your subjects?

2   When prewriting for a comparison or contrast paper, divide your document or sheet of paper into two columns: one for each side of your comparison or contrast. List or freewrite for one side (or for one of your subjects) in one column, and for your other side in the other column.

3   Decide whether your paragraph will compare or contrast either both sides of your subject or both of your subjects. Prewrite, using the two-column method, to accumulate enough details for both sides of your paper. Then revise your prewriting to be sure one side's points of comparison or contrast have "matching" points for the other side. Eliminate any details or points that cannot apply to both sides.

4   Decide which method of development best suits your subject: one side at a time, or point by point. Set up your outline to reflect the format you choose. (See the outlines for the two paragraphs on page 224 for examples of both.) Begin your outline by stating your reason for making a comparison or contrast, and state this point, as well as whether you will compare or contrast your two sides, in a trial topic sentence. In the body of your outline, create subtopics or groupings for your major points of comparison or contrast. Under each subtopic (base for comparison or contrast), list details for each side.

5   As you create drafts based on your outline, be sure to use transitional words and phrases (see page 233) appropriate to comparing or contrasting to assist your readers and to clarify the point your paragraph will make.

6   Be sure to write a conclusion that reaffirms the point of your comparison or contrast, based on the information your paragraph has presented.

■ **Writing Assignment 1**

Write a comparison or contrast paragraph on one of the topics below.

Two holidays	Two jobs
Two instructors	Two characters in the same TV show
Two children	Two homes
Two kinds of eaters	Two neighbourhoods
Two drivers	Two video games
Two classmates	Two cars
Two members of a team	Two friends
Two singers or groups	Two crises
Two pets	Two bosses or supervisors
Two parties	Two magazines

Prewriting

a Choose your topic, the two subjects you will write about.

b Decide whether your paragraph will *compare* the two subjects—discuss their similarities—or *contrast* them—discuss their differences. Students most often choose to write about differences. For example, you might write about how a musical group you enjoy differs from a musical group you dislike. You might discuss important differences between two employers you have had or between two neighbourhoods you have lived in. You might contrast a job you have had in a factory with a job you've had as a receptionist.

c Write a direct topic sentence for your paragraph. Here's an example: "My job in a car-parts factory was very different from my job as a receptionist."

d Come up with at least three strong subtopics to support your topic sentence. If you are contrasting two jobs, for example, your points might be that they differed greatly (1) in their physical settings, (2) in the skills they required, and (3) in the people they brought you into contact with.

e Use your topic sentence and subtopics to create a basic outline for your paragraph. Leave lots of space under each point you list. For the jobs paragraph, the outline might start out like this.

Topic sentence: My job in a car-parts factory was very different from my job as a receptionist.

1. The jobs differed in physical setting.
2. The jobs differed in the skills required.
3. The jobs differed in the people they brought me into contact with.

f Under each of your subtopics, jot down as many details as occur to you. Don't worry yet about whether the details all fit perfectly or whether you will be able to use them all. Your goal is to generate a wealth of material to draw on. An example:

<u>Topic Sentence</u>: My job in a car-parts factory was very different from my job as a receptionist.

1. <u>The jobs differed in physical setting</u>
   Factory loud and dirty
   Office clean and quiet
   Factory full of machines, hunks of metal, tools
   Office full of desks, computers, files
   Factory smelled like oil
   Office smelled like new carpet
   Windows in factory too high and dirty to look out of
   Office had big windows along walls

2. <u>The jobs differed in the skills and behaviour they required</u>
   Factory required physical strength and speed
   Office needed mental activity
   Didn't need to be polite in factory
   Had to be polite in office
   Didn't need to think much for myself in factory
   Constantly had to make decisions in the office

3. <u>The jobs differed in the people they brought me into contact with</u>
   In factory, worked with same crew every day
   In office, saw a constant stream of new customers
   Most co-workers in factory had high school or less
   Many co-workers and clients in office well educated
   Co-workers in factory spoke a lot of different languages
   Heard mostly English in the office

g   Decide which format you will use to develop your paragraph: one side at a time or point by point. Either is acceptable; it is up to you to decide which you prefer and which suits your subject better. The important thing is to be consistent: whichever format you choose, be sure to use it throughout the entire paragraph.

h   Write the first draft of your paragraph.

Revising

Put your writing away for a day or so. You will return to it with a fresh perspective and a better ability to critique what you have done.

Reread your work with these questions in mind:

- Does my topic sentence make it clear what two things I am comparing or contrasting?

- Have I compared or contrasted the subjects in at least three important ways?

- Have I provided specific details that effectively back up my subtopics?

- If I have chosen the point-by-point format, have I consistently discussed a point about one subject, then immediately discussed the same point about the other subject before moving on to the next point?

- If I have chosen the one-side-at-a-time format, have I discussed every point about one of my subjects, then discussed the same points in the same order about the second subject?

- Have I used appropriate transitions, such as *first, in addition, also,* and *another way* or any reasonable choices from the box below, to help readers follow my train of thought?

- Have I carefully proofread my paragraph, using the list on the inside front cover of this book, and corrected all sentence-skills mistakes, including spelling errors?

Continue revising your work until you can answer yes to all these questions.

Transitions for Comparison or Contrast Papers

Comparison Transitions	*Contrast Transitions*
just as, just like	on the other hand
like, likewise	in contrast to, contrasting
similarly, in a similar way, similar to	as opposed to, in opposition to
also, too, again	although, even though
moreover, further, furthermore	whereas, while
	but, still, nonetheless, nevertheless, yet

Writing Assignment 2

Write a paragraph in which you compare or contrast your life in the real world with your life in an imagined "perfect world." Your paragraph may be humorous or serious.

Prewriting

a Because your "real life" and "perfect world" are too broad for a paragraph, decide on three specific areas to focus on. Select any of the areas below, or think of others yourself.

Work	Physical location	Possessions
Money	Personal appearance	Housing
Romance	Friends	Talents

b Write the name of one of your three areas (for example, "Work") across the top of a page. Divide the page into two columns. Label one column "Real Life" and the other column "Perfect World." Under "Real Life," write down as many details as you can think of that describe your real-life work situation. Under "Perfect World," write down details that describe what your perfect work life would be like. Repeat the process on separate pages for your other two major areas.

c Write a topic sentence for your paragraph. Here is an example: "In my perfect world, my life would be quite different in the areas of work, money, and housing."

d Decide which approach you will take: one side at a time or point by point.

e Write a quick outline that reflects the format you have selected. The outline for a point-by-point format would look like this.

> <u>Topic sentence</u>: In my perfect world, my life would be quite different in the areas of work, money, and housing.
>
> 1. Work
>   a. Real-life work
>   b. Perfect-world work
>
> 2. Money
>   a. Real-life money
>   b. Perfect-world money
>
> 3. Housing
>   a. Real-life housing
>   b. Perfect-world housing

The outline for a one-side-at-a-time format would look like this.

> <u>Topic sentence</u>: In my perfect world, my life would be quite different in the areas of work, money, and housing.
>
> 1. Real life
>   a. Work
>   b. Money
>   c. Housing
>
> 2. Perfect world
>   a. Work
>   b. Money
>   c. Housing

f Drawing from the three pages of details you generated in step *b*, complete your outline by jotting down your strongest supporting details for each point.

g Write the first draft of your paragraph.

Revising

Reread your paragraph, then show it to a friend who will give you fair feedback. You should both review it with these questions in mind:

■ Does the topic sentence make it clear what three areas of your life are being compared or contrasted?

■ Does the paragraph follow a consistent format: point by point or one side at a time?

- Does the paragraph provide specific details that describe both the "real life" and the "perfect world"?
- Does the paragraph include transitional words and phrases that make it easy to follow?
- Have all the sentence-skills mistakes, including spelling errors, been corrected?

Continue revising your work until you and your reader can answer yes to all these questions.

■ Writing Assignment 3

Write a contrast paragraph on one of the topics below.

Neighbourhood stores versus a shopping mall
Driving on an expressway versus driving on side roads
Shift versus *Wired* (or any other two popular magazines)
Working parents versus stay-at-home parents
Last year's fashions versus this year's
Shopping in stores versus shopping online
CD players versus MP3 players
Hip hop versus R&B, electronica, or another music style
News in a newspaper versus news on television or online
Yesterday's toys versus today's
One Canadian TV series versus a similar U.S. network series
"Winning" locker room after a game versus "losing" locker room
Ad on television versus ad (for the same product) in a magazine
Your values versus those of your parents and their generation

Follow the directions for prewriting and revising in Writing Assignment 2.

■ Writing Assignment 4

You have volunteered to contribute a monthly column to the students' section of your college's website. You are asked to post on your links page helpful advice and information about various issues of interest to your peers. This month's column is dedicated to first-semester students.

Write an open letter comparing or contrasting *specific aspects* of two sides of one of the following subjects:

- life as a first-semester college student versus life as a working person (*or* a high-school student or other option)
- issues faced by the "mature student" versus those faced by the "just-out-of-high-school student"

■ Writing Assignment 5

Television talk shows share certain features, but they also differ in significant ways. Write a paragraph contrasting two talk shows. In preparation, watch two different talk shows, taking some notes on various aspects of the shows. Then arrange the details of your notes into a few categories, such as the performance of the hosts, the types of guests, and the behaviour of their audiences. Use your notes to help you decide on a point of view to take in your topic sentence, which might be similar to this one.

While _____ (*name of show*) aims to help its viewers, _____ (*name of other show*) is more interested in satisfying viewers' desire for dramatic conflict.

Once you decide on your topic sentence, use only those details that support it. Then decide which method of organization you will use, and prepare your outline. Since readers will focus mainly on your subjects and contrasts, write in the third person. Be sure to use transition words and to edit your next-to-final draft carefully.

Writing Assignment 6

Writing about a Reading Selection: Read the selection "Are We Raising Morally Illiterate Kids?" on pages 552-55. Then consider a situation in your life when you were confronted by the need to make a choice between two courses of action. One option open to you was likely "wrong" by most ethical standards, and the other option was probably the "right" moral choice. Which course of action did you choose, and why? Write a paragraph that examines your situation and decision by comparing or contrasting the appeals, rewards, or problems of each possible course of action.

To get started, write a brief description of your decision and its circumstances at the top of a sheet of paper. Under that description, make two lists: one containing the appealing aspects and problems of making the "wrong" choice, and one containing the appeals, difficulties, and rewards of making the "right" choice. You may want to further subdivide the lists into headings such as "short-term" and "long-term," or "personal" and "affecting others," depending on your situation and decision.

Next, decide whether you will use a side-by-side or point-by-point method of development. Whichever method you use, counter each point for the "wrong" side with a comparable point for the "right" side. If you use the side-by-side method, be sure to use transitions to remind readers of your first side's points as you cover the points for the other side of your moral issue.

REVIEWING THE LEARNING OUTCOMES FOR COMPARISON OR CONTRAST WRITING

After completing one of the writing assignments in this chapter, review your work to see how well it meets the following tests.

1   Does your paragraph compare or contrast two sides of an idea or two subjects that have a logical reason to be considered together? Does a worthwhile point emerge from the activity of comparing or contrasting the two parts of your topic?

2 Do you open with a topic sentence that states (1) both parts of your subject, (2) your intention to either compare or contrast, and (3) the point your paragraph makes by comparing or contrasting your two subjects?

3 Have you carefully and consistently used the method most appropriate to your subject matter? If you have many specific details on each side, have you used the point-by-point format? If you wished to pursue each side in some depth, have you used the one-side-at-a-time format?

4 Within either format, are your points of comparison or contrast and your supporting details for each relatively equal and balanced for both sides or both subjects?

5 Do you conclude with a summing-up of the points you have made in your paragraph and an indication of how these points reaffirm and strengthen your main point?

Visit the *English Skills with Readings* Online Learning Centre at **www.mcgrawhill.ca/college/langan** to access self-quizzes, bonus material on study and research skills, web resources, and other learning and study tools.

learning a Process · *Examining Cause and Effect* · *Comparing or Contrasting* · *Defining*
viding and classifying · *Describing a Scene or Person* · *Narrating an Event* · *Arguing a P*
xplaining a Process · *Examining Cause and Effect* · *Comparing or Contrasting* · *Defining*
viding and classifying · *Describing a Scene or Person* · *Narrating an Event* · *Arguing a P*
Explaining a Process · *Examining Cause and Effect* · *Compari*

CHAPTER 14

Defining a Term

LEARNING OUTCOMES

By working through this chapter's activities and completing one or more of its writing assignments, you will write a definition paragraph that

- sets its subject in an appropriately focused category of similar subjects and then sets its subject apart from other members of that category with adequate explanations of how the subject differs from them;
- begins with a topic sentence placing the subject in its category, setting out the subject as somehow unique, and indicating the relative degree of formality or objectivity involved in the definition to follow;
- offers at least three subtopics (or one extended subtopic) to clarify and limit the meaning of its subject; such points may be examples, brief anecdotes, or comparisons or contrasts with other closely related concepts;
- offers meanings appropriate both to the subject and to the needs of the reader for either an objective or a personal and subjective definition; and
- concludes with a summary of the meaning of the term and its significance, based on what has been stated in the paragraph.

Defining is essential to clear communication. Unless people agree on what a speaker or writer means by a given term, misunderstandings occur, and communication may fail. Definition paragraphs explain the meaning of some term or concept; they are forms of extended definitions—extended beyond the limited definitions found in dictionaries. Although a paragraph defining some concrete or abstract term may initially use elements of a dictionary definition, such a paragraph's purpose is to state fully the writer's sense of that term's meaning. The writer's task, in defining, is to do three things: (1) to *classify* the subject appropriately in terms of other items of its type, (2) to *make specific* his or her explanation of the subject's meaning by limiting that meaning, and (3) to offer meanings *relevant to the needs of the readers* of the paragraph.

Every day we offer informal definitions to explain what we mean by a particular term. We may say, "Mario is an anxious person." Then, without pausing, we try to be more exact about what we mean by *anxious*. We expand on our definition by giving *examples*: "He's always worrying about the future. Yesterday he was talking about how many bills he'll have this year." Or we offer a *story* to show Mario's anxiety in a specific circumstance. Or perhaps we may *compare or contrast* Mario's anxiety with what we feel in similar situations. We even describe the stages in the *process* by which Mario became so anxious. Our aim is to *set limits* around exactly what we mean by *anxious* in the *context of our conversation*, as opposed to what a dictionary may mean by *anxious* or what a psychologist may mean by the term. Even in ordinary conversations, we use the same assortment of methods for defining that we use in writing definition papers.

The word *definition*, as derived from its Latin origin, refers to putting "fines," or limits, around a subject. This boundary-setting happens every time you define any subject. You will work with and create definitions for many purposes in your life; as language and situations change, so does the way words are used. Misunderstandings may be remedied quickly in conversation, but there is little tolerance for misunderstanding or not knowing a term in career contexts. The growth of technology has obviously increased the need for definitions of new words and of existing words with new meanings; business constantly creates its own terminologies, and careers in human and social services rely on precise definitions for terms in reports and studies.

In this section, you will be asked to write a paragraph in which you define a term. The two student paragraphs below are examples of definition writing. Read them, and then answer the questions that follow.

PARAGRAPHS TO CONSIDER

Luck

[1]Luck is putting $1.75 into a vending machine and getting the money back with your snacks. [2]It is an instructor's decision to give a retest on a test where you first scored thirty. [3]Luck refers to moments of good fortune that happen in everyday life. [4]It is not going to the dentist for two years and then going and finding out that you do not have any cavities. [5]It is calling up a plumber to fix a leak on a day when the plumber has no other work to do. [6]Luck is finding a used car for sale at a good price at exactly the time when your car rolls its last kilometre. [7]It is driving into a traffic bottleneck and choosing the lane that winds up moving most rapidly. [8]Luck is being late for work on a day when your boss arrives later than you do. [9]It is having a new checkout aisle at the supermarket open up just as your cart arrives. [10]The best kind of luck is winning a new TV set with a raffle ticket for which you paid only a quarter.

Disillusionment

[1]Disillusionment is the feeling of having one of our most cherished beliefs stolen from us. [2]I learned about disillusionment first-hand the day Mr. Khalid, our grade eight teacher, handed out the marks on our class biology projects. [3]I had worked hard to assemble what I thought was the best insect collection

any school had ever seen. [4]For weeks, I had set up homemade traps around our house, in the woods, and in vacant lots. [5]At night, I would stretch a white sheet between two trees, shine a lantern on it, and collect the night-flying insects that gathered there. [6]With my own money, I had bought killing jars, insect pins, gummed labels, and display boxes. [7]I carefully arranged related insects together, with labels listing each scientific name and the place and date of capture. [8]Slowly and painfully, I processed and printed the report that accompanied my project at the Moose Jaw school science fair. [9]In contrast, my friend Michael did almost nothing for his project. [10]He had his father, a doctor, build an impressive maze complete with live rats and a sign that read, "You are the trainer." [11]A person could lift a little plastic door, send a rat running through the maze, and then hit a button to release a pellet of rat food as a reward. [12]This exhibit turned out to be the most popular one at the fair. [13]I felt sure that our teacher would know that Michael could not have built it, and I was certain that my hard work would be recognized and rewarded. [14]Then the marks were finally handed out, and I was crushed. [15]Michael had an A+, but my mark was a B. [16]I suddenly realized that honesty and hard work don't always pay off in the end. [17]The idea that life is not fair hit me with such force that I felt sick. [18]I will never forget that moment.

◼ Questions

About Unity

1. Which paragraph places its topic sentence within the paragraph rather than, more appropriately, at the beginning?

   _____

2. Which sentence in "Disillusionment" is somewhat repetitious and might be revised for paragraph unity? (*Write the sentence number here.*) _____

About Support

3. Which paragraph develops its definition through a series of short examples?

   _____

4. Which paragraph develops its definition through a single extended example?

   _____

About Coherence

5. Which paragraph uses emphatic order, saving its best detail for last?

   _____

6. Which paragraph uses time order to organize its details?

   _____

DEVELOPING A DEFINITION PARAGRAPH

Development through Prewriting

When Thuyen, a biochemistry student and the author of "Disillusionment," started working on her assignment, she did not know what she wanted to write about. She looked around her room for inspiration. Her cats chasing each other around the furniture made her think about defining "energy." The way she felt near the end of the semester made her think she might write about "exhaustion." Still not sure of a topic, she looked over her notes from that day's class. Her instructor had listed some terms on the whiteboard, saying, "Maybe you could focus on what one of these words has meant in your own life." Thuyen scanned the words she had copied down: *honesty, faith, betrayal, disillusionment...* "When I got to the word *disillusionment*, my grade eight science fair flashed into my mind," Thuyen said. "That was a bitter experience that definitely taught me what disillusionment was all about."

Because the science fair had occurred years before, Thuyen had to work to remember it clearly. She decided to try questioning herself to come up with the details of what really had happened. Here are the questions Thuyen asked herself and the answers she wrote.

When did I learn about disillusionment?
When I was in grade eight

Where did it happen?
At the school science fair

Who was involved?
Me, Michael Schmidt and his father, and Mr. Khalid

What happened?
I had worked really hard on my insect collection. Michael had done almost nothing but he had a rat maze that his father had built. I got a B on my project while Michael got an A.

Why was the experience so disillusioning?
I thought my hard work and my interest would be rewarded. I was sure Mr. Khalid would know that I had put far more effort into my project than Michael had. When he won, I learned that cheating can pay off and honest work isn't always recognized.

How did I react?
I felt sick to my stomach. I wanted to confront Mr. Khalid and Michael and make them see how unfair the grades were. But I knew I'd just look like a whiner, so I didn't do anything.

Based on this experience, how would I define disillusionment?
It's finding out that something you really believed in isn't true.

Drawing from the ideas she came up with in her self-questioning, Thuyen wrote an outline, then the following first draft.

> Disillusionment is finding out that one of your most important beliefs isn't true. I used to want to be an entomologist, and science was always my favourite subject. In my grade eight science fair, I learned all about disillusionment. I had worked very hard on my project, an insect collection. I was sure it would get an A. I had worked so hard on it, even spending nights outside making sure it was very good. My friend Michael also did a project, but he barely worked on his at all. Instead, he had his father build a maze for a rat to run through. The trainer lifted a little plastic door to let the rat into the maze, and if it completed the maze, the trainer could release a food pellet for it to eat. It was a nice project, but the point is that Michael hadn't made it. He just made things like the banner that hung over it. Mr. Khalid was our science teacher. He gave Michael an A+ and me just a B. So that really taught me about disillusionment.

Development through Revising

The next class, Thuyen's instructor divided the class up into groups of three. The groups reviewed each member's paragraph. Thuyen was grouped with Stefanie and Trevor. After reading through Thuyen's paragraph, the group had a discussion.

"My first reaction is that I want to know more about your project," said Stefanie. "You say a lot about Michael's, but not much about your own. What was so good about it? Is an entomologist somebody who studies bugs? You need to show us why your project was so incredible, not just tell us. Also, you say how hard you worked, but you don't show us how hard."

"Yeah, you're right," said Thuyen. "I remember my project clearly, but I guess somebody reading this has to know what it was like and how much effort went into it."

Trevor said, "I like your topic sentence, but when I finished the paragraph, I wasn't sure what 'important belief' you'd learned wasn't true. What was the thing you believed in so much?"

Thuyen thought a minute. "I was brought up to believe that honest hard work would always be rewarded. I found out it doesn't always happen that way, and that cheaters can actually win."

Trevor nodded. "So put that in your paper."

Stefanie added, "I know I'd have been really angry if I got that mark. So I guess I think you should say how you felt after you saw your mark. If you don't explain that a bit, your paragraph kind of ends abruptly."

Thuyen agreed with her classmates' suggestions. After she had gone through several revisions, she produced the paragraph that appears on pages 239-40.

WRITING A DEFINITION PARAGRAPH

How to Write a Definition Paragraph

1   Looking at the subject for your paragraph, first ask yourself this question: Is your subject a *concrete* thing or an *abstract* concept? Concrete objects, like dogs or computers, have precise basic (denotative) definitions, to which personal experience-based shadings (connotative descriptions) may be added. Abstract ideas like honour or ambition are defined almost completely according to personal interpretations and understandings of their meaning. Some terms occupy a "middle space" between the concrete and the abstract, like "an ideal employee."

2   Next, consider the degree of objectivity most suitable to defining your subject. Is your paragraph a personal definition of some abstract subject or quality best explained by your own experience with that quality, or is it an extended definition of some concrete subject where more objective details, even scientific or factual ones, are required? Although the methods for writing a definition are the same for both types of subjects, the tones, points of view, types of details, and needs of readers differ.

3   Prewrite to accumulate as many details as possible of any sort about your subject. As you prepare to create an outline for your paragraph, consider the methods that will best define your subject: examples, comparing or contrasting with other subjects of its type, brief anecdotes, or a description of how your subject works. Decide on a method of development for your definition and create an outline based on that method.

4   Write a topic sentence that places your subject in a logical category and includes at least one specific detail that distinguishes your subject. Include an indication of the nature and tone of your definition: subjective and personal, or objective and factual.

5   Be sure that the body of your definition truly clarifies the meaning of your subject and does not merely repeat itself or offer unclear synonyms as alternative definitions. Make sure that your examples or distinguishing details are vivid and logically connected. The details or support for your definition may also state what your subject is by setting out what it is not.

6   Conclude with a summation of your understanding of your term, and its significance.

■   **Writing Assignment 1**

Write a paragraph that defines the term *TV addict*. Base your paragraph on the topic sentence and three subtopics below.

Topic sentence: Television addicts are people who will watch all the programs they can, for as long as they can, rather than do anything else.

1. TV addicts, first of all, will watch anything on the tube, no matter how bad it is ...

2. In addition, addicts watch TV more hours than normal people do ...

3. Finally, addicts feel that TV is more important than other people or any other activities or events that might be going on. ...

Prewriting

a Generate as many examples as you can for each of the three qualities of a TV addict. You can do this by asking yourself the following questions:

- What are some of the truly awful shows that I (or TV addicts I know) watch just because the television is on?
- What are some examples of the large amounts of time that I (or TV addicts I know) spend watching television?
- What are some examples of ways that I (or TV addicts I know) neglect people or give up activities in order to watch TV?

Write down every answer you can think of for each question. At this point, don't think about writing full sentences or about grammar or spelling. Just get your answers down on the screen or on paper.

b Look over the list of examples you have accumulated. Select the strongest examples you have thought of. You should have at least two or three for each quality. If not, ask yourself the questions in step *a* again.

c Write out the examples you will use, this time expressing them in full, grammatically correct sentences. Look for possible comparisons or contrasts within your examples—these can be useful ways to limit and clarify a point. For example, how much TV does an addict watch, compared with someone else?

d Start with the topic sentence and the three subtopics provided in the assignment. Fill in the examples you've generated to support each subtopic. You now have a very complete sentence-form outline, and you are ready to write a first draft of your paragraph.

Revising

Put your first draft away for as long as possible. When you come back to it, reread it critically, asking yourself these questions:

- Have I used the topic sentence and the three subtopics that were provided?
- Have I backed up each subtopic with at least two examples?
- Does each of my examples truly illustrate the point it backs up?
- Have I used appropriate transitional language (*another, in addition, for example, in contrast to*) to tie my thoughts together?
- Have I proofread my paragraph and corrected any sentence-skills errors, including spelling mistakes?

Keep revising your paragraph until you can answer yes to each question.

■ **Writing Assignment 2**

Our conversations are full of labels for people. These labels are a convenient kind of verbal shorthand, but how often do people know exactly what we mean by our terms? Write a paragraph that states your definition of what is meant by one of these labels. Each term refers to a certain kind of person.

Big-mouth	Clown	Pessimist
Charmer	Jellyfish	Hypocrite
Loser	Leader	Perfectionist
Lazybones	Nerd	Pack rat
Con artist	Good neighbour	Hard worker
Fair-weather friend	Optimist	Team player

Prewriting

a Write a topic sentence for your definition paragraph. This is a two-part process:

■ First, place the term in a class, or category. For example, if you are writing about a certain kind of person, the general category is *person*. If you are describing a type of friend, the general category is *friend*.
■ Second, describe what you consider the special feature or features that set your term apart from other members of its class. For instance, say what *kind* of person you are writing about or what *type* of friend.

In the following topic sentence, try to identify three things: the term being defined, the class it belongs to, and the special feature that sets the term apart from other members of its class.

A chocoholic is a person who craves chocolate.

The term being defined is *chocoholic*. The category it belongs to is *person*. The words that set *chocoholic* apart from any other person are *craves chocolate*.

Below is another example of a topic sentence for this assignment. It is a definition of a *whiner*. The class, or category, is underlined: a whiner is a type of person. The words that set the term *whiner* apart from other members of the class are double-underlined.

A whiner is a <u>person</u> who feels <u><u>wronged by life</u></u>.

In the following sample topic sentences, underline the class and double-underline the special features.

A clotheshorse is a person who needs new clothes to be happy.
The class clown is a student who gets attention through silly behaviour.
A worrywart is a person who sees danger everywhere.

b Develop your definition by using one of the following methods.

Examples: Give several examples that support your topic sentence.
Extended example: Use one longer example to support your topic sentence.

Contrast: Support your topic sentence by showing what your term is *not.* For instance, you may want to define a *fair-weather friend* by contrasting his or her actions with those of a true friend.

c Write an outline. Once you have created a topic sentence and decided how to develop your paragraph, write an outline. This step is especially important if you are using a contrast method of development.

d Write a first draft of your paragraph

Revising

As you revise your paragraph, keep these questions in mind:

- Does my topic sentence (1) place my term in a class and (2) name some special features that set it apart from its class?
- Have I made a clear choice to develop my topic sentence through either several examples, one extended example, or contrast?
- If I have chosen to illustrate my topic through contrast, have I consistently followed either a point-by-point or a one-side-at-a-time format?
- Have I used appropriate transitions (*another, in addition, in contrast, for example*) to tie my thoughts together?
- Is my paragraph free of sentence-skills errors, including spelling mistakes?

Continue revising until you can answer yes to all these questions.

■ Writing Assignment 3

Write a paragraph that defines one of the abstract terms below.

Persistence	Responsibility	Fear
Rebellion	Insecurity	Arrogance
Sense of humour	Assertiveness	Conscience
Escape	Jealousy	Class
Danger	Nostalgia	Innocence
Curiosity	Gentleness	Freedom
Common sense	Depression	Violence
Family	Obsession	Shyness
Practicality	Self-control	

As a guide in writing your paper, use the suggestions for prewriting and revising in Writing Assignment 2. Remember to place your term in a class or category and to describe what you feel are the distinguishing features of that term.

After writing your topic sentence, check that it is complete and correct for a definition paragraph by doing the following:

- Single-underline the category of the term you're defining.
- Double-underline the term's distinguishing characteristic or characteristics.

Here are three sample topic sentences.

Laziness is the <u>trait</u> of <u><u>resisting all worthwhile work as much as possible.</u></u>

> Jealousy is the <u>feeling</u> of <u>wanting a possession or quality someone else has</u>.
> A family is a <u>group</u> whose <u>members are related to one another in some way</u>.

Defining an abstract term or concept requires you to select certain specific examples or circumstances that make your view of that term's meaning clear to your reader. Definition papers make use of many methods of paragraph development.
Here are several approaches to writing such a paper.

- Begin with an objective definition of your concept, then compare or contrast that meaning with your own specific experiences with or knowledge of that concept.
- Consider explaining what your concept or term means by using *negation*; explain what something is by stating clearly what it is *not* or need not be.
- Sometimes using an anecdote, or brief story, can vividly show an abstract quality in action.
- Dividing your abstract quality into different aspects or categories, with examples for each, often makes a broad concept clearer to readers.

■ Writing Assignment 4

Since it affects all of us to some degree, stress is a useful subject to explore. Write a paragraph defining that word. Organize your paragraph in one of these ways:

- Use a series of examples (see Chapter 10) of stress.
- Use narration (see Chapter 8) to provide one longer example of stress: create a hypothetical person (or use a real person) and show how this person's typical morning or day illustrates your definition of stress.

Using strategies described on the Online Learning Centre, research the topic of stress. Narrow down your findings to support the person or examples you have decided on.

Note: Do not simply write a series of general, abstract sentences that repeat and reword your definition. If you concentrate on your topic sentence and on providing specific support for it, you will avoid the common trap of getting lost in a maze of generalities.

■ Writing Assignment 5

Option 1: At the place where you work, one employee has just quit, creating a new job opening. Since you have been working there for a while, your boss has asked you to write a job description of the position. That description, which is really a detailed definition of the job, will be sent to employment agencies. These agencies will be responsible for interviewing candidates. Choose any position you know about, and write a job description for it. First, give the purpose of the job, and then list its duties and responsibilities. Finally, give the qualifications for the position.
Here is a sample topic sentence for this assignment.

> Purchasing department clerk is a <u>position</u> in which someone <u>provides a variety of services to the purchasing-department managers</u>.

In a paragraph with this topic sentence, the writer would go on to list and explain the various services the clerk must provide.

Option 2: Alternatively, imagine that your boss has asked you to explain *team spirit* to a new worker. The purpose of your explanation will be to give the newcomer an idea of the teamwork that is expected in this workplace. Write a paragraph that defines in detail what your boss means by *team spirit*. Use examples or one extended example to illustrate your general statements.

■ Writing Assignment 6

Writing about a Reading Selection: Read the selection "Shopping: The Oldest Profession" by Candace Fertile on pages 583-88. The author defines shopping as one of mankind's oldest behaviours—and refers to it as a "profession." Think about something you particularly enjoy, and imagine doing this for a living. Write a definition paragraph on your activity as "the perfect profession." Your topic sentence might be "Playing pool is the perfect profession—it offers challenges, physical activity, and companionship."

Prewrite to come up with reasons why your chosen activity would make such an ideal job for you. How do these define your "perfect profession"? Then decide on the order in which to present your subtopics, making sure to use appropriate transitions to indicate relative importance.

REVIEWING THE LEARNING OUTCOMES FOR DEFINITION WRITING

After completing any of the writing assignments in this chapter, review your work to see how well it meets the following tests.

1   Does your paragraph open with a topic sentence that both places your subject to be defined in an appropriate category and sets it off from other members of that category?

2   Does your topic sentence indicate your paper's tone and the degree of objectivity or subjectivity with which you will define your subject?

3   Do you offer at least three subtopics and details for your definition of your subject? Are your points and details specific, and does each directly support your topic sentence's point about your subject?

4   Have you used a method of development for your supporting material that is appropriate to the subject you define: examples, comparison or contrast, negation, or anecdote?

5   Does your paper conclude with a summary of your meanings, a reminder of your topic sentence's point, and a suggestion of the significance of your definition?

Visit the *English Skills with Readings* Online Learning Centre at **www.mcgrawhill.ca/college/langan** to access self-quizzes, bonus material on study and research skills, web resources, and other learning and study tools.

plaining a Process · Examining Cause and Effect · Comparing or Contrasting · Defining
rm · Dividing and Classifying · Describing a Scene or Person · Narrating an Event · Arguir
Position · Explaining a Process · Examining Cause and Effect · Comparing or Contrasting
fining a Term · Dividing and Classifying · Describing a Scene or Person · Narrating a
ent · Arguing a Position · Explaining a Process · Examining Cause and Effect · Compari

CHAPTER 15

Dividing and Classifying

LEARNING OUTCOMES

By working through this chapter's activities and completing at least one of its writing assignments, you will write a classification and division paragraph that

- divides its subject according to a consistent classifying principle logically related to your purpose in analyzing that subject;

- arranges its categories or subject divisions in a sequence that best supports the point and purpose of the paper;

- begins with a topic sentence that states the paper's subject, the divisions of its subject, and your point in making those divisions;

- offers a balanced number of specific and adequate details for each subtopic or subject division; and

- concludes with a return to your subject as a whole and offers a closing thought based on your paragraph's examination of your subject divisions.

Dividing a subject into classes or categories occurs constantly in everyday life. People break groups of things or ideas into subgroups, based on some purpose or need, hoping to manage situations or understand ideas more easily. The process of dividing and classifying seeks to create order out of apparent confusion and often leads to decision making. Division and classification paragraphs imitate a natural human tendency to divide up a subject or to open it up and examine its parts according to some logical pattern.

If you were doing the laundry, you would probably separate the clothing into piles. If your purpose was to decide when to use bleach, you would sort all the whites into one pile and all the colours into another. If your purpose was to see how many types of washing cycles were needed, you might put all cottons in one pile, polyesters in another, silks in a third, and so on. Such ordinary processes of sorting according to various principles demonstrate how we organize and order our environment in order to make decisions.

Classifying and dividing are two separate and different processes. *Classifying* is the process of taking many things and separating them into categories. We generally classify to better manage or understand many things. Music stores classify CDs into many different genres such as hip hop, dance, electronica, and so on, so that customers can find the artists they enjoy. Librarians classify books into groups (novels, travel, health, etc.) to make them easier to find. *Dividing*, in contrast, is taking one thing and breaking it down into parts. We often divide, or analyze, to better understand, teach, or evaluate something. For example, a botanist divides a tree into its parts to explain their functions. A music reviewer may analyze the elements of a band's performance—for example, the skill of the lead guitarist, rapport with the audience, songs chosen, and so on.

In short, if you are classifying, you are sorting *numbers of things* into categories. If you are dividing, you are breaking *one thing* into parts. It all depends on your purpose—you might classify flowers into various types or divide a single flower into its parts.

Division and classification activities are ongoing parts of your college and career communications tasks. Sorting a mass of consumers into demographic groups to examine and report on buying patterns; dividing components of a software program into categories to analyze their effectiveness: these involve the same set of structuring and analyzing skills.

In this chapter, you will be asked to write a paragraph in which you divide or classify a subject according to a single principle. To prepare for this assignment, first read the division and classification paragraphs below and then work through the questions and the activity that follow.

PARAGRAPHS TO CONSIDER

Studying for a Test

[1]Phase 1, often called the "no problem" phase, runs from the day the test is announced to approximately forty-eight hours before the dreaded exam is passed out. [2]During phase 1, the student is carefree, smiling, and kind to helpless animals and small children. [3]When asked by classmates if he or she has studied for the test yet, the reply will be an assured "No problem." [4]During phase 1, no actual studying takes place. [5]Phase 2 is entered two days before the test. [6]For example, if the test is scheduled for 9 a.m. Friday, phase 2 begins at 9 a.m. Wednesday. [7]During phase 2, again, no actual studying takes place. [8]Phase 3, the final phase, is entered twelve hours before "zero hour." [9]This is the acute phase, characterized by sweaty palms, nervous twitches, and confused mental patterns. [10]For a test at nine o'clock on Friday morning, a student begins exhibiting these symptoms at approximately nine o'clock on Thursday night. [11]Phase 3 is also termed the "shock" phase, since the student is shocked to discover the imminent nature of the exam and the amount of material to be studied. [12]During this phase, the student will probably be unable to sleep and will mumble meaningless phrases like "$a^2 + c^2$." [13]This phase will not end until the exam is over. [14]If the cram

session has worked, the student will fall gratefully asleep. [15]On waking up, he or she will be ready to go through the whole cycle again with the next test.

Three Kinds of Dogs

[1]A city walker will notice that most dogs fall into one of three categories. [2]First there are the big dogs, which are generally harmless and often downright friendly. [3]They walk along peacefully with their owners, their tongues hanging out and big goofy grins on their faces. [4]Apparently, they know they're too big to have anything to worry about, so why not be nice? [5]Second are the spunky medium-sized dogs. [6]When they see a stranger approaching, they go on alert status. [7]They prick up their ears, they raise their hackles, and they may growl a lillle, deep in their throats. [8]"I don't know you," they seem to be saying, "so be careful what you do." [9]Unless the walker confronts their owners, these dogs usually won't do anything more than threaten. [10]The third category is made up of the shivering, neurotic little yappy dogs whose shrill barks could shatter glass and whose needle-like little teeth are ready to sink into a friendly outstretched hand. [11]Strollers always wonder about these dogs: don't they know that anyone who really wanted to could pick them up in one hand and growl right back at them? [12]Apparently they do not, because of all the dogs a walker meets, these are the most irritating. [13]Such dogs are only one of the potential hazards a city walker meets.

▨ Questions

About Unity

1. Which paragraph lacks a topic sentence?

    _____

2. Which sentence in "Three Kinds of Dogs" should be eliminated in the interest of paragraph unity? (*Write the sentence number here.*) _____

About Support

3. Which of the three phases in "Studying for a Test" lacks specific details?

    _____

About Coherence

4. Which paragraph uses time order to organize its details?

    _____

5. Which paragraph uses emphatic order to organize its details?

    _____

6. What words in the emphatic-order paragraph signal the most important detail?

    _____

Activity

This activity will sharpen your sense of the classifying process.

Classification *always* divides items in a group according to some criterion, or *principle of classification*. This principle is used both for *dividing* a group into its members and for maintaining *unity* of the classifications. In each of the following ten groups, cross out the one item that has not been classified on the same basis as the other three. Also, indicate in the space provided the single *principle of classification* used for the three items. Note the examples.

Examples

Water
a. Cold
b. ~~Lake~~
c. Hot
d. Lukewarm
Unifying principle:

temperature

Household pests
~~a. Mice~~
b. Ants
c. Roaches
d. Flies
Unifying principle:

insects

1. Eyes
   a. Blue
   b. Nearsighted
   c. Brown
   d. Hazel
   Unifying principle:

   _____

2. Mattresses
   a. Double
   b. Twin
   c. Queen
   d. Firm
   Unifying principle:

   _____

3. Zoo animals
   a. Flamingo
   b. Peacock
   c. Polar bear
   d. Ostrich
   Unifying principle:

   _____

4. Vacation
   a. Summer
   b. Holiday
   c. Seashore
   d. Weekend
   Unifying principle:

   _____

5. College classes
   a. Enjoy
   b. Dislike
   c. Tolerate
   d. Morning
   Unifying principle:

   _____

6. Wallets
   a. Leather
   b. Plastic
   c. Stolen
   d. Fabric
   Unifying principle:

   _____

7. Newspaper
   a. Wrapping garbage
   b. Editorials
   c. Making paper planes
   d. Covering floor while painting
   Unifying principle:

   _____

8. Music
   a. Metal
   b. Country
   c. Melodic
   d. R & B
   Unifying principle:

   _____

9. Exercise
   a. Running
   b. Swimming
   c. Gymnastics
   d. Fatigue
   Unifying principle:

   _____

10. Leftovers
   a. Cold chicken
   b. Feed to dog
   c. Reheat
   d. Use in a stew
   Unifying principle:

   _____

DEVELOPING A DIVISION AND CLASSIFICATION PARAGRAPH

Development through Prewriting

Adam walked home from his bus stop, thinking about the assignment to write a division and classification paragraph. As he strolled along his familiar route, his observations made him think of a few possibilities. "First I thought of writing about the businesses in my neighbourhood, dividing them into the kinds of customers they attract," he said. "When I stopped in at my favourite coffee place, I thought about dividing the people who hang out there. There is a group of men who sit with cups of espresso and play cards, and there are some students like me, but there didn't seem to be a clear third category and I wasn't sure two would be enough. As I continued walking home, I saw a dog walker with four dogs on a joined leash. Then I saw Mr. Kobielski with his big golden Lab and a lady with two nervous little dogs that acted as if they wanted to eat me, and I thought, 'Dogs! I can classify different kinds of dogs.'"

But how would he classify them? Thinking further, Adam realized that he thought of dogs as having certain personalities depending on their sizes. "I know there are exceptions, of course, but since this was going to be a comical paragraph, I thought it would be all right if I exaggerated a bit." He wrote down his three categories.

> Big dogs
> Medium-sized dogs
> Small dogs

Under each division, he wrote down as many characteristics as he could think of.

> <u>Big dogs</u>
>   calm
>   friendly
>   good-natured
>   lazy
>   slow-moving
>
> <u>Medium-sized dogs</u>
>   spunky
>   energetic
>   ready for a challenge
>   protective
>   friendly if they know you

<u>Small dogs</u>
nervous
trembling
noisy
yappy
snappy
annoying

Adam then wrote a topic sentence: "Dogs seem to fall into three categories." Using that topic sentence and the rough outline he'd just produced, he wrote the following first draft.

Most dogs seem to fall into one of three categories. First there are the big slow-moving friendly dogs. They give the impression of being sweet and your best friend in the world. One example of this kind of dog is Lucy. She's a golden Lab belonging to a man in my neighbourhood. Lucy goes everywhere with Mr. Kobielski. She doesn't even need a leash but just follows him. Dogs like Lucy never bother you. She just lies at Mr. K's feet when he stops to talk to anyone. The guy who runs every day near here has a spunky medium-sized dog. Once the dog knows you he's friendly and even playful. But he's always on the lookout for a stranger who might mean trouble. For a dog who's not very big he can make himself look pretty fierce if he wants to. Then there are my least favourite kind of dogs. Little nervous yappy ones. My aunt used to have a Pomeranian like that. It smelled, too. It knew me for nine years and still went crazy shaking and yipping at me every time we met. She loved that dog but I can't imagine why. If I had a dog it would definitely come from category 1 or 2.

Development through Revising

Adam traded his first draft with a fellow student, Rachel, and asked her to give him feedback. Here are the comments Rachel wrote on his paper.

Most dogs seem to fall into one of three categories. First there are the big slow-moving friendly dogs. They give the impression of being sweet and your best friend in the world. One example of this kind of dog is Lucy. She's a golden Lab belonging to a man in my neighbourhood. Lucy goes everywhere with Mr. Kobielski. She doesn't even need a leash but just follows him. Dogs like Lucy never bother you. She just lies at Mr. K's feet when he stops to talk to anyone. The guy who runs every day near here has a spunky medium-sized dog. Once the dog knows you he's friendly and even playful. But he's always on the lookout for a stranger who might mean trouble. For a dog who's not very big he can make himself look pretty fierce if he wants to. Then there are my least favourite kind of dogs. Little nervous yappy ones. My aunt used to have a Pomeranian like that. It smelled, too. It knew me for nine years and still went

This is a change in point of view —you weren't using "you" before.

Is this a new category? That's not clear.

Not a sentence

You've gone from third person to "you" to "me."

Adam—I think you need to make your three categories clearer. Your first one is OK—"big dogs," which you say are friendly—but categories 2 & 3 aren't stated as clearly.

It's distracting to have your point of view change from third person to "you" to "we" and "me."

Since you're trying to divide and classify all dogs, I'm not sure it's a good thing to talk only about three individual dogs. This way it sounds like you're just describing those three dogs instead of putting them into groups.

crazy shaking and yipping at me every time we met. She loved that dog but I can't imagine why. If I had a dog it would definitely come from category 1 or 2.

When Adam thought about Rachel's comments and reread his own paragraph, he agreed with what she'd written. "I realized it was too much about three particular dogs and not enough about the categories of dogs," he said. "I decided to revise it and focus on the three classes of dogs."

Adam then wrote the version that appears on page 251.

WRITING A DIVISION AND CLASSIFICATION PARAGRAPH

How to Write a Division and Classification Paragraph

1 As you begin your prewriting, think about your reason or purpose for dividing up your subject. Consider your audience: who are your readers, and what would they want to know about your subject? What do you know about your subject, and how will that help you to divide and classify your subject into interesting and appropriate categories? Write down your purpose and subject in a trial topic sentence at the top of your prewriting page.

2 Divide your subject into at least three groups and set up your prewriting as three columns, one for each of your groups. Be sure that your groups all follow a single principle for classification. List, freewrite, or question until you have fairly equal numbers of details for each of your categories.

3 Read over and revise your prewriting to discover the clear *point* that emerges from your divisions and details: what are you saying about your subject? Edit any details that do not directly support your point as well as your purpose for dividing and classifying your subject. State your point about your subject, your purpose for dividing it as you do, and your divisions or categories in a topic sentence. Proceed to create a detailed outline, showing each division and its supporting details.

4 As you write your drafts based on your outline, be sure that each point and its support (each division or category and details) relate clearly to your subject as a whole and the point you make about your subject.

5 Conclude by refocusing your reader on your subject as a whole and on the significance of what your dividing and classifying has shown about your subject.

■ **Writing Assignment 1**

Below are four possible division and classification writing assignments, along with possible divisions or subtopics. Choose *one* of them to develop into a paragraph.

Option A

Supermarket shoppers
1. Slow, careful
2. Average
3. Rushed, hurried

Option B

Eaters
1. Super-conservative
2. Typical
3. Adventurous

Option C

Types of housekeepers
1. Those who never clean
2. Those who clean regularly
3. Those who clean constantly

Option D

Attitudes toward money
1. Tight-fisted
2. Sometimes splurge
3. Spendthrift

Prewriting

a Begin by doing some prewriting on the topic you have chosen. For ten minutes, simply write down everything that comes into your head when you think about "types of housekeepers," "attitudes toward money," or whichever option you choose. Don't worry about grammar, spelling, or organization—just write.

b Now that you've loosened up your brain a little, try some second-stage prewriting. Try asking yourself questions about the topic and writing down your answers. If you are writing about supermarket shoppers, for instance, you might ask questions like these.

How do the three kinds of shoppers pick out the items they want?
How many aisles will each type of shopper visit?
Which shoppers bring lists, calculators, coupons, cellphones, and so on?
How much time does it take each type of shopper to finish shopping?

Decide on an appropriate order for your details.

c Take a new sheet of paper or open a new document on your screen. Divide your page or screen into three columns (use the tables tool to do so on your computer). Label each column with one of your categories and fill in each column with appropriate items from your prewriting and questioning.

d Reread the material in your three columns. If some of the details you have written make you think of even better ones, add them. Select the details that best support your three points.

e Make decisions about the exact information you will use to support each point. Number the details within each classification *1, 2, 3,* and so on, in the order you will present them. To ensure a balanced paragraph, try to have roughly the same number of supporting details for each of your three classifications.

f Restate your topic as a grammatically correct sentence. For example, if you are writing about eaters, your topic sentence might be "Eaters can be divided into three categories." Turn each of your three subtopics at the tops of your columns into a full sentence as well.

g   Using your topic sentence and three supporting subtopic sentences and adding the details you have generated, write the first draft of your paragraph.

Revising

Put away your work for a day or so. Reread it with a critical eye, asking yourself these questions:

- Does my paragraph include a complete topic sentence and three subtopics?
- Have I backed up each subtopic or category with strong, specific details?
- Does my paragraph hold together in terms of unity, support, and coherence?
- Have I edited my paragraph and corrected sentence-skills mistakes, including spelling errors?

Continue revising your work until you can answer yes to all these questions.

Writing Assignment 2

Write a division and classification paragraph on one of the following topics.

Instructors	Drivers
Sports fans	Mothers or fathers
Eating places	Women's or men's magazines
Attitudes toward life	Presents
Commercials	Neighbours
Employers	Rock, pop, rap, or country singers
Jobs	Amusement parks or rides
Bars	Guests or company
Family get-togethers	Ways to get an A (or an F) in a course
Shoes	Car accessories

Prewriting

a   Choose a single logical principle for dividing your subject. The first step in writing a division and classification paragraph is to divide your tentative topic into three reasonably complete parts. *Always use a single principle of division* when you form your three parts. For example, if your topic was "automobile drivers" and you divided them into slow, moderate, and fast drivers, your single basis for division would be "rate of speed." It would be illogical, then, to have as a fourth type "teenage drivers" (the basis of such a division would be "age") or "female drivers" (the basis of such a division would be "sex"). You could probably classify automobile drivers on the basis of age or sex or another division, for almost any subject can be analyzed in more than one way. What is important, however, is that *in any single paper you choose only one basis for division and stick to it.* Be consistent.

In "Studying for a Test," the writer divides the process of studying into three time phases: from the time the test is announced to forty-eight hours before the test; the two days before the test; and the final twelve hours before the test.

b Decide on your purpose for making such a decision. Remember that your topic sentence and your paragraph must *make a point*. It is not enough simply to *announce,* "There are three categories of shoes." *What point* do you wish to make by dividing up your topic? Do you wish to *explain* more about your topic, to *describe* each classification in greater detail? As part of your prewriting, aim at discovering your point.

c Freewrite to accumulate details about your subtopics or divisions. Divide your page into three columns, each headed by the name of one of your divisions. List details for each division under your headings for ten minutes.

d Expand your topic into a fully stated topic sentence.

e At this point, you have all three elements of your paragraph: the topic sentence, the three main points or categories, and the details needed to support each point. You are ready to outline your paragraph.

To ensure a clear three-part division in your own paragraph, fill in the outline below before starting to write and make sure you can answer yes to the questions that follow. You should expect to do a fair amount of thinking before coming up with a logical plan.

Topic (subject, point, and divisions): _____

Three-part division of the topic and purpose: _____

(1) _____

(2) _____

(3) _____

Is there a single basis of division for the three parts? _____

Is the division reasonably complete? _____

f Now expand your outline to include all your supporting details and write your first draft.

Revising

Do not attempt to revise your paragraph right away. Put it away for a while; if possible, leave it until the next day. When you reread it, try to be as critical of it as you would be if someone else had written it. As you go over the work, ask yourself these questions:

- Have I divided my topic into three distinct parts?
- Is each of those parts based on the same principle of division?
- Have I given each of those parts approximately equal weight? In other words, have I spent about the same amount of time discussing each part?
- Have I provided effective details to back up each of my three points?
- Does my paragraph satisfy the requirements of unity, coherence, and support?

- Have I edited my paragraph for sentence-skills mistakes, including spelling errors?

Continue revising until you are sure the answer to each question is yes.

■ Writing Assignment 3

There are many ways you could classify the students around you. Pick out one of your courses and write a paragraph in which you classify the students in that class according to one principle. You might want to categorize the students according to one of the principles of division below.

Attitude toward class	Level of confidence
Participation in the class	Performance during oral reports,
Method of taking notes in class	speeches, presentations, lab
Punctuality	sessions
Attendance	

If you decide, for instance, to classify students according to their attitudes toward class, you might come up with these three categories.

Students actually interested in learning the material

Students who know they need to learn the material but don't want to overdo it

Students who find class a good opportunity to catch up on lost sleep

Of course, you may use any other principle of division that seems appropriate. Follow the directions for prewriting and revising for Writing Assignment 2.

■ Writing Assignment 4

Along with students from other colleges and universities in your area, you have been invited to be part of a panel speaking to graduating students at local high schools. You are to give your audience an overview of student life at your college, or at your campus of your college.

Write a script for a brief presentation that discusses aspects of "Life at _____ _____ College." Divide the college experience into three categories you feel would be of use and interest to your audience. Be sure to (1) indicate your purpose in having chosen each aspect of college life you include in your presentation, and (2) include enough specifics about each aspect to help and inform students who have not yet had any experience of post-secondary education.

■ Writing Assignment 5

Write a review of a restaurant by analyzing its (1) food, (2) service, and (3) atmosphere. For this assignment, try to do some field research by visiting a restaurant. Take a notebook with you and write down observations about such elements as:

Quantity of food you receive	Attitude of servers
Taste of the food	Efficiency of servers

Temperature of the food	Decor
Freshness of the ingredients	Level of cleanliness
How the food is presented	Noise level and music, if any
(garnishes, dishes, and so on)	

Feel free to write about details other than those listed above. Just be sure each detail fits into one of your three categories: food, service, or atmosphere.

For your topic sentence, rate the restaurant by giving it from one to five stars, on the basis of your overall impression. Include the restaurant's name and location in your topic sentence. Here are some examples.

Borsalino, an Italian restaurant in North Vancouver, deserves three stars.
The Tim Hortons near Winston Churchill and Dundas barely merits two stars.
Frank's Noodle Parlour and Internet Café is a five-star favourite with downtown students.

Writing Assignment 6

Writing about a Reading Selection: Read the selection "Letter" on pages 500-1, and consider what the author has to say about generosity and its rewards. Using the concept of charity (or generosity) as your topic, and basing your work on your own experience, write a paragraph that divides charity into different types or forms according to the classifying principle of the rewards involved.

To get started, think carefully about two things: the forms of generosity or charity you have offered to others and those you have received from others. Start your prewriting with whichever form of charity you find easiest to write about. Write only and specifically about your own experience; do not generalize. Focus on one specific situation and the rewards that arose from it, and look for headings under which to classify those rewards: possibilities might be "personal rewards," "material rewards," "unexpected rewards," and so on. As in the reading selection, look for an overall "lesson" or summarizing statement about your experience and its meaning with which to conclude your paragraph.

REVIEWING THE LEARNING OUTCOMES FOR CLASSIFICATION AND DIVISION WRITING

After completing any of the writing assignments in this chapter, review your work to see how well it meets the following tests.

1 Do the divisions in your paragraph's subject follow a consistent principle? Is this dividing principle logically related to your purpose in examining your subject? Does it lead to new and interesting information about your subject?

2 Does your paragraph open with a topic sentence that states your purpose for dividing and classifying your subject, your point about doing so, and your categories or divisions?

3 Do your divisions and supporting details appear in an order that makes your point most strongly?

4 Do you have a balanced number of supporting details for each subject division, and is each detail closely related to your point about your subject?

5 Does your conclusion remind readers of your opening point about your subject and reinforce whatever has been shown in examining your divisions of your subject?

Visit the *English Skills with Readings* Online Learning Centre at **www.mcgrawhill.ca/college/langan** to access self-quizzes, bonus material on study and research skills, web resources, and other learning and study tools.

Explaining a Process • Examining Cause and Effect • Comparing or Contrasting • Defining a Term • Dividing and Classifying • Describing a Scene or Person • Narrating an Event • Arguing a Position • Explaining a Process • Examining Cause and Effect • Comparing or Contrasting • Defining a Term • Dividing and Classifying • Describing a Scene or Person • Narrating an Event • Arguing a Position • Explaining a Process • Examining Cause and Effect • Compar

CHAPTER 16

Arguing a Position

LEARNING OUTCOMES

By completing this chapter's activities and at least one of its writing assignments, you will write an argumentation paragraph that

- **opens with a clear and definite statement of the point to be argued;**
- **shows in its opening section, based on some knowledge of its audience, possible counter-arguments and responses to them;**
- **uses a method of development most appropriately suited to stating logical and well-reasoned points and details to support the point to be argued;**
- **shows logic and knowledge of the specifics of its subject in its subtopics and details;**
- **argues its point and support cleanly, without slanting its point with emotional appeals or insulting its audience; and**
- **concludes by reaffirming its point, as justified by the evidence presented in the paragraph.**

A paragraph whose main purpose is to argue a point, or to persuade, aims to influence the thought and action of the reader. Since responding to persuasion or to an argument usually involves some degree of emotion, many people assume that a paragraph arguing a position will use non-rational techniques to sway its readers. The opposite is actually true for an effective piece of argumentation. Logic, reason, and knowing the interests of the audience are the most potent tactics for effectively arguing a point.

Every day, on the basis of feelings, we make general statements of opinion. In the ordinary course of things, we do not expect to be challenged, so we do not exercise our ability to defend a point very often. Occasionally, though, someone will greet one of our statements with the question "Why do you say that?" or "What are your reasons for saying that?" Our questioner then listens carefully as we work to muster our reasons, waiting to see if we really do have solid evidence to support our point of view. Such a questioner may make us feel nervous, but we may also feel grateful to him or her for helping us think through our opinions.

The ability to advance sound and compelling arguments is an important skill in everyday life. We may use persuasion to get an extension on a term paper or convince an employer that we are the right person for a job. Understanding persuasion based on clear, logical reasoning can also help develop critical awareness of arguments advanced by advertisers, artists, editors, and politicians. Argumentation skills are essential to college and career communications needs. Oral and written presentations are generally persuasive in nature, and proposals and reports often require competent use of the skills and techniques of argumentation and persuasion.

In this chapter, you will be asked to argue a position and defend it with a series of solid reasons. You are in a general way doing the same thing—making a point and then supporting it—with all the paragraphs in this book. The difference is that here, in a more direct and formal manner, you will advance a point about which you feel strongly and seek to persuade others to agree with you.

PARAGRAPHS TO CONSIDER

"Teensploitation" Insults Teenagers

[1]Some people my age never question all the "teensploitation" movies and TV shows these days, but I believe they are insulting to the audiences they are made for. [2]One reason is that the creators of these movies and programs present unrealistic main characters, teenagers who are all good-looking, well off, and basically idle, self-centred consumers. [3]Teen watchers are separated into "the ones who idolize the characters" and "the ones who feel inadequate because they're not Britney or Paris Hilton." [4]Being either of those types of watchers can cause any sensitive young person to feel dissatisfied and unhappy with himself or herself after a while. [5]Another problem is that these movies and shows suggest that high school is the most important stage in life, an unreal stage that never ends. [6]Many Canadian teenagers cope with very real financial pressures and demanding family and home situations every day; to them, endless worries about a dance or riding around in a friend's Humvee seem as unrealistic as Paris Hilton's rural adventures. [7]These shows and movies are candy-coloured dreams that leave many young people feeling lied to and miserable when they consider their own lives by comparison. [8]Perhaps the main reason "teensploitation" entertainment is so insulting is that it assumes that teenagers are empty-headed, waiting to be told what is good or bad. [9]Also, teens are assumed to be so dull and gullible that they want only sequels or copies of the last ten successful teen movies or TV shows. [10]Creators of these repetitive "copycat" products insult their teen audiences by boring them to death. [11]Teens and college-age audiences are not so stupid that new or interesting ideas must be sugar-coated with new titles, flashy settings, and renamed characters played by Ashton Kutcher or the Olsen twins. [12]In fact, teens often end up watching the shows and movies they do simply because there don't seem to be any other choices available. [13]Moreover, teenagers and young people are no different from other consumers: they buy what is advertised—every teen mag and every entertainment TV show and magazine promotes "teensploitation" stars, shows, and movies. [14]No one can resist forever, especially teens who already feel pressure to conform to the

tastes of their peers and the media. [15]For all these reasons, creators of entertainment for young people should stop insulting and maybe damaging their target audiences.

Living Alone

[1]Living alone is quite an experience. [2]People who live alone, for one thing, have to learn to do all kinds of tasks by themselves. [3]They must learn—even if they have had no experience—to reset circuit breakers, put up curtains and shades, temporarily dam an overflowing toilet, cook a meal, and defrost a refrigerator. [4]When there are no fathers, husbands, mothers, or wives to depend on, a person can't fall back on the excuse "I don't know how to do that." [5]Those who live alone also need the strength to deal with people. [6]Alone, singles must face noisy neighbours, unresponsive property managers, and dishonest repair people. [7]Because there are no buffers between themselves and the outside world, people living alone have to handle every visitor—friendly or unfriendly—alone. [8]Finally, singles need a large dose of courage to cope with occasional panic and unavoidable loneliness. [9]That weird thump in the night is even more terrifying when there is no one in the next bed or the next room. [10]Frightening weather or unexpected bad news is doubly bad when the worry can't be shared. [11]Even when life is going well, little moments of sudden loneliness can send shivers through the heart. [12]Struggling through such bad times taps into reserves of courage that people may not have known they possessed. [13]Facing everyday tasks, confronting all types of people, and handling panic and loneliness can shape singles into brave, resourceful, and more independent people.

■ Questions

About Unity

1. The topic sentence in "Living Alone" is too broad. Circle the letter of the topic sentence below that states accurately what the paragraph is about.

   a. Living alone takes courage.

   b. Living alone can create feelings of loneliness.

   c. Living alone should be avoided.

2. Which sentence in "Teensploitation Insults Teens" should be eliminated in the interest of paragraph unity? (*Write the sentence number here.*) _____

About Support

3. How many reasons are given to support the topic sentence in each paragraph?

   a. In "Teensploitation Insults Teens":

   _____ one   _____ two   _____ three   _____ four

b. In "Living Alone":

_____ one   _____ two   _____ three   _____ four

4. After which sentence in "Teensploitation Insults Teens" are more specific details needed? _____

About Coherence

5. Why is emphatic order the most logical choice for both paragraphs?

_____

6. What are the three main transition words in "Living Alone"?
    a. _____   b. _____   c. _____

Activity

Complete the outline below of a paragraph about "a terrible vacation." Summarize in a few words the primary and secondary supporting material that fits under the topic sentence. Two items have been done for you as examples.

Topic sentence: Despite much advertising to the contrary, taking a cruise is a terrible way to spend a vacation.

1. _____
    a. _____
    b. _____
2. _____
    a. _____
    b. *Little room for jogging*
3. _____
    a. _____
    b. *Dull conversations with other passengers*
    c. _____

DEVELOPING AN ARGUMENT PARAGRAPH

Development through Prewriting

Amanda is the student author of "Teensploitation Insults Teenagers." She decided on her topic after an evening with friends. They had held a movie marathon, renting an assortment of DVDs. They watched a Hilary Duff movie, two teen-oriented horror movies, and *Scooby-Doo*, among others. Amanda found she wasn't enjoying the get-together as much as her friends, and she decided that something about the movies was the problem. She sat down and tried to write about what was on her mind.

I started thinking about the movies we usually rent together. They all show us as idiots most of the time. Or as characters who are so unrealistic that we can't relate to them at all. We're always these stereotypes—the blond girl, the nerdy guy, the stud, the brown-haired sidekick girl, and, of course, the party animal. I understand that TV and movies simplify things, but I'm getting sick of it. Some of the people I know actually see these characters as role models, and that is really wrong. They can't ever be Britney or Avril Lavigne, and after a while, I think they start disliking themselves for falling short of their idols. Shows like <u>Popstars</u> and <u>Canadian Idol</u> just encourage people my age to believe that they can be someone famous, even if they don't have any talent. But they just keep making the same movies, videos, and TV shows, all aimed at me and my age group. Nobody ever asks if this is what we want. If you show us something often enough, I guess it will end up being what we want.

A week or so later, Amanda's English instructor assigned an argument paragraph. Amanda felt as if she was already prepared with a good topic. Although she had no idea how to gather up her ideas into a neat package, she thought that she would start by looking back at the note she'd written to herself. She then tried some point-form list making. Here is the list Amanda came up with.

—characters in "TS" are unrealistic; they always have money and are well dressed and good-looking—TV or movies
—teens see actors and singers as idols, someone they can never be
—teens and twentysomethings know real life and school aren't like what they see—so these movies and shows assume we're stupid
—TV shows and movies for us are nearly always set in "forever" high school or in fancy locations—does high school ever end?
—Characters in TS have no real pressures or ordinary problems—who pays their college tuition? —and even parents' divorces are glamorous
—TV shows, DVDs, CDs, movies are advertised everywhere—can't get away from it, so you start wanting it
—teens and college students feel like this is all there is, there's nothing much else to choose from except for stuff like the <u>Lord of the Rings</u> movies, so they react to the hype and peer pressure and go with it
—TS is insulting to teens and young people—tries to tell us what we want, how we should look, and what we can understand

Next, Amanda put her list away for a couple of days. She felt as if she still didn't have a clear focus, and she hoped one would come to her. Although she did not enjoy outlining, she felt very strongly about her subject and wanted to do it justice, so she decided to sort through her list and make a clear outline. She recalled that her instructor had said that the most powerful reason should appear last, so she started by trying to put her points in order and making notes to herself.

Am I talking about TV or movies, or videos?

1. Characters—least important?
    —Britney and Paris Hilton—they come across as mindless
    —other TV shows—nobody I know has that much time or money

—these aren't supposed to be "fantasy" people, like in LotR—supposed to
be real, so people my age feel bad compared with them and their lives
—in fact, nobody is like teens in TV and movies—who has that many
clothes?
Would we watch them if they were like us? Another argument? (Joan of
Arcadia—Joan is sort of "idealistic")

2. Settings—unrealistic
    —high school lasted forever on most shows—actors look too old, look at
    Smallville, unbelievable—don't look like college students either, when
    they go to college
    —the characters all have these great jobs, if they work—isn't anybody a
    cashier?—look at The O.C.
    —the problems and situations are stupid, teens are not that dumb
    —shows insult teens, with fairy-tale lives, cars, and belongings that never
    change or get worse

3. TS is just about all we're offered—there's not much choice
    —movies and shows are advertised everywhere—end up watching
    —sequels and copies—how many Jasons will there be?—don't young peo-
    ple want something new or different?
    —if friends watch something, we'll eventually want to—peer pressure &
    media uses this
    —dumbed-down versions of Shakespeare and novels—candy coated (not
    O, though—it was good)

What order do I put these details in?

Even though she still felt her thoughts were a bit muddled, Amanda was running out of time, so she wrote the following first draft of her paragraph.

A lot of people my age never question the movies and TV shows they
watch. Maybe they don't realize how different they are from the characters
they like so much. Not one of my friends has as many clothes as Britney,
Hilary Duff, or Paris Hilton. These are supposed to be realistic characters,
not fantasies like Bilbo in Lord of the Rings or Luke Skywalker. If young
people compare themselves with TV and movie characters, they could feel
bad about themselves and their lives. The settings and situations are
unrealistic, too. High school seems to go on forever, and the actors look too
old even when they're supposed to be in college. If they have to work, then
they get jobs that are glamorous. Nobody is ever a cashier in a discount store.
Again, if somebody knows they're supposed to think Stiffler is realistic, how
can they not be insulted? The biggest problem is that the media uses the
thing we're supposed to ignore against us—peer pressure. Because we go to
and rent a lot of movies and watch TV, movies and shows targeted at us are
advertised everywhere. We end up watching just because we see so many ads
in the magazines we read and even on the sides of buses. And over half the
time, movies are just sequels, too. Young people are victims of our own
power, and we're being insulted because of it.

Development through Revising

Amanda's instructor reviewed her first draft and made these comments.

> *It's obvious you feel very strongly about your point, and it is an interesting one. The first thing I notice is that you're working on offering balanced supporting details for each point. You may want to add a few more illustrations and examples, especially for your third subtopic.*
>
> *Although you make good use of emphatic order by ending with "The biggest problem is...," you need more transitions to make your argument's buildup stronger and your paragraph clearer.*

With these comments in mind, Amanda revised her paragraph until she produced the version that appears on pages 263-64.

WRITING AN ARGUMENT PARAGRAPH

How to Write an Argument Paragraph

1   If your topic is one with which you are not very familiar, or one for which you will need more facts to support your viewpoint, take some time to look up some information on your topic at the library or on a search engine. Try to read both supporting and opposing views of your topic so that you can anticipate likely counter-arguments and your own responses. Be sure you are firm in your point of view on your subject.

2   Prewrite, using as many methods as needed to accumulate as many facts as possible to support your viewpoint on your topic. Add any points you may have found during research.

3   Begin your outline by looking for the main points to support your viewpoint. Rank your main points (subtopics) in order of increasing importance, or emphatic order. Under each point, note any examples, details, facts or statistics, or anecdotes to support that point. Compose a trial topic sentence that states your topic and your viewpoint; many such topic sentences use the words *should, must*, and *ought*.

4   Look over your outline and think about your audience. How much does your reader know about your subject? If you feel that your reader will be more ready to accept your views if you supply some information, do so. What will be your reader's attitude toward your topic? Think of any possible objections your reader might have, and counter these with appropriate facts as part of the first section of your paper.

5   Be prepared to work on your drafts until you are satisfied that your audience will see your viewpoint as clearly as you do. Make sure all the facts and details that support your argument follow logically from one another.

6   Conclude with a statement that both reinforces your viewpoint and is justified by the facts you have presented.

▨ Writing Assignment 1

Develop an argument paragraph based on one of the statements that follow. Make sure that you have three separate and distinct reasons for each statement.

1. Condoms should [*or* should not] be made available in schools.

2. _____ (*name a specific hockey team*) should win the Stanley Cup.

3. The computer is one of the best [*or* worst] inventions of this century.

4. _____ are the best [*or* worst] pets.

5. All cigarette and alcohol advertising should be banned.

6. Canadian immigration laws should be changed.

7. _____ is one public figure today who can be considered a hero.

8. This college needs a better cafeteria [*or* library *or* student centre *or* marks policy *or* attendance policy].

Prewriting

a Make up brief outlines for any three of the eight statements above. Make sure you have three separate and distinct reasons or subtopics for each statement. Below is an example of a brief outline for a paragraph making another point.

> Toronto should ban passenger cars.
> 1.   Cut down on pollution
> 2.   Cut down on noise
> 3   Make more room for pedestrians and bikes

b Decide, perhaps through discussion with your instructor or classmates, which of your outlines is the most promising for development into a paragraph. Make sure your subtopics are logical by asking yourself in each case, "Does this item truly support my topic sentence?"

c Do some prewriting. Prepare a list of all the details you can think of that might actually support your point. Don't limit yourself; include more details than you can actually use. Here, for example, are details generated by the writer of "Living Alone."

Deal with power failures	Noisy neighbours
Nasty owners	Develop courage
Scary noises at night	Do all the cooking
Dishonest repair people	Weird phone calls
Spiders	Home repairs
Lightning storms	Loneliness

d Decide which details you will use to develop your paragraph. Number the details in the order in which you will present them. Because presenting the strongest reason last (emphatic order) is the most effective way to organize an argument paragraph, be sure to save your most powerful reason for last. Here is how the author of "Living Alone" made decisions about details.

    1 Deal with power failures
    4 Nasty owners
    7 Scary noises at night
    6 Dishonest repair people
    ~~Spiders~~
    8 Lightning storms
    5 Noisy neighbours
    10 Develop courage
    2 Do all the cooking
    ~~Weird phone calls~~
    5 Home repairs
    9 Loneliness

e Write the first draft of your paragraph. As you write, develop each subtopic with specific details. For example, in "Living Alone," notice how the writer makes the experience of living alone come alive with phrases like "that weird thump in the night" or "little moments of sudden loneliness can send shivers through the heart."

Revising

- Put your paragraph away for at least a day. When you reread it, imagine that your audience is a jury that will ultimately render a verdict on your argument. Have you presented a convincing case? If you were on the jury, would you be favourably impressed with this argument?
- As you work on subsequent drafts of your paragraph, keep in mind unity, support, and coherence.
- Edit the next-to-final draft of your paper for sentence-skills mistakes, including spelling errors. Use the list on the inside front cover of this book.

▪ Writing Assignment 2

Write a paragraph in which you take a stand on one of the controversial subjects below. As a lead-in to this writing project, your instructor might give the class a chance to "stand up for what they believe in." One side of the front of the room should be designated *strong agreement* and the other side *strong disagreement,* with the space between for intermediate degrees of agreement or disagreement. As the class stands in front of the room, the instructor will read one value statement at a time from the list below, and students will move to the appropriate spot, depending on their degree of agreement or disagreement. Some time will be allowed for students to discuss with those near them the reasons they are standing where they are and to state to those at the other end of the scale the reasons for their position.

1. Students should not be required to attend high school.

2. Prostitution should be legalized.

3. Recreational drugs should be legalized.

4. Casinos and legalized gambling benefit provincial economies.

5. Gay couples should receive the same benefits and legal status as heterosexual couples.

6. Federal prisons should be co-ed, and prisoners should be allowed to marry.

7. Parents of girls under eighteen should be informed if their daughters receive birth control aids.

8. The government should legalize euthanasia.

9. Canada should have one official language only, and all signs and publications should be in this language.

10. Parents should never hit their children.

Prewriting

a Begin your paragraph by writing a sentence that expresses your attitude toward one of these value statements. For example, "I feel that prostitution should be legalized."

b Outline the reason or reasons you hold the opinion that you do. Your support may be based on your own experience, the experience of someone you know, logic, or research. For example, this is an outline of a paragraph based on one student's logic.

I feel that prostitution should be legalized for the following reasons:
1. Prostitutes would then have to pay their fair share of income tax.
2. Government health centres would administer regular checkups and thus help prevent the spread of STDs.
3. Prostitutes would be able to work openly and independently and would not be subject to exploitation by others.
4. Most of all, prostitutes would no longer be regarded so much as social outcasts—an attitude that is psychologically damaging to those who may already have emotional problems.

Another outline, based on experience, proceeded as follows.

I do not feel that prostitution should be legalized, because of a woman I know who was once a prostitute.
1. The attention Linda received as a prostitute prevented her from seeing and working on her personal problems.
2. She became embittered toward all men, whom she always suspected of wanting to exploit her.
3. She developed a negative self-image and felt that no one could love her.

c Use your outline as the basis for writing a paragraph, providing specific details to back up each point in your outline.

Revising

Put your paragraph away for a while, ideally at least a day. Ask a friend whose judgment you trust to read and critique it. Your friend should consider each of these questions as he or she reads:

- Does the topic sentence clearly state the writer's opinion on a controversial subject?
- Does the paragraph include at least three separate and distinct reasons that support the author's argument?
- Is each of the three reasons or subtopics backed up by specific, relevant evidence?
- Has the author saved the most powerful reason for last?
- Is the paragraph free of spelling errors and other sentence-skills mistakes listed on the inside front cover of this book?

Continue revising your work until you and your reader can answer yes to all these questions.

■ Writing Assignment 3

You have finally met Mr. or Ms. Right—but your parents don't approve of him or her. Specifically, they are against your doing one of the following.

Continuing to see this person
Going steady
Moving in together
Getting married at the end of the school year

Write a letter to your parents explaining in a fully detailed way why you have made your choice. Do your best to convince them that it is a good choice.

■ Writing Assignment 4

Where do you think it is best to bring up children—in the country, the suburbs, or the city? Write a paragraph in which you argue that one of those three environments is best for families with young children. Your argument should cover two types of reasons: (1) the advantages of living in the type of environment you've chosen and (2) the disadvantages of living in the other places. Use the following, or something much like it, for your topic sentence.

For families with young children, the country [or the suburbs or the city] is the best place to live.

For each reason you advance, include at least one persuasive example. For instance, if you argue that the cultural life in the city is one important reason to live there, you should explain in detail just how going to a science museum is interesting and helpful to children. After deciding on your points of support, arrange them in an outline, saving your strongest point for last. In your paragraph, introduce each of your reasons with an addition transition, such as *first of all*, *another*, *also*, and *finally*.

■ Writing Assignment 5

Write a paper in which you use research findings to help support one of the following statements.

> Many people do not need vitamin supplements.
> Disposable cans and bottles should be banned.
> Everyone should own a pet.
> Mandatory retirement ages should be abolished.
> Advertising should not be permitted on Saturday-morning cartoon shows.

Using strategies described on the Online Learning Centre, research the topic you have chosen. Reading material on your topic will help you think about that topic. See if you can then organize your paper in the form of three reasons that support the topic. Put these reasons into a short-form outline, and use it as a guide in writing your paragraph. Here is an example.

> Many people do not need vitamin supplements.
> 1. Some vitamins, taken in high dosages, are actually harmful.
> 2. Other vitamins do not clearly improve health in any specific way.
> 3. Most Canadians' diets provide enough of daily vitamin requirements.

Note that statistics could support these reasons. Do not hesitate to cite studies and other data in a limited way; they make your argument more objective and compelling.

■ Writing Assignment 6

Writing about a Reading Selection: Read the selection "Language Out, Style In" by Jerry Amernic on pages 559-61. Then write an argumentation paragraph in which you agree or disagree with one of the following statements from Amernic's article.

> Author Tom Wolfe calls the Internet a "great time waster." (paragraph 4)
> The result [of education's neglect of language skills] is an entire generation of people who aren't up to snuff on the basics. (paragraph 2)

Your topic sentence could be something like the following.

> The Internet is not a "time waster"—it is humanity's most useful invention, offering improved global communication, simplified research, and instantly accessible information.

REVIEWING THE LEARNING OUTCOMES FOR ARGUING A POSITION

After completing any of the writing assignments in this chapter, review your work to see how well it meets the following tests.

1   Does your paragraph open with a clear statement of your viewpoint on the topic to be argued?

2   Does your paragraph acknowledge and counter any opposing viewpoints close to its beginning?

3   Do you use a method of development appropriate to the type of argument you have chosen (facts and statistics for a logical argument, anecdotes or examples for an experience-based argument)?

4   Does each subtopic and detail clearly support your expressed viewpoint in a logical way?

5   Is your concluding statement justified by the evidence you have presented in the body of your paragraph?

Visit the *English Skills with Readings* Online Learning Centre at **www.mcgrawhill.ca/college/langan** to access self-quizzes, bonus material on study and research skills, web resources, and other learning and study tools.

PREVIEW

Section Three moves from the single-paragraph paper to the several-paragraph essay. The differences between a paragraph and an essay are explained and then illustrated with a paragraph that has been expanded into an essay. You are shown how to begin an essay, how to tie its supporting paragraphs together, and how to conclude it. Three student essays are presented, along with questions to increase your understanding of the essay form. Finally, directions on how to plan an essay are followed by a series of essay writing assignments.

Explaining a Process • Examining Cause and Effect • Comparing or Contrasting • Defini Term • Dividing and Classifying • Describing a Scene or Person • Narrating an Event • Arg a Position • Explaining a Process • Examining Cause and Effect • Comparing or Contrast Defining a Term • Dividing and Classifying • Describing a Scene or Person • Narratin Event • Arguing a Position • Explaining a Process • Examining Cause and Effect • Compa

C H A P T E R   1 7

Writing the Essay

LEARNING OUTCOMES

After working through this chapter's activities, you will be ready to write an effective essay that

- contains an opening paragraph that attracts a reader's interest and presents a solid thesis statement;

- is *unified* because it opens with a clear, focused thesis in the introduction and reinforces this thesis with each following paragraph's topic sentences, subtopics, and supporting details;

- shows *adequate and specific support* for the viewpoint of the thesis in the body paragraphs, with each one offering distinct and sufficient supporting details to clarify or explain the thesis point made in its topic sentence;

- demonstrates *coherence* because (1) you have chosen a definite, clear method of organization appropriate to the subject matter, and (2) you have used transitional sentences and phrases to link paragraphs and help readers follow your ideas;

- contains a conclusion that sums up the overall point of your thesis and then offers a parting thought to round off the essay and signal completion; and

- communicates ideas easily and smoothly because of *effective use of sentence skills.*

WHAT IS AN ESSAY?

DIFFERENCES BETWEEN AN ESSAY AND A PARAGRAPH

An essay is an expanded, more detailed form of the paragraph that you have learned to write in the preceding chapters. An essay is a paper of several paragraphs, each of which supports and explains a single aspect of the essay's main point. Therefore, an essay offers the opportunity to explore a subject more fully than a single-paragraph paper could.

You will now use the skills you have acquired and practised in creating effective paragraphs as you learn to organize, outline, and write a successful essay. You will discover and state your main idea: your viewpoint on some subject. In an essay, the main idea—the point of view and subject that you will develop—is called the *thesis statement*. Like the *topic sentence* in a paragraph, the thesis statement appears at the beginning, in the introductory paragraph; your idea is developed and explored in the supporting paragraphs that follow. Your essay ends with a brief concluding paragraph.

Begin your approach to essay writing by looking at the form of an essay, below. Compare this structure with the Paragraph Outline Form in Chapter 2, on page 28. Note that the supporting paragraphs all echo the format for paragraph construction you have already learned. You will be expanding on skills here rather than acquiring totally new ones.

THE FORM OF AN ESSAY

Introductory Paragraph

Introduction
Thesis statement
Plan of development:
Supporting points 1, 2, 3

The *introduction* attracts the reader's interest.

The *thesis statement* states the main idea advanced in the paper.

The *plan of development* is a list of points that support the thesis. The supporting points are presented in the order in which they will be developed in the essay.

First Supporting Paragraph

Topic sentence (point 1)
Subtopics
Supporting details

The topic sentence advances the first supporting point for the thesis. The subtopics and supporting details explain or defend that first thesis point, as presented in the topic sentence.

Second Supporting Paragraph

Topic sentence (point 2)
Subtopics
Supporting details

The topic sentence advances the second supporting point for the thesis. The subtopics and supporting details explain or defend that second thesis point, as presented in the topic sentence.

Third Supporting Paragraph

Topic sentence (point 3)
Subtopics
Supporting details

The topic sentence advances the third supporting point for the thesis. The subtopics and supporting details explain or defend that third thesis point, as presented in the topic sentence.

Concluding Paragraph

Summary, conclusion, or both

A *summary* is a brief restatement of the thesis and its main points. A *conclusion* is a final thought or two stemming from the subject of the paper, perhaps placing those thoughts in a wider context.

A MODEL ESSAY

Alexa, the writer whose paragraph "Torture by Telephone" described her nightly ritual of working as a telemarketer (page 77), later decided to develop her subject more fully and change her method of organization. Here is the essay that resulted.

Tele-Torture

INTRODUCTORY PARAGRAPH

[1]When I left high school in grade eleven, I became an expert in the field of awful short-term jobs. [2]I have worked nine-hour holiday shifts as a sales clerk—a job where counting inventory in freezing stockrooms feels like a relief from picky customers. [3]I have also pushed the limits of my patience babysitting a four-month-old boy and his three-year-old sister—she called me "the bad lady" and liked to bite me. [4]I have been a fairground fry cook, making chips and Beaver Tails, with oil-burn scars on both arms that kept me in bandages all summer. [5]But none of these jobs came close to the torture of my only office job, telemarketing. [6]The hours messed up my life; the office and the equipment were miserable; and, worst of all, the people I worked with were scary robots.

FIRST SUPPORTING PARAGRAPH

[7]First, I did not work day shifts; I worked late hours that taught me how to really waste my life. [8]My workday started at five in the evening and ended at eleven o'clock at night. [9]This schedule turned me into a slug. [10]Because I was getting home after midnight, I started sleeping in until after noon, waking up feeling anxious about the coming shift. [11]Then I would start worrying about what to wear, fiddling with my school clothes, making an effort not to look like a seventeen-year-old who is "just in it for the money." [12]I never caught up on the things I intended to do during the day, like seeing my friends or registering for correspondence courses—all I had the energy for was watching soap operas and reading magazines. [13]My routine felt like sleepwalking: any skills I'd had disappeared, now that I was programmed only to sell credit cards over the phone. [14]I gave up all my habits and plans, just to make "easy money."

SECOND SUPPORTING PARAGRAPH

[15]Although I might have got used to the late shift eventually, the equipment I used and the office itself made every hour misery. [16]I sat under glaring lights in a little cubicle. [17]The lights made my eyes water as I strained to read my sales script from the computer screen, and the chairs were the wrong height, so my back stiffened up from hours of hunching over. [18]The phone headset burst out in static every time I moved my head, and I often couldn't hear the person I'd called. [19]To make matters worse, the program that guided me through each call was slow, and I would start babbling nervously at

the person I'd called while waiting for my next screen to appear. [20]Babblers don't make sales, and I grew frustrated and nervous.

THIRD
SUPPORTING
PARAGRAPH

[21]But more than the physical discomfort, what upset me most about the job was the supervisors. [22]I felt they were there to judge my every call. [23]Their real job was to motivate the telemarketers and to help us when we had problems. [24]In fact, they behaved like robots who had scripts like our computer programs. [25]Over and over they told me to "sound positive," to beware of "not living up to my potential," and to always "smile and dial." [26]They thought women should "act perky" and flirt with male customers. [27]As a result, I became so upset that I started speed-talking, and that was usually the moment when supervisors would monitor my calls. [28]I could not "calm down, slow down," and be "perky" when these robots were whispering in one ear and a customer was hanging up in my other ear. [29]I never felt so pressured in my life.

CONCLUDING
PARAGRAPH

[30]I lasted for two months as a telemarketer—the hours, the office, and the supervisors made it the hardest money I ever earned. [31] By the time I quit, I questioned my sanity, my decision to leave school, and my urge for an office job with "easy money."

IMPORTANT POINTS ABOUT THE ESSAY

The essay is a longer writing format than the paragraph. On a page, an essay appears as a piece of text with distinct breaks in it. The "breaks" are the spatial divisions between paragraphs; a line of text ends and a new line begins with an indentation, as you see here in what you are reading. The trick with an essay or any longer piece of writing is to transform those "breaks" into "pauses," while keeping the reader following the path you create as a writer.

Essays give you the opportunity to pursue your ideas at greater length and in more detail in separate paragraphs. Because these separate paragraphs take readers more deeply into your paths of thought, essays also present some challenges. Your first challenge is maintaining *unity*—keeping a strong, clear relationship from paragraph to paragraph through to your conclusion.

You can begin to create a unified essay by following tested, straightforward methods, beginning with your first paragraph.

INTRODUCTORY PARAGRAPH

An introductory paragraph has certain purposes or functions and can be constructed using various methods.

Purposes of the Introduction

An introductory paragraph should do three things:

1 Attract the reader's *interest.* Use one of the suggested methods of introduction described below to help draw the reader into your paper.

2   Present a *thesis statement*—a clear, direct statement of the central idea that you will develop in your paper. The thesis statement, like a topic sentence, should have a keyword or key phrase reflecting your attitude about the subject. For example, in the essay on the telemarketing job, the keyword is *torture.*

3   Indicate a *plan of development,* a list or *preview* of the *major points* that will support your thesis statement, listed *in the order in which they will be presented.* A more specific way to indicate your method of development for the paragraphs to follow is to use keywords identifying that method: for example, *a description, a comparison* (or *contrast), the causes* (or *effects), the advantages* (or *disadvantages), a definition,* or *an analysis* or *examination.* In some cases, the thesis statement and the plan of development may appear in the same sentence. In other cases, the plan of development may be omitted.

Activity

1. In "Tele-Torture," which sentences are used to attract the reader's interest?

    _____ sentences 1 to 3   _____ 1 to 5   _____ 1 to 6

2. The thesis in "Tele-Torture" is presented in

    _____ sentence 4   _____ sentence 5   _____ sentence 6

3. The thesis is followed by a plan of development.

    _____ Yes   _____ No

4. Which words in the plan of development announce the three major supporting points in the essay? Write them below.

    a. _____

    b. _____

    c. _____

Common Methods of Introduction

Here are some common methods of introduction. Use any one method or a combination of methods to introduce your subject in an interesting way.

■   **Broad statement.** Begin with a broad, general statement of your topic and narrow it down to your thesis statement. Broad, general statements ease the reader into your thesis statement by providing a background for it. In "Tele-Torture," Alexa opens with a general statement on the topic of unpleasant jobs and then narrows her focus to a specific job that was the worst of them all.

■   **Background information or context.** In many college and career writing tasks, you will write about subjects unfamiliar to general readers. You will need to offer some background information to make your meaning clear to readers. Opening with a few sentences to "set up" or explain your subject or situation is a useful method of introduction. Whenever you write about a subject that is not considered common knowledge, use this approach. If you must explain some technical process or a complicated situation, always give enough background information to make your thesis and supporting statements clear and understandable to readers. Here is an introductory paragraph that presents background information.

Canadians usually think of DVDs as something they rent instead of videotapes. Well, DVDs have certainly replaced analog tapes for movies, but they are much more than a new kind of shiny disk. DVD now means "digital versatile disk," and it really lives up to its name. A DVD is a CD-size disk that can hold up to 17 GB of visual and sound information; it works with computers or players; in fact, it is the fastest-growing electronics format available today. DVD-ROMs are replacing CD-ROMs; they hold games that are more realistic and interesting to play—games that can run on the computer rather than only on consoles like the Xbox. DVD Audio is becoming popular with music fans because it can offer surround sound with visuals of bands and performers. Now there are recordable DVDs, too, for use as higher-capacity backup disks for computer data and as alternatives to videotapes for recording TV programs. DVDs truly are versatile items—as small and convenient as CDs, but with much larger capacities and more diversified uses.

- **Contrast.** Start with an idea or situation that is the opposite of the one you will develop. This approach works because your readers will be surprised, and then intrigued, by the contrast between the opening idea and the thesis that follows it. Here is an example of a "contrast" introduction.

When I was a girl, I never argued with my parents about differences between their attitudes and mine. My father would deliver his judgment on an issue, and that was usually the end of the matter. Discussion seldom changed his mind, and disagreement was not tolerated. But the situation is different with today's parents and children. My husband and I have to contend with radical differences between what our children think about a given situation and what we think about it.

- **Relevance.** Explain the importance of your topic. If you can convince your readers that the subject applies to them in some way, or is something they should know more about, they will want to continue reading. The introductory paragraph of "Consuming Canadians" (pages 288-89) provides an example of a "relevance" introduction.

- **Anecdote.** Use an incident or brief story. Stories are naturally interesting. They appeal to a reader's curiosity. In your introduction, an anecdote will grab the reader's attention right away. The story should be brief and should be related to your central idea. The incident in the story can be something that happened to you, something that you may have heard about, or something that you have read about in a newspaper or magazine. Here is an example of a paragraph that begins with a story.

Down in the basement lived a monster. He squatted right in the centre of his dark, cement-walled cave and stretched his huge metal arms right up into the ceiling. The big metal monster was old; he had once eaten coal, we were told, and was probably mean from surviving through decades of northern Ontario winters. Now the monster was tamed and attached to the oil tank that leaned against the side of the house, so at least we knew he could not mysteriously move and come creaking after us. But he was still a monster; this we knew from his grated mouth, right in the middle of his steely face—behind those grates blazed infernal fires, day and night. This monster, the furnace, was part of a story invented by our father, and such stories are typical of "real" fairy tales, told not so much to scare children as to teach some important lessons needed for survival.

- **Questions.** Ask your readers one or more questions. These questions catch the readers' interest and make them want to read on; they serve as a lead-in to the thesis. Here is an example of a paragraph that begins with questions.

  What would happen if we were totally honest with ourselves? Would we be able to stand the pain of giving up self-deception? Would the complete truth be too much for us to bear? Such questions will probably never be answered, for in everyday life we protect ourselves from too much reality. All of us cultivate defence mechanisms that prevent us from seeing, hearing, or feeling too much. Included among such defence mechanisms are rationalization, reaction formation, and substitution.

  Note, however, that the thesis itself must not be a question.

- **Quotation.** A quotation can be something you have read in a book or an article. It can also be something that you have heard: a popular saying or proverb ("Never give advice to a friend"); a current or recent advertising slogan ("Reach out and touch someone"); a favourite expression used by your friends or family ("My father always says …"). Using a quotation in your introductory paragraph lets you add someone else's voice to your own. Here is an example of a paragraph that begins with a quotation.

  "Evil," wrote Martin Buber, "is lack of direction." In my school days as a fatherless boy, with a mother too confused by her own life to really care for me, I strayed down a number of paths. Before my eighteenth birthday, I had been thrown out of school, fired from jobs, and put into a group home.

THE THESIS STATEMENT

An essay's thesis statement is like a paragraph's topic sentence: it contains two elements, the essay's subject and your position or viewpoint on that subject. As a topic sentence does with a paragraph, a thesis statement previews the essay's content. The thesis guides readers on what to expect from the paragraphs that follow. To write a strong thesis statement, follow these steps.

1 To develop an effective thesis, begin by working out a focus on your subject. Narrow a general subject to find your focus.

   Refer back to pages 56-63 on writing an effective topic sentence for additional help with writing your thesis statement, since a thesis and a topic sentence are the same in principle: they should not be announcements, and they should be neither too broad nor too narrow.

A focused subject for an essay will help you write a good thesis statement. Your goal is to find a focused view of your subject that is (1) clear, (2) specific, and (3) a suitable size to develop in three supporting paragraphs. (Some essays will have only two supporting paragraphs; others, four or more.)

Alexa, the student who wrote about telemarketing, was assigned the general subject of "part-time jobs." She did some prewriting and, in doing so, came up with details about four or five part-time jobs she had worked at. No single focus appeared right away. Rereading her material, she found herself returning to the idea of job routines, so that became the focus of the paragraph on page 77. When she returned to her subject weeks later, it was because she had been assigned the task of turning her paragraph into an essay. She changed her focus and considered some other possibilities before deciding to write about one particularly awful job.

> *An unclear focus:* part-time jobs are awful
>
> *A non-specific focus:* students and part-time jobs
>
> *A focus that is too broad for an essay:* profiles of students in telemarketing
>
> *A clearly focused subject:* telemarketing, and why it was so awful

One good way to find a focus is to brainstorm or prewrite on the one aspect of your general subject to which you relate most easily. Write about what you know. Alexa's thought processes, in narrowing her subject, might have gone like this:

> Part-time jobs → jobs I've held → what was good or bad about them → telemarketing was the worst

2 Write a sentence about your narrowed, focused subject that expresses a single viewpoint or position. The viewpoint you express in your thesis is your attitude toward your subject—the limits you place around your coverage of it. As with writing a topic sentence, use keywords to express your attitude or position (page 59). Do not offer more than one viewpoint on your subject in your thesis.

> *A thesis that offers more than one viewpoint or attitude:* Telemarketing is depressing work, but it pays well.
>
> *A thesis that is too general:* Telemarketing is the kind of job that students all across Canada take.
>
> *A thesis that is too narrow and a dead-end statement:* Telemarketing is a typical part-time job.
>
> *An effective thesis statement:* Telemarketing was the worst job I have ever had.

Write a thesis statement that is general enough to cover each of your supporting points, but not so general that it uses wordings or ideas such as "All over the world" or refers to what "everyone" knows, thinks, or does. Specify your focus on your subject.

3   Suggest or list your supporting points as part of your thesis statement. The attitude or viewpoint stated in your thesis may be enough to imply the nature of your supporting evidence, but some effective thesis statements offer or preview these points as well.

> *A thesis that presents its supporting points:* Three types of people end up working in telemarketing: starving students, out-of-work actors, and social misfits.

4   If you are writing an essay using a specific method of development, your thesis should suggest that method with related keywords.

> *A thesis for a division and classification essay:* First-semester students can be divided into three groups: the eager beavers, the frankly frightened, and the "too cool for school."
>
> *A thesis for a definition essay:* The meaning of pollution is clear all along Toronto's waterfront.

Activity

Following is one general subject and a list of narrowed or focused subjects that fit under that general term. Write a thesis statement for one of each group of narrowed subjects. Ask yourself what point you wish to make about the narrowed subject you choose in each case, so that your thesis statements show a clear, single attitude.

1. *General subject:* School clothes
    - Showing too much skin
    - Suits and career wear
    - Comfort clothes
    - Personalities of wearers
    - Good taste

    Your thesis statement: _____

2. *General subject:* Music today
    - Downloading songs
    - Rap videos
    - NuPunk
    - Songs on the radio
    - Concert behaviour

    Your thesis statement: _____

3. *General subject:* Food
    - Fast food
    - Vegetarianism
    - Comfort foods
    - Healthy eating
    - Eating on a budget

    Your thesis statement: _____

4. *General subject:* Grooming
   - Manicures and pedicures
   - Cost of products
   - Hair obsessions
   - Professional appearance
   - Piercings and tattoos

Your thesis statement: _____

SUPPORTING PARAGRAPHS

Many college essays have three supporting points, developed in three separate paragraphs. Each of the supporting paragraphs should begin with a topic sentence that states the point to be detailed in that paragraph. Just as the thesis provides a focus or controlling idea for the entire essay, the topic sentence provides a focus for each supporting paragraph.

Activity

1. What is the topic sentence for the first supporting paragraph of "Tele-Torture"? (*Write the sentence number here.*) _____

2. What is the topic sentence for the second supporting paragraph? _____

3. What is the topic sentence for the third supporting paragraph? _____

As you compose each supporting paragraph, you will find it helpful to review Chapters 3 and 4 in this book. Your topic sentences focus each paragraph and help unify your essay by referring to your thesis and continuing its train of thought. Now, as you work on the body of your essay, keep in mind the guiding principle of providing *adequate and specific support.* Be certain that every supporting paragraph explains or proves the point stated in its topic sentence thoroughly, illustrating its meaning with specific ideas and phrases. Your supporting paragraphs should be roughly equal in length, so that your essay is balanced in content and appearance.

Structuring Supporting Paragraphs

In an essay, each supporting point for the thesis becomes the topic of one of the essay's body paragraphs—each supporting paragraph's topic sentence presents one of the points of the thesis. Each supporting paragraph then follows the structure you have learned in earlier chapters of this book. Writers do not always need three subtopics for every supporting paragraph of every essay, however. Sometimes a supporting point may be best explained with one extended discussion containing strong specific details or examples. Two natural subtopics may be a realistic number for other essays; your content will guide you as you create an internal structure for your supporting paragraphs.

Activity

1. What details explain the topic sentence in the first supporting paragraph of "Tele-Torture"? Which seem most effective to you, and why? Are there details that might be more specific?
2. How many subtopics are there in the second supporting paragraph?
3. Which details in the third supporting paragraph explain the idea that the supervisors were like "robots"?

TRANSITIONS AND TRANSITIONAL SENTENCES

In Chapter 4, you learned to use a clear method of organization and transitional words and devices within your paragraphs to achieve the goal of *coherence*, to help readers follow your thinking. You should organize your supporting paragraphs according to a definite method and provide transitional words and cues to link your sentences and show their relationship to one another.

Activity

1. In the first supporting paragraph of "Tele-Torture," how many transitional words or phrases are used? What type of transition is each one?
2. Where is the transitional phrase within the second supporting paragraph? Could another transitional word be used in this paragraph? If so, what kind of transition, and where would it appear?
3. What types of transitions are used in the third supporting paragraph?

These transitions and other connective devices (pages 78-79) help to create smoothly flowing paragraphs that are *coherent* to readers.

Similarly, in an essay, *transitional sentences* are used to help tie the supporting paragraphs together. Such transitional sentences usually occur near the end of one paragraph or the beginning of the next.

In "Tele-Torture," the first transitional sentence is:

> Although I might have got used to the late shift eventually, the equipment I used and the office itself made every hour misery.

In this sentence, the keywords *late shift* remind us of the point of the first supporting paragraph, while the words *equipment, office,* and *misery* tell us the point to be developed in the second supporting paragraph.

Activity

Here is the other transitional sentence in "Tele-Torture":

> But more than the physical discomfort, what upset me most about the job was the supervisors.

Note: Notice that the dependent or subordinate first part of the sentence refers to the previous paragraph, and the independent (or main) part of the sentence takes the reader into the paragraph to follow.

Complete the following statement: In the sentence above, the keywords _____ _____ echo the point of the second supporting paragraph, and the keywords _____ announce the topic of the third supporting paragraph.

CONCLUDING PARAGRAPH

The concluding paragraph often summarizes the essay by briefly restating the thesis and, at times, the main supporting points of the essay. Also, the conclusion brings the paper to a natural and graceful end, sometimes leaving the reader with a final thought on the subject.

Activity

1. Which sentence in the concluding paragraph of "Tele-Torture" restates the thesis and supporting points of the essay? _____

2. Which sentence contains the concluding thought of the essay? _____

ESSAYS TO CONSIDER

Read the three student essays below and then answer the questions that follow.

Starting Over and Over Again

[1]Before I came into class last Tuesday, I heard two people talking in the hall. [2]One student asked another one, "Why did you start all over again?" [3]A year ago, I would have had no answer to that question. [4]I felt as if I had made one too many mistakes, beginning with coming to Canada. [5]I could not work in my profession here, so I had to take terrible jobs, and I wasn't even good at them. [6]Although I am glad now that I didn't give up and I started college, there were a lot of reasons why I hated starting anything all over again.

[7]First of all, I gave up a lot when I left the Philippines, mainly my pride. [8]I knew that my architect's degree would not be accepted in Canada, but I was sure I could get work drafting. [9]As soon as I began looking for a position, I found out that construction business was slow and there were few jobs available. [10]Because my English was poor, I did so badly at interviews that I was never called back. [11]I was just another face with a Spanish accent, no experience, and no Canadian references on my resumé. [12]Starting over in a new country was starting to look hopeless.

[13]My next reason to dislike starting over was the kind of job I had to take to support my family. [14]Before I left Manila, I thought I knew something about the cost of living in Canadian cities. [15]But trying to survive in Vancouver with no income was hard. [16]Our money ran out fast, so I registered with employment agencies, looked for signs in store windows, and sent out more resumés. [17]Finally I got a job as the night manager of a convenience store.

[18]I never saw my wife and son, and the owner took advantage of my situation. [19]He expected me to do all the cleaning for the day and night shifts as well as manage the store. [20]I had to wash out the coffee machine and freezers, clean up rotten vegetables, mop the floor, restock the shelves, and at the same time, try to work the cash. [21]Each morning when I left the store, I hated myself and the job more. [22]But what could I do?

[23]What I did was what I feared most about starting over—I failed. [24]When a family friend heard about my situation, he took pity on me and gave me a job. [25]He ran a shipping company, and he put me in charge of one of the offices. [26]I was so happy to put on a suit, all ready to work normal hours for more money. [27]My family would not starve or go home in disgrace. [28]Unfortunately, I did not realize how unprepared I was for sorting out forwarding problems and talking to customers and suppliers. [29]My English was not up to business standards, and I knew nearly no Canadian geography. [30]Every day, I tried so hard to do well, and every day I made more and more mistakes. [31]Customers yelled at me because I was so slow and packages sometimes went to the wrong destinations. [32]After three weeks, my boss sadly said he had to let me go. [33]I was ready to give up on starting over.

[34]Only now, a year later, do I understand something about starting over again. [35]I realize that I learned from each experience, even if I was unhappy at the time. [36]I used to believe that all I learned was not to give up. [37]But now I think I learned something else—how important it is to prepare for new beginnings—and that's what led me to this new start, at college.

Consuming Canadians

[1]Canadians are consumed by consuming. [2]They shop all the time for just about anything. [3]They shop instead of doing just about anything else. [4]Shopping is a pretty innocent, ordinary activity—everyone needs things, and people enjoy buying something new. [5]But Canadians, especially those who live in cities, now spend far too much of their daily lives being consumers. [6]They think about shopping every day; they spend weekends at the mall, and then they go online and shop some more.

[7]Constant advertising everywhere makes Canadians believe that they need to buy or consume something every single day. [8]What they need is not just something, but a brand-name something that they saw on TV, on a website banner, at the movies, on a billboard, in a magazine, in the paper, on a bus-shelter wall, or even on a taxicab's hubcap covers. [9]If people want their daily cups of coffee, they go to Timothy's, Second Cup, or Starbucks for some frothy, flavoured four-dollar beverage in a trademarked cup. [10]When Canadians want some exercise, do they just step out the door for a walk? [11]No, they go to a well-advertised sportswear store to buy a brand-name outfit and shoes. [12]Or they remember that fitness club they liked the ad for, and spend a few hundred on a membership and workout clothes they may not make much use of. [13]People would rather buy things than actually do things.

[14]Shopping has also replaced socializing, hobbies, and other weekend activities. In fact, going to the mall is now considered a "weekend activity."

[15]Canadians claim they prefer going to malls because of the convenience or because they can avoid bad weather. [16]But the fact is that families don't spend weekend time mowing the lawn, washing the windows, hiking, playing games, or going to the museum—they go to the mall. [17]Teenagers don't just spend weekends shopping at malls; malls are their social centres, where they meet friends, eat, go to movies, and generally hang out in groups like mall rats, not leaving until they're forced to.

[18]Just how good Canadians are at consuming shows most of all when they go online. [19]The Internet is a huge international communications medium, but ads, banners, and pop-ups have turned it into an advertising and shopping system. [20]When people go home in the evening and open up their personal e-mail, their in-boxes are full of advertising—promotional posts from Bell or Rogers or e-mail "coupons" from stores like Staples or Shoppers Drug Mart, and of course spam advertisements. [21]Canadians respond so well that major U.S. online retailers like Ebay and Amazon have opened Canadian sites. [22]Every major Canadian store chain, like the Bay, Chapters, and Canadian Tire, is open for business 24/7 to catch every possible customer. [23]In fact, people must be too busy even to shop for food in person, because Canadians lead the world in online use of sites like Grocery Gateway. [24]Shopping by computer supposedly saves time, but what are Canadians saving that time for? [25]Probably more "real-time" shopping.

[26]Canadians really do seem to live to consume. [27]Perhaps they really believe all the advertising they're surrounded by. [28]Perhaps twenty-first-century life will be just a cycle of working and shopping. [29]Whatever the reason, Canadians do "shop 'til they drop."

An Interpretation of <u>Lord of the Flies</u>

[1]Modern history has shown us the evil that exists in human beings. [2]Assassinations are common, governments use torture to discourage dissent, and six million Jews were exterminated during World War II. [3]In <u>Lord of the Flies</u>, William Golding describes a group of schoolboys shipwrecked on an island with no authority figures to control their behaviour. [4]One of the boys soon yields to dark forces within himself, and his corruption symbolizes the evil in all of us. [5]First, Jack Merridew kills a living creature; then, he rebels against the group leader; and finally, he seizes power and sets up his own murderous society.

[6]The first stage in Jack's downfall is his killing of a living creature. [7]In Chapter 1, Jack aims at a pig but is unable to kill. [8]His upraised arm pauses "because of the enormity of the knife descending and cutting into living flesh, because of the unbearable blood," and the pig escapes. [9]Three chapters later, however, Jack leads some boys on a successful hunt. [10]He returns triumphantly with a freshly killed pig and reports excitedly to the others, "I cut the pig's throat." [11]Yet Jack twitches as he says this, and he wipes his bloody hands on his shorts as if eager to remove the stains. [12]There is still some civilization left in him.

[13]After the initial act of killing the pig, Jack's refusal to cooperate with Ralph shows us that this civilized part is rapidly disappearing. [14]With

no adults around, Ralph has made some rules. [15]One is that a signal fire must be kept burning. [16]But Jack tempts the boys watching the fire to go hunting, and the fire goes out. [17]Another rule is that at a meeting, only the person holding a special seashell has the right to speak. [18]In Chapter 5, another boy is speaking when Jack rudely tells him to shut up. [19]Ralph accuses Jack of breaking the rules. [20]Jack shouts: "Bollocks to the rules! We're strong—we hunt! If there's a beast, we'll hunt it down! We'll close in and beat and beat and beat—!" [21]He gives a "wild whoop" and leaps off the platform, throwing the meeting into chaos. [22]Jack is now much more savage than civilized.

[23]The most obvious proof of Jack's corruption comes in Chapter 8, when he establishes his own murderous society. [24]Insisting that Ralph is not a "proper chief" because he does not hunt, Jack asks for a new election. [25]After he again loses, Jack announces, "I'm going off by myself. . . . Anyone who wants to hunt when I do can come too." [26]Eventually, nearly all the boys join Jack's "tribe." [27]Following his example, they paint their faces like savages, sacrifice to "the beast," brutally murder two of their schoolmates, and nearly succeed in killing Ralph as well. [28]Jack has now become completely savage— and so have the others.

[29]Through Jack Merridew, then, Golding shows how easily moral laws can be forgotten. [30]Freed from grown-ups and their rules, Jack learns to kill living things, defy authority, and lead a tribe of murdering savages. [31]Jack's example is a frightening reminder of humanity's potential for evil. [32]The "beast" the boys try to hunt and kill is actually within every human being.

■ Questions

1. In which essay does the thesis statement appear in the last sentence of the introductory paragraph?

   _____

2. In the essay on *Lord of the Flies,* which sentence of the introductory paragraph contains the plan of development? _____

3. Which method of introduction is used in "Starting Over and Over Again"?
   a. Broad statement   c. Anecdote
   b. Relevance   d. Questions

4. Complete the following brief outline of "Starting Over and Over Again." Starting over and over again was hard for three reasons:

   a. _____

   b. _____

   c. _____

5. Which *two* essays use a transitional sentence between the first and second supporting paragraphs?

   _____

   _____

6. Complete the following statement: Emphatic order is shown in the last supporting paragraph of "Starting Over and Over Again" with the words "what I feared most"; in the last supporting paragraph of "Consuming Canadians" with the words _____; and in the last supporting paragraph of "An Interpretation of *Lord of the Flies*" with the words _____.

7. Which essay uses time order as well as emphatic order to organize its three supporting paragraphs? _____

8. List four major transitions used in the supporting paragraphs of "An Interpretation of *Lord of the Flies*."

   a. _____   c. _____

   b. _____   d. _____

9. Which *two* essays include a sentence in the concluding paragraph that summarizes the three supporting points?

   _____

   _____

10. Which essay includes two final thoughts in its concluding paragraph?

    _____

PLANNING THE ESSAY

As you prepare to write an essay, first refer to the four-step sequence for effective writing in Chapter 2.

Begin by prewriting to discover the point you wish to make about your subject. As you are considering your thesis, remember that each supporting point for the view expressed in your thesis will now be explained in an entire paragraph.

You will find that the prewriting stage will take more time now—after all, an essay has many paragraphs. Be sure to allow yourself enough prewriting time to discover (1) strong supporting points for your thesis and (2) enough specific details to explain or prove those supporting points.

OUTLINING THE ESSAY

Because an essay's structure and content are more complex than those of a single paragraph, planning is essential for success, and outlining is absolutely crucial to creating a solid essay. You should plan your essay by outlining in two ways:

1 Prepare a brief outline. This should consist of a short statement of the thesis followed by the main supporting points for the thesis. Here is Alexa's outline for her essay on the telemarketing job:

Telemarketing was an awful job.
1. Night shifts
2. Office and equipment
3. Supervisors

Do not underestimate the value of this initial outline—or the work involved in achieving it. Be prepared to do a good deal of plain hard thinking at this first and most important stage of your writing.

2   Prepare a more detailed outline. The Essay Outline Form that follows will serve as a guide. Your instructor may ask you to submit a copy of this form either before you write an essay or along with your finished essay.

ESSAY OUTLINE FORM

Photocopy this outline form, or create your own on disk by setting it up and saving it as a blank document. Each time you are ready to outline, just paste your outline document onto a new document page.

Introductory Paragraph

Introduction: _____

Thesis Statement: _____

Plan of Development: _____

   Supporting Point 1: _____

   Supporting Point 2: _____

   Supporting Point 3: _____

First Supporting Paragraph

Topic Sentence: _____

Subtopic 1: _____

   Supporting Details:

      a. _____

      b. _____

      c. _____

Subtopic 2: _____

   Supporting Details:

      a. _____

      b. _____

      c. _____

Subtopic 3: _____

   Supporting Details:

      a. _____

      b. _____

      c. _____

Second Supporting Paragraph

Topic Sentence: _____

Subtopic 1: _____

   Supporting Details:

     a. _____

     b. _____

     c. _____

Subtopic 2: _____

   Supporting Details:

     a. _____

     b. _____

     c. _____

Subtopic 3: _____

   Supporting Details:

     a. _____

     b. _____

     c. _____

Third Supporting Paragraph

Topic Sentence: _____

Subtopic 1: _____

   Supporting Details:

     a. _____

     b. _____

     c. _____

Subtopic 2: _____

   Supporting Details:

     a. _____

     b. _____

     c. _____

Subtopic 3: _____

   Supporting Details:

     a. _____

     b. _____

     c. _____

Concluding Paragraph

Summary, conclusion, or both _____

ESSAY WRITING ASSIGNMENTS

Hints: Keep the following points in mind when writing an essay on any of the topics below.

1   As you prewrite to develop your thesis and support, remember that your essay will be longer and more detailed than a single paragraph. Allow yourself more time or perhaps more sessions for the prewriting stage.

2   After leaving your prewriting for a day, or at least a few hours, prepare to plan your essay. Begin with a brief outline of its thesis and main supporting points; then create a more detailed outline using the Essay Outline Form above.

3   While writing your essay, use the checklist below to make sure your essay touches all four bases of effective writing.

Base 1: Unity

_____   Clearly stated thesis in the introductory paragraph of your paper

_____   All the supporting paragraphs on target in backing up your thesis

Base 2: Support

_____   Three separate supporting points for your thesis

_____   *Specific* evidence for each of the three supporting points

_____   *Plenty* of specific evidence for each supporting point

Base 3: Coherence

_____   Clear method of organization

_____   Transitions, other connecting words, or transitional sentences

_____   Effective introduction and conclusion

Base 4: Sentence Skills

_____   Clear, error-free sentences (use the checklist on the inside front cover of this book)

■ 1 Your House or Apartment

Write an essay on the advantages *or* disadvantages (not both) of the house, apartment, or residence room where you live. In your introductory paragraph, briefly describe the place you plan to write about. End the paragraph with your thesis statement and a plan of development. Here are some suggestions for thesis statements.

The best features of my apartment are its large windows, roomy closets, and great location.

The drawbacks of my house are its unreliable oil furnace, tiny kitchen, and old-fashioned bathroom.

An inquisitive property manager, sloppy neighbours, and troops of mice came along with our rented house.

My apartment has several advantages, including friendly neighbours, lots of storage space, and a good security system.

2 A Big Mistake

Write an essay about the biggest mistake you made within the past year. Describe the mistake and show how its effects have convinced you that it was the wrong thing to do. For instance, if you write about "taking on a full-time job while going to school" as your biggest mistake, show the problems it caused. (You might discuss such matters as low grades, constant exhaustion, and poor performance at work, for example.)

To get started, make a list of all the things you did last year that, with hindsight, now seem to be mistakes. Then pick out the action that has had the most serious consequences for you. Make a brief outline to guide you as you write, as in the examples below.

Thesis: Breaking up with my girlfriend was the worst mistake I made last year.
1. Didn't know what to do by myself
2. Had to leave lots of my stuff at her place
3. Loneliness

Thesis: Buying a used car to commute to school was the worst mistake of last year.
1. Unreliable—late for class or missed class
2. Expenses for insurance, repairs
3. Led to an accident

3 A Valued Possession

Write an essay about a valued material possession. Here are some suggestions.

Car	Book
TV set	Photograph album
Piece of furniture	Piece of clothing
Piece of jewellery	Sound system (car or home)
Camera	Piece of hobby equipment

In your introductory paragraph, describe the possession: tell what it is, when and where you got it, and how long you have owned it. Your thesis statement should centre on the idea that there are several reasons this possession is so important to you. In each of your supporting paragraphs, provide details to back up one of the reasons.

For example, here are the three supporting points of an essay written about a leather jacket:

1. It is comfortable.
2. It wears well.
3. It makes me look and feel good.

■ 4 An Essay Based on a Reading Selection

Write an essay based on the selection "Power Learning" on pages 529-35. Read the selection through several times, noting its main points about study skills. You may wish to write this essay from the third-person point of view, as in the sample introductory paragraph below.

Choose three topics for your supporting paragraphs from among the article's suggested study skills. Select the three suggestions that relate best to your own experience as a student. Do not simply copy words or phrases from the selection— that would be plagiarism. (Refer to the Online Learning Centre for more information on using sources effectively.) Express your own responses to the article's ideas in your own words.

One possible introductory paragraph and possible topic sentences for the supporting paragraphs are provided below. In addition to developing the supporting paragraphs, you should write a brief conclusion for the essay.

Introductory Paragraph

Using Study Skills

Why do some students in a college class receive As, while others get Ds and Fs? Are some people just naturally smarter? Are other students doomed to failure? Motivation—willingness to do the work—is a factor in good grades. But the main difference between successful and unsuccessful students is that the ones who do well have mastered the specific skills needed to handle college work. Fortunately, these skills can be learned by anyone. Doing well in college depends on knowing how to … *(Complete this sentence with the three study skills you decide to write about.)*

Possible Topic Sentences for Three Supporting Paragraphs

Time control is one aid to success as a student.
Another aid is the use of memory techniques.
Knowing how to concentrate is another essential skill.
Studying a textbook effectively is another key to success.
Perhaps the most crucial step of all is effective classroom note-taking.

■ 5 Single Life

Write an essay using the third-person point of view on the advantages or drawbacks of single life. (See the model essay "Consuming Canadians" for an example of third-person point of view, pages 288-89.) To get started, make a list of all the advantages and drawbacks you can think of. Advantages might include:

Fewer expenses
Fewer responsibilities

More personal freedom
More opportunities to move or travel

Drawbacks might include:

Parental disapproval
Being alone at social events
No companion for shopping, movies, and so on
Sadness at holiday time

After you make up two lists, select the thesis for which you feel you have more supporting material. Then organize your material into a brief outline. Be sure to include an introduction, a clear topic sentence for each supporting paragraph, and a conclusion.

Alternatively, write an essay on the advantages or drawbacks of married life. Follow the directions given above.

6 Influences on Your Writing

Are you as good a writer as you want to be? Write an essay analyzing the reasons you have become a good writer or explaining why you are not as good as you'd like to be. Begin by considering some factors that may have influenced your writing ability.

Your family background: Did you see people writing at home? Did your parents respect and value the ability to write?

Your school experience: Did you have good writing teachers? Did you have a history of failure or success with writing? Was writing fun, or was it a chore? Did your school emphasize writing?

Social influences: How did your school friends do at writing? What were your friends' attitudes toward writing? What feelings about writing did you pick up from TV or the movies?

You might want to organize your essay by describing the three greatest influences on your writing skill (or lack of writing skill). Show how each of these has contributed to the present state of your writing.

7 A Major Decision

All of us come to various crossroads in our lives, times when we must make an important decision about which course of action to follow. Think about a major decision you had to make (or one you are planning to make). Then write an essay on the reasons for your decision. In your introduction, describe the decision you have reached or are contemplating. Each of the supporting paragraphs that follow should fully explain one of the reasons for your decision. Here are some examples of major decisions that often confront people.

Enrolling in or dropping out of college
Accepting or quitting a job
Breaking up with a boyfriend or girlfriend
Having a baby
Moving away from home

Student papers on this topic include the essay on pages 287-88 and the paragraphs on pages 50-51.

■ 8 Reviewing a TV Show or Movie

Write an essay about a television show or movie you have seen very recently. The thesis of your essay will be that the show (or movie) has both good and bad features. (If you are writing about a TV series, be sure that you evaluate only one episode. Remember also to see page 408 for correct formatting of titles of movies, TV shows, and episodes.)

In your first supporting paragraph, briefly summarize the episode of the show or the movie. Don't get bogged down in small details here; just give an overview, describe briefly the major characters and give the highlights of the action.

In your second supporting paragraph, explain what you feel are the best features of the show or movie. Listed below are some examples of good features you might write about.

Suspenseful, ingenious, or realistic plot
Good acting
Good scenery or special effects
Surprise ending
Good music
Believable characters

In your third supporting paragraph, explain what you feel are the worst features of the show or movie. Here are some possibilities.

Far-fetched, confusing, or dull plot
Poor special effects
Bad acting
One-dimensional characters
Unrealistic dialogue

Remember to cover only a few features in each paragraph; do not try to include everything. Use your concluding paragraph to sum up your overall positive or negative view of the show or movie, based on your three previous paragraphs.

■ 9 Your High School

Imagine that you are an outside consultant called in as a neutral observer to examine the high school you attended. After your visit, you must send the school board a five-paragraph letter in which you describe the most striking features (good, bad, or a combination of both) of the school and the evidence for each of these features.

In order to write the letter, you may want to think about the following features of your high school.

Attitude of the teachers, student body, or administration
Condition of the buildings, classrooms, recreational areas, and so on
Curriculum
How classes are conducted

Extracurricular activities

Crowded or uncrowded conditions

Be sure to include an introduction, a clear topic sentence for each supporting paragraph, and a conclusion.

REVIEWING THE LEARNING OUTCOMES FOR ESSAY WRITING

After working through this chapter's activities and completing one of its essay assignments, review your final draft to see how well your essay responds to the following questions.

1   Does your essay attract the reader's interest with its introduction? Does your introduction clearly relate to your thesis?

2   Does your introductory paragraph contain a clear thesis statement and some indication of the method of organization you will use?

3   Does each supporting paragraph open with a topic sentence that relates to one of the supporting points for your thesis?

4   Does each supporting paragraph contain enough specific and separate explanatory and supporting details to clarify that paragraph's point and thus reinforce your thesis?

5   Are your supporting paragraphs linked smoothly to one another by transitional devices or transitional sentences? Do the sentences within each supporting paragraph show effective use of transitional words where needed?

6   Does your conclusion return the reader to the point of your thesis? Does it sum up the meaning and evidence supplied in the body of your essay? Do you leave the reader with a parting thought to signal completion or suggest wider meaning?

7   Have you revised your essay carefully to avoid errors in spelling and other mechanics?

Visit the *English Skills with Readings* Online Learning Centre at **www.mcgrawhill.ca/college/langan** to access self-quizzes, bonus material on study and research skills, web resources, and other learning and study tools.

Handbook of Sentence Skills

PREVIEW

You can refer to Section Four of this book at any time when you need help with grammar or sentence skills.

In Section One, you first encountered the four steps to, or bases for, effective writing. Section Four is a handbook that focuses on the *fourth step: writing clear, error-free sentences.* Turn to Section Four whenever you are uncertain about a point of grammar or punctuation, or when a sentence "seems wrong." Most of all, turn to this handbook when you are revising and proofreading your work.

To help you make the best use of Section Four, the opening chapter contains a diagnostic test to help you in two areas. First, you will see how well you currently handle and understand sentence skills. Next, you will learn to identify and name the areas of grammar and sentence skills that challenge you. Knowing the usual labels for important sentence-skills concepts helps you find the relevant chapters within Section Four.

The chapters on sentence skills deal with grammar, mechanics, punctuation, and word use. Chapter 41 presents pointers and brief activities for ESL students. Next come mastery tests and editing tests that reinforce basic writing skills and give you practice in editing and proofreading. Finally, an achievement test helps you measure your improvement in important sentence skills. After working with Section Four, try the achievement test, and compare your new results with the results you obtained in Chapter 18's diagnostic test.

Explaining a Process · Examining Cause and Effect · comparing or Contrasting · Definin
rm · Dividing and Classifying · Describing a Scene or Person · Narrating an Event · Argu
Position · Explaining a Process · Examining Cause and Effect · comparing or Contrastin
efining a Term · Dividing and Classifying · Describing a Scene or Person · Narrating
vent · Arguing a Position · Explaining a Process · Examining Cause and Effect · Compar

CHAPTER 18

Sentence-Skills Diagnostic Test

PART 1

This diagnostic test will help you check your knowledge and awareness of important sentence skills. Each section of the test begins with a heading, such as "Fragments" or "Run-ons and Comma Splices." The heading alerts you to the name or label usually given to the area of sentence skills, grammar, or mechanics that this section of the test deals with. The headings also give you clues to the type of mistakes to look for. But you can find your mistakes even if you do not yet understand the meaning of the heading or label. What you are checking for now is your own sense of what constitutes effective written English.

Each heading is followed by a number of word groups. Certain parts of these word groups are underlined. Write *X* in the answer space to the left of the word group if you think a mistake appears in the underlined part. Write *C* in the answer space if you think the underlined part is correct.

When you have completed the diagnostic test and checked your results (see page 600), note the names of the areas of sentence skills, grammar, or punctuation where you had the most difficulty. These will be the areas to work on as you proceed through the semester and the areas to check most carefully as you revise and proofread your papers.

Faulty Parallelism (pages 95-96)

1. Ben enjoys cross-country skiing, socializing with friends, and <u>to read comics.</u>

2. The recipe instructed me to chop onions, to peel carrots, and <u>to boil a pot of water.</u>

3. When I saw my roommate with my girlfriend, I felt worried, angry, and <u>embarrassment as well.</u>

4. Francine enjoys shopping for new clothes, <u>trying different cosmetics,</u> and reading fashion magazines.

Consistent Verb Tense (pages 96-98)

_____   5. I played some CDs and watched television before I <u>decide</u> to do some homework.

_____   6. The first thing Scott does every day is weigh himself. The scale <u>informs</u> him what kind of meals he can eat that day.

_____   7. Sandy eats a nutritious breakfast, <u>skips</u> lunch, and then enjoys a big dinner.

_____   8. His parents stayed together for his sake; only after he <u>graduates</u> from college were they divorced.

Pronoun Point of View (pages 98-99)

_____   9. I work at a clothes shop where <u>you</u> do not get paid for all the holidays I should.

_____   10. I enjoy movies like *The Ring* that frighten <u>me</u>.

Fragments (Chapter 21)

_____   11. <u>Because Tom had eaten and drunk too much.</u> He had to leave the party early. His stomach was like a volcano ready to erupt.

_____   12. <u>After I slid my aching bones into the hot water of the tub, I realized there was no soap.</u> I did not want to get out again.

_____   13. I spent two hours on the phone yesterday. <u>Trying to find a garage to repair my car.</u> Eventually I had to have the car towed to a garage in another town.

_____   14. <u>Sweating under his heavy load.</u> Brian staggered up the stairs to his apartment. He felt as though his legs were crumbling beneath him.

_____   15. <u>I love to eat and cook Italian food, especially lasagna and ravioli.</u> I make everything from scratch.

_____   16. One of my greatest joys in life is eating desserts. <u>Such as blueberry cheese-cake and cannoli.</u> Almond fudge cake makes me want to dance.

Run-ons and Comma Splices (Chapter 22)

_____   17. She decided to drive to <u>Port Dover, because</u> she wanted to sit on the beach.

_____   18. The window shade snapped up like a <u>gunshot her</u> cat leaped a metre off the floor.

_____   19. Billy is the meanest little kid on his <u>block, he</u> eats only the heads of animal crackers.

_____   20. He knew he had flunked the driver's <u>exam, he</u> ran over a stop sign.

_____   21. My first boyfriend was five years <u>old. We</u> met every day in the playground sandbox.

_____   22. Luisa wanted to go <u>dancing, Terrell</u> preferred going to a movie.

Irregular Verbs (Chapter 23)

_____ 23. I <u>knowed</u> her from somewhere, but I couldn't remember just where.

_____ 24. I had <u>eaten</u> so much food at the buffet dinner that I went into the bathroom just to loosen my belt.

_____ 25. When the mudslide started, the whole neighbourhood <u>began</u> going downhill.

____ _____ 26. Julio has <u>rode</u> the bus to school for two years while saving for a car.

Subject-Verb Agreement (Chapter 24)

_____ 27. There <u>is</u> long lines at the checkout counter.

_____ 28. The baby <u>have</u> a painful ear infection.

_____ 29. One of the files <u>was</u> infected by a worm.

_____ 30. The bugs behind my stove <u>gets</u> high on Raid.

Pronoun Agreement and Reference (Chapter 25)

_____ 31. Every guest at the costume party dressed like <u>their</u> favourite cartoon character.

_____ 32. Persons camping in those woods should watch <u>their</u> step because of poison ivy.

____ _____ 33. Angry because he had struck out, Mark hurled the baseball bat at the fence and broke <u>it</u>.

_____ 34. I love feta cheese, but <u>it</u> does not always agree with me.

Pronoun Types (Chapter 26)

_____ 35. Randy and <u>me</u> take turns driving to college.

_____ 36. No one is a better cook than <u>she</u>.

_____ 37. Brent does not know, because <u>him</u> and I arrived late.

Adjectives and Adverbs (Chapter 27)

_____ 38. Tranh ran <u>quick</u> up the steps, taking them two at a time.

____ _____ 39. Justin is <u>more better</u> than I am at darts.

Misplaced Modifiers (Chapter 28)

_____ 40. He swatted the wasp that stung him <u>with a newspaper</u>.

_____ 41. Maria returned the hamburger <u>that was spoiled</u> to the supermarket.

_____ 42. My aunt once met Mike Myers at a benefit, <u>whom she found to be a very engaging person</u>.

_____ 43. I adopted a dog from the pound <u>which is very close to my heart</u>.

Dangling Modifiers (Chapter 29)

_____ 44. <u>Tapping a marker on the table</u>, Ms. Rinaldi asked for the class's attention.

_____ 45. <u>Flunking out of school</u>, my parents demanded that I get a job.

_____ 46. <u>While I was waiting for the bus</u>, rain began to fall.

_____ 47. <u>Braking the car suddenly</u>, the shopping bags tumbled onto the floor.

Capital Letters (Chapter 31)

_____ 48. Joon was falling asleep at the wheel, so he was glad to see a <u>tim hortons</u> sign ahead.

_____ 49. During <u>july</u>, Frank's company works a four-day week.

_____ 50. I asked my dad, <u>"When's</u> Uncle Bill getting his toupee?"

_____ 51. On <u>Summer</u> days I like to sit in the backyard and sunbathe.

Apostrophe (Chapter 33)

_____ 52. The <u>Wolfman's</u> bite is worse than his bark.

_____ 53. <u>Alans</u> quick hands reached out to break his son's fall.

_____ 54. I'll be with you shortly if <u>youll</u> just wait a minute.

_____ 55. You <u>shouldn't</u> drink any more if you intend to drive home.

Quotation Marks (Chapter 34)

_____ 56. Someone once said, <u>"Canadians sing about the North but live as far south as possible."</u>

_____ 57. Say something tender to me, <u>"whispered Sean to Ina."</u>

_____ 58. <u>"I hate that commercial, he muttered."</u>

_____ 59. "If you don't leave soon," he warned, <u>"you'll be late for work."</u>

Comma (Chapter 35)

_____ 60. Jeremy's favourite bands include <u>Sum 41 Nickelback the White Stripes and Linkin Park</u>.

_____ 61. Although I have a black belt in <u>karate</u> I decided to go easy on the demented bully who had kicked sand in my face.

_____ 62. All the tree branches, <u>which were coated with ice</u>, glittered like crystal.

_____ 63. We could always tell when our instructor felt <u>disorganized for</u> his shirt would not be tucked into his pants.

_____ 64. <u>You, my friend</u>, are going to get yours.

_____ 65. His father <u>shouted</u> "Why do you never close the garage door?"

Commonly Confused Words (Chapter 39)

_____   66. Some stores will accept your credit cards but not you're cheque.

_____   67. That issue is to hot for any politician to handle.

_____   68. They're planning to trade in their old car.

_____   69. Its important to get this job done properly.

_____   70. Will you except this job if it is offered to you, or will you keep looking?

_____   71. Who's the culprit who left the paint can on the table?

Effective Word Choice (Chapter 40)

_____   72. I comprehended her statement.

_____   73. The movie was a real bomb, so we left early.

_____   74. The victims of the car accident were shaken but none the worse for wear.

_____   75. Anne is of the opinion that her children should go to private schools.

Answers are on page 600.

PART 2 (OPTIONAL)

Do Part 2 at your instructor's request. This second part of the test will provide more detailed information about skills you need to know. On a separate piece of paper, number and correct all the items you have marked above with an *X*. For example, suppose you had marked the following word groups with an *X*. (Note that these examples are not taken from the test.)

4. If football games disappeared entirely from television. I would not even miss them. Other people in my family would perish.

7. The kitten suddenly saw her reflection in the mirror, she jumped back in surprise.

15. The tree in my cousins front yard always sheds its leaves two weeks before others on the street.

29. When we go out to a restaurant we always order something we would not cook for ourselves.

Here is how you should write your corrections on a separate sheet of paper.

4. television, I

7. mirror, and she

15. cousin's

29. restaurant, we

There are over forty corrections to make in all.

Explaining a Process • Examining Cause and Effect • Comparing or Contrasting • Defini
Term • Dividing and Classifying • Describing a Scene or Person • Narrating an Event • Arg
a Position • Explaining a Process • Examining Cause and Effect • Comparing or Contrasti
Defining a Term • Dividing and Classifying • Describing a Scene or Person • Narrating
Event • Arguing a Position • Explaining a Process • Examining Cause and Effect • Compa

CHAPTER 19

Subjects and Verbs

The building blocks of English sentences are subjects and verbs. Understanding them is an important first step toward mastering many sentence skills.

Every sentence has a subject and a verb. Who or what the sentence speaks about is called the <u>subject</u>; what the sentence says about the subject is called the <u>verb</u>.

The <u>children</u> <u>laughed</u>.
Several <u>branches</u> <u>fell</u>.
Most <u>students</u> <u>passed</u> the test.
That <u>man</u> <u>is</u> a crook.

A SIMPLE WAY TO FIND A SUBJECT

To find a subject, ask *who* or *what* the sentence is about. As shown below, your answer is the subject.

Who is the first sentence about? <u>Children</u>
What is the second sentence about? Several <u>branches</u>
Who is the third sentence about? Most <u>students</u>
Who is the fourth sentence about? That <u>man</u>

A SIMPLE WAY TO FIND A VERB

To find a verb, ask what the sentence *says about* the subject. As shown below, your answer is the verb.

What does the first sentence *say about* the children? They <u>laughed</u>.
What does the second sentence *say about* the branches? They <u>fell</u>.
What does the third sentence *say about* the students? They <u>passed</u>.
What does the fourth sentence *say about* that man? He <u>is</u> (a crook).

A second way to find the verb is to put *I, you, we, he, she, it,* or *they* (whichever form is appropriate) in front of the word you think is a verb. If the result makes sense, you have a verb. For example, you could put *they* in front of *laughed* in the first sentence above, with the result—*they laughed*—making sense. Therefore you know that *laughed* is a verb. You could use *they* or *he,* for instance, to test the other verbs as well.

Verbs of Action and Linking Verbs

It helps to remember that most verbs show action. In the sentences already considered, the three action verbs are *laughed, fell,* and *passed.* Certain other verbs, known as *linking verbs,* or *verbs of appearance or perception,* do not show action. They do, however, give information about the subject. In "That man is a crook," the linking verb *is* tells us that the man is a crook. Other common linking verbs include *am, are, was,* and *were.* Verbs indicating appearance or perception include *feel, appear, look, become,* and *seem.*

Activity

In each of the following sentences, draw one line under the subject and two lines under the verb.

1. The heavy backpack cut into my shoulders.

2. Small stones pinged onto the windshield.

3. The test directions confused the students.

4. Cotton shirts feel softer than polyester ones.

5. The fog rolled into the cemetery.

6. Sparrows live in the eaves of my porch.

7. A green fly stung her on the ankle.

8. Every other night, garbage trucks rumble down my street on their way to the dump.

9. The family played badminton and volleyball, in addition to a game of softball, at the picnic.

10. With their fingers, the children drew pictures on the steamed window.

MORE ABOUT SUBJECTS AND VERBS

1 A noun is often the subject of a sentence. The words in the four examples on page 306, *children, branches, students,* and *man,* are called *nouns.* The word *noun* comes from the Latin word *nomen,* meaning "name." Nouns *name* an object, a place, a person, or another living thing. *Proper nouns* are those which are used for people's names or for place names, such as *Mr. Khan* or *Windsor. Abstract nouns* identify an idea, condition, or state of being: *truth, beauty,* or *honesty,* for instance.

2 A pronoun (a word like *he, she, it, we, you,* or *they* used in place of a noun) can serve as the subject of a sentence.

He seems like a lonely person.
They both like to gamble.

Without a surrounding context (so that we know who *he* or *they* refers to), such sentences may not seem clear, but they *are* complete.

3   A sentence may have more than one verb, more than one subject, or several subjects and verbs.

My heart skipped and pounded.
The radio and CD player were stolen from the car.
Minh and Elsa prepared the report together and presented it to the class.

4   The subject of a sentence never appears within a prepositional phrase. A *prepositional phrase* is simply a group of words that begins with a preposition. Nouns and pronouns *follow* prepositions in prepositional phrases. Because nouns and pronouns appear as the subjects of sentences, confusion may arise when they also appear in a prepositional phrase at the beginning of a sentence. A noun or a pronoun following a preposition is the *object* of a preposition; it completes the "positioning" thought begun by the preposition.

Note: The word *preposition* contains the word *position*; many prepositions indicate positions in time or space. Below is a list of common prepositions.

about	before	by	inside	over
above	behind	during	into	through
across	below	except	of	to
among	beneath	for	off	toward
around	beside	from	on	under
at	between	in	onto	with

Cross out prepositional phrases when looking for the subject of a sentence.

~~Under my pillow~~ I found a quarter left by the tooth fairy.
One ~~of the yellow lights at the school crossing~~ began flashing.
The comics section ~~of the newspaper~~ disappeared.
~~In spite of my efforts,~~ Derek dropped out of school.
~~During a rainstorm,~~ I sat in my car reading magazines.

5   Many verb forms consist of more than one word. Here, for example, are some of the many forms of the verb *smile*.

to smile	smiled	should smile
smiles	were smiling	will be smiling
does smile	have smiled	can smile
is smiling	had smiled	could be smiling
are smiling	had been smiling	must have smiled

Notes

a Words like *not, just, never, only,* and *always* are not part of the verb, although they may appear between parts of the verb.

> Larry did not finish the paper before class.
> The road was just completed last week.

b No verb preceded by *to*—the infinitive form of a verb—is ever the verb of a sentence. The infinitive form (for example, *to do, to make*) is the beginning point for all other forms of a verb. The infinitive form never changes but is used in combination with other verb forms, as in the following examples.

> My car suddenly began to sputter on the highway.
> I swerved to avoid a squirrel on the road.

c No *-ing* word *by itself* is ever the verb of a sentence. (It may be part of the verb, but it must have a helping verb in front of it.)

> They leaving early for the game. (This is not a sentence, because the verb is not complete.)
> They are leaving early for the game. (This is a sentence.)

Activity

Draw a single line under the subjects and a double line under the verbs in the following sentences. Be sure to include all parts of the verb.

1. A burning odour from the wood saw filled the room.

2. At first, sticks of gum always feel powdery on your tongue.

3. Vampires and werewolves are repelled by garlic.

4. Three people in the long bank lineup looked impatiently at their watches.

5. The driving rain had pasted wet leaves all over the car.

6. She has decided to buy a condominium.

7. The trees in the mall were glittering with tiny white lights.

8. The puppies slipped and tumbled on the vinyl kitchen floor.

9. Tanya and Luis ate at Swiss Chalet and then went to a movie.

10. We have not met our new neighbours in the apartment building.

■ Review Test

Draw a single line under subjects and a double line under verbs. Crossing out prepositional phrases may help to find the subjects.

1. A cloud of fruit flies hovered over the bananas.

2. Candle wax dripped onto the table and hardened into pools.

3. Nick and Chan are both excellent Frisbee players.

4. The leaves of my dying rubber plant resembled limp brown rags.

5. During the first week of vacation, Kevin slept until noon every day.

6. They have just decided to start working out together.

7. Psychology and digital animation are my favourite subjects.

8. The sofa in the living room has not been cleaned for over a year.

9. The water stains on her suede shoes did not disappear with brushing.

10. Kieran stayed in bed too long and, as a result, arrived late for work.

Visit the *English Skills with Readings* Online Learning Centre at **www.mcgrawhill.ca/college/langan** to access self-quizzes, bonus material on study and research skills, web resources, and other learning and study tools.

plaining a Process • Examining Cause and Effect • comparing or contrasting • Defining
rm • Dividing and Classifying • Describing a Scene or Person • Narrating an Event • Argui
Position • Explaining a Process • Examining Cause and Effect • comparing or contrastin
fining a Term • Dividing and Classifying • Describing a Scene or Person • Narrating
ent • Arguing a Position • Explaining a Process • Examining Cause and Effect • Compari

CHAPTER 20

Sentence Sense

WHAT IS SENTENCE SENSE?

You already possess a very valuable writing and revising skill. As someone who speaks English all or some of the time in your everyday life, you often communicate effectively, and often in complete sentences. Canadian college students come from many cultures and many linguistic backgrounds, but you all have a gift you learned "by ear." You have *sentence sense*—an instinctive feel for where a sentence begins, where it ends, and how it can be developed. You learned sentence sense automatically and naturally, as part of learning the English language, and you have practised it through however many years you have been speaking English. It is as much a part of you as your ability to speak and understand English is a part of you.

Sentence sense can help you recognize and avoid fragments and run-ons, two of the most common and serious sentence-skills mistakes in written English. Sentence sense will also help you to place commas, spot awkward and unclear phrasings, and add variety to your sentences.

You may ask, "If I already have this 'sentence sense,' why do I still make mistakes in punctuating sentences?" One answer could be that your past school experiences in writing were unrewarding or unpleasant. English may have been a series of dry writing topics and heavy doses of "correct" grammar and usage, or it may have devoted no time at all to sentence skills. Or perhaps you studied English primarily as a written language and had little opportunity to practise speaking English every day before coming to Canada. For any of these reasons, or perhaps for other reasons, the instinctive sentence skills you practise while *speaking* may turn off when you start *writing*. The very act of picking up a pen or touching a keyboard may shut down your whole natural system of language abilities and skills.

TURNING ON YOUR SENTENCE SENSE

Chances are you don't read a paper aloud after you write it, or you don't do the next best thing: read it "aloud" in your head. But reading aloud is essential to turn on the natural language system within you. By reading aloud, you will be able to hear the points where your sentences begin and end. In addition, you will be able to pick up any trouble spots where your thoughts are not communicated clearly and well.

The activities that follow will help you turn on and rediscover the enormous language power within you. You will be able to see how your built-in sentence sense can guide your writing just as it does your speaking.

Activity

Each item that follows lacks basic sentence punctuation. There is no period to mark the end of one sentence and no capital letter to mark the start of the next. Read each item aloud (or in your head) so that you hear where each sentence begins and ends. Your voice will tend to drop and pause at the point of each sentence break.

■ Put a light slash mark (/) at every point where you hear a break.

Then go back and read over the item a second time. If you are now sure of each place where a split occurs, insert a period and change the first small letter after it to a capital. Minor pauses are often marked in English by commas; these are already inserted. Part of item 1 is done for you as an example.

1. I take my dog for a walk on Saturdays in the big park by the lake I do this very early in the morning before children come to the park. That way I can let my dog run freely he jumps out the minute I open the car door and soon sees the first innocent squirrel then he is off like a shot and doesn't stop running for at least half an hour.

2. Anna hates huge tractor-trailers that sometimes tailgate her Honda the enormous smoke-belching machines seem ready to swallow her small car she shakes her fist at the drivers, and she lets fly a lot of angry words recently she had a very satisfying dream she broke into a party supply store and stole fireworks she then became the first person in history to illuminate a truck

3. When I sit down to write, my mind is blank all I can think of is my name, which seems to me the most boring name in the world often I get sleepy and tell myself I should take a short nap other times I start daydreaming about things I want to buy sometimes I decide I should make a telephone call to someone I know the piece of paper in front of me is usually still blank when I leave to watch my favourite television show

4. One of the biggest regrets of my life is that I never told my father I loved him I resented the fact that he had never been able to say the words "I love you" to his children even during the long period of my father's illness, I

remained silent and unforgiving then one morning he was dead, with my words left unspoken a guilt I shall never forget tore a hole in my heart I determined not to hold in my feelings with my daughters they know they are loved, because I both show and tell them this all people, no matter who they are, want to be told that they are loved

5. Two days ago, Greg killed several flying ants in his bedroom he also sprayed a column of ants forming a colony along the kitchen baseboard yesterday, he picked the evening newspaper off the porch and two black army ants scurried onto his hand this morning, he found an ant crawling on a lollipop he had left in his shirt pocket if any more insects appear, he is going to call an exterminator he feels like the victim in a horror movie called *The Ants* he is half afraid to sleep tonight he imagines the darkness will be full of tiny squirming things waiting to crawl all over him

SUMMARY: USING SENTENCE SENSE

You probably did well in locating the end stops in these selections, proving to yourself that you *do* have sentence sense. This instinctive sense will help you deal with sentence fragments and run-ons, perhaps the two most common sentence-skills mistakes.

Remember the importance of *reading your paper aloud.* By doing so, you turn on the natural language skills that come from all your experience of speaking English. The same sentence sense that helps you communicate effectively in speaking will help you communicate effectively in writing.

Online *Learning* Centre

Visit the *English Skills with Readings* Online Learning Centre at **www.mcgrawhill.ca/college/langan** to access self-quizzes, bonus material on study and research skills, web resources, and other learning and study tools.

Explaining a Process · Examining Cause and Effect · Comparing or Contrasting · Defini
erm · Dividing and Classifying · Describing a Scene or Person · Narrating an Event · Argu
· Position · Explaining a Process · Examining Cause and Effect · Comparing or Contrasti
Defining a Term · Dividing and Classifying · Describing a Scene or Person · Narratin
Event · Arguing a Position · Explaining a Process · Examining Cause and Effect · Compa

C H A P T E R   2 1

Fragments

Introductory Project

Every sentence must have a subject and a verb and must express a complete thought. A word group that lacks a subject or a verb and that does not express a complete thought is a *fragment*. Underline the statement in each numbered item that you think is *not* a complete sentence.

1. Because I could not sleep. I turned on my light and read.
2. Calling his dog's name. Todd walked up and down the street.
3. My little sister will eat anything. Except meat, vegetables, and fruit.
4. The reporter turned on her laptop computer. Then began to type quickly.

Understanding the answers: Read and complete each explanation.

1. *Because I could not sleep* is an incomplete sentence. The writer does not complete the

   _____ by telling us what happened because he could not sleep.
   Correct the fragment by joining it to the sentence that follows it:

   Because I could not sleep, I turned on my light and read.

2. *Calling his dog's name* is not a complete sentence. The word group lacks both a

   _____ and a verb, and it does not express a complete thought.
   Correct the fragment by adding it to the sentence that follows it:

   Calling his dog's name, Todd walked up and down the street.

3. *Except meat, vegetables, and fruit* is not a complete sentence. Again, the word group lacks a

   subject and a _____, and it does not express a complete thought.
   Correct the fragment by adding it to the sentence that comes before it:

   My little sister will eat anything except meat, vegetables, and fruit.

4. *Then began to type quickly* is not a complete sentence. The word group lacks a

   _____. One way to correct the fragment is to add the subject *she*:

   Then she began to type quickly.

Answers are on page 601.

WHAT ARE FRAGMENTS?

Every sentence must have a subject and a verb and must express a complete thought. A word group that lacks a subject or a verb and that does not express a complete thought is a *fragment*. The most common types of fragments are:

1   Dependent-word fragments

2   *-ing* and *to* fragments (participal and infinitive fragments)

3   Added-detail fragments

4   Missing-subject fragments

Once you understand the specific kind or kinds of fragments that you may write, you should be able to eliminate them from your writing. The following pages explain all four types of fragments.

1   DEPENDENT-WORD FRAGMENTS

Some word groups that begin with a dependent word are fragments. Here is a list of common dependent words.

Dependent Words		
after	if, even if	when, whenever
although, though	in order that	where, wherever
as	since	whether
because	that, so that	which, whichever
before	unless	while
even though	until	who, whoever
how	what, whatever	whose

Whenever you start a sentence with one of these words, you must be careful that a fragment does not result.

The word group beginning with the dependent word *after* in the example below is a fragment.

<u>After I learned the price of new cars</u>. I decided to keep my old Toyota.

A *dependent statement*—one starting with a dependent word like *after*—cannot stand alone. It *depends on* another statement to complete the thought. "After I learned the price of new cars" is a dependent statement. It leaves us hanging. We expect in the same sentence to find out *what happened after* the writer learned the price of new cars. When a writer does not follow through and complete a thought, a fragment results.

To correct the fragment, follow through and complete the thought.

After I learned the price of new cars, I decided to keep my old Toyota.

Remember, then, that dependent statements *by themselves* are fragments. They must be *attached* to a statement that makes sense standing alone.

Here are two other examples of dependent-word fragments.

My daughter refused to stop smoking. <u>Unless I quit also.</u>
Bill asked for a loan. <u>Which he promised to pay back in two weeks.</u>

"Unless I quit also" is a fragment; it does not make sense standing by itself. We want to know—in the same statement—*what would not happen unless* the writer quit also. The writer must complete the thought. Likewise, "Which he promised to pay back in two weeks" is not in itself a complete thought. We want to know in the same statement what *which* refers to.

Correcting a Dependent-Word Fragment

In most cases you can correct a dependent-word fragment by attaching it to the sentence that comes after it or the sentence that comes before it.

After I learned the price of new cars, I decided to keep my old Toyota. (The fragment has been attached to the sentence that comes after it.)
My daughter refused to quit smoking unless I quit also. (The fragment has been attached to the sentence that comes before it.)
Bill asked for a loan which he promised to pay back in two weeks. (The fragment has been attached to the sentence that comes before it.)

Another way of correcting a dependent-word fragment is simply to eliminate the dependent word by rewriting the sentence.

I learned the price of new cars and decided to keep my old Toyota.
She wanted me to quit also.
He promised to pay it back in two weeks.

Do not use this method of correction too frequently, however, for it may cut down on interest and variety in your writing style.

Notes

1   Use a comma if a dependent-word group comes at the beginning of a sentence (also see page 413).

After I learned the price of new cars, I decided to keep my old Toyota.

However, do not generally use a comma if the dependent-word group comes at the end of a sentence.

My daughter refused to stop smoking unless I quit also.
Bill asked for a loan which he promised to pay back in two weeks.

2   Sometimes the dependent words *who, that, which,* and *where* are not at the very start of a word group but are near the start. A fragment often results.

The city council decided to put more lights on South Street. <u>A place where several people have been harassed.</u>

"A place where several people have been harassed" is not in itself a complete thought. We want to know in the same statement *where the place was* where several people were harassed. The fragment can be corrected by attaching it to the sentence that comes before it.

> The city council decided to put more lights on South Street, a place where several people have been harassed.

Activity 1

Turn each of the following dependent-word groups into a sentence by adding a complete thought. Put a comma after the dependent-word group if a dependent word starts the sentence.

Examples   Although I arrived in class late
        Although I arrived in class late, I still did well on the test.

        The little boy who plays with our daughter
        The little boy who plays with our daughter just came down with
        German measles.

1. Because the weather is bad

    _____

    _____

2. If I lend you twenty dollars

    _____

    _____

3. The car that we bought

    _____

    _____

4. Since I was tired

    _____

    _____

5. Before the instructor entered the room

    _____

    _____

Activity 2

Underline the dependent-word fragment or fragments in each item. Then correct each fragment by attaching it to the sentence that comes before or the sentence that comes after, whichever sounds more natural. Put a comma after the dependent-word group if it starts the sentence.

1. Whenever our front and back doors are open. The air current causes the back door to slam shut. The noise makes everyone in the house jump.

   _____

   _____

   _____

2. Chris always watches *Breakfast Television* in the morning to see the traffic reports. He wants to see how driving conditions are on Highway 400. Before he gets on with his day.

   _____

   _____

   _____

3. Since the line at the driver's licence office crawls at a snail's pace. Eng waited two hours there. When there was only one person left in front of him. The office closed for the day.

   _____

   _____

   _____

4. My dog ran in joyous circles on the wide beach. Until she found a dead fish. Before I had a chance to drag her away. She began sniffing and nudging the smelly remains.

   _____

   _____

   _____

5. When the air conditioner broke down. The temperature was over thirty degrees. I then found an old fan. Which turned out to be broken also.

   _____

   _____

   _____

2 *-ING* AND *TO* FRAGMENTS

When an *-ing* word (the present participle form of a verb) appears at or near the start of a word group, a fragment may result. Such fragments often lack a subject and part of the verb. Underline the word groups in the examples below that contain *-ing* words. Each is a fragment.

Example 1

I spent almost two hours on the phone yesterday. Trying to find a garage to repair my car. Eventually I had to have it towed to a garage across the city.

Example 2

Anita was at first happy with the blue hatchback she had bought for only five hundred dollars. Not realizing until a week later that the car averaged twenty litres of gas per hundred kilometres.

Example 3

He looked forward to the study period at school. It being the only time he could sit unbothered and dream about his future. He imagined himself as a lawyer with lots of money, a huge office, and great clothes.

People sometimes write *-ing* fragments because they think the subject in one sentence will work for the next word group as well. Thus, in the first example, the writer thinks that the subject *I* in the opening sentence will also serve as the subject for "Trying to find a garage to repair my car." But the subject must actually be *in* the sentence.

Correcting *-ing* Fragments (Participial Fragments)

1 Attach the *-ing* fragment to the sentence that comes before it or the sentence that comes after it, whichever makes sense. Example 1 could read: "I spent two hours on the phone yesterday, trying to find a garage to repair my car."

2 Add a subject and change the *-ing* verb part to the correct form of the verb. Example 2 could read: "She realized only a week later that the car averaged twenty litres of gas per hundred kilometres."

3 Change *being* to the correct form of the verb *be (am, are, is, was, were)*. Example 3 could read: "It was the only time he could sit unbothered and dream about his future."

Correcting *to* Fragments (Infinitive Fragments)

When *to* appears at or near the start of a word group, a fragment sometimes results.

> I plan on working overtime. To get this job finished. Otherwise, my boss may get angry with me.

The second word group is a fragment and can be corrected by adding it to the preceding sentence.

> I plan on working overtime to get this job finished.

Activity 1

Underline the *-ing* fragment in each of the items that follow. Then make it a sentence by rewriting it, using the method described in parentheses.

Example   A thunderstorm was brewing. A sudden breeze shot through the windows. <u>Driving the stuffiness out of the room.</u> (*Add the fragment to the preceding sentence.*)

A sudden breeze shot through the windows, driving the stuffiness out of the room.

(In the example, a comma is used to set off "driving the stuffiness out of the room," which is extra material placed at the end of the sentence.)

1. Sweating under his heavy load. Brian staggered up the stairs to his apartment. He felt as though his legs were crumbling beneath him. (*Add the fragment to the sentence that comes after it.*)

   _____

   _____

2. He works ten hours a day. Then going to class for three hours. It is no wonder he writes sentence fragments. (*Correct the fragment by adding the subject* he *and changing* going *to the proper form of the verb*, goes.)

   _____

   _____

3. Jennifer loved the movie *The Red Violin*, but Mark hated it. His chief objection being that it had no action sequences. (*Correct the fragment by changing* being *to the proper verb form*, was.)

   _____

   _____

Activity 2

Underline the *-ing* or *to* fragment or fragments in each item. Then rewrite each item, correcting the fragments by using one of the three methods of correction described on page 319.

1. A mysterious disk appeared in my backpack yesterday. Having no label on it. I was too worried about viruses to open it.

   _____

   _____

2. Jeff bundled up and went outside on the bitterly cold day. To saw wood for his fireplace. He returned half frozen with only two logs.

   _____

   _____

3. Looking tired and drawn. The little girl's parents sat in the waiting room. The operation would be over in a few minutes.

   _____

   _____

4. Sighing with resignation. Teresa switched on her television. She suspected there would be no picture. Her cable being off at that time.

   _____

_____

_____

_____

5. Jabbing the ice with a screwdriver. Luis attempted to speed up the defrosting process in his freezer. However, he used too much force. The result being a freezer compartment riddled with holes.

_____

_____

_____

3 ADDED-DETAIL FRAGMENTS

Added-detail fragments lack a subject and a verb. They often begin with one of the following words.

also	except	including
especially	for example	such as

See if you can locate and underline the one added-detail fragment in each of these examples.

Example 1

I love to cook and eat Italian food. Especially spaghetti and lasagna. I make everything from scratch.

Example 2

The class often starts late. For example, yesterday at a quarter after nine instead of at nine sharp. Today the class started at five after nine.

Example 3

He failed a number of courses before he earned his diploma. Among them English I, Economics, and Introductory Marketing.

   People often write added-detail fragments for much the same reason they write _-ing_ fragments. They think the subject and verb in one sentence will serve for the next word group as well. But the subject and verb must be in _each_ word group.

Correcting Added-Detail Fragments

1 Attach the fragment to the complete thought that precedes it. Example 1 could read, "I love to cook and eat Italian food, especially spaghetti and lasagna."

2   Add a subject and a verb to the fragment to make it a complete sentence. Example 2 could read, "The class often starts late. For example, yesterday it began at a quarter after nine instead of at nine sharp."

3   Change words as necessary to make the fragment part of the preceding sentence. Example 3 could read, "Among the courses he failed before he earned his diploma were English I, Economics, and Introductory Marketing."

Activity 1

Underline the fragment in each of the items below. Then make it a sentence by rewriting it, using the method described in parentheses.

Example   I am always short of pocket money. Especially for everyday items like magazines and pop. Luckily my friends often have change. (*Add the fragment to the preceding sentence.*)

I am always short of pocket money, especially for everyday items like magazines and pop.

1. Nina is trying hard for a promotion. For example, taking night classes and a public speaking course. She is also working overtime for no pay. (*Correct the fragment by adding the subject and verb* she is.*)

_____

_____

2. I could feel Sean's anger building. Like a land mine ready to explode. I was silent because I didn't want to be the one to set it off. (*Add the fragment to the preceding sentence.*)

_____

_____

3. We went on vacation without several essential items. Among other things, our running shoes and fleece jackets. (*Correct the fragment by adding the subject and verb* we forgot.*)

_____

_____

Activity 2

Underline the added-detail fragment in each item. Then rewrite part of the item to correct the fragment. Use one of the three methods of correction described above.

1. It's always hard for me to get up for work. Especially on Mondays after a holiday weekend. However, I always wake up early on days with no classes and no work.

_____

_____

2. Tony has enormous endurance. For example, the ability to run seven kilometres in the morning and then play basketball all afternoon.

_____

_____

3. A counsellor gives you a chance to talk about your problems. With your family or the boss at work. You learn how to cope better with life.

_____

_____

4. Phil and Maria do most of their shopping at online sites. Especially the Grocery Gateway and Chapters sites.

_____

_____

5. One of my greatest joys in life is eating desserts. Such as cherry cheesecake and vanilla cream puffs. Almond fudge cake makes me want to dance.

_____

_____

4 MISSING-SUBJECT FRAGMENTS

In each example below, underline the word group in which the subject is missing.

Example 1

The truck skidded on the rain-slick highway. But missed a telephone pole on the side of the road.

Example 2

Michelle tried each of the appetizers on the table. And then found that, when the dinner arrived, her appetite was gone.

People write missing-subject fragments because they think the subject in one sentence will apply to the next word group as well. But the subject, as well as the verb, must be in each word group to make it a sentence.

Correcting Missing-Subject Fragments

1 Attach the fragment to the preceding sentence. Example 1 could read, "The truck skidded on the rain-slick highway but missed a telephone pole on the side of the road."

2 Add a subject (which can often be a pronoun standing for the subject in the preceding sentence). Example 2 could read, "She then found that, when the dinner arrived, her appetite was gone."

Activity

Underline the missing-subject fragment in each item. Then rewrite that part of the item as needed to correct the fragment. Use one of the two methods of correction described above.

1. I tried on an old suit hanging in our basement closet. Then discovered, to my surprise, that it was too tight to button.

    _____

    _____

    _____

    _____

2. When Tina had a sore throat, friends told her to gargle with salt water. Or suck on an ice cube. The worst advice she got was to avoid swallowing.

    _____

    _____

    _____

    _____

3. One of my elementary-school teachers embarrassed us with her sarcasm. Also, seated us in rows from the brightest students to the dumbest. I can imagine the pain the student in the last seat must have felt.

    _____

    _____

    _____

    _____

A Review: How to Check for Fragments

1 Read your paper aloud from the *last* sentence to the *first.* You will be better able to see and hear whether each word group you read is a complete thought.

2 If you think a word group is a fragment, ask yourself: Does this contain a subject and a verb and express a complete thought?

3 More specifically, be on the lookout for the most common fragments:

- Dependent-word fragments (starting with words like *after, because, since, when,* and *before*)
- *-ing* and *to* fragments (*-ing* or *to* at or near the start of a word group)
- Added-detail fragments (starting with words like *for example, such as, also,* and *especially*)
- Missing-subject fragments (a verb is present but not the subject)

■ Review Test 1

Turn each of the following word groups into a complete sentence. Use the spaces provided.

Examples   With sweaty palms

With sweaty palms, I walked in for the job interview.

Even when it rains

The football teams practise even when it rains.

1. When the alarm sounded

   _____

2. In order to save some money

   _____

3. Was late for the game

   _____

4. To pass the course

   _____

5. Peter, who is very impatient

   _____

6. During the holiday season

   _____

7. The store where I worked

   _____

8. Before the movie started

   _____

9. Down in the basement

   _____

10. Feeling very confident

   _____

■ Review Test 2

Each word group in the student paragraph below is numbered. In the space provided, write *C* if a word group is a *complete sentence;* write *F* if it is a *fragment.* You will find seven fragments in the paragraph.

A Disastrous First Date

1. _____
2. _____
3. _____
4. _____
5. _____
6. _____
7. _____
8. _____
9. _____
10. _____
11. _____
12. _____
13. _____
14. _____
15. _____
16. _____
17. _____
18. _____
19. _____
20. _____

[1]My first date with Elaine was a disaster. [2]I decided to take her to a small Italian restaurant. [3]That my friends told me had reasonable prices. [4]I looked over the menu and realized I could not pronounce the names of the dishes. [5]Such as "saltimbocca" and "gnocchi verdi." [6]Then, I noticed a burning smell. [7]The candle on the table was starting to blacken. [8]And scorch the back of my menu. [9]Trying to be casual, I quickly poured half my glass of water onto the menu. [10]When the waiter returned to our table. [11]He asked me if I wanted to order some wine. [12]I ordered a bottle of Baby Duck. [13]The only wine that I had heard of and could pronounce. [14]The waiter brought the wine, poured a small amount into my glass, and waited. [15]I said, "You don't have to stand there. We can pour the wine ourselves." [16]After the waiter put down the wine bottle and left. [17]Elaine told me I was supposed to taste the wine. [18]Feeling like a complete fool. [19]I managed to get through the dinner. [20]However, for weeks afterward, I felt like jumping out a tenth-storey window.

On a separate piece of paper, correct the fragments you have found. Attach each fragment to the sentence that comes before or after it, or make whatever other change is needed to turn the fragment into a sentence.

■ **Review Test 3**

Underline the two fragments in each item. Then rewrite the item in the space provided, making the changes needed to correct the fragments.

Example   The people at the restaurant save money. <u>By watering down the coffee. Also, using the cheapest grade of hamburger.</u> Few people go there any more.

The people at the restaurant save money by watering down the

coffee. Also, they use the cheapest grade of hamburger.

1. Gathering speed with enormous force. The plane was suddenly in the air. Then it began to climb sharply. And several minutes later levelled off.

    _____

    _____

    _____

2. Before my neighbours went on vacation. They asked me to watch their house. I agreed to check the premises once a day. Also, to take in their mail.

    _____

    _____

    _____

3. Running untouched into the end zone. The halfback raised his arms in triumph. Then he slammed the football to the ground. And did a little victory dance.

    _____

    _____

    _____

4. It's hard to keep up with bills. Such as the telephone, gas, and electricity. After you finally mail the cheques. New ones seem to arrive a day or two later.

    _____

    _____

    _____

5. While a woman ordered ten kilograms of cold cuts. Customers at the deli counter waited impatiently. The woman explained that she was in charge of a school picnic. And apologized for taking up so much time.

    _____

    _____

    _____

■ **Review Test 4**

Write quickly for five minutes about what you like to do in your leisure time. Don't worry about spelling, punctuation, finding exact words, or organizing your thoughts. Just focus on writing as many words as you can without stopping.

After you have finished, go back and make whatever changes are needed to correct any sentence fragments in your writing.

Visit the *English Skills with Readings* Online Learning Centre at **www.mcgrawhill.ca/college/langan** to access self-quizzes, bonus material on study and research skills, web resources, and other learning and study tools.

plaining a Process · Examining Cause and Effect · Comparing or Contrasting · Defining
rm · Dividing and Classifying · Describing a Scene or Person · Narrating an Event · Argui
Position · Explaining a Process · Examining Cause and Effect · Comparing or Contrastin
fining a Term · Dividing and Classifying · Describing a Scene or Person · Narrating
ent · Arguing a Position · Explaining a Process · Examining Cause and Effect · Compari

CHAPTER 22

Run-ons and Comma Splices

Introductory Project

A run-on (or fused sentence) occurs when two sentences are run together with no punctuation to mark the break between them. A comma splice occurs when two sentences are joined together with only a comma, which is insufficient punctuation. Shown below are four examples of run-ons or comma splices and four correctly punctuated sentences. See if you can complete the statement that explains how each sentence error is corrected.

1. He is the meanest little kid on his block he eats only the heads of animals crackers. (*Run-on or fused sentence*)

    He is the meanest little kid on his block. He eats only the heads of animal crackers. (*Correct*)

    The run-on or fused sentence has been corrected by using a _____ and a capital letter to separate the two complete thoughts.

2. Josh Evans likes to gossip about other people, he doesn't like them to gossip about him. (*Comma splice*)

    Josh Evans likes to gossip about other people, but he doesn't like them to gossip about him. (*Correct*)

    The comma splice has been corrected by using a joining word, _____ , to connect the two complete thoughts.

3. The chain on my bike likes to chew up my pants, it leaves grease marks on my ankle as well. (*Comma splice*)

    The chain on my bike likes to chew up my pants; it leaves grease marks on my ankle as well. (*Correct*)

    The comma splice has been corrected by using a _____ to connect the two closely related thoughts.

4. The window shade snapped up like a gunshot, her cat leaped a metre off the floor. (*Comma splice*)

    When the window shade snapped up like a gunshot, her cat leaped a metre off the floor. (*Correct*)

    The run-on has been corrected by using the subordinating word _____ to connect the two closely related thoughts.

Answers are on page 601.

WHAT ARE RUN-ONS AND COMMA SPLICES?

A *run-on* is two complete thoughts that are run together with no punctuation to mark the break between them.* They are also known as *fused sentences:* they are fused or joined together as if they were only one thought.

Run-ons or Fused Sentences

My grades are very good this semester my social life rates only a C.
Our father was a madman in his youth he would do anything on a dare.

In *comma splices,* a comma is used to connect or "splice" together the two complete thoughts. However, a comma alone is *not enough* to connect two complete thoughts. Some stronger connection than a comma alone is needed.

Comma Splices

My grades are very good this semester, my social life rates only a C.
Our father was a madman in his youth, he would do anything on a dare.

Comma splices are common mistakes. Students sense that some kind of connection is needed between two thoughts, and so they put a comma at the dividing point. But the comma alone is not sufficient, and a stronger, clearer mark between the two thoughts is needed.

Words That Can Lead to Run-ons and Comma Splices: People often write run-ons when the second complete thought begins with one of the following words.

I	we	there	now
you	they	this	then
he, she, it		that	next

Remember to be on the alert for run-ons whenever you use one of these words in a series of sentences.

CORRECTING RUN-ONS AND COMMA SPLICES

Here are four common methods of correcting a run-on or a comma splice.

1   Use a period and a capital letter to break the two complete thoughts into separate sentences.

---

*Note: Some instructors refer to each complete thought in a run-on as an *independent clause*. A *clause* is simply a group of words having a subject and a verb. A clause may be *independent* (expressing a complete thought and able to stand alone) or *dependent* (not expressing a complete thought and not able to stand alone). A run-on is two independent clauses that are run together with no punctuation to mark the break between them.

> My grades are very good this semester. My social life rates only a C.
>
> Our father was a madman in his youth. He would do anything on a dare.

2 Use a comma plus a joining word (*and, but, for, or, nor, so, yet*) to connect the two complete thoughts.

> My grades are very good this semester, but my social life rates only a C.
>
> Our father was a madman in his youth, for he would do anything on a dare.

3 Use a semicolon to connect the two complete thoughts.

> My grades are very good this semester; my social life rates only a C.
>
> Our father was a madman in his youth; he would do anything on a dare.

4 Use subordination.

> Although my grades are very good this semester, my social life rates only a C.
>
> Because my father was a madman in his youth, he would do anything on a dare.

The following pages will give you practice in all four methods of correcting a run-on or a comma splice. The use of subordination is explained further on page 104, in the section about sentence variety.

Method 1: Period and a Capital Letter

One way of correcting a run-on or a comma splice is to use a period and a capital letter at the break between the two complete thoughts. Use this method especially if the thoughts are not closely related or if another method would make the sentence too long.

Activity 1

Locate the split in each of the following word groups. Each is a *run-on* or *fused sentence*; that is, each consists of two sentences that are fused or joined together with no punctuation between them. Reading each fused sentence aloud will help you "hear" where a major break or split in the thought occurs. At such a point, your voice will probably drop and pause.

Correct the run-on by putting a period at the end of the first thought and a capital letter at the start of the next thought.

Example   Marta shuffled around the apartment in her slippers. *H*̷her husband couldn't stand their slapping sound on the floor.

1. The goose down jacket was not well made little feathers leaked out of the seams.

2. Liam cringed at the sound of the dentist's drill it buzzed like a twenty-kilogram mosquito.

3. Last summer no one swam in the lake a little boy had dropped his pet piranhas into the water.

4. A horse's teeth never stop growing they will eventually grow outside the horse's mouth.

5. Sue's doctor told her he was an astrology nut she did not feel good about learning that.

6. Ice water is the best remedy for a burn using butter is like adding fat to a flame.

7. In the apartment the air was so dry that her skin felt parched the heat was up to thirty degrees.

8. My parents bought me an ant farm it's going to be hard to find tractors that small.

9. Lobsters are cannibalistic this is one reason they are hard to raise in captivity.

10. Julia placed an egg timer next to the phone she did not want to talk more than three minutes on her long-distance calls.

Activity 2

Locate the split in each of the following word groups. Some of these word groups are *run-ons*, and some of them are *comma splices*, independent clauses spliced or joined together with only a comma. Correct each item by putting a period at the end of the first thought and a capital letter at the start of the next thought.

1. A bird got into the house through the chimney we had to catch it before our cat did.

2. Some so-called health foods are not so healthy, many are made with oils that raise cholesterol levels.

3. We sat only a few metres from the magician, we still couldn't see where all the birds came from.

4. Mohammed needs only five hours of sleep each night his wife needs at least seven.

5. Our image of dentistry will soon change dentists will use lasers instead of drills.

6. Halina entered her apartment and jumped with fright someone was leaving through her bedroom window.

7. There were several unusual hair styles at the party one woman had bright green braids.

8. Jeremy saves all of his magazines, once a month, he takes them to a nearby nursing home.

9. The doctor seemed to be in a rush, I still took time to ask all the questions that were on my mind.

10. When I was little, my brother tried to feed me flies, he told me they were raisins.

Activity

Write a second sentence to go with each of the sentences that follow. Start the second sentence with the word given in the margin. Your sentences can be serious or playful.

> ***Example***   she   Jackie works for the phone company. *She climbs telephone poles in all kinds of weather.*

it   1. The alarm clock is unreliable. _____

_____

he   2. My uncle has a peculiar habit. _____

_____

then   3. Tatiana studied for the math test for two hours. _____

_____

it   4. I could not understand why the car would not start. _____

_____

there   5. We saw all kinds of litter on the highway. _____

_____

Method 2: Comma and a Joining Word

A second way of correcting a run-on or a comma-splice error is to use a comma *plus* a joining word to connect the two complete thoughts. Joining words (also called *conjunctions*) include *and, but, for, or, nor, so,* and *yet.* Here is what the four most common joining words mean.

and   in addition to, along with

His feet hurt from the long hike, and his stomach was growling.

(*And* means "in addition": His feet hurt from the long hike; *in addition,* his stomach was growling.)

but   however, except, on the other hand, just the opposite

I remembered to get the cocoa, but I forgot the marshmallows.

(*But* means "however": I remembered to get the cocoa; *however,* I forgot the marshmallows.)

for   because, the reason why, the cause of something

She was afraid of not doing well in the course, for she had always struggled with English before.

(*For* means "because" or "the reason why": She was afraid of not doing well in the course; *the reason why* was that she had always struggled with English before.)

Note: If you are not comfortable using *for*, you may want to use *because* instead of *for* in the activities that follow.

so   as a result, therefore

> The windshield wiper was broken, so she was in trouble when the rain started.

(*So* means "as a result": The windshield wiper was broken; *as a result,* she was in trouble when the rain started.)

Activity 1

Insert the joining word (*and, but, for, so*) that logically connects the two thoughts in each sentence.

1. The couple wanted desperately to buy the house, _____ they did not qualify for a mortgage.

2. A lot of men today get their hair streaked, _____ they use cologne and other cosmetics as well.

3. Winston asked his wife if she had any bandages, _____ he had just sliced his finger with a paring knife.

4. He failed the vision part of his driver's test, _____ he did not get his driver's licence that day.

5. The restaurant was beautiful, _____ the food was overpriced.

Activity 2

Add a complete and closely related thought to go with each of the following statements. Use a comma plus the joining word in the margin when you write the second thought.

Example   for   Ayesha spent the day walking barefoot, *for the heel of one of her shoes had come off.*

but   1. She wanted to go to the party _____

_____

and   2. Terry washed his car in the morning _____

_____

so   3. The day was dark and rainy _____

_____

for   4. I'm not going to eat in the school cafeteria any more _____

_____

but   5.   I asked my brother to get off the telephone _____

Method 3: Semicolon

A third method of correcting a run-on or a comma splice is to use a semicolon to mark the break between two thoughts. A *semicolon* (;) is made up of a period above a comma. The semicolon signals more of a pause than a comma alone but not quite the full pause of a period.

Semicolon Alone: Here are some earlier sentences that were connected with a comma plus a joining word. Notice that a semicolon, unlike the comma alone, can be used to connect the two complete thoughts in each sentence.

> A lot of men today get their hair streaked; they use cologne and other cosmetics as well.
>
> She was afraid of not doing well in the course; she had always struggled with English before.
>
> The restaurant was beautiful; the food was overpriced.

The semicolon can add to sentence variety. For some people, however, the semicolon is a confusing mark of punctuation. Keep in mind that if you are not comfortable using it, you can and should use one of the first two methods of correcting a run-on or comma splice.

Activity

Insert a semicolon where the break occurs between the two complete thoughts in each of the following run-ons.

Example   I missed the bus by seconds; there would not be another for half an hour.

1. I spend eight hours a day in a windowless office it's a relief to get out into the open air after work.

2. The audience howled with laughter the comedian enjoyed a moment of triumph.

3. It rained all week parts of the highway were flooded.

4. Tony never goes to a certain gas station any more he found out that the service manager overcharged him for a valve job.

5. The washer shook and banged with its unbalanced load then it began to walk across the floor.

Semicolon with a Transitional Word: A semicolon is sometimes used with a transitional word and a comma to join two complete thoughts.

We were short of money; therefore, we decided not to eat out that weekend.

The roots of a geranium have to be crowded into a small pot; otherwise, the plant may not flower.

I had a paper to write; however, my brain had stopped working for the night.

Following is a list of common transitional words (also known as *adverbial conjunctions*). Brief meanings are given for the words.

Transitional Word	*Meaning*
however	but
nevertheless	but
on the other hand	but
instead	as a substitute
meanwhile	in the intervening time
otherwise	under other conditions
indeed	in fact
in addition	and
also	and
moreover	and
furthermore	and
as a result	in consequence
thus	as a result
consequently	as a result
therefore	as a result

Activity 1

Choose a logical transitional word from the list in the box above and write it in the space provided. Put a semicolon *before* the connector and a comma *after* it.

Example   Exams are over _____; however,_____ I still feel tense and nervous.

1. I did not understand her point _____ I asked her to repeat it.

2. With his thumbnail, Jason tried to split open the cellophane covering on the new video game _____ the cellophane refused to tear.

3. Post offices are closed for today's holiday _____ no mail will be delivered.

4. They decided not to go to the movie _____ they went to play miniature golf.

5. I had to skip lunch _____ I would have been late for class.

Activity 2

Punctuate each sentence by using a semicolon and a comma.

Example   My brother's asthma was worsening; as a result, he tried a new medication.

1. Manny ate an entire pizza for supper in addition he had a big chunk of pound cake for dessert.

2. The man leaned against the building in obvious pain however no one stopped to help him.

3. Our instructor was absent therefore the test was postponed.

4. I had no time to process the paper instead I printed it out neatly in black ink.

5. Benita loves the velvety texture of mango pudding morcover she loves to squish it between her teeth.

Method 4: Subordination

A fourth method of joining related thoughts is to use subordination. *Subordination* is a way of showing that one thought in a sentence is not as important as another thought or depends on it.

Here are three earlier sentences that have been recast so that one idea is subordinated to (made less important than) the other idea.

> When the window shade snapped up like a gunshot, her cat leaped a metre off the floor.
>
> Because it rained all week, parts of the highway were flooded.
>
> Although my grades are very good this semester, my social life rates only a C.

Notice that when we subordinate, we use dependent words like *when, because,* and *although*. Here is a brief list of common dependent words.

Common Dependent Words		
after	before	unless
although	even though	until
as	if	when
because	since	while

Subordination is explained further on page 104.

Activity

Choose a logical dependent word from the box on page 337 and write it in the space provided.

Example   _____Because_____ I had so much to do, I never even turned on the TV last night.

1. _____ we emerged from the darkened theatre, it took several minutes for our eyes to adjust to the light.

2. _____ "All Natural" was printed in large letters on the yogourt container, the fine print listing the ingredients told a different story.

3. I can't study for the test this weekend _____ my boss wants me to work overtime.

4. _____ the vampire movie was over, my children were afraid to go to bed.

5. _____ you have a driver's licence and two major credit cards, that store will not accept your cheque.

A Review: How to Check for Run-ons and Comma Splices

1 To see if a sentence is a run-on or a comma splice, read it aloud and listen for a break between two complete thoughts. Your voice will probably drop and pause at the break.

2 To check an entire paper, read it aloud from the *last* sentence to the *first*. Doing so will help you hear and see each complete thought.

3 Be on the lookout for words that can lead to run-on sentences and comma splices:

I	he, she, it	they	this	then
you	we	there	that	next

4 Correct run-on sentences and comma splices by using one of the following methods:
- Period and capital letter
- Comma and joining word (*and, but, for, or, nor, so, yet*)
- Semicolon
- Subordination

■ Review Test 1

Some of the word groups in the items that follow are run-ons or fused sentences, having no punctuation between the two complete thoughts; others are comma splices, having only a comma between the two complete thoughts. Correct the run-ons and comma splices by using one of these three methods:

- Period and capital letter

- ■ Comma and joining word
- ■ Semicolon

Do not use the same method of correction for every sentence.

                                      but

Example   Three people did the job, I could have done it alone.

1. The impatient driver tried to get a jump on the green light he kept edging his car into the intersection.

2. The course on the history of UFOs sounded interesting, it turned out to be very dull.

3. That clothing store is a strange place to visit you keep walking up to mannequins that look like real people.

4. Everything on the menu sounded delicious they wanted to order the entire menu.

5. Chung pressed a cold washcloth against his eyes, it helped relieve his headache.

6. Marc used to be a fast-food junkie now he eats only vegetables and sunflower seeds.

7. I knew my term paper was not very good, I placed it in a shiny plastic cover to make it look better.

8. Elaine enjoys watching a talk show, Jared prefers watching a movie channel.

9. My boss does not know what he is doing half the time then he tries to tell me what to do.

10. In the next minute, 100 people will die, over 240 babies will be born.

■ Review Test 2

Correct each comma splice by using subordination. Choose from among the following dependent words.

after	before	unless
although	even though	until
as	if	when
because	since	while

Example   My eyes have been watering all day, I can tell the pollen count is high.

         Because my eyes have been watering all day, I can tell the pollen

         count is high.

1. There are a number of suits and jackets on sale, they all have very noticeable flaws.

_____

_____

2.   Rust has eaten a hole in the muffler, my car sounds like a motorcycle.

3.   I finished my household chores, I decided to do some shopping.

4.   The power went off for an hour during the night, all the clocks in the house must be reset.

5.   Electric cars eliminate exhaust pollution, the limited power of the car's battery is a serious problem.

■ Review Test 3

There are two sentence errors in each passage; some are run-ons, and some are comma splices. Correct them by using one of the following methods:

- ■ Period and capital letter
- ■ Comma and one of these joining words: *and, but,* or *so*
- ■ One of these dependent words: *although, because,* or *when*

1.   The dog raced into the house it was happy to be among people. Its owner bent down to pet it he drew back in disgust. The dog had rolled in something with a horrible smell.

2.   Small feet were admired in ancient China, some female infants had their feet tightly bound. The feet then grew into a tiny, deformed shape. The women could barely walk their feet were crippled for life.

3. The four friends were losing touch with one another they decided to start a chain letter. Each woman receives the letter, she adds a page and then sends it on to the next friend. Each person has to write only one letter to keep the other three informed.

_____

_____

_____

4. A stimulating scent such as peppermint can help people concentrate better. The idea has practical applications, studies have shown students do better on tests when peppermint is in the air. Students' performance improves in a scented atmosphere, it might help office workers be more alert, too.

_____

_____

_____

◼ Review Test 4

Write quickly for five minutes about what you did this past weekend. Don't worry about spelling, punctuation, finding exact words, or organizing your thoughts. Just focus on writing as many words as you can without stopping.

After you have finished, go back and make whatever changes are needed to correct any run-ons or comma splices in your writing.

Visit the *English Skills with Readings* Online Learning Centre at **www.mcgrawhill.ca/college/langan** to access self-quizzes, bonus material on study and research skills, web resources, and other learning and study tools.

*xplaining a Process · Examining Cause and Effect · Comparing or Contrasting · Defining
rm · Dividing and Classifying · Describing a Scene or Person · Narrating an Event · Argu
Position · Explaining a Process · Examining Cause and Effect · Comparing or Contrasting
efining a Term · Dividing and Classifying · Describing a Scene or Person · Narrating
vent · Arguing a Position · Explaining a Process · Examining Cause and Effect · Compar

C H A P T E R   2 3

Irregular Verbs

Introductory Project

You may already have a sense of which common English verbs are regular and which are not. To test yourself, fill in the past tense and past participle of the verbs below. Five are regular verbs and so take *-d* or *-ed* in the past tense and past participle. Five are irregular verbs and will probably not sound right when you try to add *-d* or *-ed*. Write *I* for *irregular* in front of these verbs. Also, see if you can write in their irregular verb forms. (The item at the top is an example.)

Present	Past	Past Participle
shout	*shouted*	*shouted*
1. crawl	_____	_____
2. bring	_____	_____
3. use	_____	_____
4. do	_____	_____
5. give	_____	_____
6. laugh	_____	_____
7. go	_____	_____
8. scare	_____	_____
9. dress	_____	_____
10. see	_____	_____

Answers are on page 601.

A BRIEF REVIEW OF REGULAR VERBS

Every verb has four principal parts: present, past, past participle, and present participle. These parts can be used to build all the verb tenses (the times shown by a verb).

The past and past participle of a regular verb are formed by adding *-d* or *-ed* to the present. The *past participle* is the form of the verb used with the helping verbs *have, has,* and *had* (or some form of *be* with passive verbs). The *present participle* is formed by adding *-ing* to the present. Here are the principal forms of some regular verbs.

Present	Past	Past Participle	Present Participle
crash	crashed	crashed	crashing
shiver	shivered	shivered	shivering
kiss	kissed	kissed	kissing
apologize	apologized	apologized	apologizing
tease	teased	teased	teasing

Most verbs in English are regular.

FORMS OF IRREGULAR VERBS

Irregular verbs have irregular forms in the past tense and past participle. For example, the past tense of the irregular verb *know* is *knew;* the past participle is *known.*

Almost everyone has some degree of trouble with irregular verbs. When you are unsure about the form of a verb, you can check the following list of irregular verbs. (The present participle is not shown on this list because it is formed simply by adding *-ing* to the base form of the verb.*) Or you can check a dictionary, which gives the principal parts of irregular verbs.

Present	Past	Past Participle
arise	arose	arisen
awake	awoke	awoken
be (am, are, is)	was (were)	been
become	became	become
begin	began	begun
bend	bent	bent
bite	bit	bitten
blow	blew	blown
break	broke	broken
bring	brought	brought

*The base form of a verb is its present-tense form. If this form of the verb ends in *e,* the *e* is removed before adding *-ing,* the present participle ending.

Present	*Past*	*Past Participle*
build	built	built
burst	burst	burst
buy	bought	bought
catch	caught	caught
choose	chose	chosen
come	came	come
cost	cost	cost
cut	cut	cut
do (does)	did	done
draw	drew	drawn
drink	drank	drunk
drive	drove	driven
eat	ate	eaten
fall	fell	fallen
feed	fed	fed
feel	felt	felt
fight	fought	fought
find	found	found
fly	flew	flown
freeze	froze	frozen
get	got	got *or* gotten
give	gave	given
go (goes)	went	gone
grow	grew	grown
have (has)	had	had
hear	heard	heard
hide	hid	hidden
hold	held	held
hurt	hurt	hurt
keep	kept	kept
know	knew	known
lay	laid	laid
lead	led	led
leave	left	left
lend	lent	lent
let	let	let
lie	lay	lain
lose	lost	lost
make	made	made
meet	met	met
pay	paid	paid
ride	rode	ridden
ring	rang	rung
run	ran	run
say	said	said
see	saw	seen

Present	Past	Past Participle
sell	sold	sold
send	sent	sent
shake	shook	shaken
shrink	shrank *or* shrunk	shrunk
shut	shut	shut
sing	sang	sung
sit	sat	sat
sleep	slept	slept
speak	spoke	spoken
spend	spent	spent
stand	stood	stood
steal	stole	stolen
stick	stuck	stuck
sting	stung	stung
swear	swore	sworn
swim	swam	swum
take	took	taken
teach	taught	taught
tear	tore	torn
tell	told	told
think	thought	thought
wake	woke *or* waked	woken *or* waked
wear	wore	worn
win	won	won
write	wrote	written

Activity 1

Cross out the incorrect verb form in each of the following sentences. Then write the correct form of the verb in the space provided.

Example _____ *drew* _____ The little boy ~~drawed~~ on the marble table with permanent ink.

_____ 1. Tomatoes were once thought to be poisonous, and they were growed only as ornamental shrubs.

_____ 2. Julio has rode the bus to school for two years while saving for a car.

_____ 3. My cats have tore little holes in all my good wool sweaters.

_____ 4. The pipes in the bathroom freezed last winter, and they burst when they thawed.

_____ 5. Every time my telephone has rang today, there has been bad news on the line.

_____ 6. Only seven people have ever knowed the formula for Coca-Cola.

_____ 7. Amy blowed up animal-shaped balloons for her son's birthday party.

_____ 8. I shaked the bottle angrily until the ketchup began to flow.

_____   9. While waiting for the doctor to arrive, I sitted in a plastic chair for over two hours.

_____   10. The pile of bones on the plate showed how much chicken the family had ate.

Activity 2

For each of the italicized verbs, fill in the three missing forms in the following order:

a Present tense, which takes an *-s* ending when the subject is *he, she, it,* or any *one person* or *thing*

b Past tense

c Past participle—the form that goes with the helping verb *have, has,* or *had*

Example   My uncle likes to *give* away certain things. He (*a*) _____*gives*_____ old, threadbare clothes to the Salvation Army. Last year he

(*b*) _____*gave*_____ me a worthless television set in which the

picture tube was burned out. He has (*c*) _____*given*_____ away stuff that a junk dealer would reject.

1. I like to *freeze* chocolate bars. A chocolate bar (*a*) _____ in

   half an hour. Once I (*b*) _____ a bottle of cola. I put it in the freezer to chill and then forgot about it. Later I opened the freezer and

   discovered it had (*c*) _____ and exploded.

2. Sue knows how to *speak* French. She (*a*) _____ Vietnamese

   too. Her late grandmother (*b*) _____ both languages and

   taught them to her. Since she was a child, Sue has (*c*) _____ them both as well as she speaks English.

3. I *know* the route from Mississauga to the Lake Erie shore better than Theo

   does. He (*a*) _____ the main roads. But I drove him down to

   Port Stanley, and he soon realized that I (*b*) _____ all the

   backroads and shortcuts. I have (*c*) _____ these shortcuts for at least ten years.

4. I *go* to parties a lot. Often Camille (*a*) _____ with me. She (*b*)

   _____ with me just last week. I have (*c*) _____ to parties every Friday for the past month.

5. My brother likes to *throw* things. Sometimes he (*a*) _____

   socks into his bureau drawer. In high school years ago he (*b*) _____

   footballs while quarterbacking the team. And he has (*c*) _____

   Frisbees in our backyard for as long as I can remember.

6. I *see* her every weekend. She (*a*) _____ her other friends during the week. We first (*b*) _____ each other on a cold Saturday night last winter, when we went for supper at an Indian restaurant. Since then we have (*c*) _____ each other every weekend except when my car was broken down.

7. I often *lie* down for a few minutes after a hard day's work. Sometimes my cat (*a*) _____ down near me. Yesterday was Saturday, so I (*b*) _____ in bed all morning. I probably would have (*c*) _____ in bed all afternoon, but I wanted to get some planting done in my vegetable garden.

8. I *do* not understand the assignment. It simply (*a*) _____ not make sense to me. I was surprised to learn that Shareen (*b*) _____ understand it. In fact, she had already (*c*) _____ the assignment.

9. I often find it hard to *begin* writing a paper. The assignment that I must do (*a*) _____ to worry me while I'm watching television, but I seldom turn off the set. Once I waited until the late movie had ended before I (*b*) _____ to write. If I had (*c*) _____ earlier, I would have gotten a decent night's sleep.

10. Alissa likes to *eat*. She (*a*) _____ all day long. Once she (*b*) _____ a large pack of cookies in half an hour. Even if she has (*c*) _____ a heavy meal, she often starts munching snacks right afterwards.

■ **Review Test 1**

Underline the correct verb in the parentheses.

1. I (*shaked, shook*) the bottle of medicine before I took a teaspoon of it.

2. Ahmed came into the gym and (*began, begun*) to practise on the parallel bars.

3. Over half the class has (*taken, took*) this course on a pass-fail basis.

4. Even though my father (*teached, taught*) me how to play baseball, I never enjoyed any part of the game.

5. Because I had (*lended, lent*) him the money, I had a natural concern about what he did with it.

6. The drugstore clerk (*gave, gived*) him the wrong change.

7. May (*brang, brought*) a sweatshirt with her, for she knew the mountains got cold at night.

8. My sister (*was, be*) at school when a stranger came asking for her at our home.

9. The mechanic (*did, done*) an expensive valve job on my engine without getting my permission.

10. The basketball team has (*broke, broken*) the school record for the most wins in one year.

11. Someone (*leaved, left*) his or her books in the classroom.

12. That jacket was (*tore, torn*) during the football game.

13. If I hadn't (*threw, thrown*) away the receipt, I could have gotten my money back.

14. I would have (*become, became*) very angry if you had not intervened.

15. As the flowerpot (*fell, falled*) from the windowsill, the little boy yelled, "Bombs away!"

■ Review Test 2

Write short sentences that use the form requested for the following irregular verbs.

Example   Past of *grow*   *I grew ten centimetres in one year.* _____

1. Past of *know* _____

2. Past of *take* _____

3. Past participle of *give* _____

4. Past participle of *write* _____

5. Past of *bring* _____

6. Past participle of *speak* _____

7. Present of *begin* _____

8. Past of *go* _____

9. Past participle of *see* _____

10. Past of *drive* _____

Visit the *English Skills with Readings* Online Learning Centre at **www.mcgrawhill.ca/college/langan** to access self-quizzes, bonus material on study and research skills, web resources, and other learning and study tools.

xplaining a Process • Examining Cause and Effect • Comparing or Contrasting • Definin
rm • Dividing and Classifying • Describing a Scene or Person • Narrating an Event • Argu
Position • Explaining a Process • Examining Cause and Effect • Comparing or Contrastin
efining a Term • Dividing and Classifying • Describing a Scene or Person • Narrating
vent • Arguing a Position • Explaining a Process • Examining Cause and Effect • Compar

C H A P T E R   2 4

Subject-Verb Agreement

Introductory Project

As you read each pair of sentences below, make a check mark beside the sentence that you think uses the underlined word correctly.

There <u>was</u> too many people talking at once. _____
There <u>were</u> too many people talking at once. _____

The green peppers on that pizza <u>gives</u> me indigestion. _____
The green peppers on that pizza <u>give</u> me indigestion. _____

The mayor and her husband <u>attends</u> neighbourhood meetings. _____
The mayor and her husband <u>attend</u> neighbourhood meetings. _____

Everything <u>seem</u> to slow me down when I'm in a hurry. _____
Everything <u>seems</u> to slow me down when I'm in a hurry. _____

Answers are on page 601.

Nouns and pronouns are generally the subjects of sentences; as words standing for single or multiple objects or beings, they may be *singular* (a single unit of something) or *plural* (more than one of something). Verbs, which show the actions or perceptions of their subjects, have corresponding singular and plural forms.

A verb must agree with its subject in number. A *singular subject* (one person or thing) takes a singular verb. A *plural subject* (more than one person or thing) takes a plural verb. Mistakes in subject-verb agreement are sometimes made in the following situations (each situation is explained on the following pages):

1   When words come between the subject and the verb
2   When a verb comes before the subject
3   With compound subjects
4   With indefinite pronouns

349

1 WORDS BETWEEN SUBJECT AND VERB

Words that come between the subject and the verb do not change subject-verb agreement. Such word groups are often prepositional phrases. In the sentence

The <u>tomatoes</u> in this salad <u>are</u> pale pink and mushy.

the subject (<u>tomatoes</u>) is plural, and so the verb (<u>are</u>) is plural. The words *in this salad,* which come between the subject and the verb, do not affect subject-verb agreement.

To help find the subject of certain sentences, you should cross out prepositional phrases (see page 308):

<u>Nell</u>, ~~with her three dogs close behind~~, runs around the park every day.
The <u>seams</u> ~~in my new coat~~ <u>have split</u> after only two wearings.

Activity

Underline the correct verb form in the parentheses.

1. The decisions of the judge (*seem, seems*) questionable.

2. The flakes in this cereal (*taste, tastes*) like sawdust.

3. The woman in the dark sunglasses (*is, are*) our mayor.

4. Many people in Europe (*speak, speaks*) several languages.

5. A salad and a small yogourt (*is, are*) my usual lunch.

6. That silk flower by the candles (*look, looks*) real.

7. One of my son's worst habits (*is, are*) leaving an assortment of dirty plates on the kitchen counter.

8. The rust spots on the back of Emma's car (*need, needs*) to be cleaned with a special polish.

9. The collection of shampoo bottles in my bathroom (*overflow, overflows*) the cabinet shelves.

10. A tired-looking student in my class often (*sleep, sleeps*) through most of the lectures.

2 VERB BEFORE SUBJECT

A verb agrees with its subject even when the verb comes *before* the subject. Words that may precede the subject include *there, here,* and, in questions, *who, which, what,* and *where.*

On Glen's doorstep <u>were</u> two <u>police officers</u>.
There <u>are</u> many pizza <u>places</u> in our town.
Here <u>is</u> your <u>receipt</u>.
Where <u>are</u> <u>they</u> <u>going</u> to sleep?

If you are unsure about the subject, look at the verb and ask *who* or *what.* With the first example above, you might ask, "*Who* were on the doorstep?" The answer, *police officers,* is the subject.

Activity

Write the correct form of the verb in the space provided.

is, are 1. What _____ your middle name?

was, were 2. Among the guests _____ a private detective.

do, does 3. Where _____ you go when you want to be alone?

is, are 4. There _____ many hungry people in Canadian cities.

rest, rests 5. In that grave _____ the bones of my great-grandfather.

was, were 6. There _____ too many people in the room for me to feel comfortable.

is, are 7. Why _____ the lights turned off?

stand, stands 8. Across the street _____ the post office.

is, are 9. Here _____ the tickets for tonight's game.

was, were 10. Stuffed into the mailbox _____ ten pieces of junk mail and three ripped magazines.

3 COMPOUND SUBJECTS

Subjects joined by *and* generally take a plural verb. These are called compound subjects.

> Maple syrup and sweet butter taste delicious on pancakes.
> Fear and ignorance have a lot to do with hatred.

When subjects are joined by *either . . . or, neither . . . nor, not only . . . but also,* the verb agrees with the subject closer to the verb.

> Either the Dixie Chicks or Shania Twain deserves the award for the best country album of the year.

The nearer subject, *Shania Twain,* is singular, and so the verb is singular.

Activity

Write the correct form of the verb in the space provided.

stays, stay 1. Our cats and dog _____ at a neighbour's house when we go on vacation.

is, are 2. _____ the birthday cake and ice cream ready to be served?

holds, hold 3. Staples and sticky tape _____ all our old photo albums together.

was, were   4. Rent and car insurance _____ my biggest expenses last month.

wants, want   5. Neither the students nor the instructor _____ to postpone the final exam till after the holidays.

is, are   6. An egg and a banana _____ required for the recipe.

was, were   7. Owning a car and having money in my pocket _____ the chief ambitions of my adolescence.

visits, visit   8. My aunt and uncle from Poland _____ us every other summer.

was, were   9. Before they saw a marriage therapist, Peter and Sylvia _____ planning to get divorced.

acts, act   10. Not only the property owner but also her children _____ unfriendly to us.

4 INDEFINITE PRONOUNS

The following words, known as *indefinite pronouns,* always take singular verbs.

(-one *words*)	(-body *words*)	(-thing *words*)	
one	nobody	nothing	each
anyone	anybody	anything	either
everyone	everybody	everything	neither
someone	somebody	something	

Note: *Both* always takes a plural verb.

Activity

Write the correct form of the verb in the space provided.

is, are   1. Everybody in my marketing class _____ friendly.

feel, feels   2. Neither of those mattresses _____ comfortable.

knows, know   3. Nobody in my family _____ how to swim.

needs, need   4. Each of the children _____ some attention.

sounds, sound   5. Something about Robbie's story _____ suspicious.

pitches, pitch   6. If each of us _____ in, we can finish this job in an hour.

was, were   7. Everybody in the theatre _____ getting up and leaving before the movie ended.

provides, provide 8. Neither of the restaurants _____ facilities for physically challenged customers.

likes, like   9. No one in our family _____ housecleaning, but we all take a turn at it.

steals, steal   10. Someone in our neighbourhood _____ vegetables from people's gardens.

■ Review Test 1

Underline the correct verb in parentheses.

1. The lettuce in most of the stores in our area now (*costs, cost*) almost two dollars a head.

2. Nobody in the class of fifty students (*understands, understand*) how to solve the equation on the whiteboard.

3. The packages in the shopping bag (*was, were*) a wonderful mystery to the children.

4. My exercise class of five students (*meets, meet*) every Thursday afternoon.

5. Anyone who (*steals, steal*) my purse won't find much inside it.

6. Business contacts and financial backing (*is, are*) all that I need to establish my career as a dress designer.

7. Each of those breakfast cereals (*contains, contain*) a high proportion of sugar.

8. The serious look in that young girl's eyes (*worries, worry*) me.

9. All of the cars on my block (*has, have*) to be moved one day a month for street cleaning.

10. Some people (*know, knows*) more about their favourite TV characters than they do about the members of their own family.

■ Review Test 2

Each of the following passages contains two mistakes in subject-verb agreement. Find these two mistakes and cross them out. Then write the correct form of each verb in the space provided.

1. Few people recalls seeing baby pigeons. The reason is simple. Baby pigeons in the nest eats a huge amount of food each day. Upon leaving the nest, they are close to the size of their parents.

   a. _____

   b. _____

2. Everything in the mall stores are on sale today. Customers from all over are crowding the aisles. There is terrific bargains in many departments.

   a. _____

   b. _____

3. All the students looks forward to the trip to Niagara Falls. Everyone packs far too many things for a three-day trip. Huge piles of backpacks and suitcases sits beside the bus waiting to be loaded.

    a. _____

    b. _____

4. The members of the swimming team paces nervously beside the pool. Finally, an official blows a whistle. Into the pool dive a swimmer with thick, tan arms. He paddles quickly through the water.

    a. _____

    b. _____

5. There are three paths through the woods. There is narrow, rocky parts on two of the paths. The hikers take the easiest one. Around a bend, someone spots a snake. It is lying in the middle of the path, sunning itself. One of the hikers fear snakes. He refuses to go on.

    a. _____

    b. _____

Visit the *English Skills with Readings* Online Learning Centre at **www.mcgrawhill.ca/college/langan** to access self-quizzes, bonus material on study and research skills, web resources, and other learning and study tools.

C H A P T E R   2 5

Pronoun Agreement and Reference

Introductory Project

Read each pair of sentences below. Then write a check mark beside the sentence that you think uses the underlined word or words correctly.

Someone in my neighbourhood lets their dog run loose. _____
Someone in my neighbourhood lets his or her dog run loose. _____

After Kieran reviewed his notes with Scott, he passed the exam with ease.
_____

After reviewing his notes with Scott, Kieran passed the exam with ease.
_____

Answers are on page 601.

Pronouns are words that take the place of nouns (persons, places, or things). In fact, the word *pronoun* means "for a noun." Pronouns are shortcuts that keep you from unnecessarily repeating words in writing. Here are some examples of pronouns.

Ivana had not finished *her* paper. (*Her* is a pronoun that takes the place of *Ivana's*.)

Brendan swung so heavily on the tree branch that *it* snapped. (*It* replaces *branch*.)

When the three little pigs saw the wolf, *they* pulled out cans of pepper spray. (*They* is a pronoun that takes the place of *pigs*.)

This section presents rules that will help you avoid two common mistakes people make with pronouns. The rules are:

1   A pronoun must agree in number with the word or words it replaces.
2   A pronoun must refer clearly to the word it replaces.

PRONOUN AGREEMENT

A pronoun must agree in number with the word or words it replaces. If the word a pronoun refers to is singular, the pronoun must be singular; if that word is plural, the pronoun must be plural. (Note that the word a pronoun refers to is also known as the *antecedent. Antecedent* means "going before" in Latin.)

> Jacquie agreed to lend me her Nickelback CDs.
> People walking the trail must watch their step because of snakes.

In the first example, the pronoun *her* refers to the singular word *Jacquie*; in the second example, the pronoun *their* refers to the plural word *people*.

Activity

Write the appropriate pronoun (*their, they, them, it*) in the blank space in each of the following sentences.

Example   I lifted the pot of rice and boiling water carefully, but _____*it*_____ slipped out of my hand.

1. The value that people receive for _____ dollars these days is rapidly diminishing.

2. Rick never misses his daily workout; he believes _____ keeps him healthy.

3. Sometimes, in marriage, partners expect too much from _____ mates.

4. For some students, college is their first experience with a less structured learning situation, and _____ are not always ready to accept the responsibility.

5. Our new neighbours moved in three months ago, but I have yet to meet _____.

Indefinite Pronouns

The following words, known as *indefinite pronouns,* are always singular.

(**-one** *words*)	(**-body** *words*)	
one	nobody	each
anyone	anybody	either
everyone	everybody	neither
someone	somebody	

If a pronoun in a sentence refers to one of the singular words above, the pronoun should be singular.

Each father felt that (his) child should have won the contest.

One of the women could not find (her) purse.

Everyone must be in (his) seat before the instructor takes attendance.

In each example, the circled possessive pronoun is singular because it refers to one of these special singular words.

Note: The last example is correct *if* everyone in the class is a man. If everyone in the class is a woman, the pronoun would be *her.* If the class has both women and men, the pronoun form would be *his or her.*

Everyone must be in his or her seat before the instructor takes attendance.

Some writers follow the traditional practice of using *his* to refer to both women and men. Many now use *his or her* to avoid an implied gender bias. To avoid using *his* or the somewhat awkward *his or her,* a sentence can often be rewritten in the plural.

Students must be in their seats before the instructor takes attendance.

Activity

Underline the correct pronoun.

1. Someone has blocked the parking-lot exit with (*his or her, their*) car.

2. Everyone in the women's group has volunteered some of (*her, their*) time for the voting drive.

3. Neither of the men arrested as terrorists would reveal information about (*his, their*) group.

4. Not one of the women coaches will be returning to (*her, their*) job next year.

5. Each of the CEO's advisers offered (*his or her, their*) opinion about the rail strike.

PRONOUN REFERENCE

A sentence may be confusing and unclear:

- if a pronoun appears to refer to more than one word, or
- if the pronoun does not refer to any specific word.

Look at this sentence:

Jeremy almost dropped out of high school, for he felt *they* emphasized discipline too much.

Who emphasized discipline too much? There is no specific word that *they* refers to. Be clear:

Jeremy almost dropped out of high school, for he felt *the teachers* emphasized discipline too much.

Here are sentences with other kinds of faulty pronoun references. Read the explanations of why they are faulty and look carefully at how they are corrected.

Faulty	*Clear*
Jade told Marisa that *she* lacked self-confidence. (*Who* lacked self-confidence: Jade or Marisa? Be clear.)	Jade told Marisa, "You lack self-confidence." (Quotation marks, which can sometimes be used to correct an unclear reference, are explained in Chapter 34.)
Nazima's mother is a hairdresser, but Nazima is not interested in *it*. (There is no specific word that *it* refers to. It would not make sense to say, "Nazima is not interested in hairdresser.")	Nazima's mother is a hairdresser, but Nazima is not interested in becoming one.
Ron blamed the police officer for the ticket, *which* was foolish. (Does *which* mean that the officer's giving the ticket was foolish, or that Ron's blaming the officer was foolish? Be clear.)	Foolishly, Ron blamed the police officer for the ticket.

Activity

Rewrite each of the following sentences to make clear the vague pronoun reference. Add, change, or omit words as necessary.

Example   Our cat was friends with our hamster until he bit him.

Until the cat bit the hamster, the two were friends.

1. Maria's mother let her wear her new earrings to school.

2. When I asked why I failed my driver's test, he said I drove too slowly.

3. Dad ordered my brother to paint the garage because he didn't want to do it.

4. Julian dropped his psychology courses because he thought they assigned too much reading.

_____

5. I love mozzarella cheese on veal, but it does not always agree with me.

_____

■ **Review Test 1**

Cross out the pronoun error in each sentence and write the correction in the space provided at the left. Then circle the letter that correctly describes the type of error that was made.

Examples

his (or her)   Each player took ~~their~~ position on the court.
           Mistake in: a. pronoun reference   ⓑ pronoun agreement

the store   I was angry when ~~they~~ wouldn't give me cash back when I returned the sweater I had bought.
           Mistake in: ⓐ pronoun reference   b. pronoun agreement

_____   1. Dan asked Mr. Lalonde if he could stay an extra hour at work today.
           Mistake in: a. pronoun reference   b. pronoun agreement

_____   2. Both the front door and the back door of the abandoned house had fallen off its hinges.
           Mistake in: a. pronoun agreement   b. pronoun reference

_____   3. I have been taking cold medicine, and now it is better.
           Mistake in: a. pronoun agreement   b. pronoun reference

_____   4. Neil was angry when they raised the provincial gasoline tax again.
           Mistake in: a. pronoun agreement   b. pronoun reference

_____   5. Every one of those musicians who played for two hours in the rain truly earned their money last night.
           Mistake in: a. pronoun agreement   b. pronoun reference

_____   6. An annual flu shot is a good idea; they will help students and the general population stay healthy.
           Mistake in: a. pronoun agreement   b. pronoun reference

_____   7. Each of the pageant contestants is asked a thought-provoking question and then judged on their answer.
           Mistake in: a. pronoun agreement   b. pronoun reference

_____   8. Ihor could not believe they had closed the Winnipeg airport again because of snow conditions.
           Mistake in: a. pronoun agreement   b. pronoun reference

_____   9. At the dental office, I asked him if it was really necessary to take X-rays of my mouth again.
           Mistake in: a. pronoun agreement   b. pronoun reference

_____ 10. Every ant in the bustling anthill has their own job to do that helps support the entire community.

Mistake in: a. pronoun agreement   b. pronoun reference

■ Review Test 2

Underline the correct word or phrase in parentheses.

1. Megan is the kind of woman who will always do (*their, her*) best.

2. Hoping to be first in line when (*they, the ushers*) opened the doors, we arrived two hours early for the concert.

3. If a person really wants to appreciate good coffee, (*he or she, they*) should drink it black.

4. Students are sometimes hooked on science fiction stories because (*they, the stories*) allow readers to escape to other worlds.

5. Tina often visits the reading centre in school, for she finds that (*they, the tutors*) give her helpful instruction.

6. Nobody seems to know how to add or subtract without (*his or her, their*) pocket calculator any more.

7. As the room grew colder, everybody wished for (*his or her, their*) coat.

8. Each of my brothers has had (*his, their*) apartment broken into.

9. If someone is going to write an essay, (*he or she, they*) should prepare at least one rough draft.

10. I've taken the car in for a tune-up, and now (*it, the car*) runs more smoothly.

Visit the *English Skills with Readings* Online Learning Centre at **www.mcgrawhill.ca/college/langan** to access self-quizzes, bonus material on study and research skills, web resources, and other learning and study tools.

plaining a Process · Examining Cause and Effect · Comparing or Contrasting · Defining
rm · Dividing and Classifying · Describing a Scene or Person · Narrating an Event · Argu
Position · Explaining a Process · Examining Cause and Effect · Comparing or Contrastin
fining a Term · Dividing and Classifying · Describing a Scene or Person · Narrating
ent · Arguing a Position · Explaining a Process · Examining Cause and Effect · Compar

CHAPTER 26

Pronoun Types

This chapter describes some common types of pronouns: subject-case and object-case pronouns, possessive pronouns, and demonstrative pronouns.

SUBJECT AND OBJECT CASES OF PRONOUNS

The form of a pronoun is called its case. *Case* means the form of a pronoun that shows its grammatical function in a sentence. Pronouns appear in the subject case, the object case, or the possessive case. Because pronouns change form, they pose challenges to speakers and writers of English.

Here is a list of subject-case and object-case pronouns.

Subject-Case Pronouns	*Object-Case Pronouns*
I	me
you	you (*no change*)
he	him
she	her
it	it (*no change*)
we	us
they	them

SUBJECT-CASE PRONOUNS

Subject-case pronouns are subjects of verbs.

> *She* is wearing blue nail polish on her toes. (*She* is the subject of the verb *is wearing*.)
>
> *They* ran up three flights of steps. (*They* is the subject of the verb *ran*.)
>
> We children should have some privacy too. (*We* is the subject of the verb *should have*.)

Rules for using subject-case pronouns and several kinds of mistakes people some-times make with them are explained below.

1   Use the subject case of a pronoun where you have a compound (more than one) subject.

Incorrect	*Correct*
Eliza and *me* are exactly the same size.	Eliza and *I* are exactly the same size.
Her and *me* share our wardrobes with each other.	*She* and *I* share our wardrobes with each other.

Hint: If you are not sure which pronoun case to use, try each pronoun by itself in the sentence. The correct pronoun will be the one that sounds right. For exam-ple, "Her shares her wardrobe" does not sound right; "She shares her wardrobe" does.

2   Use the subject case of a pronoun after forms of the verb *be*. Forms of *be* include *am, are, is, was, were, has been,* and *have been.*

It was *I* who called you a minute ago and then hung up.

It may be *they* entering the coffee shop.

It was *he* who put the white tablecloth into the washing machine with a red sock.

The sentences above may sound strange and stilted to you because they are seldom used in conversation. When we speak with one another, forms such as "It was me," "It may be them," and "It's her" are widely accepted. In formal writing, however, the grammatically correct forms are still preferred.

Hint: To avoid having to use the subject-case pronoun after *be*, you can reword a sentence. Here is how the examples above could be reworded.

I was the one who called you a minute ago and then hung up.

They may be the people entering the coffee shop.

He put the white tablecloth into the washing machine with a red sock.

3   Use subject-case pronouns after *than* or *as*. The subject case is used because a verb is understood after the pronoun.

Mark can hold his breath longer than *I* (can). (The verb *can* is understood after *I*.)

Her thirteen-year-old daughter is as tall as *she* (is). (The verb *is* is understood after *she*.)

You drive much better than *he* (drives). (The verb *drives* is understood after *he*.)

Hint: Avoid mistakes by mentally adding the "missing" verb at the end of the sentence.

OBJECT-CASE PRONOUNS

The object case of pronouns (*me, him, her, us, them*) is used for the objects of verbs or prepositions. (*Prepositions* are connecting words like *for, at, about, to, before, with,* and *of.* See also page 308.) An object, in grammatical terms, receives the action of a verb or completes a prepositional phrase.

> Lee pushed *me.* (*Me* is the object of the verb *pushed.*)
>
> We dragged *them* all the way home. (*Them* is the object of the verb *dragged.*)
>
> She wrote all about *us* in her diary. (*Us* is the object of the preposition *about.*)
>
> Vera passed a note to *him* as she walked to the pencil sharpener. (*Him* is the object of the preposition *to.*)

People are sometimes uncertain about which pronoun to use when two objects follow the verb.

Incorrect	*Correct*
I argued with his sister and *he.*	I argued with his sister and *him.*
The cashier cheated Connor and *I.*	The cashier cheated Connor and *me.*

Hint: If you are not sure which pronoun to use, try each pronoun by itself in the sentence. The correct pronoun will be the one that sounds right. For example, "I argued with he" does not sound right; "I argued with him" does.

Activity

Underline the correct subject-case or object-case pronoun in each of the following sentences. Then show whether your answer is a subject-case or an object-case pronoun by circling *S* or *O* in the margin. The first one is done for you as an example.

(S) O   1. (*She,* Her) and Darcy kept dancing even after the band stopped playing.

S   O   2. The letters Mom writes to Stella and (*I, me*) are always printed in red.

S   O   3. Pilar drove to Thunder Bay but her sister, who took the bus, got there faster than (*she, her*).

S   O   4. Their relay team won because they practised more than (*we, us*).

S   O   5. (*We, Us*) choir members get to perform for the premier of the province.

S   O   6. The rest of (*they, them*) came to the wedding by train.

S   O   7. (*She, Her*) and Sammy got divorced and then remarried.

S   O   8. Since we were both taking a tough statistics course, it was a long, hard semester for my best friend and (*me, I*).

S   O   9. (*He, Him*) and Terrell look a lot alike, but they're not even related.

S   O   10. Our neighbours asked Rosa and (*I, me*) to help with their parents' surprise party.

POSSESSIVE PRONOUNS

Pronouns in the possessive case—possessive pronouns—show ownership or possession.

Using a small branch, Siu wrote *his* initials in the wet cement.

The furniture is *mine,* but the car is hers.

Here is a list of possessive pronouns.

my, mine	our, ours
your, yours	your, yours
his	their, theirs
her, hers	
its	

Note: A possessive pronoun *never* uses an apostrophe. (Also see page 399.)

Incorrect	*Correct*
That earring is *hers'* (or *her's*).	That earring is *hers.*
The orange cat is *theirs'* (or *their's*).	The orange cat is *theirs.*

Activity

Cross out the incorrect possessive pronoun form in each of the sentences below. Write the correct form in the space at the left.

Example   _____*hers*_____   Those gloves are ~~hers'~~.

1. A porcupine has no quills on it's belly.

2. The Power Book on that table is theirs'.

3. You can easily tell which team is our's by when we cheer.

4. The car with the leather seats is hers'.

5. My experience with the power blackout in 2003 was nothing compared with your's.

DEMONSTRATIVE PRONOUNS

Demonstrative pronouns point to or single out a person or thing. Demonstrative pronouns do not have cases, but they do change in singular and plural forms. There are four demonstrative pronouns.

this	these
that	those

Generally speaking, *this* and *these* refer to things close at hand; *that* and *those* refer to things farther away.

> *This* is the milk that has gone sour.
>
> *These* are the computer magazines that my son insists on saving.
>
> *That* is the roller skate that I almost tripped on at the bottom of the stairs.
>
> *Those* are the plants in the corner that don't get enough light.

These four pronouns are commonly used as demonstrative adjectives as well.

> *This* milk has gone sour.
>
> My son insists on saving all *these* computer magazines.
>
> I almost tripped on *that* roller skate at the bottom of the steps.
>
> *Those* plants in the corner don't get enough light.

■ Review Test

Underline the correct word in the parentheses.

1. If I left dinner up to (*he*, *him*), we'd have Shreddies every night.

2. Julia's words may have come from the script, but the smile is all (*hers'*, *hers*).

3. My boyfriend offered to drive his mother and (*I*, *me*) to the mall to shop for his birthday present.

4. (*Them*, *Those*) little marks on the floor are scratches, not crumbs.

5. I took a picture of my brother and (*I*, *me*) looking into the hallway mirror.

6. When (*she*, *her*) and Lin drove back from the airport, they talked so much that they missed their exit.

7. (*That there*, *That*) orange juice box says "Fresh," but the juice is made from concentrate.

8. The night before Irina was injured in a car accident, Eliot swears, he dreamt about (*she*, *her*) and a speeding car .

9. The server brought our food to the people at the next table and gave (*theirs*, *theirs'*) to us.

10. Since it was so hot out, (*he*, *him*) and Lee Ann felt they had a good excuse to study at the beach.

Explaining a Process · Examining Cause and Effect · Comparing or Contrasting · Defini·
·Term · Dividing and Classifying · Describing a Scene or Person · Narrating an Event · Arg·
·a Position · Explaining a Process · Examining Cause and Effect · Comparing or Contrasti·
Defining a Term · Dividing and Classifying · Describing a Scene or Person · Narrating·
Event · Arguing a Position · Explaining a Process · Examining Cause and Effect · Compa·

CHAPTER 27

Adjectives and Adverbs

ADJECTIVES

What Are Adjectives?

Adjectives describe nouns (names of persons, places, or things) or pronouns.

Emil is a *rich* man. (The adjective *rich* describes the noun *man.*)

He is also *generous.* (The adjective *generous* describes the pronoun *he.*)

Our *grey* cat sleeps a lot. (The adjective *grey* describes the noun *cat.*)

She is *old.* (The adjective *old* describes the pronoun *she.*)

Adjectives usually come before the words they describe (as in *rich man* and *grey cat).* But they also come after forms of the verb *be* (*is, are, was, were,* and so on). They also follow verbs of appearance or perception such as *look, appear, seem, become, sound, taste,* and *smell.*

That speaker was *boring.* (The adjective *boring* describes the speaker.)

The Petersons are *homeless.* (The adjective *homeless* describes the Petersons.)

The soup looked *good.* (The adjective *good* describes the soup.)

But it tasted *salty.* (The adjective *salty* describes the pronoun *it.*)

USING ADJECTIVES TO COMPARE

For all one-syllable adjectives and some two-syllable adjectives, add *-er* when comparing two things and *-est* when comparing three or more things.

My sister's handwriting is *neater* than mine, but Mother's is the *neatest.*

Canned or boxed juice is sometimes *cheaper* than fresh juice, but frozen juice is often the *cheapest.*

For some two-syllable adjectives and all longer adjectives, add *more* when comparing two things and *most* when comparing three or more things.

> Typing something is *more efficient* than writing it by hand, but the *most efficient* way to write is on a computer.

> Jeans are generally *more comfortable* than slacks, but sweat pants are the *most comfortable* of all.

You can usually tell when to use *more* and *most* by the sound of a word. For example, you can probably tell by its sound that "carefuller" would be too awkward to say and that *more careful* is thus correct. But there are many words for which both *-er* or *-est* and *more* or *most* are equally correct. For instance, either "a more fair rule" or "a fairer rule" is correct.

To form negative comparisons, use *less* and *least*.

> When I slipped on the black ice, I tried to look *less* hurt than I felt.

> Many people say men gossip *less* than women do, but I don't believe it.

> Suzanne is the most self-centred, *least* thoughtful person I know.

Points to Remember about Comparing

1 Use only one form of comparison at a time. In other words, do not use both an *-er* ending and *more* or both an *-est* ending and *most*.

Incorrect	*Correct*
My Newfoundland accent is always *more stronger* after I visit my family in Bonavista.	My Newfoundland accent is always *stronger* after I visit my family in Bonavista.
My *most luckiest* day was the day I met my wife.	My *luckiest* day was the day I met my wife.

2 Learn the irregular forms of the words shown below.

	Comparative (for Comparing Two Things)	*Superlative (for Comparing Three or More Things)*
bad	worse	worst
good, well	better	best
little (in amount)	less	least
much, many	more	most

Do not use both *more* and an irregular comparative or *most* and an irregular superlative.

Incorrect	*Correct*
It is *more better* to stay healthy than to have to get healthy.	It is *better* to stay healthy than to have to get healthy.

Yesterday I went on the *most best* date of my life—and all we did was go on a picnic.

Yesterday I went on the *best* date of my life—and all we did was go on a picnic.

Activity

Add to each sentence the correct form of the word in the margin.

bad

Examples   The_____*worst*_____ scare I ever had was when I thought my son was on an airplane that crashed.

wonderful

The day of my divorce was even ___*more wonderful*___ than the day of my wedding.

good

1. The Juno awards are given to the _____ Canadian recording artists of each year.

popular

2. Vanilla ice cream is even _____ than chocolate ice cream.

bad

3. One of the _____ things you can do to people is ignore them.

light

4. A kilogram of feathers is no _____ than a kilogram of stones.

little

5. The _____ expensive way to accumulate a wardrobe is by buying used clothing whenever possible.

ADVERBS

What Are Adverbs?

Adverbs describe verbs, adjectives, or other adverbs. They usually end in *-ly.*

The referee *suddenly* stopped the fight. (The adverb *suddenly* describes the verb *stopped.*)

Her yellow rosebushes are *absolutely* beautiful. (The adverb *absolutely* describes the adjective *beautiful.*)

The auctioneer spoke so *extremely* fast that I couldn't understand him. (The adverb *extremely* describes the adverb *fast.*)

A Common Mistake with Adverbs and Adjectives

People often mistakenly use an adjective instead of an adverb after a verb.

Incorrect	*Correct*
I jog *slow.*	I jog *slowly.*
The nervous witness spoke *quiet.*	The nervous witness spoke *quietly.*
The first night after I left home, I wanted to call *bad.*	The first night after I left home, I wanted to call *badly.*
Reid is *real* sneaky.	Reid is *really* sneaky.

Activity

Underline the adjective or adverb needed. (Remember that adjectives describe nouns, and adverbs describe verbs or other adverbs.)

1. During a quiet moment in class, my stomach rumbled (*loud, loudly*).

2. I'm a (*slow, slowly*) reader, so I have to put aside more time to study than some of my friends.

3. Thinking no one was looking, the young man (*quick, quickly*) emptied his car's ashtray onto the parking lot.

4. The cottage mice wait (*patient, patiently*) in the shadows; at night they'll have the place to themselves.

5. I hang up the phone (*immediate, immediately*) whenever the speaker is a recorded message.

Comparative and Superlative Forms of Adverbs

Adverbs, like adjectives, have comparative and superlative forms. Comparative or superlative forms of adverbs, except for common irregular adverbs such as *well*, are formed by adding *more* or *most* before the adverb. Examples are *more slowly*, *most carefully*, and so on.

Well and Good

Two words that are often confused are *well* and *good*. *Good* is an adjective; it describes nouns. *Well* is usually an adverb, but it is also used as an adjective when referring to a person's health. The opposite of *well* in this sense is *unwell* (not *bad* or *badly*).

Activity

Write *well* or *good* in each of the sentences that follow.

1. I could tell by the broad grin on Delia's face that the news was _____.

2. They say he sang so _____ that even the wind stopped to listen.

3. The food at the salad bar must have been too heavy because I didn't sleep _____ that night.

4. When I want to do a really _____ job of washing the floor, I do it on my hands and knees.

5. The best way to get along _____ with our boss is to stay out of his way.

■ Review Test

Underline the correct word in the parentheses.

1. In Egypt, silver was once (*more valued, most valued*) than gold.

2. After seeing Ben get sick, I felt (*badly, unwell*) myself.

3. The (*littler, less*) coffee I drink, the better I feel.

4. Light walls make a room look (*more large, larger*) than dark walls do.

5. One of the (*unfortunatest, most unfortunate*) men I know is a millionaire.

6. The moths' (*continuous, continuously*) thumping against the screen got on my nerves.

7. Some Mennonite groups manage (*good, well*) without radios, telephones, or television.

8. A purple crocus had burst (*silent, silently*) through the snow outside our window.

9. It is (*good, better*) to teach people to fish than to give them fish.

10. Today a rocket can reach the moon more (*quick, quickly*) than a stagecoach can travel from one end of England to the other.

Visit the *English Skills with Readings* Online Learning Centre at **www.mcgrawhill.ca/college/langan** to access self-quizzes, bonus material on study and research skills, web resources, and other learning and study tools.

plaining a Process • Examining Cause and Effect • Comparing or Contrasting • Definin

m • Dividing and Classifying • Describing a Scene or Person • Narrating an Event • Argui

Position • Explaining a Process • Examining Cause and Effect • Comparing or Contrasting

fining a Term • Dividing and Classifying • Describing a Scene or Person • Narrating a

ent • Arguing a Position • Explaining a Process • Examining Cause and Effect • Compari

C H A P T E R 2 8

Misplaced Modifiers

Introductory Project

Because of misplaced words, each of the sentences below has more than one possible meaning. In each case, see if you can explain the intended meaning and the unintended meaning. Also, circle the words that you think create the confusion because they are misplaced.

1. The sign in the restaurant window reads, "Wanted: Young Man—To Open Oysters with References."

    Intended meaning: _____

    Unintended meaning: _____

2. Carlo and Charlotte decided to have two children on their wedding day.

    Intended meaning: _____

    Unintended meaning: _____

3. Marissa eats only chocolates with hazelnut filling.

    Intended meaning: _____

    Unintended meaning: _____

Answers are on page 601.

WHAT MISPLACED MODIFIERS ARE AND HOW TO CORRECT THEM

Modifiers are descriptive words. *Misplaced modifiers* are words or groups of words that, because of awkward placement, do not describe the words the writer intended them to describe. Misplaced modifiers often obscure the meaning of a sentence. To avoid them, place words as close as possible to what they describe.

Misplaced Words	*Correctly Placed Words*
Alex bought an old car from a crooked dealer *with a faulty transmission.* (The dealer had a faulty transmission?)	Alex bought an old car with a faulty transmission from a crooked dealer. (The words describing the old car are now placed next to *car.*)
I *nearly* earned a hundred dollars last week. (You just missed earning a hundred dollars, but in fact earned nothing?)	I earned nearly a hundred dollars last week. (The meaning—that you earned a little under a hundred dollars—is now clear.)
We could see the football stadium *driving across the bridge.* (The stadium was driving?)	Driving across the bridge, we could see the football stadium. (The words describing us are placed next to *we.*)

Activity

Underline the misplaced word or words in each sentence. Then rewrite the sentence, placing related words together and thereby making the meaning clear.

Example   The suburbs <u>nearly</u> had ten centimetres of rain.

The suburbs had nearly ten centimetres of rain.

1. During the city workers' strike, I saw mountains of uncollected garbage walking along the streets.

   _____

2. I almost had a dozen job interviews after I sent out my résumé.

   _____

3. Clark swatted the wasp that stung him with a newspaper.

   _____

4. Joanne decided to live with her grandparents when she attended college to save money.

   _____

5. Paula returned the yogourt to the supermarket with mould on top.

   _____

6. Roger visited the old house still weak with the flu.

   _____

7. The phone almost rang fifteen times last night.

   _____

8. My uncle saw a kangaroo at the window under the influence of whisky.

_____

9. We decided to send our daughter to college on the day she was born.

_____

10. Farid always opens the bills that arrive in the mailbox with a sigh.

_____

■ **Review Test**

Write _M_ for _misplaced_ or _C_ for _correct_ in front of each sentence.

_____   1. Rita found it difficult to mount the horse wearing tight jeans.

_____   2. Rita, wearing tight jeans, found it difficult to mount the horse.

_____   3. I noticed a crack in the window walking into the delicatessen.

_____   4. Walking into the delicatessen, I noticed a crack in the window.

_____   5. A well-worn track shoe was found on the locker bench with holes in it.

_____   6. A well-worn track shoe with holes in it was found on the locker bench.

_____   7. I almost caught a hundred lightning bugs.

_____   8. I caught almost a hundred lightning bugs.

_____   9. In a second-hand store, Josh found a television set that had been stolen from me last month.

_____   10. Josh found a television set in a second-hand store that had been stolen from me last month.

_____   11. Josh found, in a second-hand store, a television set that had been stolen from me last month.

_____   12. There were four cars parked outside the café with Alberta licence plates.

_____   13. There were four cars with Alberta licence plates parked outside the café.

_____   14. The prime minister was quoted on the CBC news as saying that the recession was about to end.

_____   15. The prime minister was quoted as saying that the recession was about to end on the CBC news.

Explaining a Process • Examining Cause and Effect • Comparing or Contrasting • Defini
Term • Dividing and Classifying • Describing a Scene or Person • Narrating an Event • Arg
Position • Explaining a Process • Examining Cause and Effect • Comparing or Contrasti
Defining a Term • Dividing and Classifying • Describing a Scene or Person • Narrating
Event • Arguing a Position • Explaining a Process • Examining Cause and Effect • Compa

CHAPTER 29

Dangling Modifiers

Introductory Project

Because of dangling words, each of the sentences below has more than one possible meaning. In each case, see if you can explain the intended meaning and the unintended meaning.

1. While smoking a pipe, my dog sat with me by the crackling fire.

    Intended meaning: _____

    Unintended meaning: _____

2. Looking at the traffic accident, his sports car went through a red light.

    Intended meaning: _____

    Unintended meaning: _____

3. After baking for several hours, Dad removed the moussaka from the oven.

    Intended meaning: _____

    Unintended meaning: _____

Answers are on page 601.

WHAT DANGLING MODIFIERS ARE AND HOW TO CORRECT THEM

Dangling modifiers are words, phrases, or clauses that modify, describe, or refer to (1) something not present in the sentence or (2) something these modifiers are not intended to describe. Often, dangling modifiers appear at the beginnings of sentences.

A modifier that opens a sentence must be *followed immediately* by the word it is meant to describe. Otherwise, the modifier will be *dangling*, and the sentence takes on an unintended meaning. For example, in the sentence

While smoking a pipe, my dog sat with me by the crackling fire.

the unintended meaning is that the *dog* was smoking the pipe. What the writer meant, of course, was that *he,* the writer, was smoking the pipe. The dangling modifier could be corrected by placing *I,* the word being described, directly after the opening modifier.

> While smoking a pipe, *I* sat with my dog by the crackling fire.

The dangling modifier could also be corrected by placing the subject within the opening word group.

> While *I* was smoking my pipe, my dog sat with me by the crackling fire.

Here are other sentences with dangling modifiers. Read the explanations of why they are dangling, and look carefully at how they are corrected.

Dangling	*Correct*
Swimming at the lake, a rock cut Samantha's foot. (*Who* was swimming at the lake? The answer is not *rock* but *Samantha.* The subject *Samantha* must be added.)	Swimming at the lake, *Samantha* cut her foot on a rock. *Or:* When *Samantha* was swimming at the lake, she cut her foot on a rock.
While eating my sandwich, five mosquitoes bit me. (*Who* is eating the sandwich? The answer is not *five mosquitoes,* as it unintentionally seems to be, but *I.* The subject *I* must be added.)	While *I* was eating my sandwich, five mosquitoes bit me. *Or:* While eating my sandwich, *I* was bitten by five mosquitoes.
Getting out of bed, the tile floor was so cold that Yoko shivered all over. (*Who* got out of bed? The answer is not *tile floor* but *Yoko.* The subject *Yoko* must be added.)	Getting out of bed, *Yoko* found the tile floor so cold that she shivered all over. *Or:* When *Yoko* got out of bed, the tile floor was so cold that she shivered all over.
To join the team, a C average or better is necessary. (*Who* is to join the team? The answer is not *C average* but *you.* The subject *you* must be added.)	To join the team, *you* must have a C average or better. *Or:* For *you* to join the team, a C average or better is necessary.

The preceding examples make clear the two ways of correcting a dangling modifier. Decide on a logical subject and do one of the following:

1 Place the subject *within* the opening word group.

> When Samantha was swimming at the lake, she cut her foot on a rock.

In some cases an appropriate subordinating word such as *when* must be added, and the verb may have to be changed slightly as well.

2   Place the subject right *after* the opening word group.

   Swimming at the lake, Samantha cut her foot on a rock.

Activity

Ask "Who?" as you look at the opening words in each sentence. The subject that answers the question should be nearby in the sentence. If it is not, provide the logical subject by using either method of correction described above.

Example   While sleeping at the campsite, a Frisbee hit Derek on the head.

   While Derek was sleeping at the campsite, a Frisbee hit him on

   the head.

   or   *While sleeping at the campsite, Derek was hit on the head by a*

   Frisbee.

1. Watching the horror movie, goosebumps came up all over me.

   _____

   _____

2. After putting on a corduroy shirt, the room didn't seem so cold.

   _____

   _____

3. Flunking out of school, my parents demanded that I get a job.

   _____

   _____

4. Covered with food stains, my brother decided to wash the tablecloth.

   _____

   _____

5. Joining several college clubs, Anton's social life became more active.

   _____

   _____

6. While visiting the African Lion Safari, a baboon scrambled onto the hood of their car.

   _____

   _____

7. Under attack by beetles, Nina sprayed her roses with insecticide.

   _____

   _____

8. Standing at the ocean's edge, the wind coated my glasses with a salty film.

   _____

   _____

9. Braking the car suddenly, my shopping bags tumbled off the seat.

   _____

   _____

10. Using binoculars, the hawk was clearly seen following its prey.

    _____

    _____

◼ Review Test

Write *D* for *dangling* or *C* for *correct* in the blank next to each sentence. Remember that the opening words are a dangling modifier if they have no nearby or logical subject to modify.

_____ 1. Advertising in the paper, Ian's car was quickly sold.

_____ 2. By advertising in the paper, Ian quickly sold his car.

_____ 3. After painting the downstairs, the house needed airing to clear out the fumes.

_____ 4. After we painted the downstairs, the house needed airing to clear out the fumes.

_____ 5. Frustrated by piles of homework, Rhonda was tempted to watch television.

_____ 6. Frustrated by piles of homework, Rhonda's temptation was to watch television.

_____ 7. After I waited patiently in the bank line, the teller told me I had filled out the wrong form.

_____ 8. After waiting patiently in the bank line, the teller told me I had filled out the wrong form.

_____ 9. When dieting, desserts are especially tempting.

_____ 10. When dieting, I find desserts especially tempting.

_____ 11. Looking through the telescope, I saw a brightly lit object come into view.

_____ 12. As I was looking through the telescope, a brightly lit object came into view.

_____ 13. Looking through a telescope, a brightly lit object came into view.

 **Online LearningCentre**

Visit the *English Skills with Readings* Online Learning Centre at **www.mcgrawhill.ca/college/langan** to access self-quizzes, bonus material on study and research skills, web resources, and other learning and study tools.

*xplaining a Process · Examining Cause and Effect · comparing or contrasting · Defini
Term · Dividing and Classifying · Describing a Scene or Person · Narrating an Event · Arg
Position · Explaining a Process · Examining Cause and Effect · comparing or Contrasti
Defining a Term · Dividing and Classifying · Describing a Scene or Person · Narrating
Event · Arguing a Position · Explaining a Process · Examining Cause and Effect · Compa

CHAPTER 30

Manuscript Form

Guidelines in this chapter are appropriate for most subjects, but instructors in some courses could have different requirements. Always check with your instructor for any special formatting preferences he or she may have.

Here are guidelines to follow when you prepare an assignment for submission.

1 Use full-size paper (21.5 by 28 cm, or 8.5 by 11 inches).

2 Leave wide margins (2.5 to 4 cm, or 1 to 1.5 inches) on all four sides of each page. In particular, do not crowd the right-hand or bottom margin. The white space makes your paper more readable and gives the instructor room for comments.

3 If you write by hand:
   a Use a blue or black pen (*not* a pencil).
   b Be careful not to overlap letters or to make decorative loops on letters. Write only on every other line.
   c Make all your letters distinct. Pay special attention to *a, e, i, o,* and *u*—five letters that people sometimes write illegibly.
   d Keep your capital letters clearly distinct from small letters. You may even want to print all the capital letters.
   e Make commas, periods, and other punctuation marks firm and clear. Leave a slight space after each punctuation mark (except an opening quotation mark or an opening parenthesis).
   f Write on one side only of each sheet of paper.
   g Number each page, and write your name, course number, section (if required), and the date in the top margin area (upper right-hand corner) of each page.

4 Centre the title of your paper on the first line of page 1. Do *not* put quotation marks around it, underline it, or put a period after it. Capitalize all the major words in a title, including the first word. Small connecting words within a title like *of, for, the, in,* and *to* are not capitalized. Skip a line between the title and the first line of your text.

5 Indent the first line of each paragraph about five spaces (1.25 cm, or half an inch) from the left-hand margin.

6 When you word-process, use double spacing between lines.

7 Whenever possible, avoid breaking (hyphenating) words at the end of lines. If you must break a word, break only between syllables. Do not break words of

one syllable. Most word-processing applications will automatically move a complete word to the next line.

8 Write your name, the date, and the course number where your instructor asks for them. Generally, these appear at the top left side of the first page.

9 Unless your professor instructs you otherwise, place your last name and the page number (Jones 2, Jones 3, and so on) in the upper right-hand corner of the pages after the first one. Use the "header" function in your word-processing application to insert your name and set the page numbering. When you do so, the pages will automatically be numbered consecutively and your name will be repeated on each page.

Also keep in mind these important points about the *title* and *first sentence* of your work:

10 The title should simply be several words that tell what the assignment is about. It should usually *not* be a complete sentence. For example, if you are writing about one of the most frustrating jobs you have ever had, the title could be "A Frustrating Job."

11 Do not rely on the title to help explain the first sentence of your assignment. The first sentence must be independent of the title. For instance, if the title is "A Frustrating Job," the first sentence should *not* be "It was working as a babysitter." Rather, the first sentence might be "Working as a babysitter was the most frustrating job I ever had."

Activity 1

Identify the mistakes in manuscript form in the following lines from a handwritten version of a student's paragraph. Explain the mistakes in the spaces provided. One mistake is described for you as an example.

		Jamie Wood 1. *Comm 101CX* *May 6, 2004*
	"an unpleasant dining companion"	
	My little brother is often an unpleasant dining companion. Last	
	night was typical. For one thing, his appearance was disgusting.	
	His shoes were not tied, and his shirt was unbuttoned and han-	
	ging out of his pants, which he had forgotten to zip up. Traces	
	of his afternoon snack of grape juice and chocolate cookies were	

1. *Hyphenate only between syllables.* _____

2. _____

3. _____

4. _____

5. _____

6. _____

Activity 2

A title should tell in several words (but *not* a complete sentence) what an essay or paragraph is about. Often a title can be based on the topic sentence—the sentence that expresses the main idea. Following are five topic sentences from student assignments. Write a suitable and specific title for each one, basing the title on the topic sentence. (Note the example.)

Example   *Compromise in a Relationship*_____

Learning how to compromise is essential to a good relationship.

1. *Title:* _____
Some houseplants are dangerous to children and pets.

2. *Title:* _____
A number of fears haunted me when I was a child.

3. *Title:* _____
To insulate a house properly, several important steps should be taken.

4. *Title:* _____
My husband is compulsively neat.

5. *Title:* _____
There are a number of drawbacks to having a roommate.

Activity 3

You must *not* rely on the title to help explain your first sentence. In four of the five sentences that follow, the writer has, inappropriately, used the title to help explain the first sentence.

Rewrite the four sentences so that they stand independent of the title. Write *Correct* under the one sentence that is independent of the title.

Example   *Title:* My Career Plans
First sentence: They have changed in the last six months.

Rewritten: *My career plans have changed in the last six months.*

1. *Title:* Contending with Dogs
First sentence: This is the main problem in my work as a mail carrier.

Rewritten: _____

_____

2. *Title:* Study Skills
    First sentence: They are necessary if a person is to do well in college.

    Rewritten: _____

    _____

3. *Title:* Summer Vacation
    First sentence: Contrary to popular belief, a summer vacation can be the most miserable experience of the year.

    Rewritten: _____

    _____

4. *Title:* Sudbury: More Than Nickeltown
    First sentence: The Big Nickel is all many people see of the city.

    Rewritten: _____

    _____

5. *Title:* Cellphones
    First sentence: Many drivers have learned first-hand just how dangerous these handy devices can be.

    Rewritten: _____

    _____

■ Review Test

In the space provided, rewrite the following sentences from a handwritten student assignment. Correct the mistakes in format.

		Sonia Seto 1.
		Eng 120 BF
		May 4, 2004
	"disciplining our children"	
	My husband and I are becoming experts in disciplining our chil-	
	dren. We have certain rules that we insist upon, and if there are	
	any violations, we are swift to act. When our son simply doesn't	
	do what he is told to do, he must write that particular action	
	twenty times. For example, if he doesn't brush his teeth, he	
	writes, "I must brush my teeth." If a child gets home after the	

 Visit the *English Skills with Readings* Online Learning Centre at **www.mcgrawhill.ca/college/langan** to access self-quizzes, bonus material on study and research skills, web resources, and other learning and study tools.

plaining a Process · Examining Cause and Effect · Comparing or Contrasting · Defining
m · Dividing and Classifying · Describing a Scene or Person · Narrating an Event · Argui
osition · Explaining a Process · Examining Cause and Effect · Comparing or Contrasting
fining a Term · Dividing and Classifying · Describing a Scene or Person · Narrating
ent · Arguing a Position · Explaining a Process · Examining Cause and Effect · Compari

C H A P T E R   3 1

Capital Letters

Introductory Project

Items 1 to 13: You probably know a good deal about the uses of capital letters. Answering the questions below will help you check your knowledge.

1. Write the full name of a person you know: _____

2. In what city and province or in what country were you born? _____

3. What is your present street address? _____

4. Name a country where you would like to travel: _____

5. Name a school that you attended: _____

6. Give the name of a store where you buy food: _____

7. Name a company where someone you know works: _____

8. Which day of the week gives you the best chance to relax? _____

9. Which holiday is your favourite? _____

10. Which brand of toothpaste do you use? _____

11. Give the brand name of a candy or gum you like: _____

12. Name a song or a television show you enjoy: _____

13. Give the title of a magazine you read: _____

Items 14 to 16: Three capital letters are needed in the lines below. Underline the words that you think should be capitalized. Then write them, capitalized, in the spaces provided.

the caped man started his sleek black car, waved goodbye, and roared out of town. My heart thrilled when i heard someone say, "that was Batman. You don't see superheroes much any more."

14. _____   15. _____   16. _____

Answers are on page 602.

MAIN USES OF CAPITAL LETTERS

Capital letters are used with:

1 The first word in a sentence or direct quotation
2 Names of persons and the word *I*
3 Names of particular places
4 Names of days of the week, months, and holidays
5 Names of commercial products
6 Names of organizations such as religious and political groups, associations, companies, unions, and clubs
7 Titles of books, magazines, newspapers, articles, stories, poems, films, television shows, songs, papers that you write, and the like

Each use is illustrated on the pages that follow.

1 First Word in a Sentence or Direct Quotation

The street person touched me and asked, "Do you have any change?"
↑   ↑
(Capitalize the first word in the   (Capitalize the first word in the
sentence.)   direct quotation.)

"If you want a ride," said Tammy, "get ready now. Otherwise, I'm going alone."
(*If* and *otherwise* are capitalized because they are the first words of sentences within a direct quotation. But *get* is not capitalized because it is part of the first sentence within the quotation.)

2 Names of Persons and the Word I

Last night I ran into Terry Kowalski and Liane Morrison.

3 Names of Particular Places

Candi graduated from St. Boniface High School in Winnipeg, Manitoba. She then moved with her parents to Red Deer, Alberta, and worked there for a time at Freda's Gift Shop. Eventually she married and moved with her husband to a Canadian Forces Base in Norfolk County, Ontario. She takes courses two nights a week at Fanshawe College. On weekends, she and her family drive to Point Pelee National Park and go birdwatching and swimming in Lake Erie. She does volunteer work at the Simcoe Hospital in connection with Holy Trinity Church. In addition, she works during the summer as a host at the Eva Brook Donly Museum and the Holiday Inn.

But: Use small letters if the specific name of a place is not given.

Candi sometimes remembers her unhappy days in high school and at the gift shop where she worked after graduation. She did not imagine then that she would one day be going to college and doing volunteer work for a church and a hospital in the community where she and her husband live.

4 Names of Days of the Week, Months, and Holidays

I was angry at myself for forgetting that Sunday was Mother's Day.

During July and August, Franco's company works a four-day week, and he has Mondays off.

Aaron still has a scar on his ankle from a firecracker that exploded near him on Victoria Day and a scar on his arm where he stabbed himself with a fishhook on Labour Day weekend.

But: Use small letters for the seasons—summer, fall, winter, spring.

5 Names of Commercial Products

Louis uses Scope mouthwash, Certs mints, and Dentyne gum to drive away the taste of the Export cigarettes and Monte Cristo cigars that he always smokes.

My sister likes to play Monopoly and Trivial Pursuit; I like chess and poker; my brother likes Scrabble, baseball, and table tennis.

But: Use small letters for the *type* of product (mouthwash, mints, gum, cigarettes, and so on).

6 Names of Organizations Such as Religious and Political Groups, Associations, Companies, Unions, and Clubs

Tom Wilcox attended the United Church for many years but converted to Catholicism when he married. Both he and his wife, Louise, are members of the Liberal Party. Both belong to the Canadian Automobile Association. Louise works part-time as a service representative at Sears. Tom is an ambulance driver and belongs to the Canadian Union of Public Employees.

Enzo met Carla when he was a Boy Scout and she was a Girl Guide; she claimed he needed some guidance.

7 Titles of Books, Magazines, Newspapers, Articles, Stories, Poems, Films, Television Shows, Songs, Papers That You Write, and the Like

On Sunday Anna read the first chapter of *Whale Music*, a book required for her writing course. She looked through her parents' copy of *The Globe and Mail*. She then read an article titled "Favourite Son" and a poem titled "Montreal Malaise" in *Saturday Night* magazine. At the same time, she played an old Stones CD, *Aftermath*. In the evening, she watched *Futurama* on television and a movie, *Black Robe*, about Jesuit explorers and Native Canadians. Then, from 11 p.m. to midnight, she worked on a paper called "Trends in Mall Occupancy in the New Century" for her retail marketing course.

Activity

Cross out the words that need capitals in the following sentences. Then write the capitalized forms of the words in the spaces provided. The number of spaces tells you how many corrections to make in each case.

Example   I brush with ~~crest~~ toothpaste but get cavities all the time. _____*Crest*_____

1. A spokesperson for general motors announced that the prices of all chevrolets will rise next year.

   _____   _____   _____

2. Steve graduated from Bishop Maroccco high school in june 1998.

   _____   _____   _____

3. The mild-mannered reporter named clark kent said to the Wolfman, "you'd better think twice before you mess with me, buddy."

   _____   _____   _____

4. While watching television, Spencer drank four pepsis, ate an entire package of ritz crackers, and finished up a bag of oreo cookies.

   _____   _____   _____

5. A voyageur bus almost ran over Tony as he was riding his yamaha to a friend's home in quebec.

   _____   _____   _____

6. Before I lent my polaroid camera to Janette, I warned her, "be sure to return it by friday."

   _____   _____   _____

7. Before christmas George took his entire paycheque, went to zellers, and bought a twenty-inch zenith television.

   _____   _____   _____

8. On their first trip to Toronto, Sam and Mattias visited the CN tower and Nathan Phillips square. They also saw the Toronto Blue jays at SkyDome.

   _____   _____   _____

9. Rob was listening to the Trews' song "Confessions," Erica was reading an article in *Chatelaine* titled "Wedding bell blues," and their son was watching *Sitting ducks* on TV.

   _____   _____   _____

10. When a sign for a tim hortons rest stop appeared on the highway, anita said, "let's stop here and stretch our legs for a bit."

    _____   _____   _____

OTHER USES OF CAPITAL LETTERS

Capital letters are also used with:

1 Names that show family relationships
2 Titles of persons when used with their names

3 Specific school courses
4 Languages
5 Geographic locations
6 Names of ships, aircraft, spacecraft, and trains
7 Historical periods and events
8 Races, nations, and nationalities
9 Openings and closings of letters

Each use is illustrated on the pages that follow.

1 Names That Show Family Relationships

I got Mother to babysit for me.
I went with Grandfather to the church service.
Uncle Carlo and Aunt Rachel always enclose five dollars with birthday cards.

But: Do not capitalize words like *mother, father, grandmother, aunt,* and so on when they are preceded by a possessive word (*my, your, his, her, our, their*).

I got my mother to babysit for me.
I went with my grandfather to the church service.
My uncle and aunt always enclose five dollars with birthday cards.

2 Titles of Persons When Used with Their Names

I wrote to Premier Laurent and Mayor Miller.
Professor Snorrel sent me to Chair Ruck, who sent me to Dean Guzzi.
He drove to Dr. Jolanda Thompson's office after the cat bit him.

But: Use small letters when titles appear by themselves, without specific names.

I wrote to the premier and the mayor.
The professor sent me to the chair, who sent me to the dean.
He drove to the doctor's office after the cat bit him.

3 Specific School Courses

I got an A in both Accounting I and Small Business Management, but I got a C in Human Behaviour.

But: Use small letters for general subject areas.

I enjoyed my business courses but not my psychology or language courses.

4 Languages

She knows German and Portuguese, but she speaks mostly Canadian slang.

5 Geographic Locations

I grew up in the Maritimes. I worked in the East for a number of years and then moved to the West Coast.

But: Use small letters in directions.

A new high school is being built at the south end of town.
Because I have a compass in my car, I know that I won't be going east or west when I want to go north.

6 Names of Ships, Aircraft, Spacecraft, and Trains

Roberta Bondar flew aboard the space shuttle *Discovery*; she was the second Canadian astronaut.

The name of the *Discovery* appears in italics; names of individual ships, aircraft, spacecraft, and trains are italicized as well as capitalized.

7 Historical Periods and Events

Mario did well answering an essay question about the Second World War, but he lost points on a question about the Great Depression.

8 Races, Nations, and Nationalities

The research study centred on Native Canadians and Québécois.
They have German knives and Danish glassware in the kitchen, an Indian wood carving in the bedroom, Mexican sculptures in the study, and a Persian rug in the living room.

9 Openings and Closings of Letters

Dear Sir:
Dear Madam:
Sincerely yours,
Truly yours,

Note: Capitalize only the first word in a closing.

Activity

Cross out the words that need capitals in the following sentences. Then write the capitalized forms of the words in the spaces provided. The number of spaces tells you how many corrections to make in each case.

1. Although my grandfather spoke german and polish, my mother never learned either language.

   _____   _____

2. The chain letter began, "dear friend—You must mail twenty copies of this letter if you want good luck."

   _____   _____

3. Tomorrow in our cultural studies class, Dr. connalley will start lecturing on the war of 1812.

   _____   _____   _____   _____

4. aunt Catherine and uncle Hank, who are mennonites, took us to their church services when we visited them on the prairies.

   _____   _____   _____   _____

5. My sister has signed up for a course titled eastern religions; she'll be studying buddhism and hinduism.

   _____   _____   _____   _____

UNNECESSARY USE OF CAPITALS

Many errors in capitalization are caused by using capitals where they are not needed.

Activity

Cross out the incorrectly capitalized words in the following sentences. Then write the correct forms of the words in the spaces provided. The number of spaces tells you how many corrections to make in each sentence.

1. Although the Commercials say that Things go better with Coke, I prefer Root Beer.

   _____   _____   _____   _____

2. The old man told the Cabdriver, "I want to go out to the Airport and don't try to cheat me."

   _____   _____

3. A front-page Newspaper story about the crash of a commercial Jet has made me nervous about my Overseas trip.

   _____   _____   _____

4. During Hurricane Hazel in the 1950s, People's Houses were flooded in the Northern Suburbs of Toronto.

   _____   _____   _____   _____

5. I asked the Bank Officer at Scotiabank, "How do I get a bank Card to use the automatic teller machines?"

   _____   _____   _____

■ Review Test 1

Cross out the words that need capitals in the following sentences. Then write the capitalized forms of the words in the spaces provided. The number of spaces tells you how many corrections to make in each sentence.

1. wendy and i agreed to meet on saturday before the hockey game.

   _____   _____   _____

2. Off the Gaspé peninsula in the gulf of St. Lawrence lies a long thin island called anticosti island.

   _____   _____   _____   _____

3. When I'm in the supermarket checkout line, it seems as if every magazine on display has an article called "how You Can Lose Ten kilograms in two weeks."

   _____   _____   _____   _____

4. At the bookstore, each student received a free sample pack of dove soap, mitchum deodorant, and alberto shampoo.

   _____   _____   _____

5. "can't you be quiet?" I pleaded. "do you always have to talk while I'm watching *general hospital* on television?"

   _____   _____   _____   _____

6. On father's day, the children drove home and took their parents out to dinner at swiss chalet.

   _____   _____   _____   _____

7. I will work at the montessori Day School on mondays and fridays for the rest of september.

   _____   _____   _____   _____

8. bank of montreal, where my sister Amber works, is paying for her night course titled business accounting I.

   _____   _____   _____   _____

9. I subscribe to one newspaper, the *sun,* and two magazines, *maclean's* and *chatelaine.*

   _____   _____   _____

10. On Father's day my brother said, "let's hurry and eat so i can go watch the soccer game on our new sony TV."

   _____   _____   _____   _____

■ **Review Test 2**

On a piece of paper, write:

1. Seven sentences demonstrating the seven main uses of capital letters.

2. Nine sentences demonstrating the nine additional uses of capital letters.

Visit the *English Skills with Readings* Online Learning Centre at **www.mcgrawhill.ca/college/langan** to access self-quizzes, bonus material on study and research skills, web resources, and other learning and study tools.

Explaining a Process · Examining Cause and Effect · Comparing or Contrasting · Defini
Term · Dividing and Classifying · Describing a Scene or Person · Narrating an Event · Arg
a Position · Explaining a Process · Examining Cause and Effect · Comparing or Contrast
Defining a Term · Dividing and Classifying · Describing a Scene or Person · Narrating
Event · Arguing a Position · Explaining a Process · Examining Cause and Effect · Compa

C H A P T E R   3 2

Numbers and Abbreviations

NUMBERS

1 Spell out numbers that can be expressed in one or two words. Otherwise, use numerals—the numbers themselves.

> During the past five years, over five hundred lampreys have been caught in the lake.
> The parking fine was twenty dollars.
> In my grandmother's attic are eighty-four pairs of old shoes.

But:

> Each year about 250 baby trout are added to the lake.
> My costs after contesting a parking fine in court were $135.
> Grandmother has 110 old copies of the Eaton's catalogue in her attic.

2 Be consistent when you use a series of numbers. If some numbers in a sentence or paragraph require more than two words, then use numerals throughout the selection.

> During his election campaign, Premier Lou Stanley went to 3 local fairs, 16 parades, 45 cookouts, and 112 club dinners and delivered the same speech 176 times.

3 Use numerals for dates, times, addresses, percentages, and parts of a book.

> The letter was dated April 3, 1872.
> My appointment was at 6:15. (*But:* Spell out numbers before *o'clock*. For example: "The doctor didn't see me until seven o'clock.")
> He lives at 212 West 19th Street.
> About 20 percent of our class has dropped out of school.
> Turn to page 179 in Chapter 8 and answer questions 1 to 10.

Activity

Cross out the mistakes in numbers and write the corrections in the spaces provided.

1. Roy was born on February fifteen, nineteen eighty.

   _____

   _____

2. When the 2 children failed to return from school, over 50 people volunteered to search for them.

   _____

   _____

3. At 1 o'clock in the afternoon last Thursday, an earthquake destroyed at least 20 buildings in the town.

   _____

   _____

ABBREVIATIONS

While abbreviations are a helpful time-saver in note-taking, you should avoid most abbreviations in formal writing. Listed below are some of the few abbreviations that can acceptably be used in compositions. Note that a period is used after most of these abbreviations.

1 Mr., Mrs., Ms., Jr., Sr., Dr. when used with proper names:

   Mr. Tibble   Dr. Stein   Ms. O'Reilly

2 Time references:

   a.m.   p.m.   B.C. or A.D., or B.C.E. and C.E.

3 First or middle name in a signature:

   Pierre E. Trudeau   Otis T. Redding   J. Alfred Prufrock

4 Organizations and common terms known primarily by their initials:

   RCMP   UN   CBC   FM   ISP

Activity

Cross out the words that should not be abbreviated and correct them in the spaces provided.

1. On a Sat. morning I will never forget, Dec. 5, 1998, at ten min. after eight o'clock, I came downstairs and discovered that I had been robbed.

   _____   _____   _____

2.   For six years I lived close to Thorncliff Pk., near Misericordia Hosp., in W. Edm., AB.

_____   _____   _____   _____   _____

3.   Before her biol. and Eng. exams, Linda was so nervous that her doc. gave her a tranq.

_____   _____   _____   _____   _____

■ **Review Test**

Cross out the mistakes in numbers and abbreviations and correct them in the spaces provided.

1.   At three-fifteen p.m., an angry caller said a bomb was planted in a bus stat. locker.

_____   _____

2.   Page eighty-two is missing from my chem. book.

_____   _____

3.   Martha has over 200 copies of *People* mag.; she thinks they may be worth money someday.

_____   _____

4.   When I was eight yrs. old, I owned three cats, two dogs, and 4 rabbits.

_____   _____

5.   Approx. half the striking workers returned to work on Jan. third, nineteen ninety-seven.

_____   _____   _____   _____

plaining a Process · Examining Cause and Effect · comparing or contrasting · Defining
rm · Dividing and classifying · Describing a Scene or Person · Narrating an Event · Argui
Position · Explaining a Process · Examining Cause and Effect · Comparing or contrastin
fining a Term · Dividing and classifying · Describing a Scene or Person · Narrating
ent · Arguing a Position · Explaining a Process · Examining Cause and Effect · Compari

C H A P T E R 3 3

Apostrophe

Introductory Project

1. Lauren's motorcycle
   my sister's boyfriend
   Grandmother's laptop
   the men's room

   What is the purpose of *'s* in the examples above?

   _____

2. They didn't mind when their dog bit people, but now they're leashing
   him because he's eating all their garden vegetables.

   What is the purpose of the apostrophe in *didn't, they're,* and *he's?*

   _____

3. I used to believe that vampires lived in the old coal bin of my cellar.
   The vampire's whole body recoiled when he saw the crucifix.
   Mark ate two baked potatoes.
   One baked potato's centre was still hard.

   In each of the sentence pairs above, why is *'s* used in the second

   sentence but not in the first? _____

   _____

Answers are on page 602.

The three main uses of the apostrophe are:

1   To show the omission of one or more letters in a contraction
2   To show ownership or possession
3   To form the plural of letters, numbers as numerals, and words used as special terms

Each of these uses of the apostrophe is explained on the pages that follow.

1 APOSTROPHE IN CONTRACTIONS

A contraction is formed when two words (often a pronoun and a verb) are combined to make one word. An apostrophe is used to show where letters are omitted in forming the contraction. Here are two contractions.

have + not = haven't (*o* in *not* has been omitted)
I + will = I'll (*wi* in *will* has been omitted)

These are some other common contractions.

I + am = I'm   it +   is = it's
I + have = I've   it +   has = it's
I + had = I'd   is +   not = isn't
who +   is = who's   could +   not = couldn't
do + not = don't   I + would = I'd
did + not = didn't   they +   are = they're

Note: Will + not has an unusual contraction: won't.

Activity 1

Combine the following words into contractions. One is done for you.

1.   we + are = ___we're___   6.   you + have = _____

2.   are + not = _____   7.   has + not = _____

3.   you + are = _____   8.   who + is = _____

4.   they + have = _____   9.   does + not = _____

5.   would + not = _____   10. there + is = _____

Activity 2

Write the contractions for the words in parentheses. One is done for you.

1.   (*Are not*) ____Aren't____ you coming with us to the concert?

2.   (*I am*) _____ going to take the car if (*it is*) _____ all right with you.

3. (*There is*) _____ an extra bed upstairs if (*you would*)

    _____ like to stay here for the night.

4. (*I will*) _____ give you the name of the human resources

    director, but there (*is not*) _____ much chance that (*he will*)

    _____ speak to you.

5. Denise (*should not*) _____ complain about the cost of vegetables

    if (*she is*) _____ not willing to grow her own by planting a back-
yard garden.

Note: Even though contractions are common in everyday speech and in written dialogue, it is usually best to avoid them in formal writing.

2 APOSTROPHE TO SHOW OWNERSHIP OR POSSESSION

To show ownership or possession, we can use such words as *belongs to, possessed by, owned by,* or (most commonly) *of.*

> the jacket that *belongs to* Terrell
> the marks *possessed by* James
> the gas station *owned by* our cousin
> the footprints *of* the animal

But the apostrophe plus *s* (if the word is singular or a plural that does not end in -*s*) is often the quickest and easiest way to show possession. Thus we can say:

> Terrell's jacket
> James's marks
> our cousin's gas station
> the animal's footprints

Points to Remember

1 The *'s* ending goes with the owner or possessor (in the examples given, *Terrell, James, cousin, animal*). What follows is the person or thing possessed (in the examples given, *the jacket, marks, gas station, footprints*).

2 When *'s* is handwritten, there should always be a break between the word and the *'s*.

Terrell's   not   *Terrells*

Correct   **Incorrect**

3 A singular word ending in -*s* (such as *James* in the earlier example) also shows possession by adding an apostrophe plus *s* (*James's*).

Activity 1

Rewrite the italicized part of each of the sentences below, using *'s* to show possession. Remember that *'s* goes with the owner or possessor.

Example   *The toys belonging to the children* filled an entire room.

   The children's toys

1. *The Rollerblades owned by Dawn* have been stolen.

2. *The visit of my cousin* lasted longer than I wanted it to.

3. *The fenders belonging to the car* are badly rusted.

4. *The prescription of a doctor* is needed for the pills.

5. *The Jeep owned by Doris* was recalled because of an engine defect.

6. Is this *the hat of somebody?*

7. The broken saddle produced a sore on *the back of the horse.*

8. *The cords coming from the computer* were so tangled that they looked like spaghetti.

9. *The skates belonging to Salé and Pelletier* are on display in the museum.

10. *The foundation of the house* is crumbling.

Activity 2

Add *'s* to each of the following words to make them the possessors or owners of something. Then write sentences using the words. Your sentences can be serious or playful. One is done for you.

1. dog _____*dog's*_____   *That dog's bite is worse than his bark.*

2. instructor _____   _____

3. Avril _____ _____

_____

4. store _____ _____

_____

5. mother _____ _____

_____

Apostrophe and Possessive Forms of Pronouns

Do not use an apostrophe with possessive forms of pronouns. They already show ownership. Possessive forms of pronouns include *his, hers, its, yours, ours,* and *theirs.*

Incorrect

The bookstore lost its' lease.
The racing bikes were theirs'.
The change is yours'.
His' problems are ours', too.
His' skin is more sunburned than hers'.

Correct

The bookstore lost its lease.
The racing bikes were theirs.
The change is yours.
His problems are ours, too.
His skin is more sunburned than hers.

Apostrophe and Plurals

Do *not* add an apostrophe to make a word plural (except in three specific instances explained on page 401). For example, the plural of the word *movie* is *movies,* not *movie's* or *movies'.* Look at this sentence:

Ina admires Martin's broad shoulders, rippling muscles, and warm eyes.

The words *shoulders, muscles,* and *eyes* are simple plurals, meaning "more than one shoulder," "more than one muscle," "more than one eye." The plural is shown by adding -*s* only. On the other hand, *'s* after *Martin* shows possession—that Martin owns the shoulders, muscles, and eyes.

Activity

In the space provided under each sentence, add the one apostrophe needed and explain why the other word or words ending in -*s* are plurals.

Example   Karens tomato plants are almost as tall as her two-year-old.

Karens: *Karen's, meaning "belonging to Karen"*

plants: *plural meaning "more than one plant"*

1. My fathers influence on his brothers has been enormous.

fathers: _____

brothers: _____

2. Ben Mulroneys job—interviewing celebrities—makes him a celebrity, too.

   Mulroneys: _____

   celebrities: _____

3. As Tinas skill at studying increased, her grades improved.

   Tinas: _____

   grades: _____

4. When I walked into my doctors office, there were six people waiting who also had appointments.

   doctors: _____

   appointments: _____

5. I asked the record clerk for several blank cassette tapes and Avril Lavignes new CD.

   tapes: _____

   Lavignes: _____

6. After six weeks without rain, the nearby streams started drying up, and the lakes water level fell sharply.

   weeks: _____

   streams: _____

   lakes: _____

7. Everyone wanted to enroll in Dr. Bodors class, but all the sections were closed.

   Bodors: _____

   sections: _____

8. When the brakes failed on Eriks truck, he narrowly avoided hitting several parked cars and two trees.

   brakes: _____

   Eriks: _____

   cars: _____

   trees: _____

9. My familys favourite breakfast is bacon, eggs, and home-fried potatoes.

   familys: _____

   eggs: _____

   potatoes: _____

10. We like British Columbias winters, but we prefer to spend the summers in Nova Scotia.

   British Columbias: _____

winters: _____

summers: _____

Apostrophe with Possessive of Plural Words

Plurals that end in *-s* show possession simply by adding the apostrophe (rather than an apostrophe plus *s*):

My *parents'* van is ten years old.
The many *students'* complaints were ignored by the high-school principal.
All the *Boy Scouts'* tents were damaged by the hailstorm.

Plurals that do not end in *-s* (*women, men, mice, geese*, and so on) show possession by adding an apostrophe plus *s*.

The *women's* files are in the library.
We were woken up by the *geese's* honking.

Activity

In each sentence, cross out the one plural word that needs an apostrophe. Then write the word correctly, with the apostrophe, in the space provided.

Example _____*soldiers'*_____ All the ~~soldiers~~ boots were polished for inspection.

1. My parents car was stolen last night.

    _____

2. The transit workers strike has just ended.

    _____

3. Two of our neighbours homes are up for sale.

    _____

4. The door to the ladies room is locked.

    _____

5. When students complaints about the cafeteria were ignored, many started to bring their own lunches.

    _____

3 APOSTROPHE TO FORM THE PLURALS OF LETTERS, NUMERALS, AND SPECIAL TERMS

Plural forms of small (lower-case) letters or characters, numerals, and words used as specialized terms or phrases are formed by adding an apostrophe plus *s*.

Dotting the *i's* and crossing the *t's* in a handwritten assignment is important.
Two *6's* were scribbled on the Post-it note.
Mike had two *Incomplete's* and three *Unsat's* on his transcript.

Do not use italics for these plurals; in the examples above, the italics are used only for emphasis.

Note: Do not use apostrophes to form the plurals of dates, capital letters, abbreviations that end in capital letters, or abbreviations that end in numerals.

1990s   CDs   MP3s   VCRs   MAs   PhDs

Activity

In each sentence, supply the correct plural form of the word shown in italics.

1. Mark typed in four bold (*X*) _____ at the end of the page.

2. During the _____ (*1970*), platform shoes were popular.

3. Remove all the _____ (*and*) from that sentence.

4. Now that I download _____ (*MP3*), I do not buy as many _____ (*CD*).

5. Fanny received two _____ (*Satisfactory*) on the last set of assignments.

■ Review Test 1

In each sentence, cross out the two words that need apostrophes. Then write the words correctly in the spaces provided.

1. The contestants face fell when she learned that all she had won was a years supply of Vim cleanser.

    _____   _____

2. Weve been trying for weeks to see that movie, but theres always a long line.

    _____   _____

3. Tams car wouldnt start until the baby-faced mechanic replaced its spark plugs and points.

    _____   _____

4. The citys budget director has trouble balancing his own familys cheque book.

    _____   _____

5. Taking Dianes elderly parents to church every week is one example of Pauls generous behaviour.

    _____   _____

6. Heres a checklist of points to follow when youre writing your class reports.

    _____   _____

7. Blair shops in the mens store for jeans and the childrens department for belts.

    _____   _____

8. The cats babies are under my chair again; I cant find a way to keep her from bringing them near me.

_____   _____

9. Because of a family feud, Jules wasnt invited to a barbecue at her cousins house.

_____   _____

10. Philomenas mark was the highest in the class, and Phil's mark was the lowest.

_____   _____

■ Review Test 2

Make the following words possessive and then use at least five of them in a not-so-serious paragraph that tells a story. In addition, use at least three contractions in the paragraph.

movies	restaurant	Laurel	student
Toronto	sister	children	vampire
duck	Mike Myers	boss	Ed the Sock
customer	bartender	police car	yesterday
instructor	someone	mob	Montreal

Quotation Marks

The two main uses of quotation marks are:

1 To set off the exact words of a speaker or a writer
2 To set off the titles of short works

Each use is explained on the pages that follow.

1 QUOTATION MARKS TO SET OFF EXACT WORDS OF A SPEAKER OR A WRITER

Use quotation marks when you want to show the exact words of a speaker or a writer.

"Say something tender to me," whispered Rachel to André. (Quotation marks set off the exact words that Rachel spoke to André.)

Leonard Cohen once wrote, "I want history to jump on Canada's spine with sharp skates." (Quotation marks set off the exact words that Leonard Cohen wrote.)

"The only dumb question," the instructor said, "is the one you don't ask." (Two pairs of quotation marks are used to enclose the instructor's exact words.)

Koji complained, "I worked so hard on this paper. I spent two days getting information in the library and two days writing it. Guess what mark I got on it." (Note that the end quotation marks do not come until the end of Koji's speech. Place quotation marks before the first quoted word of a speech and after the last quoted word. As long as no interruption occurs in the speech, do not use quotation marks for each new sentence.)

Elaine exclaimed, "You're stepping on the cat's tail!" (Quotation marks set off Elaine's exclamation.)

Adam asked, "Why is this test necessary?" (Quotation marks set off Adam's question.)

Punctuation with Quotations

- A comma is used to set off a quotation from the rest of a sentence.
- Commas and periods go *inside* the quotation marks.
- Semicolons and colons appear *outside* the quotation marks in a sentence.

  I just heard about the provincial government's proposal to charge a "health premium"; is that a tax or not?

  Here is "the truth, the whole truth, and nothing but the truth": I don't know the answer.

- Exclamation marks and question marks that belong to the quotations go inside the quotation marks. But these marks go outside the quotation marks when they belong to the sentence, not the quotation.

  She begged for a clear answer, but all he said was, "Maybe"!

  Can you believe Mom said, "Do whatever you want"?

Complete the following statements explaining how capital letters, commas, and periods are used in quotations. Refer to the examples as guides.

1. Every quotation begins with a _____ letter.

2. When a quotation is split (as in the sentence about dumb questions), the second part does not begin with a capital letter unless it

   is a _____ sentence and follows a period.

3. _____ are used to separate the quoted part of a sentence from the rest of the sentence.

4. Commas and periods that come at the end of a quotation should go

   _____ the quotation marks.

The answers are *capital, new, Commas,* and *inside.*

Activity 1

Place quotation marks around the exact words of a speaker or writer in the sentences that follow.

1. Try zinc lozenges and vitamin C for your cold, Anna told Dylan.

2. How are you doing in school? my uncle always asks me.

3. An epitaph on a tombstone in Nova Scotia reads, I told you I was sick!

4. Dave said, Let's walk faster. I think the game has already started.

5. Marshall McLuhan wrote, The medium is the message.

6. Cheryl said, My brother is so lazy that if opportunity knocked, he'd resent the noise.

7. Wayne Gretzky may be the best Canadian hockey player to your generation, the coach said. Still, I don't think we should forget Maurice Richard.

8. Ice-cold drinks! shouted the vendor selling lukewarm drinks.

9. Be careful not to touch the fence, the guard warned. It's electrified.

10. Just because I'm deaf, Lin said, many people treat me as if I were stupid.

Activity 2

1. Write a sentence in which you quote a favourite expression of someone you know. Identify the relationship of the person to you.

   Example   *One of my father's favourite expressions is, "Don't sweat the*

   small stuff."

   _____

   _____

   _____

2. Write a quotation that contains the words *Dylan asked Anna.* Write a second quotation that includes the words *Anna replied.*

_____

_____

_____

_____

3. Copy a sentence or two that interests you from a book or magazine article. Identify the title and author of the work.

Example   <u>In "Hockey and Culture," Gary Genosko writes, "Hockey was, in</u>

<u>fact, the last North American sport to have black athletes enter</u>

<u>its ranks."</u>

_____

_____

_____

_____

Indirect Quotations

An indirect quotation is a rewording of someone else's statement, rather than a word-for-word direct quotation. The word *that* often signals an indirect quotation. Quotation marks are *not* used with indirect quotations.

Direct Quotation	*Indirect Quotation*
Sean said, "The distributor cap on my car is cracked." (Sean's exact spoken words are given, so quotation marks are used.)	Sean said that the distributor cap on his car was cracked. (We learn Sean's words indirectly, so no quotation marks are used.)
Alexandra's note to Jay read, "I'll be working late. Don't wait up for me." (The exact words that Alexandra wrote in the note are given, so quotation marks are used.)	Alexandra left a note for Jay saying she would be working late and he should not wait up for her. (We learn Alexandra's words indirectly, so no quotation marks are used.)

Activity

Rewrite the following sentences, changing words as necessary to convert the sentences into direct quotations. The first one is done for you as an example.

1. Matt asked Luisa if she had tickets to the Sum 41 concert.

   <u>*Matt asked Luisa, "Do you have tickets to the Sum 41 concert?"*</u>

2. Luisa said she did not think there were any left.

_____

3. Matt replied that a whole new block of tickets was on sale on Ticketmaster.

    _____

4. Luisa said that as long as she could use her mother's credit card, she would order two tickets.

    _____

5. Matt said that he hoped she would be able to go to the concert.

    _____

2 QUOTATION MARKS TO SET OFF TITLES OF SHORT WORKS

When referred to in sentences, titles of short works are usually set off by quotation marks, while titles of long works are underlined. Use quotation marks to set off the titles of such short works as articles in books, newspapers, or magazines; chapters in a book; short stories; poems; and songs.

On the other hand, you should underline or italicize the titles of books, newspapers, magazines, plays, movies, music albums, and television shows.

Quotation Marks	*Underlines or Italics*
the article "Yes, There Are Canadian Comics"	in the book *Canuck Comics*
the article "A Day at the Beach"	in the newspaper <u>The Vancouver Sun</u>
the article "Biters' Banquet"	in the magazine *Canadian Geographic*
the chapter "Mila, the Movie"	in the book <u>More Than a Rose</u>
the story "Blossom"	in the book *Sans Souci*
the poem "Suzanne"	in the book <u>The Spice-Box of Earth</u>
the song "Closing Time"	on the CD *The Future*
the episode "Life Is Messy"	from the TV series <u>Train 48</u>
	the movie *The Red Violin*

Note: In printed works, titles of books, newspapers, and so on are set off by italics—slanted type that looks *like this*—instead of being underlined.

Activity

Use quotation marks or underlines as needed.

1. Spending Smart is the title of the fourth chapter of Dian Cohen's book Money.

2. No advertising is permitted in Consumer Reports, a non-profit consumer magazine.

3. I cut out an article from Maclean's called Canadian Universities: Rankings for 2004 to use in my sociology report.

4. Vince's favourite television show is Angel, and his favourite movie is The Ring.

5. Our instructor gave us a week to buy the textbook titled Personal Finance and to read the first chapter, Work and Income.

6. Every holiday season, our family watches the movie A Christmas Carol on television.

7. Allen bought Chatelaine because he wanted to read the cover article, titled Secrets Men Never Tell You.

8. Edgar Allan Poe's short story The Murders in the Rue Morgue and his poem The Raven are in a paperback titled Great Tales and Poems of Edgar Allan Poe.

9. When Victoria got her Starweek TV Magazine, she read an article titled The New Comedians and then thumbed through the listings to see when Pop-Up Video would be on that week.

10. The night before his exam, he discovered with horror that the chapter Becoming Mature was missing from Childhood and Adolescence, the psychology text that he had bought second-hand.

OTHER USES OF QUOTATION MARKS

1 Quotation marks are used to set off special words or phrases from the rest of a sentence.

> Many people spell the words "a lot" as *one* word, "alot," instead of correctly spelling them as two words.
> I have trouble telling the difference between "their" and "there."

Note: In printed works, *italics* are often used to set off special words or phrases. That is usually done in this book, for example.

2 Single quotation marks are used to mark off a quotation within a quotation.

> The instructor said, "Know the chapter titled 'Status Symbols' in *Adolescent Development* if you expect to pass the test."
> Kyra said, "One of my favourite Mae West lines is 'I used to be Snow White, but I drifted.'"

▨ Review Test 1

Insert quotation marks where needed in the sentences that follow.

1. Don't you ever wash your car? Carly asked Jesse.

2. When the washer tilted and began to buzz, Zena shouted, Let's get rid of that blasted machine!

3. Take all you want, read the sign above the cafeteria salad bar, but please eat all you take.

4. After scrawling formulas all over the board with lightning speed, my math instructor was fond of asking, Any questions now?

5. Move that heap! the truck driver yelled. I'm trying to make a living here.

6. I did a summary of an article titled Adolescent Anxiety in the latest issue of Canadian Living.

7. Writer's block is something that happens to everyone at times, the instructor explained. You simply have to keep writing to break out of it.

8. A passenger in the car ahead of Kim threw food wrappers and empty cups out the window. That man, said Kim to his son, is a human pig.

9. If you are working during the day, said the counsellor, the best way to start college is with a night course or two.

10. I told the dentist that I wanted Novocaine. Don't be a sissy, he said. A little pain won't hurt. I told him that a little pain wouldn't hurt him, but it would bother me.

◼ Review Test 2

Go through the comics section of a newspaper to find a comic strip that amuses you. Be sure to choose a strip where two or more characters are speaking to each other. Write a full description that will enable people who have not read the comic strip to visualize it clearly and appreciate its humour. Describe the setting and action in each panel, and enclose the words of the speakers in quotation marks.

Visit the *English Skills with Readings* Online Learning Centre at **www.mcgrawhill.ca/college/langan** to access self-quizzes, bonus material on study and research skills, web resources, and other learning and study tools.

plaining a Process • Examining Cause and Effect • Comparing or Contrasting • Defining
m • Dividing and Classifying • Describing a Scene or Person • Narrating an Event • Argu
osition • Explaining a Process • Examining Cause and Effect • Comparing or Contrasting
fining a Term • Dividing and Classifying • Describing a Scene or Person • Narrating
nt • Arguing a Position • Explaining a Process • Examining Cause and Effect • Compari

C H A P T E R   3 5

Comma

Introductory Project

Commas often (but not always) signal a minor break or pause in a sentence. Each of the six pairs of sentences below illustrates one of the six main uses of the comma. Read each pair of sentences aloud and place a comma wherever you feel that a slight pause occurs.

1. a. Many college students must balance coursework with part-time jobs family responsibilities and some social activities.
    b. Days in winter are short cold and dark.

2. a. Although David Miller is the new mayor of Toronto he has been in municipal politics for some time.
    b. To open the cap of the Aspirin bottle you must first press down on it.

3. a. Avril Lavigne and Deryck Whibley Canada's leading punk stars arrived at the awards show together.
    b. Melanie who lives next door to me refused to go to the hospital during the SARS outbreak.

4. a. The wedding was scheduled for four o'clock but the bride changed her mind at two.
    b. Franka took three coffee breaks before lunch and then she went on a two-hour lunch break.

5. a. Delia's mother asked her "What time do you expect to get home?"
    b. "Don't bend over to pat the dog" I warned "or he'll kiss you."

6. a. Benjie ate seventeen hamburgers on July 29 1998 and lived to tell about it.
    b. Benjie lives at 817 Ouellette Avenue Windsor Ontario.

Answers are on page 602.

SIX MAIN USES OF THE COMMA

Commas are used mainly:

1 To separate items in a series
2 To set off introductory material
3 Before and after words that interrupt the flow of thought in a sentence
4 Between two complete thoughts connected by *and, but, for, or, nor, so, yet*
5 To set off a direct quotation from the rest of a sentence
6 For certain everyday material

Each use is explained on the pages that follow.

You may find it helpful to remember that the comma often marks a slight pause or break in a sentence. Read aloud the sentence examples given for each rule, and listen for the minor pauses or breaks that are signalled by commas.

1 Comma between Items in a Series

Use commas to separate items in a series.

Do you drink tea with milk, lemon, or honey?

Today the dishwasher stopped working, the garbage bag split, and the oven door fell off.

The television talk shows enraged him so much he did not know whether to laugh, cry, or scream.

Reiko awoke from a restless, nightmare-filled sleep.

Notes

a The final comma in a series of three or more items is optional, but it is generally used.

b A comma is used between two adjectives (descriptive words) in a series only if *and* inserted between the words sounds natural. You could say:

Reiko awoke from a restless *and* nightmare-filled sleep.

But notice in the following sentence that the descriptive words do not sound natural when *and* is inserted between them. In such cases, no comma is used.

Barbara drove a shiny blue Saturn. (A shiny *and* blue Saturn doesn't sound right, so no comma is used.)

Activity

Place commas between items in a series.

1. Godzilla lives for revenge violence and destruction.

2. My father taught me to swim by talking to me in a calm manner holding my hand firmly and throwing me into the pool.

3. Enzo added white wine mushrooms salt pepper and oregano to his spaghetti sauce.

4. Baggy threadbare jeans feel more comfortable than pyjamas to me.

5. Carmen grabbed a tiny towel bolted out of the bathroom and ran toward the ringing phone.

2 Comma after Introductory Material

Use a comma to set off introductory material. *Introductory material* may be clauses, phrases, or words.

> After punching the alarm clock with his fist, Bill turned over and went back to sleep.
> Looking up at the sky, I saw a man who was flying faster than a speeding bullet.
> Holding a baited trap, Jesse cautiously approached the gigantic mouse hole.
> In addition, he held a broom in his hand.
> Also, he wore a football helmet in case a creature should leap out at his head.

Notes

a If the introductory material is brief, the comma is sometimes omitted. In the activities here, you should use the comma.

b A comma is also used to set off extra material at the end of a sentence. Here are two sentences where this comma rule applies.

> A sudden breeze shot through the windows, driving the stuffiness out of the room.
> I love to cook and eat Italian food, especially penne and lasagna.

Activity

Place commas after introductory material.

1. When the movie started the theatre quieted down.

2. Feeling brave and silly at the same time Bernie volunteered to go on stage and help the magician.

3. While I was eating my tuna sandwich the cats circled my chair like hungry sharks.

4. Because my parents died when I was young I have learned to look after myself. Even though I am now independent I still carry a special loneliness within me.

5. At first putting extra hot pepper flakes on the pizza seemed like a good idea. However I felt otherwise when flames seemed about to shoot out of my mouth.

3 Comma around Words Interrupting the Flow of Thought

Use commas before and after words or phrases that interrupt the flow of thought in a sentence.

> My brother, a sports nut, owns over five thousand hockey cards.

That game show, at long last, has been cancelled.

The children used the old Buick, rusted from disuse, as a backyard clubhouse.

Phrases and clauses that interrupt a sentence's flow or rhythm are called *non-essential* (or non-restrictive). Such phrases or clauses are not essential to the sentence, which means that they are not needed for its meaning to be clear.

Usually you can "hear" words that interrupt the flow of thought in a sentence. However, if you are not sure that certain words are interrupters, remove them from the sentence. If it still makes sense without the words, you know that the words are interrupters and the information they give is non-essential. Such non-essential information is set off with commas. In the sentence

Doris Thompson, who lives next door, won the javelin-throwing competition.

the words *who lives next door* are extra information, not needed to understand the subject of the sentence, *Doris Thompson*. Put commas around such non-essential information.

On the other hand, some phrases and clauses are *essential* in order for the reader to grasp the meaning of a sentence. In the sentence

The woman who lives next door won the javelin-throwing competition.

the words *who lives next door* supply essential information—information needed for us to identify the woman being spoken of. If the words were removed from the sentence, we would no longer know who won the competition. Commas are *not* used around such essential information.

Here is another example, this time of a non-essential clause.

Wilson Hall, which the hurricane destroyed, was ninety years old.

Here the words *which the hurricane destroyed* are extra information, not needed to identify the subject of the sentence, *Wilson Hall*. Commas go around such non-essential information. On the other hand, in the sentence

The building that the hurricane destroyed was ninety years old.

the words *that the hurricane destroyed* are needed to identify the building. Commas are *not* used around such essential information. The word *that* is generally used to introduce an essential clause, as in the example above. In the preceding example about Wilson Hall, the word *which* is used; *which* is generally used to introduce non-essential clauses. Clauses beginning with *who*, however, may be either essential or non-essential.

As noted above, however, most of the time you will be able to "hear" words that interrupt the flow of thought in a sentence and will not have to think about whether the words are essential or non-essential.

Activity

Use commas to set off interrupting words.

1. On Friday my day off I went to get a haircut.

2. Dracula who had a way with women is Lyle's favourite movie hero. He feels that the Wolfman on the other hand showed no class in handling women.

3. Many people forget that Mackenzie King one of our most effective prime ministers also talked to his dead mother.

4. Mowing the grass especially when it is three centimetres high is my least favourite job.

5. A jar of chicken noodle soup which was all there was in the refrigerator did not make a very satisfying meal.

4 Comma between Complete Thoughts

Use a comma between two complete thoughts or independent clauses connected by coordinating conjunctions: *and, but, for, or, nor, so, yet.*

The wedding was scheduled for four o'clock, but the bride changed her mind at two.

We could always tell when our instructor felt disorganized, for his shirt would not be tucked in.

Amelia has to work some nights, so she tapes the hockey games on her VCR.

Notes

a The comma is optional when the complete thoughts are short.

Grace's skin tans and Mark's skin freckles.

Her pop was flat but she drank it anyway.

The day was overcast so they didn't go swimming.

b Be careful not to use a comma in sentences having *one* subject and a *double* verb. The comma is used only in sentences made up of two complete thoughts (two subjects and two verbs). In the following sentence, there is only one subject (*Kevin*) with a double verb (*will go* and *forget*). Therefore, no comma is needed.

Kevin will go partying tonight and forget all about tomorrow's exam.

Likewise, the following sentence has only one subject (*Rita*) and a double verb (*was* and *will work*); therefore, no comma is needed.

Rita was a server at the Banff Hotel last summer and probably will work there this summer.

Activity

Place a comma before a joining word that connects two complete thoughts (two subjects and two verbs). Remember, do *not* place a comma within sentences that have only one subject and a double verb.

1. The oranges in the refrigerator were covered with blue mould and the potatoes in the cupboard felt like sponges.

2. All the jeans in the shop were on sale but not a single pair was my size.

3. Phil often window shops in the malls for hours and comes home without buying anything.

4. Zeeshan left the dentist's office with his mouth still numb from Novocaine and he talked with a lisp for two hours.

5. I covered the walls with three coats of white paint but the purple underneath still showed through.

6. The car squealed up the on-ramp and sped recklessly out onto the Gardiner Expressway.

7. Winters in Vancouver are much milder than winters in Winnipeg and snow rarely sits long on the ground.

8. The singer in the group kept jumping into the audience but they kept throwing him back up on stage.

9. I felt that I did not belong in the statistics course but did not dare to admit it.

10. Emil claims he wants to succeed in college but he has missed classes all semester.

5 Comma with Direct Quotations

Use a comma to set off a direct quotation from the rest of a sentence.

> His father shouted, "Why don't you go out and get a job?"
> "Our modern world has lost a sense of the sacredness of life," the speaker said.
> "No," said Celia to Jerry. "I won't go to the bingo hall with you."
> "Money," wrote Marshall McLuhan, "is the poor people's credit card."

Note: Commas and periods at the end of a quotation go inside quotation marks. See also page 405.

Activity

Use commas to set off quotations from the rest of the sentence.

1. Hassan appeared at the door and called out "Welcome to my home!"

2. My partner on the dance floor said "Don't be so stiff. You look as if you'd swallowed an umbrella."

3. The question on the anatomy test read "What human organ grows faster than any other, never stops growing, and always remains the same size?"

4. The student behind me whispered "The skin."

5. "My stomach hurts" Bruce said "and I don't know whether it was the hamburger or the math test."

6 Comma with Everyday Material

Use a comma with certain everyday material.

Persons Spoken To, or Direct Address

> Tina, go to bed if you're not feeling well.
> Aaron, where did you put my shoes?
> Are you coming with us, Omar?

When a sentence is directly addressed to someone, separate the name or identifying noun from the rest of the sentence with a comma.

Dates

> July 1, 1867, is the date of Confederation.

Addresses

> Tony's grandparents live at 183 Roxborough Avenue, Toronto, Ontario
> M4S 1V3.

Note: No comma is used to mark off the postal code (Canada) or Zip code (U.S.).

Openings and Closings of Letters

> Dear Santa,
> Dear Larry,
> Sincerely yours,
> Truly yours,

Note: In formal letters, a colon is used after the opening: Dear Sir: *or* Dear Madam:

Numbers

Place a comma before each group of three digits.

> The dishonest dealer turned the used car's odometer from 98,170 kilometres to 39,170 kilometres.

Activity

Place commas where needed.

1. I expected you to set a better example for the others Michel.

2. Janet with your help I passed the test.

3. Andre DaCosta and Jason Peters started college on September 2 2003 and shared an apartment at 346 Pembina Highway Winnipeg Manitoba for two semesters.

4. The winner of the first *Canadian Idol* competition Ryan Malcolm received over 50000 fan letters during the first few weeks after he took the title.

5. The new computers for the software design program were purchased on March 12 2003 and cost the college $15000.

■ Review Test 1

Insert commas where needed. In the space provided below each sentence, summarize briefly the rule that explains the use of the comma or commas.

1. Mike Myers said Canada's main exports are wheat bauxite hockey players and comedians.

   _____

2. Because we got in line at dawn we were among the first to get tickets for the Toronto International Film Festival.

   _____

3. "When will someone invent a telephone" Elise asked "that will ring only at convenient moments?"

   _____

4. Without opening his eyes Simon stumbled out of bed and opened the door for the whining dog.

   _____

5. I think Chris that you had better ask someone else for your $2500 loan.

   _____

6. Sushi was not a big favourite in the college cafeteria for most students preferred pizza or sandwiches.

   _____

7. Tax forms though shortened and revised every year never seem to get any simpler.

   _____

8. Sandra may decide to go to college full-time or she may enrol in a couple of evening courses.

   _____

9. I remember how with a longing gaze Chris examined the poster for the new Grand Theft Auto game.

   _____

10. Although Alexa's website won several awards she still is not satisfied with it.

   _____

■ Review Test 2

Insert commas where needed.

1. My dog who is afraid of the dark sleeps with a night light.

2. "There is just no way" said the nutritionist "that you can convince me that poutine is an essential food group."

3. The designer-label sweater looked like a bargain but it was not pure cotton.

4. Janice attended class for four hours worked at the hospital for three hours and studied at home for two hours.

5. The patient as he gasped for air tried to assure the hospital clerk that he had his provincial health card somewhere.

6. Blaine and Kristina sat down to watch the hockey game with two orders of nachos four hot dogs and two large diet colas.

7. Although I knew exactly what was happening the solar eclipse gave me a strong feeling of anxiety.

8. The company agreed to raise a senior bus driver's salary to $42000 by January 1 2000.

9. Even though the martial arts expert was jumping from rooftop to rooftop his arch-enemy the evil overlord kept shouting at him "I will defeat you!"

10. Navel oranges which Melanie as a little girl called belly-button oranges are her favourite fruit.

■ Review Test 3

On a separate piece of paper, write six sentences, each of them demonstrating one of the six main comma rules.

Visit the *English Skills with Readings* Online Learning Centre at **www.mcgrawhill.ca/college/langan** to access self-quizzes, bonus material on study and research skills, web resources, and other learning and study tools.

xplaining a Process · Examining Cause and Effect · Comparing or Contrasting · Defini
erm · Dividing and Classifying · Describing a Scene or Person · Narrating an Event · Argu
Position · Explaining a Process · Examining Cause and Effect · Comparing or Contrasti
efining a Term · Dividing and Classifying · Describing a Scene or Person · Narrating
vent · Arguing a Position · Explaining a Process · Examining Cause and Effect · Compa

CHAPTER 36

Other Punctuation Marks

Introductory Project

Each of the sentences below needs one of these punctuation marks:

   ;   —   -   ( )   :

See if you can insert the correct mark in each sentence. Each mark should be used once.

1. The following holiday plants are poisonous and should be kept away from children and pets holly, mistletoe, and poinsettias.

2. The freeze dried soups and casseroles sealed in plastic bags that we took to Algonquin Park tasted worse than they looked.

3. William Shakespeare 1564-1616 married a woman eight years his senior when he was eighteen.

4. Grooming in space is more difficult than on Earth no matter how much Marc Garneau combed his hair, for instance, it still tended to float loosely around his head.

5. I opened the front door, and our cat walked in proudly with a live mouse hanging from his mouth.

Answers are on page 602.

COLON (:)

A colon in a sentence signals two things: a distinct pause and a pause that precedes the introduction of something. Colons also have numeric and mathematical significance; they are used when writing numerals indicating time and ratios.

Colons Used with Numerals

Use a colon between the numbers used to show the hour and the numbers used to show minutes (and seconds, if necessary) when writing times of day.

9:30 a.m.   11:05 p.m.   8:27:35

Use a colon between numerals indicating a ratio of one thing to another.

The ratio of students to tutors in the lab is 1:7.

Colons Used in Sentence Punctuation

A colon functions like an equal sign in arithmetic; it appears between an introductory independent clause (a complete statement) and a list, explanation, or long quotation. The colon signals that the material following it is equivalent to or explains the content of the independent clause preceding it.

Be sure that an independent clause appears before a colon within a sentence. These examples show correct and incorrect uses of the colon.

Colon Introducing a List

Incorrect	*Correct*
Marino's favourite things are: sleeping late, noisy parties, and extensions on deadlines.	Marino's favourite things are easy to name: sleeping late, noisy parties, and extensions on deadlines.
("Marino's favourite things are" is not a complete statement.)	

A colon should not appear between a linking verb and the words that describe the subject.

Incorrect	*Correct*
Kathy's shopping list for the party includes: dip, bottled water, and paper towels.	Kathy's shopping list for the party includes dip, bottled water, and paper towels.
("Kathy's shopping list for the party includes" is not a complete statement.)	

A colon should not appear between a verb and its object.

Colon Introducing an Explanation

Incorrect	*Correct*
Brent based his research report on: the effect of federal and provincial sales taxes on fast-food sales.	Brent based his research report on one idea: the effect of federal and provincial sales taxes on fast-food sales.
("Brent based his research report on" is not a complete statement.)	

A colon should not appear between a preposition and its object.

Colon Introducing a Long Quotation

Incorrect	*Correct*
In his essay "The Role of New Media in Social Change," Marshall McLuhan wrote: "The average distance from the page of children in the first three grades is ... 6 1/2 inches. The children seem to be striving to do a version of their relation to the TV image."	In his essay "The Role of New Media in Social Change," Marshall McLuhan discusses the effects of television watching on children's reading habits: "The average distance from the page of children in the first three grades ... is 6 1/2 inches. The children seem to be striving to do a version of their relation to the TV image."

The introductory statement before the colon must be complete and independent.

Activity

Place colons where needed.

1. Foods that are high in cholesterol include the following eggs, butter, milk, cheese, shrimp, and well-marbled meats.

2. All the signs of the flu were present hot and cold spells, heavy drainage from the sinuses, a bad cough, and an ache through the entire body.

3. A new study published online, *Canadian College Student Finance*, makes college students' money problems sound tolerable "Over three-quarters of college students report spending less than $5,000 on education-related expenses (tuition, fees, books and supplies) for one year."

SEMICOLON (;)

A semicolon signals more of a break in a sentence than a comma but less of an interruption than a colon. Its main function is to join independent clauses or to mark a break between them, as explained on page 335. Another use of the semicolon is to mark off items in a series when the items themselves contain commas. Here are some examples.

> Winning prizes at the national flower show were Roberta Collins, British Columbia, azaleas; Sally Hunt, Alberta, roses; and James Weber, Ontario, shasta daisies.
>
> The following books must be read for the course: *The Handmaid's Tale*, by Margaret Atwood; *The English Patient*, by Michael Ondaatje; and *Man's Search for Meaning*, by Viktor Frankl.

Activity

Place semicolons where needed.

1. The specials at the restaurant today are eggplant Parmesan, for $5.95 black beans and rice, for $4.95 and chicken burritos, for $6.95.

2. The top of the hill in France offered an awesome view of the Canadian soldiers' cemetery thousands of headstones were arranged in perfect rows.

3. Curtis's favourite older movies are *Psycho*, starring Anthony Perkins and Janet Leigh *Alien*, the first movie in the *Alien* series and *Fast Times at Ridgemont High*, with Sean Penn.

DASH (—)

A dash signals a pause longer than a comma but not as complete as a period. Use a dash to set off words for dramatic effect.

I didn't go out with him a second time—once was more than enough.
Some of you—I won't mention you by name—cheated on the test.
It was so windy that the Mini passed him on the highway—overhead.

Notes

a The dash is formed on a keyboard by striking the hyphen twice (--). In handwriting, the dash is as long as two letters would be.

b Be careful not to overuse dashes.

Activity

Place dashes where needed.

1. Riding my bike, I get plenty of exercise especially when dogs chase me.

2. I'm advising you in fact, I'm telling you not to bother me again.

3. The package finally arrived badly damaged.

HYPHEN (-)

A hyphen is created with a single strike of the hyphen key. Hyphens are used when joining two words to create a descriptive phrase, when forming compound words, when joining letters and words, and when dividing words at the end of a line of text.

1 Use a hyphen with two or more words that act as a single unit describing a noun.

The fast-talking journalist was so ambitious that she went into local politics. (*Fast* and *talking* combine to describe the journalist.)
Vince was a little naive and starry-eyed when he began his internship at CTV.
When Neo removed his narrow black-tinted sunglasses, he looked a lot less mysterious and sort of good-natured.

2   Use a hyphen to form some familiar compound words.

> Marisa's great-great-grandmother celebrated her ninetieth birthday with a helicopter ride.
> Sam's father-in-law was adamant about his son-in-law carrying on the family restaurant business.
> The best buy at the flea market was a ten-year-old portable stereo that was still in its box.

3   Use a hyphen to form words that are combinations of letters and words.

> The T-shirts at the Smashmouth concert were overpriced.
> Rose was so anxious that she made a U-turn on a one-way street in downtown Hamilton.
> The V-shaped tear in the convertible top would be expensive to repair.

4   Use a hyphen to divide a word at the end of a line of writing or keyed text. When you need to divide a word at the end of a line, divide it between syllables. Use a dictionary to be sure of correct syllable divisions.

> When Tom lifted up the hood of his Toyota, he realized that one of the radiator hoses had broken.

Notes

a   Do not divide words of one syllable.

b   Do not divide a word if you can avoid doing so.

Activity

Place hyphens where needed.

1. High flying jets and gear grinding trucks are constant sources of noise pollution in our neighbourhood, and consequently we are going to move.

2. When Linda turned on the porch light, ten legged creatures scurried everywhere over the crumb filled floor.

3. Scott had ninety two dollars in his pocket when he left for the supermarket, and he had twenty two dollars when he got back.

PARENTHESES ( )

Parentheses are used to set off extra or incidental information from the rest of a sentence.

> The section of that book on the dangers of eating disorders (pages 35 to 72) is outdated.
> Yesterday at Pizza Nova (my favourite pizza place), the guy behind the counter asked me to go out with him.

Note: Do not use parentheses too often in your writing.

Activity

Add parentheses where needed.

1. Certain sections of the novel especially Chapter 5 made my heart race with suspense.

2. Did you hear that George Linda's first husband just remarried?

3. Sigmund Freud 1856-1939 was the founder of psychoanalysis.

■ Review Test

At the appropriate spot or spots, place the punctuation mark shown in the margin.

; 1. Ella's savings have dwindled to nothing she's been borrowing from me to pay her rent.

— 2. There's the litterbug I'd know him anywhere who dumped garbage on our front lawn.

– 3. Today's two career couples spend more money on eating out than their parents did.

: 4. Britney Spears's statement in a recent interview showed off her knowledge of geography "The good thing about going on tour is getting to go overseas to places like Canada."

( ) 5. One-fifth of our textbook pages 401 to 498 consists of footnotes and a bibliography.

Online *Learning* Centre

Visit the *English Skills with Readings* Online Learning Centre at **www.mcgrawhill.ca/college/langan** to access self-quizzes, bonus material on study and research skills, web resources, and other learning and study tools.

xplaining a Process • *Examining Cause and Effect* • *Comparing or Contrasting* • *Definiti*
rm • *Dividing and Classifying* • *Describing a Scene or Person* • *Narrating an Event* • *Arg*
Position • *Explaining a Process* • *Examining Cause and Effect* • *Comparing or Contrasti*
efining a Term • *Dividing and Classifying* • *Describing a Scene or Person* • *Narrating*
vent • *Arguing a Position* • *Explaining a Process* • *Examining Cause and Effect* • *Compa*

C H A P T E R   3 7

Improving Spelling

Spelling is a code, a pattern of letter arrangements, which both writers and readers understand when it is correct. Every time a word is misspelled, the reader's attention is pulled away from the meaning of the document. If spellings are too difficult to follow, or if there are too many misspelled words, readers will not grasp the meaning of a written text or will simply give up trying to decode its sense.

Incorrect spelling results from a number of educational and life experiences. Some native English speakers were educated during periods when spelling was de-emphasized in Canadian schools and so are not as aware of spelling as they might be. Sometimes spelling in a second language causes difficulties. Whatever the causes, spelling problems are certainly remediable. Awareness of the correct appearance of words is always the first step in the remediation process, and improvement nearly always follows awareness.

Spelling is mainly a matter of pattern memory, and spelling correctly is definitely a learnable skill, just like writing well. Not only can you learn to spell correctly, but you will see instant improvement in your spelling by following the tips in this chapter. The rewards go beyond better marks to a lifetime of clear documents that your readers understand readily.

If you are like most people, you approach writing tasks in a hurry. You want to get words down as quickly as possible—partly to get the task over with, and partly to capture your thoughts before they escape from your mind. When you are brainstorming or writing first drafts, you are writing for yourself, so your hasty spelling choices are allowable, so long as *you* understand what you write. But remember that your "personal spelling code" works only if you are the only audience and if you know what you mean by it.

So the first tip for improving your spelling is a simple one: slow down.

STEP 1: SLOW DOWN AND BECOME AWARE OF THE LOOK OF WORDS

Once you have pinned your ideas down, it's time to slow down. Be prepared to look closely at your writing and check the spelling of any word you are unsure of. As you do so, you are training your mind and beginning to replace your memory of an incorrect spelling with a correct one. You will become increasingly aware of the correct spelling patterns, of the look of words, each time you practise reading over your writing, and you will be more focused on how words should be spelled. When you write for any other reader, always write at least two drafts.

You can train your memory for correct spelling by working with the next seven steps as often as possible.

STEP 2: RELY ON THE DICTIONARY EACH TIME YOU PROOFREAD

Buy a good Canadian dictionary and use it each time you write. Your dictionary is the single most reliable source of correct spelling, and the more often you consult it, the faster your searches will become. Moreover, each time you see a correct spelling of a word in the dictionary, you are more likely to spell it correctly on your own in the future. An excellent way to strengthen your memory of a word's spelling is to look up a word, then look away from the dictionary page and visualize the word in your mind. Then look back at the correct form on the page, visualize it again, and jot it down a few times on a scrap of paper. You are locking the image or pattern of the word's appearance in your mind. An added benefit of dictionary use is that you will make better choices from the words offered in your computer's spell checker.

When you write a paper, allow yourself time to look up the spelling of all the words you are unsure about. Do not overlook the value of this step just because it is such a simple one. By using the dictionary, you can probably make yourself a 95 per cent better speller.

STEP 3: USE THE SPELL CHECKER IN YOUR WORD-PROCESSING APPLICATION

Whenever you are writing on the computer, use its spell checker function. But do so with some caution. Most spell checkers are available in British, Canadian, or American spellings; set yours to Canadian, if possible, and use it consistently. Fast and easy to use as spell-checking tools are, they can actually create some spelling errors instead of eliminating them. Use the spell checker only with your dictionary open beside the keyboard.

Spell-checking tools are lists of frequently used words. A spell checker works by highlighting words that do not match its word list. It simply matches the letters in some word you have typed with words with similar letter sequences from its word list. As a result, for each word highlighted, you face a menu of spelling options that may or may not include the correct word or spelling. Ironically, you must know the correct spelling of any word in order to choose that correct spelling from the menu screen. Therefore, the spell checker's main virtue is to alert you to a word that may be misspelled; you still need the dictionary to make the right choice.

Because spell checkers simply match groups of letters, they cannot differentiate between meanings of words that look similar. People who misspell the word *definitely* as *definately* may be offered the word *defiantly* as the correct spelling, although the meanings of the two words are quite different. It's important for writers of English to know that spell-checking systems cannot differentiate between unintentional mistakes in word usage. "Same sound" words, homonyms like *its* and *it's* or *there*, *their*, and *they're*, cannot be corrected by a spell checker when they are spelled correctly but used incorrectly. You may want to highlight these words on your screen and double-check your intended meaning and spelling with the dictionary.

STEP 4: KEEP A PERSONAL SPELLING LIST

Keep a list of words you misspell, and study these words regularly. Use the Spelling List on the Online Learning Centre as a starter. When you accumulate additional words, write them on the back page of a frequently used notebook or on a separate sheet of paper titled "Personal Spelling List."

To master the words on your list, follow these tips:

1   Write down any hint that will help you remember the spelling of a word. For example, you might want to note that *occasion* is spelled with two *c*'s, or that *all right* is two words, not one word.

2   Study a word by looking at it, saying it, and spelling it. You may also want to write out the word one or more times, or "air-write" it with your finger in large, exaggerated motions.

3   When you have trouble spelling a long word, try to break the word down into syllables and see whether you can spell the syllables. For example, *inadvertent* can be spelled easily if you can hear and spell in turn its four syllables: *in ad ver tent.* Or the word *consternation* can be spelled easily if you hear and spell in turn its four syllables: *con ster na tion.* Remember: try to see, hear, and spell long words syllable by syllable.

4   Keep in mind that review and repeated self-testing are the keys to effective learning. When you are learning a series of words, go back after studying each new word and review all the preceding ones.

STEP 5: MASTER COMMONLY CONFUSED WORDS

Master the meanings and spellings of the commonly confused words on pages 439-47. Your instructor may assign twenty words for you to study at a time and give you a series of quizzes until you have mastered the words.

STEP 6: LEARN KEYWORDS IN MAJOR SUBJECTS

Make up and master lists of words central to the vocabulary of your major subjects. For example, a list of keywords in business might include *economics, management, resources, scarcity, capitalism, decentralization, productivity, enterprise,* and so on; in psychology, *behaviour, investigation, experimentation, frustration, cognition, stimulus, response, organism,* and so on. Add words from your course-specific lists and any words you consistently have trouble spelling to the "custom dictionary" listing in your spell checker, or set aside a specific portion of each of your course notebooks to be used only for such lists.

STEP 7: UNDERSTAND BASIC SPELLING RULES

Explained briefly here are three rules that may improve your spelling. While exceptions sometimes occur, the rules hold true most of the time.

1 ***Changing* y *to* i.** When a word ends in a consonant plus *y*, change *y* to *i* when you add an ending.

try + ed = tried	easy + er = easier
defy + es = defies	carry + ed = carried
ready + ness = readiness	penny + less = penniless

2 ***Final silent* e.** Drop the final *e* before an ending that starts with a vowel (the vowels are *a, e, i, o,* and *u*).

create + ive = creative	believe + able = believable
nerve + ous = nervous	share + ing = sharing

Keep the final *e* before an ending that starts with a consonant.

extreme + ly = extremely	life + less = lifeless
hope + ful = hopeful	excite + ment = excitement

3 ***Doubling a final consonant.*** * Double the final consonant of a word when all three of the following are true:
   a   The word is one syllable or is accented on the last syllable.
   b   The word ends in a single consonant preceded by a single vowel.
   c   The ending you are adding starts with a vowel.

shop + er = shopper	thin + est = thinnest
strip + ed = stripped	submit + ed = submitted
swim + ing = swimming	drag + ed = dragged

Activity

Combine the following words and endings by applying the three rules above.

1. worry   + ed   = _____

2. write   + ing   = _____

3. marry   + es   = _____

4. run   + ing   = _____

5. terrify + ed   = _____

6. dry   + es   = _____

7. forget   + ing   = _____

8. care   + ful   = _____

---

*In addition, Canadian spelling usually doubles the final *l* in many words that do not match these conditions. See "Canadian Spelling, Consistent Spelling, and Communicating Effectively" on page 433.

9. control + ed   = _____

10. debate + able = _____

STEP 8: STUDY A BASIC WORD LIST

Study the spellings of the words in the following list. They are five hundred of the words most often used in English. Your instructor may assign twenty-five or fifty words for you to study at a time and give you a series of quizzes until you have mastered the list.

Five Hundred Basic Words

ability	approach	bottle	city
absent	approve	bottom	close
accept	argue	brake	clothing
accident	around	breast	coffee
ache	arrange	breathe	collect
across	attempt	brilliant	college
address	attention	brother	colour
advertise	August	building	come
advice	automobile	bulletin	comfortable
after	autumn	bureau	company **100**
again	avenue	business	condition
against	awful	came	conversation
agree	awkward	can't	copy
all right	back	careful	daily
almost	balance	careless **75**	danger
a lot	bargain	cereal	daughter
already	beautiful	certain	daybreak
also	because	chair	dear
although	become	change	death
always	been **50**	charity	December
amateur	before	cheap	decide
among	begin	cheat	deed
amount	being	cheek	dentist
angry	believe	chicken	deposit
animal **25**	between	chief	describe
another	bicycle	children	did
answer	black	choose	died
anxious	blue	church	different
appetite	board	cigarette	dinner
apply	borrow	citizen	direction

discover	forward	into	men
disease	found	iron	middle
distance	fourteen	itself	might
doctor	Friday	January	million
does **125**	friend	July	minute
dollar	from	June	mistake
don't	gallon	just	Monday **250**
doubt	garden	kindergarten	money
down	general	kitchen	month
dozen	get	knock	more
during	good	knowledge	morning
each	grammar	labour	mother
early	great	laid	mountain
earth	grocery **175**	language	mouth
easy	grow	last	much
education	guess	laugh	must
eight	half	learn	nail
either	hammer	led	near
empty	hand	left	needle
English	handkerchief	leisure	neighbour
enough	happy	length	neither
entrance	having	lesson	never
evening	head	letter **225**	newspaper
everything	heard	life	nickel
examine	heavy	light	niece
except	high	listen	night
exercise	himself	little	ninety
exit	hoarse	loaf	noise
expect	holiday	loneliness	none
fact **150**	home	long	not
factory	hospital	lose	nothing
family	house	made	November **275**
far	however	making	now
February	hundred	many	number
few	hungry	March	ocean
fifteen	husband	marry	o'clock
fight	instead	match	October
flower	intelligence	matter	offer
forehead	interest **200**	may	often
foreign	interfere	measure	old
forty	interrupt	medicine	omit

once	pursue	sight	theatre
one	put	since	them
only	qualify	sister	there
operate	quarter	sixteenth	therefore
opinion	quick	sleep	they
opportunity	quiet	smoke	thing
optimist	quit	soap	thirteen
original	quite	soldier	this
ought	quiz	something 375	though
ounce	raise	sometimes	thousand
overcoat	read	soul	thread
pain	ready	soup	three
paper	really	south	through
part	reason	stamp	Thursday
peace	receive	state	ticket
pear 300	recognize	still	time
pencil	refer	stockings	tired
penny	religion	straight	today 425
people	remember	street	together
perfect	repeat	strong	tomorrow
period	resource	student	tongue
person	restaurant	studying	tonight
picture	ribbon	such	touch
piece	ridiculous	suffer	toward
pillow	right 350	sugar	travel
place	said	suit	trouble
plain	same	summer	trousers
please	sandwich	Sunday	truly
pocket	Saturday	supper	twelve
policeman	say	sure	uncle
possible	school	sweet	under
post office	scissors	take	understand
potato	season	teach	unique
power	see	tear 400	until
prescription	sentence	telegram	upon
president	September	telephone	used
pretty	service	tenant	usual
probably	seventeen	tenth	valley
promise	several	than	value
psychology	shoes	Thanksgiving	variety
public 325	should	that	vegetable

very	warning	whether **475**	work
view **450**	watch	which	world
villain	water	while	worth
visitor	wear	white	would
voice	weather	whole	writing
vote	Wednesday	whose	written
wage	week	wife	wrong
wagon	weigh	window	year
waist	welcome	winter	yesterday
wait	well	without	yet
wake	went	woman	young
walk	were	wonder	your
warm	what	won't	you're **500**

Note: Two spelling mistakes that students often make are to write *a lot* as one word ("alot") and to write all right as one word ("alright"). Do not write either *a lot* or *all right* as one word.

CANADIAN SPELLING, CONSISTENT SPELLING, AND COMMUNICATING EFFECTIVELY

Canadian spelling is a contentious subject. Canadian spelling is neither British nor American spelling; it is a hybrid of the two, and spellings of certain words may vary from one printed source to another. It is understandable that students may be confused.

Check with your instructor for his or her preference, but choose *one* spelling system, and *be consistent*. Choose a Canadian dictionary, such as *The Canadian Oxford Dictionary*, which this text uses, or *Gage*.

The main differences between American and Canadian spellings are in *-or/-our* endings (*honour, neighbour, labour, flavour*), *-er/-re* endings (*theatre, litre, centre, fibre*), and *-se/-ce* endings (*defence, licence, offence*).

Canadian spelling also includes more doubled *l*'s than does U.S. spelling. These double *l*'s appear in nouns such as *traveller* and *counsellor*, and in present and past participle forms of verbs such as *levelling, panelling, cancelled*, and *counselled*. Whichever form your dictionary uses, remember that consistent spelling is important.

Correct spelling requires patience and attention to seemingly small details. But correct spelling is no minor issue—it is an essential part of the image you present of yourself to the outside world. You can train your memory to spell words correctly in a relatively brief time, if you persist with the steps in this chapter.

The increasing use of text-dependent media such as e-mail and online chat in social communication probably means you write more often than you may have even five years ago. But you may write in another type of "personal spelling code" when you are online with friends. Chat-screen windows and related social e-mail have created their own casual shorthand spellings such as *u* rather than *you* and abbreviations like *LOL*. These spellings and expressions belong only in personal online contexts; their use is unacceptable in "real world" communication.

The Internet and online communication present challenges to everyone because of their various levels and forms of content. Be aware of your writing situation—of your audience and context—when you write for any purpose online.

International communications systems are integral parts of your personal and professional future. Clear and understandable communication relies on standardized spelling. Individual illiteracy, bounced off satellites and transmitted digitally through fibre optic cable, becomes an obstacle to information transmission and an international liability to employers and private citizens alike.

Visit the *English Skills with Readings* Online Learning Centre at **www.mcgrawhill.ca/college/langan** to access self-quizzes, bonus material on study and research skills, web resources, and other learning and study tools.

plaining a Process • Examining Cause and Effect • Comparing or Contrasting • Defining
m • Dividing and Classifying • Describing a Scene or Person • Narrating an Event • Argui
osition • Explaining a Process • Examining Cause and Effect • Comparing or Contrasting
ining a Term • Dividing and Classifying • Describing a Scene or Person • Narrating a
nt • Arguing a Position • Explaining a Process • Examining Cause and Effect • Compari

C H A P T E R   3 8

Vocabulary Development

A good vocabulary is a vital part of effective communication. A command of many words will make you a better writer, speaker, listener, and reader. Studies have shown that students with a strong vocabulary and students who work to improve a limited vocabulary are more successful in school. And one research study found that *a good vocabulary, more than any other factor, was common to people enjoying successful careers.* This section will describe three ways of developing your word power: (1) regular reading, (2) vocabulary word sheets, and (3) vocabulary study tools. You should keep in mind from the start, however, that none of the approaches will help unless you truly decide that vocabulary development is an important goal. Only when you have this attitude can you begin doing the sustained work needed to improve your word power.

REGULAR READING

Through reading a good deal, you will learn words by encountering them a number of times in a variety of sentences. Repeated exposure to a word in context will eventually make it a part of your working language.

You may, at this point, spend much of your time reading textbooks and websites. Reading text from a computer screen, however, will probably not expand your vocabulary in the same way as reading from pages. Screens are more difficult to read, partly because of their physical position in relation to your eyes, and people tend to read webpages more quickly and less carefully than they read print pages. You are less likely to pay attention to a word you do not understand or look it up when you read online text. Therefore, to improve your vocabulary, you should develop the habit of reading a daily newspaper and one or more Canadian magazines like *Maclean's,* as well as magazines suited to your interests. In addition, you should try to read some books for pleasure. This may be especially difficult at times when you also have textbook reading to do. Try, however, to redirect a regular period, half an hour to one hour, of your recreational time to reading books rather than watching television. You may eventually reap the rewards of an improved vocabulary *and* discover that reading can be truly enjoyable. If you would like some recommendations, ask your instructor for a copy of the "List of Interesting Books" in the Instructor's Manual of *English Skills with Readings,* Third Canadian Edition.

VOCABULARY WORD SHEETS

Vocabulary word sheets are another means of vocabulary development. Whenever you read, you should mark words that you want to learn. After you have accumulated a number of words, sit down with a dictionary and look up basic information about each of them. Put this information on a word sheet like the one shown below. Be sure also to write down a sentence in which each word appears. A word is always best learned in the context of surrounding words.

To study each word, start by making sure you can correctly pronounce the word and its derivations. The dictionary pronunciation key will help you pronounce each word properly. Next, study the main meanings of the word until you can say them without looking at them. Finally, spend a moment looking at the example of the word in context. Follow the same process with the second word. Then, after testing yourself on the first and second words, go on to the third word. After you learn each new word, remember to continue to test yourself on all the words you have studied. Repeated self-testing is a key to effective learning.

Activity

In your reading, locate four words that you would like to master. Enter them in the spaces on the vocabulary word sheet below and fill in all the needed information. Your instructor may then check your word sheet and perhaps give you a quick oral quiz on selected words.

You may receive a standing assignment to add five words a week to a word sheet and to study the words. You can create your own word sheets using loose-leaf paper, or your instructor may give you copies of the word sheet that appears below.

Vocabulary Word Sheet

1. Word: _____*formidable*_____   Pronunciation: *(fôr' mi d b l)*

    Meanings: ____*1. feared or dreaded*_____

    _____*2. extremely difficult*_____

    _____*ə ə*____

    Other forms of the word: _____*formidably   formidableness*_____

    Use of the word in context: ____*Several formidable obstacles stand between*____

    *Matt and his goal.*_____

2. Word: _____   Pronunciation: _____

    Meanings: _____

    _____

    _____

    Other forms of the word: _____

    Use of the word in context: _____

    _____

3. Word: _____ Pronunciation: _____

    Meanings: _____

    _____

    _____

    Other forms of the word: _____

    Use of the word in context: _____

    _____

4. Word: _____ Pronunciation: _____

    Meanings: _____

    _____

    _____

    Other forms of the word: _____

    Use of the word in context: _____

    _____

5. Word: _____ Pronunciation: _____

    Meanings: _____

    _____

    _____

    Other forms of the word: _____

    Use of the word in context: _____

    _____

VOCABULARY STUDY BOOKS AND ONLINE RESOURCES

A third way to increase your word power is to use vocabulary study books. Many vocabulary books and programs are available. The best are those that present words in one or more contexts and then provide several reinforcement activities for each word. These books will help you increase your vocabulary if you have the determination required to work with them on a regular basis.

You may also find vocabulary improvement websites valuable and fun to use. Some Canadian colleges have writing-skills sites with vocabulary and word-use pages, and there are many general audience sites, too; some are career-oriented, and some are geared to second-language audiences, but most are useful. Here is a site where you can start your online explorations: https://www.vocabvitamins.com/.

Visit the *English Skills with Readings* Online Learning Centre at **www.mcgrawhill.ca/college/langan** to access self-quizzes, bonus material on study and research skills, web resources, and other learning and study tools.

Explaining a Process · Examining Cause and Effect · Comparing or Contrasting · Defini
Term · Dividing and Classifying · Describing a Scene or Person · Narrating an Event · Arg
a Position · Explaining a Process · Examining Cause and Effect · Comparing or contrastin
Defining a Term · Dividing and Classifying · Describing a Scene or Person · Narratin
Event · Arguing a Position · Explaining a Process · Examining Cause and Effect · compa

C H A P T E R   3 9

Commonly Confused Words

Introductory Project

Circle the five words that are misspelled in the following passage. Then see if you can write the correct spellings in the spaces provided.

> You're mind and body are not as separate as you might think. Their is a lot of evidence, for instance, that says if you believe that a placebo (a substance with no medicine) will help you, than it will. One man is said too have rapidly recovered from an advanced case of cancer after only one dose of a drug that he believed was highly effective. Its not clear just how placebos work, but they do show how closely the mind and body are related.

1. _____

2. _____

3. _____

4. _____

5. _____

Answers are on page 602.

HOMONYMS

The commonly confused words on the following pages have the same sounds but different meanings and spellings; such words are known as *homonyms*. Complete the activity for each set of homonyms, and check off and study the words that give you trouble.

a lot   a fair quantity
allot   give a share or portion to

> I wish the person who schedules our timetables would *allot* more than one period in the middle of the day for lunch; I need *a lot* more time than just one hour.

Fill in the blanks: Fahrid needs _____ more webspace for his site than the

college will _____ each student.

Note: "alot" is not a word.

all ready   completely prepared
already   previously; before

> We were *all ready* to start the play, but the audience was still being seated.
> I have *already* called the police.

Fill in the blanks: I am _____ for the economics examination

because I have _____ studied the chapter three times.

brake   stop; the stopping device in a vehicle
break   come apart

> His car bumper has a sticker reading, "I *brake* for animals."
> "I am going to *break* up with Bill if he keeps seeing other women," said Rita.

Fill in the blanks: When my car's emergency _____ slipped,

the car rolled back and demolished my neighbour's rose garden, causing a

_____ in our good relations with each other.

coarse   rough
course   part of a meal; a school subject; direction; certainly (in *of course*)

> By the time the server offered the customers the second *course* of the meal, she was aware of their *coarse* eating habits.

Fill in the blanks: Theo felt that the fitness instructor's humour was too

_____ for his taste and was glad when he finished the _____.

complement add to, fill out, go well with
compliment praise

> Van's navy sweater *complemented* his khaki pants and pea jacket; he received several *compliments* on his outfit.

Fill in the blanks: The coconut rice _____ the curried chicken that you plan to serve for dinner; you will probably get some _____ on your cooking.

hear perceive with the ear
here in this place

> "The salespeople act as though they don't see or *hear* me, even though I've been standing *here* for fifteen minutes," the woman complained.

Fill in the blanks: "Did you _____ about the distinguished visitor who just came into town and is staying _____ at this very hotel?"

hole an empty spot
whole entire

> "I can't believe I ate the *whole* pizza," moaned Raphael. "I think it's going to make a *hole* in my stomach lining."

Fill in the blanks: The _____ time I was at the party I tried to conceal the _____ I had in my sweater.

its belonging to it
it's shortened form of *it is* or *it has*

> The car blew *its* transmission (the transmission belonging to it, the car).
> *It's* (it has) been raining all week and *it's* (it is) raining now.

Fill in the blanks: _____ hot and unsanitary in the restaurant kitchen I work in, and I don't think the restaurant deserves _____ good reputation.

knew past form of *know*
new not old

> "I had *new* wallpaper put up," said Sarah.
> "I *knew* there was some reason the place looked better," said Bill.

Fill in the blanks: Lisa _____ that getting her hair cut would give her face a _____ look.

know   understand
no   a negative

> "I don't *know* why my dog Fang likes to attack certain people," said Kerry. "There's *no* one thing the people have in common."

Fill in the blanks: I _____ of _____ way of telling whether the politician is honest.

pair   set of two
pear   fruit

> "What a great *pair* of shorts Tim bought," said Keesha to Nora. Tim didn't hear her, for he was feeling very sick after munching on an unripe *pear*.

Fill in the blanks: In his lunch box was a _____ of

_____ s.

passed   went by; succeeded in; handed to
past   time before the present; beyond, as in "We worked past closing time"

> Someone *passed* him a wine bottle; it was the way he chose to forget his unhappy *past*.

Fill in the blanks: I walked _____ the instructor's office but was afraid to ask her whether I had _____ the test.

peace   calm
piece   part

> Nations often risk world *peace* by fighting over a *piece* of land.

Fill in the blanks: Helen did not have any _____ until she gave her dog a _____ of her meat loaf.

plain   simple; flat area
plane   aircraft

> The small, *plain* snacks and meals that airlines serve on *planes* these days are not worth eating.

Fill in the blanks: The game-show contestant opened the small box wrapped in _____ brown paper and found inside the keys to his own jet _____.

pore   opening in skin or other surface; look at intently
pour   flow; cause something to flow

> *Pour* boiling water into a bowl; put a towel over your head, then lean over the bowl. The steam will open your *pores.*

Fill in the blanks: The soup _____ all over the counter because of the tiny

_____ in the strainer that Willie ignored as he _____ over the recipe

book.

principal   main; a person in charge of a school
principle   law, standard, or rule

> Pete's high school *principal* had one *principal* problem: Pete. This was because there were only two *principles* in Pete's life: rest and relaxation.

Fill in the blanks: The _____ reason she dropped out of school was

that she believed in the _____ of complete freedom of choice.

Note: It might help to remember that the *e* in *principle* is also in *rule*—the meaning of *principle.*

right   correct; opposite of left
write   convey thoughts in words in print
wright   a builder or craftsperson, a maker of something

> "You are *right* to watch while I *write* this," said the play*wright.*

Fill in the blanks: Dimitri thinks I am strange because I make a check mark in

the air every time I am _____ when I _____ an answer that I

am not sure about.

stationary   still or not moveable
stationery   paper and envelopes

> Denise spent ten minutes in a *stationary* position in the lineup while she waited to buy printer paper and other *stationery.*

Fill in the blanks: Put the _____ that you have chosen for your

wedding invitations into the box carefully so that it remains _____

while it is being shipped.

than   used in comparisons
then   at that time

> When we were kids, my friend Shannon had prettier clothes *than* I did. I really envied her *then.*

Fill in the blanks: Carol thought she was better _____ the rest of us,

but _____ she got the lowest grade on the accounting test.

Note : It might help to remember that th*e*n (with an *e*) is also a tim*e* signal.

their   belonging to them
there   at that place; neutral word used with verbs like *is, are, was, were, have,* and *had*
they're shortened form of *they are*

> Two people own that van over *there* (at that place). *They're* (they are) going to move out of *their* apartment (the apartment belonging to them) and into the van, in order to save money.

Fill in the blanks: _____ not going to invite us to _____

table because _____ is no room for us to sit down.

threw   past form of *throw*
through from one side to the other; finished

> The fans *threw* so much litter onto the field that the teams could not go *through* with the game.

Fill in the blanks: When Shereen was _____ with her juice bottle, she

_____ it in the recycling bin.

to   verb part, as in *to smile;* toward, as in "I'm going *to* Montreal"
too   overly, as in "The pizza was *too* hot"; also or as well, as in "The coffee was hot, *too*"
two   number 2

> Kyle drove *to* the park *to* be alone with Cheryl. (The first *to* means "toward"; the second *to* is a verb part that goes with *be.*)
>
> Kyle's shirt is *too* tight; his pants are tight, *too.* (The first *too* means "overly"; the second *too* means "also.")
>
> You need *two* hands (2 hands) to handle a floor sander.

Fill in the blanks: _____ times tonight, you have been _____

ready _____ make assumptions without asking questions first.

wear   to have on
where   in what place

> Tino wanted to *wear* his light jacket on the hot day, but he didn't know *where* he had put it.

Fill in the blanks: Exactly _____ on my leg should I _____

this elastic bandage?

weather   atmospheric conditions
whether   if it happens that; in case; if

> Some people go on vacations *whether* or not the *weather* is good.

Fill in the blanks: I always ask Bill _____ we're going to have a storm,

for his bad knee can feel rainy _____ approaching.

whose   belonging to whom
who's   shortened form of *who is* and *who has*

> *Who's* the instructor *whose* students are complaining?

Fill in the blanks: _____ ready to leave, and _____ car is closest to

the exit?

your   belonging to you
you're   shortened form of *you are*

> *You're* (meaning "you are") not going to the fair unless *your* brother (the
> brother belonging to you) goes with you.

Fill in the blanks: _____ going to have to put aside individual

differences and play together for the sake of _____ team.

OTHER WORDS FREQUENTLY CONFUSED

Following is a list of other words that people frequently confuse. Complete the
activities for each set of words, and check off and study the words that give you
trouble.

a, an   Both *a* and *an* are used before other words to mean, approximately, "one."

Generally you should use *an* before words starting with the sound of a vowel (*a,
e, i, o, u*).

> an ache   an experiment   an elephant   an idiot   an ox

Generally you should use *a* before words starting with the sound of a consonant (all
other letters).

> a card   a brain   a cheat   a television   a gambler

Fill in the blanks: The girls had _____ argument over _____

former boyfriend.

accept (ăk sĕpt′)   receive; agree to
except (ĕk sĕpt′)   exclude; but

> "I would *accept* your loan," said Nga to the his uncle, "*except* that I'm not
> ready to pay 25 percent interest."

Fill in the blanks: _____ for the fact that she can't _____

any criticism, Lori is a good friend.

advice (ăd vīs′)   noun meaning "an opinion"
advise (ăd vīz′)   verb meaning "to counsel, to give advice"

   I *advise* you to take the *advice* of your friends and stop working so hard.

Fill in the blanks: I _____ you to listen carefully to any

_____ you get from your boss.

affect (uh fĕkt′)   verb meaning "to influence"
effect (ĭ fĕkt′)   verb meaning "to bring about something"; noun meaning
                      "result"

   The full *effects* of marijuana and alcohol on the body are only partly known;
   however, both drugs clearly *affect* the brain in various ways.

Fill in the blanks: The new tax laws go into _____ next month, and

they are going to _____ your income tax deductions.

among   implies three or more
between implies only two

   We had to choose from *among* 125 shades of paint but *between* only two
   fabrics.

Fill in the blanks: The layoff notices distributed _____ the unhappy

workers gave them a choice _____ working for another month at

full pay and leaving immediately with two weeks' pay.

anyone   some item or person out of a number; not a particular one
any one any person

   Any one of the computer stations is ready for *anyone* who wants to work.

Fill in the blanks: Is _____ available for tutorial help? I have more

assignments due than _____ student can handle.

beside   along the side of
besides in addition to

   I was lucky I wasn't standing *beside* the car when it was hit.
   Besides being unattractive, these uniforms are impractical.

Fill in the blanks: _____ the colour printer Jeff bought recently, he

also has a scanner _____ his computer.

conscience   sense of right and wrong
conscious   aware or awake

> Once Brian was *conscious* of where he was, his *conscience* told him he should not be there.

Fill in the blanks: Your _____ may be ready to guide you, but you must be _____ of what it is saying to you.

desert (dĕz′ ert)   stretch of dry land; (di zûrt′) to abandon one's post or duty
dessert (dĭ zûrt′)   last part of a meal

> Sweltering in the *desert,* I was tormented by the thought of an icy *dessert.*

Fill in the blanks: At the buffet, André said, "Now is not the time to _____ me, just when I'm lining up for _____!"

disinterested   impartial or unbiased
uninterested   not interested

> Sam was *uninterested* in participating in the student survey, but he did think that a *disinterested* committee should examine the results.

Fill in the blanks: Try appointing a _____ third party to judge the contest, even if everyone seems _____.

fewer   used with things that can be counted
less   refers to amount, value, or degree

> There were *fewer* than seven people in all my classes today.
> I seem to feel *less* tired when I exercise regularly.

Fill in the blanks: With _____ people driving large cars, Canadians are using _____ gas than they used to.

loose (loos)   not fastened; not tight-fitting
lose (looz)   misplace; fail to win

> Phil's belt is so *loose* that he always looks ready to *lose* his pants.

Fill in the blanks: At least once a week our neighbours _____ their dog because they let him run _____.

precede   come before, go before
proceed   go ahead, move on

> Rajiv *preceded* Kim out of the room, after the fire-drill announcement told people to *proceed* to the closest exit doors.

Fill in the blanks: "The *i* _____ the *j* in my name," said Alicija, and she

_____ to write her name on the board to demonstrate.

quiet (kwī′ ĭt)   peaceful
quite (kwīt)   entirely; really; rather

> After a busy day, the children are now *quiet,* and their parents are *quite* tired.

Fill in the blanks: The _____ halls of the church become

_____ lively during swing dance evenings.

though (thō)   despite the fact that
thought (thôt)   past form of *think*

> Even *though* she worked, she *thought* she would have time to go to school.

Fill in the blanks: Yoshiko _____ she would like her job, but even

_____ the pay was good, she hated the travelling involved.

■ Review Test 1

Underline the correct word in the parentheses. Don't try to guess. If necessary, look back at the explanations of the words.

1. Please take my (*advice, advise*) and (*where, wear*) something warm and practical, rather (*than, then*) something fashionable and flimsy.

2. Glen felt that if he could (*loose, lose*) ten kilograms, the (*affect, effect*) on his social life might be dramatic.

3. (*Their, There, They're*) going to show seven horror films at (*their, there, they're*) Halloween night festival; I hope you'll be (*their, there, they're*).

4. (*Your, You're*) going to have to do (*a, an*) better job on (*your, you're*) final exam if you expect to pass the (*coarse, course*).

5. Those (*to, too, two*) issues are (*to, too, two*) hot for any politician (*to, too, two*) handle.

6. Even (*though, thought*) the (*brakes, breaks*) on my car were worn, I did not have (*quiet, quite*) enough money to get them replaced (*right, write*) away.

7. (*Accept, Except*) for the fact that my neighbour prowls the halls in his boxer shorts in (*plain, plane*) view of all the other students, he is (*know, no*) stranger (*than, then*) anyone else in this residence.

8. Because the Randalls are so neat and fussy, (*its, it's*) hard (*to, too, two*) feel comfortable when (*your, you're*) in (*their, there, they're*) house.

9. (*Whose, Who's*) the culprit who left the paint can on the table? The paint has ruined a (*knew, new*) tablecloth, and (*its, it's*) soaked (*threw, through*) the linen and (*affected, effected*) the finish on the table.

10. I would have been angry at the car that (*passed, past*) me at one hundred kilometres an hour on the highway, (*accept, except*) that I (*knew, new*) it would not get (*passed, past*) the speed trap (*to, too, two*) kilometres down the road.

■ Review Test 2

On a separate piece of paper, write short sentences using the ten words shown below.

their	principal
its	except
you're	past
too	through
then	who's

Visit the *English Skills with Readings* Online Learning Centre at **www.mcgrawhill.ca/college/langan** to access self-quizzes, bonus material on study and research skills, web resources, and other learning and study tools.

plaining a Process • Examining Cause and Effect • Comparing or Contrasting • Defini

rm • Dividing and Classifying • Describing a Scene or Person • Narrating an Event • Argue

Position • Explaining a Process • Examining Cause and Effect • Comparing or Contrastin

fining a Term • Dividing and Classifying • Describing a Scene or Person • Narrating

ent • Arguing a Position • Explaining a Process • Examining Cause and Effect • Compare

CHAPTER 40

Effective Word Choice

Introductory Project

Put a check beside the sentence in each pair that you feel makes more effective use of words.

1. I'm totally bummed that I missed the concert. _____

    I'm really disappointed that I missed the concert. _____

2. Doctors as dedicated as Dr. Khan are few and far between. _____

    Doctors as dedicated as Dr. Khan are rare. _____

3. Yesterday I ascertained that Elena and Wes broke up. _____

    Yesterday I found out that Elena and Wes broke up. _____

Now see if you can circle the correct number in each case:

    Pair (1, 2, 3) contains a sentence with slang.

    Pair (1, 2, 3) contains a sentence with a cliché.

    Pair (1, 2, 3) contains a sentence with a pretentious word.

Answers are on page 602.

Choose your words carefully when you write. Once you are revising your work, take the time to think about your word choices, rather than simply using the first words that come to mind. Give your ideas the settings they deserve—the words and phrases that truly express what you mean.

Always keep two criteria in mind when you revise the wording of any piece of writing:

■ Your purpose: what are you trying to say, and why? Which words best carry the meaning you intend so that your writing fulfills your goals for it?

■ Your audience: to whom are you writing, and what word choices will best carry your meaning most accurately to him or her?

Your main writing goal is always clarity; your writing should explain your ideas as exactly as possible. One concrete first step to making your words work effectively for you and your readers is to avoid slang, clichés, and pretentious words.

SLANG

We often use slang expressions when we talk because they are so vivid and colourful. However, slang is usually out of place in formal writing. Here are some examples of slang expressions.

My friend in the statistics class *gave me the 411* on the assignments.
The atmosphere in the club was *way cool*; everybody was *just chillin'*.
His skateboard was *totally rad*.

Slang works against clear expression of meaning for three reasons:

- Slang depends on its trendiness, on being current. As a result, it goes out of date quickly and can cause confusion for readers.
- Slang expressions arise from some group's desire to have a "private code" or language not understood by the general public. Therefore, using slang runs counter to communicating clearly to most audiences.
- Slang is habit-forming in speech; current expressions become overused very quickly, and then they are annoying. In print, the risk of annoyance to reading audiences from frequent use of slang is significantly higher.

But, most important, using slang is generally an evasion, a way of avoiding specific, careful details that are often needed to make one's meaning clear in writing. For example, in "The tires on the SUV make the car look like something else," the writer has not provided the specific details about the tires necessary for us to understand the statement clearly. In general, then, you should avoid slang in your writing. If you are in doubt about whether an expression is slang, it may help to check a recently published dictionary.

Activity

Rewrite the following sentences, replacing the italicized slang words with more standard ones.

Example   The movie was *the bomb,* so we *hit replay.*

The movie was excellent, so we watched it again.

1. My roommate told me he was going to Vancouver for study week, but later he admitted he was just *messing with my head.*

_____

_____

2. Once Mikela and her friends *scoped the place out,* they decided to stay.

_____

_____

3. If the instructor stops *hassling* me, I am going to *get my act together* in the course.

_____

_____

CLICHÉS

A cliché is an expression that has been worn out through constant use. Some typical clichés are listed in the box.

Clichés	
all work and no play	saw the light
at a loss for words	short but sweet
better late than never	sigh of relief
drop in the bucket	singing the blues
easier said than done	taking a big chance
had a hard time of it	time and time again
in the nick of time	too close for comfort
in this day and age	too little, too late
it dawned on me	took a turn for the worse
it goes without saying	under the weather
last but not least	where he (she) is
make ends meet	coming from
on top of the world	word to the wise
sad but true	work like a dog

Clichés are common in speech but make your writing seem tired and stale. Also, clichés—like slang—are often a way of evading the specific details that you must work to provide in your writing. You should avoid clichés and try to express your meaning in fresh, original ways.

Activity

Underline the cliché in each of the following sentences. Then substitute specific, fresh words for the trite expression.

Example   I passed the test <u>by the skin of my teeth</u>.

I barely passed the test.

1. Anyone turning in a paper late is throwing caution to the winds.

_____

2. Yolanda doesn't make any bones about her ambition.

_____

3. I met with my instructor to try to iron out the problems in my paper.

_____

PRETENTIOUS WORDS

Some people feel they can improve their writing by using fancy and elevated words rather than simple and natural words. They use artificial and stilted language that more often obscures their meaning than communicates it clearly.

Here are some unnatural-sounding sentences.

I comprehended her statement.

While partaking of our morning meal, we engaged in an animated conversation.

I am a stranger to excessive financial sums.

Law enforcement officers directed traffic when the lights malfunctioned.

The same thoughts can be expressed more clearly and effectively by using plain, natural language.

I understood what she said.

While eating breakfast, we had a lively talk.

I have never had much money.

Police officers directed traffic when the lights stopped working.

Activity

Cross out the artificial words in each sentence. Then substitute clear, simple language for the artificial words.

Example   The manager ~~reproached~~ me for my ~~tardiness~~.

The manager criticized me for being late.

1. One of Irina's objectives in life is to accomplish a large family.

    _____

    _____

2. Upon entering our residence, we detected smoke in the atmosphere.

    _____

    _____

3. I am not apprehensive about the test, which encompasses five chapters of the book.

    _____

    _____

■ Review Test 1

Certain words are italicized in the following sentences. In the space provided, identify the words as *slang* (S), *clichés* (C), or *pretentious words* (PW). Then rewrite the sentences, replacing the words with more effective diction.

_____   1. We're *psyched* for tonight's White Stripes concert, which is going to be *totally awesome.*

_____   2. Getting good marks in college courses is sometimes *easier said than done.*

_____   3. I *availed myself* of the chance to *participate* in the computer course.

_____   4. The victims of the car accident were shaken but *none the worse for wear.*

_____   5. My roommate *pulled an all-nighter* and almost *zoned out* during the exam.

_____   6. Be sure to *deposit* your garbage in the appropriate *receptacle.*

_____   7. Carlos has to *work like a dog* on his international marketing presentation.

_____   8. Winter in Winnipeg *drives me up the wall.*

_____   9. Every October, my whole family *congregates* at Melissa's house for a Thanksgiving *repast.*

_____   10. Nicole *totally lost it* when she could not find her cellphone for three days.

Visit the *English Skills with Readings* Online Learning Centre at **www.mcgrawhill.ca/college/langan** to access self-quizzes, bonus material on study and research skills, web resources, and other learning and study tools.

xplaining a Process · Examining Cause and Effect · Comparing or Contrasting · Definin
rm · Dividing and Classifying · Describing a Scene or Person · Narrating an Event · Argi
Position · Explaining a Process · Examining Cause and Effect · Comparing or Contrastin
efining a Term · Dividing and Classifying · Describing a Scene or Person · Narrating
vent · Arguing a Position · Explaining a Process · Examining Cause and Effect · Compai

C H A P T E R   4 1

E S L   P o i n t e r s

You may have turned to this chapter because English is your second or third language. Or you may have spoken English all your life but want further information on points of usage and grammar. This chapter offers detailed explanations of points and rules of common usage and English idiomatic structures that most native speakers of English take for granted.

ARTICLES

Articles often come before nouns in English. Many other languages do not use articles the same way, so learning how to use them correctly in English may take some time.

There are two kinds of articles: indefinite and definite.

Indefinite Articles: *a* and *an*

Generally, an indefinite article does not specify a particular item.

- Use *a* before a word that begins with a consonant sound.

  a carrot, *a* pig, *a* uniform (An *a* is used before *uniform* because the *u* in that word sounds like the consonant *y* plus *u*, not the vowel sound of the letter *u*.)

- Use *an* before a word beginning with a vowel sound.

  an answer, *an* excuse, *an* onion, *an* umbrella, *an* honour (The word *honour* sounds as if it begins with a vowel because the *h* is silent.)

The Definite Article: *the*

The definite article specifies one item or particular items.

  the fan, *the* lemons

Placement of Articles

An article may come directly before a noun.

  a circle, *the* summer

Or an article may be separated from the noun by adjectives (words that describe the noun).

a large circle, *the* hot, humid summer

Articles with Count and Non-Count Nouns

To know whether to use an article with a noun and which article to use, you must learn to recognize count and non-count nouns. A *noun* names a person, place, thing, or concept.

Count nouns name people, places, things, or ideas that can be counted. Therefore, count nouns can be made into plurals: *window* (*one window, three windows*); *table* (*a table, some tables*); *principal* (*one principal, four principals*).

Non-count nouns name things or ideas that cannot be counted and thus cannot be made into plurals, such as *weather, anger, flour,* and *happiness*. The box below lists common types of non-count nouns.

Common Non-Count Nouns

Abstractions and emotions: anger, bravery, health, humour, pride, truth
Activities: baseball, jogging, reading, teaching, travel
Foods: bread, broccoli, chocolate, cheese, flour, rice
Gases and vapours: air, helium, oxygen, smoke, steam
Languages and areas of study: Korean, Spanish, algebra, history, physics
Liquids: blood, gasoline, lemonade, tea, water
Materials that come in bulk form: aluminum, cloth, dust, sand, soap
Natural occurrences: magnetism, moonlight, rain, snow, thunder
Other things that cannot be counted: clothing, furniture, homework, machinery, money, news, transportation, vocabulary, work

---

The quantity of a non-count noun (or a count noun) can be expressed with a word or words called a **quantifier**, such as *some, a lot of, a unit of,* and so on. (In the following two examples, the quantifiers are shown in *italic* type, and the non-count nouns are shown in **boldface** type.)

Please have *some* **patience**.
We need to buy *two bags of* **flour** today.

Some words can be either count or non-count nouns depending on whether they refer to one or more individual items or to something in general.

Certain *cheeses* give some people headaches. (This sentence refers to individual cheeses; *cheese* in this case is a count noun.)
The yearly *rains* in India are called monsoons. (This sentence refers to specific, individual rains; *rains* in this case is a count noun.)

Cheese is made in almost every country where milk is produced. (This sentence refers to cheese in general; in this case, *cheese* is a non-count noun.)

Rain is something farmers cannot do without. (This sentence refers to rain in general; in this case, *rain* is a non-count noun.)

Using *a* or *an* with Non-Specific Singular Count Nouns

Use *a* or *an* with singular nouns that are non-specific. A noun is *non-specific* when the reader doesn't know its specific identity.

A left-handed person faces special challenges with right-handed tools. (The sentence refers to any left-handed person, not a specific one.)

Today, our cat proudly brought *a* baby bird into the house. (The reader isn't familiar with the bird. This is the first time it is mentioned.)

Using *the* with Specific Nouns

In general, use *the* with all specific nouns—specific singular, plural, and non-count nouns.

A noun is specific—and therefore requires the article *the*—in the following cases:

- When it has already been mentioned once

    Today, our cat proudly brought a baby bird into the house. Luckily, *the* bird was still alive.

  The is used with the second mention of *bird*.

- When it is identified by a word or phrase in the sentence

    The pockets in the boy's pants are often filled with sand and dirt.

  Pockets is identified by the words *in the boy's pants*.

- When its identity is suggested by the context

    At Willy's Diner last night, *the* service was terrible and *the* food was worse.

  Service and *food* are identified as belonging to the context of Willy's Diner.

- When it is unique

    Scientists are concerned about the growing hole in *the* ozone layer.

  Earth has only one ozone layer.

- When it is preceded by a superlative adjective (*best, biggest, wisest*)

    The best way to store broccoli is to refrigerate it in an open plastic bag.

Omitting Articles

Omit articles with non-specific plurals and non-count nouns. Plurals and non-count nouns are non-specific when they refer to something in general.

Pockets didn't exist until the end of the 1700s.

Service is as important as *food* to a restaurant's success.

Iris serves her children homemade *lemonade.*

Using *the* with Proper Nouns

Proper nouns name particular people, places, things, or ideas and are always capitalized. Most proper nouns do not require articles; those that do, however, require *the.* Following are general guidelines about when and when not to use *the.*

Do not use *the* for most singular proper nouns, including names of the following:

- *People and animals* (Paul Martin, Fido)
- *Continents, provinces or states, cities, streets,* and *parks* (North America, Canada, Alberta, Lethbridge, Portage Street, Banff National Park)
- *Most countries* (France, Mexico, Russia)
- *Individual bodies of water, islands, and mountains* (Lake Erie, Prince Edward Island, Mount Everest)

Use *the* for the following types of proper nouns:

- *Plural proper nouns* (the Turners, the United States, the Great Lakes, the Rocky Mountains)
- *Names of large geographic areas, deserts, oceans, seas,* and *rivers* (the South, the Gobi Desert, the Atlantic Ocean, the Black Sea, the Don River)
- *Names with the format* the _____ of _____ (the People's Republic of China, the University of Manitoba)

Activity

Underline the correct form of the noun in parentheses.

1. (*A library, Library*) is a valuable addition to a neighbourhood.

2. This morning, the mail carrier brought me (*a letter, the letter*) from my cousin.

3. As I read (*a letter, the letter*), I began to laugh at what my cousin wrote.

4. Every night we have to do lots of (*homework, homeworks*).

5. We are going to visit our friends in (*the British Columbia, British Columbia*) next week.

6. Cats are known for having a great deal of (*curiosity, the curiosity*).

7. The soldiers in battle showed a great deal of (*courage, courages*).

8. A famous park in Toronto is (*High Park, the High Park*).

9. My son would like to eat (*the spaghetti, spaghetti*) at every meal.

10. It is dangerous to stare directly at (*the sun, sun*).

SUBJECTS AND VERBS

Avoiding Repeated Subjects

In English, a particular subject must be used only once in each clause, or word group with a subject and verb. Do not repeat a subject in the same clause by following a noun with a pronoun.

> *Incorrect:* The *manager he* asked Devon to lock up tonight.
> *Correct:* The **manager** asked Devon to lock up tonight.
> *Correct:* **He** asked Devon to lock up tonight.

Even when the subject and verb are separated by a long word group, the subject should not be repeated in the same clause.

> *Incorrect:* The *girl* that danced with you *she is* my cousin.
> *Correct:* The **girl** that danced with you **is** my cousin.

Including Pronoun Subjects and Verbs

Some languages may omit a pronoun as a subject, but in English, every clause and every sentence other than a command must have a subject. (In a command, the subject *you* is understood: [**You**] Hand in your papers now.)

> *Incorrect:* The Yellowhead Highway is in central Alberta. Runs across the province.
> *Correct:* The Yellowhead Highway is in central Alberta. **It** runs across the province.

Every English clause and sentence must also have a verb, even when the meaning of the clause or sentence is clear without the verb.

> *Incorrect:* Angelita's piano teacher very patient.
> *Correct:* Angelita's piano teacher **is** very patient.

Including *there* and *here* at the Beginning of Clauses

Some English sentences begin with *there* or *here* plus a linking verb (usually a form of *be*: *is*, *are*, and so on). In such sentences, the verb comes before the subject.

> **There are** masks in every culture on earth. (The subject is the plural noun *masks*, so the plural verb *are* is used.)

> **Here is** your driver's licence. (The subject is the singular noun *licence*, so the singular verb *is* is used.)

In sentences like the ones above, remember not to omit *there* or *here*.

> *Incorrect:* *Are* several chickens in the Bensons' yard.
> *Correct:* **There are** several chickens in the Bensons' yard.

Avoiding the Progressive (or Continuous) Tenses of Certain Verbs

The progressive (or continuous) tenses are made up of forms of *be* plus the *-ing* form of the main verb (the present participle). They express actions or conditions that have a definite beginning and a definite end.

George **will be taking** classes this summer.

However, verbs for mental states, the senses, possession, and inclusion are generally not used in the progressive tense.

Incorrect: Luisa *is seeming* to be ill.
Correct: Luisa **seems** to be ill.

Incorrect: That box *is containing* a surprise for Paulo.
Correct: That box **contains** a surprise for Paulo.

Using Only Transitive Verbs for the Passive Voice

Only *transitive* verbs—verbs that need direct objects to complete their meaning—can have a passive form (one in which the subject receives the action instead of performing it). Intransitive verbs cannot be used in the passive voice.

Incorrect: If you don't fix those brakes, an accident *may be happened.*

Happen is an intransitive verb—no object is needed to complete its meaning.

Correct: If you don't fix those brakes, an accident **may happen.**

If you are not sure whether a verb is transitive or intransitive, check your dictionary. Transitive verbs are indicated with an abbreviation such as *v.tr.* or *v.t.* Intransitive verbs are indicated with an abbreviation such as *v.intr.* or *v.i.*

Using Gerunds and Infinitives after Verbs (Idiomatic Verb Structures)

A gerund is the *-ing* form of a verb that is used as a noun.

Complaining is Ian's favourite activity. (*Complaining* is the subject of the sentence.)

An *infinitive* is *to* plus the basic form of the verb (the form in which the verb is listed in the dictionary); for example, *to eat, to stand, to revise.* The infinitive can function as an adverb, an adjective, or a noun.

We decided **to eat** dinner on the porch. (*To eat dinner on the porch* functions as an adverb that describes the verb *decided.*)

Aaron built a shelf **to hold** his DVD collection. (*To hold his DVD collection* functions as an adjective describing or modifying the noun *shelf.*)

To have a good time is the best we can expect. (*To have a good time* functions as a noun: the subject of the verb *is.*)

Some verbs can be followed by only a gerund or only an infinitive; other verbs can be followed by either. Examples are given in the following lists. You will encounter many others in your reading.

Verb + gerund   (*admit + stealing*)
Verb + preposition + gerund   (*apologize + for + yelling*)

Some verbs can be followed by a gerund but not by an infinitive. In many cases, there is a preposition (such as *for, in,* or *of*) between the verb and the gerund. Here are some verbs and verb/preposition combinations that can be followed by gerunds but not by infinitives.

admit	deny	look forward to
apologize for	discuss	postpone
appreciate	dislike	practise
approve of	enjoy	suspect of
avoid	feel like	talk about
be used to	finish	thank for
believe in	insist on	think about

Incorrect: He must *avoid to jog* until his knee heals.
Correct: He must **avoid jogging** until his knee heals.

Incorrect: The instructor *apologized for to be* late to class.
Correct: The instructor **apologized for** being late to class.

Verb + infinitive   (*agree + to leave*)

These common verbs can be followed by an infinitive but not by a gerund.

agree	expect	plan
arrange	have	refuse
claim	manage	wait
decide		

Incorrect: The students *refuse staying* after class.
Correct: The students **refuse to stay** after class.

Verb + noun or pronoun + infinitive   (*cause + them + to flee*)

These common verbs are followed first by a noun or pronoun and then by an infinitive (not a gerund).

cause	force	remind
command	persuade	warn

Incorrect: The coach *persuaded Mario studying* harder.
Correct: The coach **persuaded Mario to study** harder.

Here are common verbs that can be followed either by an infinitive alone or by a noun or pronoun and an infinitive.

ask	need	want
expect	promise	would like

Dena **asked to have a day** off next week.

Her boss **asked her to work** on Saturday.

Verb + gerund or infinitive   (*begin + packing* or *begin + to pack*)

These verbs can be followed by either a gerund or an infinitive.

begin	hate	prefer
continue	love	start

The meaning of each of the above verbs remains the same or almost the same whether a gerund or an infinitive is used.

Zoe **hates being** late.

Zoe **hates to be** late.

With the verbs below, the gerunds and the infinitives have very different meanings.

forget	remember	stop

Esta **stopped to call** home. (*Meaning:* She interrupted something to call home.)

Esta **stopped calling** home. (*Meaning:* She discontinued calling home.)

Activity

Underline the correct form in parentheses.

1. The doctor (*asked me, she asked me*) if I smoked.

2. The coffee is very fresh. (*Is, It is*) strong and delicious.

3. (*Are mice, There are mice*) living in our kitchen.

4. The box (*is containing, contains*) a beautiful necklace.

5. Unless you take your foot off the brake, the car will not (*be going, go*).

6. Most basketball players (*very tall, are very tall*).

7. Many people (*enjoy to spend, enjoy spending*) a day in the city.

8. The teacher (*plans taking, plans to take*) us on a field trip tomorrow.

9. Some old men in my neighbourhood (*play cards, they play cards*) every afternoon.

10. When I am happy, I feel like (*to sing, singing*).

ADJECTIVES

Following the Order of Adjectives in English

Adjectives modify nouns and pronouns. In English, an adjective usually comes directly before the word it describes or after a linking verb (a form of *be* or a verb of appearance or perception such as *look*, *seem*, or *taste*), in which case it modifies the subject. In each of the following two sentences, the adjective is **boldfaced** and the noun it describes is *italicized*.

That is a **false** *story*.
The *story* is **false**.

When more than one adjective modifies the same noun, the adjectives are usually stated in a certain order, though there are often exceptions. The box shows the typical order of English adjectives.

Typical Order of Adjectives in a Series

1 **An article or other determiner***: a, an, the, Lee's, your, some, this, three, another

2 **Opinion adjective**: dull, handsome, unfair, useful

3 **Size**: big, huge, little, tiny

4 **Shape**: long, short, round, square

5 **Age**: ancient, medieval, old, new, young

6 **Colour**: blue, green, scarlet, white

7 **Nationality**: Italian, Korean, Mexican, Vietnamese

8 **Religion**: Buddhist, Catholic, Jewish, Muslim

9 **Material**: cardboard, gold, marble, silk

10 **Noun used as an adjective**: house (as in *house call*), tea (as in *tea bag*), wall (as in *wall hanging*), or **participle as an adjective**: rocking (as in *rocking chair*), watering (as in *watering can*)

---

* These are the categories of *determiners*, with examples of each:

- *Possessive forms of nouns:* Karen's, the college's
- *Possessive pronouns:* my, your, our
- *Quantifiers:* some, several, many, a few of, a lot of
- *Demonstrative adjectives:* this, these

- *Numbers:* one, ten, 120
- *Indefinite pronouns:* another, both, few

Here are some examples of the order of adjectives.

> **a long cotton** scarf
>
> **the beautiful little silver** cup
>
> **your new lavender evening** gown
>
> **Anna's sweet Italian** grandmother

In general, use no more than *two or three* adjectives after the article or other determiner. Numerous adjectives in a series can be awkward: **the beautiful big new blue cotton** sweater.

Using the Present and Past Participles as Adjectives

The present participle ends in *-ing*. Past participles of regular verbs end in *-ed* or *-d*; a list of the past participles of many common irregular verbs begins on page 343. Both types of participles may be used as adjectives. A participle used as an adjective may come before the word it describes.

> It was a **boring** *program.*

A participle used as an adjective may also follow a linking verb and describe the subject of the sentence.

> The *program* was **boring**.

While both present and past participles of a particular verb may be used as adjectives, their meanings differ. Use the *present participle* to describe whoever or whatever *causes* a feeling.

> a **surprising** *conversation* (The conversation *caused* the surprise.)

Use the *past participle* to describe whoever or whatever *experiences* the feeling.

> a **surprised** cashier (The cashier *is* surprised.)

Here are two more sentences that illustrate the differing meanings of present and past participles.

> The horror movie was **frightening**; the audience was **frightened**. (The movie *caused* the fear; the audience *experienced* the fear.)

Following are pairs of present and past participles with similar distinctions.

annoying / annoyed	exhausting / exhausted
boring / bored	fascinating / fascinated
confusing / confused	frightening / frightened
depressing / depressed	surprising / surprised
exciting / excited	

Activity

Underline the correct form in parentheses.

1. The Johnsons live in a (*stone big, big stone*) house.

2. Mr. Kim runs a (*popular Korean, Korean popular*) restaurant.

3. For her party, the little girl asked if her mother would buy her a (*beautiful long velvet, beautiful velvet long*) dress.

4. When their son didn't come home by bedtime, Mr. and Mrs. Singh became (*worried, worrying*).

5. The constant humming of the laboratory equipment is very (*annoyed, annoying*).

PREPOSITIONS USED FOR TIME AND PLACE

The use of prepositions in English is often idiomatic, not based on their usual meanings, and exceptions to general rules are common. Therefore, correct preposition use must be learned gradually through experience. The box shows how three of the most common prepositions are used in some customary references to time and place.

The Use of on, in, *and* at *to Refer to Time and Place*

Time

    On *a specific day:* on Monday, on January 1, on your anniversary

    In *a part of a day:* in the morning, in the daytime (but *at* night)

    In *a month or a year:* in December, in 1867

    In *a period of time:* in an hour, in a few days, in a while

    At *a specific time:* at 10:00 a.m., at midnight, at sunset, at dinnertime

Place

    On *a surface:* on the desk, on the counter, on a ceiling

    In *a place that is enclosed:* in my room, in the office, in the box

    At *a specific location:* at the mall, at his house, at the ballpark

---

Activity

Underline the correct preposition in parentheses.

1. Can you babysit for my children (*on, at*) Thursday?

2. Please come to my office (*on, at*) 3:00 p.m.

3. You will find some computer disks (*in, on*) the desk drawer.

4. Miguel will begin his new job (*in, at*) two weeks.

5. People like to feed the ducks (*on, at*) the park.

Review Test

Underline the correct form in parentheses.

1. During the storm, I was startled by the loud (*thunder, thunders*).

2. (*Is, Here is*) your new textbook.

3. The ending of the movie was very (*surprised, surprising*).

4. Liane (*postponed to go, postponed going*) on vacation because she broke her ankle.

5. (*The people, People*) in the photograph are my mother's relatives.

6. The city streets were full of (*big yellow, yellow big*) taxis.

7. My friend and I (*are usually agreeing, usually agree*) with each other.

8. In the West, New Year's Day is celebrated (*in, on*) January 1.

9. If the weather is nice tomorrow, let's (*think about to go, think about going*) to the city ourselves.

10. Most (*cheese, cheeses*) are made from cow's milk, but others are made from the milk of sheep or goats.

Visit the *English Skills with Readings* Online Learning Centre at **www.mcgrawhill.ca/college/langan** to access self-quizzes, bonus material on study and research skills, web resources, and other learning and study tools.

Explaining a Process • Examining Cause and Effect • Comparing or Contrasting • Defin
Term • Dividing and Classifying • Describing a Scene or Person • Narrating an Event • Arg
Position • Explaining a Process • Examining Cause and Effect • Comparing or Contrast
efining a Term • Dividing and Classifying • Describing a Scene or Person • Narrating
vent • Arguing a Position • Explaining a Process • Examining Cause and Effect • Compa

CHAPTER 42

Combined Mastery Tests

SENTENCE FRAGMENTS AND RUN-ONS

■ **Combined Mastery Test 1**

1. _____
2. _____
3. _____
4. _____
5. _____
6. _____
7. _____
8. _____
9. _____
10. _____
11. _____
12. _____
13. _____
14. _____
15. _____
16. _____
17. _____
18. _____
19. _____
20. _____

The word groups below are numbered 1 through 20. In the space provided for each, write *C* if a word group is a complete sentence, write *F* if it is a fragment, write *R-O* if it is a run-on, and write *CS* if it is a comma splice. Then correct the errors.

¹I had a frightening dream last night, I dreamed that I was walking high up on an old railroad trestle. ²It looked like the one I used to walk on recklessly. ³When I was about ten years old. ⁴At that height, my palms were sweating, just as they did when I was a boy. ⁵I could see the ground out of the corners of my eyes, I felt a swooning, sickening sensation. ⁶Suddenly, I realized there were rats below. ⁷Thousands upon thousands of rats. ⁸They knew I was up on the trestle, they were laughing. ⁹Because they were sure they would get me. ¹⁰Their teeth glinted in the moonlight, their red eyes were like thousands of small reflectors. ¹¹That almost blinded my sight. ¹²Sensing there was something even more hideous behind me. ¹³I kept moving forward. ¹⁴Then I realized that I was coming to a gap in the trestle. ¹⁵There was no way I could stop or go back I would have to cross over that empty gap. ¹⁶I leaped out in despair. ¹⁷Knowing I would never make it. ¹⁸And felt myself falling helplessly down to the swarm of rejoicing rats. ¹⁹I woke up bathed in sweat. ²⁰Half expecting to find a rat in my bed.

Score Number correct _____ × 5 = _____ per cent

SENTENCE FRAGMENTS AND RUN-ONS

■ Combined Mastery Test 2

The word groups below are numbered 1 through 20. In the space provided for each, write *C* if a word group is a complete sentence, write *F* if it is a fragment, and write *CS* if it is a comma splice. Then correct the errors.

1. _____

2. _____

3. _____

4. _____

5. _____

6. _____

7. _____

8. _____

9. _____

10. _____

11. _____

12. _____

13. _____

14. _____

15. _____

16. _____

17. _____

18. _____

19. _____

20. _____

[1]My sister asked my parents and me to give up television for two weeks. [2]As an experiment for her psychology class. [3]We were too embarrassed to refuse, we reluctantly agreed. [4]The project began on a Monday morning. [5]To help us resist temptation. [6]My sister unplugged the living room set. [7]That evening the four of us sat around the dinner table much longer than usual, we found new things to talk about. [8]Later we played board games for several hours, we all went to bed pleased with ourselves. [9]Everything went well until Thursday evening of that first week. [10]My sister went out after dinner. [11]Explaining that she would be back about ten o'clock. [12]The rest of us then decided to turn on the television. [13]Just to watch the CBC news. [14]We planned to unplug the set before my sister got home. [15]And pretend nothing had happened. [16]We were settled down comfortably in our respective chairs, unfortunately, my sister walked in at that point and burst out laughing. [17]"Ah ha! I caught you," she cried. [18]She explained that part of the experiment was to see if we would stick to the agreement. [19]Especially during her absence. [20]She had predicted we would weaken, it turned out she was right.

Score   Number correct _____ × 5 = _____ per cent

VERBS

■ **Combined Mastery Test 3**

Each sentence contains a mistake involving (1) irregular verb forms, (2) subject-verb agreement, or (3) consistent verb tense. Circle the letter that identifies the mistake. Then cross out the incorrect verb and write the correct form in the space provided.

_____ 1. One of my apartment neighbours always keep the radio on all night.
Mistake in: a. Subject-verb agreement   b. Verb tense

_____ 2. The more the instructor explained the material and the more he wroted on the board, the more confused I got.
Mistake in: a. Irregular verb form   b. Verb tense

_____ 3. I grabbed the last carton of skim milk on the supermarket shelf, but when I checks the date on it, I realized it was not fresh.
Mistake in: a. Subject-verb agreement   b. Verb tense

_____ 4. This morning my parents argued loudly, but later they apologized to each other and embrace.
Mistake in: a. Subject-verb agreement   b. Verb tense

_____ 5. When the bell rang, Abdul takes another bite of his sandwich and then prepared for class.
Mistake in: a. Irregular verb form   b. Verb tense

_____ 6. Someone called Marlene at the office to tell her that her son had been bit by a stray dog.
Mistake in: a. Irregular verb form   b. Verb tense

_____ 7. Because I throwed away the sales slip, I couldn't return the microwave.
Mistake in: a. Irregular verb form   b. Verb tense

_____ 8. My dog and cat usually ignores each other, but once in a while they fight.
Mistake in: a. Subject-verb agreement   b. Verb tense

_____ 9. From the back of our neighbourhood bakery comes some of the best smells in the world.
Mistake in: a. Subject-verb agreement   b. Verb tense

_____ 10. The cost of new soles and heels are more than those old shoes are worth.
Mistake in: a. Subject-verb agreement   b. Verb tense

***

Score   Number correct _____ × 10 = _____ per cent

VERBS

■ **Combined Mastery Test 4**

Each sentence contains a mistake involving (1) irregular verb forms, (2) subject-verb agreement, or (3) consistent verb tense. Circle the letter that identifies the mistake. Then cross out the incorrect verb and write the correct form in the space provided.

_____ 1. My friend's bitter words had stinged me deeply.
    Mistake in: a. Irregular verb form   b. Verb tense

_____ 2. After she poured the ammonia into the bucket, Karen reels backward because the strong fumes made her eyes tear.
    Mistake in: a. Subject-verb agreement   b. Verb tense

_____ 3. Flying around in space is various pieces of debris from old space satellites.
    Mistake in: a. Subject-verb agreement   b. Verb tense

_____ 4. Ella watched suspiciously as a strange car drived back and forth in front of her house.
    Mistake in: a. Irregular verb form   b. Verb tense

_____ 5. Both crying and laughing helps us get rid of tension.
    Mistake in: a. Subject-verb agreement   b. Verb tense

_____ 6. All my clothes were dirty, so I stayed up late and wash a load for tomorrow.
    Mistake in: a. Subject-verb agreement   b. Verb tense

_____ 7. McDonald's has selled enough hamburgers to reach to the moon.
    Mistake in: a. Irregular verb form   b. Verb tense

_____ 8. When Chen peeled back the bedroom wallpaper, he discovered another layer of wallpaper and uses a steamer to get that layer off.
    Mistake in: a. Subject-verb agreement   b. Verb tense

_____ 9. Pina searched for the fifty-dollar bill she had hid somewhere in her dresser.
    Mistake in: a. Irregular verb form   b. Verb tense

_____ 10. The realistic yellow tulips on the gravestone is made of weather-resistant fabric.
    Mistake in: a. Subject-verb agreement   b. Verb tense

> *Score*   Number correct _____ × 10 = _____ per cent

CAPITAL LETTERS AND PUNCTUATION

■ **Combined Mastery Test 5**

Each of the following sentences contains an error in capitalization or punctuation. Refer to the box below and write, in the space provided, the letter identifying the error. Then correct the error.

a. missing capital	c. missing quotation mark
b. missing apostrophe	d. missing comma

_____ 1. Nicole's aerobics class has been cancelled this week so she's decided to go running instead.

_____ 2. "One of the striking differences between a cat and a lie, wrote Mark Twain, "is that a cat has only nine lives."

_____ 3. My uncles cheques are printed to look like Monopoly money.

_____ 4. Did you know someone is turning the old school on ninth Street into a restaurant named Home Economics?

_____ 5. My parents always ask me where Im going and when I'll be home.

_____ 6. She doesn't talk about it much, but my aunt has been a member of alcoholics Anonymous for ten years.

_____ 7. The sweating straining horses neared the finish line.

_____ 8. Whenever he gave us the keys to the car, my father would say, Watch out for the other guy."

_____ 9. If you're going to stay up late be sure to turn down the heat before going to bed.

_____ 10. I decided to have a glass of apple juice rather than order a pepsi.

Score Number correct _____ × 10 = _____ per cent	

CAPITAL LETTERS AND PUNCTUATION

■ **Combined Mastery Test 6**

Each of the following sentences contains an error in capitalization or punctuation. Refer to the box below and write, in the space provided, the letter identifying the error. Then correct the error.

a. missing capital	c. missing quotation mark
b. missing apostrophe	d. missing comma

_____ 1. Even though I hadn't saved the receipt I was able to return the blender to the Bay.

_____ 2. "The diners food is always reliable," said Stan. "It's consistently bad."

_____ 3. Some people are surprised to hear that vancouver is not on Vancouver Island.

_____ 4. "To love oneself, said Oscar Wilde, "is the beginning of a lifelong romance."

_____ 5. The airplane was delayed for more than three hours and the passengers were getting impatient.

_____ 6. Lydia said to the woman behind her in the theatre, "will you stop talking, please?"

_____ 7. Walters arthritis is as good a predictor of the weather as the TV weather report.

_____ 8. "Before you can reach your goals," says my grandfather, you have to believe you can reach them."

_____ 9. There is little evidence that king Arthur, the legendary hero, really existed.

_____ 10. My cousin learned to cook when he was head chef in a b.C. logging camp.

Score   Number correct _____ × 10 = _____ per cent

WORD USE

■ **Combined Mastery Test 7**

Each of the following sentences contains a mistake identified in the margin. Underline the mistake and then correct it in the space provided.

slang

1. Because Maxine has a lot of pull at work, she always has first choice of vacation time.

   _____

cliché

2. Kate hoped her friends would be green with envy when they saw her new boyfriend.

   _____

pretentious language

3. Bret utilizes old coffee cans to water his house plants.

   _____

adverb error

4. The sled started slow and then picked up speed as the icy hill became steeper.

   _____

error in comparison

5. When the weather is dry, my sinus condition feels more better.

   _____

confused word

6. If you neglect your friends, their likely to become former friends.

   _____

confused word

7. She's the neighbour who's dog is courting my dog.

   _____

confused word

8. If you don't put cans, jars, and newspapers on the curb for recycling, the city won't pick up you're garbage.

   _____

confused word

9. "Its the most economical car you can buy," the announcer said.

   _____

confused word

10. Although Evan knew he had alot of CDs, he never counted them.

    _____

Score   Number correct _____ × 10 = _____ per cent

WORD USE

■ Combined Mastery Test 8

Each of the following sentences contains a mistake identified in the margin. Underline the mistake and then correct it in the space provided.

slang

1. After coming in to work late all last week, Sheila was canned.

_____

cliché

2. Jan and Alan knew they could depend on their son in their hour of need.

_____

pretentious language

3. I plan to do a lot of comparison shopping before procuring a new dryer.

_____

adverb error

4. The children sat very quiet as their mother read the next chapter of *Charlie and the Chocolate Factory.*

_____

error in comparison

5. The respectfuller you treat people, the more they are likely to deserve your respect.

_____

confused word

6. The dog has lost its' flea collar.

_____

confused word

7. "My advise to you," said my grandmother, "is to focus on your strengths, not your fears."

_____

confused word

8. The principle advantage of the school cafeteria is that it's three blocks from a Harvey's.

_____

confused word

9. My parents mean well, but there goals for me aren't my goals.

_____

confused word

10. Lenka's conscious told her that lying about where she had been was wrong.

_____

Score   Number correct _____ × 10 = _____ per cent

CHAPTER 43

Editing Tests

EDITING AND PROOFREADING FOR SENTENCE-SKILLS MISTAKES

The twelve tests in this chapter will give you practice in proofreading and revising for sentence-skills mistakes.

Remember that each time you submit a piece of written work, if you do not edit and revise carefully, you risk sabotaging the work you have put into that assignment. When readers see too many surface flaws, they often assume you do not place much value on what you have to say, and they may not give your ideas a fair hearing. Moreover, mechanical and language errors constitute "noise," in communications terms; such errors distract readers and obscure the meaning of your content. Worse yet, readers may simply give up on writing that is troublesome to read and understand, so that your work may be rejected or left unread. Revising to eliminate sentence-skills errors is one of the most essential parts of communicating effectively. Revision is a necessity, not an option. A lifetime of readers will rely on you to revise your writing.

People find it hard to proofread and revise their work carefully. They have put so much work into their writing, or perhaps so little, that it is almost painful for them to look at their writing one more time. In the beginning, you may have to *force* yourself to proofread and revise your writing. As you get into the habit of checking your writing, you will be rewarded by writing better sentences and practising revising skills more accurately, with better results.

Here are five hints that can help you edit the next-to-final drafts of your assignments for sentence-skills mistakes.

Editing Hints

1 The first tip is a familiar one to readers of this book: *slow down*. Editing and revising take time and require a calm, focused mind. Locating and correcting errors uses a lot of mental energy and cannot be rushed.

2 Have at hand two essential tools: a good dictionary (see page 427) and a grammar handbook (you can use Chapter 5 and Section Four of this book).

3 Use a sheet of paper to cover your paragraph or essay so that you expose only one sentence at a time. Look for errors in grammar, spelling, and typing. It may help to read each sentence out loud. If a sentence does not read clearly and

smoothly, chances are that something is wrong, either with the content or with the grammar or mechanics.

4 Pay special attention to the kinds of errors you tend to make. For example, if you tend to write run-ons or fragments, be especially on the lookout for those errors. The tests in Chapters 42, 43, and 44 will help you to identify by name the writing problems you face most frequently.

5 These proofreading symbols may be helpful.

℮	omit	in the ~~the~~ meantime
∧	insert missing letter or word	bel∧eve
Cap + ≡	change lower case letter to capital	my p̲e̲rsian cat
lc + /	change capital letter to lower case	an April S̸hower

In this chapter, the errors in half of the tests are underlined, so your job is to identify and correct each error. In the other tests, you must locate the errors as well as identifying and correcting them.

■ Editing Test 1

Identify the five mistakes in manuscript form in the student paragraph that follows. From the box below, choose the letters that describe the five mistakes and write those letters in the spaces provided.

a.	The title should not be underlined.
b.	The title should not be set off in quotation marks.
c.	There should not be a period at the end of the title.
d.	All the major words in the title should be capitalized.
e.	The title should be a phrase, not a complete sentence.
f.	The first line of the paper should stand independent of the title.
g.	A line should be skipped between the title and the first line of the paper.
h.	The first line of the paper should be indented.
i.	The right-hand margin should not be crowded.
j.	Hyphenation should occur only between syllables.

	"my candy apple adventure"
	It was the best event of my day. I loved the sweetness that
	filled my mouth as I bit into the sugary coating. With my second
	bite, I munched contentedly on the apple underneath. Its
	crunchy tartness was the perfect balance to the smooth sweet-
	ness of the outside. Then the apple had a magical effect on me.
	Suddenly I remembered when I was seven years old, walking
	through the local fair grounds, holding my father's hand. We
	stopped at a refreshment stand, and he bought us each a
	candy apple. I had never had one before, and I asked him what it
	was. "This is a very special fruit," he said. "If you ever feel sad,
	all you have to do is eat a candy apple, and it will bring you
	sweetness." Now, years later, his words came back to me, and
	as I ate my candy apple, I felt the world turn sweet once more.

1. _____   2. _____   3. _____   4. _____   5. _____

■ Editing Test 2

Identify the sentence-skills mistakes at the underlined spots in the paragraph that follows. From the box below, choose the letter that describes each mistake and write it in the space provided. The same mistake may appear more than once.

a. fragment	d. apostrophe mistake
b. comma splice	e. faulty parallelism
c. mistake in subject-verb agreement	

Looking Out for Yourself

It's sad but true that "if you don't look out for yourself, no one else will."

For example, some people have a false idea about the power of a college

diploma, they think that once they possesses the diploma, the world will be
      1   2

waiting on their doorstep. In fact, nobody is likely to be on their doorstep

unless, through advance planning, they has prepared themselves for a career.
                                                3

The kind in which good job opportunities exist. Even after a person has landed
                     4

a job, however, a healthy amount of self-interest is needed. People who hide

in corners or with hesitation to let others know about their skills doesn't get
                       5   6

promotions or raises. Its important to take credit for a job well done, whether
                   7

it involves writing a report, organized the office filing system, or calming down
                                8

an angry customer. Also, people should feel free to ask the boss for a raise.

If they work hard and really deserve it. Those who look out for themselves get
                       9

the rewards, people who depend on others to help them along get left behind.
       10

1. _____   3. _____   5. _____   7. _____   9. _____

2. _____   4. _____   6. _____   8. _____   10. _____

■ Editing Test 3

Identify the sentence-skills mistakes at the underlined spots in the paragraph that follows. From the box below, choose the letter that describes each mistake and write it in the space provided. The same mistake may appear more than once.

a. fragment	e. missing commas around an interrupter
b. run-on	
c. mistake in verb tense	f. mistake with quotation marks
d. irregular verb mistake	g. apostrophe mistake
	h. comma splice

Deceptive Appearances

Appearances can be deceptive. While looking through a library window yesterday, I saw a neatly groomed woman walk by. Her clothes were skilfully <u>tailored her</u> makeup was perfect. <u>Then thinking no one was looking she</u>
      1   2
crumpled a piece of paper in her hand. <u>And tossed it into a nearby hedge.</u>
                                             3
Suddenly she no longer <u>looks</u> attractive to me. On another occasion, I started
                          4
talking to a person in my psychology class named Eric. Eric seemed to be a great person. He always got the class laughing with his <u>jokes, on the days</u>
                                                  5
when Eric was absent, I think even the professor missed his lively personality. Eric asked me <u>"if I wanted to get a pop in the cafeteria,"</u> and I felt happy
                                            6
he had <u>chose</u> me to be a friend. <u>While we were sitting in the cafeteria.</u> Eric
       7   8
admitted something that really surprised me. "You think I'm so funny?" he asked. "I've been depressed for most of my life. I still see my doctor about once a month." My jaw almost <u>dropped, I</u> was so startled. <u>Erics</u> lively
                                        9   10
personality was a product of his struggle against sadness.

1. _____   3. _____   5. _____   7. _____   9. _____

2. _____   4. _____   6. _____   8. _____   10. _____

■ Editing Test 4

Identify the sentence-skills mistakes at the underlined spots in the paragraph that follows. From the box below, choose the letter that describes each mistake and write it in the space provided. The same mistake may appear more than once.

a. fragment	e. apostrophe mistake
b. comma splice	f. dangling modifier
c. irregular verb mistake	g. missing quotation marks
d. missing comma after introductory words	

A Horrifying Moment

The most horrifying moment in my life occurred in the dark hallway.

<u>Which led to my apartment house</u>. Though the hallway light was <u>out I</u>
  1   2

managed to find my apartment door. However, I could not find the keyhole

with my door key. I then pulled a book of matches from my pocket. <u>Trying to</u>
                                                                        3

<u>strike a match</u>, the entire book of matches <u>bursted</u> into flames. I flicked the
                                                    4

matches away but not before my coat sleeve <u>catched</u> fire. Within seconds, my
                                                 5

arm was like a torch. <u>Struggling to unsnap the buttons of my coat</u>, flames
                                            6

began to sear my skin. I was quickly going into shock. <u>And began screaming</u>
                                                              7

<u>in pain</u>. A <u>neighbours</u> door opened and a voice cried out, <u>My God!</u> I was pulled
   8   9

through an apartment and put under a bathroom shower, which extinguished

the flames. I suffered third-degree burns on my <u>arm, I</u> felt lucky to escape
                                                      10

with my life.

1. _____   3. _____   5. _____   7. _____   9. _____

2. _____   4. _____   6. _____   8. _____   10. _____

■ Editing Test 5

Identify the sentence-skills mistakes at the underlined spots in the paragraph that follows. From the box below, choose the letter that describes each mistake and write it in the space provided. The same mistake may appear more than once.

a. fragment	e. faulty parallelism
b. run-on	f. apostrophe mistake
c. missing capital letter	g. missing quotation mark
d. mistake in subject-verb agreement	h. missing comma after introductory words
	i. comma splice

Why I Didn't Go to Church

I almost never attended church in my boyhood years. There was an

unwritten code that the guys on the corner <u>was</u> not to be seen in <u>churches'</u>.
                                              1   2

Although there <u>was</u> many days when I wanted to attend a church, I felt I had
                 3

no choice but to stay away. If the guys had heard I had gone to church, they

would have said things like, <u>"hey</u>, angel, when are you going to <u>fly?</u> With my
                              4   5

group of friends, <u>its</u> amazing that I developed any religious feeling at all.
                   6

Another reason for not going to church was my father. When he was around

the <u>house he</u> told my mother, "Tim's not going to church. No boy of mine is a
     7

sissy." My mother and sister went to <u>church I</u> sat with my father and read the
                                       8

Sunday paper or <u>watching television</u>. I did not start going to church until years
                  9

later. <u>When I no longer hung around with the guys on the corner or let my</u>
                                      10

<u>father have power over me.</u>

1. _____   3. _____   5. _____   7. _____   9. _____

2. _____   4. _____   6. _____   8. _____   10. _____

■ Editing Test 6

Identify the sentence-skills mistakes at the underlined spots in the paragraph that follows. From the box below, choose the letter that describes each mistake and write it in the space provided. The same mistake may appear more than once.

a. fragment	f. missing comma between two
b. comma splice	complete thoughts
c. faulty parallelism	g. missing comma after
d. missing apostrophe	introductory words
e. missing quotation mark	h. misspelled word

Anxiety and the Telephone

Not many of us would want to do without our <u>telephones but</u> there are
<u>1</u>

times when the phone is a source of anxiety. For example, you might be

walking up to your front door. <u>When you hear the phone ring.</u> You struggle to
<u>2</u>

find your key, to unlock the door, and <u>getting to the phone quickly.</u> You know
<u>3</u>

the phone will stop ringing the instant you pick up the <u>receiver, then you</u>
<u>4</u>

wonder if you missed the call that would have made you a <u>millionare</u> or
<u>5</u>

introduced you to the love of your life. Another time, you may have called in

sick to work with a phony excuse. All day long, <u>youre</u> afraid to leave the house
<u>6</u>

in case the boss calls back. <u>And asks himself why you were feeling well</u>
<u>7</u>

<u>enough to go out.</u> In addition, you worry that you might unthinkingly pick up

the phone and say in a cheerful voice, <u>"Hello,</u> completely <u>forgeting</u> to use
<u>8</u>   <u>9</u>

your fake cough. In cases like <u>these having</u> a telephone is more of a curse
<u>10</u>

than a blessing.

1. _____   3. _____   5. _____   7. _____   9. _____

2. _____   4. _____   6. _____   8. _____   10. _____

■ Editing Test 7

See if you can locate and correct the ten sentence-skills mistakes in the following passage. The mistakes are listed in the box below. As you locate each mistake, write the number of the word group containing that mistake. Use the spaces provided. Then (on a separate piece of paper) correct the mistakes.

---

5 fragments

_____   _____   _____   _____   _____

5 comma splices

_____   _____   _____   _____   _____

Family Stories

¹When I was little, my parents invented some strange stories to explain everyday events to me, my father, for example, told me that trolls lived in our house. ²When objects such as scissors or pens were missing. ³My father would look at me and say, "The trolls took them." ⁴For years, I kept a flashlight next to my bed. ⁵Hoping to catch the trolls in the act as they carried away our possessions. ⁶Another story I still remember is my mother's explanation of pussy willows. ⁷After the fuzzy grey buds emerged in our backyard one spring. ⁸I asked Mom what they were. ⁹Pussy willows, she explained, were cats who had already lived nine lives, in this tenth life, only the tips of the cats' tails were visible to people. ¹⁰All the tails looked alike. ¹¹So that none of the cats would be jealous of the others. ¹²It was also my mother who created the legend of the birthday fairy, this fairy always knew which presents I wanted. ¹³Because my mother called up on a special invisible telephone. ¹⁴Children couldn't see these phones, every parent had a direct line to the fairy. ¹⁵My parents' stories left a great impression on me, I still feel a surge of pleasure when I think of them.

Editing Test 8

See if you can locate and correct the ten sentence-skills mistakes in the following passage. The mistakes are listed in the box below. As you locate each mistake, write the number of the word group containing that mistake. Use the spaces provided. Then (on a separate piece of paper) correct the mistakes.

<table>
<tr><td>1 fragment _____</td><td>2 missing commas between items</td></tr>
<tr><td>1 run-on _____</td><td>in a series _____ _____</td></tr>
<tr><td>1 non-standard verb _____</td><td>2 apostrophe mistakes _____</td></tr>
<tr><td>1 missing comma around</td><td>_____</td></tr>
<tr><td>an interrupter _____</td><td>1 capital letter mistake _____</td></tr>
<tr><td></td><td>1 homonym mistake _____</td></tr>
</table>

Search for Order

[1]I had an odd boss in my job as an Inventory clerk at Canadian Tire. [2]Jerrys obsessions about numbers and order were irritating bizarre and interesting. [3]Jerry, a thirty-year-old management trainee was a fanatic about details and order. [4]He seemed to think that unless he had an exact, double-checked count of everything, disasters would happen. [5]He would dig out everyones inventory sheets and sneak around the warehouse recounting as many items as he could. [6]And look for errors in there counts and figuring. [7]Other times, he would ask us to count how many markers and notebooks we had in our jackets and our lockers. [8]He would make us empty our pockets and shake out our cases. [9]Some days, I'd come upon two or three of the fellows I worked with standing at attention at their lockers I'd know Jerry was counting markers and notebooks again. [10]He were tireless in his need for perfect counts and records of everything. [11]It was a need he would never completely satisfy.

■ Editing Test 9

See if you can locate and correct the ten sentence-skills mistakes in the following passages. The mistakes are listed in the box below. As you locate each mistake, write the number of the word group containing that mistake. Use the spaces provided. Then (on a separate piece of paper) correct the mistakes.

2 fragments _____ _____	1 missing comma after
1 comma splice _____	introductory words _____
1 irregular verb mistake _____	2 apostrophe mistakes _____
1 missing comma between	_____
items in a series _____	1 faulty parallelism _____
	1 missing quotation mark _____

Franco's Funeral

¹Sometimes when Franco feels undervalued and depression, he likes to imagine his own funeral. ²He pictures all the people who will be there. ³He hears their hushed words sees their tears, and feels their grief. ⁴He glows with a warm sadness as the priest begins a eulogy by saying, Franco Corelli was no ordinary man. . . ." ⁵As the minister talks on Francos eyes grow moist. ⁶He laments his own passing and feels altogether appreciated and wonderful.

Feeding Time

⁷Recently I was at the cat house in the zoo. ⁸Right before feeding time. ⁹The tigers and lions were lying about on benches and little stands. ¹⁰Basking in the late-afternoon sun. ¹¹They seemed tame and harmless. ¹²But when the meat was brung in, a remarkable change occurred. ¹³All the cats got up and moved toward the food. ¹⁴I was suddenly aware of the rippling muscles' of their bodies and their large claws and teeth. ¹⁵They seemed three times bigger, I could feel their power.

Editing Test 10

See if you can locate and correct the ten sentence-skills mistakes in the following passage. The mistakes are listed in the box below. As you locate each mistake, write the number of the word group containing that mistake. Use the spaces provided. Then (on a separate piece of paper) correct the mistakes.

1 comma splice _____	1 missing comma between
1 mistake in subject-verb	items in a series _____
agreement _____	2 apostrophe mistakes _____
1 missing comma after	_____
introductory words _____	2 missing quotation marks
2 missing commas around an	_____ _____
interrupter _____ _____	

Walking Billboards

¹Many Canadians have turned into driving, walking billboards. ²As much as we all claim to hate commercials on television we dont seem to have any qualms about turning ourselves into commercials. ³Our car bumpers for example advertise resorts brands of sunglasses, and radio stations. ⁴Also, we wear clothes marked with other peoples initials and slogans. ⁵Our fascination with the names of designers show up on the backs of our hats, our running shoes, and our backpacks. ⁶And we wear T-shirts filled with all kinds of advertising messages. ⁷For instance, people are willing to wear shirts that read, "Dillon Construction," "Nike," or even I Got Crabs at Ed's Seafood Palace. ⁸In conclusion, we say we hate commercials, we actually pay people for the right to advertise their products.

■ **Editing Test 11**

See if you can locate and correct the ten sentence-skills mistakes in the following passage. The mistakes are listed in the box below. As you locate each mistake, write the number of the word group containing that mistake. Use the spaces provided. Then (on a separate piece of paper) correct the mistakes.

3 fragments _____ _____ _____	1 mistake in pronoun point of view _____
1 run-on _____	1 dangling modifier _____
1 comma splice _____	1 missing comma between two complete thoughts _____
1 irregular verb mistake _____	
1 faulty parallelism _____	

Too Many Cooks

¹The problem in my college cafeteria was the succession of incompetent cooks who were put in charge. ²During the time I worked there, I watched several cooks come and go. ³The first of these was Irving. ⁴He was skinny and greasy like the undercooked bacon he served for breakfast. ⁵Irving drank by late afternoon he begun to sway as he cooked. ⁶Once, he looked at the brightly coloured photograph on the orange juice machine. ⁷And asked why the TV was on. ⁸Having fired Irving, Marky was hired. ⁹Marky had a soft, round face that resembled a marshmallow but he had the size and temperament of a large bear. ¹⁰He'd wave one paw and growl if you entered the freezers without his permission. ¹¹He also had poor eyesight. ¹²This problem caused him to substitute flour for sugar and using pork for beef on a regular basis. ¹³After Marky was fired, Enzo arrived. ¹⁴Because he had come from Italy less than a year previously. ¹⁵He spoke little English. ¹⁶In addition, Enzo had trouble with seasoning and spices. ¹⁷His vegetables were too salty, giant bay leaves turned up in everything. ¹⁸Including the scrambled eggs. ¹⁹The cooks I worked for in the college cafeteria would have made any chef go into shock.

■ **Editing Test 12**

See if you can locate and correct the ten sentence-skills mistakes in the following passage. The mistakes are listed in the box below. As you locate each mistake, write the number of the word group containing that mistake. Use the spaces provided. Then (on a separate piece of paper) correct the mistakes.

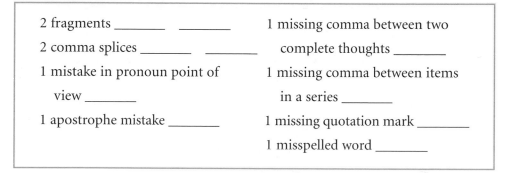

2 fragments _____ _____	1 missing comma between two
2 comma splices _____ _____	complete thoughts _____
1 mistake in pronoun point of	1 missing comma between items
view _____	in a series _____
1 apostrophe mistake _____	1 missing quotation mark _____
	1 misspelled word _____

My Ideal Date

¹Here are the ingredients for my ideal date, first of all, I would want to look as stunning as possible. ²I would be dressed in a black velvet dress. ³That would fit me like a layer of paint. ⁴My acessories would include a pair of black patent sandels a diamond hair clip, and a full-length black satin coat. ⁵My boyfriend, Gene, would wear a sharply tailored black tuxedo, a white silk shirt, and a bow tie. ⁶The tux would emphasize Gene's broad shoulders and narrow waist, and you would see his chest muscles under the smooth shirt fabric. ⁷Gene would pull up to my house in a long, shiny limousine, then the driver would take us to the most exclusive club in Vancouver. ⁸All eyes would be on us as we entered and photographers would rush up to take our picture for *The Sun*. ⁹As we danced on the lighted floor of the club, everyone would step aside to watch us perform our moves. ¹⁰After several bottles of champagne, Gene and I would head for an intimate restaurant on Granville Island. ¹¹As we gazed out over the lights' of the city, Gene would hand me a small velvet box containing a ten-carat ruby engagement ring. ¹²And ask me to marry him. ¹³I would thank Gene for a lovely evening and tell him gently, "Gene, I don't plan to marry until I'm thirty.

*xplaining a Process • Examining Cause and Effect • Comparing or Contrasting • Defini
erm • Dividing and Classifying • Describing a Scene or Person • Narrating an Event • Arg
Position • Explaining a Process • Examining Cause and Effect • Comparing or Contrasti
efining a Term • Dividing and Classifying • Describing a Scene or Person • Narratin
vent • Arguing a Position • Explaining a Process • Examining Cause and Effect • Compa

C H A P T E R   4 4

Sentence-Skills Achievement Test

PART 1

This test will help you measure your improvement in important sentence skills. Certain parts of the following word groups are underlined. Write *X* in the answer space if you think a mistake appears at the underlined part. Write *C* in the answer space if you think the underlined part is correct.

The headings ("Faulty Parallelism," "Consistent Verb Tense," and so on) will give you clues to the mistakes to look for.

Faulty Parallelism

_____ 1. Much of my boyhood was devoted to getting into rock fights, crossing railway trestles, and the <u>hunt for rats in drainage tunnels</u>.

_____ 2. I put my books in my locker, changed into my gym clothes, and <u>hurried to the playing field</u>.

_____ 3. Ruth begins every day with warm-up exercises, a half-hour run, and <u>taking a hot shower</u>.

_____ 4. In the evening I plan to write a paper, <u>watch a movie</u>, and read two chapters in my biology text.

Consistent Verb Tense

_____ 5. Kyra wanted to watch the late movie, but she was so tired she <u>falls</u> asleep before it started.

_____ 6. When the mail carrier arrived, I <u>hoped</u> the latest issue of *Spin* magazine would be in her bag.

_____ 7. Michelle ran down the hall without looking and <u>trips</u> over the toy truck sitting on the floor.

_____   8. Debbie enjoys riding her bike in the newly built park, which <u>features a</u> special path for bikers and runners.

Pronoun Point of View

_____   9. At the Saturday afternoon movie we went to, children were making so much noise that <u>you</u> could not relax.

_____   10. Tom installed so much software that <u>you</u> could do almost anything on his computer.

_____   11. When students start cooking courses, <u>they</u> tend to forget about cleaning up.

Fragments

_____   12. <u>After a careless driver hit my motorcycle, I decided to buy a car.</u> At least I would have more protection against other careless drivers.

_____   13. I was never a good student in high school. <u>Because I spent all my time socializing with my group of friends.</u> Good grades were not something that my group really valued.

_____   14. The elderly couple in the supermarket were not a pleasant sight. <u>Arguing with each other.</u> People pretended not to notice them.

_____   15. <u>Using a magnifying glass, the little girls burned holes in the dry leaf.</u> They then set some tissue paper on fire.

_____   16. My brother and I seldom have fights about what to watch on television. <u>Except with baseball games.</u> I get bored watching this sport.

_____   17. My roommate and I ate, talked, danced, and sang at a party the other night. <u>Also, we played cards until 3 a.m.</u> As a result, we both slept until noon the next day.

Run-ons and Comma Splices

_____   18. She decided to quit her high-pressure <u>job, she</u> didn't want to develop heart trouble.

_____   19. His car's wheels were not balanced <u>properly, for</u> the car began to shake when he drove over sixty kilometres an hour.

_____   20. I got through the interview without breaking out in a sweat <u>moustache I</u> also managed to keep my voice under control.

_____   21. The craze for convenience in North America has gone too <u>far. There</u> are drive-in banks, restaurants, and even churches.

_____   22. My most valued possession is my <u>crockpot, I</u> can make entire meals in it at a low cost.

_____   23. The shopping carts outside the supermarket seemed welded <u>together Rita</u> could not separate one from another.

Irregular Verbs

_____ 24. I learned that Dennis had <u>began</u> to see someone else while he was still going out with me.

_____ 25. That woman has never <u>ran</u> for political office before.

_____ 26. I <u>knowed</u> the answer to the question, but I was too nervous to think of it when the instructor called on me.

_____ 27. They had <u>ate</u> the gallon of natural vanilla ice cream in just one night.

Subject-Verb Agreement

_____ 28. Her watchband <u>have</u> to be fixed.

_____ 29. There <u>is</u> two minutes left in the hockey game.

_____ 30. He believes films that feature violence <u>is</u> a disgrace to our society.

_____ 31. The slipcovers that she bought <u>have</u> begun to fray.

Pronoun Agreement and Reference

_____ 32. We did not return to the amusement park, for <u>we</u> had to pay too much for the rides and meals.

_____ 33. Drivers should check the oil level in <u>their</u> cars every three months.

_____ 34. In the hall outside the exam room, I saw a student and his friends frantically thumbing through their textbooks, hoping <u>he</u> would find the answers.

_____ 35. Sharon's mother was overjoyed when <u>she</u> became pregnant.

_____ 36. You must observe all the rules of the game, even if you do not always agree with <u>it</u>.

Pronoun Types

_____ 37. Nancy and <u>her</u> often go to swing music bars.

_____ 38. No one in the class is better at computers than <u>he</u>.

Adjectives and Adverbs

_____ 39. The little girl spoke so <u>quiet</u> I could hardly hear her.

_____ 40. Kerry looks <u>more better</u> than Gina in a leather coat.

Misplaced Modifiers

_____ 41. I saw sharks <u>scuba-diving</u>.

_____ 42. <u>With a mile-wide grin</u>, Jessica turned in her winning lottery ticket.

_____ 43. I bought a beautiful blouse in a local store with <u>long sleeves and French cuffs</u>.

_____ 44. I first spotted the turtle <u>playing tag on the back lawn</u>.

Dangling Modifiers

_____ 45. <u>When seven years old</u>, Jeff's father taught him to play ball.

_____ 46. <u>Running across the field</u>, I caught the Frisbee.

_____ 47. <u>Turning on the ignition</u>, the car backfired.

_____ 48. <u>Looking at my watch</u>, a taxi nearly ran me over.

Capital Letters

_____ 49. When the can of <u>drano</u> didn't unclog the sink, Rob called a plumber.

_____ 50. I asked Bonita, "<u>what</u> time will you be leaving?"

_____ 51. I have to get an allergy shot once a <u>Week</u>.

_____ 52. Mother ordered the raincoat online on <u>Monday</u>, and it arrived four days later.

Apostrophe

_____ 53. I asked the clerk if the store had <u>Nickelbacks</u> latest CD.

_____ 54. <u>He's</u> failing the course because he doesn't have any confidence in his ability to do the work.

_____ 55. David was incensed at the dentist who charged him fifty dollars to fix his <u>son's</u> tooth.

_____ 56. I <u>cant</u> believe that she's not coming to the dance.

Quotation Marks

_____ 57. <u>"Don't forget to water the grass, my sister said</u>.

_____ 58. June said to Ward at bedtime, "Why is it that men's pyjamas always have such baggy <u>bottoms?" "You</u> look like a circus clown in that flannel outfit."

_____ 59. The red sign on the door <u>read, "Warning</u>—open only in case of an emergency."

_____ 60. "I can't stand that commercial," said Sue. "<u>Do you mind if I turn off the television?</u>"

Comma

_____ 61. Hard-luck Sam needs a <u>loan, a well-paying job, and</u> someone to show an interest in him.

_____ 62. Even though I was <u>tired I</u> agreed to go shopping with my parents.

_____ 63. <u>Power, not love or money, is</u> what most politicians want.

_____ 64. The heel on one of Halina's shoes came <u>off, so</u> she spent the day walking barefoot.

_____ 65. "Thank goodness I'm almost <u>done</u>" I said aloud with every stroke of the broom.

_____ 66. I hated to ask <u>Anita who is a very stingy person</u> to lend me the money.

Commonly Confused Words

_____ 67. To succeed in the job, you must learn how to control <u>your</u> temper.

_____ 68. Fortunately, I was not driving very fast when my car lost <u>it's</u> brakes.

_____ 69. Put your packages on the table over <u>their.</u>

_____ 70. There are <u>too</u> many steps in the math formula for me to understand it.

_____ 71. The counselling centre can <u>advise</u> you on how to prepare for an interview.

_____ 72. <u>Who's</u> white Lexus is that in front of the house?

Effective Word Use

_____ 73. The teacher called to discuss Ron's <u>social maladjustment difficulties.</u>

_____ 74. I thought the course would be a <u>piece of cake</u>, but a ten-page essay was required.

_____ 75. When my last class ended, I felt <u>as free as a bird.</u>

_____ 76. Spike gave away his television <u>owing to the fact that</u> it distracted him from studying.

PART 2 (OPTIONAL)

Do Part 2 at your instructor's request. This second part of the test will provide more detailed information about your improvement in sentence skills. On a separate piece of paper, number and correct all the items in this chapter that you have marked with an *X*. For example, suppose you had marked the word groups below with an *X*. (Note that these examples are not taken from the test.)

4. <u>If baseball games disappeared entirely from television.</u> I would not even miss them. Other people in my family would perish.

7. The kitten suddenly saw her reflection in the <u>mirror, she</u> jumped back in surprise.

15. The tree in my <u>cousins</u> front yard always sheds its leaves two weeks before others on the street.

29. When we go out to a <u>restaurant we</u> always order something we would not cook for ourselves.

Here is how you should write your corrections on a separate sheet of paper.

4. television, I

7. mirror, and she

15. cousin's

29. restaurant, we

There are over forty corrections to make in all.

Visit the *English Skills with Readings* Online Learning Centre at **www.mcgrawhill.ca/college/langan** to access self-quizzes, bonus material on study and research skills, web resources, and other learning and study tools.

Fifteen
Reading Selections

PREVIEW

This book assumes that writing and reading are closely connected skills, so that practising one helps the other and neglecting one hurts the other. Section Five will enable you to work on becoming a better reader as well as a stronger writer. Following an introductory section that offers a series of tips on effective reading, there are fifteen reading selections. Each selection begins with a preview that supplies background information about the piece. After the selection are ten questions to give you practice in key reading comprehension skills. A set of discussion questions is also provided, both to deepen your understanding of the selection and to point out basic writing techniques used in the essay. Then come several writing assignments, along with guidelines to help you think about the assignments and get started working on them.

Introduction to the Readings

You will find fifteen readings in Section Five: they are presented for you to enjoy and to help you find topics for writing. These selections deal in various ways with interesting, often thought-provoking concerns or experiences of contemporary life. Subjects of the essays and articles include the creation of virtual communities, raising children with ethical standards, shopping as a genetically encoded trait, the damage done by bullying, and the challenge of managing anxiety. Readings about our values offer a new way of looking at mild depression, one writer's thoughts about charity, and a lighthearted look at our urban animal companions. Selections on the subject of education present useful, direct information about how to study more efficiently, how to write a test, how to write clearly, and how to decide on a career. The final set of readings look outward at various Canadian communities and interests; some of these selections are humorous, such as Tony Wong's consideration of his lack of mathematical ability or Joe Fiorito's musings on Canadian culture and Canadian refrigerator contents. All selections are quite current and most are Canadian. All should inspire lively class discussions as well as some individual thought. The selections should also provide interesting material for a wide range of writing assignments.

The selections serve another purpose as well. They will help develop reading skills, with direct benefits to you as a writer. First, through close reading, you will learn how to recognize the thesis or point of a selection and how to identify and evaluate the supporting material that develops the thesis. In your writing, you will aim to achieve the same essential structure: an overall thesis followed by detailed and valid support for that point. Second, close reading will help you explore a selection and its possibilities thoroughly. The more you understand about what is said in a piece, the more ideas and feelings you may have about writing on an assigned topic or a related topic of your own. A third benefit of close reading is becoming more aware of authors' stylistic devices—for example, their introductions and conclusions, their ways of presenting and developing a point, their use of transitions, and their choice of language to achieve a particular tone. Recognizing these devices in other people's writing will help you enlarge your own range of writing techniques.

THE FORMAT OF EACH SELECTION

Each selection begins with a short overview that gives helpful background information as well as a brief idea of the topic of the reading. The selection is then followed by two sets of questions.

- First, there are ten reading comprehension questions to help you measure your understanding of the material. These questions involve several important reading skills: recognizing a subject or topic, determining the thesis or main idea, identifying key supporting points, making inferences, and understanding vocabulary in context. Answering the questions will enable you and your instructor to check your basic understanding of a selection quickly. More significantly, as you move from one selection to the next, you will sharpen your reading skills as well as strengthening your thinking skills— two key factors in making you a better writer.
- Following the comprehension questions are several discussion questions. In addition to dealing with issues of content, these questions focus on matters of structure, style, and tone. *Structure* refers to the ways in which the author has given shape to the work; *style* refers to word choice and the technical skills used by the writer; and *tone* is the "feeling" of a piece of work: whether it is serious, light, or comic.

The assignments range from personal narratives to expository and persuasive essays about issues in Canada and the world at large. Many assignments provide detailed guidelines on how to proceed, including suggestions for prewriting and appropriate methods of development. A number of new essay assignments require the use of Internet research. When writing your paragraph and essay responses to the readings, you will have opportunities to apply all the methods of development presented in Section Two as well.

HOW TO READ WELL: FOUR GENERAL STEPS

Skilful reading is an important part of becoming a skilful writer. Following are four steps that will make you a better reader—both of the selections here and in your reading at large.

1 Concentrate as You Read

To improve your concentration, follow these tips.

- First, read in a place where you can be quiet and alone. Don't choose a spot where a TV or stereo is on or where friends or family are talking nearby.
- Next, sit in an upright position when you read. If your body is in a completely relaxed position, sprawled across a bed or nestled in an easy chair, your mind is also going to be completely relaxed. The light muscular tension that comes from sitting in an upright chair promotes concentration and keeps your mind ready to work.
- Finally, consider using your index finger (or a pen) as a pacer while you read. Lightly underline each line of print with your index finger as you read down a page. Hold your hand slightly above the page and move your finger at a speed that is a little too fast for comfort. This pacing with your index finger, like sitting upright on a chair, creates a slight physical tension that will keep your body and mind focused and alert.

2 Skim Material Before You Read It

In skimming, you spend about two minutes rapidly surveying a selection, looking for important points and skipping secondary material. Follow this sequence when skimming:

- Begin by reading the overview that precedes the selection.
- Then study the title of the selection for a few moments. A good title is the shortest possible summary of a selection; it often tells you in several words what a selection is about. For example, the title "Welcome to the Matrix" suggests that you're going to read about an alternative world because of its reference to the *Matrix* movies.
- Next, form a basic question (or questions) out of the title. For instance, for the selection titled "Welcome to the Matrix," you might ask, "What exactly does the author mean by 'the Matrix'? Is he referring to the movie? If so, what is his reason for referring to *The Matrix*? Is the event he is writing about like the movie's world?" Forming questions out of the title is often a key to locating a writer's main idea—your next concern in skimming.
- Read the first two or three paragraphs and the last two or three paragraphs in the selection. Very often a writer's main idea, *if* it is directly stated, will appear in one of these paragraphs and will relate to the title. For instance,

in "Why Should We Hire You?" the author states in the final paragraph, "You need to work hard in order to find the work you desire. That means knowing the reasons you should be hired and taking the steps needed to prepare a solidly based answer before you are asked The Question."

- Finally, look quickly at the rest of the selection for other clues to important points. Are there any subheadings you can relate in some way to the title? Are there any words the author has decided to emphasize by setting them off in *italic* or **boldface** type? Are there any major lists of items signalled by words such as *first, second, also, another*, and so on?

3 Read the Selection Straight Through with a Pen Nearby

Read the selection without slowing down or turning back; just aim to understand as much as you can the first time through. Place a check or star beside answers to basic questions you formed from the title and beside other ideas that seem important. Number the important points *1, 2, 3*, and so on. Circle words you don't understand. Put question marks in the margin next to passages that are unclear and that you will want to reread.

4 Work with the Material

Now go back and reread passages that were not clear the first time through. Look up words that block your understanding of ideas and write their meanings in the margin. Also, reread carefully the areas you identified as most important; doing so will enlarge your understanding of the material. Now that you have a sense of the whole, prepare a short outline of the selection by answering the following questions on a sheet of paper:

- What is the thesis?
- What key points support the thesis?
- What seem to be other important points in the selection?

By working with the material in this way, you will significantly increase your understanding of a selection. *Effective reading, just like effective writing, does not happen all at once.* Rather, it is a *process*. Often you begin with a general impression of what something means, and then, by working at it, you move to a deeper level of understanding of the material.

How to Answer the Comprehension Questions: Specific Hints

Several important reading skills are involved in the ten reading comprehension questions that follow each selection. The skills are:

- Summarizing the selection by providing a title for it
- Determining the main idea
- Recognizing key supporting details
- Making inferences
- Understanding vocabulary in context

The following hints will help you apply each of these reading skills:

- **_Subject or title._** Remember that the title should accurately describe the _entire_ selection. It should be neither too broad nor too narrow for the material in the selection. It should answer the question "What is this about?" as specifically as possible. Note that you may at times find it easier to answer the "title" question _after_ the "main idea" question.
- **_Main idea._** Choose the statement that you think best expresses the main idea or thesis of the entire selection. Remember that the title will often help you focus on the main idea. Then ask yourself, "Does most of the material in the selection support this statement?" If you can answer yes to this question, you have found the thesis.
- **_Key details._** If you were asked to give a two-minute summary of a selection, the major details would be the ones you would include in that summary. To determine the key details, ask yourself, "What are the major supporting points for the thesis?"
- **_Inferences._** Answer these questions by drawing on the evidence presented in the selection and on your own common sense. Ask yourself, "What reasonable judgments can I make on the basis of the information in the selection?"
- **_Vocabulary in context._** To decide on the meaning of an unfamiliar word, consider its context. Ask yourself, "Are there any clues in the sentence that suggest what this word means?"

On page 603 is a chart on which you can keep track of your performance as you answer the ten questions for each selection. The chart will help you identify reading skills you may need to strengthen.

Explaining a Process • Examining Cause and Effect • Comparing or Contrasting • Defin
Term • Dividing and Classifying • Describing a Scene or Person • Narrating an Event • Arg
a Position • Explaining a Process • Examining Cause and Effect • Comparing or Contrast
Defining a Term • Dividing and Classifying • Describing a Scene or Person • Narratin
Event • Arguing a Position • Explaining a Process • Examining Cause and Effect • Comp

Knowing Ourselves and Our Values

LETTER

Judith MacKenzie

In all of our lives, there have been times when we survived some difficult situation not because of our own efforts or toughness but because of the kindness, grace, or generosity of others. There are also times in our lives when we are privileged to be able to help others. Both giving and receiving such generosity are our finest moments as humans: the "gift" gives to both giver and receiver endlessly. This "mystery" that is "charity" is the essence of human goodness. Sometimes highly publicized, it also occurs unnoted every day; in fact, it is often overlooked or dismissed by those too cynical to believe in it, or by those who see only the arithmetic of "give something; get something in return." In "Letter," Judith MacKenzie contemplates two intertwined personal experiences with the mysterious and life-enriching nature of charity in action.

When I was eight years old, my father, a union organizer in the forties and fifties, was blacklisted, accused of communist activities. It meant no work—with a vengeance. My mother, then in her forties, had twin boys that spring—premature, and in premedicare times you can imagine the devastating costs for their care. I was hungry that year, hungry when I got up, hungry when I went to school, hungry when I went to sleep. In November I was asked to leave school because I only had boys' clothes to wear—hand-me-downs from a neighbour. I could come back, they said, when I dressed like a young lady. 1

The week before Christmas, the power and gas were disconnected. We ate soup made from carrots, potatoes, cabbage and grain meant to feed chickens, cooked on our wood garbage burner. Even as an eight-year-old, I knew the kind of hunger we had was nothing compared to people in India and Africa. I don't think we could have died in our middle-class Vancouver suburb. But I do know that the pain of hunger 2 is intensified and brutal when you live in the midst of plenty. As Christmas preparations increased, I felt more and more isolated, excluded, set apart. I felt a deep, abiding hunger for more than food. Christmas Eve day came, grey and full of the bleak sleety rain of a west-coast winter. Two women, strangers, struggled up our driveway, loaded down with bags. They left before my mother answered the door. The porch was full of groceries—milk, butter, bread, cheese and Christmas oranges. We never knew who they were, and after that day, pride being what it was, we never spoke of them again. But I'm forty-five years old, and I remember them well.

Since then I've crafted a life of joy and independence, if not of financial security. Several years ago, living in Victoria, my son and I were walking up the street, once more in west-coast sleet and rain. It was just before Christmas and we were, as usual, counting our pennies to see if we'd have enough for all our festive treats, juggling these against the necessities. A young man stepped in front of me, very pale and carrying an old sleeping bag, and asked for spare change—not unusual in downtown Victoria. No, I said, and walked on. Something hit me like a physical blow about a block later. I left my son and walked back to find the young man. I gave him some of our Christmas luxury money—folded into a small square and tucked into his hand. It wasn't much, only ten dollars, but as I turned away, I saw the look of hopelessness turn into amazement and then joy. Well, said the rational part of my mind, Judith, you are a fool, you know he's just going up the street to the King's Hotel and spend it on drink or drugs. You've taken what belongs to your family and spent it on a frivolous romantic impulse. As I was lecturing myself on gullibility and sensible charity, I noticed the young man with the sleeping bag walking quickly up the opposite side of the street, heading straight for the King's. Well, let this be a lesson, said the rational Judith. To really rub it in, I decided to follow him. Just before the King's, he turned into a corner grocery store. I watched through the window, through the poinsettias and the stand-up Santas. I watched him buy milk, butter, bread, cheese and Christmas oranges. 3

Now, I have no idea how that young man arrived on the street in Victoria, nor will I ever have any real grasp of the events that had led my family to a dark and hungry December. But I do know that charity cannot be treated as an RRSP. There is no best-investment way to give, no way to insure value for our dollar. Like the Magi, these three, the two older women struggling up the driveway and the young man with the sleeping bag, gave me, and continue to give me, wonderful gifts— the reminder that love and charity come most truly and abundantly from an open and unjudgemental heart. 4

■ **Reading Comprehension Questions**

1. Which of the following would be the best alternative title for the selection?
    a. Christmas Gifts
    b. Giving Is the Best Gift of All
    c. Charity Begins at Home
    d. Lessons in Life

2. Which sentence best expresses the main idea of the selection?
    a. Learning to give is a lifelong process.

   b. People never really know the suffering of others.

   c. Memories of generosity can make us generous.

   d. Giving freely rewards both giver and receiver.

3. At age eight the author felt her family's situation most acutely when

   a. she was constantly hungry and was not allowed to go to school.

   b. she realized there would be no Christmas gifts.

   c. her family was so poor they had to take handouts.

   d. she was embarrassed by the women bringing food.

4. *True or false?* _____ The author and her son were no better off than her family was during her childhood.

5. The author argues with herself about giving the young street person money because

   a. she resented people begging on the street.

   b. her past had made her prone to giving in to foolish impulses.

   c. she wanted to be logical and sensible, but remembered her own past.

   d. she was ashamed of looking stingy in front of her son.

6. The author implies that

   a. she was ashamed of wearing boys' clothes to school.

   b. school regulations of the time were cruel and unreasonable.

   c. wearing used "charity" clothes was painful to her.

   d. she enjoyed dressing like a "tomboy."

7. The author implies that the worst part of being hungry was

   a. the awfulness of eating food cooked on a garbage burner.

   b. her shame at starving like people in Third World countries.

   c. that the family's health was at risk because of their poor diet.

   d. feeling set apart by their deprivation in the midst of a comfortable society.

8. From the selection, we can infer that the author feels that

   a. sometimes our best actions are impulsive, rather than rational.

   b. we never understand the situations in which we find ourselves.

   c. the best gifts are those we give away.

   d. we should do without to learn the true meaning of charity.

9. The word *abiding* in "I felt a deep, abiding hunger for more than food" (paragraph 2) means

   a. gnawing.

   b. annoying.

   c. enduring.

   d. grinding.

10. The word *gullibility* in "As I was lecturing myself on gullibility and sensible charity" (paragraph 3) means

    a. stupidity.

    b. naïveté.

    c. practicality.

    d. generosity.

■ **Discussion Questions**

About Content

1. What were the reasons for the author's family's poverty during her childhood? Why was there "no work—with a vengeance" (paragraph 1) for her father?

2. Why, as Christmas approached, did the author feel a "hunger for more than food" (paragraph 2)?

3. What specific elements of the setting, the characters, and their actions make the visit of the women to the family so magical and unexpected?

4. What are the author's reasons for saying to herself in paragraph 3, "Judith, you are a fool," and what is she "rub[bing] in" as she follows the young man?

About Structure

5. "Letter" is primarily a narrative selection, and generally a brief narrative covers only a single event. However, two situations are narrated in "Letter" rather than one. Why might MacKenzie have decided to include two events?

6. Where in the selection do you find the best statement of the author's thesis? Write the sentence(s) in the space below:

    _____

    _____

    Why has MacKenzie chosen this position for her thesis?

7. Narratives are mostly structured in *time order*. "Letter" uses transitional words and phrases to "set the stage" for each paragraph. List words and phrases that show readers when each paragraph occurs:

    a. _____

    b. _____

    c. _____

    d. _____

About Style and Tone

8. The author offers several parallel elements, as well as some elements that differ, in the two major "scenes" of her narrative. Which elements are similar in the two situations, and which are different? What is achieved by the parallels and differences?

9. "Letter" is perhaps an odd title for an essay. Why do you think MacKenzie chose this title? One element common to good personal letters and this selection is the inclusion of finely drawn details, probably aimed at evoking an emotional response. Which two of the selection's details do you find most effective, and why?

■ **Writing Assignments**

Assignment 1: Writing a Paragraph

An assignment based on this selection appears on page 260.

Assignment 2: Writing a Paragraph

Some ancient cultures believed that beggars must always be treated kindly because they might be gods in disguise. Judith MacKenzie's reaction to the street person in Victoria is probably typical of most people in today's cities: she feels torn between reason, cynicism, and sympathy. What is your reaction to being approached by one of the growing number of homeless people in Canadian cities? What would you say to someone like the young man in "Letter"?

Write a paragraph in the form of a letter, either to the person in MacKenzie's essay or to a real person who has approached you for a handout. What would you give such a person, either as advice or as direct help, or as both? Why?

Assignment 3: Writing an Essay

Charity, or unselfish, active love for fellow humans, is held as the highest good by most of the world's cultures and religions. Indeed, in classical Judaism, the best form of charity is that where the receiver never knows the giver. Not all charity is public or even acknowledged by others. In our society, there are many types of charity, from well-publicized corporate, tax-deductible donations to the personal gift of one's time and energy to help another person.

What, to you, is the finest form of charity, and why? In an essay that explains its point with examples, discuss why one specific type of generosity is most beneficial. Think of people who exemplify human generosity or charity, or of several instances of a single person's generosity; think of situations where someone or some group of people acted unselfishly for another's good; such self-questioning will lead you to the specific and well-explained examples you need to argue your point of view.

HERE'S TO A LONG AND UNHAPPY LIFE

Lisa Gabriele

In many cultures, old age is associated with calmness and wisdom. In Lisa Gabriele's case, old age means cranky behaviour and complaining; apparently, for women, these are essentials for a long life. Mild depression and associated behaviours, however unpleasant, may be a kind of safety valve that works as a release and an escape from major sources of stress. How often does each of us, female or male, use this defence mechanism without realizing it? Perhaps we should reconsider our reactions next time we visit a bad-natured elderly woman relative—crankiness may be her lifeline.

Last week, a bunch of people forwarded to me a copy of a study done on older   1
women and longevity. It found that those who were mildly, though markedly,
depressed tended to live longer. Big surprise, I thought, tossing the balled-up clip-
ping over my shoulder. That's up there with "money eases stress," "liars make good
writers" and "philanderers make even better liars." (On the other hand, researchers
found that depression had no influence on the mortality of men. That's because
when asked "So, what's wrong?" all the men circled "Nothing", really, really hard.)

Most of us know an old aunt, a lonely grandmother, or a widowed neighbour-   2
lady who's a little depressed about life. Maybe we'd spend more time with them if
they'd just stop complaining about their backs, the noise, their pensions, the pollution, all these foreigners. Sometimes we tune out their depression, thinking, I
cannot believe she is still around, this Energizer Bunny in support hose.

My own nana finally died after suffering for decades from strokes and diabetes.   3
For the last 10 years of her life, she sat paralyzed in an adult diaper on the chronic-
care floor of an excellent hospital. She was almost 100 years old, and for most of
this century, she was pretty much happy about pretty much nothing. My spry, per-
petually young mother visited her often, more often than we did, her churlish
grandkids. Poor Nana bitched constantly, and sank sullenly into her own shoulders every time we asked her how she was doing. Terrible, she'd say. How do you
think I'm doing?

Who can blame her? Two World Wars, the Depression, a long marriage to a dif-   4
ficult man, children accidentally born to her in her forties, during the Forties. At
the end of her harrowing life, to wind up sharing a room with bawling strangers,
baring her withered body to impatient nurses for tepid sponge baths would render any Pollyanna somewhat depressed, no?

But we all agreed that sparring with us, and nurses, kept Nana alert, treacly   5
soap operas kept her agitated, and the absence of her ungrateful, lazy grandkids
kept her permanently dissatisfied. Things that caused her to sigh heavily depressed
her, yes, but they also kept her wilfully (woefully) alive.

When my mother would return from one of her exhausting visits, she'd always   6
say she never, ever wanted to grow old like Nana. Last year, she sadly got her wish,
far too soon, living just over half as long as the woman who bore her.

It is no coincidence that my mother worked as a private, uncomplaining nurse   7
for old, depressive ladies. But she loved her job, loved caring for those sick, deflated
people. Loved making their grey, bleak lives a little cheerier. She'd throw up their
dusty blinds, fluff their musty pillows, serve their canned fruit cocktail, read to
them, iron for them, and try her best to cheer them up. Her last client, an elegant,
whiny, rich lady, still alive in her early nineties, did not send flowers to my mother's
funeral. My mother was devoted to this woman, so my nickname for her became
"That Miserable Old Bitch."

In *The Corrections*, author Jonathan Franzen superbly captures the stamina of   8
these mildly depressed old ladies. His main character, Enid Lambert, suffers from
a depression that acts as a kind of invisible force field, unconsciously repelling
everyone away from her fragile core. Enid complains and sulks, manipulates and
cajoles, in order to assuage her fundamental dissatisfaction. Many chapters later,
most around her fall like diseased trees. Enid, however, picks up her skirts, and tip-
toes around the proverbial corpses. Enid survives—thrives even. She remains intact

because her depression protects her from ever truly suffering, the way those around her must. What doesn't kill you, it seems, moves on to more stubborn quarry.

9   Contrast Enid with young Lily Bart from Edith Wharton's *House of Mirth*. Lily is stoic, idealistic, and intrepid. She complains about nothing and accepts her lot in life as fate. Lily dies broke and alone at thirtysomething. If only she could have collapsed into her sadness, she might have died broke and alone at eightysomething.

10   So, hit the snooze, the bottle or the skids. Resume bitching, chin down, carry the hatchet, under rug nothing. Life is hard and then you ... sigh. Heavily. And frankly, this comes as a relief to me. I've never pictured myself living in a candy-coloured retirement villa, wearing skorts, cheerfully participating in activities, embarking on a late-in-life spiritual awakening. I always saw myself in a ratty lawn chair, frowning amidst overgrown crabgrass, a small rifle propped up against the armrest to keep racoons away from my sweet, old cats. I am possibly chewing tobacco, and complaining, to my grown daughter, or her husband, or whoever the hell picked up the phone, about my own lazy-ass husband, or whoever the hell's making all that bloody noise down in the basement. So goodbye beta blockers, nicotine gum, and yoga. This the first day of the rest of my miserable, long, life.

■ **Reading Comprehension Questions**

1. Which of the following would make the best alternative title for the selection?
   a. Survival Is a Nasty Business
   b. The Misery of Retirement Homes
   c. Depression Is a Woman's Best Defence
   d. Grandmothers, Mothers, and Daughters

2. Which sentence best expresses the selection's main point?
   a. Low-level depression seems to distract women from stresses that could shorten their lives.
   b. Grandmothers of the last few generations led very hard lives, so they had reason to complain.
   c. Caring for an elderly parent is dangerously stressful.
   d. Depression is not as dangerous or serious as people believe it to be.

3. The author suggests that complaining elders
   a. should be dealt with by tuning them out.
   b. tend to be unpleasant to visit.
   c. are sad and lonely.
   d. all talk about the same things.

4. *True or false?* _____ The main problem that the author's grandmother endured was the poor quality of the care facility where she lived.

5. Gabriele feels that her grandmother
   a. had a loving family and no real reason to be depressed.
   b. was depressed because she did not live with her family.

    c. was depressed because she had to share a room and had unpleasant
       nurses.

    d. had led a difficult life whose circumstances were depressing.

6. We can conclude that the author's mother
    a. worked hard and endured exactly the type of stress that the grandmother
       avoided.
    b. was a saint who selflessly sacrificed herself for her own mother.
    c. worked at a demanding and draining job because she had a death wish.
    d. was treated badly by all her elderly patients.

7. The author's fundamental recommendation to her female readers who want
to live longer lives is to
    a. drink heavily, smoke, and carry weapons.
    b. reserve a space in a care facility as soon as possible.
    c. stop suffering in silence and internalizing stress.
    d. sit in their backyards, acquire cats, and offend others.

8. We can infer from most of the examples provided by the author that
    a. women work far harder than people realize.
    b. caring for others leads to fulfillment in life.
    c. only the good die young.
    d. suffering and suppressing strong emotion are destructive.

9. The word *philanderers* in "philanderers make even better liars" (paragraph 1)
means
    a. writers.
    b. researchers.
    c. adulterers.
    d. women.

10. The word *tepid* in "tepid sponge baths" (paragraph 4) means
    a. chilly.
    b. lukewarm.
    c. scalding.
    d. unsatisfying.

■ Discussion Questions

About Content

1. According to paragraph 1 of this selection, what is the source for the
author's article? What is Gabriele's reaction to this information? Why does
she react this way?

2. Does the author believe that her grandmother's unhappiness may have been
justified? Why or why not?

3. What seems contradictory about the feelings and behaviours that the
author's grandmother demonstrated in her last ten years?

4. How do details provided about Gabriele's grandmother contrast with details that portray the author's mother?

About Structure

5. In which paragraph does Gabriele move from her more general introduction into her first specific example? How many paragraphs are devoted to this first example? Which paragraph serves as a transitional paragraph to Gabriele's second example?

6. Where do you find a transition that indicates the author's use of comparison or contrast structure? In what specific details does the example following this transition differ from the character example of the previous paragraph? Where else in the selection do you find evidence of the comparison or contrast method of development?

7. What concluding transitional word opens the final paragraph? In which ways does this paragraph return to the character and content of the opening paragraph?

About Style and Tone

8. Which words and phrases do you find most effective in the author's descriptions of the people she includes in the selection? Why?

9. How does Gabriele shift the tone of her article in paragraph 3? What in the content leads her to change her tone? Where else in the selection do you find a marked change of tone? How successful, in both cases, is the author in using this mixture of comic and serious tones?

10. Two examples in this selection are from novels that some of the audience may not have read. How successful is the author in using these examples? Do they further explain and clarify her thesis?

■ Writing Assignments

Assignment 1: Writing a Paragraph

Stress is unavoidable, unpleasant, and, according to some, essential to provoking us into action sometimes. Write a paragraph about one of the most stressful experiences in your life. To select an experience to write about, try asking yourself these three sets of questions:

- ■ Which situations or experiences stand out in my mind as very stressful?

- ■ What specific aspects of these experiences stand out in my mind as causes of stress for me? Did interactions with others increase my stress?

- ■ What were the results of my feeling such stress? How did I react to it? Did I learn something from the experience?

To get started, do a second stage in your prewriting. Use freewriting to add to the answers you noted for the questions above. Your goal in freewriting is to help you remember specific details, and to record these as accurately as possible.

When you are ready to write a first draft, consider a topic sentence like one of the following:

> A small event during recess in grade six caused me more stress than anything I have had to face since then.

> Leaving my daughter in daycare for the first time was the most stressful thing I have ever done.

Use concrete, specific details—actions, descriptions of emotions, situations, and people—to help your readers see what caused your stress and how it felt.

Assignment 2: Writing a Paragraph

Apparently, Lisa Gabriele's grandmother mastered the art of annoying people. Many of us are still amateurs at this art but manage to be annoying sometimes anyway. Mastering anything requires learning its fine points, and some practice as well.

Write a process paragraph in which you instruct your readers on how to annoy people. First, think of a situation where you have been annoyed by someone or know how to be annoying yourself: is it a classroom, a lineup somewhere, a movie theatre, or some other ordinary situation? Make a list of situations where you have either seen someone causing annoyance or caused annoyance yourself. Once you have chosen the situation which stands out most for you, think about what the person causing the irritation did (even if you were that person). Break his or her actions, attitude, and words into stages, noting the results of each stage. Now, consider who your most likely audience would be. Who might want to learn your lesson: classmates, shoppers, moviegoers? Teach them the benefits, comic or serious, of annoying others in the specific situation you have selected.

Assignment 3: Writing an Essay

People deal with life's challenges by using many kinds of adaptive and self-protective techniques. Gabriele's grandmother discovered one that worked for her—accepting her unhappiness and giving vent to it. Think about one person of any age whom you know well. What personal quality or characteristic defines this person for you? Do you know someone who is flexible and willing to adapt to circumstances easily? Do you have a relative or friend whose cheerfulness or optimism colours everything he or she does? Or perhaps you, like the author of this selection, know a chronic complainer who finds fault with nearly everything. Choose a person who consistently displays a particular quality as your essay's subject.

Write an essay in which you define the quality or characteristic you see in this person, and provide three main examples that illustrate this quality. In preparation for writing, think of key moments in this person's life when he or she displayed this characteristic. List as many details about these key moments as you can, details that will clarify your definition for readers. Your thesis statement should suggest how this person is a "living definition" of this particular behaviour, personal quality, or characteristic. Here are two possible thesis statements for such an essay.

My uncle Julio has shown determination in every difficulty he has ever faced—that is why he has the nickname "Bulldog."

Even though my friend Thea's name starts with a *T*, she would be found under *P* for "pessimist" in the dictionary.

Your conclusion for this essay might summarize the ways in which this person's actions and words act as definitions of the quality he or she demonstrates most often.

Assignment 4: Writing an Essay Using Internet Research

Lisa Gabriele examines some women and the ways in which they adapt to the stresses of aging—some successfully, some not. What can people do, both mentally and physically, to make their later years active and happy? Use the Internet to discover what some authorities suggest. Then write an essay on three ways in which people can cope well with old age.

Use Google or another good search engine, and try keywords and phrases such as the following:

happy healthy aging
elderly people and healthy living
active aging and attitudes

Try variations on these and other keywords until you find two or three websites whose main focus is these concepts. Be sure to use sites whose text you find easy to understand as well. Write down the names of the sites you find most useful and the other information noted at the Online Learning Centre as essential when using an online source. Take care to distinguish between quoting directly from a site's text and paraphrasing its content as well. Finally, review the sections at the Online Learning Centre on introducing quotations and paraphrases correctly before you write your final drafts.

MRS. SQUIRREL AND I NEGOTIATED TERMS

Margot Devlin

City dwellers tend to see wild animals as enemies or annoyances. Wild creatures fascinate and delight us, so long as they are on television; people watch the Outdoor Living Network and wildlife programs avidly. Once in a while, though, a neighbourhood wild creature may endear itself to us, as Margot Devlin's squirrel does. How do we define our relationships with our non-human neighbours? When does annoyance become affection?

My husband and I recently moved from the suburbs to the city.   1

I was sitting in my den reading a couple of weeks ago when I heard a large com-   2
motion. In order to defend the matrimonial home from intruders, I picked up my
lethal defence weapon (broom) and proceeded cautiously downstairs.

I went outside to see if I could determine from whence the intruder was enter-   3
ing my home. As I was stumbling about, I saw the culprit emerging from the roof
of my porch. It was not a 50-pound raccoon as I had imagined from the noise, but
a half-pound grey fluffy squirrel. I shooed her away with my broom but the next
day I heard her again.

After researching squirrels on the Internet, I found that because squirrels are   4
rodents, their teeth keep growing; thus they have to constantly chew on things to
shorten their teeth. Chewing on wires is common, I learned, and thus there are
dangers of house fires. This was disturbing so I asked the Vice-President (my husband) to call some wildlife control people. On Saturday, he called the first company, and arranged for a time on Thursday. Then he called another company who
said they could send someone on Monday morning.

On Monday morning two smokers showed up. They finished their cigarettes   5
and then swaggered up to my front porch. "Well, li'l lady," one of them said in his
best John Wayne impression, "Where's the varmint?"

I pointed uneasily to the hole in my porch roof, which now had a small wel-   6
come mat out front. I had visions of the baby nursery inside and these ruffians tossing the little ones out in the snow. I confirmed that they would not harm her.

"We are recommended by the Humane Society," they said in a huff, but I   7
noticed that they put their Tasers back in their truck. Instead, they brought out
some spring-scented deodorizer and sprayed it into the squirrel's home. They told
me she would not like the smell and would leave. I had some doubt about that as
it had a pleasant aroma.

There was no sign of Mrs. Squirrel, so they barricaded the hole, took my   8
cheque for $250 and left in a trail of smoke. They gave me a guarantee, so I, being
the gullible sort, thought I was dealing with an honourable company.

Shortly after they left, Mrs. Squirrel returned from her shopping expedition.   9
She was very upset about being evicted and I believe the scent emanating from her
home acted like catnip on her senses. She began feverishly clawing at the porch
roof. Huge hunks of wood were flying everywhere. In order to stop the destruction
of my home, I went out with the broom and shooed her away again. I reported this
to the Vice-President. He asked me to monitor the situation and prepare a presentation with PowerPoint slides for when he got home.

In the evening, after he took in my animated report, he said he would defer the   10
matter for future consideration. He called the first company to cancel the Thursday
morning appointment.

Each day thereafter, Mrs. Squirrel continued her attack on my property. There   11
were so many wood chips on the porch by now that I had to shovel them away.
Once again, I called the Vice-President to report. He asked me if I wanted him to
come home from his very important work to board up a squirrel hole. As he is the
sole breadwinner at this time and as I like to eat, I sighed and said, "No, that's all
right."

12   I then hauled out the wildlife company's guarantee. I called them to report that "SHE'S BAAAAAACK..." The receptionist at the company told me that if Mrs. Squirrel had managed to find another way into the porch roof, it would be a new charge. I replied that I could not ethically continue contributing my husband's hard-earned income to the smoking addictions of her wildlife experts and hung up.

13   I went out to the porch and banged on the roof. Mrs. Squirrel came out and glared at me. We negotiated some terms, came to a mutually agreeable arrangement and went back into our respective homes.

14   The next day, I saw the first company's truck pull up. As we had cancelled, I ran out to see why he was here. I did not want to be charged for this smoker's visit. (Apparently, all wildlife experts smoke due to the stress of the job.) I explained to him that my husband had called to cancel. As I was standing on my porch talking to him, Mrs. Squirrel strolled by, dragging a huge piece of insulation for her home renovations. She and I nodded to each other, as the terms of our accord call for graciousness. The fellow looked at her as she wrestled the material on to my porch roof and then he looked at me. I smiled uneasily and ran inside before he could say anything.

15   All is quiet these days, although I noticed that large quantities of insulation appear to have been removed from my garage wall and my neighbour's daughter claims that some of her doll-house furniture has vanished. I still intend to evict Mrs. Squirrel, but I will wait until it is warmer and hopefully until after the birth of the wee ones. It may be lonely without my industrious neighbour, however, so I am considering the presentation of a business proposal to the Vice-President. Eco-condos with low maintenance fees. After all, she has done all the construction and renovations—a regular Bob Vila of the squirrel population.

■ Reading Comprehension Questions

1. Which of the following would make the best alternative title for the selection?
   a. Pest Problems
   b. Familiarity Breeds Fondness
   c. Exterminating the Enemy
   d. Women in Conflict

2. Which sentence best expresses the selection's main point?
   a. Devlin cannot wait to be rid of the squirrel.
   b. The author has learned to love wildlife.
   c. The author learns affection and respect for the squirrel and enjoys her company.
   d. Getting rid of pests in the city is expensive and time-consuming.

3. Devlin learned from the Internet that the main problem with squirrels is that
   a. they may chew electrical wiring.
   b. they are rodents, and can carry diseases.
   c. their teeth grow continuously.
   d. they are difficult to exterminate.

4. *True or false?* _____ The pest control people are equipped only with items that do not harm animals.

5. Devlin's husband, after being told about the squirrel's reaction to the spraying,
   a. watched a PowerPoint presentation about the pest situation.
   b. stopped thinking about it at all.
   c. decided his wife was overreacting.
   d. thought their squirrel problems were over.

6. The pest control company's guarantee may not hold because
   a. the Devlins' cheque was not good.
   b. the squirrel has created another entrance to its nest.
   c. exterminators and pest control companies are dishonest.
   d. they do not know how to get rid of rodents.

7. The author runs indoors after talking with the pest control worker from the first company because
   a. she is ashamed to send him away.
   b. she cannot afford another service call.
   c. she likes the squirrel.
   d. her husband had cancelled the appointment.

8. *True or false?* _____ Devlin has firmly decided that the squirrel will have to be removed.

9. The word *emanating* in "I believe the scent emanating from her home acted like catnip on her senses" (paragraph 9) means
   a. attracting.
   b. circulating.
   c. coming out.
   d. fading.

10. The word *defer* in "he said he would defer the matter for future consideration" (paragraph 10) means
   a. decide on.
   b. think about.
   c. forget about.
   d. put off.

■ Discussion Questions

About Content

1. What incident sets off the events in Devlin's narrative? What is her first reaction to her discovery?
2. Why is the author concerned about the two pest control workers who arrive at her home? What do they offer her as reassurance?
3. What does the squirrel do when it returns to its deodorized home? Why do you think it reacts this way?

4. What is the squirrel adding to its nest after the second pest control call, and why?

5. How has the author's attitude toward the squirrel changed by the end of the selection?

About Structure

6. What method does the author use to introduce this selection?
   a. Contrast.
   b. Broad statement.
   c. Anecdote.
   d. Question.

7. Which method of organization does Devlin use in her selection?

8. Which paragraphs open with transitional words and phrases? What are these words and phrases? How do they support the author's choice of organizational method?

About Style and Tone

9. The author's tone can be described as
   a. comic.
   b. serious.
   c. concerned.
   d. informative.

   Give two examples that illustrate your choice.

10. Devlin uses the literary device of *personification* to describe the squirrel. In which paragraph do you find the first use of this device? Which words or phrases help to continue the personification the squirrel after this first use of the device?

11. How does personifying the squirrel affect the author's presentation of (a) the pest control workers and (b) her own relationship with the animal?

12. Where has the author intentionally exaggerated persons and situations in the selection? Why has she done so?

■ Writing Assignments

Assignment 1: Writing a Paragraph

Write a paragraph in which you use narrative to recount a conflict with some person, animal, or object, a conflict that results in something learned. As with Devlin's article, the conflict need not be a serious one; you may write about struggling with an appliance, a sibling, some piece of technology, or a pet. Focus on the stages of development in your conflict and on what resulted from your involvement with your opponent. Your topic sentence should present both your opponent and the nature of the conflict you will explore, as in the following example: "Trying to train a monitor lizard is a huge challenge; Renaldo resisted every lesson I tried to teach him."

Assignment 2: Writing a Paragraph

We live in a society that depends on services to take care of many aspects of daily life. Apparently people do not have the time or know-how to deal with some tasks on their own, so Canadians purchase the services of dog walkers, pet daycare, pest control, lawn care, online grocery stores, frozen-meal delivery services, exterminators, housecleaners, and so on. Is our reliance on such services a good thing or not?

Write a paragraph in the third-person point of view in which you argue for or against three such currently popular services.

Assignment 3: Writing an Essay

Do you live in a town or city? Most Canadians do, and, according to news reports, most do not know their neighbours very well. Does this result in people feeling lonely or isolated and perhaps even helpless occasionally? Or are we happier without intrusive or gossipy neighbours? What does knowing our neighbours add to or detract from our lives?

Write an essay that explains, with examples, what makes a "good neighbour" or, by contrast, a "bad neighbour."

ANXIETY: CHALLENGE BY ANOTHER NAME

James Lincoln Collier

What is your basis for making personal decisions? Do you aim to rock the boat as little as possible, choosing the easy, familiar path? There is comfort in sticking with what is safe and well-known, just as there is comfort in eating mashed potatoes. But James Lincoln Collier, author of numerous articles and books, decided soon after leaving college not to live a mashed-potato sort of life. In this essay, first published in *Reader's Digest*, he tells how he learned to recognize the marks of a potentially exciting, growth-inducing experience, to set aside his anxiety, and to dive in.

Between my sophomore and junior years at college, a chance came up for me to spend the summer vacation working on a ranch in Argentina. My roommate's father was in the cattle business, and he wanted Ted to see something of it. Ted said he would go if he could take a friend, and he chose me.

The idea of spending two months on the fabled Argentine pampas* was exciting. Then I began having second thoughts. I had never been very far from New England, and I had been homesick my first weeks at college. What would it be like

1

2

*A vast plain in south-central South America.

in a strange country? What about the language? And besides, I had promised to teach my younger brother to sail that summer. The more I thought about it, the more the prospect daunted me. I began waking up nights in a sweat.

3   In the end I turned down the proposition. As soon as Ted asked somebody else to go, I began kicking myself. A couple of weeks later I went home to my old summer job, unpacking cartons at the local supermarket, feeling very low. I had turned down something I wanted to do because I was scared, and I had ended up feeling depressed. I stayed that way for a long time. And it didn't help when I went back to college in the fall to discover that Ted and his friend had had a terrific time.

4   In the long run that unhappy summer taught me a valuable lesson out of which I developed a rule for myself: *do what makes you anxious, don't do what makes you depressed.*

5   I am not, of course, talking about severe states of anxiety or depression, which require medical attention. What I mean is that kind of anxiety we call stage fright, butterflies in the stomach, a case of nerves—the feelings we have at a job interview, when we're giving a big party, when we have to make an important presentation at the office. And the kind of depression I am referring to is that downhearted feeling of the blues, when we don't seem to be interested in anything, when we can't get going and seem to have no energy.

6   I was confronted by this sort of situation toward the end of my senior year. As graduation approached, I began to think about taking a crack at making my living as a writer. But one of my professors was urging me to apply to graduate school and aim at a teaching career.

7   I wavered. The idea of trying to live by writing was scary—a lot more scary than spending a summer on the pampas, I thought. Back and forth I went, making my decision, unmaking it. Suddenly, I realized that every time I gave up the idea of writing, that sinking feeling went through me; it gave me the blues.

8   The thought of graduate school wasn't what depressed me. It was giving up on what deep in my gut I really wanted to do. Right then I learned another lesson. To avoid that kind of depression meant, inevitably, having to endure a certain amount of worry and concern.

9   The great Danish philosopher Søren Kierkegaard believed that anxiety always arises when we confront the possibility of our own development. It seems to be a rule of life that you can't advance without getting that old, familiar, jittery feeling.

10   Even as children we discover this when we try to expand ourselves by, say, learning to ride a bike or going out for the school play. Later in life we get butterflies when we think about having that first child, or uprooting the family from the old hometown to find a better opportunity halfway across the country. Any time, it seems, that we set out aggressively to get something we want, we meet up with anxiety. And it's going to be our traveling companion, at least part of the way, in any new venture.

11   When I first began writing magazine articles, I was frequently required to interview big names—people like Richard Burton, Joan Rivers, sex authority William Masters, baseball great Dizzy Dean. Before each interview I would get butterflies and my hands would shake.

12   At the time, I was doing some writing about music. And one person I particularly admired was the great composer Duke Ellington. On stage and on television,

he seemed the very model of the confident, sophisticated man of the world. Then I learned that Ellington still got stage fright. If the highly honored Duke Ellington, who had appeared on the bandstand some ten thousand times over thirty years, had anxiety attacks, who was I to think I could avoid them?

I went on doing those frightening interviews, and one day, as I was getting onto   13
a plane for Washington to interview columnist Joseph Alsop, I suddenly realized to my astonishment that I was looking forward to the meeting. What had happened to those butterflies?

Well, in truth, they were still there, but there were fewer of them. I had bene-   14
fited, I discovered, from a process psychologists call "extinction." If you put an individual in an anxiety-provoking situation often enough, he will eventually learn that there isn't anything to be worried about.

Which brings us to a corollary to my basic rule: *you'll never eliminate anxiety*   15
by avoiding the things that caused it. I remember how my son Jeff was when I first began to teach him to swim at the lake cottage where we spent our summer vaca-tions. He resisted, and when I got him into the water he sank and sputtered and wanted to quit. But I was insistent. And by summer's end he was splashing around like a puppy. He had "extinguished" his anxiety the only way he could—by con-fronting it.

The problem, of course, is that it is one thing to urge somebody else to take on   16
those anxiety producing challenges; it is quite another to get ourselves to do it.

Some years ago I was offered a writing assignment that would require three   17
months of travel through Europe. I had been abroad a couple of times on the usual "If it's Tuesday this must be Belgium"* trips, but I hardly could claim to know my way around the continent. Moreover, my knowledge of foreign languages was lim-ited to a little college French.

I hesitated. How would I, unable to speak the language, totally unfamiliar with   18
local geography or transportation systems, set up interviews and do research? It seemed impossible, and with considerable regret I sat down to write a letter beg-ging off. Halfway through, a thought—which I subsequently made into another corollary to my basic rule—ran through my mind: *you can't learn if you don't try.*
So I accepted the assignment.

There were some bad moments. But by the time I had finished the trip I was   19
an experienced traveler. And ever since, I have never hesitated to head for even the most exotic of places, without guides or even advance bookings, confident that somehow I will manage.

The point is that the new, the different, is almost by definition scary. But each   20
time you try something, you learn, and as the learning piles up, the world opens to you.

I've made parachute jumps, learned to ski at forty, flown up the Rhine in a bal-   21
loon. And I know I'm going to go on doing such things. It's not because I'm braver or more daring than others. I'm not. But I don't let the butterflies stop me from doing what I want. Accept anxiety as another name for challenge, and you can accomplish wonders.

---

*Reference to a film comedy about a group of American tourists who visited too many European countries in too little time.

■ Reading Comprehension Questions

1. The word *daunted* in "The more I thought about [going to Argentina], the more the prospect daunted me. I began waking up nights in a sweat" (paragraph 2) means
   a. encouraged.
   b. interested.
   c. discouraged.
   d. amused.

2. The word *corollary* in "Which brings us to a corollary to my basic rule: *you'll never eliminate anxiety by avoiding the things that caused it*" (paragraph 15) means
   a. an idea that follows from another idea.
   b. an idea based on a falsehood.
   c. an idea that creates anxiety.
   d. an idea passed on from one generation to another.

3. Which of the following would be the best alternative title for this selection?
   a. A Poor Decision
   b. Don't Let Anxiety Stop You
   c. Becoming a Writer
   d. The Courage to Travel

4. Which sentence best expresses the main idea of the selection?
   a. The butterflies-in-the-stomach type of anxiety differs greatly from severe states of anxiety or depression.
   b. Taking on a job assignment that required traveling helped the author get over his anxiety.
   c. People learn and grow by confronting, not backing away from, situations that make them anxious.
   d. Anxiety is a predictable part of life that can be dealt with in positive ways.

5. When a college friend invited the writer to go with him to Argentina, the writer
   a. turned down the invitation.
   b. accepted eagerly.
   c. was very anxious about the idea but went anyway.
   d. did not believe his friend was serious.

6. *True or false?* _____ As graduation approached, Collier's professor urged him to try to make his living as a writer.

7. *True or false?* _____ The philosopher Søren Kierkegaard believed that anxiety occurs when we face the possibility of our own development.

8. "Extinction" is the term psychologists use for
   a. the inborn tendency to avoid situations that make one feel very anxious.
   b. a person's gradual loss of confidence.
   c. the natural development of a child's abilities.
   d. the process of losing one's fear by continuing to face the anxiety-inspiring situation.

9. The author implies that
   a. it was lucky he didn't take the summer job in Argentina.
   b. his son never got over his fear of the water.
   c. Duke Ellington's facing stage fright inspired him.
   d. one has to be more daring than most people to overcome anxiety.

10. The author implies that
    a. anxiety may be a signal that one has an opportunity to grow.
    b. he considers his three-month trip to Europe a failure.
    c. facing what makes him anxious has eliminated all depression from his life.
    d. he no longer has anxiety about new experiences.

■ Discussion Questions

About Content

1. Collier developed the rule "Do what makes you anxious; don't do what makes you depressed." How does he distinguish between feeling anxious and feeling depressed?

2. In what way does Collier believe that anxiety is positive? How, according to him, can we eventually overcome our fears? Have you ever gone ahead and done something that made you anxious? How did it turn out?

About Structure

3. Collier provides a rule and two corollary rules that describe his attitude toward challenge and anxiety. Below, write the location of that rule and its corollaries.

   Collier's rule: paragraph _____
   First corollary: paragraph _____
   Second corollary: paragraph _____

   How does Collier emphasize the rule and its corollaries?

4. Collier uses several personal examples in his essay. Find three instances of these examples and explain how each helps Collier develop his main point.

About Style and Tone

5. In paragraph 3, Collier describes the aftermath of his decision not to go to Argentina. He could have just written, "I worked that summer." Instead he writes, "I went home to my old summer job, unpacking cartons at the local supermarket." Why do you think he provides that bit of detail about his job? What is the effect on the reader?

6. Authors often use testimony by authorities to support their points. Where in Collier's essay does he use such support? What do you think it adds to his piece?

7. In the last sentence of paragraph 10, Collier refers to anxiety as a "traveling companion." Why do you think he uses that image? What does it convey about his view of anxiety?

8. Is Collier just telling about a lesson he has learned for himself, or is he encouraging his readers to do something? How can you tell?

■ Writing Assignments

Assignment 1: Writing a Paragraph

Collier explains how his life experiences made him view the term *anxiety* in a new way. Write a paragraph in which you explain how a personal experience of yours has given new meaning to a particular term. Following are some terms you might wish to consider for this assignment.

> Failure
> Friendship
> Goals
> Homesickness
> Maturity
> Success

Here are two sample topic sentences for this assignment.

> I used to think of failure as something terrible, but thanks to a helpful boss, I now think of it as an opportunity to learn.

> The word *creativity* has taken on a new meaning for me ever since I became interested in dancing.

Assignment 2: Writing a Paragraph

The second corollary to Collier's rule is "You can't learn if you don't try." Write a paragraph using this idea as your main idea. Support it with your own experience, someone else's experience, or both. One way of developing this point is to compare two approaches to a challenge: one person may have backed away from a frightening opportunity while another person decided to take on the challenge. Or you could write about a time when you learned something useful by daring to give a new experience a try. In that case, you might discuss your reluctance to take on the new experience, the difficulties you encountered, and your eventual success. In your conclusion, include a final thought about the value of what was learned.

Listing a few skills you have learned will help you decide on the experience you wish to write about. To get you started, below is a list of things adults often need to go to some trouble to learn.

> Driving with a stick shift
> Taking useful lecture notes
> Knowing how to do well on a job interview
> Asking someone out on a date
> Making a speech
> Standing up for your rights

Assignment 3: Writing an Essay

Collier describes three rules he follows when facing anxiety. In an essay, write about one or more rules, or guidelines, that you have developed for yourself through experience. If you decide to discuss two or three such guidelines, mention or refer to them in your introductory paragraph. Then go on to discuss each in one or more paragraphs of its own. Include at least one experience that led you to develop a given guideline, and tell how it has helped you at other times in your life. You might end with a brief summary and an explanation of how the guidelines as a group have helped. If you decide to focus on one rule, include at least two or three experiences that help to illustrate your point.

To prepare for this assignment, spend some time freewriting about the rules or guidelines you have set up for yourself. Continue writing until you feel you have a central idea for which you have plenty of interesting support. Then organize that support into a rough outline, such as this one:

Thesis: I have one rule that keeps me from staying in a rut: Don't let the size of a challenge deter you; instead, aim for it by making plans and taking steps.

Topic sentence 1: I began to think about my rule one summer in high school when a friend got the type of summer job that I had only been thinking about.

Topic sentence 2: After high school, I began to live up to my rule when I aimed for a business career and entered college.

Topic sentence 3: My rule is also responsible for my having the wonderful boyfriend [or girlfriend or job] I now have.

BULLIES IN SCHOOL

Kathleen Berger

How serious a problem is bullying in schools? Is it a rite of passage, a normal part of childhood that every kid has to go through? Should adults intervene, or is the bully-victim relationship something children need to work out for themselves? And what influences create a bully or a victim? In this selection, Kathleen Berger reports on the work of a researcher who has come up with some surprising—even alarming—findings about bullies. Read it and see if the researcher's conclusions correspond with what you have observed or experienced.

Bullying was once commonly thought to be an unpleasant but normal part of children's play, not to be encouraged, of course, but of little consequence in the   1 long run. However, developmental researchers who have looked closely at the society of children consider bullying to be a very serious problem, one that harms both the victim and the aggressor, sometimes continuing to cause suffering years after the child has grown up.

2   One leading researcher in this area is Dan Olweus, who has studied bullying in his native country of Norway and elsewhere for twenty-five years. The cruelty, pain, and suffering that he has documented in that time are typified by the examples of Linda and Henry:

> Linda was systematically isolated by a small group of girls, who pressured the rest of the class, including Linda's only friend, to shun her. Then the ringleader of the group persuaded Linda to give a party, inviting everyone. Everyone accepted; following the ringleader's directions, no one came. Linda was devastated, her self-confidence "completely destroyed."
>
> Henry's experience was worse. Daily, his classmates called him "Worm," broke his pencils, spilled his books on the floor, and mocked him whenever he answered a teacher's questions. Finally, a few boys took him to the bathroom and made him lie, face down, in the urinal drain. After school that day he tried to kill himself. His parents found him unconscious, and only then learned about his torment.

3   Following the suicides of three other victims of bullying, the Norwegian government asked Olweus in 1983 to determine the extent and severity of the problem. After concluding a confidential survey of nearly all of Norway's 90,000 school-age children, Olweus reported that the problem was widespread and serious; that teachers and parents were "relatively unaware" of specific incidents of bullying; and that even when adults noticed bullying, they rarely intervened. Of all the children Olweus surveyed, 9 percent were bullied "now and then"; 3 percent were victims once a week or more; and 7 percent admitted that they themselves sometimes deliberately hurt other children, verbally or physically.

4   As high as these numbers may seem, they are equaled and even exceeded in research done in other countries. For instance, a British study of eight- to nine-year-olds found that 17 percent were victims of regular bullying and that 13 percent were bullies. A study of middle-class children in a university school in Florida found that 10 percent were "extremely victimized." Recently, American researchers have looked particularly at sexual harassment, an aspect of childhood bullying ignored by most adults. Fully a third of nine- to fifteen-year-old girls say they have experienced sexual teasing and touching sufficiently troubling that they wanted to avoid school, and, as puberty approaches, almost every boy who is perceived as homosexual by his peers is bullied, sometimes mercilessly.

5   Researchers define bullying as repeated, systematic efforts to inflict harm on a particular child through physical attack (such as hitting, punching, pinching, or kicking), verbal attack (such as teasing, taunting, or name-calling), or social attack (such as deliberate social exclusion or public mocking). Implicit in this definition is the idea of an unbalance of power: victims of bullying are in some way weaker than their harassers and continue to be singled out for attack, in part because they have difficulty defending themselves. In many cases, this difficulty is compounded by the fact that the bullying is being carried out by a group of children. In Olweus's research, at least 60 percent of bullying incidents involved group attacks.

As indicated by the emphasis given to it, the key word in the preceding defin- 6
ition of bullying is "repeated." Most children experience isolated attacks or social
slights from other children and come through them unscathed. But when a child
must endure such shameful experiences again and again—being forced to hand
over lunch money, or to drink milk mixed with detergent, or to lick someone's
boots, or to be the butt of insults and practical jokes, with everyone watching and
no one coming to the child's defense—the effects can be deep and long-lasting. Not
only are bullied children anxious, depressed, and underachieving during the
months and years of their torment, but even years later, they have lower self-esteem
as well as painful memories.

The picture is somewhat different, but often more ominous, for bullies. 7
Contrary to the public perception that bullies are actually insecure and lonely, at
the peak of their bullying they usually have friends who abet, fear, and admire
them, and they seem brashly unapologetic about the pain they have inflicted, as
they often claim, "all in fun." But their popularity and school success fade over the
years, and especially if they are boys, they run a high risk of ending up in prison.
In one longitudinal study done by Olweus, by age twenty-four, two-thirds of the
boys who had been bullies in the second grade were convicted of at least one felony,
and one-third of those who had been bullies in the sixth through the ninth grades
were already convicted of three or more crimes, often violent ones. International
research likewise finds that children who are allowed to regularly victimize other
children are at high risk of becoming violent offenders as adolescents and adults.

Unfortunately, bullying during middle childhood seems to be universal: it 8
occurs in every nation that has been studied, is as much a problem in small rural
schools as in large urban ones, and is as prevalent among well-to-do majority children as among poor immigrant children. Also quite common, if not universal, is
the "profile" of bullies and their victims. Contrary to popular belief, victims are
not distinguished by their external traits: they are no more likely to be fat, skinny,
or homely, or to speak with an accent, than nonvictims are. But they usually are
"rejected" children, that is, children who have few friends because they are more
anxious and less secure than most children and are unable or unwilling to defend
themselves. They also are more often boys than girls and more often younger
children.

Bullies have traits in common as well, some of which can be traced to their 9
upbringing. The parents of bullies often seem indifferent to what their children do
outside the home but use "power-assertive" discipline on them at home. These children are frequently subjected to physical punishment, verbal criticism, and displays
of dominance meant to control and demean them, thereby giving them a vivid
model, as well as a compelling reason, to control and demean others. Boys who are
bullies are often above average in size, while girls who are bullies are often above
average in verbal assertiveness. These differences are reflected in bullying tactics:
boys typically use force or the threat of force; girls often mock or ridicule their victims, making fun of their clothes, behavior, or appearance, or revealing their most
embarrassing secrets.

What can be done to halt these damaging attacks? Many psychologists have 10
attempted to alter the behavior patterns that characterize aggressive or rejected
children. Cognitive interventions seem particularly fruitful: some programs teach

social problem-solving skills (such as how to use humor or negotiation to reduce a conflict); others help children reassess their negative assumptions (such as the frequent, fatalistic view of many rejected children that nothing can protect them, or the aggressive child's typical readiness to conclude that accidental slights are deliberate threats); others tutor children in academic skills, hoping to improve confidence and short-circuit the low self-esteem that might be at the root of both victimization and aggression.

11   These approaches sometimes help individuals. However, because they target one child at a time, they are piecemeal, time-consuming, and costly. Further, they have to work against habits learned at home and patterns reinforced at school, making it hard to change a child's behavior pattern. After all, bullies and their admirers have no reason to learn new social skills if their current attitudes and actions bring them status and pleasure. And even if rejected children change their behavior, they still face a difficult time recovering accepted positions in the peer group and gaining friends who will support and defend them. The solution to this problem must begin, then, by recognizing that the bullies and victims are not acting in isolation but, rather, are caught up in a mutually destructive interaction within a particular social context.

12   Accordingly, a more effective intervention is to change the social climate within the school, so that bully-victim cycles no longer spiral out of control. That this approach can work was strikingly demonstrated by a government-funded aware-ness campaign that Olweus initiated for every school in Norway. In the first phase of the campaign, community-wide meetings were held to explain the problem; pamphlets were sent to all parents to alert them to the signs of victimization (such as a child's having bad dreams, having no real friends, and coming home from school with damaged clothes, torn books, or unexplained bruises); and videotapes were shown to all students to evoke sympathy for victims.

13   The second phase of the campaign involved specific actions within the schools. In every classroom, students discussed reasons for and ways to mediate peer conflicts, to befriend lonely children, and to stop bullying attacks whenever they saw them occur. Teachers were taught to be proactive, organizing coopera-tive learning groups so that no single child could be isolated, halting each inci-dent of name-calling or minor assault as soon as they noticed it, and learning how to see through the bully's excuses and to understand the victim's fear of reprisal. Principals were advised that adequate adult supervision during recess, lunch, and bathroom breaks distinguished schools where bullying was rare from those where bullying was common.

14   If bullying incidents occurred despite such measures, counselors were urged to intervene, talking privately and seriously with bullies and their victims, coun-seling their parents, and seeking solutions that might include intensive therapy with the bully's parents to restructure family discipline, reassigning the bully to a different class, grade, or even school, and helping the victim strengthen skills and foster friendships.

15   Twenty months after this campaign began, Olweus resurveyed the children in forty-two schools. He found that bullying had been reduced overall by more than 50 percent, with dramatic improvement for both boys and girls at every grade level. Developmental researchers are excited because results such as these, in which

a relatively simple, cost-effective measure has such a decided impact on a developmental problem, are rare. Olweus concludes, "It is no longer possible to avoid taking action about bullying problems at school using lack of awareness as an excuse. . . . it all boils down to a matter of will and involvement on the part of the adults." Unfortunately, at the moment, Norway is the only country to have mounted a nationwide attack to prevent the problem of bullying. Many other school systems, in many other nations, have not even acknowledged the harm caused by this problem, much less shown the "will and involvement" to stop it.

■ Reading Comprehension Questions

1. The word *compounded* in " victims of bullying . . . continue to be singled out for attack, in part because they have difficulty defending themselves. In many cases, this difficulty is compounded by the fact that the bullying is being carried out by a group of children" (paragraph 5) means
    a. reduced.
    b. increased.
    c. solved.
    d. forgiven.

2. The word *unscathed* in "Most children experience isolated attacks . . . from other children and come through them unscathed. But when a child must endure such shameful experiences again and again . . . the effects can be deep and long-lasting" (paragraph 6) means
    a. unharmed.
    b. unpleasant.
    c. unknown.
    d. uncertain.

3. Which of the following would be the best alternative title for the selection?
    a. Bullies: Why Do They Act That Way?
    b. The Pain of Being Bullied
    c. Bullies in Norway
    d. Bullying: A Problem Too Serious to Ignore

4. Which sentence best expresses the selection's main point?
    a. Certain types of children are inclined to become either bullies or victims.
    b. To combat the problem of bullying in Norway, a researcher designed an innovative program for all of its schools.
    c. Researchers consider bullying a very serious problem, one that harms both victims and bullies.
    d. Researchers have concluded that bullying is a very serious problem that can be solved only by changing the social climate in which it develops.

5. One thing many bullies have in common is that they
    a. are harshly punished at home.
    b. have few friends.
    c. are often apologetic after they've acted in a bullying way.
    d. are often from poor immigrant families.

6. *True or false?* _____ Victims of bullies tend to be physically unattractive.

7. Parents of a bully
    a. are usually anxious to stop their child's bullying behavior.
    b. were often victims of bullies themselves.
    c. often seem unconcerned about their child's behavior away from home.
    d. actively encourage their child to be a bully.

8. A study done by Dan Olweus of what happens in later years to boys who are bullies showed that
    a. a high proportion become teachers.
    b. a high percentage end up in prison.
    c. they have trouble finding and keeping jobs.
    d. their suicide rate is higher than average.

9. Boy and girl bullies
    a. differ: girls tend to mock their victims, while boys are more likely to use force.
    b. bully their victims in just about the same ways.
    c. differ: girls tend to be bigger than average, while boys are more verbally assertive than average.
    d. differ: girls tend to use force on their victims, while boys are more likely to mock them.

10. If a teacher witnessed an incident of bullying, we can infer that Olweus (the designer of the Norwegian program) would advise him or her to
    a. ignore it, letting the students involved settle the matter themselves.
    b. privately encourage the victim to fight back.
    c. transfer the victim to another class.
    d. immediately confront the bully.

■ Discussion Questions

About Content

1. Olweus describes two specific incidents of bullying, involving Linda and Henry. Did those incidents remind you of anything that ever occurred at your own school? Who were the bullies? Who were the victims? Describe the incident. What role, if any, did you play in such events?

2. What are some of the measures Olweus recommends be taken in a school and community to stop bullying? Do you think such measures would have been helpful in your school? If you are a parent, would you support such programs in your child's school?

3. Olweus concludes that bullying is a very serious problem, with effects that carry over for years into the lives of both bullies and victims. Do you agree? Or do you think Olweus is exaggerating the problem?

4. Olweus reports that, although bullying is a widespread and serious problem, most teachers and parents are "relatively unaware" of bullying going on. How can this be? What is it about the dynamics of the relationship between bully and victim that can make it both a serious problem and one that is nearly invisible to adults?

About Structure

5. What combination of methods does Berger use to introduce this selection?
    a. Broad statement; quotation.
    b. Anecdote; questions.
    c. Contrast; anecdote.
    d. Quotation; questions.

    Is this introduction effective? Why or why not?

6. This selection can be divided into five parts. Fill in the blanks to show which paragraphs are included in each part.
    (1) Berger's introduction of the topic: paragraph _____
    (2) Two examples of bullying typical of the consequences Olweus reports on: paragraph _____
    (3) Findings of Olweus's government-sponsored study and other research: paragraphs _____ to _____
    (4) Ways to halt bullying: paragraphs _____ to _____
    (5) Olweus's follow-up study and the author's brief conclusion: paragraph _____

About Style and Tone

7. Find three places in the selection where statistics are cited. Why would a selection like this use so many statistics? What do statistics accomplish that anecdotes cannot?

8. The author's tone can be described as a combination of
    a. horror and fear.
    b. concern and objectivity.
    c. bewilderment and pleading.
    d. curiosity and excitement.

Find examples in the selection that illustrate this tone.

■ Writing Assignments

Assignment 1: Writing a Paragraph

Write a paragraph describing a bully you have been acquainted with. Focus on three aspects of the person: his or her appearance, actions, and effects on others. Help your reader vividly imagine the bully by providing concrete details that illustrate each aspect. Your topic sentence might be similar to this: "In junior high school, I became familiar with a bully and the pain he caused one student."

Assignment 2: Writing a Paragraph

The social aspect of school is hard for many students, even if they are not victims of bullies. Write a paragraph about another reason or reasons that school was difficult for you or for people you observed. Was it the pressure to wear a certain kind of clothing? Be involved in sports? Use drugs and drink? Become sexually active? Hang out with a "cool" crowd? Provide details that help your reader understand how difficult pressures at school can be.

Assignment 3: Writing an Essay

Think of a time when you were on the giving end or the receiving end of an act of bullying. (The incident could fall into any of the categories mentioned in paragraph 5 of the reading—a physical, verbal, or social attack.) If you cannot think of an incident that involved you, think of one that you witnessed. Write an essay describing the incident. In your essay, be sure to cover the following points: How did the bully behave? How did the victim respond? And how did any onlookers react to what was going on? For an example of one author's clear, detailed narrative writing about situations and the feelings they evoke, read Judith MacKenzie's "Letter" (pages 500-1).

Assignment 4: Writing an Essay Using Internet Research

Victims of bullying often need help for two reasons. They have to stand up to the bullies who are tormenting them, and they also have to deal with negative feelings about themselves. Use the Internet to research methods recommended by experts for helping victims of bullying. Then write an essay that describes in detail three methods that can help victims cope with their own negative self-image or with the bullies themselves.

To access the Internet, use the search engine Google (www.google.com) or one of the other search engines listed at the Online Learning Centre. Try one of the following phrases or some related phrase:

coping with bullies
victims of bullying
bullies and coping and victims

You may, of course, use a single keyword such as *bullies*, but that will bring up too many items. By using a phrase such as one of the above, you can begin to limit your search. As you proceed, you'll develop a sense of how to track down and focus a topic by adding more information to your search words and phrases.

plaining a Process · Examining Cause and Effect · Comparing or Contrasting · Definin
m · Dividing and Classifying · Describing a Scene or Person · Narrating an Event · Argu
osition · Explaining a Process · Examining Cause and Effect · Comparing or Contrastin
fining a Term · Dividing and Classifying · Describing a Scene or Person · Narrating
ent · Arguing a Position · Explaining a Process · Examining Cause and Effect · Compar

Education and Self-Improvement

POWER LEARNING

Sheila Akers

For many students, cramming for tests, staying up late to do assignments, and having an incomplete grasp of information are a natural part of college life. After all, there is so much to do, and almost none of it is easy. If you are one of those students who never seem able to catch up, you may find the following selection a revelation. It might convince you that even though you study hard in school, you may need to learn more about how to study better.

Jill had not been as successful in high school as she would have liked. Since college involved even more work, it was no surprise that she was not doing any better there. 1

The reason for her so-so performance was not a lack of effort. She attended most of her classes and read her textbooks. And she never missed handing in any assignment, even though it often meant staying up late the night before homework was due. Still, she just got by in her classes. Before long, she came to the conclusion that she just couldn't do any better. 2

Then one day, one of her instructors said something to make her think otherwise. "You can probably build some sort of house by banging a few boards together," he said. "But if you want a sturdy home, you'll have to use the right techniques and tools. Building carefully takes work, but it gets better results. The same can be said of your education. There are no shortcuts, but there are some proven study skills that can really help. If you don't use them, you may end up with a pretty flimsy education." 3

Prompted by this advice, Jill signed up for a course in study skills at her school. She then found out a crucial fact—that learning how to learn is the key to success in school. There are certain dependable skills that have made the difference between 4

529

disappointment and success for generations of students. These techniques won't free you from work, but they will make your work far more productive. They include three important areas: time control, classroom note-taking, and textbook study.

Time Control

5   Success in college depends on time control. Time control means that you deliberately organize and plan your time, instead of letting it drift by. Planning means that you should never be faced with a night-before-the-test "cram" session or an overdue term paper.

6   There are three steps involved in time control. The *first step* is to prepare a large monthly calendar. Buy a calendar with a large white block around each date, or make one yourself. At the beginning of the college semester, circle important dates on this calendar. Circle the days on which tests are scheduled; circle the days when papers are due. This calendar can also be used to schedule study plans. You can jot down your plans for each day at the beginning of the week. An alternative method would be to make plans for each day the night before. On Tuesday night, for example, you might write down "Read Chapter 5 in psychology" in the Wednesday block. Be sure to hang this calendar in a place where you will see it every day— your kitchen, your bedroom, even your bathroom!

7   The *second step* in time control is to have a weekly study schedule for the semester. To prepare this schedule, make up a chart that covers all the days of the week and all the waking hours in each day. Part of one student's schedule is shown [below]. On your schedule, mark in all the fixed hours in each day—hours for meals, classes, job (if any), and travel time. Next, mark in time blocks that you can *realistically* use for study each day. Depending on the number of courses you are taking and the demands of the courses, you may want to block off five, ten, or even twenty or more hours of study time a week. Keep in mind that you should not block off time for study that you do not truly intend to use for study. Otherwise, your schedule will be a meaningless gimmick. Also, remember that you should allow time for rest and relaxation in your schedule. You will be happiest, and able to accomplish the most, when you have time for both work and play.

Time	Monday	Tuesday	Wednesday	Thursday	Friday	Saturday	Sunday
6:00 A.M.							
7:00	*B*	*B*	*B*	*B*	*B*		
8:00	*Math*	*STUDY*	*Math*	*STUDY*	*Math*		
9:00	*STUDY*	*Biology*	*STUDY*	*Biology*	*STUDY*	*Job*	
10:00	*Psychology*	↓	*Psychology*	↓	*Psychology*		
11:00	*STUDY*	*English*		*English*			
12:00 NOON	*L*		*L*	↓	*L*	↓	

The *third step* in time control is to make a daily or weekly "to do" list. This may   **8** be the most valuable time-control method you ever use. On this list, you write down the things you need to do for the following day or the following week. If you choose to write a weekly list, do it on Sunday night. If you choose to write a daily list, do it the night before. You may use a three- by five-inch notepad or a small spiral-bound notebook for this list. Carry the list around with you during the day. Always concentrate on doing first the most important items on your list. Mark high-priority items with an asterisk and give them precedence over low-priority items in order to make the best use of your time. For instance, you may find yourself wondering what to do after dinner on Thursday evening. Among the items on your list are "Clean inside of car" and "Review chapter for math quiz." It is obviously more important for you to review your notes at this point; you can clean the car some other time. As you complete items on your "to do" list, cross them out. Do not worry about unfinished items. They can be rescheduled. You will still be accomplishing a great deal and making more effective use of your time. Part of one student's daily list is shown below.

> *To Do*   *Tuesday*
> *1. Review biology notes before class*
> *2. Proof-read English paper due today*
> 3. See Dick about game on Friday*
> *4. Gas for car*
> 5. Read next chapter of psychology text

Classroom Note-Taking

One of the most important single things you can do to perform well in a college   **9** course is to take effective class notes. The following hints should help you become a better note-taker.

First, attend class faithfully. Your alternatives—reading the text or someone   **10** else's notes, or both—cannot substitute for the experience of hearing ideas in person as someone presents them to you. Also, in class lectures and discussions, your instructor typically presents and develops the main ideas and facts of the course—the ones you will be expected to know on exams.

Another valuable hint is to make use of abbreviations while taking notes. Using   **11** abbreviations saves time when you are trying to get down a great deal of information. Abbreviate terms that recur frequently in a lecture and put a key to your abbreviations at the top of your notes. For example, in a sociology class, *eth* could stand for *ethnocentrism*; in a psychology class, *STM* could stand for *short-term memory*. (When a lecture is over, you may want to go back and write out the terms you have abbreviated.) In addition, abbreviate words that often recur in any lecture. For instance, use *ex* for *example*, *def* for *definition*, *info* for *information*, + for *and*, and so on. If you use the same abbreviations all the time, you will soon develop a kind of personal shorthand that makes taking notes much easier.

12   A third hint when taking notes is to be on the lookout for signals of importance. Write down whatever your instructor puts on the board. If he or she takes
the time to put material on the board, it is probably important, and the chances
are good that it will come up later on exams. Always write down definitions and
enumerations. Enumerations are lists of items. They are signaled in such ways as:
"The four steps in the process are …"; "There were three reasons for …"; "The two
effects were …"; "Five characteristics of …"; and so on. Always number such enumerations in your notes (1, 2, 3, etc.). They will help you understand relationships
among ideas and organize the material of the lecture. Watch for emphasis words—
words your instructor may use to indicate that something is important. Examples
of such words are "This is an important reason …"; "A point that will keep coming up later …"; "The chief cause was …"; "The basic idea here is …"; and so on.
Always write down the important statements announced by these and other
emphasis words. Finally, if your instructor repeats a point, you can assume it is
important. You might put an R for *repeated* in the margin, so that later you will
know that your instructor has stressed it.

13   Next, be sure to write down the instructor's examples and mark them with an
X. The examples help you understand abstract points. If you do not write them
down, you are likely to forget them later when they are needed to help make sense
of an idea.

14   Also, be sure to write down the connections between ideas. Too many students
merely copy the terms the instructor puts on the board. They forget that, as time
passes, the details that serve as connecting bridges between ideas quickly fade. You
should, then, write down the relationships and connections in class. That way
you'll have them to help tie your notes together later on.

15   Review your notes as soon as possible after class. You must make them as clear
as possible while they are fresh in your mind. A day later may be too late, because
forgetting sets in very quickly. Make sure that punctuation is clear, that all words
are readable and correctly spelled, and that unfinished sentences are completed (or
at least marked off so that you can check your notes with another student's). Add
clarifying or connecting comments whenever necessary. Make sure important ideas
are clearly marked. Improve the organization if necessary, so that you can see at a
glance main points and relationships among them.

16   Finally, try in general to get down a written record of each class. You must do
this because forgetting begins almost immediately. Studies have shown that within
two weeks you are likely to have forgotten 80 percent or more of what you have
heard. And in four weeks you are lucky if 5 percent remains! This is so crucial that
it bears repeating: to guard against the relentlessness of forgetting, it is absolutely
essential to write down what you hear in class. Later on you can concentrate on
working to understand fully and to remember the ideas that have been presented
in class. And the more complete your notes are at the time of study, the more you
are likely to learn.

Textbook Study

17   In many college courses, success means being able to read and study a textbook
skillfully. For many students, unfortunately, textbooks are heavy going. After an

hour or two of study, the textbook material is as formless and as hard to understand as ever. But there is a way to attack even the most difficult textbook and make sense of it. Use a sequence in which you preview a chapter, mark it, take notes on it, and then study the notes.

Previewing. Previewing a selection is an important first step to understanding. Taking the time to preview a section or chapter can give you a bird's-eye view of the way the material is organized. You will have a sense of where you are beginning, what you will cover, and where you will end.   18

There are several steps in previewing a selection. First, study the title. The title   19
is the shortest possible summary of a selection and will often tell you the limits of the material you will cover. For example, the title "FDR and the Supreme Court" tells you to expect a discussion of President Roosevelt's dealings with the Court. You know that you will probably not encounter any material dealing with FDR's foreign policies or personal life. Next, read over quickly the first and last paragraphs of the selection; these may contain important introductions to, and summaries of, the main ideas. Then examine briefly the headings and subheadings in the selection. Together, the headings and subheadings are a brief outline of what you are reading. Headings are often main ideas or important concepts in capsule form; subheadings are breakdowns of ideas within main areas. Finally, read the first sentence of some paragraphs, look for words set off in **boldface** or *italics*, and look at pictures or diagrams. After you have previewed a selection in this way, you should have a good general sense of the material to be read.

Marking. You should mark a textbook selection at the same time that you read   20
it through carefully. Use a felt-tip highlighter to shade material that seems important, or use a regular ballpoint pen and put symbols in the margin next to the material: stars, checks, or NBs (for *nota bene*, a Latin phrase meaning "note well"). What to mark is not as mysterious as some students believe. You should try to find main ideas by looking for the following clues: definitions and examples, enumerations, and emphasis words.

1 *Definitions and examples:* Definitions are often among the most important   21
    ideas in a selection. They are particularly significant in introductory courses
    in almost any subject area, where much of your learning involves mastering
    the specialized vocabulary of that subject. In a sense, you are learning the "lan-
    guage" of psychology or business or whatever the subject might be.

    Most definitions are abstract, and so they usually are followed by one or   22
    more examples to help clarify their meaning. Always mark off definitions and
    at least one example that makes a definition clear to you. In a psychology text,
    for example, we are told that "rationalization is an attempt to reduce anxiety
    by deciding that you have not really been frustrated." Several examples follow,
    among them: "A young man, frustrated because he was rejected when he asked
    for a date, convinces himself that the woman is not very attractive and is much
    less interesting than he had supposed."

2 *Enumerations:* Enumerations are lists of items (causes, reasons, types, and so   23
    on) that are numbered 1, 2, 3, … or that could easily be numbered in an out-

line. They are often signaled by addition words. Many of the paragraphs in a textbook use words like *first of all, another, in addition,* and *finally* to signal items in a series. This is a very common and effective organizational method.

24   3 *Emphasis words:* Emphasis words tell you that an idea is important. Common emphasis words include phrases such as *a major event, a key feature, the chief factor, important to note, above all,* and *most of all.* Here is an example: "The most significant contemporary use of marketing is its application to non-business areas, such as political parties."

25   **Note-Taking.** Next, you should take notes. Go through the chapter a second time, rereading the most important parts. Try to write down the main ideas in a simple outline form. For example, in taking notes on a psychology selection, you might write down the heading "Kinds of Defense Mechanisms." Below the heading you would number and describe each kind and give an example of each.

Defense Mechanisms

a. *Definition: Unconscious attempts to reduce anxiety*
b. *Kinds:*

(1) *Rationalization: Attempt to reduce anxiety by deciding that you have not really been frustrated*
Example: Man turned down for a date decides that the woman was not worth going out with anyway

(2) *Projection: Attributing to other people motives or thoughts of one's own*
Example: Wife who wants to have an affair accuses her husband of having one

26   **Studying Notes.** To study your notes, use the method of repeated self-testing. For example, look at the heading "Kinds of Defense Mechanisms" and say to yourself, "What are the kinds of defense mechanisms?" When you can recite them, then say to yourself, "What is rationalization?" "What is an example of rationalization?" Then ask yourself, "What is projection?" "What is an example of projection?" After you learn each section, review it, and then go on to the next section.

Do not simply read your notes; keep looking away and seeing if you can recite them to yourself. This self-testing is the key to effective learning.

28   In summary, remember this sequence in order to deal with a textbook: previewing, marking, taking notes, studying the notes. Approaching a textbook in this methodical way will give you very positive results. You will no longer feel bogged down in a swamp of words, unable to figure out what you are supposed to know. Instead, you will understand exactly what you have to do and how to go about doing it.

■

29   Take a minute now to evaluate your own study habits. Do you practise many of the above skills in order to control your time, take effective classroom notes, and learn

from your textbooks? If not, perhaps you should. The skills are not magic, but they are too valuable to ignore. Use them carefully and consistently, and they will make academic success possible for you. Try them, and you won't need convincing.

■ Reading Comprehension Questions

1. Which of the following would be the best alternative title for this selection?
   a. The Importance of Note-Taking
   b. Good Study Skills: The Key to Success
   c. Easy Ways to Learn More
   d. How to Evaluate Your Study Habits

2. Which sentence best expresses the main idea of the selection?
   a. Good study skills can increase academic success.
   b. Note-taking is the best way to study difficult subjects.
   c. More and more schools are offering courses on study skills.
   d. Certain study techniques make college work easy for everyone.

3. Which of these is *not* a good way to organize your time?
   a. Make a monthly calendar.
   b. Keep a weekly study schedule.
   c. Prepare a "to do" list.
   d. Always use extra time for studying.

4. Which is the correct sequence of steps in studying from a textbook?
   a. Preview, self-test, take notes.
   b. Take notes, preview, mark, self-test.
   c. Take notes, mark, preview, self-test.
   d. Preview, mark, take notes, self-test.

5. When marking the textbook for main ideas, do *not*
   a. mark it while you are previewing.
   b. highlight definitions and examples.
   c. include lists of items.
   d. look for "emphasis" words.

6. *True or false?* _____ The author implies that it is better to write too much rather than too little when taking classroom notes.

7. The author implies that one value of class attendance is that you
   a. need to get the next assignment.
   b. will please the instructor, which can lead to better grades.
   c. can begin to improve your short-term memory.
   d. increase your understanding by hearing ideas in person.

8. *True or false?* _____ The author implies that studying does not require any memorization.

9. The word *abstract* in "The examples help you understand abstract points" (paragraph 13) means
   a. simple.

       b. difficult.

       c. ordinary.

       d. correct.

10. The word *capsule* in "Headings are often main ideas or important concepts in capsule form" (paragraph 19) means

       a. adjustable.

       b. larger.

       c. complicated.

       d. abbreviated.

■ Discussion Questions

About Content

1. Evaluate Jill's college coursework. What was she doing right? What was she probably doing wrong?

2. When taking notes in class, how can we tell what information is important enough to write down?

3. What are the three steps in time control? Which do you think would be most helpful to you?

4. What are some of the ways you can spot main ideas when marking a textbook chapter?

About Structure

5. Does Akers use time order or emphatic order in presenting the three study skills?

6. Write down seven different transitional words and phrases used in "Classroom Note-Taking":

   _____

   _____

   _____

   _____

7. Akers tells us that emphasis words (paragraphs 12 and 24) are keys to important ideas. What are three emphasis words or phrases that she herself uses at different places in the article?

   _____ (paragraph _____)

   _____ (paragraph _____)

   _____ (paragraph _____)

About Style and Tone

8. Why has Akers chosen to present most of her essay in the second person— "you"? Why didn't she continue to use Jill, or another student, as an example?

■ Writing Assignments

Assignment 1: Writing a Paragraph

A writing assignment based on this selection is on pages 205-6.

Assignment 2: Writing a Paragraph

Akers says, "A third hint when taking notes is to be on the lookout for signals of importance" (paragraph 12). Pay close attention to these signals in your classes over the next few days. Watch for use of the board, for definitions, for enumerations, and for other ways your instructors might stress information. On a special sheet of paper, keep track of these signals as they occur. Then use your notes to write a paragraph on ways that your instructors signal that certain ideas are important. Be sure to provide specific examples of what your instructors say and do. A possible topic sentence for this paragraph might be "My psychology instructor has several ways of signalling important points in her lectures" or "My instructors use several signals in common to let students know that ideas are important."

Assignment 3: Writing an Essay

For many students, the challenge of college is not just to learn good study skills. It is also to overcome the various temptations that interfere with study time. What pulls you away from success at school? Time with friends or family? Video games? Extracurricular activities? TV? Time spent daydreaming or listening to music? An unneeded part-time job?

Make a list of all the temptations that distract you from study time. Then decide on the three that interfere most with your studying time. Use these three as the basis for an essay titled "Temptations in College Life."

Here is one student's partial outline for an essay.

Thesis statement: The local coffee shop, television, and my girlfriend often tempt me away from what I should be doing in school.

Topic sentence 1: The time I spend at the coffee shop interferes with school in three ways.
a. Skipping classes
b. Going right after class, instead of checking notes
c. Long lunches with friends, instead of studying

Topic sentence 2: I also find that the time I spend watching television interferes with school.
a. Time away from study because of sports and other shows
b. Getting to sleep too late because of late-night TV

Topic sentence 3: Finally, I am often with my girlfriend, who is not a student and does not need to study.
a. Time spent together on non-school activities
b. Studying poorly when she is around

In your final paragraph, include one or two sentences of summary and, perhaps, comment on any changes you plan to make to improve your study time.

As an alternative, you may want to write generally (rather than personally) about "temptations faced by college students." In such a paper, you will use a third-person point of view rather than the first person, and you will provide examples based on your observations of others.

HOW TO WRITE A TEST

Eileen A. Brett

Writing tests never seems as trying for some students as it does for others. A few are calm, plan their attack, and finish on time. Many, however, perspire on their exam books, chew their pens, and never complete a test. If you, like the Canadian author of this text, belong to the latter group, Eileen A. Brett has some sensible, down-to-earth advice about approaching and managing test-taking. Brett, a student at the University of British Columbia, writes with a light touch about a subject of serious concern. Both her recommendations and her information are concrete, specific, and, hopefully, valuable and interesting to you.

1   It is the day of the final exam or perhaps it is just a unit quiz. (Of course, in today's academic courses, when entire grades are sometimes comprised of quiz marks, there is no such thing as a mere quiz.) Whether quiz, test, or examination, does the very suggestion of being tested induce fear and panic? Rest assured; writing tests need not be a frightening experience. If you sit in a place without distractions, bring the right tools, relax, think positively, and organize yourself, you will survive the experience. You may even surprise yourself by doing well on the test.

2   As you enter the classroom the day of the test, your first priority should be to choose where to sit. The important point here is not to find the most comfortable seat but to avoid windows. When a task of importance is unpleasant, eyes tend to wander toward windows and scenes of interest outside. When this happens, inevitably, concentration is relaxed. Equally distracting can be a seat at the back of the room where the back view of any number of attractive blondes or rugged athletes will be in your direct line of vision. Always choose a seat in the front row.

3   To be prepared you will have brought with you at least two pens and one pencil accompanied by a bottle of correction fluid, an eraser, and a watch. Often I have forgotten this last item and suffered tremendously from judging incorrectly how much time remained. These are the essential tools of any test. The pencil may be used substantially more than the pen, for reasons that will be discussed later. One pencil is sufficient, since the walk to the pencil sharpener provides a practical excuse to exercise leg muscles. I stress, however, that this is not an opportunity to

cheat. The walk over to the pencil sharpener is not only a form of physical release, it is also a "brain break." However short this walk may be, the brain welcomes the chance to escape deep mental concentration for the non-strenuous act of sharpening a pencil.

Many students spend the remaining few minutes before the test cramming crucial bits of information into their heads. This effort is wasteful since, in my experience, last minute cramming serves to confuse and is not actually remembered anyway. Why not, instead, spend those moments in mental relaxation and deep breathing? At the same time, analyze the mood in the room. If absolutely everyone else, not having read these helpful hints, is deeply engrossed in last minute preparation, this is a fairly positive indication that the exam will be a difficult one. In this case, it is best that you breathe deeply rather than analyze. If, on the other hand, the majority is calm, cool, and collected, either the test is going to be easy or you have got the date wrong. In both cases, you have nothing to worry about.   4

The interval between the time the test is placed in front of you and the time you are told you may begin is the time to take the Attitude Adjustment Approach, which concerns the mindset in which you will commence writing the exam. During this time, students who want only to scrape by will decide to put minimum effort into the exam. In contrast, students who want a good, if not exceptional, grade will use this time to prepare mentally for the challenge ahead.   5

As the examination begins, take a moment to glance through the test. The decision as to where to start is yours. However, a word to the wise: multiple choice questions should be attacked first for two reasons. First, tidbits of information can often be gleaned from them and then reworked to fit nicely (and inconspicuously) into sentence answers or essays. Second, since the answer is right in front of you, multiple choice questions are the least painful way of easing into the task ahead.   6

In examinations, an organized student has the advantage over a disorganized student. An organized system for writing tests involves using a pen or pencil, depending on how confident you are with the material. Those answers of which you are fairly certain should be answered in pen. Otherwise, pencils are ideal for answering tests because answers can be changed easily. However, since numerous studies have found that, particularly with multiple choice, the first answer chosen is most often the correct one, be 110 percent sure before you change an answer. Should time permit double-checking, it will be necessary to review only those answers in pencil as answers in pen are likely to be correct. If an answer is elusive, make a mark beside the question so you will be able to quickly identify those questions to which you did not know the answers. Then move on and go back to them later.   7

A few techniques have been developed for writing essays. Of course, understanding exactly what the question is asking is essential. If, for example, there is more than one essay question, ideas may flow more freely if you switch back and forth among them. When I begin to get frustrated for lack of ideas, often new thoughts will surface as I answer another question and I will quickly jot them down. Still, other people find staying with one essay until it is completed more beneficial. If all else fails, use the technique of free-writing: write on anything that is even remotely connected with the essay topic until you feel inspired. But perhaps you should take a brain break.   8

9   The technique you choose is of less importance, though, than the interest level of your essays. Not many teachers enjoy perusing forty essay exams on "The Effect of Green Pesticides on Small Herbivores." If you want a good mark, you will strive to keep the professor not only awake but also excited at your discussion of genetic differences in field mice. Imagination is a wonderful asset, but if it is not one of yours, description or examples are also effective. Easy reading is also enhanced by grammatically correct writing.

10   Before you finish the exam, remember to finish those multiple choice questions that you had found impossible to answer. If the process of elimination does not yield an answer that is satisfactory, depending on the amount of time remaining, one of two options is open: count up how many *A* answers you have, how many *B*, etc., and choose the letter that has the least number of answers; or take a reasonable guess. If all else fails, write your professor a note telling him or her of the immense satisfaction and enjoyment you derived from doing the exam, and extend holiday greetings. Then, with hope, you wait for the results and you trust that:

(a)   Without your knowledge, your teacher has sent in several of your essays from the examination to Mensa, which extends the honour of membership to you.
(b)   The test was for the government, which does not care anyway.
(c)   The teacher appreciated your note.

■ Reading Comprehension Questions

1.   Which of the following would be the best alternative title for the selection?
    a.   Seven Steps to Success
    b.   Foolproof Ways to Pass
    c.   Tested Techniques for Taking Tests
    d.   Easy Ways to Ace Exams

2.   Which sentence best expresses the main idea of the selection?
    a.   Mental and physical strategies and organization help you to handle tests better.
    b.   Bringing the right equipment to an exam is half the battle.
    c.   Writing entertaining essay answers and using a clever system for multiple-choice answers guarantee exam success.
    d.   A positive mental attitude and last-minute extra studying can ensure a passing grade.

3.   Which of these is *not* a good idea when you enter the exam room?
    a.   Finding a chair or desk that feels comfortable.
    b.   Sitting away from the window.
    c.   Taking a seat at the front of the room.
    d.   Bringing enough pens.

4.   Brett suggests that cramming just before a test is pointless
    a.   because you can't analyze the mood in the exam room.
    b.   because it adds to your mental clutter and you won't remember those facts.
    c.   because you can overprepare and go to the wrong location in your confusion.
    d.   because you can't meditate and practise deep breathing as you cram.

5. The most important steps in approaching a test are
   a. choosing a good seat, bringing lots of equipment, and having the right attitude.
   b. arriving on time, going to the right location, and handling multiple-choice questions correctly.
   c. choosing the right location and materials, being calm enough to write in an organized way, and knowing how to write a good essay answer.
   d. remembering your watch, keeping your pencils sharp, and using the information from multiple-choice questions in your essays.

6. The author implies that
   a. intense total concentration is the best mental state for dealing with a test.
   b. test results may benefit from brief pauses in concentration.
   c. large muscle exercise is necessary to do well on tests.
   d. several short strolls through the exam room are advisable.

7. *True or false?* _____ Brett implies that final marks are partly the result of decisions made by the student as he or she first looks at the exam.

8. You may conclude that
   a. a good essay answer depends on your ability to amuse the professor.
   b. a good essay answer may result from the use of correct grammar and spelling.
   c. a good essay answer results from an innovative approach, solid content, and attention to language usage.
   d. a good essay answer will result from exciting new discoveries you make in your subject area.

9. The word *gleaned* in "tidbits of information can often be gleaned from them and then reworked to fit nicely (and inconspicuously) into sentence answers or essays" (paragraph 6) means
   a. stolen.
   b. sneaked.
   c. rewritten.
   d. picked up.

10. The word *herbivores* in "The Effect of Green Pesticides on Small Herbivores" (paragraph 9) means
    a. field mice.
    b. plant-eating animals.
    c. houseflies.
    d. rodents.

Discussion Questions

About Content

1. What are Eileen A. Brett's five recommendations for writing better tests? Which of the five have you tried? Have any that you practise worked for you? Why?

2. Why should you bring only one pencil? Are you going to use the pencil more or less often than your pen? Why?

3. What is the "Attitude Adjustment Approach"? Why is this important?

4. What is the point of doing any multiple-choice questions first? Why bother to use two different writing implements?

About Structure

5. What method of ordering, common to all process writing, is used for this essay? In the opening paragraph, which elements recommended by this text for the first paragraphs of process writing do you find?

6. How many paragraphs does the author devote to each of the five steps she lists as parts of the process? List the stages or steps and the numbers of the paragraphs in which they are discussed.

    Step 1 _____ (paragraph _____)

    Step 2 _____ (paragraph _____)

    Step 3 _____ (paragraph _____)

    Step 4 _____ (paragraph _____)

    Step 5 _____ (paragraph _____)

    Which of the steps receives the most attention from the author? Why?

7. How does the writer link the stages in her process? Does she use transition words, "time marker" words and phrases, and/or repetition of important ideas? Which of these devices do you find in which paragraphs? Where are the transition devices placed?

About Style and Tone

8. The author uses some humorous phrases and a tone that is upbeat and lively. What is the effect on you as a reader of the mixture of a light tone with serious subject matter?

9. Where do you find examples of Brett's sense of humour? Some techniques to look for include (1) exaggeration, (2) unlikely combinations of ideas, and (3) unexpected ideas or turns of phrase.

    List an example of each of these below:

    1. _____

    2. _____

    3. _____

■ Writing Assignments

Assignment 1: Writing a Paragraph

Brett notes that the result of not knowing how to take tests is panic. She suggests that such tension may be the result of many factors, such as disorganization, last-minute cramming, mental attitude, and lack of understanding of test design and marking.

Write a paragraph about one memorable exam or test experience of your own. Decide while you are prewriting whether you have more bad or good experiences to list. Your point of view or attitude expressed will result from the list which is longer and contains clearer details or memories. Your paragraph may reflect details and suggestions from Brett's essay. A good exam experience of your own may or may not be the result of having followed some of the author's suggestions, while suffering through a particularly terrible test may bring back some very vivid details. Such strong memories may produce a good paragraph.

Your paragraph should isolate the *causes* of such a good or bad test-writing experience. The end result will be a topic sentence such as "The worst exam I ever wrote was the result of three problems: _____."

Assignment 2: Writing a Paragraph

Should such techniques as note-taking, test-writing, time management, and study skills in general be part of your college's course offerings? Many students arrive at post-secondary education without much knowledge of such skills. Do you believe that a half-semester course covering these areas would be of use to you?

Write a paragraph that argues for or against such a course, covering *three* skills areas you believe would help you most. Be sure to choose three skills you would most like to acquire, and for each of these, list the reasons you feel these should or should not be part of college curricula. If you wish to dispute the value of such a course, you may find justification in the availability of articles such as Eileen A. Brett's, or Sheila Akers's "Power Learning," or other personal experiences which have helped your study skills.

Assignment 3: Writing an Essay

Taking tests and exams is only one of life's challenges. We all face situations and personal trials where a bit of advice or someone else's experience and techniques could prove useful. How-to books are among the best-selling titles in any bookstore.

Here is a list of ordinary social situations with which you may have some experience. What these situations have in common is the often unspoken set of rules governing what to do. Select one of these topics and begin to draft an outline, listing your own set of steps for a process essay that tells someone how to handle just such an event or problem.

1. Attending the funeral of someone to whom you are not closely attached
2. Giving a speech at a wedding reception
3. Looking after someone else's child for a day
4. Saying thank you for a gift you disliked
5. Saying no to a particularly forceful salesperson
6. Refusing a date or invitation from someone you like but are not that fond of
7. Getting out of attending a family dinner or major family celebration
8. Being best man or maid/matron of honour at a friend's wedding

You may want to refer to the chapter on process writing (pages 194-206) for a review of how to construct a process essay. In your outline, be sure to include in the opening paragraph the final result of the process and whatever benefits you think will result from following your procedures. Indicate roughly how many steps will be involved and any anticipated difficulties, as well as any equipment or materials needed to complete the process.

Divide your list of steps or stages into three sections, and give precise details of how to complete each step successfully. Try not to omit any necessary steps, or leave room for mistakes caused by omitting complete instructions. Be sure to make good use of transitions to help your reader through the process.

Finish your essay with a summary of what the reader has now accomplished and a parting thought on the value of such an achievement. You may treat your subject with humour, if you are comfortable doing so.

WHY SHOULD WE HIRE YOU?

Jim Maloney

The workplace of the third millennium is a new place: perhaps a not-so-pleasant prospect for the college student and a place of decreasing possibilities for the already-employed individual. Neither "a job for a lifetime" nor the chance of steady advancement in a field of personal expertise can be expected, much less taken for granted by anyone. A diploma, a degree, and a snappy resumé are no guarantees of a lifetime's steady employment. Instead, a sense of direction, steady and careful academic preparation, and active job research during the college years are needed to face the realities of the twenty-first-century job market. Jim Maloney, coordinator of the Technical Communication program at Seneca College in Toronto and a long-time expert in career-based areas of writing, poses student readers "The Question"—a question he faced, and a question most companies' human resources personnel will ask any student reading this essay: "Why should we hire you?"

I

1   "Why should we hire you for this position?"

2   I remember the first time I was asked that question. I remember it the same way I remember the first time a police officer asked to see my driver's licence and registration. I was no more prepared to be caught speeding than I was prepared to explain why I should be permanently employed teaching English at a community college. In both cases, I experienced a sinking feeling in my stomach, and a quickening of my pulse: the sensations that come with being caught.

3   I got a speeding ticket, but I didn't get the job.

Looking back at the difficulty I had with that basic question, I can't believe that   **4**
I approached the interview so badly prepared. If I had been as prepared for the job
interview as I was for doing the job, I would have felt no surprise. I had had a number of previous jobs where I was hired only for my ability to perform physical tasks,
so the interviews for these jobs were far less crucial than was the simple ability to
do the work. However, just as exceeding the speed limit will, when traffic police
are performing properly, lead to a speeding ticket, so being interviewed for an
attractive career-entry position will, when the interviewer knows what to look for,
lead directly or indirectly to the question "Why should we hire you?"

The question is a significant one, not just because you will encounter it, in   **5**
some form, as part of a job interview, along with other "open-ended" queries
designed to uncover your understanding of the position and of the suitability of
your qualifications. The question is also important to consider in preparing your
resume and application letter—documents crucial to creating possible interviews.
Moreover, the question is relevant to you, who haven't yet finished your postsecondary career preparation and, therefore, won't be immediately facing interviews
for positions in your chosen field. For you at this stage, the question "Why should
we hire you?" may seem pointless, premature, or irrelevant. Try turning the question around: "Why should *I* be hired?" Now the question may have more meaning to you. Indeed, considered in this form, the question can guide you towards
preparing for a career. So, thinking about how you will answer such a question will
help you not only to understand the significance of the question but also to back
up your answers with the right credentials, skills, and experiences.

II

Too frequently, students seem to take for granted their right, or even their access,   **6**
to interviews and to jobs needed to begin their careers. Such optimism can no
longer be justified. Ten years ago, graduating students were warned that continued
employment in one field for one company for one's entire working life was increasingly becoming a thing of the past. Students could expect three or four career
shifts. Today, many college or university graduates will never have the chance even
to begin careers in their chosen fields. Others may find only part-time or contract
work. The last decade has produced enormous changes in the way business and
industry operate in North America, and in the ways in which people are employed.

Corporate downsizing—reductions in the workforce needed by a company   **7**
for operating purposes—has been a fact in business life for some time now. Global
competition is usually given as the reason for smaller workforce requirements,
while, it is claimed, technological developments, especially computerization, have
led to massive employee lay-offs with no loss to productivity. Of course, there is
an alternative view of downsizing: that remaining employees are expected to be
more productive—to work longer and harder—to pick up the slack. A consequence of downsizing and technological change is a reduced full-time workforce,
many of whom either handle more tasks or perform more specialized technological activities. In some companies, another consequence of a smaller workforce is
the replacement of permanent full-time employees who receive higher salaries and
significant benefit packages with part-time or contract workers who are offered

lower salaries and few, if any, benefits. Some companies have virtually nothing to offer but these limited, rather unpromising positions.

8   These changes are not limited to the private sector. Recently, the governments of Alberta and Ontario initiated large-scale downsizing projects in their civil services. Many job lay-offs in health care, education, and local governments have resulted from such funding cuts. For someone wishing to begin a new career, the prospects are starting to look nasty and brutish, and the immediate picture is distinctly short of jobs, hours, and rewards for new employees. Quite simply, there may not be jobs for college and university graduates who don't know how they fit into this brave new workworld.

9   Consequently, it is now more important than ever for you to consider and act on The Question while there is still time for you to learn the needs of employers and to make yourself capable of meeting those needs.

III

10   There are numerous reasons why students may not be seriously addressing The Question. Many students place so much trust in the educational system that they fail to look onward to life beyond graduation. Often, the very fact that students are attending college or university may be the reason they don't take advantage of their school years to prepare themselves effectively for the next step. Some students make the error of seeing an employment ad's requirement of a postsecondary diploma or degree as a guarantee of entry into that career. These students may be so impressed by their status as college or university students that they are complacent about their futures. Unfortunately, being a student is not a career and, with few exceptions, is not very profitable. Other students may find their academic work difficult and demanding enough without adding the headache of anticipating yet more demands. Still others may trust their chosen vocationally based academic program to put them on the correct job track. The problem is that they may not actually know where it is that they are going. I am amazed every semester by the number of students in specialized programs who are utterly unaware of jobs that may be available to them, of skills needed and of the actual nature of duties they may be expected to perform. Clueless in an academic fool's paradise, all of these students are caught in wishful rather than realistic thinking.

11   But what *actual* difference will it make to familiarize yourself with job specifications and employment prospects during your education instead of when you graduate? Preparing yourself to be desirable to prospective employers can have clear advantages during your college or university years. Even if there were no other consequences, a sense of the ultimate purpose of your studies should make your efforts more significant, less abstract—less academic. Being aware of the competition you face in your chosen field could certainly make the pursuit of good grades more meaningful. If you are in a program with a variety of optional courses, your knowledge of the job market's demands will help you to make more informed decisions. Should you be registered in a more rigidly structured program, knowing that the real requirements of the job you want differ from your program's offerings could indicate that you should supplement your education with additional courses beyond your curriculum. Reading job descriptions during your

school years will teach you that certain types of work experience are desired, even for entry-level positions. Therefore, choosing summer or part-time work in an area related to your chosen career, even if the pay is less attractive, may ultimately be more rewarding. Most career-advice agencies now recommend volunteer work, and many students volunteer their time to organizations connected to their career paths. In the cases of both occasional and volunteer work, the contacts made and the experience gained can be very valuable. Finally, you may never need a total personality make-over, but you should think about personal characteristics of successful people in your chosen field.

IV

With all these advantages to be gained from planning ahead for employment, how do you go about finding out what employers want? **12**

One place to start is within your school. Many vocationally based programs have a faculty member responsible for student employment. Some of your instructors may be actively involved in their fields; others may have informal but vital contacts with employers or former students in business and technology. You may discover that it is quite easy to gain insight into your field of interest just by sounding out your teachers. Yet another source of information is your school's student employment office. As well as placing graduating students, this facility usually offers a range of services including personality testing, career counselling, information resources on companies, and job profiles. Graduation is too late to find out what your school has to offer. **13**

Don't feel limited to these paths as you try to discover a career direction. Find out requirements for actual jobs in order to become the candidate you want to be. Even though you are not applying for a permanent position now, make a habit of following not only jobs listed in your school's employment office but also those advertised in newspapers, professional journals, or occupational periodicals. Best of all, visit human resources offices of major employers in your field; check job requirements for current or future positions; meet personnel officers, and read any information available about their companies. The time spent will pay off in your career. **14**

At this point, you may be ready to get in touch with someone already working in your chosen field to gain first-hand knowledge of positions you would like. You don't need to know personally someone who fits this description; one of your teachers or friends may know someone you can contact. Alternatively, speaking with or writing to an employer in your field may help you to find a person suitably placed to answer your questions about qualifications, duties, and responsibilities. You would be surprised by how easy it is to get information, even from a stranger. If you try some of these approaches, you are on your way to a personal network. **15**

Today, you need to work hard to find the work you desire. That means knowing the reasons you should be hired and taking the steps needed to prepare a solidly based answer before you are asked The Question. **16**

■ **Reading Comprehension Questions**

1. Which of the following would be the best alternative title for this selection?
   a. Diplomas and Dim Prospects

    b. Prepare to Work to Find Work
    c. Career Confusion
    d. The Best Degree Is No Guarantee

2. Which sentence best expresses the main idea of the selection?
    a. Intelligent choices of the right courses give students fair chances of getting work on graduation.
    b. The workplace is a crowded "buyer's market," and students must work to prepare themselves to be the "right product."
    c. Today's students must expect several changes in career paths, and several different employers in their professional futures.
    d. Technological developments have eliminated many traditional job opportunities.

3. Maloney believes that
    a. students should concentrate on the employer's viewpoint as they acquire education, skills, and experience.
    b. concentrating on writing good resumés and cover letters will ensure job interviews.
    c. students can focus on career goals from the beginning of their college experience.
    d. due to changes in business and industry, finding a job in the next few years is a hopeless task.

4. Corporate downsizing has led to
    a. a need for more highly trained technological workers.
    b. a mixture of highly versatile and very specialized workers.
    c. companies consisting only of part-time workers.
    d. changes only in the private sector.

5. *True or false?* _____ Maloney believes that choice of a diploma program in a developing area of industry and careful attention to course work can maximize chances for full-time future employment.

6. The author implies that
    a. looking toward the employment market involves looking at all aspects of oneself.
    b. looking forward to job interviews is pointless and terrifying.
    c. it is never too early to start preparing a good resumé and cover letter.
    d. looking for work in the public sector is a waste of time.

7. The essay suggests that
    a. being in focused vocational training is a demanding occupation and gives students enough of an advantage in the job search.
    b. a sense of future job needs may motivate students toward better performance, better course choices, and the acquisition of suitable experience.
    c. knowing which skills will be needed and what jobs may be available will lead to success.
    d. becoming "the ideal lab technician" or "the perfect accountant" while in college is the only way to ensure job interviews.

8. *True or false?* _____ Professional contacts, college student employment offices, "go-see" interviews, and daily reading of employment ads are enough to guarantee a shot at the ideal job.

9. The word *crucial* in "documents crucial to creating possible interviews" (paragraph 5) means
   a. special.
   b. justifiable.
   c. reasonable.
   d. important.

10. The word *anticipating* in "without adding the headache of anticipating yet more demands" (paragraph 10) means
    a. awaiting.
    b. worrying about.
    c. denying.
    d. looking ahead to.

■ Discussion Questions

About Content

1. Why does Professor Maloney recall so vividly the first time he heard the question "Why should we hire you?"

2. The essay's proposed strategy for early focusing on future work is opposed to some traditional thinking which saw college years as a time for discovering yourself and your goals. Do you agree with Maloney's suggestions? What do you think of such "one-track" end-directed approaches to your college experience?

3. What are the early advantages the author sees for the student who is aware of future job needs and possibilities?

4. What resources are available to students within their own colleges?

About Structure

5. The thesis of many essays is found near the beginning or the end. Locate the thesis statement of "Why Should We Hire You?" and write it here.

   _____

6. Which method(s) of introduction does the author use in this selection?
   a. Broad statement
   b. Relevance
   c. Anecdote
   d. Contrast

7. What methods of achieving transitions between paragraphs does Maloney
    use more than once in this selection?
    a. Repetition of keywords
    b. Transitional phrases
    c. Questions followed by explanations

    Find examples of at least three of these, and note them below, with the
    appropriate paragraph numbers.

    _____   (paragraph _____)

    _____   (paragraph _____)

    _____   (paragraph _____)

About Style and Tone

8. Maloney begins his essay with a highly personal and directly voiced confes-
    sion containing a comparison between two apparently dissimilar events.
        How does the tone of the opening three paragraphs compare with that
    of the rest of the essay? What do you learn about the author, and how does
    what you discover affect your connection with him as a writer? Does it make
    the information in the essay more or less credible? Why?

9. After the introductory paragraphs, the essay is divided into three sections.
    How would you subtitle each of these sections?

    1. _____

    2. _____

    3. _____

    What general method of organization do your subtitles seem to suggest?

■ Writing Assignments

Assignment 1: Writing a Paragraph

Jim Maloney describes three types of attitudes prevalent among students. Choose
the attitude that most closely resembles your own and write a paragraph that
defends your position.

Assignment 2: Writing a Paragraph

Put yourself in Jim Maloney's position as he begins his essay. Imagine you have successfully graduated from your current program, have your resumé in hand, and are
sitting in a job interview. Now answer "The Question" posed by the essay's title.
Start with a specific job you may have in mind or may have read about in the paper.
Now, list what you think the employer may be looking for in skills, academic training, and part-time experience. Your paragraph should answer "The Question." You
may want to begin with a topic sentence like "Working in fire protection has been
a lifelong goal of mine, and I've done a lot of academic and practical preparation
to get ready to enter the field." Make use of the groups of details you have listed
under the headings above to build up your paragraph.

Assignment 3: Writing an Essay

You are an employer in the year 2005. *You* ask "The Question." You are a human resources officer in a company, and *you* must write the job description to be read by all those eager college graduates.

Write an essay that follows the format of a job description for a position for which your diploma is preparing you. To see examples of these, go to your student services office or look at some periodicals special to your area of study for employers' advertisements. Your mission is to find and persuade that "ideal candidate" that this job is what that person is after. Be as specific in your details as possible. You can't offer "the world on a string"; you have limited salary and promotion possibilities in this uncertain economy. But you are going to be facing hundreds of applicants.

Make an outline similar to the following:

Thesis/Introduction: Omnitech Incorporated is looking for an energetic and ambitious entry-level _____. The successful candidate will have three main qualifications: _____, _____, and especially _____. [Also include a brief company description and approximate salary range, as well as any special requirements, such as a willingness to travel.]

Topic Sentence 1: Your background and education will include

a. _____
b. _____
c. _____

Topic Sentence 2: The skills we are looking for are

a. _____
b. _____
c. _____

Topic Sentence 3: The types of experience we prefer are

a. _____
b. _____
c. _____

Conclude by summarizing your needs, emphasizing that the successful applicant will come close to or exceed all the requirements listed, and stating that only resumés received within a certain time frame will be considered.

ARE WE RAISING MORALLY ILLITERATE KIDS?

Caroline Medwell

Talk of morality in youth and adult behaviour is everywhere today. Are we any more or less moral than our grandparents were? Has everyone ceased to care what is good or bad, or is the "bad apple" count the same as it ever was? People are the same mixed lot from one generation to another, so what changes in the past twenty-five years might have affected ethics and behaviour? Well, there are at least two generations now who are predominantly products not of "ideal" two-parent nuclear families but of single-parent or two-working-parent families. And most people in these generations grew up with TV as a constant in their lives. Is there any single cause of "moral illiteracy"? Are children and young adults actually "morally illiterate"? Weigh your own views and experiences against those of Caroline Medwell as you read the following selection.

1   The two boys were about eight years old. Derek looked athletic and confident. Adam seemed more fragile, his thin shoulders hunched up around his ears. On "Go!" they plunged into the water and began their race to the far end of the pool and back. The shrieks of their classmates bounced off the walls—most were cheering for the obvious favorite: "Derek! Derek!"

2   Adam kept his head down, concentrating on the shallow-end wall where they were to turn. Derek kept a close eye on the teacher. When she turned to talk to the lifeguard, Derek, quick as a wink, spun around and started back toward the starting point, shaving about six metres off the prescribed distance. Adam turned at the shallow-end wall, as instructed, now far behind his opponent.

3   The crowd of boys watching from the deck fell silent for a moment, as they digested the fact that Derek had cheated. Some then resumed cheering for Derek, now almost guaranteed to win. But others hesitated, then moved over to Adam's lane to lend him new-found encouragement and support.

4   Although Derek did reach the finish first, it was, unbelievably, a close race. The teacher, sensing something amiss, declared the result to be a tie. Derek argued loudly against that verdict, insisting that he had won. Adam wrapped himself in his towel and walked slowly back to the dressing room, a contented little smile on his face.

5   For some reason, this small incident took on almost epic proportions in my mind; a representation, I thought, of the struggle between the desire to win and the ability and willingness to play fair. That it had been enacted by two small boys was unaccountably depressing.

6   A short while later, I turned on the radio to hear the announcer introduce a program "Is TV Turning Kids into Violent Criminals?" The psychiatrist being interviewed described "desensitized" children, who are "more likely to use violence" as a result of television viewing. He cited the example of a three-year-old Washington child who found his father's gun, picked it up, pointed it at his two-year-old playmate and shot him dead. The weekend newspaper carried an article

on children who are pushed to succeed so hard by their parents that they become "problems, not prodigies."

The only item publicized that weekend indicating any kind of adult attention to the needs of children highlighted the National Campaign to Save Lemon Yellow, a U.S. parent group who are fighting hard to save "eight classic crayon colors" from the Crayola 64-pack.   7

I couldn't help myself. I saw Nero fiddling while Rome burned.   8

To my mind, the morality of today's children looms as a more important issue than discontinued crayon colors. Are our kids equipped with a solid set of values? A conscious code of ethics? A healthy respect for the people and the world around them? Or are they a generation of violent, stressed-out human beings, whose main objective is to win at any cost? Are they a generation saddled by "moral illiteracy"?   9

Moral illiteracy is a term coined by Burle Summers, president of the Ontario Moral/Values Education Association, a volunteer group of parents, teachers and university professors. Concerned that traditional values are giving way to the fast track, the quick promotion and a "me first" attitude, members promote the teaching of qualities such as honesty, respect, courtesy, generosity, responsibility and self-discipline.   10

Summers cautions, however, against too literal an interpretation of the phrase "morally illiterate." "I'm not saying kids are immoral," says Summers. "I am saying that they don't have the same background, the same set of rules as before." The result, he says, is five-year-olds who don't know how to share and to whom "please" and "thank you" are foreign words, 10-year-olds who laugh and chatter in the movies and put their feet up on occupied theatre seats, teens who speak rudely to store clerks and loll about on public transit seats while their elders stand precariously. The reason for such behavior, says Summers, is an "absence of certitude"— a kind of moral vacuum that creates a need to explore potential substitutes for values which were instilled in the previous generation but seem to have gone missing in our kids.   11

It's true that many of us adults were raised in stable nuclear families, where issues were discussed together around the family dinner table, and our parents took the time to school us in manners and good grace. Even our TV viewing revolved around such wholesome shows as *Ozzie and Harriet, Father Knows Best,* and *Leave It To Beaver*—which, if anything, erred on the side of idealism in depicting family life. Our upbringing may not have been perfect, but most of us matured with finely tuned notions of right and wrong.   12

Our children are not so lucky. They live in a complex world, where truth, goodness and respect are often hard to find. They spend almost as much time during the year watching TV as they do in school, and their heroes include Bart Simpson and the Teenage Mutant Ninja Turtles. Role models like Ben Johnson and Pete Rose have been barred from their respective sports for breaking the rules—and kids have noticed that this only happened after they were caught publicly. Our children live in a country which has been torn apart over the Constitution and—incredibly— embroiled in a world war.   13

Today's children probably have more intense life experiences every day than we would have faced in a year at their age. And, at the end of these intense days,   14 many children don't have the opportunity to discuss these experiences with their parents and, in doing so, receive guidance. One of the reasons is that many modern families are often just too busy to talk. Some families sit down to only one meal together a week, and for others, there are few social situations where children can intermingle with adults to converse, interact—and learn.

15   Instead, children spend a lot of time interacting with electronic gadgets. Walkmans drown out the sounds of the surrounding world, running interference against two-way conversations. Video games enable children to play for hours without another human being in sight. Television, which 97 per cent of Canadian children watch for an average of 20 hours per week, offers a third form of solitary entertainment. Through that screen, children see and learn from a variety of characters. Bart Simpson, the bratty, brazen star of *The Simpsons* does say grace before dinner, but this is how it goes: "Dear God, we paid for all this stuff ourselves, so thanks for nothing." His father, Homer hears that the nuclear plant where he works is "contaminating the planet" and responds "Well, nobody's perfect."

16   Antonia Coffman, publicist for *The Simpsons*, points out that the characters "aren't meant to be role models. The show is meant to entertain, it's not a message show." Coffman adds that both children and adults like the Simpsons because they're more realistic than the "perfect family" portrayed, for example, on *The Cosby Show*. Coffman credits kids these days with being "smarter, more savvy. They love the edge—and can see, for the most part, what's right and wrong."

17   Maybe so—but it may not always be the right lessons that are sinking in, especially if children absorb too much of this material alone or without discussion.

18   Marcia Williamson, a Toronto grade 2 teacher, is one of many educators who is rising to the challenge of teaching values along with the regular subjects in the curriculum. Avoiding "really scary" issues like nuclear warfare, Williamson concentrates on helping her kids learn cooperation and non-violence—and how to react to everyday situations peacefully and positively. She uses films, followed by discussion, and the lessons learned are repeated around the classroom on large, colorful pieces of paper. Topics include sharing, learning from disappointment and good manners. At this level, says Williamson, you can't expect kids to perfect these skills. "All I'm doing is planting the seeds." Parent participation is crucial, so Williamson sends information home and discusses her program with the families. Without their support, she asserts, her efforts "just won't stick as well."

19   According to Burle Summers, "open, honest dialogue" among family members is also a crucial component of values education. With respect to promoting it in the home, his advice is threefold. To start, he says, we must "sort out what's important to us—what we'd live and die for—and encourage others to reflect with us." Then, we must consider what we are doing, as a family unit or on our own, to develop respect for the individual, society, the environment, and how that respect is extended to the community around us. Thirdly, Summers asks us to "invite kids to participate in life decisions and life behavior." Do this on a daily basis, says Summers, using practical, realistic examples.

20   A factor Summers perceives as inhibiting the effectiveness of values education is today's focus on self. "Kids are emerging from a 'me first' society," he says, "and considering the needs and rights of others can be difficult for them." It's true that children need a strong sense of themselves, and what they stand for and believe in,

before they can extend or express those feelings to the world around them. Unfortunately, too many children have not been taught how to move beyond the self, and this "me first" attitude can make life difficult for those around them. Said one veteran teacher: "Teachers have a hard time these days with the lack of respect from kids—and you feel like they're getting that attitude from home." While none of the teachers I spoke with regret the freer, more open education system that we have now, most point out that it has its price.

I have three children, and I know it's not easy, and occasionally impossible, to con- 21 sistently offer them the kind of time and dialogue that the experts have described. My kids can squabble like masters, and I can be crankier sometimes than I like to imagine. But, in the interest of honesty, and inspired by my conversations with people like Burle Summers and Marcia Williamson, I decided to put into practice some of their peacemaking, thoughtful philosophies.

When my kids erupted over possession of a cereal box prize, I resisted the urge 22 to make a snap decision on who got what. Instead, I let each of them have their say, without interruption, and then asked for their solution. This turned out to be giving that particular item to the youngest ("I didn't really like it anyway," mut-tered one of the empty-handed two) and adding a piece of paper to the fridge door, on which we will record receipt of all such things from now on—and in doing so, know whose turn is next. And each day, I made sure I spent time with each of them, just talking about whatever was on our minds.

The results weren't always picture-perfect. I sometimes became impatient with 23 the peacemaking process and jumped ahead to a ruling on the matter. And I'll con-fess that when we played the one cooperative board game that we have, I found it less exciting than, say, Snakes and Ladders.

But then something happened which gave me hope. I came home yesterday 24 to find an addition to our message board. Written in a child's hand, shining out from the list of that day's activities, were the words, "Peace, Flower Power, Saving the World."

It's a start, I thought, a good start. 25

■ Reading Comprehension Questions

1. Which of the following would be the best alternative title for the selection?
   a. Media Make Children Monsters
   b. Why Morals May Be Puzzling to Kids
   c. Why Schools Can't Cope with Children Today
   d. Today's Immoral Children

2. Which sentence best expresses the main idea of the selection?
   a. Children live in a complex world full of diverse influences and little guidance and are less morally certain than earlier generations.
   b. Media have failed to provide positive role models for children and thus encourage violence and selfishness.
   c. Families no longer offer the consistent patterns and guidance needed to raise children with sound ethics.
   d. Ethics and morality are no longer important in today's society or in its choice of role models.

3. "Moral illiteracy," according to Burle Summers, means
   a. children do not understand what morality means.
   b. children have no role models and simply imitate society's current lack of ethics.
   c. children have not learned values and are uncertain of right and wrong.
   d. children misbehave because they prefer to challenge standards and rules.

4. Medwell believes she and her generation have a strong sense of ethics primarily because
   a. they were brought up very well.
   b. they watched only wholesome TV shows.
   c. they all grew up in two-parent nuclear families.
   d. families communicated well and taught ethical lessons.

5. The appeal of *The Simpsons*, according to its publicist, lies in the fact that
   a. it reflects reality more accurately than shows with ideal families.
   b. its characters live "on the edge" of acceptable behaviour.
   c. its wisecracking characters always deliver a good message.
   d. it makes fun of everything.

6. The article implies that
   a. the media sensationalize and exaggerate child-morality issues.
   b. the media care about selling products more than about providing children with suitable role models.
   c. the media teach children violence and selfishness.
   d. the media prefer trivial items about children rather than problematic or complex stories.

7. The article implies that
   a. electronic toys and TV create aggressive tendencies and ignorance of ethics in children.
   b. children cannot develop an ethical sense in the absence of social interaction.
   c. today's active and busy families are to blame for not teaching children moral values.
   d. children isolate themselves from reality and problems with technology and entertainment.

8. From the article, we can conclude that
   a. learning and practising ethics is best done at home.
   b. children have too little respect for others to learn from them.
   c. learning and practising ethics must be interactive and family-, community-, and school-based.
   d. children already have a sense of ethics but cannot express it.

9. The word *prodigies* in "pushed to succeed so hard by their parents that they become 'problems, not prodigies'" (paragraph 6) means
   a. monsters.
   b. underachievers.

    c. geniuses.

    d. smart alecks.

10. The word *embroiled* in "torn apart over the Constitution and—incredibly —embroiled in a world war" (paragraph 13) means

    a. attacked.

    b. overcooked.

    c. manipulated.

    d. involved.

■ Discussion Questions

About Content

1. Where in the opening anecdote do you see examples of "the desire to win" and "the ability and willingness to play fair" (paragraph 5)? Could these events have happened in any decade, or are they typical only of today's children? Are there situations in your life when you have taken part in or witnessed such a struggle? How did your observations or experience affect you?

2. What examples of "moral illiteracy" among today's children and teens does Burle Summers offer? Does such behaviour confirm a judgment of today's children as "a generation of violent, stressed-out human beings, whose main objective is to win at any cost" (paragraph 9)? Why or why not? Is such behaviour prevalent, in your experience?

3. What factors, according to author Caroline Medwell, contribute to the "complex world" in which today's children live? What other factors might make their world complex as well?

4. What three recommendations does Burle Summers give for families who wish to create opportunities for dialogue about values? Are these recommendations realistic or achievable? Why or why not?

About Structure

5. What method is used to introduce and conclude the selection?

    a. Explaining the importance of the subject.

    b. Situation opposite to the one to be developed.

    c. Anecdote related to the thesis.

    d. Asking a question.

    Which standard of effective writing is achieved by the author's use of the same method for both sections?

6. Although Medwell's essay may be primarily persuasive in intention, she uses other subsidiary patterns to develop and set out her ideas. The cause-and-effect structure is one such pattern within the essay. Where in the selection do you find the cause-and-effect pattern used? Note the paragraph groups where this pattern is used, and note in a few words the causes and effects mentioned.

7. Where in the selection do you find the following transitional devices used to link the end of one paragraph to the beginning of another? Note the words and paragraph numbers.
    a. Repetition of a keyword or phrase.
    b. Change-of-direction word or phrase.

About Style and Tone

8. "Are We Raising Morally Illiterate Kids?" is written from two points of view: the first person (*I, we*) and the third person (*he/she*). Which paragraphs are written in the first person, and which in the third person? In which point of view are more paragraphs written? What is the content of the paragraphs in each point of view? Compare the first-person paragraphs and the third-person paragraphs; how effectively does the author make her point in each set of paragraphs?

▦ Writing Assignments

Assignment 1: Writing a Paragraph

An assignment based on this selection appears on page 236.

Assignment 2: Writing a Paragraph

Are you and your friends "stressed-out human beings" (paragraph 9)? What are the specific sources of stress felt by college students at the beginning of the twenty-first century? Why is your generation's stress level different from that of your parents? Do the stresses you feel affect the ethical choices you make? How, specifically?

Write a paragraph in which you defend or argue against the following statement: "College students today face pressures and temptations that make conventionally moral choices difficult."

Assignment 3: Writing an Essay

Everyone today lives in a media-generated environment, made of TV programming, the Internet, music videos, song lyrics, advertising, movies, and magazines. Some people feel that the media adversely inform and influence audiences, to the point of stimulating or causing violent or anti-social behaviour. Such people would inevitably cite the U.S. and Alberta high-school shooting tragedies as examples of media influencing young minds. "Are We Raising Morally Illiterate Kids?" suggests that media do offer questionable role models, such as Bart and Homer Simpson, while other people feel that viewers actually use media to help them make better moral choices.

Write an essay that looks at specific ways in which three TV shows you watch convey fair ethical standards in their characters and plot lines. Be honest; do not use overly wholesome programs you never watch. It is entirely possible to argue that *The Simpsons*, *Smackdown Raw*, and *General Hospital* display reasonable ethics and moral values.

LANGUAGE OUT, STYLE IN

Jerry Amernic

A recent television commercial for a major car company had a text screen that read, "First in it's class." Do you see a problem in that sentence? If not, you are not alone. Thousands of North Americans, like the Canadian students Jerry Amernic discusses in this selection, seem oblivious to spelling and grammatical errors. Why did no one at the advertising agency that created the car commercial catch the error? Are literacy skills lower than ever, now that communication technology is more pervasive than ever? Consider what Amernic, who teaches corporate communications at a college, has to say.

We all know the most famous line in movies when Rhett Butler said to Scarlett O'Hara, "Frankly, my dear, I don't give a damn," but another Butlerian comment to that same southern belle carries a lot more meaning. "What most people don't seem to realize is that there is just as much money to be made out of the wreckage of a civilization as from the upbuilding of one... I'm making my fortune out of the wreckage." 1

Today, as we close out the millennium in a time of prosperity, it's clear that the wreckage of society is coming in many forms, among them the continual erosion of language. Indeed, language skills are at their lowest ebb ever. For the past 30 years, educators have come up with every reason why *not* to teach spelling, grammar, and punctuation in favour of a "holistic" approach to learning. The result is an entire generation of people who aren't up to snuff on basics. Item. Earlier this year, an American TV news announcer—whose name I didn't catch—was commenting on the Senate impeachment hearings, and what she said still boggles my mind. "It's just getting interesting-er and interesting-er." 2

Now she was young and pretty and if those were the only requirements for a TV news announcer in the '90s, terrific, but it would be nice if they knew something about words too. With her hair neatly coiffed and her colours perfectly co-ordinated for the camera, she had the temerity to coin a comparative right up there with *fascinatinger, remarkabler,* and *tremendouser* and if we made these words superlatives, we'd have *fascinatingest, remarkablest,* and *tremendousest.* 3

She's not alone. Spelling errors and bad grammar are increasingly common in ads and newspapers, never mind the Internet, which is the best place to learn how *not* to spell. Author Tom Wolfe calls the Internet a "great time waster," but he's 68 and what does he know? Maybe more than we think. His colleague, Gore Vidal, once said: "Fewer and fewer young people are addicted to reading. If they don't get into it from the time they are ten or 12 years old, they'll never enjoy reading, and if you don't enjoy reading, there goes literature. Literature is still the most profound of arts, but its prognosis is very bad." Vidal said this five years ago when the Internet was just coming out of the embryo and now that it's a child, our young read even less than they did back in '94, opting to surf instead. 4

5   In the middle of the last century, Alexis de Tocqueville wrote in **Democracy in America** that the future would result in an egalitarian dismissal of excellence. Well, guess what? The future is here! While companies like Microsoft and IBM keep telling us about the benefits of the Internet, who stops to think that maybe no one is really benefiting—except Microsoft and IBM?

6   Any parent with kids in high school knows that standards aren't what they used to be. I teach writing to public relations students in college, some of them with university degrees and many from other countries. Without fail, the ones with the worst proficiency in English are those who were educated in Canada. Not Jamaica, Algeria or Russia. Canada. A Canadian-educated student up on grammar is a diamond in the rough; it's usually due to a grade 9 English teacher who went against the grain and stressed what the curriculum abandoned.

7   What do you do with 20-year-olds who are just learning the basics? I give them some standard punctuation and the parts of speech, tell them to toss 'spellcheck' and 'grammarcheck' out the window, and take a look at George Orwell's "Six Rules of Good Writing." (Some of them have actually heard of Orwell.) Come to think of it, professionals could use these rules too.

8   *1. **'Never use a figure of speech which you are used to seeing in print.'** This brings to mind tech-ies who use "connectivity," "multi-tasking," and "design methodology" when they should just try to speak plain English.*

9   *2. **'Never use a long word where a short one will do.'** A popular phrase like "home sweet home" would never have lasted if the original was "residence sweet residence."*

10   *3. **'If it's possible to cut out a word, always cut it out.'** Lawyers are especially guilty of breaking this rule. Example. "If the company revises this policy form with respect to policy revisions, endorsements or rules by which the insurance hereunder could be extended or broadened without additional premium charge, such insurance as is afforded hereunder shall be so extended or broadened effective immediately upon approval or acceptance of such revision during the policy by the appropriate insurance supervisory authority." Doesn't it work better this way? "We will automatically give you the benefits of any extension of this policy if the change doesn't require additional cost." By the way, the word count dropped from 59 to 20, so a pox on all those history and English majors who think it's better to use more words.*

11   *4. **'Never use the passive where you can use the active.'** This is any politician's pet peeve; be vague and don't take responsibility for anything (and your writing will be as exciting as a Hansard debate).*

12   *5. **'Never use a foreign phrase, a scientific word or a jargon word if you can think of an everyday English equivalent.'** (See lawyer example in No. 3).*

13   *6. **'Break any of these rules sooner than say anything outright barbarous.'** In other words, a good lead with 18 words is still better than a bad one with 15, but we should still strive to say more with less.*

14   Rules aside, it is also a good idea to study both good and bad communicators. Former U.S. Secretary of State Alexander Haig ("a dialectic fashion at one end of the spectrum"), aspiring presidential candidate Dan Quayle ("We Republicans understand the importance of bondage between a mother and child"), and many of our leaders in Canada (anything Jean Chrétien says) are all poor

communicators. Winston Churchill and Martin Luther King, on the other hand, were wonderful. Unfortunately, male cadavers are unyielding of testimony. Huh? Sorry. I mean, "Dead men don't talk." But that's not really true. Their speeches survive. Why not have a look?

■ **Reading Comprehension Questions**

1. Which of the following would make the best alternative title for the selection?
    1. Education Neglects Literacy
    2. The End of Excellence
    3. The Internet and Illiteracy
    4. Reading, Writing, and Miscommunication

2. Which sentence best expresses the selection's main point?
    a. Media are responsible for careless language use.
    b. The decline in language skills is symptomatic of wider social disintegration.
    c. The Canadian educational system has left students weak in literacy skills.
    d. Corporate interests work against literacy.

3. Why does Amernic find fault with the American news announcer he mentions in paragraphs 2 and 3?
    a. She is commenting on serious news but is unable to speak correctly.
    b. She is too attractive to be a news commentator.
    c. She is too young to know any better.
    d. She reflects network hiring practices.

4. *True or false?* _____ The Internet, which forces people to read text screens, encourages literacy, according to the author.

5. A Canadian student who has a good grasp of grammar probably
    a. learned from students from other countries.
    b. worked hard in English classes.
    c. had a teacher who ignored the standard curriculum.
    d. uses spell-checking and grammar-checking tools regularly.

6. *True or false?* _____ Rules for good writing apply to everyone, not just students.

7. We learn from this article that
    a. the author recommends staying up to date on new word uses.
    b. the author recommends breaking grammatical rules occasionally.
    c. the author dislikes those with English degrees.
    d. the author values clear, straightforward writing.

8. We can conclude from this article that Amernic believes that
    a. politicians and public figures are poor communicators.
    b. people can learn from poor and effective communicators.
    c. the only good politician or public figure is a dead one.
    d. Canadian politicians are especially poor communicators.

9. The word *prognosis* in "Literature is still the most profound of the arts, but its prognosis is very bad" (paragraph 4) means
   a. effectiveness.
   b. market share.
   c. history or track record.
   d. future or predictable outlook.

10. The word *cadavers* in "Unfortunately, male cadavers are unyielding of testimony" (paragraph 14) means
    a. corpses.
    b. politicians.
    c. celebrities.
    d. communicators.

■ Discussion Questions

About Content

1. What does the author mean by a "'holistic' approach to learning" (paragraph 2)? Which subject areas has such an approach affected most? How does your own educational experience compare with what Amernic describes?

2. Why does the author call the Internet "the best place to learn how *not* to spell"? Where, in online communication, do you see proof of this statement?

3. What is the risk if children are not strong readers by a certain age, according to author Gore Vidal? What is potentially lost if this possibility becomes the norm?

4. Who does Amernic see as making their "fortune out of the wreckage" (paragraph 1) of today's society? Why does he say so? Do you agree or not, and why?

5. What are the author's methods for teaching language and writing skills to his students? How do these differ from the way you are learning to write?

About Structure

6. What purposes are served by Amernic's introduction?

7. Where in the selection do you find the clearest statement of the author's thesis? Why does it appear in this position?

8. How many paragraphs does the author use to provide supporting evidence for his first point about the decline in language-use standards? How many examples does he provide in these paragraphs? Which are most effective, and why?

About Style and Tone

9. Amernic includes George Orwell's "Six Rules of Good Writing" in their entirety, with his own commentary added beneath each rule. What is the

effect of including the full text of Orwell's rules in a short selection? Should Amernic have paraphrased the rules? Does the author's commentary on each rule lessen the effectiveness of the rules or explain their meaning more fully?

10. Does the author's use of a slightly comic tone strengthen or weaken his point? Why?

◼ Writing Assignments

Assignment 1: Writing a Paragraph

In 2003, Bruce Sterling wrote an article called "10 Technologies That Deserve to Die," about pieces of technology that are annoying or ineffective. Try your own, language-based version of this topic: "Three [or some other number] Words That Deserve to Disappear."

To begin, make a list of words that particularly annoy you. Then consider the *reasons why* these words should disappear. Come up with three words that fit into a single category, such as "words that are impossible to spell," "words that don't mean anything," "trendy words I don't understand," or "words that always upset me." Explain, with examples, why that word really fits the category into which you have placed it. Your topic sentence could be something like one of these.

> When people are dating, they use words that should disappear forever from the English language because of the arguments these words cause.

> There are three words that never mean what they say in advertisements: "new," "free," and "improved."

Assignment 2: Writing a Paragraph

"Internetspeak" or "chat language" is an English teacher's nightmare. Is there a place in the development of English for Internet-based usages such as "IMO" or "BTW," or for "chat code" spellings like "u r the best—c u b4 tuesday" that ignore case and spelling rules completely?

Write a paragraph in which you argue that certain specific Internet spelling and language changes should or should not be considered acceptable written English. If you argue for these new spellings and word patterns, in which situations would they be appropriate, and why? Would everyone who reads text written this way understand it? Why is it preferable to current standard English?

Assignment 3: Writing an Essay

Writing well is the subject of this book as well as of Amernic's article. All of us, at one time or another, in some language, and for some reason, have written something that we feel is very good. This piece of writing could be a note on a birthday card to a friend or parent, a story you wrote as a child, or a letter of application for college or a job.

Write a narrative-style essay in which you relate the story of one piece of writing of which you are proud. Your thesis statement could involve what you learned from writing it, what it means to you, or what the effect of your writing was on the person who read it. In your opening paragraph, set up the background or context needed for readers to understand your point. Your body paragraphs could describe the circumstances prompting you to create your piece of writing, the process of writing it, or the significance of doing so. Here is one student's partly completed outline.

<u>Thesis Statement:</u> My first resumé might be the best thing I have ever written.

<u>Topic Sentence 1:</u> I wanted to get a good summer job, so I knew my resumé needed to be impressive.
—never had jobs where I needed one before
—wanted a job where I wasn't doing physical labour

<u>Topic Sentence 2:</u> I had no idea how to lay out or write a resumé, so it took a lot of work.
—I nearly paid for a resumé service to write one for me
—I wanted to prove to myself I could do it
—Learned a lot about formatting documents

<u>Topic Sentence 3:</u> It worked—I got a job at my local cable station.
—the interviewer complimented me on my resumé
—have to write memos sometimes, so the practice was good?

Assignment 4: Writing an Essay Using Internet Research

The Internet is actually a source of some good information about writing well. Use Google or another search engine to look up a few webpages about good writing. Try keywords such as *rules for good writing*, *writing well*, and other combinations, until you find at least five pages whose main content is how to write effectively. Good sites include http://www.uniquecritique.net/AspiringWriters.html and http://palc.sd40.bc.ca/palc/StudentWriting/tipsforgood.htm, and there are many others, including some sponsored by colleges and universities.

Choose two sites about writing well and write an essay that compares them, based on their usefulness to you. In your prewriting, begin with two columns, one for each site. List the items you found most or least helpful on the sites. In a second stage of prewriting, add notes that explain why you chose your helpful or unhelpful list items. Next, for your outline, select three comparable items for each site, so that the body of your essay is balanced.

plaining a Process · Examining Cause and Effect · Comparing or Contrasting · Defining
m · Dividing and classifying · Describing a Scene or Person · Narrating an Event · Argu
osition · Explaining a Process · Examining Cause and Effect · Comparing or Contrastin
fining a Term · Dividing and classifying · Describing a Scene or Person · Narrating
ent · Arguing a Position · Explaining a Process · Examining Cause and Effect · Compar

Human Groups and Society

HAVE YOU SEEN MY MISSING MATH GENE?

Tony Wong

One of Canada's favourite stereotypes is that of the Asian math and computer whiz. As high-school and college students, we automatically assume that the Asian student next to us will get an A in Accounting and can probably program our PC to do everything but cook dinner. All nations and peoples are prone to stereotyping; it's one of the ways in which our brains learn to classify and sort information. However, when we apply these categorizing principles to people, the results can range from silly social mistakes to deep-seated and harmful prejudices that lead to movements such as neo-Nazism and apartheid. Tony Wong, a reporter for *The Toronto Star*, takes a light-hearted look at the Canadian perception of the typical Asian: its origins in economic necessity and its effects on him and his non-typical brother and cousin.

1   It seems every year I am asked to speak to Asian kids about alternate careers.

2   An alternate career for an Asian child being defined as anything but a doctor, dentist, pharmacist, accountant or any vocation requiring addition.

3   I am uniquely qualified to give these seminars, it seems, because I must be one of the few Asians, according to programs like *60 Minutes* (which once did a segment on why so many Asians are taking over the medical schools of America), who cannot add. Or subtract or multiply.

4   I also stink at chess and have trouble turning on my computer.

5   To this day I have not figured out how to properly program my VCR, although I have cleverly got rid of the flashing 12 o'clock sign by pasting electrical tape over it. So you see, I am not bereft of resources.

6   If there is a math gene for Chinese folk, I have somehow missed out.

7   Philippe Rushton would have a field day with me, and I have not even got into the issue of Asian versus Black versus Caucasian penis size, which has been—for goodness sake—the topic of the good professor's latest research. I already have enough of a complex, thank you.

8   But do not despair for me, for I have been living a fulfilling life despite my handicap, although my job has been made more difficult with China's win this summer at, what else, the International Math Olympiad, where, to top things off, Canada's top-gun was Chinese Canadian.

9   This leaves folks like me in a precarious situation, burdened with trying to lead Asian youth out of their computer and slide rule-induced stupor.

10   I remember one year where Metro Councillor Olivia Chow and I were dragged out as mathematically challenged role models for a workshop on alternate career skills for teens.

11   Olivia, who can actually add but faked it for my benefit, seemed doubly qualified for this job as she started life as an artist before becoming a high-powered politician.

12   For the occasion, I wrote a skit to demonstrate the pressures faced by Asian kids at home. Olivia kindly agreed to play my mom, while I played a bratty kid who wants to be an artist. I gave Olivia all the good lines.

13   Olivia: "Jimmy Li got into pharmacy. His mother said he got scholarship, too."

14   Me: "That's nice, Mom. I think I'll continue practising my Spider-Man doodle. You never know when Marvel will call."

15   Actually my own segue into the writing life wasn't so difficult. My brother Victor inadvertently paved the way when he decided to be an artist.

16   When my mother got a look at his work, which included the influences of Matisse and Rubens with a little *Playboy* thrown in, she was not amused.

17   She seemed relieved when I told her I just wanted to be a starving writer.

18   She changed her tune, though, after a visit to the Barnes exhibition at the Art Gallery of Ontario.

19   "That looks like something your brother would draw," she would exclaim seeing Matisse's dance of life which consists of a bunch of fat nudes frolicking. It was then she figured that my poor brother had not been "marketed" properly, especially after seeing that a bunch of naked people dancing in a park by a dead guy could fetch so much money. Moreover, my brother is alive to boot.

20   It reminded me of the time my cousin Walter, a photographer who had shot covers for all the top international fashion magazines, including *Vogue*, *Elle* and *Cosmopolitan*, was told by his mother that he shouldn't have a studio upstairs where no one could see him.

21   After all, suppose someone wanted to get a passport picture? He would lose business. It was the ever-pragmatic Asian philosophy at work. Don't forget the walk-by traffic. At that time, national media profiles pegged his daily fee at $50,000. But, as my aunt would say, you never know when another $9.95 might come in handy.

22   So you see, there can be life after math. Diversity is the name of the game. And stereotypes, like bad clichés, just won't hold any water—at least if you don't subscribe to them.

■ Reading Comprehension Questions

1. Which of the following would be the best alternative title for this article?
   a. Adding Up Those Accurate Asians
   b. A Writer of a Different Colour
   c. Asians and the Arts
   d. Sticky Stereotypes and Tricky Truisms

2. Which sentence best expresses the main idea of the selection?
   a. Asian students are driven by their families into science-based careers.
   b. Tony Wong comes from an artistically gifted family.
   c. People of any racial group are prone to vary in their gifts and abilities.
   d. Asians are basically practical in their view of valuable life skills.

3. The stereotype of Asians as gifted only in areas of technical expertise
   a. is part of our social fabric and further exploited by media and academics.
   b. is probably true because of Chinese students' abilities in math and medicine.
   c. is a product of the Western drive for economic success.
   d. makes life almost impossible for Chinese young people gifted in other areas.

4. The author found that starting a career as a writer was less difficult because
   a. he was mathematically challenged anyway.
   b. his brother had already become an artist.
   c. his mother thought it was better than being a cartoonist.
   d. there wasn't much Asian competition in the field.

5. Wong's aunt believed that his cousin should have a street-level office
   a. because her own view of economics suggested that he might miss out on daily customers.
   b. because she wanted him to take passport pictures.
   c. because she didn't know what he really did for a living.
   d. because upstairs offices are bad for business.

6. The author implies that
   a. he feels threatened by Chinese abilities in technical fields.
   b. Asian students are perhaps not encouraged toward less practical careers.
   c. he is so inept that he had to become a writer to explain himself.
   d. a sense of humour is not appreciated in Asian cultures.

7. *True or false?* _____ Wong's mother's main objection to Victor Wong's career as an artist was that he painted mostly naked women.

8. Paragraphs 19 to 21 imply that Tony Wong
   a. finds the Asian culture too money-conscious.
   b. thinks his mother's values are out of touch with reality.
   c. respects the survival instinct in his culture but sees the irony in it.
   d. envies those more successful than he is.

9. The word *precarious* in "This leaves folks like me in a precarious situation, burdened with trying to lead Asian youth out of their computer and slide rule-induced stupor" (paragraph 9) means

      a. uncertain.

      b. scary.

      c. impossible.

      d. overworked.

10. The word *pragmatic* in "It was the ever-pragmatic Asian philosophy at work" (paragraph 21) means

      a. changing.

      b. working.

      c. stubborn.

      d. realistic.

■ Discussion Questions

About Content

1. What careers does Tony Wong give as those expected of Asian students? Why?

2. What reasons does the author offer for being "uniquely qualified" to give seminars on "alternate careers" for Asian students? How serious is he, do you think? Why?

3. What made Wong's mother decide that his brother's choice of career was not so stupid? What did she decide was the problem with his being an artist?

About Structure

4. Wong's article has three sections, with an introductory and a concluding paragraph. What subtitles would you give these sections? Fill in the spaces below with appropriate subtitles.

    Paragraphs 2 to ?_____

    Paragraphs ? to 14_____

    Paragraphs 15 to ?_____

    Why have you chosen your subtitles? What is the subject of each of these sections? How does each section advance Wong's main idea?

5. In which paragraph do you find the author's thesis? Why has he chosen this position for his thesis?

6. What is the keyword in the author's thesis statement? What examples in the essay support this keyword? Which examples seem to contradict the idea implied by this word?

About Style and Tone

7. Tony Wong is evidently a writer with a sense of humour. Some techniques natural to the comic writer or comedian include the following: exaggeration, understatement or deflation, unlikely comparisons, shifts in vocabulary levels, and the use of surprising punch lines.

Find examples of four of these comic techniques in the article, and list the phrases after the paragraph number in which you find the example required.

Exaggeration _____ (paragraph _____)

Understatement _____ (paragraph _____)

Shift in vocabulary level _____ (paragraph _____)

Unexpected punch line _____ (paragraph _____)

8. What type of publication would you expect to find this selection in: a weekly magazine or daily newspaper, a scholarly journal on sociology, or a text on race relations in Canada?

    What do the word choices, subject matter, and tone suggest about the audience Wong is writing for?

■ Writing Assignments

Assignment 1: Writing a Paragraph

Tony Wong feels he is missing a math gene. Write a descriptive paragraph about some aspect of *you* that seems to be missing, dormant, or undiscovered. Your paragraph may be humorous or straightforward in approach.

Assignment 2: Writing a Paragraph

People often surprise us because they don't always conform to the stereotypes or judgments we have developed about them on the basis of appearances. Either their behaviour or their reasons for their actions do not follow our preconceived notions. Tony Wong's mother and his aunt are examples of apparent adherence to the Asian stereotype of practicality, but both manage to adapt to their offspring's radical career choices. Wong himself, his brother, his cousin Victor, and the politician Olivia Chow are contradictions to the stereotypical Asian.

Write a paragraph about a person whose appearance completely misled you (or someone else) at first. Describe the person's appearance and characteristics in some detail, and contrast them with what you found to be the person's underlying character. Be sure to be precise in your choice of details and to contrast them with details that relate to your first impressions, so that the reader will follow your discovery of the difference between appearance and reality.

You might want to begin with a topic sentence like this one, which gives a remembered first or dominant impression of the subject, based solely on what the writer first observed.

Jim's three earrings, Metallica T-shirt, ripped black jeans, and shaved head had him marked as one mean punk in my mind, and the silver skull on his belt buckle did nothing to change my opinion.

Conclude your paragraph with a summary of what you learned and a statement of your current feelings about this person.

Assignment 3: Writing an Essay

Tony Wong mentions in his seventh paragraph a controversial professor from an Ontario university, Philippe Rushton. Rushton studies racial and genetic patterns in human beings. His findings about human intelligence have prompted criticism of his supposed racist views. When carried to an extreme, or when misapplied, judgments or findings based on race, religion, or culture are always questionable and have led to horrendous social problems, persecution, and such atrocities as Nazism and terrorist activities around the world.

Although stereotyping or classifying is indeed a standard part of the process by which humans learn to distinguish one thing from another and to group similar ideas, it is very dangerous when applied to people. Most Canadian students attend colleges and universities where diversity in the classroom is the rule, not the exception. Moreover, our laws and college charters guarantee the rights of all Canadians. A fast glance at any major Canadian city's newspaper will, unfortunately, disabuse us of the notion that we have created the "perfect egalitarian society"; various racial groups continue to labour under stereotypes, and factions that support racist views continue to form.

Write an essay that tackles an experience of your own with stereotyping, whether on your part or as applied to you by someone else. Make use of the cause-and-effect format for your essay. What caused you or someone else to make a premature judgment, and what were the consequences? You may choose a lighthearted approach, as Tony Wong did, or you may treat the subject seriously.

Opening sentences in the paragraph that includes your thesis statement could be like these.

> Because I am a female student of Italian descent, people sometimes assume I must be a good cook, interested in babies, and intensely religious. Are they in for some surprises!

> When I registered in my first course in chemical engineering and answered to the name "Littlefeather, Jim" on the attendance list, the student in the next chair raised his hand to me and said, "How." I said, "I don't know; do you?"

> Arriving from Beijing was difficult enough, but registering in a new school system, dealing with an unfamiliar language, and trying to understand the other students' behaviour all seemed just too much.

THE IMPORTANCE OF COOKING DINNER

Nancy Eng

Do you remember the first time you tried to cook a meal? Cooking is never as easy as recipes or relatives make it seem. Food, its preparation, and the rituals of the table are important parts of our daily social and family lives. In the twenty-first century, it seems that everyone is interested in food, if not in cooking. But despite the advances of feminist advice, statistics show that most cooking is still done by women and is regarded (other than in the elevated realm of the great chefs) as part of essential female knowledge and skills. Nancy Eng, an English student at the University of British Columbia, takes issue with the idea that the honourable womanly place in the kitchen is somehow genetically inherited.

This was not to be just any dinner. This meal was to be a part of my rites of passage, another step into womanhood. Like the first pair of pantyhose, the first teetering steps on high heels, and the first taste of lipstick, an entire dinner prepared on one's own has always been an initiation into the adult female ranks. Despite all the advances women have made in this male-dominated world, despite the inspiration of the Sandra Day O'Connors, the Pat Carneys, and the Sally Rides, woman continues to carry certain limiting connotations. When one thinks of women, terms like *gentle, maternal,* and *domestic* still spring even to some of the most liberal minds. No matter how capable a woman is in the work world, it is still difficult to shake the time-honoured tradition of Mom baking cookies for her family, or Grandma fixing turkey for the clan. So, as I entered the kitchen that fateful day of my fifteenth year, armed with *The Joy of Cooking* and enshrouded in a "Kiss the Cook" apron, I was ready to tackle green salad, roast chicken, and chocolate mousse. I rolled up my sleeves, took a deep breath, and went to work.   1

The salad was easy enough. For that, I didn't even need to consult the cooking bible. I managed to wash and tear up a quantity of lettuce, and I threw in a variety of appropriately coloured vegetables so that my bowl more or less resembled green salad. This accomplished, I moved on with an air of confidence to the next course.   2

The chicken sat in all its slimy glory on a roasting pan, awaiting an expert touch. Cold and slippery in my hands, it was placid and cooperative as I dangled it awkwardly from one of its slick little limbs, trying to decide which end was up. I viewed my fowl friend from several angles, puzzled as to where exactly its head had been during its previous life. The directions called for stuffing the animal, so I located my box of Stouffer's Stovetop and contemplated where it belonged. Flipping the chicken around a few more times, I finally discovered an opening. I peered into its damp darkness, feeling slightly perverse about my actions, and hoping the chicken didn't mind this kind of intrusion. I couldn't see how I was going to hold that small hole open wide enough to fill the creature up, until I spied a funnel hanging invitingly from its hook in the cupboard. Inserting the funnel's tip into the bird, I poured in the contents of the box of stuffing, not realizing the dry, crumbly mess I was forcing in was meant to be cooked first. The chicken soon bulged slightly with uncooked stuffing and the innards, which I had not bothered to remove. Pleased with its bumpy plumpness, I went on to basting.   3

"Butter outer chicken generously," the book directed. I partially unwrapped a cold block of margarine, hoping such a substitution wouldn't offend anyone too much, and proceeded to rub the block over the surface of the equally cold, nubbly chicken skin with as much generosity as I could muster toward raw poultry. Large clots of yellow stuck here and there on the uneven epidermis, along with some bits   4 of gold foil from the margarine wrapper. Good enough, I thought as I flicked off some of the larger, more conspicuous pieces of foil, time for seasoning. Nothing warms the heart of an inexperienced cook more than a spice rack chock full of multicoloured substances that one can sprinkle and toss with a certain chef-like finesse. I sprinkled and tossed to my heart's content until, inspecting my master-piece, I discovered that I had liberally covered my poor chicken with cinnamon, garlic powder, and sugar. Quickly, I snapped out of my Julia Child act and reme-died my mistake by attempting to wipe off my wrongs with a paper towel. Shreds of tissue now decorated the main course, alongside the already present foil. As din-nertime was nearing, I tried to hurry myself along and ended up dusting the bird with allspice, something that sounded like a good general spice to me, but which I later discovered to be the chief flavouring for gingerbread and apple and pump-kin pies. Being behind schedule, I didn't bother with any more fancy stuff; I popped the chicken into the oven and cranked the temperature up to 500° to speed up the cooking time.

5   Finally, it was time to prepare the dessert. A cinch, I said: no problem. Setting a large pot on the burner, I began to throw in haphazardly whatever the recipe called for: squares of semisweet chocolate, cream, butter, three separated eggs. Separated from what? I wondered; from their shells, I guess. Happy with my con-clusion, I continued, smashing the eggs along the rim of the pot, and watching the bright yellow yolks float on top of the chocolate with only a few bits of shell mix-ing in with them. I stirred the concoction vigorously, but it failed to resemble the light, fluffy delicacy from the glossy picture in the cookbook. Since the recipe said that this dessert was supposed to set awhile before serving, I left it on the stove, assuming it would magically take on the appearance of the cookbook picture by the time I spooned it out. Satisfied with my efforts, I left my dinner roasting and setting while I wandered off to watch *Donahue*.

6   In the middle of "Bisexual Men and Voodoo Priestesses—Compatible Marriages?" a crescendo of domestic noise swelled in my ears. The smoke alarm wailed, the oven bell clanged, and the stove crackled and sputtered. Something had gone terribly wrong. Sprinting into the kitchen, I leaped up toward the smoke alarm, waving my arms frantically in an attempt to clear the smoke and shut off the ear-piercing screech. A sharp rap with a broom handle finally silenced that con-traption and allowed me to attend to what was left of dinner. The chicken was charred beyond recognition, with the bits of paper towel burning brightly and the foil glinting mockingly at me. The mousse had not transformed itself into a dessert delight that would elicit praise from my family; instead, it had melded itself to the bottom of the pot, hardening to the point where it had become an immovable part of the metal. Even my previously trouble-free salad had succumbed to the disaster surrounding it. Left sitting on the stove, the lettuce had wilted and turned an unsightly brown around its edges. As I stood in the midst of this catastrophe, in came my mother, two aunts, and my grandmother. They shook their heads sadly, and I think I actually saw tears welling up in the eyes of my grandmother. I had failed the initiation; I would never be a traditional female. No one would savour my cookies or ask for second helpings at supper. Somehow, I'd proven myself incomplete.

Suddenly, in the midst of this horrible, laughable affair, it dawned on me that   7
I didn't really mind. I didn't care. This was not the be-all and end-all; I would be
a woman yet. Culinary skills or not, I would amount to something. I would be one
of the new breed of women who throw aside tradition to be themselves. My heart
lightened. I threw off my baking mitts, untied the apron, tossed them to my grandmother, and yelled, "Call Pizza Pizza."

■ Reading Comprehension Questions

1. Which of the following would be the best alternative title for the selection?
   a. Dinner, Denial, and Disaster
   b. Chicken à la Nancy
   c. The Importance of Poisoning Your Family
   d. Cooking Means Caring

2. Which sentence best expresses the main idea of the selection?
   a. Cooking, like caring and cleaning, is seemingly inseparable from the idea
      of womanhood.
   b. Cooking dinner for the family is a time-honoured coming-of-age ritual
      for all women.
   c. With the right cookbook, equipment, and ingredients, anyone can prepare
      a dinner.
   d. Failing at cooking dinner for the author meant failure in the traditional
      arts of womanhood.

3. The concept of womanhood, according to Nancy Eng,
   a. has changed radically because of a female judge, a female politician, and a
      female astronaut.
   b. is still narrowed by expectations of nurturing, gentleness, and domesticity.
   c. carries a double burden: workplace success and kitchen miracles.
   d. necessitates the wearing of high heels, lipstick, and an apron.

4. *True or false?* _____ The author messed up the initial preparation of every course in her meal.

5. Eng's main problem with preparing the chicken was
   a. not knowing which end to stuff.
   b. not removing the heart, liver, and gizzards prior to stuffing the bird.
   c. leaving foil and paper towel on its skin.
   d. all of the above, and more.

6. The author implies that
   a. she had at least read the recipes before trying to cook dinner.
   b. she had watched female relatives cook enough to know the basics.
   c. she had looked at the cookbook and examined her materials in advance.
   d. she mistook dressing for the event and grabbing a book for cooking.

7. Eng implies that she believed
   a. that the rules and techniques for cooking weren't that important.
   b. that all good women take time for a TV break during meal preparation.

     c. she would never be a real woman.

     d. dinner would somehow be edible, if not praiseworthy.

8. *True or false?* _____ The author implies that her attempt at cooking has been a real life crisis, as well as a rite of passage (paragraph 1) for her.

9. The word *enshrouded* in "So, as I entered the kitchen that fateful day of my fifteenth year, armed with *The Joy of Cooking* and enshrouded in a 'Kiss the Cook' apron" (paragraph 1) means
     a. dressed.
     b. disguised.
     c. wrapped up.
     d. trapped.

10. The word *crescendo* in "a crescendo of domestic noise swelled in my ears" (paragraph 6) means
     a. rumblings.
     b. buildup.
     c. shriek.
     d. cacophony.

■ Discussion Questions

About Content

1. What characteristics of womanhood does Eng list as persisting into modern times? Do you agree with her? Are these innate aspects of all women?

2. Why does the author feel "slightly perverse" (paragraph 3) about what she was doing with the stuffing mix?

3. Do you agree with Nancy Eng that "nothing warms the heart of an inexperienced cook more than a spice rack chock full of multicoloured substances" (paragraph 4)? Why do people feel this way? What's the problem with this feeling?

4. What happened to each of the author's dishes? Why, in each case?

About Structure

5. How does the author link her title with the content of her essay in the opening paragraph? Which sentences support and expand on the meaning of the title? List the number of the sentence, note the appropriate phrase, and briefly explain how each connects to the title.

    Sentence _____ Phrase _____

    Sentence _____ Phrase _____

    Sentence _____ Phrase _____

6. This is a comic version of a process essay. Generally, such essays contain transitional words and phrases to direct and assist the reader in following the process. Do you think that Nancy Eng wants you to follow her process?

There are, in fact, *two* types of process essays: prescriptive (how-to), and descriptive (telling how by describing). Which type of process essay is "The Importance of Cooking Dinner"? Why?

7. The transitions in this essay are unusually placed. They are more like "time marker" phrases, which indicate the progress of an event or process.

    Where do you find such phrases in paragraphs 2 to 5? What are the phrases, and what do they have in common?

About Style and Tone

8. The chicken is clearly an object for the author to contend with. Which of the rhetorical comic devices listed below does Eng use to make her description in paragraph 3 of her struggles with the bird so funny?

    a. Personification (giving an object human qualities) _____

    b. Alliteration (beginning closely placed words with the same letter) _____

    c. Exaggeration _____

    d. Puns or wordplay _____

    List examples of any of these comic devices which you find, and suggest why they are amusing in the context of the essay.

9. For what type of publication (and its reading audience) would such an article be likely to be written? Why?
    a. a feminist magazine
    b. a cookbook or cooking magazine
    c. a general-interest monthly magazine
    d. a sociology text

Writing Assignments

Assignment 1: Writing a Paragraph

There are "rites of passage" for every person: special (although sometimes quite mundane) activities, which, when first performed, have time-marking significance for all of us. These actions or events signal some change or turning point in our lives. Some are gender-specific, such as shaving the face (as opposed to shaving the legs, which would be a female "rite of passage"), and some transcend gender boundaries, such as learning to drive.

Write a paragraph about "the importance of...." Describe a particular "first" coming-of-age ritual which you experienced. Why was it important to you? What was its importance to that stage in your life? Consider the first time you played a game of pool, your first date, the first time you changed the oil or a tire, or some such turning point.

As Eng does, begin with some background information about yourself and the importance of the event. Then describe the stages in the process you went through in your personal "rite of passage." Be sure to use very specific details so that readers may re-experience the event along with you. Conclude with a statement of the significance, or lack thereof, that this "rite" had for you.

Assignment 2: Writing a Paragraph

We have all tried to cook something. Our first attempts may not have been as disastrous as Nancy Eng's; in fact, some of us are natural cooks, and those first scrambled eggs may have been quite edible. Write a paragraph in which you describe your first try at cooking for other people. If your first meal was suitable only for a decent burial, give the causes for the awful results; on the other hand, if you succeeded in not making your family or guests ill, make sure your paragraph tells clearly *why* you managed to cook reasonably well.

Follow the cause-and-effect format on pages 213-16 as you structure your paragraph. Begin with what you achieved; then explain the reasons for the meal that resulted, whether it was good or bad.

Assignment 3: Writing an Essay

Will you, like Nancy Eng, be among the "new breed" of men or women who have left behind the expectations and stereotypes of previous generations? Is this possible, or are certain characteristics innate within each gender? Do we want to disturb all fundamental male and female qualities as we know them?

Write a prescriptive (how-to) process essay about *your* views on "the new man" or "the new woman." Does each really exist? Do you know any examples of either? What elements would make up such creatures? Would there be changes in personality, in behaviour, in appearance? How much do we really want men and women to change, and why?

Here is your chance to play Dr. Frankenstein: Construct a new being. Tell your readers how to become "the new man" or "the new woman" in the traditional "three easy steps." Because this is a direct-advice process essay, address your reader directly as "you." If there are things you would rather not change about the gender in question, say so, but tell the reader how and why he or she should retain an existing quality you value.

Before beginning your outline, review the chapter on process writing (pages 194-206). Decide on your viewpoint first of all. You may take a reverse or comic view, and give instructions on how to become "a traditional gentleman" (which may, in fact, be a new creature) or "a real lady" (perhaps equally mythic). Consider what ingredients may be needed. In either case, list your steps, then group them into logical stages that become your three body paragraphs, and flesh out your instructions with careful details about becoming the "gender-perfect creature." Watch out for potential pitfalls or problems in your stages, and give lots of transitional help. Remember, you may be creating a new being.

WELCOME TO THE MATRIX

San Grewal

People who play video games may not consider the idea that gaming is part of a whole interconnected new world. In fact, most of us who e-mail friends and use the Internet for a variety of reasons may not think that our online time makes us members of communities, much less citizens of a virtual world. San Grewal writes about this new world that coexists with our physical world but occupies no space—except perhaps in our minds and on our computer screens. Is this new world a dark, corrupt illusion like the Matrix or a brave new place with no national boundaries?

1 The fastest growing city in the world isn't in Mexico, China or even Southern Ontario. It's in a place that can't be defined by geography, doesn't have any concrete, bricks or mortar. Its infrastructure is fibre optic cable and wireless technology, the highways and byways of what has become the Digital City.

2 Millions of inhabitants enter the Digital City every minute, searching for the virtual communities and neighbourhoods that have become their home away from their physical home. Gamers, hackers, bloggers, DJs, animators, activists, chatters, designers, artists and architects have created their own virtual city, using technology that is the building block of their world.

3 Unlike future depictions of technology in movies like *Blade Runner*, *Minority Report* and *A.I.*, which convey a message of gloom and doom, citizens of the Digital City find relief from the "physical" world in what has become a real-life Matrix.

4 It's not just pop-culture that doesn't seem to understand the upside of digital life. In his 1992 book *Technopoly*, communication theorist Neil Postman wrote, "(Technology) destroys the vital sources of our humanity. It creates a culture without a moral foundation. It undermines certain mental processes and social relations that make human life worth living."

5 A year later the "social relations" Postman thought would disappear began to flourish when the foundation for the Digital City was laid. Mosaic, the browser software that made the Web accessible to anyone with a connection, was released. A year after that the software developers who designed Mosaic created a company called Netscape Inc. and citizens of the Digital City were invited in from every corner of the globe.

6 Today, 80 per cent of North Americans access the Internet. Computers, video games, cellular phones and the Internet now occupy more of the average North American teenager's time than any other activity, including school. They shop, listen to music, do their homework, play and communicate online.

7 What has been created isn't the dark realm of technology predicted by pop culture and intellectuals.

8 "The Internet saved me," says Ejovi Nuwere, author of *Hacker Cracker*. "A few months after I was hospitalized for trying to commit suicide when I was 12 I was introduced to the Internet."

9 Nuwere was one of the presenters at Digifest 2003, an international festival of online and digital culture held recently in downtown Toronto, which focused on the future of the Electronic City.

10   Video game developers, digital artists, hackers and others from around the world challenged the idea that virtual environments are potentially dangerous places where people are led astray by sex, violence, bad ethics and escapist fantasies.

11   "The festival is an attempt to answer questions," says John Sobol, one of the event's organizers. "How is the definition of a city changing with the integration of wired technology? How do people live, what are the moral questions, how are communities formed and enhanced in a virtual wired city?"

12   For Nuwere, who grew up in the Bedford-Stuyvesant area of Brooklyn, in a neighborhood dominated by housing projects and gang violence, the Internet offered a new life. His drug-addicted mother had spent most of her time in prison. His father passed away before Nuwere got to know him.

13   His physical environment, the city in which he lived, was a desperate place. "It was hard to see past life on the street, but the Internet and the world of hacking became a world that removed me from the desperation."

14   Nuwere became a self-taught programmer and hacker, learning on the computer his uncle had bought for college in 1993.

15   "I would sit on my uncle's computer for hours and be anyone I wanted to. I could go anywhere—it was addictive. I became immersed in the cyber-world."

16   Hacking has taken on an entirely negative connotation, but that was the community he entered. In 1995, when he was 15, after he breached a company's security system, gaining access to almost all of its files, instead of using his skills to do wrong, he called up the company. He told them what he had done and gave them his name and number in case they wanted to talk.

17   They called back an hour later and offered to set up a job interview.

18   He now travels the world—on-line and physically—consulting companies about their computer security systems and appears regularly on CNN and other networks, talking about the risks of cyber-terrorism.

19   "I got acceptance in the hacking culture. Technology gave me a sense of power and freedom that I felt I didn't have in my life. It's the same for millions of other kids around the world, whether they're hackers, bloggers or gamers."

20   Participants in virtual worlds don't accept the argument that digital lives are constructed, imaginary representations of life, realities created in violent video games such as *Vice City*. That type of Matrix-like paranoia may be something those on the sidelines worry about, but gamers don't.

21   "The popularity of gaming is a comment on the outside world," says filmmaker and game designer Tim Carter, another presenter at Digifest. "People want control and accountability. But the question that should be asked is how are gaming communities and the games themselves fostering a participation in the digital world that inspires humane values?"

21   Gamers say they know the difference between what's real and what's not real. And they should. After all, they grew up in—and helped build—the Digital City. Once dominated by boys, staring glassy-eyed into cathode blue monitors, while shooting anything that moved on screen, the gaming industry is now going through an adult revolution.

23   Role-playing games such as the Sims (20 million copies sold world-wide) and Counter-Strike (15 million copies) have become a way of life for players. The reason they play is what interests Carter.

After his presentation, a teenager, who had been lingering around to ask Carter **24** a question—"What's the main reason you play: for the kills or the sense of community?"—seemed certain of the answer.

The look on his face—blank with his head slightly turned—revealed his **25** surprise.

"I told him the same thing I tell others," Carter says. "Every boy who has access **26** to a computer has played this game, some girls too. It's like a religion. They stay up till four in the morning at gaming centres, they play in their rooms, they enter tournaments, but the real experience is outside the game."

Getting to cap someone with a semi-automatic may be the draw, for some, to **27** the Digital City, but it's not why they stay.

Carter is an avid player of Counter-Strike, a first-person shooter game with the **28** essential goal of killing your opponent, played either online, with teams up to 50 a side, or on separate gaming consoles. His presentation was about Counter-Strike culture as a model for positive values—cooperation, advancement based on skill and merit, discipline.

"The need for a sense of community, to play a game by the rules, to be good **29** at something, to succeed as a group is why you think shooting an opponent is fun. The sophisticated graphics and the level of programmed control over decisions is the game. But the reason kids do it for eight hours a day has very little to do with killing opponents.

"It's like a martial art, people who don't do it think it's all about the kicking **30** and the punching."

Carter says the gaming industry is in its nascent stage. Till now most games **31** have focussed on "High Twitch" reactions to the violent or fast paced confusion that takes place on screen. But as programming and artificial intelligence get more sophisticated, the gaming industry will change, just as Hollywood did.

"Action movies, westerns, that was the easy way to attract an audience. You still **32** have them, but you also get films about real life, that represent the whole spectrum of what their audiences relate to. A game like The Sims, using artificial intelligence, gives players an interactive ability to 'play' the game of life, hard decisions and all. The industry is becoming more responsive to the demands of digital communities."

Gamers aren't the only digital community drawn to virtual worlds because of **33** the potential to express things they can't in the real world, says Sobol.

"Blogging (Web logging) is a reaction to the way the mainstream media works. **34** Young people expect that communication is interactive—every event invites multiple perspectives, multiple directions. Others have become used to responding passively to fixed descriptions of events."

Matt Jones, an information architect who has worked for the BBC, the Times **35** of London and other companies, says the key for virtual environments to flourish is access. And ultimate access means not being tied down to a time and place. The Digital City is open 24/7.

"Wireless technology, the ability to use hand-held devices anywhere, any time **36** to connect with online communities, is the future," says Jones, who was part of the "warchalking" movement. The idea behind warchalking was to create an awareness of wireless urban spaces, virtual bubbles that could be created and used by people to connect online: No wire, no fee.

37   "The idea of free wireless spaces scared telcom companies and media companies that have been buying up the platforms for bandwidth delivery. They have it all backwards."

38   Wireless technology is used by 80 per cent of the teenagers in downtown Tokyo today, members of a "Thumb Tribe" that use cell phones to send text messages any time of the day. Successful Japanese Web sites use text in the same clipped, shorthand that one-hand typists can easily send back and forth to friends.

39   "In Japan, companies realize that if you give people access, they will create digital communities that become important to them. Once the demand is created, without prohibitive connection fees, companies can come up with a number of creative ways to profit," Jones explains.

40   "In South Korea, professional gamers are respected and revered as sports stars. They're able to attract huge numbers. The idea of society is changing. South Korean gamers have more in common with Canadian gamers than they do with people from their own culture.

41   "Digital Cities are only just starting to influence the way a younger generation defines their idea of what a community is.

42   "I hope they get to shape the future of what Digital Cities will look like."

■ Reading Comprehension Questions

1. Which of the following would make the best alternative title for the selection?
   a. Virtual Life Takes Over
   b. Video Game Addiction
   c. Virtual Culture and Virtual Communities
   d. Online Salvation

2. Which sentence best expresses the selection's main point?
   a. Freedom of expression is the main appeal of virtual realities.
   b. The Internet and wireless technology have created lively, interactive, international communities.
   c. Video games are more than simply violent entertainment.
   d. Virtual reality may replace religion and other cultural bonds.

3. "Digital City" is made of
   a. bricks, buildings, roads, and highways.
   b. gamers getting together for conventions.
   c. new communities joined by fibre optic cable and wireless technology.
   d. fearful young people needing relief from the real world.

4. *True or false?* _____ Movies like *The Matrix* are similar to the online community experience.

5. Author Neil Postman feared that technology would
   a. dehumanize culture and human interaction.
   b. make people less intelligent.
   c. encourage immorality.
   d. create new social relationships.

6. According to attendees at Digifest 2003 in Toronto,
   a. the virtual future represents an escape from reality.
   b. hackers are no longer criminals.
   c. virtual technology is causing society to redefine itself.
   d. there are no longer any risks involved in virtual environments.

7. The reason for the powerful appeal of gaming, to Tim Carter, is
   a. the thrill of shooting as many opponents as possible.
   b. the appeal of the graphics and sense of control.
   c. that gaming is not understood by outsiders.
   d. that skill and group interaction are involved.

8. *True or false?* _____ Gamers are products of their national cultures.

9. The word *accountability* in "People want control and accountability" (paragraph 20) means
   a. bookkeeping.
   b. responsibility.
   c. power.
   d. respectability.

10. The word *avid* in "Carter is an avid player of Counter-Strike" (paragraph 27) means
    a. violent.
    b. skilful.
    c. enthusiastic.
    d. frequent.

■ Discussion Questions

About Content

1. Who are the inhabitants of Digital City? What is Digital City made of?

2. What was created in 1993 that changed the way the world communicates? How did developments stemming from this creation differ from Neil Postman's 1992 predictions?

3. Why does Tim Carter say that, for players of Counter-Strike, "the real experience is outside the game" (paragraph 25)? Do you agree with Carter?

About Structure

4. In which paragraph do you find the clearest expression of the author's thesis? Why did Grewal place his thesis in this position, judging by the selection's content?

5. The selection can be divided into seven parts. Fill in the following blanks to show which paragraphs are included in each part.

   • Grewal's introduction of the topic: paragraphs _____

- First example of the importance of virtual culture: paragraphs
  _____

- Transitional paragraph that takes readers to the next example: paragraph
  _____

- Second example of a significant part of virtual culture: paragraphs
  _____

- Transitional paragraph that leads readers to the next example: paragraph
  _____

- Third example of another alternative aspect of digital culture: paragraphs
  _____

- Concluding paragraphs that sum up points from the selection's examples:
  paragraphs _____

About Style and Tone

6. Where in the selection are statistics used? Why does the author offer statistical proof?

7. How many speakers are there in this selection? Who is each person who speaks in the article? What does each speaker contribute to the example that the author is presenting?

8. Where do explanations or definitions appear in this selection? Judging by the presence of these definitions and the subject matter of the piece, what kind of audience would this selection be aimed at?

■ Writing Assignments

Assignment 1: Writing a Paragraph

If you play video games, share files with others, take online courses, or contribute to online mailing lists or chat rooms, you may be part of at least one online community already. What makes up a community, whether it is a "real world" community or a virtual one?

Write a paragraph in which you define the idea of a community. Begin your paragraph with a topic sentence that gives a clear statement of your overall concept and suggests your supporting details. In your paragraph, follow Grewal's method of development and provide examples to support and explain your definition of a community.

Assignment 2: Writing a Paragraph

According to San Grewal, you spend more time interacting with various forms of technology than you do participating in any other single aspect of your life. What does this reliance on technology mean? Have we become so dependent on keyboards and screens that we are already detached from ordinary life experiences and pleasures?

In a third-person paragraph that uses division and classification structure, discuss some of the pros and cons of society's current reliance on technology.

Assignment 3: Writing an Essay

Is gaming an activity that develops personal and group skills, or is it a mind-numbing habit? Is chatting online a harmless pastime or a potentially dangerous way of exposing personal information to others? Are online courses more stimulating and more fun than classroom subjects, or do they isolate students and offer too little feedback? Write an essay in which you defend one virtual-world activity that many people oppose or have given little thought to.

Develop your essay by presenting detailed support for three reasons why some virtual-world or online experience offers definite benefits that might not otherwise be available. Your supporting paragraphs may be organized in time order, demonstrating the order in which you learned about the benefits you describe, or they may be organized in order of importance, either beginning with or ending with your most important point.

Here is a sample outline for one such essay.

<u>Thesis Statement:</u> Online courses offer some unexpected benefits to college students.

<u>Topic Sentence 1:</u> Students have the freedom to do assignments whenever it is convenient to them.

<u>Topic Sentence 2:</u> Students can save money on transportation, parking, and gas by working at home.

<u>Topic Sentence 3:</u> Students who are shy or quiet in classrooms feel more confident in online courses.

THE OLDEST PROFESSION: SHOPPING

Candace Fertile

Most people think of shopping as a modern activity; after all, where were the malls in the Middle Ages? Candace Fertile maintains that there is nothing current about going out to bring things home. She believes that shopping, in fact, can be traced back to the earliest stages of human behaviour, to our most primitive survival instincts. Is it possible that we are simply imitating the hunting and gathering behaviours of our distant ancestors when we go to the store? Read on and decide for yourself.

My shopping career began in earnest when I was seven. My currency was time and   1
deceit. My boutiques were the garbage cans in the alley behind our apartment house in Edmonton.

2   I could not believe that people threw out such wonderful stuff. What a deal— something for nothing. Perhaps like the first-time gambler who wins and is for- ever hooked on that adrenaline rush, my love of shopping began with that first magical exposure, on a day when I was wandering home from school, taking my usual route through back alleys. To my extreme delight, I saw peeking out of a gal- vanized-steel garbage pail what looked like a blue three-ring binder. Acquisition grabbed my seven-year-old soul, and to this day it hasn't let go, fuelled no doubt by relentless advertising and the creation of more and more stuff that announces to the world who we are. Or perhaps who we want to be.

3   In that alley, my paper-loving self honed in on that blue binder like a cat streak- ing up from the basement at the sound of a can opener, and I started to under- stand the power of objects. As a second-grader, I was (unjustly, I thought) required to use despised scribblers. The covers were barely more substantial than the rather nasty paper within them. The booklets had three staples in the middle holding the whole ugly mess together. I hated these scribblers, and I hated their name. And I particularly hated the fact that the teacher would stalk around the room, checking to see if we were properly holding our pencils (another affront—I longed to use a pen). Periodically she would sneak up and grab our yellow HBs to make sure that we were not gripping them too tightly. Her actions made me clutch my pencil as if it were keeping my heart pumping. And the choke-hold I had on my pencil meant that I frequently made holes in the flimsy paper of the scribbler. With grim regularity the teacher and I would get into a tug-of-war over my pencil.

4   It was after such a dismal war (I always had to lose) that the bright blue plas- tic corner of the binder caught my eye. I debated for some time about whether or not I was allowed to look in the can, or if taking something from a garbage can was stealing. I should mention: not only was I polite, but I was also Catholic. I knew God was watching my every move, and should I be so vile as to commit a mortal sin, lightning bolts would descend and incinerate my evil little soul, so that all that would be transported to Hell would be something the size of a barbecue briquette. The possibility of owning a binder seemed worth the risk.

5   I inched closer, then looked up and down the alley to make sure no one was watching me. I carefully removed the lid, which was already precariously perched to one side, and laid it on the ground. A perfect, blue, three-ring binder glowed at me. I was in Heaven. I picked it up and with disbelief discovered an unopened packet of three-hole paper inside. The narrow blue (not even the more babyish wide) lines on the stark white paper with the margins marked with a thin pink line were everything my crummy scribbler wasn't. This paper and binder were for grownups, not little kids.

6   I could hardly wait to write in my new binder. With a pen. I felt instantly grown-up, more important, more substantial, the tug-of-war over my pencil for- gotten. I had gained a new status. And this emotional boost into the stratosphere was accomplished by the simplest of means: I had acquired a new object. And it was free. No drug would ever reproduce the rush I felt as my concept of myself and the world tilted.

7   On subsequent shopping expeditions down the back alleys I never found any- thing as great as the binder and paper, but sometimes I found stuff for my little brother. At two, he would play with just about anything. I enjoyed his delight, and

finding free stuff meant saving my allowance. I now suspect my kid-sized version of dumpster-diving sparked my career as a bargain shopper.

Once I found a scarf—a sophisticated, almost sheer, leopard-spotted scarf. It spoke of glamour, beauty, and fashion, with just an edge of wildness. It was a scarf worn by elegant and capable women on television. It was perfect for my mother, who set off for work each morning with her matching high heels and handbag.   8

Maybe the scarf wasn't even supposed to have been thrown out, but there it was, dangling from a garbage can a few blocks away from home. (In the space of a few weeks, I had increased my territory substantially.) My mother would love this scarf, I thought, but I had no idea how I would explain the acquisition of such a treasure. I didn't have that kind of money. I had finally revealed the binder to her, as it was too difficult trying to write in it without being found out. Even that was hard, as I'd had to commit what I hoped was a venial sin by lying that a friend's older sister had given me the stuff. I knew that wouldn't work again with a scarf. And I still felt a bit singed around the edges from the lie. For a week I had imagined everyone thought I smelled like a campfire. And while I knew what the wrath of God entailed, I was absolutely sure that the wrath of my mother was worse.   9

I decided to come clean. I took the scarf home, and when my mother got home from work, I presented it to her. She was astonished, and then asked where I got it. I told her. To my bafflement, she burst into gales of laughter, nearly hiccupping herself into a coma while trying to catch her breath.   10

When she regained control, she announced that my garbage-looting days were over. Nice girls didn't do such things. And there could be dangerous things in the garbage. Like what, I wanted to know, but she wouldn't tell me. These events happened decades ago—I'm sure my mother was worried I'd cut myself on a tin can or broken bottle, not get jabbed by some hypodermic needle. Garbage was safer then, but not safe enough for my mother's daughter to play in it.   11

But what sticks indelibly in my mind is that my mother carefully washed and ironed the scarf and wore it faithfully, even proudly, a splash of jungle against her ever-so-fashionable green wool coat with the fur around the sleeves. She would fling one end over her shoulder as she headed out the door in the morning, as if to announce her formidable presence in the universe.   12

Scavenging no longer an option, I had to find another way to satisfy the desire for acquisition now flowing through my veins. Little did I know that I was turning into a good little twentieth-century consumer. According to Lauren Langman, an academic who studies human development: 13

> In the contemporary world, the signifying and celebrating edifice of consumer culture has become the shopping mall which exists in [a] pseudo-democratic twilight zone between reality and a commercially produced fantasy world of commodified goods, images, and leisure activities that gratify transformed desire and provide packaged self-images to a distinctive form of subjectivity. (40)   14

Langman's thesis certainly helps to explain not only the label consciousness of shoppers but also the desire of many shoppers to become apparent walking billboards for name-brand products. How much difference, if any, is there between my girlish desire for white go-go boots and the current stampede to wear T-shirts emblazoned with "Roots" or "Nike"?   15

16   I prefer to think the difference is significant. I could be wrong, in which case, Langman's argument is unassailable. But another academic offers me some hope. In an article in *Vogue* titled "The Professor Wore Prada," Elaine Showalter, professor of English at Princeton and recently president of the Modern Language Association, comments on her love of fashion and shopping. She does so in a humorous way, defending her intellectualism, femininity, and feminism. As she says, "For years I have been trying to make the life of the mind coexist with the day at the mall, and to sneak the *femme* back into feminist" (80). Showalter delineates the various ways female academics (herself included) have dressed in an effort to be taken seriously, and ends her essay by saying, "if you want to deconstruct my feminist criticism, go right ahead.But you'd better not sneer at my angel backpack or step on my blue suede shoes. I've paid my dues dressing 'feminist,' and now I'm going to wear what I like" (92). Showalter's essay is full of the pleasure one can gain from shopping, both the activity of looking and actual purchase. Throughout history and likely before, human beings have been drawn to objects of beauty (although certainly the concepts of beauty change).

17   The acquisition of objects, beautiful or otherwise, is usually an economic transaction. As a child prevented from plundering garbage bins, I needed a new way to get the stuff I wanted. So from time and deceit as currency, I turned to the more usual one: money. Getting that required work. My first job was ironing for my mother. I had seen a T-shirt in Sears, and my mother refused to buy it for me because, as she said, "You don't need it." It's no wonder that nowadays when I buy yet another object I don't need I think of King Lear's "Oh, reason not the need." The other object that captured my fancy was a particular lava lamp. I loved that lava lamp, but it was out of the realm of financial possibility. And my mother was right about the T-shirt. I didn't need it. I wore a uniform to school, and I had sufficient play clothes. Incessant pestering of my mother resulted in the ironing agreement. I ironed like a demon, encouraging my beleaguered mother to change clothes frequently so I could have something to iron. Eventually I saved enough to buy the T-shirt, and I wore it to shreds. It was the first thing I bought for myself with my own money, and I remember it in every detail. Still. It had short white sleeves, a white back, and a front in four coloured squares of red, yellow, blue, and green. If I had had white go-go boots to match, life would have achieved its pinnacle. (Elaine Showalter, by the way, wore white go-go boots to her Ph.D. defence.)

18   Since those very early days, my shopping has expanded in terms of money, objects, and range. Like many middle-class Canadians, I have more material goods than some small nations, and I am constantly acquiring more. What is interesting is that none of us needs all these things, but lemming-like we hurl ourselves at the nearest mall, which has acquired the status of a cathedral for some. Or else we seek out independent and unique shops in downtowns and other shopping areas. We go to outlets and discount centres. We are the consumer society of which much has been written. Thorstein Veblen's *The Theory of the Leisure Class* (1934), Christopher Lasch's *The Culture of Narcissism* (1979), and Hilary Radner's *Shopping Around: Feminine Culture and the Pursuit of Pleasure* (1995) are just three of the many works written to explore humans' need to shop even when we are way beyond buying what is necessary for our survival. Veblen's term "conspicuous consumption" indicates that the purchase of many unnecessary items is a perfor-

mance. It's interesting to imagine what the performance means. If we examine advertising, which certainly fuels consumer desire, we see that Langman's view of buying an identity is accurate. To wear a certain brand (a "Roots" or "Nike" T-shirt is infinitely more desirable to certain groups than, say, a "K-Mart" T-shirt) or to drive a certain car or to drink a certain beer is presumably a statement of who we are. Or is it?

In his essay "The Individual, Consumption Cultures and the Fate of Community," Rob Shields attends to the performative aspect of purchasing and gives consumers some credit: "Many consumers are now ironic, knowing shoppers, conscious of the inequalities of exchange and the arbitrary nature of exchange value. As social actors, they attempt to consume the symbolic values of objects and the mall environment while avoiding the inequalities of exchange" (100). Shields's essay notes that public spaces have changed and that the mall serves as a gathering place. Thus, the activity of shopping (whether or not a purchase is made) plays a significant social role. Shields argues: "It is necessary to recognize that consumption itself is partly determined by the non-rational, cultural element of society. Shopping is not just a functional activity. Consumption has become a communal activity, even a form of solidarity" (110). It appears to me that shopping plays a number of roles, and one of these is certainly a communal one, as Shields argues. But it can also be said that in addition to having a connective importance, shopping—and more specifically the purchased goods—can fulfill people's desires both to join a group and to differentiate themselves from one another. For example, clothing choices are laden with meaning, even if the message is inaccurate.   19

Shoppers, as Shields notes, are becoming more sophisticated and particular, if the growth in thrift stores is any indication. A CBC newscast in July 1998 noted that the thrift store business is so popular that charities depending on donations have to be much more competitive. We are still conspicuously consuming, but we want a bargain. Certain sections of the population have always needed to shop for sale goods, but the practice is now losing any stigma it might have had. In fact, getting a bargain, or a "steal," marks one as a consummate shopper. Getting a deal has become a selling point for much commercial activity. I'd like to mention sales, for example. Anyone in western Canada familiar with Woodward's $1.49 Day will remember the thrust and parry of grabbing for the goodies on this once-a-month sale extravaganza. The deals were often extraordinary, and people didn't want to miss this opportunity. Encountering sharp elbows was common. In contrast, the former frenzy of Bay Day has abated now that the sale lasts for ages and has lost any special air. No need to dive in a scrum for the merchandise. No, it's all there in stacks, and then we stand in line to pay. Infrequent sales events such as Boxing Day sales create line-ups hours before the stores open. The sale must appear to be an unusual event or it garners little excitement. I once worked at Harrods, and the annual sale was marked by the sound of crashing crockery as maniacal shoppers stormed the aisles.   20

But what are we doing when we shop, and why do I refer to it as the oldest profession? The answer is simple. Well, sort of. In *Shopping Around: Feminine Culture and the Pursuit of Pleasure*, Hilary Radner argues the following: "Feminine culture emphasizes a process of investment and return, of negotiation, in which the given articulation of pleasure is always measured against its costs, the inevitable price of   21 an invitation that is never extended freely, never absolutely, the terms of which change from day to day, from place to place" (178). While the terms and values change, it is surely the case that a shopper considers the relative costs (whether in time, effort, or money) and the benefits of the object gained. And these judgments will differ from person to person even within the same socio-economic group.

22   Shopping is our contemporary form of hunting and gathering. Men may have hunted, and women may have gathered, but both processes resulted in maintaining life. And if the effort expended exceeded what was gained—the result was death. Such an obvious relationship between acquisition (shopping in a sense) and survival is still evident in the world today. But in rich countries like Canada, hunting and gathering is largely done at the mall, and our survival is not in question. In "Dressed to Kill," Don Gillmor makes fun of men at a clothing sale, and he uses the metaphor of the hunt:

23   The big game is on the suit rack, though. Some of the men simply drape a dozen business suits over one arm and then try to find a little room in which to sort and sniff them, like lions defending their kill. But to bring down a three-button, blue wool crepe 42R Donna Karan (reg. $2,295, now $395) in open country requires keen eyesight, stealth, and a burst of cheetah-like speed. . . . [Men] are taking home cashmere and silk and cotton that feels like whipped butter. They have hunted well and they are filled with the self-knowledge that comes with risk and death and loss and dramatic savings. (75)

24   Whether the hunting is done in an exclusive boutique or a thrift store, it's the thrill of the chase that drives shoppers. It could be the lure of low prices, or exclusive merchandise, or the media-created buzz about something completely useless like Cabbage Patch Dolls or Beanie Babies that gets everyone out there, roaming, foraging, stalking, pouncing, occasionally even wrestling another shopper for the item.

25   Then we bag our prize and take it back to our cave, er, home. I bet those cave-people never stopped and said to each other, "Listen, honey, I think we have too many acorns or dried fish or fur blankets." I think they were out there scooping up whatever they thought might come in handy for survival.

26   And so while many of us shop for a variety of reasons, including pleasure, but rarely need (even grocery stores are full of stuff no one needs to survive; in fact, some of that junk probably shortens lives), perhaps somewhere at the heart of the endeavour is a genetic link to our past, when tracking and locating food was essential for survival. Now different needs drive our shopping expeditions. And survival is perceived in ways beyond the merely physical.

REFERENCES

Gillmor, Don. "Dressed to Kill: What Really Happens When Men Go Hunting for Deep Discounts." *Saturday Night* 113, no. 5 (June 1998): 75.

Langman, Lauren. "Neon Cages: Shopping for Subjectivity." In *Lifestyle Shopping: The Subject of Consumption,* ed. Rob Shields, 40–82. London: Routledge, 1992.

Radner, Hilary. *Shopping Around: Feminine Culture and the Pursuit of Pleasure.* New York: Routledge, 1995.

Shields, Rob. "The Individual, Consumption Cultures and the Fate of Community." In *Lifestyle Shopping: The Subject of Consumption,* ed. Rob Shields, 99–113. London: Routledge, 1992.

Showalter, Elaine. "The Professor Wore Prada." *Vogue,* December 1997: 80, 86, 92.

■ **Reading Comprehension Questions**

1. Which of the following would make the best alternative title for the selection?
    a. Addicted to Acquiring Things
    b. Canadian Consumer Patterns
    c. Shopping and Survival Instincts
    d. Feminism and Fashion

2. Which sentence best expresses the selection's main point?
    a. Shopping is a way of defining who we are and who we dream of being.
    b. Shopping may be a remnant of primitive instinctual drives.
    c. Shopping is a way of showing off, of performing or acting a role.
    d. Shopping is all about the thrill of finding that special item.

3. The author and her grade two teacher were in conflict because
    a. the author tore holes in her notebook.
    b. the teacher terrorized students.
    c. the author would not let go of her pencil.
    d. the author held her pencil too tightly.

4. *True or false?* _____ The author never told her mother how she acquired the blue binder.

5. We can conclude that the author's mother
    a. prized the scarf her daughter fished out of the garbage.
    b. was disgusted by her daughter's garbage picking.
    c. thought that taking things from the garbage was a sin.
    d. felt ill at the thought of her daughter picking through garbage.

6. *True or false?* _____ Brand-name and logo-printed clothing and accessories are just "wearable advertising."

7. According to Rob Shields, shopping
    a. is an irrational activity.
    b. is an unfair activity.
    c. is a social activity.
    d. is a necessity.

8. We can conclude that the author believes
    a. we shop even though we don't need to do so.
    b. we shop because we hope to find a bargain.
    c. we shop because we are driven to search for things.
    d. all of the above.

9. The word *precariously* in "the lid, which was already precariously perched to one side" (paragraph 5) means
    a. definitely.
    b. uncertainly.
    c. wildly.
    d. specially.

10. The word *incessant* in "Incessant pestering of my mother resulted in the ironing agreement" (paragraph 17) means
   a. rude.
   b. noisy.
   c. whiny.
   d. constant.

■ **Discussion Questions**

About Content

1. What were the reasons why the author was so excited about the blue binder that she found?

2. What did the author's garbage picking lead to in adulthood? Does this make sense to you? Why or why not?

3. What two seemingly opposite things does Professor Showalter wish to reconcile within herself, according to the quotation from her article in *Vogue*? Why might it be hard for these opposites to coexist?

4. How did the desire for a particular object change the author's behaviour after she was forbidden to root through garbage cans?

About Structure

5. Where in this selection do you find the clearest statement of the author's thesis? Why, judging by the article's content, do you believe Fertile chose this position?

6. How many paragraphs of "The Oldest Profession: Shopping" use narrative as their main method of development? Which paragraphs are these?

7. Where in this selection does the author refer to her title? Why might she have chosen this particular location to do so? To what does the title refer, and how does Fertile connect this idea to shopping?

About Style and Tone

8. This selection contains, as well as narrative sections, paragraphs with a distinctly scholarly flavour. Which paragraphs demonstrate the author's research into her subject? What stylistic aspects and forms of support used in these paragraphs make their tone different from the narrative sections of the article?

9. Candace Fertile uses figures of speech in this selection. She uses metaphors such as "My currency was time and deceit." What does she mean by this metaphor? She also uses similes such as this one from paragraph 2: "like the first-time gambler who wins and is forever hooked on that adrenaline rush." Find another such simile and explain its meaning.

10. There are many effective descriptive passages in "The Oldest Profession: Shopping." Choose one such passage and explain why it is effective. One aspect of good writing, and of good descriptive writing in particular, is the

writer's choice of interesting and appropriate verbs. In this selection, examples are "stalk," "sneak up," and "clutch" in paragraph 3. Find three examples of striking verb use and explain their effect on you as a reader.

■ Writing Assignments

Assignment 1: Writing a Paragraph

Childhood memories can be funny or painful, and they may often be tied to a particular object, like the scribbler that Candace Fertile describes. Generally, we learn something from memories that cluster around such objects. Choose an object you remember from childhood and write a descriptive paragraph about it.

Remember that your topic sentence should give some idea of why this object is significant and should also begin the "picture in words" that your paragraph will create of this object. Sample topic sentences could be similar to these:

> A grubby one-eared plush bunny that still sits on my dresser takes me back to the day my family arrived in Canada.

> A little box containing curly-edged brown pieces of fabric—my Brownie badges—turned out to be a box of bad memories.

Assignment 2: Writing a Paragraph

Do you shop to live or live to shop? Do you even enjoy shopping? Write a third-person paragraph in which you take a definite position on shopping. Such a position stated as a topic sentence could be like one of the following: "Shopping is one of life's great pleasures" or "Shopping is an expensive waste of time."

As well as arguing your position, use a cause *or* effect method to develop your paragraph. In other words, if you choose to write about the reasons why shopping is such a pleasure, you have chosen to write a "causes" paragraph that looks at what causes shopping to be so pleasant for you. If, on the other hand, you choose to discuss the negative results of shopping, you are writing an "effects" paragraph, one that explains effects only.

Assignment 3: Writing an Essay

Sociologists, psychologists, and advertisers use the concept of "social validation" to describe the persuasive power behind clothing and accessories that display their brand names or logos prominently. Social validation involves people's need to do or wear what they hope will get approval from some chosen group, rather than thinking for themselves.

Look around your classroom. How many people are wearing ball caps with logos; how many T-shirts have a band's name on them; how many hoodies or pairs of sweatpants have designers' names or brands displayed on them? What do all these signatures, these pieces of "free advertising," say about us? From whom are people looking for approval? Whose "world" or fantasy do the logos associate the wearers with?

Choose one such type of apparel, or one such brand name or logo, and write an essay that explains what this type of garment or brand identification says about the wearers—their interests, the ideas they wish to be identified with, and the sort of person they hope to appeal to.

Here is a thesis statement for such an essay: "Phat Pharm and other hip-hop-style clothing say that the wearer dreams of being an urban character, a tough dude of either gender, and very, very edgy."

WHAT'S IN YOUR FRIDGE

Joe Fiorito

Food and what we eat are interesting to just about everyone. We must eat, and some of us enjoy cooking, but what do our food choices and eating habits say about us? Joe Fiorito, a Toronto-based writer, takes an affectionate look at how our national identity is reflected in the contents of our refrigerators. "What's in Your Fridge" is light in tone, but consider what refrigerator contents would say about Argentinians, Germans, Hong Kong residents, or Australians. Occasionally, something apparently trivial tells us many things.

1   "Tell me what you eat and I will tell you who you are." Oh, bosh, don't give me that old swill. Brillat-Savarin never left a head of lettuce in the crisper so long it melted in a puddle; better he should have said, "Tell me what's wilting in your fridge and I will tell you who you are."

2   My own personal refrigerator—a noisy, expensive, enamelled, cartoon-covered compost bin—is known around here as the place where lemons go to die.

3   I took a sample of Canadian fridges recently. If we really are what we eat, then the national unity debate is over for good. We're Mexican. We all have plenty of jars of salsa, bottles of hot sauce, bags of jalapeños.

4   We're perfectly multicultural. We eat tofu and chutney and olives, baba ganoush and antipasto. We use tandoori paste. We eat mangoes and pierogies. We have wrinkled kiwis. We're also fussy and slightly paranoid; we have the most plentiful supply of fresh water on the planet, but we don't trust what flows from our taps, so our fridges are full of designer water.

5   Half of the people in my little survey keep baking soda in the fridge to sop up odours; half don't bother. We all keep a little maple syrup, even if we don't make as many pancakes as we should.

6   We keep our bagels cool, the lesser of two evils, since a cold bagel is only marginally more acceptable than a stale one. And that's what's wrong with the coun-

try today—we can't get a good fresh bagel when we want, unless we live in Montreal.

We keep sliced bread in the fridge. We shouldn't keep bread in the fridge, but we do. It's easier than buying it fresh. We like prepared foods. We'd probably buy frozen toast—just pop it in the toaster!—if it were available. 7

Our fridges are frost-free, even if our country is not, and it's forever spring-time in the vegetable bin. Peppers of all colours, all the time. Melons and berries whenever we want. When our sidewalks are covered with snow, our snow peas are spoiling in the crisper. 8

We feel guilty about that. 9

The average item in our fridge has travelled more than a thousand kilometres to reach us; on the other hand, if we ate locally, in most parts of the country, it'd be nothing but turnips from September to July. 10

We ought to have plenty of little stores closer us, instead of whopping great supermarkets a mile away where we buy mass quantities once a week. We'd eat better, and the icebox wouldn't look so wilted of a Thursday. 11

We keep our coffee in the freezer, a debatable practice; if a frost-free fridge extracts moisture from the air, and if coffee contains aromatic oils...well, let's just say we'd be better off if we kept our java unground, airtight, and in the cupboard. 12

We are turophiles: we love cheese—cheddar, parmigiano, feta, havarti. But we're bad to our cheese—we keep the mozzarella near the blue-veined gorgonzola, and then wonder why the mozzarella gets mouldy. 13

We still make homemade jelly, which we give away to our friends. We freeze saskatoon berries on the prairies, blueberries in northern Ontario, raspberries everywhere else. 14

In the far north, our fridges are equally exotic, but with more caribou and char; as for the char, we freeze it whole, and clean it only when it's fully thawed. It tastes better that way. 15

We keep tomatoes in the fridge, although the only ones that can really stand the cold are plum tomatoes, and only if they haven't been cut. 16

Some of us keep leftovers in plastic tubs with lids. Others, me included, think the invention of plastic wrap is a modern miracle because it allows you to see what it is wedged in behind that jar of mayo. 17

We like mayo. 18

Also mustard, horseradish and tabasco, worcestershire and wasabi, dills and beets and cornichons. We're watching our cholesterol. We go easy on the butter. We drink skim milk. We're concerned that we don't get enough calcium. We have three containers of flavoured yogurt. 19

We like eggs. 20

And finally, we don't just use the fridge for food. I know a women who keeps a bottle of nail polish on a shelf in the fridge door; I know a man whose fur hat spends the summers in the freezer in a plastic bag; my dearest friend keeps her Mont Blanc cartridges next to the sambal oelek. 21

What does this tell us about who we are? 22

Close the fridge door, he explained. 23

■ Reading Comprehension Questions

1. Which of the following would make the best alternative title for the selection?
   a. Canadian Content
   b. Stupid Storage Habits
   c. Our Fridges, Ourselves
   d. Wasteful Canadians

2. Which sentence best expresses the selection's main point?
   a. Refrigerator contents show that Canadians have varied diets and illogical habits.
   b. Canadians' refrigerator contents indicate that we are overfed and wasteful.
   c. What we have in our refrigerators shows that we do not know how to store food.
   d. Canadians are better off not thinking about what is in their refrigerators.

3. Fiorito says "the national unity debate is over for good" (paragraph 3) because
   a. if we are what we eat, Canadians are more like Mexicans than French or English Canadians.
   b. if we are what we eat, Canadians are so multicultural that they don't know what country they belong to.
   c. Canadians cannot make up their minds about anything, much less food.
   d. Canadians do not care much about politics any more.

4. *True or false?* _____ Canadians drink bottled water because most of our water sources are polluted.

5. Canadians tend to shop in supermarkets, so items they keep in the refrigerator are
   a. fresh foods that are in season and need refrigerating.
   b. fancy imported foods they don't really need.
   c. lots of prepared packaged meals.
   d. imported fruits and vegetables that they buy in large quantities.

6. In spite of our short growing season and busy lives, our fridges show that
   a. we try to cook vegetables we are not familiar with.
   b. we make homemade preserves and freeze berries.
   c. we buy produce, then have to use it when it's spoiling.
   d. we buy a lot of imported tomatoes.

7. *True or false?* _____ Coffee keeps best sealed, at room temperature.

8. Apparently, Canadian refrigerators also show that
   a. we buy cheese but do not really like it.
   b. we are health-conscious and enjoy condiments.
   c. we do not know how to store leftovers.
   d. we do not eat balanced diets.

9. The word *paranoid* in "We're also fussy and slightly paranoid" (paragraph 4) means
   a. wasteful.
   b. distrustful.
   c. neurotic.
   d. extravagant.

10. The word *marginally* in "since a cold bagel is only marginally more acceptable than a stale one" (paragraph 6) means
    a. slightly.
    b. substantially.
    c. exceptionally.
    d. partly.

■ Discussion Questions

About Content

1. In which countries do the foods listed in paragraph 4 originate? What does the presence of these foods in our refrigerators say about us as a people? With how many of these foods are you familiar?

2. Why does the author say, in paragraph 9, "We feel guilty about that"?

3. Where does Fiorito find fault with Canadian shopping habits? Do these habits reflect your own patterns or your family's?

4. How many food items mentioned in the selection are indigenous to Canada? Which of these items are commonly found in meals in your part of Canada?

5. Which products do Canadians not know how to handle or keep properly? What is the author saying about us by including each of these items?

About Structure

6. What methods of introduction does the author use in this selection?
   a. Broad statement; questions.
   b. Anecdote; relevance.
   c. Quotation; contrast.
   d. Anecdote; broad statement.

   Is Fiorito's introduction effective? Why or why not?

7. Instead of opening some paragraphs with typical transitional words and phrases, the author creates coherence with another method. Fiorito opens paragraphs with repeated words. How many paragraphs open with the same word? What effect does this repetition have on you as a reader? Which paragraphs open with something other than this repeated word? What is the significance of the author's variation from repetition in these openings? How many paragraphs begin with standard transitions? Why, in each case?

8. How many paragraphs make up the conclusion of the selection? Which of the following best describes the conclusion, and why?
   a. It just stops.
   b. It restates the point of the selection and signals completion.
   c. It focuses on possible future outcomes.
   d. It presents a viewpoint that is the opposite of the views in the body of the selection.

About Style and Tone

9. Why might Fiorito have mentioned wilting and rotting food in his first paragraph, then revealed potentially embarrassing details about his own refrigerator in paragraph 2? How does his self-revelation affect the way you regard the author and what he has to say?

10. The author intentionally uses slang and casual wordings ("Oh, bosh," "sop up"), simple words, short sentences, and even a sentence fragment. In which paragraph do you find a fragment? Why, given Fiorito's general intention for the piece and its tone, does he use these techniques?

11. How many one-sentence paragraphs are in the selection? Why is each one used?

■ Writing Assignments

Assignment 1: Writing a Paragraph

Television watchers know the Brillat-Savarin saying with which Joe Fiorito opens his first paragraph—"Tell me what you eat and I will tell you who you are"—from *Iron Chef*. How often, though, do we check to see who *we* are, based on our food choices?

Write a paragraph that explains, based on either what you like to eat or what is in your refrigerator, who you are. Your topic sentence will give an overall sense of you; then each food choice will be a subtopic that says something specific about you. Here are two sample topic sentences.

> My diet of instant mac and cheese and fast foods demonstrates that I am a nutritionist's nightmare and a person with too much to do.

> Large cans of protein supplements and packages of chicken in the refrigerator show that my kitchen belongs to a bodybuilder.

Assignment 2: Writing a Paragraph

Canada may be unique among nations because of its multicultural character. More than just the foods in our refrigerators demonstrates the dynamic and varied nature of this country. Consider the number of festivals and holidays that are celebrated, or the makeup of the average classroom or neighbourhood, or even the variety of takeout foods available. Think about three ways in which cultural diversity enriches or affects your everyday life and use these as the basis for a division and classification paragraph.

Assignment 3: Writing an Essay

Family dinners, holiday celebrations, romantic dinners, picnics: some meals have extra significance for us or mark special events in our lives. The meanings of such meals go beyond the food that is served; meanings are based on the company, the occasion, the location, the atmosphere, or some combination of these things.

Write an essay about one such meal that has particular meaning for you. Your essay should start with the effect or result that this meal was important, then look at the causes or reasons why this meal was so memorable. Remember that *memorable* need not mean something positive; you may write about an unforgettable dinner that was a disaster. Your thesis statement for such an essay might be similar to one of these.

> Most people would not cherish the memory of a cheeseburger eaten in the car during a rainstorm, but those people have never met my boyfriend Adam.

> My last Chinese New Year's dinner with my family brought me more good luck than I ever expected.

Assignment 4: Writing an Essay Using Internet Research

Joe Fiorito mentions a wide variety of foods and condiments in this selection. Many foods have interesting histories: for example, potatoes were considered poisonous at one time. Write an essay that explains the history of one particular food, condiment, or seasoning. Consider ketchup: we see it everywhere, but do you know where and when ketchup first appeared?

Use a search engine like Google, and start with the keywords *ketchup* (or the name of the food you are interested in) and *history*. Try a few keywords until you find sites whose main content is information about the origins of your food or seasoning. You will require only one or two sites. Before you write your essay, see the Online Learning Centre for advice on quoting, paraphrasing, and citing your webpage sources.

Your thesis statement might suggest why you chose the item you did or what you found most interesting about its origins. Supporting points could be three distinct stages in the product's history, three interesting facts about the food or seasoning, or three ways in which the product changed as it developed into its current form.

Credits

Answers to Sentence-Skills Diagnostic Test and Introductory Projects

SENTENCE-SKILLS DIAGNOSTIC TEST (PAGES 301-5)

Faulty Parallelism

1. X
2. C
3. X
4. C

Consistent Verb Tense

5. X
6. C
7. C
8. X

Pronoun Point of View

9. X
10. C

Fragments

11. X
12. C
13. X
14. X
15. C
16. X

Run-ons and Comma Splices

17. C
18. X

19 X
20. X
21. C
22. X

Irregular Verbs

23. X
24. C
25. C
26. X

Subject-Verb Agreement

27. X
28. X
29. C
30. X

Pronoun Agreement and Reference

31. X
32. C
33. X
34. C

Pronoun Types

35. X
36. C
37. X

Adjectives and Adverbs

38. X
39. X

Misplaced Modifiers

40. X
41. C
42. X
43. X

Dangling Modifiers

44. C
45. X
46. C
47. X

Capital Letters

48. X
49. X
50. C
51. X

Apostrophe

52. C
53. X
54. X
55. C

Quotation Marks

56. C
57. X
58. X
59. C

Comma

60. X
61. X
62. C
63. X
64. C
65. X

Commonly Confused Words

66. X
67. X
68. C
69. X
70. X
71. C

Effective Word Use

72. X
73. X
74. X
75. X

INTRODUCTORY PROJECTS

Fragments (page 314)

1. thought
2. subject
3. verb
4. subject

Run-ons and Comma Splices (page 329)

1. period
2. *but*
3. semicolon
4. *when*

Irregular Verbs (page 342)

1. crawled, crawled (regular)
2. brought, brought (irregular)
3. used, used (regular)
4. did, done (irregular)
5. gave, given (irregular)
6. laughed, laughed (regular)
7. went, gone (irregular)
8. scared, scared (regular)
9. dressed, dressed (regular)
10. saw, seen (irregular)

Subject-Verb Agreement (page 349)

The second sentence in each pair is correct.

Pronoun Agreement and Reference (page 355)

The second sentence in each pair is correct.

Misplaced Modifiers (page 371)

1. Intended: A young man with references is wanted to open oysters.
   Unintended: The oysters have references.
2. Intended: On their wedding day, Carlo and Charlotte decided they would have two children.
   Unintended: Carlo and Charlotte decided to have two children who would magically appear on the day of their wedding.
3. Intended: Hazelnut chocolates are the only chocolates Marissa eats.
   Unintended: Hazelnut chocolates are Marissa's entire diet.

Dangling Modifiers (page 374)

1. Intended: My dog sat with me as I smoked a pipe.
   Unintended: My dog smoked a pipe.
2. Intended: He looked at a traffic accident as he drove his sports car through a red light.
   Unintended: His sports car looked at a traffic accident.
3. Intended: The moussaka baked for several hours.
   Unintended: Dad baked for several hours.

Capital Letters (page 383)

All the answers to questions 1 to 13 should be in capital letters.
14. The   15. I   16. "That . . ."

Apostrophe (page 395)

1. The purpose of the *'s* is to show possession (Lauren owns the motorcycle, the boyfriend belongs to the sister, Grandmother owns the laptop, the room belongs to the men).
2. The purpose of the apostrophe is to show the omission of one or more letters in a contraction—two words shortened to form one word.
3. In each of the second sentences, the *'s* shows possession: the body of the vampire; the centre of the baked potato. In each of the first sentences, the *s* is used to form a simple plural: more than one vampire; more than one potato.

Quotation Marks (page 404)

1. The purpose of quotation marks is to set off the exact words of a speaker. (The words that Mike actually spoke aloud are set off with quotation marks, as are the words that Derrick spoke aloud.)
2. Commas and periods go inside quotation marks.

Comma (page 411)

1. a.   Many college students must balance coursework with part-time jobs, family responsibilities, and some social activities.
   b.   Days in winter are short, cold, and dark.
2. a.   Although David Miller is the new mayor of Toronto, he has been in municipal politics for a long time.
   b.   To open the cap of the Aspirin bottle, you must first press down on it.
3. a.   Avril Lavigne and Deryck Whibley, Canada's leading punk stars, arrived at the awards show together.
   b.   Melanie, who lives next door to me, refused to go to the hospital during the SARS outbreak.
4. a.   The wedding was scheduled for four o'clock, but the bride changed her mind at two.
   b.   Franka took three coffee breaks before lunch, and then she went on a two-hour lunch break.
5. a.   Delia's mother asked her, "What time do you expect to get home?"
   b.   "Don't bend over to pat the dog," I warned, "or he'll kiss you."
6. a.   Benjie ate seventeen hamburgers on July 29, 1998, and lived to tell about it.
   b.   Benjie lives at 817 Ouellette Avenue, Windsor, Ontario.

Other Punctuation Marks (page 420)

1. pets: holly
2. freeze-dried
3. Shakespeare (1564-1616)
4. Earth; no
5. proudly—with

Commonly Confused Words (page 438)

Your mind and body. . . . *There* is a lot of evidence. . . .
then it will. . . . said *to* have. . . . *It's* not clear

Effective Word Choice (page 449)

1. "Caved" is slang.
2. "Few and far between" is a cliché.
3. "Ascertained" is a pretentious word.

READING COMPREHENSION CHART

Write an X through the numbers of any questions you missed while answering the comprehension questions for each selection in Section Five, "Fifteen Reading Selections." Then write in your comprehension score. (To calculate your score for each reading, give yourself 10 points for each item that is *not* crossed out.) The chart will make clear any skill question you get wrong repeatedly, so that you can pay special attention to that skill in the future.

Selection	Subject or Title	Thesis or Main Idea	Key Details			Inferences			Vocabulary in Context		Comprehension Score
MacKenzie	1	2	3	4	5	6	7	8	9	10	%
Gabriele	1	2	3	4	5	6	7	8	9	10	%
Devlin	1	2	3	4	5	6	7	8	9	10	%
Collier	1	2	3	4	5	6	7	8	9	10	%
Berger	1	2	3	4	5	6	7	8	9	10	%
Akers	1	2	3	4	5	6	7	8	9	10	%
Brett	1	2	3	4	5	6	7	8	9	10	%
Maloney	1	2	3	4	5	6	7	8	9	10	%
Medwell	1	2	3	4	5	6	7	8	9	10	%
Amernic	1	2	3	4	5	6	7	8	9	10	%
Wong	1	2	3	4	5	6	7	8	9	10	%
Eng	1	2	3	4	5	6	7	8	9	10	%
Grewal	1	2	3	4	5	6	7	8	9	10	%
Fertile	1	2	3	4	5	6	7	8	9	10	%
Fiorito	1	2	3	4	5	6	7	8	9	10	%

Index